THE OXFORD
CONCISE CONCORDANCE
TO THE
REVISED STANDARD VERSION
OF THE HOLY BIBLE

COMPILED BY
BRUCE M. METZGER
AND
ISOBEL M. METZGER

LONDON
OXFORD UNIVERSITY PRESS
NEW YORK TORONTO MELBOURNE

Oxford University Press, Ely House, London W. 1

GLASGOW NEW YORK TORONTO MELBOURNE WELLINGTON
CAPE TOWN SALISBURY IBADAN NAIROBI LUSAKA ADDIS ABABA
BOMBAY CALCUTTA MADRAS KARACHI LAHORE DACCA
KUALA LUMPUR SINGAPORE HONG KONG TOKYO

First published 1962
Reprinted 1966 and 1969

SET IN THE UNITED STATES OF AMERICA
AND PRINTED LITHOGRAPHICALLY IN GREAT BRITAIN
BY VIVIAN RIDLER AT THE
UNIVERSITY PRESS, OXFORD

FOREWORD

THIS CONCORDANCE is intended to meet the needs of the general reader of the Bible. Within the limits of the space available, those nouns, verbs, adjectives, and adverbs were chosen for inclusion which will be of interest to a variety of users. In the selection of context lines containing these words, preference was given to passages which are intrinsically significant or which, for some other reason, can be regarded as noteworthy. Proper names, instead of standing in a separate list, are included in alphabetical order within the concordance itself, thus facilitating their consultation. References to many of the more important persons and places mentioned in the Bible are set forth in the form of brief digests of salient biographical or geographical details.

ABBREVIATIONS

Acts	The Acts of the Apostles	Jude	Jude
Am.	Amos	1 Kg.	1 Kings
1 Chr.	1 Chronicles	2 Kg.	2 Kings
2 Chr.	2 Chronicles	Lam.	Lamentations
Col.	Colossians	Lev.	Leviticus
1 Cor.	1 Corinthians	Lk.	Luke
2 Cor.	2 Corinthians	Mal.	Malachi
Dan.	Daniel	Mic.	Micah
Dt.	Deuteronomy	Mk.	Mark
Ec.	Ecclesiastes	Mt.	Matthew
Eph.	Ephesians	Nah.	Nahum
Est.	Esther	Neh.	Nehemiah
Ex.	Exodus	Num.	Numbers
Ezek.	Ezekiel	Ob.	Obadiah
Ezra	Ezra	1 Pet.	1 Peter
Gal.	Galatians	2 Pet.	2 Peter
Gen.	Genesis	Phil.	Philippians
Hab.	Habakkuk	Philem.	Philemon
Hag.	Haggai	Pr.	Proverbs
Heb.	Hebrews	Ps.	Psalms
Hos.	Hosea	Rev.	Revelation
Is.	Isaiah	Rom.	Romans
Jas.	James	Ru.	Ruth
Jer.	Jeremiah	1 Sam.	1 Samuel
Jg.	Judges	2 Sam.	2 Samuel
Jl.	Joel	S. of S.	Song of Solomon
Jn.	John	1 Th.	1 Thessalonians
1 Jn.	1 John	2 Th.	2 Thessalonians
2 Jn.	2 John	1 Tim.	1 Timothy
3 Jn.	3 John	2 Tim.	2 Timothy
Job	Job	Tit.	Titus
Jon.	Jonah	Zech.	Zechariah
Jos.	Joshua	Zeph.	Zephaniah

CONCORDANCE

AARON
appointed to be Moses' spokesman, Ex.4.14–16, 27; appeals to Pharaoh, Ex.5.1,4; his rod becomes a serpent, Ex.7.10; changes water into blood, Ex.7.20; causes the plagues of frogs, lice, flies, Ex.8.5, 17, 24; with Hur holds up Moses' hands, Ex.17.12; set apart for priest's office, Ex.28; makes the golden calf, Ex.32.4; his excuse to Moses, Ex.32.22; consecration, Ex.29; Lev.8; speaks against Moses, Num.12.1; his rod sprouted, and is kept in ark for a token, Num.17.8; Heb.9.4; for unbelief excluded from the promised land, Num.20.12; dies on Mount Hor, Num.20.28

ABASE
God *a.* the proud, but he saves	Job 22.29
a. that which is high	Ezek.21.26
who walk in pride he is able to *a.*	Dan.4.37
I know how to be *a.*, and I	Phil.4.12

ABEDNEGO
Dan.1.7; 2.49; 3.12–30

ABEL
second son of Adam, Gen.4.2; his offering accepted, Gen.4.4; slain by Cain, Gen.4.8; righteous, Mt.23.35; 1 Jn.3.12; blood of, Lk. 11.51; Heb.12.24; faith of, Heb.11.4

ABHOR
All my intimate friends *a.* me	Job 19.19
I hate and *a.* falsehood	Ps.119.163
who *a.* justice and pervert all	Mic.3.9
You who *a.* idols, do you rob . . . ?	Rom.2.22

ABIDE
shall not *a.* in man for ever	Gen.6.3
their heritage will *a.* for ever	Ps.37.18
my hand shall ever *a.* with him	Ps.89.21
who *a.* in the shadow of the Almighty	Ps.91.1
admonition will *a.* among the wise	Pr.15.31
the arrogant man shall not *a.*	Hab.2.5
A. in me, and I in you	Jn.15.4
If you *a.* in me, and my words *a.*	Jn.15.7
So faith, hope, love *a.*	1 Cor.13.13
the word of the Lord *a.* for ever	1 Pet.1.25
how does God's love *a.* in him?	1 Jn.3.17
if we love . . . God *a.* in us	1 Jn.4.12
and he who *a.* in love *a.* in God	1 Jn.4.16

ABILITY
I have given to all able men *a.*	Ex.31.6
LORD has put *a.* and intelligence	Ex.36.1
men of *a.*, had the oversight	1 Chr.26.30
to each according to his *a.*	Mt.25.15
every one according to his *a.*	Acts 11.29

ABIMELECH
(1) king of Gerar; reproved by God about Abraham's wife, Gen.20.2–3; rebukes Abraham and restores Sarah, Gen.20.9,14; healed at Abraham's prayer, Gen.20.17; (2) king of the Philistines, Gen.26.1; Isaac rebuked by, Gen.26.9–10; covenants with Isaac, Gen.26.28; (3) king at Shechem; son of the judge Gideon, Jg.8.31; murders his brethren, Jg.9.5; his death, Jg.9.54

ABLE
every man shall give as he is *a.*	Dt.16.17
no man has been *a.* to withstand	Jos.23.9
a. to stand before the LORD	1 Sam.6.20
so that none is *a.* to withstand	2 Chr.20.6
The LORD is *a.* to give you much	2 Chr.25.9
believe that I am *a.* to do this?	Mt.9.28
Are you *a.* to drink the cup that I	Mt.20.22
God is *a.* from these stones to raise	Lk.3.8
that God was *a.* to do what he had	Rom.4.21
will be *a.* to separate us from	Rom.8.39
that you may be *a.* to endure it	1 Cor.10.13
within us is *a.* to do far more	Eph.3.20
that God was *a.* to raise men even	Heb.11.19
Now to him who is *a.* to keep you	Jude 24

ABNER
cousin of Saul, commander of his army, 1 Sam. 14.50; reproved by David, 1 Sam.26.5,14; makes Ish-bosheth king, 2 Sam.2.8–9; comes to David, 2 Sam.3.20; slain by Joab, 2 Sam.3.27; mourned by David, 2 Sam.3.31

ABODE (noun)
I will make my *a.* among you	Lev.26.11
His *a.* has been established	Ps.76.2
From thy lofty *a.* thou waterest	Ps.104.13
he blesses the *a.* of the righteous	Pr.3.33

ABOMINABLE
You shall not eat any *a.* thing	Dt.14.3
she had an *a.* image made	1 Kg.15.13
put away the *a.* idols from all	2 Chr.15.8
less one who is *a.* and corrupt	Job 15.16
they do *a.* deeds, there is none that	Ps.14.1
are corrupt, doing *a.* iniquity	Ps.53.1
they made their *a.* images	Ezek.7.20

ABOMINATION
that is an *a.* to the Egyptians	Gen.43.32
for it is an *a.* to the LORD	Dt.7.25
are an *a.* to the LORD your God	Dt.25.16
perverse man is an *a.* to the LORD	Pr.3.32
Lying lips are an *a.* to the LORD	Pr.12.22
sacrifice of the wicked is an *a.*	Pr.21.27

incense is an *a.* to me — Is.1.13
ashamed when they committed *a.*? — Jer.6.15
is an *a.* in the sight of God — Lk.16.15

ABOUND
faithful man will *a.* with blessings — Pr.28.20
continue in sin that grace may *a.*? — Rom.6.1
so that . . . you may *a.* in hope — Rom.15.13
always *a.* in the work of the Lord — 1 Cor.15.58
be abased, and I know how to *a.* — Phil.4.12
increase and *a.* in love to one — 1 Th.3.12

ABRAHAM
blessed by God, and sent to Canaan, Gen.12.2–5;
goes down to Egypt, Gen.12.10; causes his
wife to pass as his sister, Gen.12.13; 20.2;
strife between him and Lot, Gen.13.7; separates from Lot, Gen.13.11; delivers Lot from
captivity, and refuses the spoil, Gen.14.16–23;
blessed by Melchizedek, king of Salem, Gen.
14.19; Heb.7.4; his faith counted for righteousness, Gen.15.6; God's covenant with, Gen.
15.18; Ps.105.9; he and house circumcised,
Gen.17; entertains angels, Gen.18; pleads for
Sodom, Gen.18.23; sends away Hagar and
Ishmael, Gen.21.14; his faith in offering Isaac,
Gen.22; sends for a wife for his son, Gen.24;
gives his goods to Isaac, Gen.25.5; dies,
Gen.25.8; his faith and works, Is.51.2; Jn.8.33;
Acts 7.2; Rom.4; Gal.3.6; Heb.11.8; Jas.2.21

ABSALOM
David's son, 2 Sam.3.3; slays Ammon, 2 Sam.
13.28; conspires against David, 2 Sam.15;
caught by head in an oak, 2 Sam.18.9; slain
by Joab, 2 Sam.18.14; mourned by David,
2 Sam.18.33; 19.1

ABSENT
when we are *a.* one from the other — Gen.31.49
For though *a.* in body I am present — 1 Cor.5.3
For though I am *a.* in body — Col.2.5

ABSTAIN
to them to *a.* from the pollutions — Acts 15.20
let not him who *a.* pass judgment — Rom.14.3
that you *a.* from immorality — 1 Th.4.3
a. from every form of evil — 1 Th.5.22

ABUNDANCE
but in an *a.* of counselors there is — Pr.11.14
a. of salvation, wisdom, and knowledge — Is.33.6
For out of the *a.* of the heart — Mt.12.34
all contributed out of their *a.* — Lk.21.4
those who receive the *a.* of grace — Rom.5.17
you with every blessing in *a.* — 2 Cor.9.8
elated by the *a.* of revelations — 2 Cor.12.7
plenty and hunger, *a.* and want — Phil.4.12

ABUNDANT
O how *a.* is thy goodness, which — Ps.31.19
according to thy *a.* mercy blot out — Ps.51.1
Great is our LORD, and *a.* in power — Ps.147.5
you know the *a.* love that I have — 2 Cor.2.4

ABUNDANTLY
to our God, for he will *a.* pardon — Is.55.7
they may have life, and have it *a.* — Jn.10.10
For as we share *a.* in Christ's — 2 Cor.1.5
is able to do far more *a.* than all — Eph.3.20

ACCEPT
A., I pray you, my gift that is — Gen.33.11
to be *a.* it must be perfect — Lev.22.21
the LORD *a.* Job's prayer — Job 42.9

A. my offerings of praise, O LORD — Ps.119.108
therefore the LORD does not *a.* them — Jer.14.10

ACCEPTABLE
the meditation of my heart be *a.* — Ps.19.14
sacrifice *a.* to God is a broken — Ps.51.17
justice is more *a.* to the LORD — Pr.21.3
Your burnt offerings are not *a.* — Jer.6.20
to proclaim the *a.* year of the Lord — Lk.4.19
Behold, now is the *a.* time — 2 Cor.6.2
offered to God a more *a.* sacrifice — Heb.11.4
let us offer to God *a.* worship — Heb.12.28
sacrifices *a.* to God through Jesus — 1 Pet.2.5

ACCOMPLISH
the LORD of hosts will *a.* this — Is.37.32
it shall *a.* that which I purpose — Is.55.11
his departure, which he was to *a.* — Lk.9.31
if only I may *a.* my course — Acts 20.24
which he *a.* in Christ when he — Eph.1.20

ACCORD
Yea, they conspire with one *a.* — Ps.83.5
the LORD and serve him with one *a.* — Zeph.3.9
But I have not come of my own *a.* — Jn.7.28
All these with one *a.* devoted — Acts 1.14
with one *a.* gave heed to what was — Acts 8.6
in *a.* with Christ Jesus — Rom.15.5
What *a.* has Christ with Belial? — 2 Cor.6.15
being in full *a.* and of one mind — Phil.2.2

ACCOUNT (noun)
Behold, I am of small *a.* — Job 40.4
men will render *a.* for every — Mt.12.36
persecution . . . on *a.* of the word — Mk.4.17
Turn in the *a.* of your stewardship — Lk.16.2
shall give *a.* of himself to God — Rom.14.12
as men who will have to give *a.* — Heb.13.17

ACCURSED
who do not know the law, are *a.* — Jn.7.49
I myself were *a.* and cut off from — Rom.9.3
has no love . . . let him be *a.* — 1 Cor.16.22
There shall no more be anything *a.* — Rev.22.3

ACCUSE
In return for my love they *a.* me — Ps.109.4
so that they might *a.* him — Mt.12.10
Do not think that I shall *a.* you — Jn.5.45
their conflicting thoughts *a.* — Rom.2.15

ACCUSER
I must appeal for mercy to my *a.* — Job 9.15
May my *a.* be put to shame — Ps.71.13
I am an object of scorn to my *a.* — Ps.109.25
Make friends quickly with your *a.* — Mt.5.25
accused met the *a.* face to face — Acts 25.16
for the *a.* of our brethren has been — Rev.12.10

ACKNOWLEDGE
In all your ways *a.* him — Pr.3.6
We *a.* our wickedness, O LORD — Jer.14.20
I also will *a.* before my Father — Mt.10.32
they did not see fit to *a.* God — Rom.1.28
fruit of lips that *a.* his name — Heb.13.15

ACT (verb)
all who *a.* dishonestly, are an — Dt.25.16
trust in him, and he will *a.* — Ps.37.5
a prudent man *a.* with knowledge — Pr.13.16
A man of quick temper *a.* foolishly — Pr.14.17
I know that you *a.* in ignorance — Acts 3.17
Did we . . . *a.* in the same spirit? — 2 Cor.12.18
that forgets but a doer that *a.* — Jas.1.25
a. as those who are to be judged — Jas.2.12

ADAM

(1) created, Gen.1; called the son of God, Lk.3.38; blessed, Gen.1.28; placed in Eden, Gen.2.8; first called Adam, Gen.2.19; creatures named by, Gen.2.19; calls his wife Eve, Gen.3.20; his fall and punishment, Gen.3; hides from God, Gen.3.8; ground cursed for his sake, Gen.3.17; his death, Gen.5.5; his transgression, Rom.5.14; the first Adam, 1 Cor.15.22,45; 1 Tim.2.13; the last Adam, 1 Cor.15.45; (2) a place, Jos.3.16

ADDER

like the deaf *a.* that stops its ear	Ps.58.4
tread on the lion and the *a.*	Ps.91.13
a serpent, and stings like an *a.*	Pr.23.32

ADJURE

I *a.* you by the living God, tell	Mt.26.63
I *a.* you by God, do not torment me	Mk.5.7
I *a.* you by the Jesus whom Paul	Acts 19.13
I *a.* you by the Lord that this	1 Th.5.27

ADMONISH

Hear, O my people, while I *a.* you	Ps.81.8
to *a.* you as my beloved children	1 Cor.4.14
you teach and *a.* one another	Col.3.16
a. the idle, encourage	1 Th.5.14

ADORN

how it was *a.* with noble stones	Lk.21.5
women . . . *a.* themselves modestly	1 Tim.2.9
they may *a.* the doctrine of God	Tit.2.10
holy women . . . used to *a.* themselves	1 Pet.3.5
as a bride *a.* for her husband	Rev.21.2

ADULLAM

Jos.12.15; 1 Sam.22.1; 2 Sam.23.13; Mic.1.15

ADULTERY

You shall not commit *a.*	Ex.20.14
If a man commits *a.* with the wife	Lev.20.10
Neither shall you commit *a.*	Dt.5.18
was said, 'You shall not commit *a.*'	Mt.5.27
committed *a.* with her in his heart	Mt.5.28
and marries another, commits *a.*	Mt.19.9
and marries another commits *a.*	Lk.16.18
woman who had been caught in *a.*	Jn.8.3
You shall not commit *a.*	Rom.13.9
They have eyes full of *a.*	2 Pet.2.14
who commit *a.* with her I will	Rev.2.22

ADVANTAGE

It is to your *a.* that I go away, for	Jn.16.7
Then what *a.* has the Jew? Or what	Rom.3.1
not seeking my own *a.*, but that	1 Cor.10.33
Christ will be of no *a.* to you	Gal.5.2

ADVERSARY

my *a.* sharpens his eyes against me	Job 16.9
Vindicate me against my *a.*	Lk.18.3
none of your *a.* will be able to	Lk.21.15
of fire which will consume the *a.*	Heb.10.27
Your *a.* the devil prowls around	1 Pet.5.8

ADVERSITY

redeemed my soul out of every *a.*	1 Kg.1.29
He thinks . . . I shall not meet *a.*	Ps.10.6
thou hast taken heed of my *a.*	Ps.31.7
and a brother is born for *a.*	Pr.17.17
and in the day of *a.* consider	Ec.7.14
the bread of *a.* and the water of	Is.30.20

AFFECTION

| love one another with brotherly *a.* | Rom.12.10 |

| all with the *a.* of Christ Jesus | Phil.1.8 |
| and godliness with brotherly *a.* | 2 Pet.1.7 |

AFFLICT

But the LORD *a.* Pharaoh and his	Gen.12.17
You shall not *a.* any widow or	Ex.22.22
the LORD has *a.* me and the Almighty	Ru.1.21
does not forget the cry of the *a.*	Ps.9.12
for I am lonely and *a.*	Ps.25.16
right of the *a.* and the destitute	Ps.82.3
It is good for me that I was *a.*	Ps.119.71
LORD maintains the cause of the *a.*	Ps.140.12
stricken, smitten by God, and *a.*	Is.53.4
he was *a.*, yet he opened not	Is.53.7
to bring good tidings to the *a.*	Is.61.1
In all their affliction he was *a.*	Is.63.9
We are *a.* in every way, but not	2 Cor.4.8
relieved the *a.*, and devoted	1 Tim.5.10
destitute, *a.*, ill-treated	Heb.11.37

AFFLICTION

the LORD has looked upon my *a.*	Gen.29.32
I have seen the *a.* of my people	Ex.3.7
the bread of *a.* – for you came out	Dt.16.3
For *a.* does not come from the dust	Job 5.6
caught in the cords of *a.*	Job 36.8
Consider my *a.* and my trouble	Ps.25.18
he raises up the needy out of *a.*	Ps.107.41
Look on my *a.* and deliver me	Ps.119.153
this is vanity; it is a sore *a.*	Ec.6.2
tried you in the furnace of *a.*	Is.48.10
Remember my *a.* and my bitterness	Lam.3.19
who comforts us in all our *a.*	2 Cor.1.4
I wrote you out of much *a.*	2 Cor.2.4
what is lacking in Christ's *a.*	Col.1.24
publicly exposed to abuse and *a.*	Heb.10.33

AFRAID

I was *a.*, because I was naked	Gen.3.10
Then Moses was *a.*, and thought	Ex.2.14
I become *a.* of all my suffering	Job 9.28
of whom shall I be *a.*?	Ps.27.1
When I am *a.*, I put my trust in thee	Ps.56.3
heart is steady, he will not be *a.*	Ps.112.8
I will trust, and will not be *a.*	Is.12.2
Fear not, nor be *a.*; have I not told	Is.44.8
Be not *a.* of them, for I am with you	Jer.1.8
Why are you *a.*, O men of little	Mt.8.26
they were *a.*, and they glorified God	Mt.9.8
so I was *a.*, and I went and hid	Mt.25.25
said to the women, "Do not be *a.*	Mt.28.5
the angel said to them, "Be not *a.*	Lk.2.10
troubled, neither let them be *a.*	Jn.14.27
Lord is my helper, I will not be *a.*	Heb.13.6

AGE

have borne him a son in his old *a.*	Gen.21.7
the harvest is the close of the *a.*	Mt.13.39
So it will be at the close of the *a.*	Mt.13.49
in the *a.* to come eternal life	Mk.10.30
she was of a great *a.*, having lived	Lk.2.36
Jesus . . . was about thirty years of *a.*	Lk.3.23
that in the coming *a.* he might show	Eph.2.7
hidden for *a.* and generations but	Col.1.26
the powers of the *a.* to come	Heb.6.5
the end of the *a.* to put away sin	Heb.9.26
are thy ways, O King of the *a.*	Rev.15.3

AGREE

| *A.* with God, and be at peace | Job 22.21 |
| if two of you *a.* on earth about | Mt.18.19 |

a. with one another . . . in peace 2 Cor.13.11
entreat Syntyche to *a.* in the Lord Phil.4.2
three witnesses . . . and these three *a.* 1 Jn.5.8

AHAB

king of Israel, 1 Kg.16.29; marries Jezebel; his
idolatry, 1 Kg.16.31; meets Elijah, 1 Kg.18.17;
defeats the Syrians, 1 Kg.20; punished for
sparing Ben-hadad, 1 Kg.20.42; takes Naboth's
vineyard, 1 Kg.21.16; his repentance, 1 Kg.
21.27; trusts false prophets, and is mortally
wounded at Ramoth-gilead, 1 Kg.22.6,34;
2 Chr.18

AHASUERUS

reigns from India to Ethiopia, Est.1.1; Vashti's
disobedience to, and divorce, Est.1.12; 2.4;
makes Esther queen, Est.2.17; promotes
Haman, Est.3.1; his decree to destroy the Jews,
Est.3.12; rewards Mordecai's loyalty, Est.6;
hangs Haman, Est.7.9; 8.7; advances Mordecai,
Est.10

AHAZ

king of Judah, 2 Kg.15.38; 16; spoils the temple,
2 Kg.16.17; his idolatry, 2 Chr.28.2; afflicted by
Syrians, 2 Chr.28.5; comforted by Isaiah, Is.7;
will not ask a sign, Is.7.12

AHAZIAH

(1) king of Israel, 1 Kg.22.40,49; his sickness
and idolatry, 2 Kg.1; his judgment by Elijah,
2 Kg.1; (2) king of Judah, his wicked reign,
2 Kg.8.25; goes with Joram to meet Jehu, 2
Kg.9.21; smitten by Jehu, 2 Kg.9.27; 2 Chr.22.9

AIM (noun)

Make love your *a.*, and earnestly 1 Cor.14.1
we make it our *a.* to please him 2 Cor.5.9
since his *a.* is to satisfy the one 2 Tim.2.4
you have observed . . . my *a.* in life 2 Tim.3.10

AIR

sea, and over the birds of the *a.* Gen.1.26
another that no *a.* can come Job 41.16
birds of the *a.* have . . . habitation Ps.104.12
and birds of the *a.* have nests Mt.8.20
I do not box as one beating the *a.* 1 Cor.9.26
you will be speaking into the *a.* 1 Cor.14.9
the prince of the power of the *a.* Eph.2.2
clouds to meet the Lord in the *a.* 1 Th.4.17

ALEXANDER

(1) Mk.15.21; (2) a member of the Sanhedrin,
Acts 4.6; (3) an Ephesian Jew, Acts 19.33;
(4) a coppersmith, 1 Tim.1.20; 2 Tim.4.14

ALIVE

Joseph my son is still *a.* Gen.45.28
but you . . . are all *a.* this day Dt.4.4
I kill and I make *a.* Dt.32.39
behold, the LORD has kept me *a.* Jos.14.10
He does not keep the wicked *a.* Job 36.6
my son was dead, and is *a.* again Lk.15.24
presented himself . . . after his Acts 1.3
dead to sin and *a.* to God in Rom.6.11
in Christ shall all be made *a.* 1 Cor.15.22
of the Lord, that we who are *a.* 1 Th.4.15
flesh but made *a.* in the spirit 1 Pet.3.18
and behold I am *a.* for evermore Rev.1.18

ALLEGORY

speak an *a.* to the house of Israel Ezek.17.2
Is he not a maker of *a.*? Ezek.20.49

utter an *a.* to the rebellious house Ezek.24.3
Now this is an *a.*: these women are Gal.4.24

ALLOW

he *a.* no one to oppress them 1 Chr.16.21
Am I not *a.* to do what I choose Mt.20.15
nor *a.* those who would enter to go Mt.23.13
Spirit of Jesus did not *a.* them Acts 16.7

ALMIGHTY

who sees the vision of the *A.* Num.24.4
for the *A.* has dealt very bitterly Ru.1.20
despise not the chastening of the *A.* Job 5.17
Can you find out the limit of the *A.*? Job 11.7
when the *A.* was yet with me Job 29.5
a faultfinder contend with the *A.*? Job 40.2
who abides in the shadow of the *A.* Ps.91.1
destruction from the *A.* . . . will come Is.13.6
like the thunder of the *A.* Ezek.1.24
the voice of God *A.* when he speaks Ezek.10.5
who was and who is to come, the *A.* Rev.1.8
Holy, holy, holy, is the Lord God *A.* Rev.4.8
Lord God *A.*, who art and who wast Rev.11.17
For the Lord our God the *A.* reigns Rev.19.6

ALMS

when you give *a.*, sound no trumpet Mt.6.2
But give for *a.* those things which Lk.11.41
Sell your possessions, and give *a.* Lk.12.33
gave *a.* liberally to the people Acts 10.2

ALONE

not good that the man should be *a.* Gen.2.18
that man does not live by bread *a.* Dt.8.3
and I *a.* have escaped to tell you Job 1.15
to him who *a.* does great wonders Ps.136.4
Man shall not live by bread *a.* Mt.4.4
Who can forgive sins but God *a.*? Mk.2.7
No one is good but God *a.* Lk.18.19
yet I am not *a.*, for the Father is Jn.16.32
by works and not by faith *a.* Jas.2.24
For thou *a.* art holy Rev.15.4

ALPHA

I am the *A.* and the Omega Rev.1.8; 21.6; 22.13

ALTAR

Then Noah built an *a.* to the LORD Gen.8.20
Abraham built an *a.* there Gen.22.9
Moses built an *a.* and called Ex.17.15
An *a.* of earth you shall make for Ex.20.24
Joshua built an *a.* in Mount Ebal Jos.8.30
built there an *a.* by the Jordan Jos.22.10
Saul built an *a.* to the LORD 1 Sam.14.35
he repaired the *a.* of the LORD 1 Kg.18.30
He made an *a.* of bronze, twenty 2 Chr.4.1
at thy *a.*, O LORD of hosts, my King Ps.84.3
are offering your gift at the *a.* Mt.5.23
We have an *a.* from which those who Heb.13.10

ALWAYS

I keep the LORD *a.* before me Ps.16.8
He will not *a.* chide, nor will he Ps.103.9
I am with you *a.*, to the close of Mt.28.20
For you *a.* have the poor with you Mk.14.7
Rejoice in the Lord *a.* Phil.4.4
Let your speech *a.* be gracious Col.4.6
We give thanks to God *a.* for you all 1 Th.1.2
To this end we *a.* pray for you, that 2 Th.1.11
I thank my God *a.* when I remember Philem. 4

AMAZIAH

(1) king of Judah, his good reign, 2 Kg.14.1;
2 Chr.25.1; defeats Edom, 2 Chr.25.11; defeated

by Joash king of Israel, 2 Chr.25.21–23; slain at Lachish, 2 Kg.14.19; (2) priest of Bethel, Am.7.10

AMAZED

all the people were *a.*	Mt.12.23
they were all *a.* and glorified God	Mk.2.12
in a white robe; and they were *a.*	Mk.16.5
he said to them, "Do not be *a.*	Mk.16.6
they were *a.* and wondered	Acts 2.7
all who heard him were *a.*	Acts 9.21

AMBASSADOR

So we are *a.* for Christ	2 Cor.5.20
for which I am an *a.* in chains	Eph.6.20
Paul, an *a.* and now a prisoner also	Philem. 9

AMEN

all the people shall say, '*A.*'	Dt.27.16
"*A.*, *A.*," lifting up their hands	Neh.8.6
let all the people say, "*A.*!"	Ps.106.48
power and the glory, for ever. *A.*	Mt.6.13
Jesus Christ be with you all. *A.*	Rom.16.24
say the "*A.*" to your thanksgiving	1 Cor.14.16
write: 'The words of the *A.*	Rev.3.14

ANANIAS

(1) (and Sapphira), their lie and death, Acts 5.1–10; (2) (disciple), sent to Paul at Damascus, Acts 9.10; 22.12; (3) (high priest), Paul brought before, Acts 22.30; rebuked by Paul, Acts 23.3

ANDREW

the Apostle, Mt.4.18; Mk.1.29; 13.3; Jn.1.40; 6.8; 12.22; Acts 1.13

ANEW

I say to you, unless one is born *a.*	Jn.3.3
I said to you, 'You must be born *a.*'	Jn.3.7
have been born *a.* to a living hope	1 Pet.1.3
You have been born *a.*	1 Pet.1.23

ANGEL

The *a.* of the LORD found her by a	Gen.16.7
the ass saw the *a.* of the LORD	Num.22.25
God sent the *a.* to Jerusalem to	1 Chr.21.15
The *a.* of the LORD encamps around	Ps.34.7
the *a.* of his presence saved	Is.63.9
God sent his *a.* and shut the lions'	Dan.6.22
He strove with the *a.* and prevailed	Hos.12.4
He will give his *a.* charge of you	Mt.4.6
the reapers are *a.*	Mt.13.39
more than twelve legions of *a.*?	Mt.26.53
the *a.* said to the women, "Do not be	Mt.28.5
And Mary said to the *a.*	Lk.1.34
an *a.* of the Lord appeared to them	Lk.2.9
suddenly there was with the *a.*	Lk.2.13
a. of God ascending and descending	Jn.1.51
But at night an *a.* of the Lord	Acts 5.19
his face was like the face of an *a.*	Acts 6.15
nor *a.*, nor principalities	Rom.8.38
not know that we are to judge *a.*?	1 Cor.6.3
in the tongues of men and of *a.*	1 Cor.13.1
Satan disguises himself as an *a.*	2 Cor.11.14
but received me as an *a.* of God	Gal.4.14
some have entertained *a.* unawares	Heb.13.2
the *a.* that did not keep their own	Jude 6
To the *a.* of the church in Ephesus	Rev.2.1
sent his *a.* to show his servants	Rev.22.6

ANGER

Cursed be their *a.*, for it is fierce	Gen.49.7
Then the *a.* of the LORD was kindled	Ex.4.14

The LORD is slow to *a.*	Num.14.18
thou art a God . . . slow to *a.*	Neh.9.17
O LORD, rebuke me not in thy *a.*	Ps.6.1
Turn not thy servant away in *a.*	Ps.27.9
For his *a.* is but for a moment	Ps.30.5
For we are consumed by thy *a.*	Ps.90.7
The LORD is . . . slow to *a.*	Ps.145.8
but a harsh word stirs up *a.*	Pr.15.1
Be not quick to *a.*	Ec.7.9
not in thy *a.*, lest thou bring me	Jer.10.24
repent and turn from his fierce *a.*	Jon.3.9
not let the sun go down on your *a.*	Eph.4.26
do not provoke your children to *a.*	Eph.6.4
slow to speak, slow to *a.*	Jas.1.19

ANGRY

Be *a.*, but sin not; commune with your	Ps.4.4
Wilt thou be *a.* with us for ever?	Ps.85.5
one who is *a.* with his brother	Mt.5.22
Now Herod was *a.* with the people	Acts 12.20
Be *a.* but do not sin; do not let	Eph.4.26

ANGUISH

will speak in the *a.* of my spirit	Job 7.11
Trouble and *a.* have come upon me	Ps.119.143
when distress and *a.* come upon you	Pr.1.27
When *a.* comes, they will seek peace	Ezek.7.25
for I am in *a.* in this flame	Lk.16.24
and unceasing *a.* in my heart	Rom.9.2
men gnawed their tongues in *a.*	Rev.16.10

ANIMAL

seven pairs of all clean *a.*	Gen.7.2
Noah . . . took of every clean *a.*	Gen.8.20
When you offer blind *a.* in sacrifice	Mal.1.8
all kinds of *a.* and reptiles and	Acts 10.12
the bodies of those *a.* whose blood	Heb.13.11
But these, like irrational *a.*	2 Pet.2.12
know by instinct as irrational *a.*	Jude 10

ANOINT

you shall *a.* Aaron and his sons	Ex.30.30
you shall not *a.* yourself with the	Dt.28.40
Wash therefore and *a.* yourself	Ru.3.3
thou *a.* my head with oil, my cup	Ps.23.5
look upon the face of thine *a.*	Ps.84.9
the LORD has *a.* me to bring good	Is.61.1
a. themselves with the finest oils	Am.6.6
a. your head and wash your face	Mt.6.17
You did not *a.* my head with oil	Lk.7.46
servant Jesus, whom thou didst *a.*	Acts 4.27
has *a.* thee with the oil of gladness	Heb.1.9

ANSWER (noun)

A soft *a.* turns away wrath, but a	Pr.15.1
a. of the tongue is from the LORD	Pr.16.1
If one gives *a.* before he hears, it	Pr.18.13
for there is no *a.* from God	Mic.3.7
were amazed at . . . his *a.*	Lk.2.47
granted us in *a.* to many prayers	2 Cor.1.11

ANSWER (verb)

he will *a.* him from his holy heaven	Ps.20.6
I cry by day, but thou dost not *a.*	Ps.22.2
When he calls to me, I will *a.* him	Ps.91.15
the LORD *a.* me and set me free	Ps.118.5
A. not a fool according to his folly	Pr.26.4
no one was able to *a.* him a word	Mt.22.46
Then the righteous will *a.* him	Mt.25.37
what you are to *a.* or what you are	Lk.12.11
to meditate beforehand how to *a.*	Lk.21.14
who are you . . . to *a.* back to God?	Rom.9.20

may be able to *a.* those who pride | 2 Cor.5.12
know how you ought to *a.* every one | Col.4.6

ANT
Go to the *a.*, O sluggard | Pr.6.6
the *a.* are a people not strong | Pr.30.25

ANTICHRIST
you have heard that *a.* is coming | 1 Jn.2.18
This is the *a.*, he who denies the | 1 Jn.2.22
This is the spirit of *a.* | 1 Jn.4.3
such a one is the deceiver and the *a.* | 2 Jn.7

ANTIOCH
(1) capital of Syria; disciples first called Christians at, Acts 11.26; Barnabas and Saul called to apostleship at, Acts 13.1–3; Paul withstands Cephas (Peter) at, Gal.2.11; (2) (Pisidia) Paul's first address at, Acts 13.14–41; Paul and Barnabas persecuted at, Acts 13.50

ANXIETY
A. in a man's heart weighs him down | Pr.12.25
in this tent, we sigh with *a.* | 2 Cor.5.4
of my *a.* for all the churches | 2 Cor.11.28
Have no *a.* about anything, but in | Phil.4.6

ANXIOUS
eating the bread of *a.* toil | Ps.127.2
do not be *a.* about your life | Mt.6.25
do not be *a.* about tomorrow | Mt.6.34
do not be *a.* beforehand what you | Mk.13.11
which of you by being *a.* can add a | Lk.12.25
the married man is *a.* about worldly | 1 Cor.7.33
be genuinely *a.* for your welfare | Phil.2.20

APART
LORD has set *a.* the godly for himself | Ps.4.3
I have no good *a.* from thee | Ps.16.2
set them *a.* for the day of slaughter | Jer.12.3
led them up a high mountain *a.* | Mt.17.1
for *a.* from me you can do nothing | Jn.15.5
set *a.* for the gospel of God | Rom.1.1
A. from the law sin lies dead | Rom.7.8
so faith *a.* from works is dead | Jas.2.26

APOLLOS
eloquent and well versed in the Scriptures, Acts 18.24; 19.1; 1 Cor.1.12; 3.4

APOSTLE
The names of the twelve *a.* are these | Mt.10.2
he was enrolled with the eleven *a.* | Acts 1.26
they arrested the *a.* and put them | Acts 5.18
The *a.* and the elders were gathered | Acts 15.6
they are men of note among the *a.* | Rom.16.7
For I am the least of the *a.* | 1 Cor.15.9
have made demands as *a.* of Christ | 1 Th.2.6
a. and high priest of our confession | Heb.3.1
O saints and *a.* and prophets | Rev.18.20
names of the twelve *a.* of the Lamb | Rev.21.14

APPEAR
one place, and let the dry land *a.* | Gen.1.9
I *a.* to Abraham, to Isaac, and to | Ex.6.3
None shall *a.* before me empty-handed | Ex.23.15
and who can stand when he *a.*? | Mal.3.2
outwardly *a.* righteous to men | Mt.23.28
then will *a.* the sign of the Son of | Mt.24.30
those in which I will *a.* to you | Acts 26.16
must all *a.* before the judgment | 2 Cor.5.10
you also will *a.* with him in glory | Col.3.4
Christ . . . will *a.* a second time, not | Heb.9.28
it does not yet *a.* what we shall be | 1 Jn.3.2

APPLY
A. your mind to instruction | Pr.23.12
When I *a.* my mind to know wisdom | Ec.8.16
be careful to *a.* themselves to good | Tit.3.8

APPOINT
to *a.* me as prince over Israel | 2 Sam.6.21
time which I *a.* I will judge | Ps.75.2
place which thou didst *a.* for them | Ps.104.8
And he *a.* twelve, to be with him | Mk.3.14
Collect no more than is *a.* you | Lk.3.13
I chose you and *a.* you that you | Jn.15.16
when they had *a.* elders for | Acts 14.23
the *a.* time has grown very short | 1 Cor.7.29
God has *a.* in the church first | 1 Cor.12.28
For this I was *a.* a preacher and | 1 Tim.2.7
whom he *a.* the heir of all things | Heb.1.2
the law *a.* men in their weakness | Heb.7.28

APPROVE
they not only do them but *a.* those | Rom.1.32
a. what is excellent | Rom.2.18
acceptable to God and *a.* by men | Rom.14.18
as we have been *a.* by God to be | 1 Th.2.4
present yourself to God as one *a.* | 2 Tim.2.15

AQUILA
(and Priscilla) go with Paul from Corinth to Ephesus, Acts 18.2,19; their constancy, Rom. 16.3–4; 1 Cor.16.19; Apollos instructed by, Acts 18.26

ARARAT
Gen.8.4; Is.37.38; Jer.51.27

ARIMATHEA
Mt.27.57; Mk.15.43; Lk.23.50; Jn.19.38

ARISE
though war *a.* against me, yet I will | Ps.27.3
A., O God, judge the earth | Ps.82.8
A., shine; for your light | Is.60.1
A., go to Nineveh, that great city | Jon.1.2
of Nineveh will *a.* at the judgment | Mt.12.41
or persecution *a.* on account of | Mt.13.21
Little girl, I say to you, *a.* | Mk.5.41
A great prophet has *a.* among us | Lk.7.16
I will *a.* and go to my father | Lk.15.18
a. from the dead, and Christ shall | Eph.5.14
priest to *a.* after . . . Melchizedek | Heb.7.11

ARK
Make yourself an *a.* of gopher wood | Gen.6.14
shall make an *a.* of acacia wood | Ex.25.10
bearing the *a.* of the covenant | Jos.3.14
he caused the *a.* of the LORD | Jos.6.11
And the *a.* of God was captured | 1 Sam.4.11
the priests took up the *a.* | 1 Kg.8.3
put out his hand to hold the *a.* | 1 Chr.13.9
the Levites took up the *a.* | 2 Chr.5.4
Put the holy *a.* in the house | 2 Chr.35.3
incense and the *a.* of the covenant | Heb.9.4
constructed an *a.* for the saving | Heb.11.7
during the building of the *a.* | 1 Pet.3.20

ARM (noun)
because of the greatness of thy *a.* | Ex.15.16
underneath are the everlasting *a.* | Dt.33.27
Have you an *a.* like God, and can | Job 40.9
Break thou the *a.* of the wicked | Ps.10.15
Thou didst with thy *a.* redeem thy | Ps.77.15
he will gather the lambs in his *a.* | Is.40.11
and his *a.* shall be against the | Is.48.14
to whom has the *a.* of the LORD been | Is.53.1

ARMAGEDDON

Let his *a*. be wholly withered	Zech.11.17
he took them in his *a*. and blessed	Mk.10.16
to whom has the *a*. of the Lord been	Jn.12.38
with uplifted *a*. he led them out	Acts 13.17

ARMAGEDDON

They assembled them at . . . *A*.	Rev.16.16

ARMOR

Saul clothed David with his *a*.	1 Sam.17.38
They put his *a*. in the temple of	1 Sam.31.10
put on the *a*. of light	Rom.13.12
Put on the whole *a*. of God	Eph.6.11
take the whole *a*. of God	Eph.6.13

ARMY

the God of the *a*. of Israel	1 Sam.17.45
Is there any number to his *a*.?	Job 25.3
A king is not saved by his great *a*.	Ps.33.16
not go forth, O God, with our *a*.	Ps.108.11
you see Jerusalem surrounded by *a*.	Lk.21.20
in war, put foreign *a*. to flight	Heb.11.34
the *a*. of heaven, arrayed in fine	Rev.19.14

ARRAY

Worship the LORD in holy *a*.	1 Chr.16.29
worship the LORD in holy *a*.	Ps.29.2
was not *a*. like one of these	Mt.6.29
a. him in a purple robe	Jn.19.2
The kings . . . set themselves in a *a*.	Acts 4.26

ARREST (verb)

he heard that John had been *a*.	Mt.4.12
But when they tried to *a*. him	Mt.21.46
in order to *a*. Jesus by stealth	Mt.26.4
but no one *a*. him, because his hour	Jn.8.20
they *a*. the apostles and put them	Acts 5.18
he proceeded to *a*. Peter also	Acts 12.3

ARROGANT

a. heart I will not endure	Ps.101.5
one who is *a*. is an abomination	Pr.16.5
he will punish the *a*. boasting of	Is.10.12
the *a*. man shall not abide	Hab.2.5
Some are *a*., as though I were not	1 Cor.4.18
love . . . is not *a*. or rude	1 Cor.13.5
he must not be *a*. or quick-tempered	Tit.1.7

ARTAXERXES

(1) (king of Persia), oppresses the Jews, Ezra 4; (2) (Longimanus), permits Ezra to restore the temple, Ezra 7; and Nehemiah to rebuild Jerusalem, Neh.2

ASA

begins his reign, 1 Kg.15.8; wars with Baasha, 1 Kg.15.16; his prayer against the Ethiopians, 2 Chr.14.11; his zeal, 2 Chr.15; seeks aid of the Syrians, 2 Chr.16.2–4; reproved by Hanani the seer, 2 Chr.16.7; reigns forty years, and dies much honored, 2 Chr.16.13

ASAPH

(1) a Levite, musical composer, and leader of David's choir, 1 Chr.6.39; 2 Chr.5.12; 29.30; 35.15; Neh.12.46; Psalms 50 and 73 to 83 are ascribed to him; (2) 2 Kg.18.18

ASCEND

Who shall *a*. the hill of the LORD?	Ps.24.3
If I *a*. to heaven, thou art there	Ps.139.8
Who has *a*. to heaven and come down?	Pr.30.4
angels of God *a*. and descending	Jn.1.51
No one has *a*. into heaven but he	Jn.3.13
I have not yet *a*. to the Father	Jn.20.17
When he *a*. on high he led a host	Eph.4.8

ASHAMED

were both naked, and were not *a*.	Gen.2.25
are you not *a*. to wrong me?	Job 19.3
let them be *a*. who are wantonly	Ps.25.3
so your faces shall never be *a*.	Ps.34.5
Fear not, for you will not be *a*.	Is.54.4
For whoever is *a*. of me and of my	Lk.9.26
For I am not *a*. of the gospel	Rom.1.16
I do not write this to make you *a*.	1 Cor.4.14
Do not be *a*. then of testifying to	2 Tim.1.8
I am not *a*., for I know whom I	2 Tim.1.12
workman who has no need to be *a*.	2 Tim.2.15
God is not *a*. to be called their	Heb.11.16
as a Christian, let him not be *a*.	1 Pet.4.16

ASHDOD

Jos.15.46; city of Philistines; the ark carried there; men of, smitten, 1 Sam.5; subdued by Uzziah, 2 Chr.26.6; predictions concerning, Jer.25.20; Am.1.8; Zeph.2.4; Zech.9.6

ASHER

(1) son of Jacob, Gen.30.13; his descendants, Num.1.40; 26.44; 1 Chr.7.30; their inheritance, Jos.19.24; Jg.5.17; *see* Ezek.48.34; Rev.7.6; Anna, prophetess, descended from, Lk.2.36; (2) a town, Jos.17.7

ASHES

I who am but dust and *a*.	Gen.18.27
and sat among the *a*.	Job 2.8
Your maxims are proverbs of *a*.	Job 13.12
I have become like dust and *a*.	Job 30.19
For I eat *a*. like bread, and mingle	Ps.102.9
He feeds on *a*.	Is.44.20
give them a garland instead of *a*.	Is.61.3
with fasting and sackcloth and *a*.	Dan.9.3
with sackcloth, and sat in *a*.	Jon.3.6
the *a*. of a heifer sanctifies	Heb.9.13

ASIA

in the New Testament not the continent, but a Roman province in the western part of Asia Minor (including the cities Ephesus, Smyrna, Pergamum, Thyatira, Sardis, Philadelphia, and Laodicea Rev.2–3), Acts 2.9; 16.6; 19.26; Rom.16.5

ASLEEP

Your shepherds are *a*., O king	Nah.3.18
in the stern, *a*. on the cushion	Mk.4.38
said to Peter, "Simon, are you *a*.?	Mk.14.37
and as they sailed he fell *a*.	Lk.8.23
Our friend Lazarus has fallen *a*.	Jn.11.11
though some have fallen *a*.	1 Cor.15.6
precede those who have fallen *a*.	1 Th.4.15
For ever since the fathers fell *a*.	2 Pet.3.4

ASS

enemy's ox or his *a*. going astray	Ex.23.4
When the *a*. saw the angel	Num.22.27
plow with an ox and an *a*. together	Dt.22.10
he found a fresh jawbone of an *a*.	Jg.15.15
the wild *a*. quench their thirst	Ps.104.11
whip for the horse, a bridle for the *a*.	Pr.26.3
and the *a*. its master's crib	Is.1.3
burial of an *a*. he shall be buried	Jer.22.19
Be like a wild *a*. in the desert	Jer.48.6
he, humble and riding on an *a*.	Zech.9.9
having an *a*. or an ox that has	Lk.14.5
found a young *a*. and sat upon it	Jn.12.14

ASSEMBLE

A. the people, men, women, and	Dt.31.12
A., all of you, and hear	Is.48.14
I will *a.* the lame and gather	Mic.4.6
when you *a.* as a church, I hear	1 Cor.11.18
to *a.* them for battle on the great	Rev.16.14

ASSEMBLY

when the whole *a.* of the congregation	Ex.12.6
Sanctify a solemn *a.* for Baal	2 Kg.10.20
Solomon and the *a.* sought the LORD	2 Chr.1.5
And all the *a.* said "Amen"	Neh.5.13
praise him in the *a.* of the elders	Ps.107.32
Sanctify a fast, call a solemn *a.*	Jl.1.14
I take no delight in your solemn *a.*	Am.5.21
it has seemed good to us in *a.* to	Acts 15.25
to the *a.* of the first-born who	Heb.12.23
in fine clothing comes into your *a.*	Jas.2.2

ASSURANCE

he has given *a.* to all men by	Acts 17.31
the full *a.* of hope until the end	Heb.6.11
a true heart in full *a.* of faith	Heb.10.22
Now faith is the *a.* of things hoped	Heb.11.1

ASTONISHED

As many were *a.* at him	Is.52.14
the crowds were *a.* at his teaching	Mt.7.28
And they were *a.* beyond measure	Mk.7.37
all were *a.* at the majesty of God	Lk.9.43
for he was *a.* at the teaching of	Acts 13.12
I am *a.* that you are so quickly	Gal.1.6

ASTRAY

They have all gone *a.*, they are	Ps.14.3
The wicked go *a.* from the womb	Ps.58.3
I have gone *a.* like a lost sheep	Ps.119.176
and your knowledge led you *a.*	Is.47.10
All we like sheep have gone *a.*	Is.53.6
their shepherds have led them *a.*	Jer.50.6
going *a.* from me after their idols	Ezek.44.10
sheep, and one of them has gone *a.*	Mt.18.12
Take heed that no one leads you *a.*	Mk.13.5
to lead *a.*, if possible, the elect	Mk.13.22
No, he is leading the people *a.*	Jn.7.12
led *a.*, slaves to various passions	Tit.3.3
They always go *a.* in their hearts	Heb.3.10

ASUNDER

I was at ease, and he broke me *a.*	Job 16.12
Let us burst their bonds *a.*	Ps.2.3
joined together, let no man put *a.*	Mt.19.6

ATHENS

Acts 17.15,16,22; 18.1; 1 Th.3.1

ATONEMENT

Aaron shall make *a.* upon its horns	Ex.30.10
the priest shall make *a.* for them	Lev.4.20
make *a.* for him before the LORD	Lev.14.29
seventh month is the day of *a.*	Lev.23.27
shall they make *a.* for the altar	Ezek.43.26
make *a.* for the house of Israel	Ezek.45.17

ATTACK (verb)

those who *a.* me with lies	Ps.69.4
the king of the south shall *a.*	Dan.11.40
a worm which *a.* the plant	Jon.4.7
no man shall *a.* you to harm you	Acts 18.10

ATTAIN

it is high, I cannot *a.* it	Ps.139.6
until we all *a.* to the unity of the	Eph.4.13
if possible . . . *a.* the resurrection	Phil.3.11
hold true to what we have *a.*	Phil.3.16

ATTENTION

O foolish men, pay *a.*	Pr.8.5
Gallio paid no *a.* to this	Acts 18.17
pay the closer *a.* to what we have	Heb.2.1
do well to pay *a.* to this as to	2 Pet.1.19

AUTHORITY

When the wicked are in *a.*	Pr.29.16
he taught them as one who had *a.*	Mt.7.29
All *a.* in heaven and on earth has	Mt.28.18
the Son of man has *a.* . . . to forgive sins	Mk.2.10
For I am a man set under *a.*	Lk.7.8
Tell us by what *a.* you do these	Lk.20.2
I can do nothing on my own *a.*	Jn.5.30
For I have not spoken on my own *a.*	Jn.12.49
let the men of *a.* among you go	Acts 25.5
For there is no *a.* except from God	Rom.13.1
Do I say this on human *a.*?	1 Cor.9.8
exhort and reprove with all *a.*	Tit.2.15
our God and the *a.* of his Christ	Rev.12.10

AVENGE

If Cain is *a.* sevenfold, truly	Gen.4.24
for he *a.* the blood of his servants	Dt.32.43
said, "May the LORD see and *a.*!"	2 Chr.24.22
he . . . *a.* him by striking the Egyptian	Acts 7.24
Beloved, never *a.* yourselves, but	Rom.12.19
thou wilt judge and *a.* our blood	Rev.6.10

AVOID

not only to *a.* God's wrath but also	Rom.13.5
A. the godless chatter and	1 Tim.6.20
A. such people	2 Tim.3.5
to *a.* quarreling, to be gentle	Tit.3.2
But *a.* stupid controversies, genealogies	Tit.3.9

AWAKE

a., O my God; thou hast appointed	Ps.7.6
A., my soul! *A.*, O harp and lyre	Ps.57.8
When I *a.*, I am still with thee	Ps.139.18
I slept, but my heart was *a.*	S.of S.5.2
A., *a.*, put on strength, O arm of	Is.51.9
who says to a wooden thing, *A.*	Hab.2.19
A., O sleeper, and arise from the	Eph.5.14
but let us keep *a.* and be sober	1 Th.5.6
A., and strengthen what remains	Rev.3.2
Blessed is he who is *a.*, keeping	Rev.16.15

AWE

as they had stood in *a.* of Moses	Jos.4.14
stand in *a.* of him, all you sons	Ps.22.23
let . . . the world stand in *a.* of him	Ps.33.8
stand in *a.* of the God of Israel	Is.29.23
the disciples . . . were filled with *a.*	Mt.17.6
not become proud, but stand in *a.*	Rom.11.20
worship, with reverence and *a.*	Heb.12.28

AXE

Abimelech took an *a.* in his hand	Jg.9.48
his *a.* head fell into the water	2 Kg.6.5
Shall the *a.* vaunt itself over him	Is.10.15
Even now the *a.* is laid to the root	Lk.3.9

AZARIAH

(1) (also called Uzziah) king of Judah, his good reign, 2 Kg.14.21; 2 Chr.26.4; his wars, 2 Chr.26.6; stricken with leprosy, 2 Kg.15.5; 2 Chr.26.20; (2) prophet, exhorts Asa, 2 Chr. 15; (3) a priest, 2 Chr. 26.17

BAAL

Israel yoked himself to *B.* of Peor	Num.25.3
the altar of *B.* which your father	Jg.6.25

saying, "O *B.*, answer us!" 1 Kg.18.26
Sanctify a solemn assembly for *B.* 2 Kg.10.20
no longer will you call me, 'My *B.*' Hos.2.16
who have not bowed the knee to *B.* Rom.11.4

BABE
by the mouth of *b.* and infants Ps.8.2
understanding and revealed them to *b.* Mt.11.25
the *b.* in my womb leaped for joy Lk.1.44
you will find a *b.* wrapped in Lk.2.12
men of the flesh, as *b.* in Christ 1 Cor.3.1
be *b.* in evil, but in thinking 1 Cor.14.20
Like newborn *b.*, long for the pure 1 Pet.2.2

BABEL
Nimrod king of, Gen.10.10; confusion of tongues at tower of, Gen.11.9

BABYLON
(1) the capital of the Babylonian Empire; ambassadors from, to Hezekiah, 2 Kg.20.12; 2 Chr.32.31; Is.39; Jewish captivity there, 2 Kg.25; 2 Chr.36; Jer.39; 52; return from, Ezra 1; Neh.2; greatness of, Dan.4.30; taken by the Medes, Dan.5.30; fall of, Is.13.14; 21.2; 47; Jer.25.12; 50; 51; church in, 1 Pet.5.13; (2) the great, Rev.14.8; 17.1–18.24

BAD
It is *b.*, it is *b.*," says the buyer Pr.20.14
and the *b.* figs very *b.*, so *b.* that Jer.24.3
make the tree *b.*, and its fruit *b.* Mt.12.33
For no good tree bears *b.* fruit Lk.6.43
B. company ruins good morals 1 Cor.15.33
will go on from *b.* to worse 2 Tim.3.13

BALAAM
requested by Balak to curse Israel, is forbidden, Num.22.5,13; his anger, Num.22.27; blesses Israel, Num.23.19; 24; his prophecies, Num. 23.9,24; 24.17; his wicked counsel, Num. 31.16; Dt.23.4; *see* Jos.24.9; Jg.11.25; Mic. 6.5; 2 Pet.2.15; Jude 11; Rev.2.14; slain, Num.31.8; Jos.13.22

BALANCE
A false *b.* is an abomination to the Pr.11.1
A just *b.* and scales are the LORD's Pr.16.11
weighed . . . the hills in a *b.*? Is.40.12
weighed in the *b.* and found wanting Dan.5.27
and its rider had a *b.* in his hand Rev.6.5

BALM
a little *b.* and a little honey Gen.43.11
Is there no *b.* in Gilead? Jer.8.22
Take *b.* for her pain; perhaps Jer.51.8
early figs, honey, oil, and *b.* Ezek.27.17

BANQUET
it was Esther's *b.* Est.2.18
Herod on his birthday gave a *b.* Mk.6.21
When you give a dinner or a *b.* Lk.14.12
none . . . invited shall taste my *b.* Lk.14.24

BAPTISM
he saw many . . . coming for *b.* Mt.3.7
The *b.* of John, whence was it? Mt.21.25
preaching a *b.* of repentance for Mk.1.4
the *b.* with which I am baptized Mk.10.38
Was the *b.* of John from heaven or Lk.20.4
beginning from the *b.* of John Acts 1.22
preached a *b.* of repentance to Acts 13.24
They said, "Into John's *b.*" Acts 19.3
baptized with the *b.* of repentance Acts 19.4
buried therefore with him by *b.* Rom.6.4

one Lord, one faith, one *b.* Eph.4.5
you were buried with him in *b.* Col.2.12
B., which corresponds to this 1 Pet.3.21

BAPTIZE
I *b.* you with water for repentance Mt.3.11
b. them in the name of the Father Mt.28.19
able . . . to be *b.* with the baptism Mk.10.38
he will *b.* you with the Holy Spirit Lk.3.16
who sent me to *b.* with water Jn.1.33
although Jesus himself did not *b.* Jn.4.2
be *b.* every one of you in the Acts 2.38
they were *b.*, both men and women Acts 8.12
had only been *b.* in the name of Acts 8.16
hearing Paul believed and were *b.* Acts 18.8
Rise and be *b.*, and wash away Acts 22.16
who have been *b.* into Christ Jesus Rom.6.3
not send me to *b.* but to preach 1 Cor.1.17
all were *b.* into Moses in the 1 Cor.10.2
we were all *b.* into one body 1 Cor.12.13
b. on behalf of the dead? 1 Cor.15.29

BARABBAS
a robber, released instead of Jesus, Mt.27.16; Mk.15.6,7; Lk.23.18; Jn.18.40

BARAK
Jg.4.6–5.15; Heb.11.32

BARE
foundations . . . were laid *b.* Ps.18.15
LORD will lay *b.* their secret parts Is.3.17
I will make you a *b.* rock Ezek.26.14
a *b.* kernel, perhaps of wheat or 1 Cor.15.37

BARN
Is the seed yet in the *b.*? Hag.2.19
but gather the wheat into my *b.* Mt.13.30
I will pull down my *b.* Lk.12.18
have neither storehouse nor *b.* Lk.12.24

BARNABAS
Levite of Cyprus, Acts 4.36; preaches at Antioch, Acts 11.22; accompanies Paul, Acts 11.30; 12.25; 13; 14; 15; 1 Cor.9.6; disagrees with Paul about John Mark, Acts 15.36–40; is misled at Antioch by Judaizing emissaries from Jerusalem, Gal.2.13

BARREN
Now Sarai was *b.*; she had no child Gen.11.30
The *b.* has borne seven, but she 1 Sam.2.5
He gives the *b.* woman a home Ps.113.9
Sing, O *b.* one, who did not bear Is.54.1
no child, because Elizabeth was *b.* Lk.1.7
they will say, 'Blessed are the *b.* Lk.23.26
O *b.* one that dost not bear Gal.4.27
that faith apart from works is *b.*? Jas.2.20

BARTHOLOMEW
Mt.10.3; Mk.3.18; Lk.6.14; Acts 1.13

BARUCH
receives Jeremiah's evidence, Jer.32.12–13; 36; discredited by Azariah, and carried into Egypt, Jer.43.2–6; God's message to, Jer.45

BASE (adjective)
b. fellows, beset the house round Jg.19.22
the wicked and *b.* fellows among 1 Sam.30.22
before my eyes anything that is *b.* Ps.101.3
the *b.* fellow to the honorable Is.3.5
God gave them up to a *b.* mind Rom.1.28
dissension, slander, *b.* suspicions 1 Tim.6.4
by teaching for *b.* gain what they Tit.1.11

BASKET

eating it out of the *b.* on my head — Gen.40.17
took for him a *b.* made of bulrushes — Ex.2.3
One *b.* had very good figs — Jer.24.2
A *b.* of summer fruit — Am.8.2
they took up twelve *b.* full of the — Mt.14.20
pieces left over, seven *b.* full — Mk.8.8
the wall, lowering him in a *b.* — Acts 9.25
let down in a *b.* through a window — 2 Cor.11.33

BATHSHEBA

wife of Uriah, taken by David, 2 Sam.11; 12;
appeals to David for Solomon against Adonijah,
1 Kg.1.15; intercedes with Solomon for Adonijah, 1 Kg.2.19

BATTLE (noun)

for the *b.* is the LORD's and he — 1 Sam.17.47
the *b.* is not yours but God's — 2 Chr.20.15
He smells the *b.* from afar — Job 39.25
gird me with strength for the *b.* — Ps.18.39
in safety from the *b.* that I wage — Ps.55.18
covered my head in the day of *b.* — Ps.140.7
nor the *b.* to the strong, nor bread — Ec.9.11
The noise of *b.* is in the land — Jer.50.22
locusts were like horses arrayed for *b.* — Rev.9.7

BEACH

the whole crowd stood on the *b.* — Mt.13.2
Jesus stood on the *b.* — Jn.21.4
kneeling down on the *b.* we prayed — Acts 21.5
they noticed a bay with a *b.* — Acts 27.39

BEAR (noun)

lion and from the paw of the *b.* — 1 Sam.17.37
two she-*b.* came out of the woods — 2 Kg.2.24
who made the *B.* and Orion — Job 9.9
Let a man meet a she-*b.* robbed — Pr.17.12
The cow and the *b.* shall feed — Is.11.7
fled from a lion, and a *b.* met him — Am.5.19

BEAR (verb)

punishment is greater than I can *b.* — Gen.4.13
then let me *b.* the blame for ever — Gen.43.9
You shall not *b.* false witness — Ex.20.16
curses his God shall *b.* his sin — Lev.24.15
I am not able alone to *b.* you — Dt.1.9
Blessed be the Lord, who daily *b.* us up — Ps.68.19
On their hands they will *b.* you up — Ps.91.12
you who *b.* the vessels of the LORD — Is.52.11
he shall *b.* their iniquities — Is.53.11
good . . . that he *b.* the yoke in his — Lam.3.27
On their hands they will *b.* you up — Mt.4.6
You shall not *b.* false witness — Mt.19.18
How long am I to *b.* with you? — Mk.9.19
B. fruits that befit repentance — Lk.3.8
but came to *b.* witness to the light — Jn.1.8
Even if I do *b.* witness to myself — Jn.8.14
Every branch of mine that *b.* no fruit — Jn.15.2
that we may *b.* fruit for God — Rom.7.4
Spirit himself *b.* witness with our — Rom.8.16
strong ought to *b.* with the failings — Rom.15.1
Love *b.* all things, believes all — 1 Cor.13.7
B. one another's burdens, and so — Gal.6.2
each man will have to *b.* his own load — Gal.6.5
I *b.* on my body the marks of Jesus — Gal.6.17
offered once to *b.* the sins of many — Heb.9.28

BEAST

And God made the *b.* of the earth — Gen.1.25
formed every *b.* of the field and — Gen.2.19
the likeness of any *b.* that is on — Dt.4.17

For every *b.* of the forest is mine — Ps.50.10
has regard for the life of his *b.* — Pr.12.10
the spirit of the *b.* goes down to — Ec.3.21
four great *b.* came up out of — Dan.7.3
I fought with *b.* at Ephesus? — 1 Cor.15.32
every kind of *b.* . . . . can be tamed — Jas.3.7
I saw a *b.* rising out of the sea — Rev.13.1

BEAT

B. your plowshares into swords — Jl.3.10
shall *b.* their swords into plowshares — Mic.4.3
winds blew and *b.* upon that house — Mt.7.25
the waves *b.* into the boat — Mk.4.37
some they *b.* and some they killed — Mk.12.5
who stripped him and *b.* him — Lk.10.30
but *b.* his breast, saying, 'God, be — Lk.18.13
have *b.* us publicly, uncondemned — Acts 16.37
I do not box as one *b.* the air — 1 Cor.9.26
Three times . . . *b.* with rods — 2 Cor.11.25
wrong and are *b.* for it you take — 1 Pet.2.20

BEAUTIFUL

but Rachel was *b.* and lovely — Gen.29.17
Let *b.* young virgins be sought out — Est.2.2
b. in elevation, is the joy of all — Ps.48.2
a *b.* woman without discretion — Pr.11.22
has made everything *b.* in its time — Ec.3.11
the branch of the LORD shall be *b.* — Is.4.2
How *b.* upon the mountains are the — Is.52.7
tombs, which outwardly appear *b.* — Mt.23.27
alms at the *B.* Gate of the temple — Acts 3.10
How *b.* are the feet of those who — Rom.10.15

BEAUTY

to behold the *b.* of the LORD, and to — Ps.27.4
Out of Zion, the perfection of *b.* — Ps.50.2
strength and *b.* are in his sanctuary — Ps.96.6
Charm is deceitful and *b.* is vain — Pr.31.30
Your eyes will see the king in his *b.* — Is.33.17
and no *b.* that we should desire him — Is.53.2
to make . . . one vessel for *b.* — Rom.9.21
flower falls, and its *b.* perishes — Jas.1.11

BED

My *b.* will comfort me, my couch — Job 7.13
chastened with pain upon his *b.* — Job 33.19
every night I flood my *b.* with tears — Ps.6.6
when I think of thee upon my *b.* — Ps.63.6
If I make my *b.* in Sheol, thou art — Ps.139.8
so does a sluggard on his *b.* — Pr.26.14
For the *b.* is too short to stretch — Is.28.20
Woe to those who lie upon *b.* of ivory — Am.6.4
Rise, take up your *b.* and go home — Mt.9.6
a vessel, or puts it under a *b.* — Lk.8.16
there will be two men in one *b.* — Lk.17.34
let the marriage *b.* be undefiled — Heb.13.4

BEELZEBUL

called the master of the house *B.* — Mt.10.25
said, "He is possessed by *B.* — Mk.3.22
And if I cast out demons by *B.* — Lk.11.19

BEFALL

Does not calamity *b.* the unrighteous — Job 31.3
no evil shall *b.* you — Ps.91.10
that nothing worse *b.* you — Jn.5.14
knowing all that was to *b.* him — Jn.18.4
not knowing what shall *b.* me — Acts 20.22

BEFIT

Praise *b.* the upright — Ps.33.1
Bear fruits that *b.* repentance — Lk.3.8
as *b.* women who profess religion — 1 Tim.2.10

teach what *b.* sound doctrine   Tit.2.1
their journey as *b.* God's service   3 Jn.6

BEG
May his children wander . . . and *b.*   Ps.109.10
the children *b.* for food, but no one   Lam.4.4
Give to him who *b.* from you   Mt.5.42
I am ashamed to *b.*   Lk.16.3
the man who used to sit and *b.?*   Jn.9.8
So I *b.* you to reaffirm your love   2 Cor.2.8
I . . . *b.* you to lead a life worthy of   Eph.4.1

BEGINNING (noun)
In the *b.* God created the heavens   Gen.1.1
And though your *b.* was small   Job 8.7
fear of the Lord . . . *b.* of wisdom   Ps.111.10
fear of the Lord is the *b.* of knowledge   Pr.1.7
The *b.* of wisdom is this: Get wisdom   Pr.4.7
Better is the end of a thing than its *b.*   Ec.7.8
but from the *b.* it was not so   Mt.19.8
The *b.* of the gospel of Jesus Christ   Mk.1.1
In the *b.* was the Word, and the Word   Jn.1.1
He was a murderer from the *b.*   Jn.8.44
he is the *b.,* the first-born from   Col.1.18
neither *b.* of days nor end of life   Heb.7.3
That which was from the *b.*   1 Jn.1.1
the devil has sinned from the *b.*   1 Jn.3.8
the Amen . . . the *b.* of God's creation   Rev.3.14
I am . . . the *b.* and the end   Rev.21.6

BEHAVIOR
who were ashamed of your lewd *b.*   Ezek.16.27
how . . . blameless was our *b.* to you   1 Th.2.10
women likewise to be reverent in *b.*   Tit.2.3
your good *b.* in Christ may be put   1 Pet.3.16

BEHEADED
they . . . slew him, and *b.* him   2 Sam.4.7
He went and *b.* him in the prison   Mk.6.27
who had been *b.* for their testimony   Rev.20.4

BEHELD
they *b.* God, and ate and drank   Ex.24.11
Thy eyes *b.* my unformed substance   Ps.139.16
Then I *b.,* and, lo, a form that had   Ezek.8.2
whenever the unclean spirits *b.* him   Mk.3.11
we have *b.* his glory, glory as of   Jn.1.14

BEHIND
But Lot's wife *b.* him looked back   Gen.19.26
b. him was a ram, caught in a   Gen.22.13
Thou dost beset me *b.* and before   Ps.139.5
I heard *b.* me the sound of a great   Ezek.3.12
said to Peter, "Get *b.* me, Satan   Mt.16.23
came up *b.* him, and touched the   Lk.8.44
the cross, to carry it *b.* Jesus   Lk.23.26
forgetting what lies *b.*   Phil.3.13
I heard *b.* me a loud voice like   Rev.1.10

BEING (noun)
and man became a living *b.*   Gen.2.7
desirest truth in the inward *b.*   Ps.51.6
praises to my God while I have *b.*   Ps.146.2
so that no human *b.* might boast   1 Cor.1.29
in bondage to *b.* that by nature are   Gal.4.8
but no human *b.* can tame the tongue   Jas.3.8

BELIEVE
they will not *b.* me or listen to my   Ex.4.1
If they will not *b.* you   Ex.4.8
I *b.* that I shall see the goodness   Ps.27.13
Who has *b.* what we have heard?   Is.53.1
Do you *b.* that I am able to do this?   Mt.9.28
repent, and *b.* in the gospel   Mk.1.15

synagogue, "Do not fear, only *b.*"   Mk.5.36
All things are possible to him who *b.*   Mk.9.23
b. that you receive it, and you will   Mk.11.24
the cross, that we may see and *b.*   Mk.15.32
that they may not *b.* and be saved   Lk.8.12
that all might *b.* through him   Jn.1.7
that whoever *b.* in him should not   Jn.3.16
He who *b.* in the Son has eternal   Jn.3.36
Unless you see . . . you will not *b.*   Jn.4.48
The Jews did not *b.* that he had   Jn.9.18
shall never die. Do you *b.* this?   Jn.11.26
b. in the light, that you may become   Jn.12.36
b. in God, *b.* also in me   Jn.14.1
B. me that I am in the Father and   Jn.14.11
we *b.* that you came from God   Jn.16.30
hear the word of the gospel and *b.*   Acts 15.7
B. in the Lord Jesus, and you   Acts 16.31
to us who *b.* in him that raised   Rom.4.24
we preach to save those who *b.*   1 Cor.1.21
Love bears all things, *b.* all things   1 Cor.13.7
since we *b.* that Jesus died and   1 Th.4.14
to God must *b.* that he exists and   Heb.11.6
Even the demons *b.*–and shudder   Jas.2.19
Abraham *b.* God, and it was reckoned   Jas.2.23

BELLY
upon your *b.* you shall go, and dust   Gen.3.14
was in the *b.* of the fish three   Jon.1.17
out of the *b.* of Sheol I cried   Jon.2.2
nights in the *b.* of the whale   Mt.12.40
destruction, their god is the *b.*   Phil.3.19

BELONG
I heard this: that power *b.* to God   Ps.62.11
for to thee *b.* all the nations   Ps.82.8
but the victory *b.* to the Lord   Pr.21.31
to the Lord our God *b.* mercy and   Dan.9.9
Deliverance *b.* to the Lord   Jon.2.9
are called to *b.* to Jesus Christ   Rom.1.6
of Christ does not *b.* to him   Rom.8.9
"I *b.* to Paul," or "I *b.* to Apollos   1 Cor.1.12
I do not *b.* to the body," that   1 Cor.12.15
To him *b.* glory and dominion for   1 Pet.4.11
and glory and power *b.* to our God   Rev.19.1

BELOVED
for he gives to his *b.* sleep   Ps.127.2
This is my *b.* Son, with whom I am   Mt.17.5
from heaven, "Thou art my *b.* Son   Mk.1.11
I will send my *b.* son; it may be   Lk.20.13
he freely bestowed on us in the *B.*   Eph.1.6
Luke the *b.* physician and Demas   Col.4.14
This is my *b.* Son, with whom I am   2 Pet.1.17
B., I am writing you no new   1 Jn.2.7
B., let us love one another   1 Jn.4.7

BELSHAZZAR
Dan.5.1,22,30; 7.1; 8.1

BELTESHAZZAR
Dan.1.7; 4.9,19; 5.12; 10.1

BENEFIT
soul, and forget not all his *b.*   Ps.103.2
A man who is kind *b.* himself   Pr.11.17
I say this for your own *b.*   1 Cor.7.35
since those who *b.* by their   1 Tim.6.2
want some *b.* from you in the Lord   Philem. 20

BENHADAD
Kings of Syria: (1) in league with Asa against
Baasha, 1 Kg.15.18; (2) wars with Ahab, 1
Kg.20; baffled by Elisha, 2 Kg.6.8–10; besieges

Samaria, 2 Kg.6.24; 7; slain by Hazael, 2 Kg.8.7–15; (3) son of Hazael, wars with Israel, 2 Kg.13.3,25

BENJAMIN
Patriarch, youngest son of Jacob, his birth at Bethlehem, Gen.35.16,18; goes into Egypt, Gen.43.15; Joseph's stratagem to detain, Gen. 44; Jacob's prophecy concerning, Gen.49.27; his descendants, Gen.46.21; 1 Chr.7.6; twice numbered, Num.1.36; 26.38; blessed by Moses, Dt.33.12; their inheritance, Jos.18.11; their wickedness chastised, Jg.20; 21; the first king chosen from, 1 Sam.9; 10; support the house of Saul, 2 Sam.2.9; afterwards adhere to that of David, 1 Kg.12.21; 1 Chr.11; the tribe of Paul, Phil.3.5

BEREFT
the woman was *b.* of her two sons   Ru.1.5
my soul is *b.* of peace   Lam.3.17
But since we were *b.* of you   1 Th.2.17
depraved . . . and *b.* of the truth   1 Tim.6.5

BESEECH
Save us, we *b.* thee, O Lord   Ps.118.25
O Lord GOD, forgive, I *b.* thee   Am.7.2
I *b.* you, do not torment me   Lk.8.28
We *b.* you on behalf of Christ   2 Cor.5.20
I *b.* you as aliens and exiles   1 Pet.2.11

BESTOW
that he may *b.* a blessing upon you   Ex.32.29
majesty thou dost *b.* upon him   Ps.21.5
the LORD God . . . *b.* favor and honor   Ps.84.11
the gifts *b.* on us by God   1 Cor.2.12
he freely *b.* on us in the Beloved   Eph.1.6
exalted him and *b.* on him the name   Phil.2.9

BETHANY
lies on the eastern shoulder of the Mount of Olives, little more than a mile east of Jerusalem; visited by Christ, Mt.21.17; 26.6; Mk.11.1; Lk.19.29; Jn.12.1; raising of Lazarus at, Jn.11.18; ascension of Christ at, Lk.24.50

BETHEL
city of Palestine, formerly Luz, named Bethel by Jacob, Gen.28.19; 31.13; eight miles north of Jerusalem; altar built by Jacob at, Gen.35.1; occupied by the house of Joseph, Jg.1.22; sons of prophets resident there, 2 Kg.2.2,3; 17.28; the king's sanctuary, Am.7.13; idolatry of Jeroboam at, 1 Kg.12.28–33; 13.1–32; reformation by Josiah at, 2 Kg.23.15–25

BETHLEHEM
about five miles south of Jerusalem; it is also called Ephrath (Gen.35.19) and Ephrathah (Mic.5.2) to distinguish it from the northern city of the same name (Jos.19.15); Naomi and Ruth return to, Ru.1–4; David anointed at, 1 Sam. 16.13; 20.6; well of, 2 Sam.23.15; 1 Chr.11.17; Christ's birth at, Mt.2.1; Lk.2.4; Jn.7.42; predicted, Mic.5.2; male children of, slain, Mt.2.16

BETHSAIDA
native place of Philip, Peter, and Andrew, Mk.6.45; Jn.1.44; 12.21; blind man cured at, Mk.8.22; condemned for unbelief, Mt.11.21; Christ feeds the five thousand at, Lk.9.10–17

BETRAY
b. one another, and hate one   Mt.24.10

of them, for your accent *b.* you   Mt.26.73
I have sinned in *b.* innocent blood   Mt.27.4
I say to you, one of you will *b.* me   Mk.14.18
you *b.* the Son of man with a kiss?   Lk.22.48
For he knew who was to *b.* him   Jn.13.11
whom you have now *b.* and murdered   Acts 7.52
on the night when he was *b.*   1 Cor.11.23

BETTER
to obey is *b.* than sacrifice   1 Sam.15.22
B. is a little that the righteous has   Ps.37.16
a day in thy courts is *b.* than   Ps.84.10
It is *b.* to take refuge in the LORD   Ps.118.9
for wisdom is *b.* than jewels   Pr.8.11
B. is a little with righteousness   Pr.16.8
It is *b.* to be of a lowly spirit   Pr.16.19
B. is a dry morsel with quiet than   Pr.17.1
There is nothing *b.* for a man than   Ec.2.24
B. is the end of a thing than its   Ec.7.8
how much *b.* is your love than   S. of S.4.10
is *b.* for you to enter life maimed   Mk.9.43
would be *b.* for him if a millstone   Lk.17.2
is *b.* to marry than to be aflame   1 Cor.7.9
count others *b.* than yourselves   Phil.2.3
as the covenant he mediates is *b.*   Heb.8.6
is *b.* to suffer for doing right   1 Pet.3.17

BEWARE
B. of practicing your piety before   Mt.6.1
B. of the leaven of the Pharisees   Mt.16.11
B. of the scribes, who like to go   Mk.12.38
b. of all covetousness   Lk.12.15
b. lest you be carried away with   2 Pet.3.17

BIND
B. them upon your heart always   Pr.6.21
B. up the testimony, seal the   Is.8.16
sent me to *b.* up the brokenhearted   Is.61.1
whatever you *b.* on earth shall be   Mt.16.19
love, which *b.* everything together   Col.3.14

BIRD
every winged *b.* according to its   Gen.1.21
every *b.* according to its kind   Gen.7.14
Flee like a *b.* to the mountains   Ps.11.1
In them the *b.* build their nests   Ps.104.17
net spread in the sight of any *b.*   Pr.1.17
Look at the *b.* of the air   Mt.6.26
the *b.* of the air devoured it   Lk.8.5
more value are you than the *b.*   Lk.12.24

BIRTH
you forgot the God who gave you *b.*   Dt.32.18
Job . . . cursed the day of his *b.*   Job 3.1
better . . . death, than the day of *b.*   Ec.7.1
Now the *b.* of Jesus Christ took   Mt.1.18
many will rejoice at his *b.*   Lk.1.14
she gave *b.* to a son   Lk.1.57
she gave *b.* to her first-born   Lk.2.7
Then desire . . . gives *b.* to sin   Jas.1.15

BIRTHRIGHT
Jacob said, "First sell me your *b.*"   Gen.25.31
Thus Esau despised his *b.*   Gen.25.34
who sold his *b.* for a single meal   Heb.12.16

BISHOP
Philippi, with the *b.* and deacons   Phil.1.1
one aspires to the office of *b.*   1 Tim.3.1
Now a *b.* must be above reproach   1 Tim.3.2
For a *b.*, as God's steward, must be   Tit.1.7

BITTER
they made life *b.* for Isaac and   Gen.26.35

why . . . life to the *b*. in soul	Job 3.20
For thou writest *b*. things against	Job 13.26
Today also my complaint is *b*.	Job 23.2
for they made his spirit *b*.	Ps.106.33
strong drink is *b*. to those who	Is.24.9
And he went out and wept *b*.	Lk.22.62
But if you have *b*. jealousy	Jas.3.14

BITTERNESS

Surely the *b*. of death is past.	1 Sam.15.32
will complain in the *b*. of my soul	Job 7.11
The heart knows its own *b*.	Pr.14.10
Remember my affliction and my *b*.	Lam.3.19
Their mouth is full of curses and *b*.	Rom.3.14
Let all *b*. and wrath and anger	Eph.4.31
that no "root of *b*." spring up	Heb.12.15

BLAMELESS

walk before me, and be *b*.	Gen.17.1
a *b*. and upright man, who fears God	Job 1.8
Then I shall be *b*., and innocent	Ps.19.13
The LORD knows the days of the *b*.	Ps.37.18
give heed to the way that is *b*.	Ps.101.2
Blessed are those whose way is *b*.	Ps.119.1
those of *b*. ways are his delight	Pr.11.20
Bloodthirsty men hate one who is *b*.	Pr.29.10
should be holy and *b*. before him	Eph.1.4
to present you holy and *b*.	Col.1.22
righteous and *b*. was our behavior	1 Th.2.10
For a bishop . . . must be *b*.	Tit.1.7

BLASPHEME

He who *b*. the name of the LORD	Lev.24.16
but he who *b*. against the Holy	Lk.12.10
tried to make them *b*.	Acts 26.11
I formerly *b*. and persecuted	1 Tim.1.13
Is it not they who *b*. that honorable	Jas.2.7

BLASPHEMY

the *b*. against the Spirit will not	Mt.12.31
It is *b*.! Who can forgive sins	Mk.2.7
We stone you . . . for *b*.	Jn.10.33
its mouth to utter *b*. against God	Rev.13.6

BLEMISH (noun)

Your lamb shall be without *b*.	Ex.12.5
See that they are without *b*.	Num.28.31
offered himself without *b*. to God	Heb.9.14
that of a lamb without *b*. or spot	1 Pet.1.19
without spot or *b*., and at peace	2 Pet.3.14
to present you without *b*. before	Jude 24

BLESS

The LORD *b*. you and keep you	Num.6.24
May the LORD *b*. his people with	Ps.29.11
I will *b*. the LORD at all times	Ps.34.1
B. the LORD, O my soul; and all	Ps.103.1
The LORD *b*. you from Zion	Ps.128.5
Come, *b*. the LORD, all you servants	Ps.134.1
Every day I will *b*. thee	Ps.145.2
shall *b*. himself by the God of truth	Is.65.16
B. are the poor in spirit, for	Mt.5.3
b. those who curse you, pray for	Lk.6.28
It is more *b*. to give than to	Acts 20.35
B. those who persecute you	Rom.12.14
When reviled, we *b*.; when	1 Cor.4.12
awaiting our *b*. hope, the appearing	Tit.2.13
With it we *b*. the Lord and Father	Jas.3.9
B. are the dead who die in the Lord	Rev.14.13

BLESSING (noun)

turned the curse into a *b*. for you	Dt.23.5
This is the *b*. with which Moses the	Dt.33.1

He will receive *b*. from the LORD	Ps.24.5
By his *b*. they multiply greatly	Ps.107.38
The *b*. of the LORD be upon you	Ps.129.8
The *b*. of the LORD makes rich	Pr.10.22
they shall be showers of *b*.	Ezek.34.26
down for you an overflowing *b*.	Mal.3.10
of service to them in material *b*.	Rom.15.27
The cup of *b*. which we bless	1 Cor.10.16
you with every *b*. in abundance	2 Cor.9.8
the same mouth come *b*. and cursing	Jas.3.10
B. and glory and wisdom	Rev.7.12

BLIND

the LORD opens the eyes of the *b*.	Ps.146.8
Then the eyes of the *b*. shall be	Is.35.5
the *b*. receive their sight and the	Mt.11.5
Let them alone; they are *b*. guides	Mt.15.14
Can a *b*. man lead a *b*. man?	Lk.6.39
the maimed, the lame, the *b*.	Lk.14.13
that though I was *b*., now I see	Jn.9.25
that you are a guide to the *b*.	Rom.2.19

BLOOD

your brother's *b*. is crying to me	Gen.4.10
Whoever sheds the *b*. of man	Gen.9.6
dipped the robe in the *b*.	Gen.37.31
that was in the Nile turned to *b*.	Ex.7.20
The *b*. shall be a sign for you	Ex.12.13
Behold the *b*. of the covenant	Ex.24.8
Moreover you shall eat no *b*. whatever	Lev.7.26
precious their *b*. in his sight	Ps.72.14
for this is my *b*. of the covenant	Mt.26.28
I am innocent of this man's *b*.	Mt.27.24
had a flow of *b*. for twelve years	Mk.5.25
and drinks my *b*. has eternal life	Jn.6.54
cup is the new covenant in my *b*.	1 Cor.11.25
we have redemption through his *b*.	Eph.1.7
peace by the *b*. of his cross	Col.1.20
more shall the *b*. of Christ	Heb.9.14
with the precious *b*. of Christ	1 Pet.1.19
the *b*. of Jesus his Son cleanses	1 Jn.1.7
by thy *b*. didst ransom men for God	Rev.5.9
them white in the *b*. of the Lamb	Rev.7.14
drunk with the *b*. of the saints	Rev.17.6

BLOT (verb)

I will *b*. out man whom I have	Gen.6.7
thy . . . mercy *b*. out my transgressions	Ps.51.1
b. out all my iniquities	Ps.51.9
be *b*. out of the book of the living	Ps.69.28
He who *b*. out your transgressions	Is.43.25
nor *b*. out their sin from thy sight	Jer.18.23
When I *b*. you out, I will cover the	Ezek.32.7
that your sins may be *b*. out	Acts 3.19
will not *b*. his name out of the book	Rev.3.5

BLOW

God made a wind *b*. over the earth	Gen.8.1
the breath of the LORD *b*. upon it	Is.40.7
b. the trumpet among the nations	Jer.51.27
B. the trumpet in Zion; sanctify a	Jl.2.15
The wind *b*. where it wills, and you	Jn.3.8

BOAST

Do not *b*. about tomorrow, for you do	Pr.27.1
Let him who *b*., *b*. of the Lord	1 Cor.1.31
lest any man should *b*.	Eph.2.9
do not *b*. and be false to the truth	Jas.3.14
As it is, you *b*. in your arrogance	Jas.4.16

BOAT

Immediately they left the *b*.	Mt.4.22

so that the *b.* was being swamped by	Mt.8.24
got into the *b.* with his disciples	Mk.8.10
he saw two *b.* by the lake	Lk.5.2
saw Jesus . . . drawing near to the *b.*	Jn.6.19
had lowered the *b.* into the sea	Acts 27.30

BOAZ

Ru.2.1; 3.2; 4.1; 1 Chr.2.12; Mt.1.5; Lk.3.32

BODY

my *b.* wasted away through my	Ps.32.3
destroy both soul and *b.* in hell	Mt.10.28
Take, eat; this is my *b.*	Mt.26.26
do not fear those who kill the *b.*	Lk.12.4
But he spoke of the temple of his *b.*	Jn.2.21
deliver me from this *b.* of death?	Rom.7.24
to present your *b.* as a living	Rom.12.1
so we . . . are one *b.* in Christ	Rom.12.5
absent in *b.* I am present in spirit	1 Cor.5.3
b. is not meant for immorality	1 Cor.6.13
your *b.* is a temple of the Holy	1 Cor.6.19
but I pommel my *b.* and subdue it	1 Cor.9.27
This is my *b.* which is for you	1 Cor.11.24
just as the *b.* is one and has	1 Cor.12.12
there are many parts, yet one *b.*	1 Cor.12.20
Now you are the *b.* of Christ	1 Cor.12.27
it is raised a spiritual *b.*	1 Cor.15.44
away from the *b.* and at home with	2 Cor.5.8
I bear on my *b.* the marks of Jesus	Gal.6.17
There is one *b.* and one Spirit	Eph.4.4
He is the head of the *b.*, the church	Col.1.18
soul and *b.* be kept sound	1 Th.5.23
offering of the *b.* of Jesus Christ	Heb.10.10
For as the *b.* apart from the spirit	Jas.2.26

BOLD

A wicked man puts on a *b.* face	Pr.21.29
but the righteous are *b.* as a lion	Pr.28.1
he had preached *b.* in the name of	Acts 9.27
He began to speak *b.* in the synagogue	Acts 18.26
though I am *b.* enough in Christ to	Philem.8

BOND

broke your yoke and burst your *b.*	Jer.2.20
will burst your *b.* asunder	Nah.1.13
you are . . . in the *b.* of iniquity	Acts 8.23
unity of the Spirit in the *b.* of peace	Eph.4.3
having canceled the *b.* which stood	Col.2.14

BONDAGE

the people . . . groaned under their *b.*	Ex.2.23
from Egypt, out of the house of *b.*	Ex.13.3
God has not forsaken us in our *b.*	Ezra 9.9
We . . . have never been in *b.* to any one	Jn.8.33
that they might bring us into *b.*	Gal.2.4
were subject to lifelong *b.*	Heb.2.15

BONE

This at last is *b.* of my *b.* and	Gen.2.23
Surely you are my *b.* and my flesh	Gen.29.14
a soft tongue will break a *b.*	Pr.25.15
came together, *b.* to its *b.*	Ezek.37.7
they are full of dead men's *b.*	Mt.23.27
a spirit has not flesh and *b.*	Lk.24.39
Not a *b.* of him shall be broken	Jn.19.36

BOOK

blot me . . . out of thy *b.* which	Ex.32.32
Take this *b.* of the law, and put it	Dt.31.26
Ezra opened the *b.* in the sight	Neh.8.5
that they were inscribed in a *b.*	Job 19.23
Of making many *b.* there is no end	Ec.12.12
read from the *b.* of the LORD	Is.34.16

is inscribed in the *b.* of truth	Dan.10.21
a *b.* of remembrance was written	Mal.3.16
not contain the *b.* that would be	Jn.21.25
whose names are in the *b.* of life	Phil.4.3
blot his name out of the *b.* of life	Rev.3.5
another *b.* was opened, which is	Rev.20.12

BORN

man is *b.* to trouble as the sparks	Job 5.7
Man that is *b.* of a woman is of few	Job 14.1
peoples, "This one was *b.* there."	Ps.87.6
a time to be *b.*, and a time to die	Ec.3.2
Cursed be the day on which I was *b.*	Jer.20.14
Now when Jesus was *b.* in Bethlehem	Mt.2.1
to you is *b.* this day in the city	Lk.2.11
unless one is *b.* anew, he cannot see	Jn.3.3
That which is *b.* of the flesh is	Jn.3.6
opened the eyes of a man *b.* blind	Jn.9.32
You were *b.* in utter sin, and would	Jn.9.34
we have been *b.* anew to a living	1 Pet.1.3
No one *b.* of God commits sin	1 Jn.3.9
For whatever is *b.* of God overcomes	1 Jn.5.4

BOSOM

by hiding my iniquity in my *b.*	Job 31.33
I bear in my *b.* the insults of the	Ps.89.50
anger lodges in the *b.* of fools	Ec.7.9
by the angels to Abraham's *b.*	Lk.16.22
who is in the *b.* of the Father, he	Jn.1.18

BOUGHT

And I *b.* the field at Anathoth	Jer.32.9
all who sold and *b.* in the temple	Mt.21.12
b. with them the potter's field	Mt.27.7
(Now this man *b.* a field with the	Acts 1.18
I *b.* this citizenship for a large	Acts 22.28
you were *b.* with a price	1 Cor.6.20
denying the Master who *b.* them	2 Pet.2.1

BOUND

Folly is *b.* up in the heart of a	Pr.22.15
cast three men *b.* into the fire?	Dan.3.24
on earth shall be *b.* in heaven	Mt.16.19
whom Satan for eighteen years	Lk.13.16
woman is *b.* by law to her husband	Rom.7.2
we are *b.* to give thanks to God	2 Th.2.13
b. him for a thousand years	Rev.20.2

BOW (noun)

I set my *b.* in the cloud, and it	Gen.9.13
for lo, the wicked bend the *b.*	Ps.11.2
he breaks the *b.*, and shatters the	Ps.46.9
the *b.* that is in the cloud	Ezek.1.28
horse, and its rider had a *b.*	Rev.6.2

BOW (verb)

you shall not *b.* down to their gods	Ex.23.24
you shall not *b.* down to them	Dt.5.9
Mordecai did not *b.* down or do	Est.3.2
shall come and *b.* down before thee	Ps.86.9
O come, let us worship and *b.* down	Ps.95.6
The evil *b.* down before the good	Pr.14.19
To me every knee shall *b.*	Is.45.23
he *b.* his head and gave up his	Jn.19.30
who have not *b.* the knee to Baal	Rom.11.4
every knee shall *b.* to me	Rom.14.11
name of Jesus every knee should *b.*	Phil.2.10

BOY

the *b.* Samuel continued to grow	1 Sam.2.26
be full of *b.* and girls playing in	Zech.8.5
the *b.* was cured instantly	Mt.17.18
immediately it convulsed the *b.*	Mk.9.20

BRANCH

a *b*. shall grow out of his roots	Is.11.1
raise up for David a righteous *B*.	Jer.23.5
a righteous *B*. to spring forth	Jer.33.15
I will bring my servant the *B*.	Zech.3.8
Every *b*. of mine that bears no fruit	Jn.15.2
the *b*. cannot bear fruit by itself	Jn.15.4
if the root is holy, so are the *b*.	Rom.11.16

BREAD

Seven days . . . eat unleavened *b*.	Ex.12.15
I will rain *b*. from heaven for you	Ex.16.4
eat up my people as they eat *b*.	Ps.53.4
Man ate of the *b*. of the angels	Ps.78.25
gave them *b*. from heaven	Ps.105.40
I will satisfy her poor with *b*.	Ps.132.15
b. eaten in secret is pleasant	Pr.9.17
B. gained by deceit is sweet	Pr.20.17
Cast your *b*. upon the waters	Ec.11.1
Man shall not live by *b*. alone	Mt.4.4
Give us this day our daily *b*.	Mt.6.11
Jesus took *b*., and blessed	Mt.26.26
command this stone to become *b*.	Lk.4.3
he took the *b*. and blessed	Lk.24.30
Jesus said . . . "I am the *b*. of life	Jn.6.35
I am the living *b*. which came down	Jn.6.51
who eats this *b*. will live for ever	Jn.6.58
The *b*. which we break, is it not a	1 Cor.10.16
as you eat this *b*. and drink the	1 Cor.11.26

BREAST

it is melted within my *b*.	Ps.22.14
a child quieted at its mother's *b*.	Ps.131.2
beat his *b*., saying, 'God, be	Lk.18.13
returned home beating their *b*.	Lk.23.48
close to the *b*. of Jesus	Jn.13.23
with a golden girdle round his *b*.	Rev.1.13

BREASTPLATE

He put on righteousness as a *b*.	Is.59.17
put on the *b*. of righteousness	Eph.6.14
put on the *b*. of faith and love	1 Th.5.8
they had scales like iron *b*.	Rev.9.9

BREATH

everything that has the *b*. of life	Gen.1.30
By the *b*. of God they perish	Job 4.9
By the *b*. of God ice is given	Job 37.10
surely every man is a mere *b*.	Ps.39.11
Man is like a *b*., his days are like	Ps.144.4
who gives *b*. to the people upon it	Is.42.5

BREATHE

they *b*. out violence	Ps.27.12
Let everything that *b*. praise the	Ps.150.6
a loud cry, and *b*. his last	Mk.15.37
he *b*. on them, and said to them	Jn.20.22

BRETHREN

one teacher, and you are all *b*.	Mt.23.8
to one of the least of these my *b*.	Mt.25.40
turned again, strengthen your *b*.	Lk.22.32
you are *b*., why do you wrong each	Acts 7.26
they gave great joy to all the *b*.	Acts 15.3
be the first-born among many *b*.	Rom.8.29
Peace to the *b*., and love	Eph.6.23
he is not ashamed to call them *b*.	Heb.2.11
made like his *b*. in every respect	Heb.2.17
to lay down our lives for the *b*.	1 Jn.3.16

BRIBE

you shall take no *b*.	Ex.23.8
a *b*. blinds the eyes of the wise	Dt.16.19

does not take a *b*. against the	Ps.15.5
he who hates *b*. will live	Pr.15.27
take a *b*., and turn aside the needy	Am.5.12

BRIDE

my *b*., you have ravished my heart	S.of S.4.9
He who has the *b*. is the bridegroom	Jn.3.29
to present you as a pure *b*.	2 Cor.11.2
prepared as a *b*. adorned for her	Rev.21.2
The Spirit and the *B*. say, "Come."	Rev.22.17

BRIDEGROOM

like a *b*. leaving his chamber	Ps.19.5
when the *b*. is taken away from them	Mt.9.15
As the *b*. was delayed, they all	Mt.25.5
Can . . . guests fast while the *b*. is with	Mk.2.19
He who has the bride is the *b*.	Jn.3.29

BRIGHT

thee, the night is *b*. as the day	Ps.139.12
b. as the sun, terrible as an army	S.of S.6.10
a *b*. cloud overshadowed them	Mt.17.5
angels . . . robed in pure *b*. linen	Rev.15.6
b. as crystal, flowing from the	Rev.22.1

BRIMSTONE

the LORD rained . . . *b*. and fire	Gen.19.24
he will rain coals of fire and *b*.	Ps.11.6
tormented with fire and *b*.	Rev.14.10
lake that burns with fire and *b*.	Rev.21.8

BROKENHEARTED

The LORD is near to the *b*.	Ps.34.18
needy and the *b*. to their death	Ps.109.16
He heals the *b*., and binds up their	Ps.147.3
he has sent me to bind up the *b*.	Is.61.1

BROOD

he said to them, "You *b*. of vipers	Mt.3.7
You *b*. of vipers! how can you	Mt.12.34
hen gathers her *b*. under her wings	Lk.13.34

BROTHER

Cain rose up against his *b*. Abel	Gen.4.8
it is when *b*. dwell in unity	Ps.133.1
a *b*. is born for adversity	Pr.17.17
friend who sticks closer than a *b*.	Pr.18.24
first be reconciled to your *b*.	Mt.5.24
B. will deliver up *b*. to death	Mt.10.21
If your *b*. sins against you, go and	Mt.18.15
Whoever does the will of God is my *b*.	Mk.3.35
if your *b*. sins, rebuke him, and if	Lk.17.3
to her, "Your *b*. will rise again."	Jn.11.23
do you pass judgment on your *b*.?	Rom.14.10
that makes your *b*. stumble	Rom.14.21
lest I cause my *b*. to fall	1 Cor.8.13
apostles except James the Lord's *b*.	Gal.1.19
as an enemy, but warn him as a *b*.	2 Th.3.15
treat younger men like *b*.	1 Tim.5.1
who hates his *b*. is in the darkness	1 Jn.2.11
one who hates his *b*. is a murderer	1 Jn.3.15

BRUISE (verb)

he shall *b*. your head, and you shall	Gen.3.15
a *b*. reed he will not break, and a	Is.42.3
he was *b*. for our iniquities	Is.53.5
was the will of the LORD to *b*. him	Is.53.10
he will not break a *b*. reed	Mt.12.20

BUILD

let us *b*. ourselves a city, and a	Gen.11.4
For the LORD will *b*. up Zion	Ps.102.16
Unless the LORD *b*. the house	Ps.127.1
those who *b*. it labor in vain	Ps.127.1
I will *b*. them up, and not tear them	Jer.24.6

on this rock I will *b*. my church	Mt.16.18
lest I *b*. on another . . . foundation	Rom.15.20
"Knowledge" puffs up, but love *b*. up	1 Cor.8.1
b. yourselves up on your most holy	Jude 20

BUILDER

the stone which the *b*. rejected	Mt.21.42
like a skilled master *b*. I laid	1 Cor.3.10
Moses as the *b*. of a house has	Heb.3.3
whose *b*. and maker is God	Heb.11.10

BUILDING (noun)

The *b*. that was facing the temple	Ezek.41.12
to him, "Do you see these great *b*.?	Mk.13.2
you are God's field, God's *b*.	1 Cor.3.9
we have a *b*. from God, a house not	2 Cor.5.1

BUILT

Then Noah *b*. an altar to the Lord	Gen.8.20
Moses *b*. an altar and called	Ex.17.15
Joshua *b*. an altar in Mount Ebal	Jos.8.30
David *b*. an altar to the	2 Sam.24.25
Wisdom has *b*. her house, she has set	Pr.9.1
foolish man who *b*. his house upon	Mt.7.26
and he *b*. us our synagogue	Lk.7.5
b. upon the foundation of the	Eph.2.20
b. up in him and established	Col.2.7

BURDEN (noun)

Cast your *b*. on the Lord, and he	Ps.55.22
yoke is easy, and my *b*. is light	Mt.11.30
you load men with *b*. hard to bear	Lk.11.46
Bear one another's *b*., and so	Gal.6.2
I do not lay upon you any other *b*.	Rev.2.24

BURN

And Aaron shall *b*. fragrant incense	Ex.30.7
Let not thy anger *b*. against me	Jg.6.39
he *b*. the chariots with fire	Ps.46.9
long will thy wrath *b*. like fire?	Ps.89.46
altars to *b*. incense to Baal	Jer.11.13
chaff he will *b*. with unquenchable	Mt.3.12
Did not our hearts *b*. within us	Lk.24.32
If any man's work is *b*. up	1 Cor.3.15
if I deliver my body to be *b*.	1 Cor.13.3
the lake that *b*. with fire and	Rev.21.8

BURNT

Your *b*. offerings are not acceptable	Jer.6.20
of God, rather than *b*. offerings	Hos.6.6
more than all whole *b*. offerings	Mk.12.33
in *b*. offerings and sin offerings	Heb.10.6

BURST

fountains of the great deep *b*. forth	Gen.7.11
Let us *b*. their bonds asunder	Ps.2.3
new wine will *b*. the skins and it	Lk.5.37
falling headlong he *b*. open in	Acts 1.18

BURY

So Joseph went up to *b*. his father	Gen.50.7
the Egyptians were *b*. all their	Num.33.4
leave the dead to *b*. their own dead	Mt.8.22
potter's field, to *b*. strangers in	Mt.27.7
anointed my body beforehand for *b*.	Mk.14.8
The rich man also died and was *b*.	Lk.16.22
Devout men *b*. Stephen, and made	Acts 8.2
We were *b*. therefore with him by	Rom.6.4
that he was *b*., that he was raised	1 Cor.15.4
and you were *b*. with him in baptism	Col.2.12

BUSH

fire out of the midst of a *b*.	Ex.3.2
Moses, in the passage about the *b*.	Mk.12.26

grapes picked from a bramble *b*.	Lk.6.44
Sinai, in a flame of fire in a *b*.	Acts 7.30

BUSHEL

light a lamp and put it under a *b*.	Mt.5.15
brought in to be put under a *b*.	Mk.4.21
puts it in a cellar or under a *b*.	Lk.11.33

BUSINESS

doing *b*. on the great waters	Ps.107.23
I have seen the *b*. that God has	Ec.3.10
also is vanity and an unhappy *b*.	Ec.4.8
to his farm, another to his *b*.	Mt.22.5

BUY

to Egypt to Joseph to *b*. grain	Gen.41.57
B. truth, and do not sell it	Pr.23.23
b. wisdom . . . and understanding	Pr.23.23
Come, *b*. wine and milk without money	Is.55.1
B. my field which is at Anathoth	Jer.32.8
no sword sell his mantle and *b*. one	Lk.22.36
those who *b*. as though they had	1 Cor.7.30
counsel you to *b*. from me gold	Rev.3.18
so that no one can *b*. or sell	Rev.13.17

CAESAR

Mt.22.17; Lk.2.1; Jn.19.12; Acts 25.12; 28.19

CAESAREA

Mt.16.13; Acts 8.40; 12.19; 21.16; 25.4

CAIN

Gen.4.1; his anger, Gen.4.5; murders Abel, Gen.4.8; 1 Jn.3.12; his punishment, Gen.4.11–12; Jude 11

CALAMITY

and all my *c*. laid in the balances	Job 6.2
Does not *c*. befall the unrighteous	Job 31.3
They came upon me in the day of my *c*.	Ps.18.18
I also will laugh at your *c*.	Pr.1.26
He who sows injustice will reap *c*.	Pr.22.8
in afflictions, hardships, *c*.	2 Cor.6.4
hardships, persecutions, and *c*.	2 Cor.12.10

CALEB

(1) faith of, Num.13.30; 14.6–10; permitted to enter Canaan, Num.26.65; 32.12; Dt.1.36; his request, Jos.14.6; his possessions, Jos.15.13; gives his daughter to Othniel as wife, Jg.1.13; (2) 1 Chr.2.18; (3) 1 Chr.2.42–50

CALF

graving tool, and made a molten *c*.	Ex.32.4
made a *c*. in Horeb and worshiped	Ps.106.19
you killed for him the fatted *c*.	Lk.15.30
And they made a *c*. in those days	Acts 7.41

CALL (noun)

his angels with a loud trumpet *c*.	Mt.24.31
gifts and the *c*. of God are	Rom.11.29
For consider your *c*., brethren	1 Cor.1.26
of the upward *c*. of God in Christ	Phil.3.14
command, with the archangel's *c*.	1 Th.4.16
God may make you worthy of his *c*.	2 Th.1.11
brethren, who share in a heavenly *c*.	Heb.3.1
to confirm your *c*. and election	2 Pet.1.10
Here is a *c*. for the endurance	Rev.13.10

CALL (verb)

Every day I *c*. upon thee, O Lord	Ps.88.9
c. upon him while he is near	Is.55.6
Before they *c*. I will answer	Is.65.24
you shall *c*. his name Jesus	Mt.1.21
for they shall be *c*. sons of God	Mt.5.9
For I came not to *c*. the righteous	Mt.9.13

all generations will *c.* me blessed	Lk.1.48
I have not come to *c.* the righteous	Lk.5.32
Why do you *c.* me 'Lord, Lord,' and	Lk.6.46
he *c.* his own sheep by name and	Jn.10.3
whoever *c.* on the name of the Lord	Acts 2.21
whom he predestined he also *c.*	Rom.8.30
every one who *c.* upon the name	Rom.10.13
For God has *c.* us to peace	1 Cor.7.15
had *c.* me through his grace	Gal.1.15

CAMEL

Now John wore a garment of *c.* hair	Mt.3.4
is easier for a *c.* to go through	Mt.19.24
out a gnat and swallowing a *c.*	Mt.23.24

CANA

Jn.2.1; 4.46; 21.2

CANAAN

land of, Ex.23.31; Jos.1.4; Zeph.2.5; promised to Abraham, Gen.12.7; 13.14–15; 17.8; inhabitants of, Ex.15.15; their wickedness at Sodom and Gomorrah, Gen.13.13; 19; Israelites not to walk in the ways of, Lev.18.3,24,30; 20.23; language of, Is.19.18; kingdoms of, Ps.135.11; king of, Jg.4.2,23,24; 5.19; wars of, Jg.3.1; dwelling of Abraham in, Gen.12.6–9; Isaac and Jacob, Gen.28; Esau, Gen.36; Joseph, Gen.37; allotted to children of Israel, Jos.14; the spies visit, and their report, Num.13; Moses sees, from Pisgah, Num.27.12; Dt.3.27; 34.1–4

CAPERNAUM

on the northwest shore of the sea of Galilee; Christ dwells at, Mt.4.13; Jn.2.12; preaches at, Mt.4.13–17; Mk.1.21; miracles at, Mt.8.5–34; Jn.6.17; parables at, Mk.4; condemned for impenitence, Mt.11.23; Lk.10.15

CAPTIVE

carried the people *c.* to Assyria	2 Kg.15.29
had carried *c.* to Babylonia	Ezra 2.1
by all those who held them *c.*	Ps.106.46
to proclaim liberty to the *c.*	Is.61.1
the LORD's flock has been taken *c.*	Jer.13.17
be led *c.* among all nations	Lk.21.24
dead to that which held us *c.*	Rom.7.6
making me *c.* to the law of sin	Rom.7.23
every thought *c.* to obey Christ	2 Cor.10.5

CAPTIVITY

for they shall go into *c.*	Dt.28.41
he took into *c.* from Jerusalem	2 Kg.24.15
my young men have gone into *c.*	Lam.1.18
went into *c.* for their iniquity	Ezek.39.23

CAPTURED

the ark of God has been *c.*	1 Sam.4.17
Then they *c.* the king, and brought	Jer.52.9
being *c.* by him to do his will	2 Tim.2.26
And the beast was *c.*, and with	Rev.19.20

CARE (noun)

but the *c.* of the world and the	Mt.13.22
him to an inn, and took *c.* of him	Lk.10.34
each man take *c.* how he builds	1 Cor.3.10
take *c.* lest this liberty of yours	1 Cor.8.9
have the same *c.* for one another	1 Cor.12.25
Take *c.*, brethren, lest there be	Heb.3.12

CARE (verb)

I will *c.* for all your wants	Jg.19.20
son of man that thou dost *c.* for him?	Ps.8.4
the shepherds who *c.* for my people	Jer.23.2
you are true . . . and *c.* for no man	Mt.22.16

Teacher, do you not *c.* if we perish?	Mk.4.38
do you not *c.* that my sister has	Lk.10.40
not that he *c.* for the poor but	Jn.12.6
how can he *c.* for God's church?	1 Tim.3.5
cast . . . anxieties on him, for he *c.*	1 Pet.5.7

CARMEL

1 Sam.15.12; 1 Kg.18.19; S.of S.7.5; Am.1.2

CARRY

you shall *c.* up my bones from	Gen.50.25
C. them in your bosom, as a nurse	Num.11.12
be thou their shepherd, and *c.* them	Ps.28.9
when he dies he will *c.* nothing	Ps.49.17
Can a man *c.* fire in his bosom and	Pr.6.27
he will *c.* them in his bosom	Is.40.11
whose sandals I am not worthy to *c.*	Mt.3.11
man they compelled to *c.* his cross	Mt.27.32
C. no purse, no bag, no sandals	Lk.10.4
died and was *c.* by the angels to	Lk.16.22
if you have *c.* him away, tell me	Jn.20.15
a man lame from birth was being *c.*	Acts 3.2
they *c.* her out and buried her	Acts 5.10
he *c.* me away in the Spirit	Rev.17.3

CASE

Moses brought their *c.* before the	Num.27.5
will you plead the *c.* for God?	Job 13.8
Argue your *c.* with your neighbor	Pr.25.9
Set forth your *c.*, says the LORD	Is.41.21
I would plead my *c.* before thee	Jer.12.1
laid Paul's *c.* before the king	Acts 25.14
you incompetent to try trivial *c.*?	1 Cor.6.2

CAST

Aaron *c.* down his rod before	Ex.7.10
C. the lot between me and my son	1 Sam.14.42
c. lots, just as their brethren	1 Chr.24.31
God had *c.* me into the mire, and I	Job 30.19
for my raiment they *c.* lots	Ps.22.18
C. me not off, forsake me not, O God	Ps.27.9
Why are you *c.* down, O my soul	Ps.42.5
Yet thou hast *c.* us off and abased us	Ps.44.9
Do not *c.* us off for ever	Ps.44.23
C. me not away from thy presence	Ps.51.11
C. your burden on the LORD	Ps.55.22
C. your bread upon the waters	Ec.11.1
And if I *c.* out demons by Beelzebul	Mt.12.27
Be taken up and *c.* into the sea	Mt.21.21
How can Satan *c.* out Satan?	Mk.3.23
Why could we not *c.* it out?	Mk.9.28
I came to *c.* fire upon the earth	Lk.12.49
who comes to me I will not *c.* out	Jn.6.37
for my clothing they *c.* lots	Jn.19.24
then *c.* off the works of darkness	Rom.13.12
C. all your anxieties on him	1 Pet.5.7
but perfect love *c.* out fear	1 Jn.4.18
c. their crowns before the throne	Rev.4.10

CATCH (verb)

A slothful man will not *c.* his prey	Pr.12.27
They set a trap; they *c.* men	Jer.5.26
henceforth you will be *c.* men	Lk.5.10
He *c.* the wise in their craftiness	1 Cor.3.19

CAUSE (noun)

multiplies my wounds without *c.*	Job 9.17
For thou hast maintained my just *c.*	Ps.9.4
He committed his *c.* to the LORD	Ps.22.8
and defend my *c.* against an ungodly	Ps.43.1
Plead my *c.* and redeem me	Ps.119.154
Who has wounds without *c.*?	Pr.23.29

to divorce one's wife for any *c.*?   Mt.19.3
They hated me without a *c.*   Jn.15.25
CAUSE (verb)
The Lord will *c.* you to be defeated   Dt.28.25
Thou dost *c.* the grass to grow for   Ps.104.14
He has *c.* his wonderful works to be   Ps.111.4
Lord God will *c.* righteousness and   Is.61.11
If your right eye *c.* you to sin   Mt.5.29
Whoever *c.* one of these little ones   Mk.9.42
What *c.* wars, and what *c.* fightings   Jas.4.1
CAVE
he may give me the *c.* of Machpelah   Gen.23.9
to David at the *c.* of Adullam   2 Sam.23.13
it was a *c.*, and a stone lay upon   Jn.11.38
in dens and *c.* of the earth   Heb.11.38
hid in the *c.* and among the rocks   Rev.6.15
CEASE
day and night, shall not *c.*   Gen.8.22
He makes wars *c.* to the end of the   Ps.46.9
grinders *c.* because they are few   Ec.12.3
steadfast love of the Lord never *c.*   Lam.3.22
the wind *c.*, and there was a . . . calm   Mk.4.39
she has not *c.* to kiss my feet   Lk.7.45
as for tongues, they will *c.*   1 Cor.13.8
day and night they never *c.* to sing   Rev.4.8
CEDAR
See now, I dwell in a house of *c.*   2 Sam.7.2
from the *c.* that is in Lebanon to   1 Kg.4.33
the Lord breaks the *c.* of Lebanon   Ps.29.5
grow like a *c.* in Lebanon   Ps.92.12
will liken you to a *c.* in Lebanon   Ezek.31.3
Wail. . . for the *c.* has fallen   Zech.11.2
CENSUS
When you take the *c.* of the people   Ex.30.12
Take a *c.* of all the congregation   Num.1.2
Then Solomon took a *c.* of all the   2 Chr.2.17
Judas . . . arose in the days of the *c.*   Acts 5.37
CENTURION
And to the *c.* Jesus said, "Go   Mt.8.13
the *c.* and those who were with   Mt.27.54
Now a *c.* had a slave who was dear   Lk.7.2
a *c.* of . . . the Italian Cohort   Acts 10.1
to a *c.* of the Augustan Cohort   Acts 27.1
CEPHAS
(Peter), Jn.1.42; 1 Cor.1.12; 3.22; 9.5; 15.5;
Gal.2.9; *see* PETER
CHAFF
like *c.* that the storm carries   Job 21.18
are like *c.* which the wind drives   Ps.1.4
Let them be like *c.* before the wind   Ps.35.5
but the *c.* he will burn with   Lk.3.17
CHAIN
Can you bind the *c.* of the Pleiades   Job 38.31
I . . . put . . . a *c.* on your neck   Ezek.16.11
a *c.* of gold was put about his neck   Dan.5.29
bind him any more, even with a *c.*   Mk.5.3
as I am–except for these *c.*   Acts 26.29
for which I am an ambassador in *c.*   Eph.6.20
in eternal *c.* in the nether gloom   Jude 6
CHANCE (noun)
time and *c.* happen to them all   Ec.9.11
by *c.* a priest was going down   Lk.10.31
on the *c.* that somehow they could   Acts 27.12
for he found no *c.* to repent   Heb.12.17
CHANGE (verb)
not fear though the earth should *c.*   Ps.46.2

has sworn and will not *c.* his mind   Ps.110.4
Can the Ethiopian *c.* his skin or   Jer.13.23
For I the Lord do not *c.*; therefore   Mal.3.6
will *c.* the customs which Moses   Acts 6.14
but we shall all be *c.*   1 Cor.15.51
are being *c.* into his likeness   2 Cor.3.18
who will *c.* our lowly body to be   Phil.3.21
has sworn and will not *c.* his mind   Heb.7.21
CHARGE (noun)
Who gave him *c.* over the earth   Job 34.13
give his angels *c.* of you to guard   Ps.91.11
He will give his angels *c.* of you   Mt.4.6
See how many *c.* they bring against   Mk.15.4
this *c.* I have received from my   Jn.10.18
Having received this *c.*, he put   Acts 16.24
Who shall bring . . . *c.* against God's   Rom.8.33
I may make the gospel free of *c.*   1 Cor.9.18
This *c.* I commit to you, Timothy   1 Tim.1.18
the flock of God that is your *c.*   1 Pet.5.2
CHARGE (verb)
Job did not . . . *c.* God with wrong   Job 1.22
Like warriors they *c.*, like soldiers   Jl.2.7
he strictly *c.* them that no one   Mk.5.43
And he *c.* them to tell no one   Mk.7.36
We strictly *c.* you not to teach   Acts 5.28
I *c.* you in the name of Jesus   Acts 16.18
I *c.* you to keep the commandment   1 Tim.6.14
I *c.* you in the presence of God   2 Tim.4.1
May it not be *c.* against them   2 Tim.4.16
CHARIOT
made him to ride in his second *c.*   Gen.41.43
picked *c.* and all the other *c.*   Ex.14.7
Sisera called out all his *c.*   Jg.4.13
A *c.* could be imported from Egypt   1 Kg.10.29
he burns the *c.* with fire   Ps.46.9
who makest the clouds thy *c.*   Ps.104.3
to Philip, "Go . . . join this *c.*"   Acts 8.29
CHASTEN
I will *c.* him with the rod of men   2 Sam.7.14
nor *c.* me in thy wrath   Ps.38.1
When thou dost *c.* man with rebukes   Ps.39.11
Blessed is the man whom thou dost *c.*   Ps.94.12
we are *c.* so that we may not be   1 Cor.11.32
CHASTISE
My father *c.* you with whips, but   1 Kg.12.11
He who chastens . . . does he not *c.*?   Ps.94.10
I will *c.* them for their wicked   Hos.7.12
I will therefore *c.* him and release   Lk.23.16
c. every son whom he receives   Heb.12.6
CHEEK
in the night, tears on her *c.*   Lam.1.2
let him give his *c.* to the smiter   Lam.3.30
one strikes you on the right *c.*   Mt.5.39
CHEERFUL
A glad heart makes a *c.* countenance   Pr.15.13
A *c.* heart is a good medicine   Pr.17.22
for God loves a *c.* giver   2 Cor.9.7
Is any *c.*? Let him sing praise   Jas.5.13
CHERUBIM
east of the garden . . . he placed the *c.*   Gen.3.24
And you shall make two *c.* of gold   Ex.25.18
He sits enthroned upon the *c.*   Ps.99.1
who art enthroned above the *c.*   Is.37.16
above it were the *c.* of glory   Heb.9.5
CHIEF (adjective)
The *c.* butler and the *c.* baker   Gen.40.2

CHILD

O Belteshazzar, c. of the magicians	Dan.4.9
assembling all the c. priests	Mt.2.4
the elders and c. priests	Mt.16.21
Iscariot, went to the c. priests	Mt.26.14
he was a c. tax collector, and rich	Lk.19.2
the c. captain Lysias came	Acts 24.7
when the c. Shepherd is manifested	1 Pet.5.4

CHILD

Shall a c. be born to a man who is	Gen.17.17
And Elijah took the c.	1 Kg.17.23
Then he went up and lay upon the c.	2 Kg.4.34
Train up a c. in the way he should	Pr.22.6
not withhold discipline from a c.	Pr.23.13
a c. left to himself brings shame	Pr.29.15
For to us a c. is born, to us a son	Is.9.6
a little c. shall lead them	Is.11.6
When Israel was a c., I loved him	Hos.11.1
search diligently for the c.	Mt.2.8
Whoever humbles himself like this c.	Mt.18.4
The c. is not dead but sleeping	Mk.5.39
And the c. grew and became strong	Lk.2.40
When I was a c., I spoke like a c.	1 Cor.13.11
Titus, my true c. in a common faith	Tit.1.4
appeal to you for my c., Onesimus	Philem.10
who loves the parent loves the c.	1 Jn.5.1

CHILDREN

in pain you shall bring forth c.	Gen.3.16
the iniquity of fathers upon c.	Num.14.18
Moses set before the c. of Israel	Dt.4.44
When your c. ask their fathers	Jos.4.21
Even young c. despise me	Job 19.18
forsaken or his c. begging bread	Ps.37.25
our fathers to teach to their c.	Ps.78.5
As a father pities his c., so the	Ps.103.13
May you see your children's c.	Ps.128.6
Her c. rise up and call her blessed	Pr.31.28
stones to raise up c. to Abraham	Mt.3.9
how to give good gifts to your c.	Mt.7.11
and c. will rise against parents	Mt.10.21
Let the c. come to me, and do not	Mt.19.14
our spirit that we are c. of God	Rom.8.16
do not be c. in your thinking	1 Cor.14.20
C., obey your parents in the Lord	Eph.6.1
obedient, do not be conformed	1 Pet.1.14
Beloved, we are God's c. now	1 Jn.3.2

CHOOSE

c. this day whom you will serve	Jos.24.15
C. a man for yourselves	1 Sam.17.8
Let us c. what is right	Job 34.4
to refuse the evil and c. the good	Is.7.15
Is not this the fast that I c.	Is.58.6
to whom the Son c. to reveal him	Lk.10.22
Did I not c. you, the twelve, and	Jn.6.70
You did not c. me, but I chose you	Jn.15.16
c. men from among them and send	Acts 15.22

CHOSE

Lot c. for himself all the . . . valley	Gen.13.11
He c. David his servant, and took	Ps.78.70
but I c. you out of the world	Jn.15.19
they c. Stephen, a man full of	Acts 6.5
God c. what is weak in the world to	1 Cor.1.27
he c. us in him before the foundation	Eph.1.4
God c. you from the beginning	2 Th.2.13

CHOSEN

your God has c. you to be a people	Dt.7.6
that you have c. the LORD	Jos.24.22

where I have c. to put my name	1 Kg.11.36
The LORD is my c. portion and my	Ps.16.5
A good name is to be c. rather than	Pr.22.1
Holy One of Israel, who has c. you	Is.49.7
For many are called, but few are c.	Mt.22.14
Mary has c. the good portion, which	Lk.10.42
is the Christ of God, his C. One	Lk.23.35
I know whom I have c.	Jn.13.18
for he is a c. instrument of mine	Acts 9.15
as God's c. ones, holy and beloved	Col.3.12
c. and destined by God the Father	1 Pet.1.2
that living stone . . . c. and precious	1 Pet.2.4
But you are a c. race, a royal	1 Pet.2.9
those . . . are called and c. and faithful	Rev.17.14

CHRIST

The book of the genealogy of Jesus C.	Mt.1.1
Jesus was born, who is called C.	Mt.1.16
You are the C., the Son of the	Mt.16.16
What do you think of the C.?	Mt.22.42
Are you the C., the Son of the	Mk.14.61
found the Messiah" (which means C.)	Jn.1.41
I believe that you are the C.	Jn.11.27
God has made him both Lord and C.	Acts 2.36
and preaching Jesus as the C.	Acts 5.42
at the right time C. died for the	Rom.5.6
separate us from the love of C.?	Rom.8.35
But put on the Lord Jesus C.	Rom.13.14
All the churches of C. greet you	Rom.16.16
to Cephas," or "I belong to C."	1 Cor.1.12
C. the power of God and the wisdom	1 Cor.1.24
But we have the mind of C.	1 Cor.2.16
For C., our paschal lamb, has been	1 Cor.5.7
followed them, and the Rock was C.	1 Cor.10.4
Be imitators of me, as I am of C.	1 Cor.11.1
God was in C. reconciling the world	2 Cor.5.19
I have been crucified with C.	Gal.2.20
C. redeemed us from the curse of	Gal.3.13
the unsearchable riches of C.	Eph.3.8
to me to live is C., and to die	Phil.1.21
but C. is all, and in all	Col.3.11
appearing of our Savior C. Jesus	2 Tim.1.10
Jesus C. is the same yesterday and	Heb.13.8
For C. also died for sins once for	1 Pet.3.18
our God and Savior Jesus C.	2 Pet.1.1
Jesus C. the faithful witness	Rev.1.5

CHRISTIAN

were for the first time called C.	Acts 11.26
you think to make me a C.	Acts 26.28
yet if one suffers as a C.	1 Pet.4.16

CHURCH

on this rock I will build my c.	Mt.16.18
listen to them, tell it to the c.	Mt.18.17
great fear came upon the whole c.	Acts 5.11
But Saul laid waste the c.	Acts 8.3
feed the c. of the Lord which he	Acts 20.28
teach them everywhere in every c.	1 Cor.4.17
to excel in building up the c.	1 Cor.14.12
head over all things for the c.	Eph.1.22
as Christ is the head of the c.	Eph.5.23
cherishes it, as Christ does the c.	Eph.5.29
He is the head of the body, the c.	Col.1.18
which is the c. of the living God	1 Tim.3.15

CIRCUMCISE

C. therefore the foreskin of your	Dt.10.16
eighth day they came to c. the child	Lk.1.59
you c. a man upon the sabbath	Jn.7.22

said, "It is necessary to *c.* them — Acts 15.5
he took him and *c.* him because of — Acts 16.3

CIRCUMCISION
Moses gave you *c.* (not that it is — Jn.7.22
And he gave him the covenant of *c.* — Acts 7.8
nor is true *c.* something external — Rom.2.28
He received *c.* as a sign or seal of — Rom.4.11
For neither *c.* counts for anything — Gal.6.15
we are the true *c.*, who worship God — Phil.3.3

CITIZEN
the ears of all the *c.* of Shechem — Jg.9.2
to one of the *c.* of that country — Lk.15.15
in Cilicia, a *c.* of no mean city — Acts 21.39
For this man is a Roman *c.* — Acts 22.26

CITY
he built a *c.*, and called — Gen.4.17
Come, let us build ourselves a *c.* — Gen.11.4
Israel, "Go every man to his *c.*" — 1 Sam.8.22
A *c.* set on a hill cannot be hid — Mt.5.14
to teach and preach in their *c.* — Mt.11.1
to upbraid the *c.* where most of — Mt.11.20
he went on through *c.* and villages — Lk.8.1
when he . . . saw the *c.* he wept — Lk.19.41
So he came to a *c.* of Samaria — Jn.4.5
was crucified was near the *c.* — Jn.19.20
the people of the *c.* were divided — Acts 14.4
they are disturbing our *c.* — Acts 16.20
for he has prepared for them a *c.* — Heb.11.16
For here we have no lasting *c.* — Heb.13.14
and the name of the *c.* of my God — Rev.3.12
I saw the holy *c.*, new Jerusalem — Rev.21.2

CLAY
Remember . . . thou hast made me of *c.* — Job 10.9
the potter be regarded as the *c.* — Is.29.16
Does the *c.* say to him who fashions — Is.45.9
we are the *c.*, and thou art our potter — Is.64.8
Jesus made *c.* and anointed my eyes — Jn.9.11
Has the potter no right over the *c.* — Rom.9.21

CLEAN (adjective)
seven pairs of all *c.* animals — Gen.7.2
can he who is born of woman be *c.*? — Job 25.4
He who has *c.* hands and a pure — Ps.24.4
Purge me with hyssop, and I shall be *c.* — Ps.51.7
Create in me a *c.* heart, O God — Ps.51.10
I will sprinkle *c.* water upon you — Ezek.36.25
that the outside also may be *c.* — Mt.23.26
(Thus he declared all foods *c.*) — Mk.7.19
behold, everything is *c.* for you — Lk.11.41
Everything is indeed *c.*, but it is — Rom.14.20

CLEANSE
first *c.* the inside of the cup and — Mt.23.26
Then said Jesus, "Were not ten *c.*? — Lk.17.17
What God has *c.*, you must not call — Acts 10.15
C. out the old leaven that you may — 1 Cor.5.7
having *c.* her by the washing of — Eph.5.26
If the worshipers had once been *c.* — Heb.10.2
C. your hands, you sinners — Jas.4.8
will forgive our sins and *c.* us — 1 Jn.1.9

CLEAR (adjective)
This is a *c.* omen to them of their — Phil.1.28
of the faith with a *c.* conscience — 1 Tim.3.9
and keep your conscience *c.* — 1 Pet.3.16
city was pure gold, *c.* as glass — Rev.21.18

CLEAR (verb)
he will by no means *c.* the guilty — Num.14.18
God will *c.* away these nations — Dt.7.22

C. thou me from hidden faults — Ps.19.12
I will not *c.* the guilty — Jl.3.21

CLEAVE
a man leaves . . . and *c.* to his wife — Gen.2.24
but *c.* to the LORD your God — Jos.23.8
Because he *c.* to me in love, I will — Ps.91.14
I *c.* to thy testimonies, O LORD — Ps.119.31
Let my tongue *c.* to the roof of my — Ps.137.6

CLEFT
I will put you in a *c.* of the rock — Ex.33.22
He *c.* rocks in the wilderness — Ps.78.15
he *c.* the rock and the water gushed — Is.48.21
hide it there in a *c.* of the rock — Jer.13.4

CLING
My soul *c.* to thee — Ps.63.8
the whole house of Judah *c.* to me — Jer.13.11
the dust of your town that *c.* to — Lk.10.11

CLOAK
a shepherd cleans his *c.* of vermin — Jer.43.12
let him have your *c.* as well — Mt.5.40
And they clothed him in a purple *c.* — Mk.15.17
takes away your *c.* do not withhold — Lk.6.29
bring the *c.* that I left . . . at Troas — 2 Tim.4.13

CLOSE (adjective)
Afflicted and *c.* to death — Ps.88.15
a whisperer separates *c.* friends — Pr.16.28
lying thus, *c.* to the breast of — Jn.13.25
I find . . . evil lies *c.* at hand — Rom.7.21

CLOSE (verb)
one of his ribs and *c.* up its place — Gen.2.21
They *c.* their hearts to pity — Ps.17.10
the pit *c.* its mouth over me — Ps.69.15
Do not *c.* thine ear to my cry — Lam.3.56
he *c.* the book, and gave it back — Lk.4.20
their eyes they have *c.* — Acts 28.27
if any one . . . *c.* his heart against — 1 Jn.3.17

CLOTH
unshrunk *c.* on an old garment — Mt.9.16
left the linen *c.* and ran away — Mk.14.52
wrapped him in swaddling *c.* — Lk.2.7
his face wrapped with a *c.* — Jn.11.44
he saw the linen *c.* lying — Jn.20.6

CLOTHE
God is *c.* with terrible majesty — Job 37.22
meadows *c.* themselves with flocks — Ps.65.13
Thou art *c.* with honor and majesty — Ps.104.1
priests be *c.* with righteousness — Ps.132.9
I *c.* the heavens with blackness — Is.50.3
will he not much more *c.* you — Mt.6.30
I was naked and you *c.* me — Mt.25.36
Now John was *c.* with camel's hair — Mk.1.6
who was *c.* in purple and fine linen — Lk.16.19
until you are *c.* with power from on — Lk.24.49
but that we would be further *c.* — 2 Cor.5.4
C. yourselves, all of you, with — 1 Pet.5.5
buy from me . . . garments to *c.* you — Rev.3.18

CLOTHING
bread to eat and *c.* to wear — Gen.28.20
Your *c.* did not wear out upon you — Dt.8.4
And why are you anxious about *c.*? — Mt.6.28
in sheep's *c.* but inwardly . . . wolves — Mt.7.15
for my *c.* they cast lots — Jn.19.24
we have food and *c.* . . . be content — 1 Tim.6.8
a poor man in shabby *c.* also comes — Jas.2.2

CLOUD
I set my bow in the *c.* — Gen.9.13

in a pillar of *c.* to lead them	Ex.13.21
And Moses entered the *c.*	Ex.24.18
a *c.* filled the house of the LORD	1 Kg.8.10
As the *c.* fades and vanishes, so he	Job 7.9
In the daytime he led them with a *c.*	Ps.78.14
C. and thick darkness are round	Ps.97.2
who makest the *c.* thy chariot	Ps.104.3
thy faithfulness reaches to the *c.*	Ps.108.4
over her assemblies a *c.* by day	Is.4.5
Your love is like a morning *c.*	Hos.6.4
a bright *c.* overshadowed them	Mt.17.5
coming on the *c.* of heaven with	Mt.24.30
When you see a *c.* rising in the	Lk.12.54
Son of man coming in a *c.* with power	Lk.21.27
our fathers were all under the *c.*	1 Cor.10.1
by so great a *c.* of witnesses	Heb.12.1
Behold, he is coming with the *c.*	Rev.1.7
he who sat upon the *c.* swung his	Rev.14.16

COAL

he will rain *c.* of fire	Ps.11.6
Let burning *c.* fall upon them	Ps.140.10
will heap *c.* of fire on his head	Pr.25.22
having in his hand a burning *c.*	Is.6.6
will heap burning *c.* upon his head	Rom.12.20

COAT

he was armed with a *c.* of mail	1 Sam.17.5
would sue you and take your *c.*	Mt.5.40
answered them, "He who has two *c.*	Lk.3.11
do not withhold your *c.* as well	Lk.6.29
c. and garments which Dorcas made	Acts 9.39

COIN

Bring me a *c.*, and let me look at	Mk.12.15
what woman, having ten silver *c.*	Lk.15.8
a poor widow put in two copper *c.*	Lk.21.2
poured out ... *c.* of ... money-changers	Jn.2.15

COLD

c. and heat, summer and winter, day	Gen.8.22
who can stand before his *c.*?	Ps.147.17
Like the *c.* of snow in the time of	Pr.25.13
Like *c.* water to a thirsty soul	Pr.25.25
gives ... even a cup of *c.* water	Mt.10.42
most men's love will grow *c.*	Mt.24.12
a charcoal fire, because it was *c.*	Jn.18.18
Would that you were *c.* or hot	Rev.3.15

COMFORT (noun)

This is my *c.* in my affliction	Ps.119.50
walking ... in the *c.* of the Holy	Acts 9.31
it is for your *c.* and salvation	2 Cor.1.6
the *c.* with which he was comforted	2 Cor.7.7
gave us eternal *c.* and good hope	2 Th.2.16

COMFORT (verb)

My bed will *c.* me, my couch will ease	Job 7.13
How then will you *c.* me with empty	Job 21.34
thy rod and thy staff, they *c.* me	Ps.23.4
LORD, hast helped me and *c.* me	Ps.86.17
be ready to *c.* me according to thy	Ps.119.76
C., *c.* my people, says your God	Is.40.1
For the LORD has *c.* his people	Is.49.13
For the LORD will *c.* Zion	Is.51.3
As one whom his mother *c.*, so I will	Is.66.13
the LORD will again *c.* Zion	Zech.1.17
who mourn, for they shall be *c.*	Mt.5.4
to *c.* those who are in any affliction	2 Cor.1.4

COMMAND (noun)

The Lord gives the *c.*; great is	Ps.68.11
stormy wind fulfilling his *c.*	Ps.148.8

by the way of concession, not of *c.*	1 Cor.7.6
I have no *c.* of the Lord, but	1 Cor.7.25
I say this not as a *c.*, but	2 Cor.8.8

COMMAND (verb)

You shall speak all that I *c.* you	Ex.7.2
he has *c.* his covenant for ever	Ps.111.9
For he *c.* and they were created	Ps.148.5
c. these stones to become loaves	Mt.4.3
to observe all that I have *c.* you	Mt.28.20
he *c.* the unclean spirits	Lk.4.36
he *c.* even wind and water	Lk.8.25
but I do as the Father has *c.* me	Jn.14.31
my friends if you do what I *c.* you	Jn.15.14
C. and teach these things	1 Tim.4.11

COMMANDMENT

those who love me and keep my *c.*	Ex.20.6
words of the covenant, the ten *c.*	Ex.34.28
you shall keep my *c.* and do them	Lev.22.31
the *c.* of the LORD is pure	Ps.19.8
Thy *c.* makes me wiser than my	Ps.119.98
My son, keep your father's *c.*	Pr.6.20
He who keeps the *c.* keeps his life	Pr.19.16
This is the great and first *c.*	Mt.22.38
they rested according to the *c.*	Lk.23.56
A new *c.* I give to you, that you	Jn.13.34
This is my *c.*, that you love one	Jn.15.12
he had given *c.* through the Holy	Acts 1.2
Beloved, I am writing you no new *c.*	1 Jn.2.7
All who keep his *c.* abide in him	1 Jn.3.24
And his *c.* are not burdensome	1 Jn.5.3

COMMEND

A man is *c.* according to his good	Pr.12.8
And now I *c.* you to God	Acts 20.32
Food will not *c.* us to God	1 Cor.8.8
Are we beginning to *c.* ourselves	2 Cor.3.1
some of those who *c.* themselves	2 Cor.10.12

COMMISSION (verb)

you shall *c.* him in their sight	Num.27.19
the LORD *c.* Joshua the son of Nun	Dt.31.23
with you in Christ, and has *c.* us	2 Cor.1.21
c. by God, in the sight of God we	2 Cor.2.17

COMMIT

You shall not *c.* adultery	Ex.20.14
to God would I *c.* my cause	Job 5.8
Into thy hand I *c.* my spirit	Ps.31.5
C. your way to the LORD; trust	Ps.37.5
C. your work to the LORD, and your	Pr.16.3
Why do you *c.* this great evil	Jer.44.7
You shall not *c.* adultery	Mt.19.18
into thy hands I *c.* my spirit	Lk.23.46
This charge I *c.* to you, Timothy	1 Tim.1.18
you *c.* sin, and are convicted by	Jas.2.9
No one born of God *c.* sin	1 Jn.3.9

COMMON

between the holy and the *c.*	Ezek.42.20
had all things in *c.*	Acts 2.44
not call any man *c.* or unclean	Acts 10.28
of the Spirit for the *c.* good	1 Cor.12.7
write to you of our *c.* salvation	Jude 3

COMPANION

his brother, and every man his *c.*	Ex.32.27
my *c.*, my familiar friend	Ps.55.13
My *c.* stretched out his hand	Ps.55.20
I am a *c.* of all who fear thee	Ps.119.63
who were Paul's *c.* in travel	Acts 19.29

COMPANY

the *c.* of the godless is barren	Job 15.34
a *c.* of evildoers encircle me	Ps.22.16
a *c.* of destroying angels	Ps.78.49
in the *c.* of the upright	Ps.111.1
not sit in the *c.* of merrymakers	Jer.15.17
the daughter . . . danced before the *c.*	Mt.14.6
Now the *c.* of those who believed	Acts 4.32
so spoke that a great *c.* believed	Acts 14.1
have enjoyed your *c.* for a little	Rom.15.24
Bad *c.* ruins good morals	1 Cor.15.33

COMPARE

none can *c.* with thee	Ps.40.5
For who . . . can be *c.* to the LORD?	Ps.89.6
nothing you desire can *c.* with her	Pr.3.15
With what can we *c.* the kingdom of	Mk.4.30
are not worth *c.* with the glory	Rom.8.18
c. themselves with one another	2 Cor.10.12

COMPASSION

Has he in anger shut up his *c.*?	Ps.77.9
let thy *c.* come speedily to meet us	Ps.79.8
his *c.* is over all that he has made	Ps.145.9
with everlasting love I will have *c.*	Is.54.8
will not pity or spare or have *c.*	Jer.13.14
I led them with cords of *c.*	Hos.11.4
He will again have *c.* upon us	Mic.7.19
he had *c.* on them, and healed	Mt.14.14
I have *c.* on the crowd, because	Mk.8.2
I will have *c.* on whom I have *c.*	Rom.9.15
c., kindness, lowliness, meekness	Col.3.12

COMPEL

men are *c.* to grind at the mill	Lam.5.13
this man they *c.* to carry his cross	Mt.27.32
c. people to come in, that my	Lk.14.23
how can you *c.* the Gentiles to live	Gal.2.14

COMPLAINT

Today also my *c.* is bitter	Job 23.2
Hear my voice, O God, in my *c.*	Ps.64.1
I pour out my *c.* before him	Ps.142.2
have a *c.* against any one	Acts 19.38
if one has a *c.* against another	Col.3.13

COMPLETE (adjective)

that the man of God may be *c.*	2 Tim.3.17
that you may be perfect and *c.*	Jas.1.4
to face, so that our joy may be *c.*	2 Jn.12
their brethren should be *c.*	Rev.6.11

COMPLETE (verb)

C. your work, your daily task, as	Ex.5.13
c. my joy by being of the same mind	Phil.2.2
in my flesh I *c.* what is lacking	Col.1.24
faith was *c.* by works	Jas.2.22

CONCEAL

slay our brother and *c.* his blood?	Gen.37.26
he will *c.* me under the cover of	Ps.27.5
I have not *c.* thy steadfast love	Ps.40.10
A prudent man *c.* his knowledge	Pr.12.23
He who *c.* his transgressions will	Pr.28.13
it was *c.* from them	Lk.9.45

CONCEIT

any who are wise in their own *c.*	Job 37.24
Lest you be wise in your own *c.*	Rom.11.25
slander, gossip, *c.*, and disorder	2 Cor.12.20
Do nothing from selfishness or *c.*	·Phil.2.3
puffed up with *c.*, and fall into	1 Tim.3.6
swollen with *c.*, lovers of pleasure	2 Tim.3.4

CONCEIVE

in sin did my mother *c.* me	Ps.51.5
young woman shall *c.* and bear a son	Is.7.14
a virgin shall *c.* and bear a son	Mt.1.23
nor the heart of man *c.*	1 Cor.2.9
desire when it has *c.*, gives birth to sin	Jas.1.15

CONDEMN

Will you *c.* him who is righteous	Job 34.17
c. the innocent to death	Ps.94.21
they will *c.* him to death	Mt.20.18
c. not, and you will not be *c.*	Lk.6.37
God sent the Son . . . not to *c.* the world	Jn.3.17
Neither do I *c.* you; go, and do not	Jn.8.11
who is to *c.*? Is it Christ	Rom.8.34
But he who has doubts is *c.*	Rom.14.23
lest you come together to be *c.*	1 Cor.11.34
whenever our hearts *c.* us	1 Jn.3.20

CONDUCT (noun)

wise *c.* is pleasure to a man of	Pr.10.23
but the *c.* of the pure is right	Pr.21.8
not a terror to good *c.*, but to bad	Rom.13.3
to give you in our *c.* an example	2 Th.3.9
be holy yourselves in all your *c.*	1 Pet.1.15
Maintain good *c.* among the	1 Pet.2.12

CONFESS

he shall *c.* the sin he has committed	Lev.5.5
I will *c.* my transgressions to the	Ps.32.5
I *c.* my iniquity, I am sorry for my	Ps.38.18
any one should *c.* him to be Christ	Jn.9.22
if you *c.* with your lips that Jesus	Rom.10.9
every tongue *c.* that Jesus Christ	Phil.2.11
c. your sins to one another	Jas.5.16
If we *c.* our sins, he is faithful	1 Jn.1.9
I will *c.* his name before my Father	Rev.3.5

CONFIDENCE

will have *c.*, because there is hope	Job 11.18
in the LORD than to put *c.* in man	Ps.118.8
I have *c.* in the Lord that you will	Gal.5.10
And we have *c.* in the Lord about	2 Th.3.4
Let us then with *c.* draw near to	Heb.4.16
Through him you have *c.* in God	1 Pet.1.21
we have *c.* before God	1 Jn.3.21
this is the *c.* which we have in him	1 Jn.5.14

CONFIDENT

though war arise . . . yet I will be *c.*	Ps.27.3
If any one is *c.* that he is Christ's	2 Cor.10.7
have been made *c.* in the Lord	Phil.1.14
C. of your obedience, I write	Philem.21

CONFIRM

will *c.* my covenant with you	Lev.26.9
c. for ever the word which thou	2 Sam.7.25
C. to thy servant thy promise	Ps.119.38
Then *c.* your vows and perform	Jer.44.25
in order to *c.* the promises given	Rom.15.8
the more zealous to *c.* your call	2 Pet.1.10

CONFORM

men who do not *c.* to thy law	Ps.119.85
predestined to be *c.* to the image	Rom.8.29
Do not be *c.* to this world but be	Rom.12.2
do not be *c.* to the passions of	1 Pet.1.14

CONFOUND

You would *c.* the plans of the poor	Ps.14.6
turned back and *c.* who devise evil	Ps.35.4
Then the moon will be *c.*	Is.24.23
All of them are put to shame and *c.*	Is.45.16

are ashamed and *c.* and cover their   Jer.14.3
c. the Jews who lived in Damascus   Acts 9.22

CONFUSION

will throw into *c.* all the people   Ex.23.27
the LORD . . . threw them into *c.*   1 Sam.7.10
hast put to *c.* those who hate us   Ps.44.7
to us *c.* of face, as at this day   Dan.9.7
the city was filled with the *c.*   Acts 19.29
is not a God of *c.* but of peace   1 Cor.14.33

CONFUTE

there was none that *c.* Job   Job 32.12
you shall *c.* every tongue that   Is.54.17
for he powerfully *c.* the Jews in   Acts 18.28
also to *c.* those who contradict   Tit.1.9

CONGREGATION

All the *c.* of the people of Israel   Ex.17.1
nor sinners in the *c.* of the righteous   Ps.1.5
in the great *c.* I will bless the   Ps.26.12
I will thank thee in the great *c.*   Ps.35.18
Bless God in the great *c.*   Ps.68.26
Sanctify the *c.*; assemble the elders   Jl.2.16
midst of the *c.* I will praise thee   Heb.2.12

CONQUER

who through faith *c.* kingdoms   Heb.11.33
he went out conquering and to *c.*   Rev.6.2
they have *c.* him by the blood   Rev.12.11
the Lamb will *c.* them   Rev.17.14
He who *c.* shall have this heritage   Rev.21.7

CONSCIENCE

to have a clear *c.* toward God   Acts 24.16
while their *c.* also bears witness   Rom.2.15
my *c.* bears me witness in the Holy   Rom.9.1
their *c.*, being weak, is defiled   1 Cor.8.7
every man's *c.* in the sight of God   2 Cor.4.2
a good *c.* and sincere faith   1 Tim.1.5
liars whose *c.* are seared   1 Tim.4.2
perfect the *c.* of the worshiper   Heb.9.9
purify your *c.* from dead works   Heb.9.14
keep your *c.* clear, so that   1 Pet.3.16

CONSECRATE

C. to me all the first-born   Ex.13.2
You shall be men *c.* to me   Ex.22.31
I will *c.* the tent of meeting and   Ex.29.44
C. yourselves therefore, and be holy   Lev.20.7
whom the Father *c.* and sent into   Jn.10.36
And for their sake I *c.* myself   Jn.17.19
husband is *c.* through his wife   1 Cor.7.14
then it is *c.* by the word of God   1 Tim.4.5

CONSIDER

C. too that this nation is thy   Ex.33.13
Have you *c.* my servant Job, that   Job 1.8
C. and answer me, O LORD my God   Ps.13.3
Blessed is he who *c.* the poor   Ps.41.1
c. well her ramparts, go through her   Ps.48.13
C. how I love thy precepts   Ps.119.159
C. the work of God; who can   Ec.7.13
C. the lilies of the field, how they   Mt.6.28
C. the ravens: they neither sow nor   Lk.12.24
For *c.* your call, brethren   1 Cor.1.26
c. Jesus, the apostle and high priest   Heb.3.1
He *c.* that God was able to raise   Heb.11.19
C. him who endured from sinners   Heb.12.3
c. the outcome of their life   Heb.13.7

CONSOLATION

Are the *c.* of God too small for you   Job 15.11
the cup of *c.* to drink for his   Jer.16.7

looking for the *c.* of Israel   Lk.2.25
for you have received your *c.*   Lk.6.24
for their upbuilding . . . and *c.*   1 Cor.14.3

CONSUME

lest I *c.* you in the way   Ex.33.3
thou dost *c.* like a moth what is   Ps.39.11
For we are *c.* by thy anger   Ps.90.7
My soul is *c.* with longing for thy   Ps.119.20
but the lips of a fool *c.* him   Ec.10.12
moth and rust *c.* and where thieves   Mt.6.19
Zeal for thy house will *c.* me   Jn.2.17
were *c.* with passion for one another   Rom.1.27
that you are not *c.* by one another   Gal.5.15
fire which will *c.* the adversaries   Heb.10.27
for our God is a *c.* fire   Heb.12.29
came down from heaven and *c.* them   Rev.20.9

CONTEMPT

He pours *c.* on princes, and looses   Job 12.21
we have had more than enough of *c.*   Ps.123.3
When wickedness comes, *c.* comes also   Pr.18.3
for the son treats the father with *c.*   Mic.7.6
treated him with *c.* and mocked him   Lk.23.11
own account and hold him up to *c.*   Heb.6.6

CONTEND

Who is there that will *c.* with me?   Job 13.19
Shall a faultfinder *c.* with the   Job 40.2
Do not *c.* with a man for no reason   Pr.3.30
I will *c.* with those who *c.* with you   Is.49.25
For I will not *c.* for ever   Is.57.16
For we are not *c.* against flesh and   Eph.6.12
appealing to you to *c.* for the faith   Jude 3

CONTENT

Be *c.* with your glory, and stay   2 Kg.14.10
Yet you were not *c.* to walk in   Ezek.16.47
and be *c.* with your wages   Lk.3.14
I am *c.* with weaknesses, insults   2 Cor.12.10
in whatever state I am, to be *c.*   Phil.4.11
be *c.* with what you have   Heb.13.5

CONTINUALLY

of his heart was only evil *c.*   Gen.6.5
as he came he cursed *c.*   2 Sam.16.5
who *c.* stand before you and hear   2 Chr.9.7
his praise shall *c.* be in my mouth   Ps.34.1
In God we have boasted *c.*   Ps.44.8
May prayer be made for him *c.*   Ps.72.15
Let them be before the LORD *c.*   Ps.109.15
I will keep thy law *c.*, for ever   Ps.119.44
And the LORD will guide you *c.*   Is.58.11
My soul *c.* thinks of it and is   Lam.3.20
justice, and wait *c.* for your God   Hos.12.6
and were *c.* in the temple blessing   Lk.24.53
Through him then let us *c.* offer up   Heb.13.15

CONTINUE

that it may *c.* for ever before   2 Sam.7.29
O *c.* thy steadfast love to those   Ps.36.10
his fame *c.* as long as the sun   Ps.72.17
but *c.* in the fear of the LORD all   Pr.23.17
all night he *c.* in prayer to God   Lk.6.12
If you *c.* in my word, you are truly   Jn.8.31
urged them to *c.* in the grace of   Acts 13.43
exhorting them to *c.* in the faith   Acts 14.22
Are we to *c.* in sin that grace may   Rom.6.1
provided that you *c.* in the faith   Col.1.23
C. steadfastly in prayer   Col.4.2
Let brotherly love *c.*   Heb.13.1

CONTRIBUTE

For they all *c.* out of their	Mk.12.44
he who *c.*, in liberality; he who	Rom.12.8
C. to the needs of the saints	Rom.12.13

CONTRIBUTION

bring the *c.* into the house of	2 Chr.31.10
make some *c.* for the poor among	Rom.15.26
concerning the *c.* for the saints	1 Cor.16.1
so that *c.* need not be made when	1 Cor.16.2
generosity of your *c.* for them	2 Cor.9.13

CONTRITE

a broken and *c.* heart, O God, thou	Ps.51.17
who is of a *c.* and humble spirit	Is.57.15
to revive the heart of the *c.*	Is.57.15
he that is humble and *c.* in spirit	Is.66.2

CONTROVERSY

LORD has a *c.* with the inhabitants	Hos.4.1
craving for *c.* and for disputes	1 Tim.6.4
to do with stupid, senseless *c.*	2 Tim.2.23
But avoid stupid *c.*, genealogies	Tit.3.9

CONVERT (noun)

Jews and devout *c.* to Judaism	Acts 13.43
Epaenetus . . . was the first *c.* in Asia	Rom.16.5
were the first *c.* in Achaia	1 Cor.16.15
He must not be a recent *c.*, or he	1 Tim.3.6

CONVINCE

he will *c.* the world of sin and of	Jn.16.8
trying to *c.* them about Jesus	Acts 28.23
fully *c.* that God was able to do	Rom.4.21
are *c.* that one has died for all	2 Cor.5.14
C. of this, I know that I shall	Phil.1.25
c., rebuke, and exhort	2 Tim.4.2

COPPER

c. is smelted from the ore	Job 28.2
nor silver, nor *c.* in your belts	Mt.10.9
came, and put in two *c.* coins	Mk.12.42
you have paid the very last *c.*	Lk.12.59

CORD

this scarlet *c.* in the window	Jos.2.18
Pleiades, or loose the *c.* of Orion?	Job 38.31
The *c.* of death encompassed me	Ps.18.4
he has cut the *c.* of the wicked	Ps.129.4
threefold *c.* is not quickly broken	Ec.4.12
before the silver *c.* is snapped	Ec.12.6
lengthen your *c.* and strengthen	Is.54.2
I led them with *c.* of compassion	Hos.11.4
making a whip of *c.*, he drove them	Jn.2.15

CORINTH

Acts 18.1; 1 Cor.1.2; 2 Cor.1.1; 2 Tim.4.20

CORNELIUS

devout centurion, Acts 10.1; his prayer answered, Acts 10.3–4; sends for Peter, Acts 10.17; is baptized, Acts 10.48

CORNER

has become the head of the *c.*	Mt.21.42
let down by four *c.* upon the earth	Acts 10.11
for this was not done in a *c.*	Acts 26.26
has become the head of the *c.*	1 Pet.2.7
at the four *c.* of the earth, holding	Rev.7.1

CORNERSTONE

a precious *c.*, of a sure foundation	Is.28.16
Out of them shall come the *c.*	Zech.10.4
Christ Jesus himself being the *c.*	Eph.2.20
a *c.* chosen and precious	1 Pet.2.6

CORRUPT

Now the earth was *c.* in God's sight	Gen.6.11
They are *c.*, they do abominable	Ps.14.1
The heart is . . . desperately *c.*	Jer.17.9
They have deeply *c.* themselves as	Hos.9.9
and is *c.* through deceitful lusts	Eph.4.22
men of *c.* mind and counterfeit	2 Tim.3.8
but to the *c.* and unbelieving	Tit.1.15

CORRUPTION

nor let thy Holy One see *c.*	Acts 2.27
the dead, no more to return to *c.*	Acts 13.34
he whom God raised up saw no *c.*	Acts 13.37
flesh will from the flesh reap *c.*	Gal.6.8
escape from the *c.* . . . in the world	2 Pet.1.4
they themselves are slaves of *c.*	2 Pet.2.19

COSTLY

the ransom of his life is *c.*	Ps.49.8
with precious stones and *c.* gifts	Dan.11.38
jar of ointment . . . very *c.*	Mk.14.3
Mary took a pound of *c.* ointment	Jn.12.3
or gold or pearls or *c.* attire	1 Tim.2.9
of ivory, all articles of *c.* wood	Rev.18.12

COUNCIL

feared in the *c.* of the holy ones	Ps.89.7
brother shall be liable to the *c.*	Mt.5.22
for they will deliver you up to *c.*	Mk.13.9
He was a member of the *c.*	Lk.23.50
called together the *c.* and all	Acts 5.21
Pharisee in the *c.* named Gamaliel	Acts 5.34
when he had conferred with his *c.*	Acts 25.12

COUNSEL (noun)

forsaking the *c.* which the old men	1 Kg.12.13
Rehoboam took *c.* with the old men	2 Chr.10.6
took *c.* with the young men	2 Chr.10.8
he has *c.* and understanding	Job 12.13
The *c.* of the wicked is far from me	Job 21.16
walks not in the *c.* of the wicked	Ps.1.1
I bless the LORD who gives me *c.*	Ps.16.7
The *c.* of the LORD stands for ever	Ps.33.11
the *c.* of the wicked are treacherous	Pr.12.5
Give *c.*, grant justice; make your	Is.16.3
counselors of Pharaoh give stupid *c.*	Is.19.11
Has *c.* perished from the prudent?	Jer.49.7
the people took *c.* against Jesus	Mt.27.1
declaring . . . the whole *c.* of God	Acts 20.27
according to the *c.* of his will	Eph.1.11

COUNSELOR

an abundance of *c.* there is safety	Pr.11.14
name will be called "Wonderful *C.*	Is.9.6
among these there is no *c.*	Is.41.28
he will give you another *C.*	Jn.14.16
But the *C.*, the Holy Spirit, whom	Jn.14.26
when the *C.* comes, whom I shall	Jn.15.26
the *C.* will not come to you	Jn.16.7
the Lord, or who has been his *c.*?	Rom.11.34

COUNT

I can *c.* all my bones–they stare	Ps.22.17
If I would *c.* them, they are more	Ps.139.18
first sit down and *c.* the cost	Lk.14.28
that they were *c.* worthy to suffer	Acts 5.41
sin is not *c.* where there is no law	Rom.5.13
but in humility *c.* others better	Phil.2.3
did not *c.* equality with God a	Phil.2.6
Indeed I *c.* everything as loss	Phil.3.8
C. it all joy, my brethren, when you	Jas.1.2

COUNTENANCE

The LORD lift up his *c.* upon you	Num.6.26
his *c.* was like the *c.* of the angel	Jg.13.6

thy arm, and the light of thy *c*.   Ps.44.3
secret sins in the light of thy *c*.   Ps.90.8
A glad heart makes a cheerful *c*.   Pr.15.13
At that saying his *c*. fell   Mk.10.22
appearance of his *c*. was altered   Lk.9.29

COUNTRY
so is good news from a far *c*.   Pr.25.25
to their own *c*. by another way   Mt.2.12
who was coming in from the *c*.   Mk.15.21
and took his journey into a far *c*.   Lk.15.13
prophet has no honor in his own *c*.   Jn.4.44
as it is, they desire a better *c*.   Heb.11.16

COURAGE
Be of good *c*., and bring some of   Num.13.20
Be strong and of good *c*., do not   Dt.31.6
Be . . . of good *c*., be not frightened   Jos.1.9
Be strong, and let your heart take *c*.   Ps.31.24
says to his brother, "Take *c*.!"   Is.41.6
Take *c*., for as you have testified   Acts 23.11
Paul thanked God and took *c*.   Acts 28.15
So we are always of good *c*.   2 Cor.5.6
we had *c*. in our God to declare to   1 Th.2.2
nor lose *c*. when you are punished   Heb.12.5

COURAGEOUS
Only be strong and very *c*.   Jos.1.7
Be *c*. and be valiant   2 Sam.13.28
His heart was *c*. in the ways of   2 Chr.17.6
in your faith, be *c*., be strong   1 Cor.16.13

COURSE
and like a strong man runs its *c*.   Ps.19.5
and the third day I finish my *c*.   Lk.13.32
as John was finishing his *c*.   Acts 13.25
accomplish my *c*. and the ministry   Acts 20.24
following the *c*. of this world   Eph.2.2

COURT
yea, faints for the *c*. of the Lord   Ps.84.2
For a day in thy *c*. is better than   Ps.84.10
Enter . . . his *c*. with praise   Ps.100.4
while you are going with him to *c*.   Mt.5.25
he entered the *c*. of the high   Jn.18.15
a member of the *c*. of Herod   Acts 13.1
judged by you or by any human *c*.   1 Cor.4.3
is it not they who drag you into *c*.?   Jas.2.6

COVENANT
I will establish my *c*. with you   Gen.6.18
a sign of the *c*. between me and   Gen.9.13
establish my *c*. . . . an everlasting   Gen.17.19
God remembered his *c*. with Abraham   Ex.2.24
Then he took the book of the *c*.   Ex.24.7
the ark of the *c*. of the Lord went   Num.10.33
the faithful God who keeps *c*.   Dt.7.9
Joshua made a *c*. with the people   Jos.24.25
he read . . . the book of the *c*. which   2 Chr.34.30
I have made a *c*. with my eyes   Job 31.1
Have regard for thy *c*.   Ps.74.20
He is mindful of his *c*. for ever   Ps.105.8
will make a new *c*. with the house   Jer.31.31
make with them an everlasting *c*.   Jer.32.40
an everlasting *c*. which will never   Jer.50.5
be an everlasting *c*. with them   Ezek.37.26
My *c*. with him was a *c*. of life   Mal.2.5
for this is my blood of the *c*.   Mt.26.28
sons . . . of the *c*. which God gave   Acts 3.25
This cup is the new *c*. in my blood   1 Cor.11.25
to be ministers of a new *c*.   2 Cor.3.6
allegory: these women are two *c*.   Gal.4.24

strangers to the *c*. of promise   Eph.2.12
Jesus the surety of a better *c*.   Heb.7.22
This is the *c*. that I will make   Heb.8.10
he is the mediator of a new *c*.   Heb.9.15
Jesus, the mediator of a new *c*.   Heb.12.24
by the blood of the eternal *c*.   Heb.13.20

COVER
O earth, *c*. not my blood   Job 16.18
thou dost *c*. him with favor   Ps.5.12
Blessed is he . . . whose sin is *c*.   Ps.32.1
who *c*. thyself with light as with   Ps.104.2
If I say, "Let only darkness *c*. me   Ps.139.11
but love . . . *c*. all offenses   Pr.10.12
shall say to the mountains, *C*. us   Hos.10.8
some began . . . to *c*. his face   Mk.14.65
Nothing is *c*. up that will not be   Lk.12.2
Blessed are those . . . whose sins are *c*.   Rom.4.7
a man ought not to *c*. his head   1 Cor.11.7
will *c*. a multitude of sins   Jas.5.20
since love *c*. a multitude of sins   1 Pet.4.8

COVERING (noun)
before God . . . Abaddon has no *c*.   Job 26.6
He made darkness his *c*. around him   Ps.18.11
He spread a cloud for a *c*.   Ps.105.39
the *c*. too narrow to wrap   Is.28.20
every precious stone was your *c*.   Ezek.28.13
her hair is given to her for a *c*.   1 Cor.11.15

COVET
shall not *c*. your neighbor's wife   Ex.20.17
you shall not *c*. the silver   Dt.7.25
They *c*. fields, and seize them   Mic.2.2
I *c*. no one's silver or gold   Acts 20.33
not have known what it is to *c*.   Rom.7.7
You shall not *c*.   Rom.13.9
you *c*. and cannot obtain   Jas.4.2

CRAFTSMAN
a thing made by the hands of a *c*.   Dt.27.15
a skilful *c*. to set up an image   Is.40.20
no little business to the *c*.   Acts 19.24
Demetrius and the *c*. with him   Acts 19.38
a *c*. . . . shall be found . . . no more   Rev.18.22

CRAFTY
Jonadab was a very *c*. man   2 Sam.13.3
He frustrates the devices of the *c*.   Job 5.12
you choose the tongue of the *c*.   Job 15.5
They lay *c*. plans against thy people   Ps.83.3
I was *c*., you say, and got the   2 Cor.12.16

CREATE
In the beginning God *c*. the heavens   Gen.1.1
So God *c*. man in his own image   Gen.1.27
C. in me a clean heart, O God   Ps.51.10
the Lord will *c*. . . . a cloud by day   Is.4.5
the Holy One of Israel has *c*. it   Is.41.20
whom I *c*. for my glory   Is.43.7
For behold, I *c*. new heavens   Is.65.17
Has not one God *c*. us?   Mal.2.10
of those who *c*. dissensions   Rom.16.17
c. in Christ Jesus for good works   Eph.2.10
c. after the likeness of God   Eph.4.24
for in him all things were *c*.   Col.1.16
For everything *c*. by God is good   1 Tim.4.4
world was *c*. by the word of God   Heb.11.3
who *c*. heaven and what is in it   Rev.10.6

CREATION
But from the beginning of *c*.   Mk.10.6
Ever since the *c*. of the world   Rom.1.20

the *c.* waits with eager longing	Rom.8.19	**CROSS** (noun)		
the whole *c.* has been groaning	Rom.8.22	not take his *c.* and follow me	Mt.10.38	
nor anything else in all *c.*	Rom.8.39	let him come down now from the *c.*	Mt.27.42	
in Christ, he is a new *c.*	2 Cor.5.17	and take up his *c.* and follow me	Mk.8.34	
nor uncircumcision, but a new *c.*	Gal.6.15	Simon of Cyrene . . . to carry his *c.*	Mk.15.21	
the first-born of all *c.*	Col.1.15	and take up his *c.* daily	Lk.9.23	
they were from the beginning of *c.*	2 Pet.3.4	he went out, bearing his own *c.*	Jn.19.17	

CREATOR
Remember also your *C.* in the days	Ec.12.1
the *C.* of the ends of the earth	Is.40.28
the *C.* of Israel, your King	Is.43.15
the creature rather than the *C.*	Rom.1.25
their souls to a faithful *C.*	1 Pet.4.19

wrote a title and put it on the *c.* — Jn.19.19
lest the *c.* of Christ be emptied — 1 Cor.1.17
the word of the *c.* is folly to — 1 Cor.1.18
except in the *c.* of our Lord Jesus — Gal.6.14
to God in one body through the *c.* — Eph.2.16
unto death, even death on a *c.* — Phil.2.8
making peace by the blood of his *c.* — Col.1.20
was set before him endured the *c.* — Heb.12.2

CREATURE
bring forth swarms of living *c.*	Gen.1.20
the man called every living *c.*	Gen.2.19
the life of every *c.* is its blood	Lev.17.14
there is not . . . a *c.* without fear	Job 41.33
the earth is full of thy *c.*	Ps.104.24
served the *c.* rather than the	Rom.1.25
preached to every *c.* under heaven	Col.1.23
And before him no *c.* is hidden	Heb.4.13
I heard every *c.* in heaven and	Rev.5.13

CROWN (noun)
good wife is the *c.* of her husband — Pr.12.4
The *c.* of the wise is their wisdom — Pr.14.24
Grandchildren are the *c.* of the aged — Pr.17.6
does a *c.* endure to all generations? — Pr.27.24
LORD of hosts will be a *c.* of glory — Is.28.5
plaiting a *c.* of thorns they — Mt.27.29
wearing the *c.* of thorns — Jn.19.5
my joy and *c.*, stand firm thus — Phil.4.1
obtain the unfading *c.* of glory — 1 Pet.5.4
and I will give you the *c.* of life — Rev.2.10
cast their *c.* before the throne — Rev.4.10
on her head a *c.* of twelve stars — Rev.12.1
with a golden *c.* on his head — Rev.14.14

CRETE
under the lee of *C.* off Salmone	Acts 27.7
a harbor of *C.*, looking northeast	Acts 27.12
This is why I left you in *C.*	Tit.1.5

CRY (noun)
God does not hear an empty *c.*	Job 35.13
attend to my *c.*! Give ear	Ps.17.1
he inclined to me and heard my *c.*	Ps.40.1
may there be no *c.* of distress in	Ps.144.14
And Jesus uttered a loud *c.*	Mk.15.37
she exclaimed with a loud *c.*	Lk.1.42
from heaven with a *c.* of command	1 Th.4.16
the *c.* of the harvesters have	Jas.5.4

CRUCIFY
to be mocked and scourged and *c.* — Mt.20.19
all the more, "Let him be *c.*" — Mt.27.23
Then two robbers were *c.* with him — Mt.27.38
And they cried out again, "*C.* him." — Mk.15.13
they cried out, "*C.* him, *c.* him!" — Jn.19.6
away with him, *c.* him — Jn.19.15
this Jesus . . . you *c.* and killed — Acts 2.23
Jesus . . . whom you *c.* . . . God raised — Acts 4.10
our old self was *c.* with him — Rom.6.6
but we preach Christ *c.* — 1 Cor.1.23
he was *c.* in weakness, but lives — 2 Cor.13.4
I have been *c.* with Christ — Gal.2.20
since they *c.* the Son of God — Heb.6.6

CRY (verb)
to my God I *c.* for help	Ps.18.6
in his temple all *c.*, "Glory!"	Ps.29.9
This poor man *c.*, and the LORD	Ps.34.6
Out of the depths I *c.* to thee	Ps.130.1
Wisdom *c.* aloud in the street	Pr.1.20
A voice *c.*: "In the wilderness	Is.40.3
A voice says, "*C.*!" And I said	Is.40.6
He will not *c.* or lift up his voice	Is.42.2
prophets . . . who *c.* "Peace"	Mic.3.5
and beginning to sink he *c.* out	Mt.14.30
they *c.* out the more, "Lord, have	Mt.20.31
Jesus *c.* with a loud voice	Mt.27.46
those who followed *c.* out, "Hosanna	Mk.11.9
they *c.* out again, "Crucify him	Mk.15.13
seizes him, and he suddenly *c.* out	Lk.9.39
who *c.* to him day and night?	Lk.18.7
the very stones would *c.* out	Lk.19.40
voice of one *c.* in the wilderness	Jn.1.23
When we *c.*, "Abba! Father!"	Rom.8.15

CRUEL
but a *c.* man hurts himself — Pr.11.17
Wrath is *c.*, anger is overwhelming — Pr.27.4
jealousy is *c.* as the grave — S.of S.8.6
daughter of my people has become *c.* — Lam.4.3

CUBIT
can add one *c.* to his span of life? — Mt.6.27

CUNNING
yea, their *c.* is in vain — Ps.119.118
we refuse to practice *c.* — 2 Cor.4.2
serpent deceived Eve by his *c.* — 2 Cor.11.3
by the *c.* of men, by their craftiness — Eph.4.14

CROOKED
are a perverse and *c.* generation	Dt.32.5
with the *c.* thou dost show	Ps.18.26
Put away from you *c.* speech	Pr.4.24
A man of *c.* mind does not prosper	Pr.17.20
The way of the guilty is *c.*	Pr.21.8
What is *c.* cannot be made straight	Ec.1.15
and the *c.* shall be made straight	Lk.3.5
yourselves from this *c.* generation	Acts 2.40
the midst of a *c.* . . . . generation	Phil.2.15

CUP
is my chosen portion and my *c.* — Ps.16.5
my head with oil, my *c.* overflows — Ps.23.5
lift up the *c.* of salvation — Ps.116.13
have drunk . . . the *c.* of his wrath — Is.51.17
give him the *c.* of consolation — Jer.16.7
gives . . . even a *c.* of cold water — Mt.10.42
to drink the *c.* that I am to drink? — Mt.20.22
you cleanse the outside of the *c.* — Mt.23.25
And he took a *c.*, and when he had — Mt.26.27
possible, let this *c.* pass from me — Mt.26.39

CURE

The *c.* of blessing which we bless	1 Cor.10.16
This *c.* is the new covenant	1 Cor.11.25
eat this bread and drink the *c.*	1 Cor.11.26
unmixed into the *c.* of his anger	Rev.14.10

CURE

He would *c.* him of his leprosy	2 Kg.5.3
he is not able to *c.* you or heal	Hos.5.13
and the boy was *c.* instantly	Mt.17.18
gave them power . . . to *c.* diseases	Lk.9.1
Jews said to the man who was *c.*	Jn.5.10
had diseases also came and were *c.*	Acts 28.9

CURSE (noun)

you this day a blessing and a *c.*	Dt.11.26
God turned the *c.* into a blessing	Dt.23.5
with all the *c.* of the covenant	Dt.29.21
God turned the *c.* into a blessing	Neh.13.2
Therefore a *c.* devours the earth	Is.24.6
I will send the *c.* upon you	Mal.2.2
began to invoke a *c.* on himself	Mt.26.74
their mouth is full of *c.* and	Rom.3.14
who rely on works . . . are under a *c.*	Gal.3.10
redeemed us from the *c.* of the law	Gal.3.13

CURSE (verb)

c. is the ground because of you	Gen.3.17
I will never again *c.* the ground	Gen.8.21
You shall not *c.* the deaf or put	Lev.19.14
his wife said, ". . . *C.* God, and die."	Job 2.9
but inwardly they *c.*	Ps.62.4
Let them *c.*, but do thou bless	Ps.109.28
C. is the man who trusts in man	Jer.17.5
fig tree which you *c.* has withered	Mk.11.21
bless those who *c.* you	Lk.6.28
bless and do not *c.* them	Rom.12.14
of God ever says "Jesus be *c.*!"	1 Cor.12.3
and with it we *c.* men	Jas.3.9

CURTAIN

stretches out the heavens like a *c.*	Is.40.22
And the *c.* of the temple was torn	Mk.15.38
the inner shrine behind the *c.*	Heb.6.19

CUSTOM

Now this was the *c.* in former times	Ru.4.7
for the *c.* of the peoples are false	Jer.10.3
as his *c.* was, he taught them	Mk.10.1
as his *c.* was, on the sabbath day	Lk.4.16
a *c.* that I should release one man	Jn.18.39
as is the burial *c.* of the Jews	Jn.19.40

CUT

So Moses *c.* two tables of stone	Ex.34.4
For the wicked shall be *c.* off	Ps.37.9
May his posterity be *c.* off	Ps.109.13
does not bear good fruit is *c.* down	Mt.3.10
c. it off and throw it from you	Mt.18.8
the man whose ear Peter had *c.* off	Jn.18.26
At Cenchreae he *c.* his hair	Acts 18.18
otherwise you too will be *c.* off	Rom.11.22

CYMBAL

Asaph was to sound the *c.*	1 Chr.16.5
with *c.*, to praise the LORD	Ezra 3.10
praise him with loud clashing *c.*	Ps.150.5
I am a noisy gong or a clanging *c.*	1 Cor.13.1

CYPRUS

Is.23.1; Ezek.27.6; Acts 11.20; 15.39; 27.4

CYRENE

Mt.27.32; Acts 2.10; 11.20; 13.1

CYRUS

king of Persia, 2 Chr.36.22; prophecies concerning, Is.44.28; 45.1; *see* Dan.6.28; 10.1; his proclamation for rebuilding the temple, 2 Chr.36.22–23; Ezra 1

DAILY

Blessed be the Lord, who *d.* bears us	Ps.68.19
Yet they seek me *d.*, and delight	Is.58.2
Give us this day our *d.* bread	Mt.6.11
take up his cross *d.* and follow me	Lk.9.23
he was teaching *d.* in the temple	Lk.19.47
they increased in numbers *d.*	Acts 16.5
examining the scriptures *d.* to see	Acts 17.11
priests, to offer sacrifices *d.*	Heb.7.27

DAMASCUS

the capital of Syria; first mentioned, Gen.14.15; subjugated by David, 2 Sam.8.6; 1 Chr.18.6; Elisha's prophecy there, 2 Kg.8.7–13; taken by Tiglath-pileser, king of Assyria, 2 Kg.16.9; restored to Israel by Jeroboam, 2 Kg.14.28; king Ahaz copies an altar there, 2 Kg.16.10; Paul's journey to, Acts 9; 22.6; Paul restored to sight, and baptized there, Acts 9.17,18; prophecies concerning, Is.7.8; 8.4; 17.1; Jer.49.23; Am.1.3

DAN

(1) son of Jacob, by Rachel's handmaid, Gen. 30.6; (2) tribe of, numbered, Num.1.39; 26.42–43; their inheritance, Jos.19.40; blessed by Jacob, Gen.49.16; blessed by Moses, Dt.33.22; win Laish, and call it Dan, Jg.18.29; set up idolatry, Jg.18.30; 1 Kg.12.29

DANCE (verb)

David *d.* before the LORD with all	2 Sam.6.14
a time to mourn, and a time to *d.*	Ec.3.4
We piped to you, and you did not *d.*	Mt.11.17
Herodias' daughter came in and *d.*	Mk.6.22
to eat and drink and rose up to *d.*	1 Cor.10.7

DANIEL

(1) (Belteshazzar), with other captives, taken from Jerusalem to Babylon, Dan.1.3–6; taught the learning of the Chaldeans, Dan.1.4; will not take the king's meat or drink, Dan.1.8; has understanding in dreams, Dan.1.17; interprets the royal dreams, Dan.2; 4, and handwriting on wall, Dan.5.17; made chief president by Darius, Dan.6.2; conspired against by the princes, Dan.6.4; idolatrous decree against, issued, Dan.6.9; cast into the lions' den, Dan. 6.16; preservation in, Dan.6.22; his visions, Dan.7–8; his prayer, Dan.9.3; promise of return from captivity, Dan.9.24; name mentioned, Ezek.14.14,20; 28.3; (2) others, 1 Chr.3.1; Ezra 8.2

DARE

nor . . . did any one *d.* to ask him any	Mt.22.46
For they no longer *d.* to ask him	Lk.20.40
none of the disciples *d.* ask him	Jn.21.12
for a good man one will *d.* even to die	Rom.5.7
does he *d.* go to law before the	1 Cor.6.1
I also *d.* to boast of that	2 Cor.11.21

DARIUS

Ezra 4.5; Neh.12.22; Dan.6.1; Hag.1.1; Zech. 1.1

DARK (noun)

They grope in the *d.* without light	Job 12.25

The murderer rises in the *d.*   Job 24.14
What I tell you in the *d.*, utter   Mt.10.27
DARK (adjective)
even the darkness is not *d.* to thee   Ps.139.12
I am very *d.*, but comely   S.of S.1.5
to the tomb . . . while it was still *d.*   Jn.20.1
as to a lamp shining in a *d.* place   2 Pet.1.19
DARKENED
Let their eyes be *d.*, so that   Ps.69.23
The sun and the moon are *d.*   Jl.2.10
after . . . those days the sun will be *d.* Mt.24.29
their senseless minds were *d.*   Rom.1.21
they are *d.* in their understanding   Eph.4.18
sun and . . . air were *d.* with the smoke   Rev.9.2
DARKNESS
d. was upon the face of the deep   Gen.1.2
and the *d.* he called Night   Gen.1.5
land of Egypt, a *d.* to be felt   Ex.10.21
as the blind grope in *d.*   Dt.28.29
the wicked shall be cut off in *d.*   1 Sam.2.9
He made *d.* around him his canopy   2 Sam.22.12
and my God lightens my *d.*   2 Sam.22.29
I am hemmed in by *d.*, and thick *d.*   Job 23.17
when I waited for light, *d.* came   Job 30.26
the Lord my God lightens my *d.*   Ps.18.28
nor the pestilence that stalks in *d.*   Ps.91.6
Let only *d.* cover me, and the light   Ps.139.11
who walked in *d.* have seen a great   Is.9.2
I form light and create *d.*   Is.45.7
For behold, *d.* shall cover the earth   Is.60.2
who makes the morning *d.*   Am.4.13
and turns deep *d.* into the morning   Am.5.8
Is not the day of the Lord *d.*   Am.5.20
who sat in *d.* have seen a great   Mt.4.16
and cast him into the outer *d.*   Mt.22.13
there was *d.* over all the land   Mt.27.45
The light shines in the *d.*   Jn.1.5
men loved *d.* rather than light   Jn.3.19
believes in me may not remain in *d.*   Jn.12.46
cast off the works of *d.* and   Rom.13.12
what fellowship has light with *d.?*   2 Cor.6.14
we are not of the night or of *d.*   1 Th.5.5
out of *d.* into his marvelous light   1 Pet.2.9
in him is no *d.* at all   1 Jn.1.5
DAUGHTER
saw that the *d.* of men were fair   Gen.6.2
and said, "Tell me whose *d.* you are   Gen.24.23.
Now the *d.* of Pharaoh came down to   Ex.2.5
When a man sells his *d.* as a slave   Ex.21.7
And she said to her, "Go, my *d.*"   Ru.2.2
Now Saul's *d.* Michal loved David   1 Sam.18.20
his sons and *d.* were eating   Job 1.13
Hear, O *d.*, consider, and incline   Ps.45.10
O *d.* of Babylon, you devastator   Ps.137.8
sons and your *d.* shall prophesy   Jl.2.28
saying, "My *d.* has just died   Mt.9.18
a *d.* against her mother, and a   Mt.10.35
the *d.* of Herodias danced before   Mt.14.6
Tell the *d.* of Zion, Behold, your   Mt.21.5
D., your faith has made you well   Mk.5.34
Fear not, *d.* of Zion   Jn.12.15
and you shall be my sons and *d.*   2 Cor.6.18
be called the son of Pharaoh's *d.*   Heb.11.24
DAVID
anointed king by Samuel, 1 Sam.16.8–13; plays
the harp before Saul, 1 Sam.16–23; his zeal and

faith, 1 Sam.17.26,34–36; kills Goliath, 1 Sam.
17.49; at first honored by Saul, 1 Sam.18.5;
Saul jealous of, tries to kill, 1 Sam.18.8–12;
afterwards persecuted by him, 1 Sam.19; 20;
loved by Jonathan, 1 Sam.18.1; 19.1; 20;
23.16; overcomes the Philistines, 1 Sam.18.27;
19.8; flees to Gath, and feigns madness, 1
Sam.21.10, 13; dwells in the cave of Adullam,
1 Sam.22; escapes Saul's pursuit, 1 Sam.23;
twice spares Saul's life, 1 Sam.24.4; 26.9–11;
dwells at Ziklag, 1 Sam.27; laments the death of
Saul and Jonathan, 2 Sam.1.17; becomes king of
Judah, 2 Sam.2.4; forms a league with Abner, 2
Sam.3.13; avenges the murder of Ish-bosheth,
2 Sam.4.9–12; becomes king of all Israel, 2
Sam.5.3; 1 Chr.11; his victories, 2 Sam.2;
5; 8; 10; 12.29; 21.15–22; 1 Chr.18–20; brings
the ark to Jerusalem, 2 Sam.6; 1 Chr.13; 15;
desires to build God a house, 2 Sam.7.2–3, and
is forbidden by Nathan, 1 Chr.17.4; God's
promises to him, 2 Sam.7.11; 1 Chr.17.10; his
prayer and thanksgiving, 2 Sam.7.18–29; 1
Chr.17.16–27; his kindness to Mephibosheth,
2 Sam.9; his sin involving Bathsheba and Uriah,
2 Sam.11; 12; repents at Nathan's parable of
the ewe lamb; 2 Sam.12; Ps.51; grieves over
Absalom's death, 2 Sam.18.33; 19.1; Sheba's
conspiracy against, 2 Sam.20; makes expiation
for the Gibeonites, 2 Sam.21; regulates the
service of the tabernacle, 1 Chr.23–26; exhorts
the congregation to fear God, 1 Chr.28; appoints Solomon his successor, 1 Kg.1; his
charge to Solomon, 1 Kg.2; 1 Chr.28.9; his last
words, 2 Sam.23; his death, 1 Kg.2; 1 Chr.
29.26–28
DAWN (verb)
and shadow of death light has *d.*   Mt.4.16
the day shall *d.* upon us from on   Lk.1.78
As day was about to *d.*, Paul urged   Acts 27.33
until the day *d.* and the morning   2 Pet.1.19
DAY
God called the light *D.*   Gen.1.5
the greater light to rule the *d.*   Gen.1.16
So God blessed the seventh *d.*   Gen.2.3
This *d.* shall be . . . a memorial *d.*   Ex.12.14
Remember the *d.* of old, consider the   Dt.32.7
This *d.* is a *d.* of good news   2 Kg.7.9
of his salvation from *d.* to *d.*   1 Chr.16.23
This *d.* is holy to the Lord your   Neh.8.9
and cursed the *d.* of his birth   Job 3.1
for our *d.* on earth are a shadow   Job 8.9
on his law he meditates *d.* and night   Ps.1.2
D. to *d.* pours forth speech   Ps.19.2
follow me all the *d.* of my life   Ps.23.6
tell . . . of thy praise all the *d.* long   Ps.35.28
Thine is the *d.*, thine also the   Ps.74.16
In the *d.* of my trouble I seek the   Ps.77.2
For a *d.* in thy courts is better   Ps.84.10
tell of his salvation from *d.* to *d.*   Ps.96.2
As for man, his *d.* are like grass   Ps.103.15
This is the *d.* which the Lord has   Ps.118.24
The sun shall not smite you by *d.*   Ps.121.6
the night is bright as the *d.*   Ps.139.12
not know what a *d.* may bring forth   Pr.27.1
the *d.* of death, than the *d.* of birth   Ec.7.1
In the *d.* of prosperity be joyful   Ec.7.14

O *D.* Star, son of Dawn! How you   Is.14.12
Cursed be the *d.* on which I was   Jer.20.14
my covenant with *d.* and night and   Jer.33.25
three times a *d.* and prayed and   Dan.6.10
For the *d.* of the LORD is near   Jl.1.15
Is not the *d.* of the LORD darkness   Am.5.20
Give us this *d.* our daily bread   Mt.6.11
own trouble be sufficient for the *d.*   Mt.6.34
more tolerable on the *d.* of judgment   Mt.10.15
and on the third *d.* be raised   Mt.16.21
of that *d.* and hour no one knows   Mt.24.36
since it was the *d.* of Preparation   Mk.15.42
born this *d.* in the city of David   Lk.2.11
When the *d.* of Pentecost had come   Acts 2.1
sealed for the *d.* of redemption   Eph.4.30
in the last *d.* . . . times of stress   2 Tim.3.1
laid up treasure for the last *d.*   Jas.5.3
both now and to the *d.* of eternity   2 Pet.3.18
was in the Spirit on the Lord's *d.*   Rev.1.10

DEACONS
Philippi, with the bishops and *d.*   Phil.1.1
D. likewise must be serious, not   1 Tim.3.8
if . . . blameless let them serve as *d.*   1 Tim.3.10
those who serve well as *d.* gain   1 Tim.3.13

DEAD
not forsaken the living or the *d.*   Ru.2.20
look upon a *d.* dog such as I?   2 Sam.9.8
out of mind like one who is *d.*   Ps.31.12
the *d.* do not praise the LORD   Ps.115.17
D. flies make the perfumer's ointment   Ec.10.1
Thy *d.* shall live, their bodies   Is.26.19
Weep not for him who is *d.*   Jer.22.10
raise the *d.,* cleanse lepers, cast   Mt.10.8
the Son of man is raised from the *d.*   Mt.17.9
he is not God of the *d.,* but of   Mt.22.32
And the *d.* man sat up, and began to   Lk.7.15
Leave the *d.* to bury their own *d.*   Lk.9.60
do you seek the living among the *d.*?   Lk.24.5
raises the *d.* and gives them life   Jn.5.21
whom God raised from the *d.*   Acts 3.15
be judge of the living and the *d.*   Acts 10.42
raised from the *d.* Jesus our Lord   Rom.4.24
consider yourselves *d.* to sin   Rom.6.11
your bodies are *d.* because of sin   Rom.8.10
Christ . . . raised from the *d.*   1 Cor.15.20
baptized in behalf of the *d.*   1 Cor.15.29
the *d.* will be raised imperishable   1 Cor.15.52
And the *d.* in Christ will rise   1 Th.4.16
repentance from *d.* works and   Heb.6.1
so faith apart from works is *d.*   Jas.2.26
Blessed are the *d.* who die in the   Rev.14.13

DEAF
be not *d.* to me, lest, if thou be   Ps.28.1
the ears of the *d.* unstopped   Is.35.5
lepers are cleansed and the *d.* hear   Mt.11.5
You dumb and *d.* spirit, I command   Mk.9.25

DEAL (verb)
May the LORD *d.* kindly with you   Ru.1.8
He does not *d.* with us according   Ps.103.10
D. bountifully with thy servant   Ps.119.17
those who *d.* with the world as   1 Cor.7.31
He can *d.* gently with the ignorant   Heb.5.2
not to *d.* with sin but to save   Heb.9.28

DEATH
I do not know the day of my *d.*   Gen.27.2
Let me die the *d.* of the righteous   Num.23.10

if even *d.* parts me from you   Ru.1.17
who long for *d.,* but it comes not   Job 3.21
Abaddon and *D.* say, 'We have heard   Job 28.22
Have the gates of *d.* been revealed   Job 38.17
For in *d.* there is no remembrance   Ps.6.5
lest I sleep the sleep of *d.*   Ps.13.3
the valley of the shadow of *d.*   Ps.23.4
D. shall be their shepherd   Ps.49.14
What man can live and never see *d.*?   Ps.89.48
hast delivered my soul from *d.*   Ps.116.8
he has not given me over to *d.*   Ps.118.18
but righteousness delivers from *d.*   Pr.11.4
for love is strong as *d.*   S.of S.8.6
We have made a covenant with *d.*   Is.28.15
my soul is . . . sorrowful, even to *d.*   Mt.26.38
darkness and in the shadow of *d.*   Lk.1.79
but has passed from *d.* to life   Jn.5.24
having loosed the pangs of *d.*   Acts 2.24
Yet *d.* reigned from Adam to Moses   Rom.5.14
The *d.* he died he died to sin, once   Rom.6.10
For the wages of sin is *d.*   Rom.6.23
deliver me from this body of *d.*?   Rom.7.24
For I am sure that neither *d.*   Rom.8.38
you proclaim the Lord's *d.* until   1 Cor.11.26
D. is swallowed up in victory   1 Cor.15.54
O *d.,* where is thy victory?   1 Cor.15.55
The sting of *d.* is sin   1 Cor.15.56
Now if the dispensation of *d.*   2 Cor.3.7
d. is at work in us, but life in   2 Cor.4.12
obedient unto *d.,* even *d.* on a cross   Phil.2.8
becoming like him in his *d.*   Phil.3.10
Put to *d.* therefore what is earthly   Col.3.5
who abolished *d.* and brought life   2 Tim.1.10
we have passed out of *d.* into life   1 Jn.3.14
He who does not love remains in *d.*   1 Jn.3.14
Be faithful unto *d.,* and I will   Rev.2.10
horse, and its rider's name was *D.*   Rev.6.8
Over such the second *d.* has no   Rev.20.6
Then *D.* and Hades were thrown into   Rev.20.14

DEBORAH
Jg.4.4–10; 5.1

DEBT
and every one who was in *d.*   1 Sam.22.2
And forgive us our *d.*   Mt.6.12
released him and forgave him the *d.*   Mt.18.27
indeed they are in *d.* to them   Rom.15.27

DECEIT
in whose spirit there is no *d.*   Ps.32.2
D. is in the heart of those who   Pr.12.20
Bread gained by *d.* is sweet to a   Pr.20.17
there was no *d.* in his mouth   Is.53.9
d., licentiousness, envy, slander   Mk.7.22
makes a prey of you by . . . empty *d.*   Col.2.8

DECEITFUL
from *d.* and unjust men deliver me   Ps.43.1
Charm is *d.,* and beauty is vain   Pr.31.30
The heart is *d.* above all things   Jer.17.9
d. workmen, disguising themselves   2 Cor.11.13
by their craftiness in *d.* wiles   Eph.4.14
by giving heed to *d.* spirits   1 Tim.4.1

DECEIVE
Why then have you *d.* me?   Gen.29.25
Every one *d.* his neighbor, and no   Jer.9.5
The pride of your heart has *d.* you   Ob.3
they use their tongues to *d.*   Rom.3.13
Let no one *d.* himself   1 Cor.3.18

serpent *d*. Eve by his cunning· 2 Cor.11.3
Let no one *d*. you with empty words Eph.5.6
we *d*. ourselves, and the truth is 1 Jn.1.8

DECLARE
to *d*. to you the word of the LORD Dt.5.5
D. his glory among the nations 1 Chr.16.24
they had *d*. Job to be in the wrong Job 32.3
The heavens *d*. his righteousness Ps.50.6
D. his glory among the nations Ps.96.3
I will *d*. thy greatness Ps.145.6
let us *d*. in Zion the work of ... God Jer.51.10
(Thus he *d*. all foods clean.) Mk.7.19
d. how much God has done for you Lk.8.39
take what is mine and *d*. it to you Jn.16.15
d. that God is really among you 1 Cor.14.25
that I may *d*. it boldly, as I ought Eph.6.20
to *d*. the mystery of Christ Col.4.3
D. these things; exhort and reprove Tit.2.15
For if the message *d*. by angels was Heb.2.2
that you may *d*. the wonderful deeds 1 Pet.2.9

DECREE (noun)
I will tell of the *d*. of the LORD Ps.2.7
Thy *d*. are very sure Ps.93.5
I have heard a *d*. of destruction Is.28.22
So the *d*. went forth that the wise Dan.2.13
In those days a *d*. went out from Lk.2.1
they know God's *d*. that those Rom.1.32

DEDICATE
the people of Israel *d*. to the LORD Lev.22.3
When a man *d*. his house to be holy Lev.27.14
these ... King David *d*. to the LORD 2 Sam.8.11
I am about to ... *d*. it to him for 2 Chr.2.4

DEDICATION
offerings for the *d*. of the altar Num.7.10
celebrated the *d*. of this house Ezra 6.16
the *d*. of the wall of Jerusalem Neh.12.27
the feast of the *D*. at Jerusalem Jn.10.22

DEED
O LORD ... terrible in glorious *d*. Ex.15.11
Tell among the peoples his *d*. Ps.9.11
By dread *d*. thou dost answer us Ps.65.5
I still proclaim thy wondrous *d*. Ps.71.17
tell ... the glorious *d*. of the LORD Ps.78.4
Praise him for his mighty *d*. Ps.150.2
what good *d*. must I do, to have Mt.19.16
mighty in *d*. and word before God Lk.24.19
because their *d*. were evil Jn.3.19
I did one *d*., and you all marvel Jn.7.21
he was mighty in his words and *d*. Acts 7.22
put to death the *d*. of the body Rom.8.13
disobedient, unfit for any good *d*. Tit.1.16
let us ... love ... in *d*. and in truth 1 Jn.3.18
Great and wonderful are thy *d*. Rev.15.3
the fine linen is the righteous *d*. Rev.19.8

DEEP (adjective)
God caused a *d*. sleep to fall upon Gen.2.21
find out the *d*. things of God? Job 11.7
O LORD! Thy thoughts are very *d*. Ps.92.5
a man's mind is like *d*. water Pr.20.5
who dwelt in a land of *d*. darkness Is.9.2
to draw with, and the well is *d*. Jn.4.11
for us with sighs too *d*. for words Rom.8.26
some call the *d*. things of Satan Rev.2.24

DEEP (noun)
darkness was upon the face of the *d*. Gen.1.2
D. calls to *d*. at the thunder of Ps.42.7

who says to the *d*., "Be dry Is.44.27
out into the *d*. and let down your Lk.5.4

DEFEND
d. my cause against an ungodly Ps.43.1
May he *d*. the cause of the poor of Ps.72.4
d. the fatherless, plead for the widow Is.1.17
he *d*. the oppressed man Acts 7.24

DEFENSE
God has shown himself a sure *d*. Ps.48.3
to make a *d*. to the people Acts 19.33
as he thus made his *d*., Festus Acts 26.24
my *d*. to those who would examine 1 Cor.9.3
put here for the *d*. of the gospel Phil.1.16

DEFILE
You shall not *d*. yourselves with Lev.11.44
You shall not *d*. the land in which Num.35.34
they have *d*. thy holy temple Ps.79.1
For your hands are *d*. with blood Is.59.3
They have *d*. my holy name by their Ezek.43.8
These are what *d*. a man Mt.15.20
his disciples ate with hands *d*. Mk.7.2
and he has *d*. this holy place Acts 21.28
their conscience, being weak, is *d*. 1 Cor.8.7
and by it the many become *d*. Heb.12.15
have not *d*. themselves with women Rev.14.4

DEITY
to think that the *D*. is like gold Acts 17.29
namely, his eternal power and *d*. Rom.1.20
whole fulness of *d*. dwells bodily Col.2.9

DELAY (verb)
saw that Moses *d*. to come down Ex.32.1
not *d*. to keep thy commandments Ps.119.60
d. not, for thy own sake, O my God Dan.9.19
My master is *d*. in coming Lk.12.45

DELIGHT (noun)
that it was a *d*. to the eyes Gen.3.6
his *d*. is in the law of the LORD Ps.1.2
For thou hast no *d*. in sacrifice Ps.51.16
LORD, but a just weight is his *d*. Pr.11.1
his *d*. shall be in the fear of the Is.11.3
then you shall take *d*. in the LORD Is.58.14
take no *d*. in your solemn assemblies Am.5.21
the *d*. in riches choke the word Mt.13.22

DELIGHT (verb)
delivered me, because he *d*. in me Ps.18.19
I *d*. to do thy will, O my God Ps.40.8
my chosen, in whom my soul *d*. Is.42.1
For I *d*. in the law of God Rom.7.22

DELIVER
I have come down to *d*. them out of Ex.3.8
I will *d*. you from their bondage Ex.6.6
the LORD will *d*. you into my hand 1 Sam.17.46
Thou dost *d*. a humble people 2 Sam.22.28
D. my life from the wicked by thy Ps.17.13
D. my soul from the sword Ps.22.20
D. me from all my transgressions Ps.39.8
Be pleased, O God, to *d*. me Ps.70.1
d. you from the snare of the fowler Ps.91.3
d. me from the hand of aliens Ps.144.11
·but righteousness *d*. from death Pr.11.4
he ... will defend and *d*. them Is.19.20
saying, "The LORD will surely *d*. us Is.36.15
who ... will *d*. you out of my hands? Dan.3.15
But *d*. us from evil Mt.6.13
Brother will *d*. up brother to death Mt.10.21
let God *d*. him now, if he desires Mt.27.43

for they will *d.* you up to councils   Mk.13.9
he who *d.* me to you has . . . greater sin   Jn.19.11
this Jesus, *d.* up according to the   Acts 2.23
the customs which Moses *d.* to us   Acts 6.14
received the law as *d.* by angels   Acts 7.53
will *d.* me from this body of death?   Rom.7.24
if I *d.* my body to be burned   1 Cor.13.3
when he *d.* the kingdom to God   1 Cor.15.24
our hope that he will *d.* us again   2 Cor.1.10
Jesus who *d.* us from the wrath to   1 Th.1.10
whom I have *d.* to Satan that they   1 Tim.1.20
and *d.* all those who through fear   Heb.2.15
was once for all *d.* to the saints   Jude 3

DELIVERER
the LORD raised up a *d.* for the people   Jg.3.9
The LORD . . . my fortress, and my *d.*   2 Sam.22.2
my *d.*, my God, my rock, in whom I   Ps.18.2
Thou art my help and my *d.*   Ps.40.17
The *D.* will come from Zion   Rom.11.26

DELUSION
men of high estate are a *d.*   Ps.62.9
Behold, they are all a *d.*   Is.41.29
you have uttered *d.* and seen lies   Ezek.13.8
God sends upon them a strong *d.*   2 Th.2.11

DEMON
sacrificed to *d.* which were no gods   Dt.32.17
sacrificed their sons . . . to the *d.*   Ps.106.37
He casts out *d.* by the prince of *d.*   Mt.9.34
and they say, 'He has a *d.*'   Mt.11.18
and the *d.* came out of him   Mt.17.18
who had the spirit of an unclean *d.*   Lk.4.33
The people answered, "You have a *d.*   Jn.7.20
Jesus answered, "I have not a *d.*   Jn.8.49
Can a *d.* open the eyes of the blind?   Jn.10.21
they offer to *d.* and not to God   1 Cor.10.20
cup of the Lord and the cup of *d.*   1 Cor.10.21
giving heed to . . . doctrines of *d.*   1 Tim.4.1
Even the *d.* believe–and shudder   Jas.2.19
has become a dwelling place of *d.*   Rev.18.2

DEN
shall be cast into the *d.* of lions   Dan.6.7
a young lion cry out from his *d.*   Am.3.4
you have made it a *d.* of robbers   Mk.11.17
in *d.* and caves of the earth   Heb.11.38

DENY
I also will *d.* before my Father who   Mt.10.33
let him *d.* himself and take up his   Mt.16.24
crows, you will *d.* me three times   Mt.26.34
Peter again *d.* it; and at once   Jn.18.27
you *d.* the Holy and Righteous One   Acts 3.14
if we *d.* him, he also will *d.* us   2 Tim.2.12
but they *d.* him by their deeds   Tit.1.16
No one who *d.* the Son has the   1 Jn.2.23
and you did not *d.* my faith even   Rev.2.13

DEPART
The scepter shall not *d.* from Judah   Gen.49.10
They say to God, '*D.* from us   Job 21.14
to *d.* from evil is understanding   Job 28.28
D. from evil and do good   Ps.34.14
D. from me, you evildoers   Ps.119.115
when he is old he will not *d.* from   Pr.22.6
shall not *d.* out of your mouth   Is.59.21
d. from me, you evildoers   Mt.7.23
D. from me, you cursed, into the   Mt.25.41
D. from me, for I am a sinful man   Lk.5.8
Gerasenes asked him to *d.* from them   Lk.8.37

d. from me, all you workers of   Lk.13.27
his hour . . . to *d.* out of this world   Jn.13.1
them not to *d.* from Jerusalem   Acts 1.4
My desire is to *d.* and be with   Phil.1.23
some will *d.* from the faith   1 Tim.4.1
Let every one . . . *d.* from iniquity   2 Tim.2.19

DEPARTURE
in glory and spoke of his *d.*   Lk.9.31
after my *d.* fierce wolves will   Acts 20.29
the time of my *d.* has come   2 Tim.4.6
that after my *d.* you may be able   2 Pet.1.15

DEPEND
on these two commandments *d.* all   Mt.22.40
That is why it *d.* on faith, in order   Rom.4.16
So it *d.* not upon man's will or   Rom.9.16
so far as it *d.* upon you, live   Rom.12.18
righteousness . . . that *d.* on faith   Phil.3.9

DEPTH
from the *d.* of the earth thou wilt   Ps.71.20
In his hand are the *d.* of the earth   Ps.95.4
Out of the *d.* I cry to thee, O LORD   Ps.130.1
to Sheol, to the *d.* of the Pit   Is.14.15
cast . . . sins into the *d.* of the sea   Mic.7.19
since they had no *d.* of soil   Mt.13.5
to be drowned in the *d.* of the sea   Mt.18.6
nor height, nor *d.*, nor anything   Rom.8.39
O the *d.* of the riches and wisdom   Rom.11.33
everything, even the *d.* of God   1 Cor.2.10
and length and height and *d.*   Eph.3.18

DESCEND
straight to the grave they *d.*   Ps.49.14
with those who *d.* into the Pit   Ezek.26.20
I saw the Spirit *d.* as a dove   Jn.1.32
something *d.*, like a great sheet   Acts 11.5
or "Who will *d.* into the abyss?"   Rom.10.7
the Lord himself will *d.* from heaven   1 Th.4.16

DESCENDANT
To your *d.* I will give this land   Gen.12.7
multiply your *d.* that they cannot   Gen.16.10
no offspring or *d.* among his people   Job 18.19
I will establish your *d.* for ever   Ps.89.4
His *d.* will be mighty in the land   Ps.112.2
I will pour my Spirit upon your *d.*   Is.44.3
We are *d.* of Abraham, and have   Jn.8.33
The promise to Abraham and his *d.*   Rom.4.13
Are they *d.* of Abraham? So am I   2 Cor.11.22
And those *d.* of Levi who receive   Heb.7.5

DESERT (noun)
often they . . . grieved him in the *d.*   Ps.78.40
He turns rivers into a *d.*, springs   Ps.107.33
the *d.* shall rejoice and blossom   Is.35.1
make straight in the *d.* a highway   Is.40.3
her *d.* like the garden of the LORD   Is.51.3
enough in the *d.* to feed so great   Mt.15.33
driven by the demon into the *d.*   Lk.8.29
wandering over *d.* and mountains   Heb.11.38

DESERTED
but a poor man is *d.* by his friend   Pr.19.4
For Gaza shall be *d.*, and Ashkelon   Zeph.2.4
are so quickly *d.* him who called   Gal.1.6
Demas . . . has *d.* me and gone to   2 Tim.4.10
no one took my part; all *d.* me   2 Tim.4.16

DESERVE
for the laborer *d.* his food   Mt.10.10
anything for which I *d.* to die   Acts 25.11
those who do such things *d.* to die   Rom.1.32

The laborer *d*. his wages	1 Tim.5.18
be *d*. by the man who has spurned	Heb.10.29
to each of you as your works *d*.	Rev.2.23

DESIGNATED

and *d*. Son of God in power according	Rom.1.4
being *d*. by God a high priest after	Heb.5.10
long ago were *d*. for this condemnation	Jude 4

DESIRE (noun)

your *d*. shall be for your husband	Gen.3.16
May he grant you your heart's *d*.	Ps.20.4
the *d*. of the wicked man comes to	Ps.112.10
He fulfils the *d*. of all who fear	Ps.145.19
a *d*. fulfilled is a tree of life	Pr.13.12
my heart's *d*. and prayer to God for	Rom.10.1
but having his *d*. under control	1 Cor.7.37
do not gratify the *d*. of the flesh	Gal.5.16
following the *d*. of body and mind	Eph.2.3
My *d*. is to depart and be with	Phil.1.23

DESIRE (verb)

More to be *d*. are they than gold	Ps.19.10
Sacrifice and offering thou dost not *d*.	Ps.40.6
upon earth that I *d*. besides thee	Ps.73.25
Do not *d*. her beauty in your heart	Pr.6.25
no beauty that we should *d*. him	Is.53.2
For I *d*. steadfast love and not	Hos.6.6
I *d*. mercy, and not sacrifice	Mt.9.13
and kings *d*. to see what you see	Lk.10.24
Father, I *d*. that they also, whom	Jn.17.24
earnestly *d*. the higher gifts	1 Cor.12.31
all who *d*. to live a godly life	2 Tim.3.12
they *d*. a better country . . . a heavenly	Heb.11.16

DESOLATE

he has made *d*. all my company	Job 16.7
He drew me up from the *d*. pit	Ps.40.2
God gives the *d*. a home to dwell in	Ps.68.6
the rights of all who are left *d*.	Pr.31.8
lay waste the earth and make it *d*.	Is.24.1
your land shall no more be termed *D*.	Is.62.4
streets of Jerusalem that are *d*.	Jer.33.10
your house is forsaken and *d*.	Mt.23.38
I will not leave you *d*.; I will come	Jn.14.18

DESOLATION

and your land shall be a *d*.	Lev.26.33
how he has wrought *d*. in the earth	Ps.46.8
It is a *d*., without man or beast	Jer.32.43
I will bring *d*. upon the land	Ezek.30.12
know that its *d*. has come near	Lk.21.20

DESPAIR (noun)

my heart, so that I am in *d*.	Ps.69.20
the prince is wrapped in *d*.	Ezek.7.27
perplexed, but not driven to *d*.	2 Cor.4.8

DESPISE

Thus Esau *d*. his birthright	Gen.25.34
How long will this people *d*. me?	Num.14.11
Even young children *d*. me	Job 19.18
I *d*. myself, and repent in dust	Job 42.6
a broken . . . heart . . . thou wilt not *d*.	Ps.51.17
son, do not *d*. the LORD's discipline	Pr.3.11
not *d*. your mother when she is old	Pr.23.22
He was *d*. and rejected by men	Is.53.3
I hate, I *d*. your feasts, and I take	Am.5.21
See that you do not *d*. one of these	Mt.18.10
devoted to the one and *d*. the other	Lk.16.13
they were righteous and *d*. others	Lk.18.9
Or do you *d*. the church of God	1 Cor.11.22
do not *d*. prophesying	1 Th.5.20

Let no one *d*. your youth, but set	1 Tim.4.12
endured the cross, *d*. the shame	Heb.12.2

DESTINED

and he is *d*. for the sword	Job 15.22
He *d*. us in love to be his sons	Eph.1.5
have been *d*. and appointed to live	Eph.1.12
For God has not *d*. us for wrath	1 Th.5.9
chosen and *d*. by God the Father	1 Pet.1.2
He was *d*. before the foundation of	1 Pet.1.20

DESTROY

I will *d*. them with the earth	Gen.6.13
neither will I ever again *d*. every	Gen.8.21
wilt thou then *d*. the place	Gen.18.24
now thou dost turn about and *d*. me	Job 10.8
D. their plans, O Lord, confuse their	Ps.55.9
The wicked lie in wait to *d*. me	Ps.119.95
not hurt or *d*. in all my holy	Is.65.25
I will utterly *d*. them, and make	Jer.25.9
I will *d*. you, O Israel	Hos.13.9
I will seek to *d*. all the nations	Zech.12.9
to search for the child, to *d*. him	Mt.2.13
fear him who can *d*. both soul and	Mt.10.28
lawful . . . to save life or to *d*. it?	Lk.6.9
D. this temple, and in three days I	Jn.2.19
d. God's temple, God will *d*. him	1 Cor.3.17
and were *d*. by the Destroyer	1 Cor.10.10
The last enemy to be *d*. is death	1 Cor.15.26
struck down, but not *d*.	2 Cor.4.9
if the earthly tent we live in is *d*.	2 Cor.5.1
through death he might *d*. him who	Heb.2.14

DESTROYER

not allow the *d*. to enter your	Ex.12.23
be a refuge to them from the *d*.	Is.16.4
suddenly the *d*. will come upon us	Jer.6.26
for a *d*. has come upon her	Jer.51.56
and were destroyed by the *D*.	1 Cor.10.10
so that the *D*. of the first-born	Heb.11.28

DESTRUCTION

Let their own eyes see their *d*.	Job 21.20
nor the *d*. that wastes at noonday	Ps.91.6
they are doomed to *d*. for ever	Ps.92.7
and delivered them from *d*.	Ps.107.20
Pride goes before *d*., and a haughty	Pr.16.18
Before . . . a man's heart is haughty	Pr.18.12
held back my life from the pit of *d*.	Is.38.17
the gate is wide . . . that leads to *d*.	Mt.7.13
the vessels of wrath made for *d*.	Rom.9.22
to Satan for the *d*. of the flesh	1 Cor.5.5
then sudden *d*. will come upon them	1 Th.5.3
the punishment of eternal *d*. and	2 Th.1.9
that plunge men into ruin and *d*.	1 Tim.6.9
of judgment and *d*. of ungodly men	2 Pet.3.7
unstable twist to their own *d*.	2 Pet.3.16

DETERMINE

I have *d*. to make an end of all	Gen.6.13
that God has *d*. to destroy you	2 Chr.25.16
Since his days are *d*.	Job 14.5
Who *d*. its measurements—surely	Job 38.5
He *d*. the number of the stars	Ps.147.4
not heard that I *d*. it long ago?	Is.37.26
The LORD *d*. to lay in ruins the wall	Lam.2.8
for what is *d*. shall be done	Dan.11.36
Son of man goes as it has been *d*.	Lk.22.22
having *d*. allotted periods and	Acts 17.26

DEVICES

He frustrates the *d*. of the crafty	Job 5.12

men in whose hands are evil *d.*	Ps.26.10		Give me children, or I shall *d.*	Gen.30.1
but a man of evil *d.* he condemns	Pr.12.2		Let me *d.* the death of . . . righteous	Num.23.10
but they have sought out many *d.*	Ec.7.29		where you *d.* I will *d.*, and there	Ru.1.17
not good, following their own *d.*	Is.65.2		integrity? Curse God, and *d.*	Job 2.9

DEVIL

the enemy who sowed them is the *d.*	Mt.13.39
prepared for the *d.* and his angels	Mt.25.41
in the wilderness, tempted by the *d.*	Lk.4.2
the twelve, and one of you is a *d.?*	Jn.6.70
give no opportunity to the *d.*	Eph.4.27
stand against the wiles of the *d.*	Eph. 6.11
reproach and the snare of the *d.*	1 Tim.3.7
power of death, that is, the *d.*	Heb.2.14
Resist the *d.* and he will flee from	Jas.4.7
the *d.* has sinned from the beginning	1 Jn.3.8
Michael, contending with the *d.*	Jude 9
who is called the *D.* and Satan	Rev.12.9

DEVISE

to *d.* artistic designs, to work in	Ex.35.32
Do they not err that *d.* evil?	Pr.14.22
for their minds *d.* violence	Pr.24.2
yet they *d.* evil against me	Hos.7.15
Woe to those who *d.* wickedness	Mic.2.1
did not follow cleverly *d.* myths	2 Pet.1.16

DEVOTE

will be *d.* to the one and despise	Lk.16.13
they *d.* themselves to the . . . teaching	Acts 2.42
But we will *d.* ourselves to prayer	Acts 6.4
that you may *d.* yourselves to	1 Cor.7.5
Practice these duties, *d.* yourself	1 Tim.4.15

DEVOTION

I remember the *d.* of your youth	Jer.2.2
your undivided *d.* to the Lord	1 Cor.7.35
a sincere and pure *d.* to Christ	2 Cor.11.3
in promoting rigor of *d.*	Col.2.23

DEVOUR

LORD was like a *d.* fire on the top	Ex.24.17
For the LORD your God is a *d.* fire	Dt.4.24
and my sword shall *d.* flesh	Dt.32.42
You love all words that *d.*	Ps.52.4
to *d.* the poor from off the earth	Pr.30.14
You *d.* men, and you bereave your	Ezek.36.13
they fly like an eagle swift to *d.*	Hab.1.8
scribes . . . who *d.* widows' houses	Mk.12.40
But if you bite and *d.* one another	Gal.5.15
lion, seeking some one to *d.*	1 Pet.5.8

DEVOUT

this man was righteous and *d.*	Lk.2.25
d. men from every nation under	Acts 2.5
D. men buried Stephen, and made	Acts 8.2
a *d.* man who feared God with all	Acts 10.2
Jews and *d.* converts to Judaism	Acts 13.43
many of the *d.* Greeks and not a	Acts 17.4
a *d.* man according to the law	Acts 22.12

DEW

God give you of the *d.* of heaven	Gen.27.28
in the morning *d.* lay round about	Ex.16.13
my speech distil as the *d.*	Dt.32.2
if there is *d.* on the fleece alone	Jg.6.37
like *d.* your youth will come to you	Ps.110.3
favor is like *d.* upon the grass	Pr.19.12
him be wet with the *d.* of heaven	Dan.4.15
like the *d.* that goes early away	Hos.6.4

DIE

that you eat of it you shall *d.*	Gen.2.17
said to the woman, "You will not *d.*	Gen.3.4

and wisdom will *d.* with you	Job 12.2
If a man *d.*, shall he live again?	Job 14.14
you shall *d.* like men, and fall like	Ps.82.7
they *d.* and return to their dust	Ps.104.29
I shall not *d.*, but I shall live	Ps.118.17
he who pursues evil will *d.*	Pr.11.19
he who hates reproof will *d.*	Pr.15.10
a time to be born, and a time to *d.*	Ec.3.2
eat and drink, for tomorrow we *d.*	Is.22.13
If I must *d.* with you, I will not	Mk.14.31
for they cannot *d.* any more	Lk.20.36
a man may eat of it and not *d.*	Jn.6.50
will seek me and *d.* in your sin	Jn.8.21
though he *d.*, yet shall he live	Jn.11.25
expedient . . . that one man should *d.*	Jn.11.50
Christ *d.* for the ungodly	Rom.5.6
one will hardly *d.* for a righteous man	Rom.5.7
How can we who *d.* to sin still live	Rom.6.2
For he who has *d.* is freed from sin	Rom.6.7
you have *d.* to the law through	Rom.7.4
according to the flesh you will *d.*	Rom.8.13
and if we *d.*, we *d.* to the Lord	Rom.14.8
For as in Adam all *d.*, so also	1 Cor.15.22
eat and drink, for tomorrow we *d.*	1 Cor.15.32
live is Christ, and to *d.* is gain	Phil.1.21
it is appointed for men to *d.* once	Heb.9.27
d. to sin and live to righteousness	1 Pet.2.24
For Christ also *d.* for sins once	1 Pet.3.18
I *d.*, and behold I am alive for	Rev.1.18
the dead who *d.* in the Lord	Rev.14.13

DIFFERENT

servants he will call by a *d.* name	Is.65.15
For who sees anything *d.* in you?	1 Cor.4.7
if you receive a *d.* spirit from	2 Cor.11.4
so quickly . . . turning to a *d.* gospel	Gal.1.6
not to teach any *d.* doctrine	1 Tim.1.3

DILIGENTLY

Only take heed, and keep your soul *d.*	Dt.4.9
You shall *d.* keep the commandments	Dt.6.17
those who seek me *d.* find me	Pr.8.17
He who *d.* seeks good seeks favor	Pr.11.27
if you will *d.* obey the voice of	Zech.6.15
Go and search *d.* for the child	Mt.2.8
sweep the house and seek *d.* until	Lk.15.8

DINNER

came to the *d.* that Esther had	Est.5.5
Better is a *d.* of herbs where love	Pr.15.17
Behold, I have made ready my *d.*	Mt.22.4
he did not first wash before *d.*	Lk.11.38
When you give a *d.* or a banquet	Lk.14.12
if one . . . invites you to *d.* and	1 Cor.10.27

DIPPED

and *d.* the robe in the blood	Gen.37.31
went down and *d.* himself seven	2 Kg.5.14
He who has *d.* his hand in the dish	Mt.26.23
when he had *d.* the morsel, he gave	Jn.13.26
He is clad in a robe *d.* in blood	Rev.19.13

DIRECT (verb)

and *d.* your heart to the LORD	1 Sam.7.3
d. their hearts toward thee	1 Chr.29.18
I *d.* my steps by all thy precepts	Ps.119.128
but the LORD *d.* his steps	Pr.16.9

DISAPPOINT

and *d.* your mind in the way	Pr.23.19
Who has *d.* the Spirit of the LORD	Is.40.13
our Lord Jesus, *d.* our way to you	1 Th.3.11
May the Lord *d.* your hearts to the	2 Th.3.5

DISAPPOINT

Behold, the hope of a man is *d.*	Job 41.9
in thee they trusted, and were not *d.*	Ps.22.5
and hope does not *d.* us	Rom.5.5

DISCERN

angel of God to *d.* good and evil	2 Sam.14.17
Cannot my taste *d.* calamity?	Job 6.30
But who can *d.* his errors?	Ps.19.12
thou *d.* my thoughts from afar	Ps.139.2
because they are spiritually *d.*	1 Cor.2.14
without *d.* the body eats and	1 Cor.11.29
d. the thoughts and intentions	Heb.4.12

DISCERNMENT

takes away the *d.* of the elders	Job 12.20
The wise of heart is . . . a man of *d.*	Pr.16.21
For this is a people without *d.*	Is.27.11
with knowledge and all *d.*	Phil.1.9

DISCIPLE

seal the teaching among my *d.*	Is.8.16
he called to him his twelve *d.*	Mt.10.1
A *d.* is not above his teacher, nor	Mt.10.24
all the *d.* forsook him and fled	Mt.26.56
and come after me, cannot be my *d.*	Lk.14.27
baptizing more *d.* than John	Jn.4.1
men will know that you are my *d.*	Jn.13.35
the *d.* whom he loved standing near	Jn.19.26
the number of the *d.* multiplied	Acts 6.7
Now there was a *d.* at Damascus	Acts 9.10
at Joppa a *d.* named Tabitha	Acts 9.36
A *d.* was there, named Timothy	Acts 16.1
Mnason of Cyprus, an early *d.*	Acts 21.16

DISCIPLINE (noun)

you hate *d.*, and you cast my words	Ps.50.17
despise not the LORD'S *d.* or be weary	Pr.3.11
He dies for lack of *d.*, and because	Pr.5.23
Whoever loves *d.* loves knowledge	Pr.12.1
Do not withhold *d.* from a child	Pr.23.13
Fathers . . . bring them up in the *d.*	Eph.6.4
do not regard lightly the *d.* of the	Heb.12.5
For the moment all *d.* seems painful	Heb.12.11

DISCIPLINE (verb)

his voice, that he might *d.* you	Dt.4.36
loves him is diligent to *d.* him	Pr.13.24
D. your son while there is hope	Pr.19.18
For the Lord *d.* him whom he loves	Heb.12.6

DISCRETION

may the LORD grant you *d.*	1 Chr.22.12
My son, keep sound wisdom and *d.*	Pr.3.21
I find knowledge and *d.*	Pr.8.12
is a beautiful woman without *d.*	Pr.11.22
but a man of *d.* is patient	Pr.14.17

DISEASE

skin of his body, it is a leprous *d.*	Lev.13.3
the priest shall examine the *d.*	Lev.13.50
By *d.* his skin is consumed	Job 18.13
who heals all your *d.*	Ps.103.3
but sent a wasting *d.* among them	Ps.106.15
healing every *d.* and every infirmity	Mt.4.23
in peace, and be healed of your *d.*	Mk.5.34
d. left them and the evil spirits	Acts 19.12
people on the island who had *d.*	Acts 28.9

DISGRACE

and thus put *d.* upon all Israel	1 Sam.11.2
All day long my *d.* is before me	Ps.44.15
for ever; let them perish in *d.*	Ps.83.17
When pride comes, then comes *d.*	Pr.11.2
Poverty and *d.* come to him who	Pr.13.18
because I bore the *d.* of my youth	Jer.31.19
So be ashamed . . . bear your *d.*	Ezek.16.52

DISGUISE (verb)

Saul *d.* himself and put on other	1 Sam.28.8
I will *d.* myself and go into	1 Kg.22.30
Satan *d.* himself as an angel	2 Cor.11.14
his servants also *d.* themselves	2 Cor.11.15

DISHONOR (noun)

May my accusers be clothed with *d.*	Ps.109.29
and with *d.* comes disgrace	Pr.18.3
worthy to suffer *d.* for the name	Acts 5.41
sown in *d.*, it is raised in glory	1 Cor.15.43
in honor and *d.*, in ill repute and	2 Cor.6.8

DISHONOR (verb)

I honor my Father, and you *d.* me	Jn.8.49
do you *d.* God by breaking the law?	Rom.2.23
with her head unveiled *d.* her head	1 Cor.11.5
But you have *d.* the poor man	Jas.2.6

DISMAY

be not frightened, neither be *d.*	Jos.1.9
thou didst hide thy face, I was *d.*	Ps.30.7
be put to shame and *d.* for ever	Ps.83.17
And your mighty men shall be *d.*	Ob.9

DISOBEDIENCE

For as by one man's *d.* many were	Rom.5.19
received mercy because of their *d.*	Rom.11.30
For God has consigned all men to *d.*	Rom.11.32
being ready to punish every *d.*	2 Cor.10.6
is now at work in the sons of *d.*	Eph.2.2
no one fall by the same sort of *d.*	Heb.4.11

DISOBEDIENT

not *d.* to the heavenly vision	Acts 26.19
inventors of evil, *d.* to parents	Rom.1.30
to a *d.* and contrary people	Rom.10.21
you were once *d.* to God but now	Rom.11.30
d. to their parents, ungrateful	2 Tim.3.2
d., unfit for any good deed	Tit.1.16
not perish with those who were *d.*	Heb.11.31

DISPUTE (noun)

both parties to the *d.* shall appear	Dt.19.17
If there is a *d.* between men	Dt.25.1
controversy and for *d.* about words	1 Tim.6.4
in all their *d.* an oath is final	Heb.6.16
It is beyond *d.* that the inferior	Heb.7.7

DISPUTE (verb)

is not able to *d.* with one stronger	Ec.6.10
The Jews then *d.* among themselves	Jn.6.52
some . . . arose and *d.* with Stephen	Acts 6.9
he . . . *d.* against the Hellenists	Acts 9.29
Michael . . . *d.* about the body of Moses	Jude 9

DISSENSION

had no small *d.* and debate with	Acts 15.2
a *d.* arose between the Pharisees	Acts 23.7
who create *d.* and difficulties	Rom.16.17
that there be no *d.* among you	1 Cor.1.10
selfishness, *d.*, party spirit	Gal.5.20
d., slander, base suspicions	1 Tim.6.4

DISTINCTION

the LORD makes a *d.* between the	Ex.11.7
have made no *d.* between the holy	Ezek.22.26

he made no *d.* between us and	Acts 15.9
there is no *d.* . . . all have sinned	Rom.3.22
no *d.* between Jew and Greek	Rom.10.12
have you not made *d.* among yourselves	Jas.2.4

DISTINGUISH
You are to *d.* between the holy and	Lev.10.10
how to *d.* between the unclean and	Ezek.44.23
the ability to *d.* between spirits	1 Cor.12.10
by practice to *d.* good from evil	Heb.5.14

DISTRESS (noun)
In my *d.* I called upon the LORD	2 Sam.22.7
d. and anguish terrify him	Job 15.24
In my *d.* I called upon the LORD	Ps.18.6
In *d.* you called, and I delivered	Ps.81.7
when *d.* and anguish come upon you	Pr.1.27
O LORD, in *d.* they sought thee	Is.26.16
great *d.* shall be upon the earth	Lk.21.23
tribulation and *d.* for every human	Rom.2.9
or *d.*, persecution, or famine	Rom.8.35
in view of the impending *d.* it	1 Cor.7.26
in all our *d.* and affliction we	1 Th.3.7

DISTRIBUTE
d. the portions to their brethren	2 Chr.31.15
duty was to *d.* to their brethren	Neh.13.13
sell all . . . and *d.* to the poor	Lk.18.22
sold their . . . goods and *d.* them	Acts 2.45
gifts . . . *d.* according to his own will	Heb.2.4

DIVINATION
any one who practices *d.*	Dt.18.10
rebellion is as the sin of *d.*	1 Sam.15.23
used *d.* and sorcery	2 Kg.17.17
worthless *d.*, and the deceit of	Jer.14.14
and uttered a lying *d.*	Ezek.13.7
slave girl who had a spirit of *d.*	Acts 16.16

DIVIDE
D. the living child in two	1 Kg.3.25
they *d.* my garments among them	Ps.22.18
Thou didst *d.* the sea by thy might	Ps.74.13
as men rejoice when they *d.* the spoil	Is.9.3
Therefore I will *d.* him a portion	Is.53.12
PERES, your kingdom is *d.* and given	Dan.5.28
Every kingdom *d.* against itself is	Mt.12.25
they *d.* his garments among them by	Mt.27.35
he *d.* the two fish among them	Mk.6.41
bid my brother *d.* the inheritance	Lk.12.13
Take . . . and *d.* it among yourselves	Lk.22.17
they cast lots to *d.* his garments	Lk.23.34
Is Christ *d.*? Was Paul crucified	1 Cor.1.13

DIVINE (adjective)
Your *d.* throne endures for ever and	Ps.45.6
because in his *d.* forbearance he	Rom.3.25
but have *d.* power to destroy	2 Cor.10.4
according to the *d.* office which	Col.1.25
the *d.* training that is in faith	1 Tim.1.4
men of old received *d.* approval	Heb.11.2
His *d.* power has granted to us	2 Pet.1.3
become partakers of the *d.* nature	2 Pet.1.4

DIVISION
Thus I will put a *d.* between my	Ex.8.23
No, I tell you, but rather *d.*	Lk.12.51
So there was a *d.* among the people	Jn.7.43
There was again a *d.* among the Jews	Jn.10.19
I hear that there are *d.* among you	1 Cor.11.18
Piercing to the *d.* of soul and	Heb.4.12

DIVORCE (noun)
he writes her a bill of *d.*	Dt.24.1
For I hate *d.*, says the LORD	Mal.2.16
let him give her a certificate of *d.*	Mt.5.31
why then . . . give a certificate of *d.*	Mt.19.7

DIVORCE (verb)
marry a woman *d.* from her husband	Lev.21.7
Joseph . . . resolved to *d.* her quietly	Mt.1.19
marries a *d.* woman commits adultery	Mt.5.32
Is it lawful to *d.* one's wife for	Mt.19.3
Whoever *d.* his wife and marries	Mk.10.11
Every one who *d.* his wife and	Lk.16.18
husband should not *d.* his wife	1 Cor.7.11

DOCTRINE
My *d.* is pure, and I am clean in	Job 11.4
opposition to the *d.* which you	Rom.16.17
carried about with every wind of *d.*	Eph.4.14
according to human precepts and *d.*	Col.2.22
not to teach any different *d.*	1 Tim.1.3
teach what befits sound *d.*	Tit.2.1
may adorn the *d.* of God our Savior	Tit.2.10
leave the elementary *d.* of Christ	Heb.6.1
does not abide in the *d.* of Christ	2 Jn.9

DOG
Am I a *d.*, that you come to me	1 Sam.17.43
who takes a passing *d.* by the ears	Pr.26.17
a living *d.* is better than a dead lion	Ec.9.4
Do not give *d.* what is holy	Mt.7.6
even the *d.* under the table eat	Mk.7.28
the *d.* came and licked his sores	Lk.16.21
Look out for the *d.*, look out	Phil.3.2
The *d.* turns back to his . . . vomit	2 Pet.2.22

DOMINION
let them have *d.* over the fish of	Gen.1.26
D. and fear are with God	Job 25.2
Thou hast given him *d.* over the	Ps.8.6
For *d.* belongs to the LORD, and he	Ps.22.28
his works, in all places of his *d.*	Ps.103.22
and thy *d.* endures throughout all	Ps.145.13
for his *d.* is an everlasting *d.*	Dan.4.34
death no longer has *d.* over him	Rom.6.9
For sin will have no *d.* over you	Rom.6.14
and authority and power and *d.*	Eph.1.21
delivered us from the *d.* of darkness	Col.1.13
To him be honor and eternal *d.*	1 Tim.6.16
glory and *d.* for ever and ever	1 Pet.4.11
to him be the *d.* for ever and	1 Pet.5.11
d., and authority, before all time	Jude 25
be glory and *d.* for ever and ever	Rev.1.6

DOOMED
preserve those *d.* to die	Ps.79.11
they are *d.* to destruction for ever	Ps.92.7
LORD our God has *d.* us to perish	Jer.8.14
rulers . . . who are *d.* to pass away	1 Cor.2.6
thus he is *d.* to be killed	Rev.11.5

DOOR
sin is couching at the *d.*	Gen.4.7
keep watch over the *d.* of my lips	Ps.141.3
As a *d.* turns on its hinges, so	Pr.26.14
make . . . Valley of Achor a *d.* of hope	Hos.2.15
shut the *d.* and pray to your Father	Mt.6.6
great stone to the *d.* of the tomb	Mt.27.60
Strive to enter by the narrow *d.*	Lk.13.24
you will . . . knock at the *d.*, saying	Lk.13.25
enters by the *d.* is the shepherd	Jn.10.2
I am the *d.*; if any one enters	Jn.10.9
The *d.* were shut, but Jesus came	Jn.20.26
opened a *d.* of faith to the Gentiles	Acts 14.27

for a wide *d*. for effective work   1 Cor.16.9
a *d*. was opened for me in the Lord   2 Cor.2.12
may open to us a *d*. for the word   Col.4.3
I have set before you an open *d*.   Rev.3.8
Behold, I stand at the *d*. and knock   Rev.3.20
and lo, in heaven an open *d*.   Rev.4.1

DORCAS
raised from death by Peter, Acts 9.36–41

DOUBT (verb)
of little faith, why did you *d*.?   Mt.14.31
if you have faith and never *d*.   Mt.21.21
they worshiped him; but some *d*.   Mt.28.17
he who *d*. is like a wave of the sea   Jas.1.6
And convince some, who *d*.   Jude 22

DOVE
Then he sent forth a *d*. from him   Gen.8.8
O that I had wings like a *d*.   Ps.55.6
My *d*., my perfect one, is only   S.of S.6.9
Spirit of God descending like a *d*.   Mt.3.16
wise as serpents and innocent as *d*.   Mt.10.16

DRAGON
the heads of the *d*. on the waters   Ps.74.13
he will slay the *d*. . . . in the sea   Is.27.1
the great *d*. that lies in the   Ezek.29.3
like a lamb and it spoke like a *d*.   Rev.13.11
seized the *d*., that ancient serpent   Rev.20.2

DRAW
D. near to me . . . set me free   Ps.69.18
the Holy One of Israel *d*. near   Is.5.19
they delight to *d*. near to God   Is.58.2
she does not *d*. near to her God   Zeph.3.2
a woman of Samaria to *d*. water   Jn.4.7
d. near to the throne of grace   Heb.4.16
through which we *d*. near to God   Heb.7.19
let us *d*. near with a true heart   Heb.10.22
whoever would *d*. near to God must   Heb.11.6
D. near to God and he will *d*. near   Jas.4.8

DREAD (noun)
the *d*. of you . . . upon every beast   Gen.9.2
the *d*. of the LORD fell upon   1 Sam.11.7
preserve my life from *d*.   Ps.64.1
for *d*. of them had fallen upon it   Ps.105.38
do not fear . . . nor be in *d*.   Is.8.12
they shall turn in *d*. to the LORD   Mic.7.17

DREAM (noun)
angel of God said to me in the *d*.   Gen.31.11
Now Joseph had a *d*., and . . . he told it   Gen.37.5
and Pharaoh told them his *d*.   Gen.41:8
LORD appeared to Solomon in a *d*.   1 Kg.3.5
They are like a *d*. when one awakes   Ps.73.20
I had a *d*., and my spirit is troubled   Dan.2.3
This *d*. I, King Nebuchadnezzar, saw   Dan.4.18
an angel . . . appeared to him in a *d*.   Mt.1.20
appeared to Joseph in a *d*. and said   Mt.2.13
and your old men shall dream *d*.   Acts 2.17

DRINK (noun)
Wine is a mocker, strong *d*. a brawler   Pr.20.1
or for rulers to desire strong *d*.   Pr.31.4
that they may run after strong *d*.   Is.5.11
valiant men in mixing strong *d*.   Is.5.22
I was thirsty and you gave me *d*.   Mt.25.35
Jesus said to her, "Give me a *d*."   Jn.4.7
if he is thirsty, give him *d*.   Rom.12.20
not to be slanderers or slaves to *d*.   Tit.2.3

DRINK (verb)
D. no wine nor strong drink   Lev.10.9

You shall *d*. from the brook   1 Kg.17.4
But David would not *d*. of it   1 Chr.11.18
wine to *d*. that made us reel   Ps.60.3
they gave me vinegar to *d*.   Ps.69.21
is thirsty, give him water to *d*.   Pr.25.21
it is not for kings to *d*. wine   Pr.31.4
Let us eat and *d*., for tomorrow we   Is.22.13
vegetables to eat and water to *d*.   Dan.1.12
be not anxious . . . what you shall *d*.   Mt.6.25
able to *d*. the cup that I am to *d*.?   Mt.20.22
D. of it, all of you   Mt.26.27
on a reed and gave it to him to *d*.   Mk.15.36
he who eats my flesh and *d*. my blood   Jn.6.54
thirst, let him come to me and *d*.   Jn.7.37
cannot *d*. the cup of the Lord   1 Cor.10.21
Do this, as often as you *d*. it   1 Cor.11.25
No longer *d*. only water, but use   1 Tim.5.23
shall *d*. the wine of God's wrath   Rev.14.10

DRIVE
For the LORD has *d*. out before you   Jos.23.9
Jehu . . . for he *d*. furiously   2 Kg.9.20
like chaff which the wind *d*. away   Ps.1.4
thou didst *d*. out the nations   Ps.80.8
D. out a scoffer, and strife will go   Pr.22.10
and began to *d*. out those who sold   Lk.19.45
D. out the wicked person from   1 Cor.5.13

DROSS
the wicked . . . thou dost count as *d*.   Ps.119.119
Take away the *d*. from the silver   Pr.25.4
Your silver has become *d*., your   Is.1.22
Because you have all become *d*.   Ezek.22.19

DRUNK
I have *d*. neither wine nor strong   1 Sam.1.15
Be *d*., but not with wine   Is.29.9
these . . . are not *d*., as you suppose   Acts 2.15
And do not get *d*. with wine   Eph.5.18
d. with the blood of the saints   Rev.17.6
nations have *d*. the wine of her   Rev.18.3

DRUNKARD
he is a glutton and a *d*.   Dt.21.20
Behold, a glutton and a *d*.   Mt.11.19
not to associate with any . . . *d*.   1 Cor.5.11
nor *d*., nor revilers, nor robbers   1 Cor.6.10
no *d*., not violent but gentle   1 Tim.3.3
must not be . . . quick-tempered or a *d*.   Tit.1.7

DRY
God called the *d*. land Earth   Gen.1.10
the midst of the sea on *d*. ground   Ex.14.22
the priests . . . stood on *d*. ground   Jos.3.17
He turned the sea into *d*. land   Ps.66.6
for his hands formed the *d*. land   Ps.95.5
the Red Sea, and it became *d*.   Ps.106.9
Nile will diminish and *d*. up   Is.19.6
I will *d*. up her sea and make her   Jer.51.36
in a *d*. and thirsty land   Ezek.19.13
And I will *d*. up the Nile   Ezek.30.12
O *d*. bones, hear the word of the   Ezek.37.4
who made the sea and the *d*. land   Jon.1.9
what will happen when it is *d*.?   Lk.23.31

DULL
The *d*. man cannot know, the stupid   Ps.92.6
his ear *d*., that it cannot hear   Is.59.1
this people's heart has grown *d*.   Mt.13.15
you have become *d*. of hearing   Heb.5.11

DUMB
Let the lying lips be *d*.   Ps.31.18

I was *d.* and silent, I held my peace Ps.39.2
the tongue of the *d.* sing for joy Is.35.6
that before its shearers is *d.* Is.53.7
a blind and *d.* demoniac was brought Mt.12.22
when they saw the *d.* speaking Mt.15.31
the deaf hear and the *d.* speak Mk.7.37
a lamb before its shearer is *d.* Acts 8.32
a *d.* ass spoke with human voice 2 Pet.2.16

DUST

formed man of *d.* from the ground Gen.2.7
you are *d.*, and to *d.* you . . . return Gen.3.19
Who can count the *d.* of Jacob Num.23.10
He raises up the poor from the *d.* 1 Sam.2.8
and wilt thou turn me to *d.* again? Job 10.9
I have become like *d.* and ashes Job 30.19
Will the *d.* praise thee? Will it Ps.30.9
Thou turnest man back to the *d.* Ps.90.3
My soul cleaves to the *d.* Ps.119.25
Shake yourself from the *d.*, arise Is.52.2
shake off the *d.* from your feet as Lk.9.5
from the earth, a man of *d.* 1 Cor.15.47

DUTY

rights and *d.* of the kingship 1 Sam.10.25
And they cast lots for their *d.* 1 Chr.25.8
for this is the whole *d.* of man Ec.12.13
we have only done what was our *d.* Lk.17.10
Practice these *d.*, devote yourself 1 Tim.4.15
Teach and urge these *d.* 1 Tim.6.2

DWELL

the father of those who *d.* in tents Gen.4.20
Who shall *d.* on thy holy hill? Ps.15.1
I shall *d.* in the house of the LORD Ps.23.6
the world and those who *d.* therein Ps.24.1
how good . . . when brothers *d.* in unity Ps.133.1
the wicked will not *d.* in the land Pr.10.30
The wolf shall *d.* with the lamb Is.11.6
justice will *d.* in the wilderness Is.32.16
I *d.* in the high and holy place Is.57.15
upon all who *d.* upon the face of Lk.21.35
the Most High does not *d.* in houses Acts 7.48
that nothing good *d.* within me Rom.7.18
if the Spirit of God really is in you Rom.8.9
and that God's Spirit *d.* in you? 1 Cor.3.16
that Christ may *d.* in your hearts Eph.3.17
word of Christ *d.* in you richly Col.3.16
O heaven and you that *d.* therein Rev.12.12

DWELLING

Where is the way to the *d.* of light Job 38.19
let them bring me . . . to thy *d.* Ps.43.3
How lovely is thy *d.* place Ps.84.1
My *d.* place shall be with them Ezek.37.27
we . . . long to put on our heavenly *d.* 2 Cor.5.2
built into it for a *d.* place of God Eph.2.22

EAGER

I am *e.* to preach the gospel Rom.1.15
the creation waits with *e.* longing Rom.8.19
e. to maintain the unity of the Eph.4.3
it is my *e.* expectation and hope Phil.1.20
searched for me *e.* and found me 2 Tim.1.17
those who are *e.* waiting for him Heb.9.28
not for shameful gain but *e.* 1 Pet.5.2
being very *e.* to write to you Jude 3

EAGLE

I bore you on *e.* wings and brought Ex.19.4
like an *e.* swooping on the prey Job 9.26

your youth is renewed like the *e.* Ps.103.5
shall mount up with wings like *e.* Is.40.31
his horses are swifter than *e.* Jer.4.13
had the face of an *e.* at the back Ezek.1.10
A great *e.* with great wings Ezek.17.3
make yourselves as bald as the *e.* Mic.1.16
there the *e.* will be gathered Mt.24.28
living creature like a flying *e.* Rev.4.7
the two wings of the great *e.* Rev.12.14

EAR

Give *e.*, O heavens, and I will Dt.32.1
Incline thy *e.*, O LORD, and hear 2 Kg.19.16
let thy *e.* be attentive, and thy eyes Neh.1.6
by the hearing of the *e.* Job 42.5
O LORD, and give *e.* to my cry Ps.39.12
We have heard with our *e.* Ps.44.1
the deaf adder that stops its *e.* Ps.58.4
He who planted the *e.*, does he not Ps.94.9
making your *e.* attentive to wisdom Pr.2.2
The hearing *e.* and the seeing eye Pr.20.12
He who closes his *e.* to the cry Pr.21.13
nor the *e.* filled with hearing Ec.1.8
did not obey or incline their *e.* Jer.7.24
two legs, or a piece of an *e.* Am.3.12
He who has *e.* to hear, let him hear Mt.11.15
high priest, and cut off his *e.* Mt.26.51
What no eye has seen, nor *e.* heard 1 Cor.2.9
If thy whole body were an *e.* 1 Cor.12.17
his *e.* are open to their prayer 1 Pet.3.12
He who has an *e.*, let him hear Rev.2.7

EARTH

God created the heavens and the *e.* Gen.1.1
wickedness . . . was great in the *e.* Gen.6.5
the covenant between me and the *e.* Gen.9.13
the Judge of all the *e.* do right? Gen.18.25
I call heaven and *e.* to witness Dt.4.26
Then the *e.* reeled and rocked 2 Sam.22.8
From going to and fro on the *e.* Job 1.7
at last he will stand upon the *e.* Job 19.25
The kings of the *e.* set themselves Ps.2.2
The *e.* is the LORD'S and the fulness Ps.24.1
Let all the *e.* fear the LORD Ps.33.8
not fear though the *e.* should change Ps.46.2
from the end of the *e.* I call to thee Ps.61.2
Thou visitest the *e.* and waterest it Ps.65.9
that thy way may be known upon *e.* Ps.67.2
In his hand are the depths of the *e.* Ps.95.4
for he comes to judge the *e.* Ps.98.9
the heavens are high above the *e.* Ps.103.11
dust returns to the *e.* as it was Ec.12.7
sits above the circle of the *e.* Is.40.22
who formed the *e.* and made it Is.45.18
the heavens are higher than the *e.* Is.55.9
I create new heavens and a new *e.* Is.65.17
for they shall inherit the *e.* Mt.5.5
I have come to bring peace on *e.* Mt.10.34
e. will pass away, but my words Mt.24.35
and on *e.* peace among men with whom Lk.2.14
I came to cast fire upon the *e.* Lk.12.49
wheat falls into the *e.* and dies Jn.12.24
my throne, and *e.* my footstool Acts 7.49
to live on all the face of the *e.* Acts 17.26
voice has gone out to all the *e.* Rom.10.18
strangers and exiles on the *e.* Heb.11.13
a new *e.* in which righteousness 2 Pet.3.13
I saw a new heaven and a new *e.* Rev.21.1

EARTHLY

If I have told you *e.* things	Jn.3.12
if the *e.* tent we live in is destroyed	2 Cor.5.1
with minds set on *e.* things	Phil.3.19
regulations for . . . an *e.* sanctuary	Heb.9.1
but is *e.*, unspiritual, devilish	Jas.3.15

EARTHQUAKE

but the LORD was not in the *e.*	1 Kg.19.11
famines and *e.* in various places	Mt.24.7
And behold, there was a great *e.*	Mt.28.2
suddenly there was a great *e.*	Acts 16.26

EASIER

For which is *e.*, to say, 'Your sins	Mt.9.5
it is *e.* for a camel to go through	Mt.19.24
But it is *e.* for heaven and earth	Lk.16.17

EAST

a garden in Eden, in the *e.*	Gen.2.8
in the land of Nod, *e.* of Eden	Gen.4.16
the LORD brought an *e.* wind upon	Ex.10.13
as far as the *e.* is from the west	Ps.103.12
house of the LORD, which faces *e.*	Ezek.11.1
God appointed a sultry *e.* wind	Jon.4.8
we have seen his star in the *E.*	Mt.2.2
And men will come from *e.* and west	Lk.13.29

EAT

You may freely *e.* of every tree	Gen.2.16
You shall not *e.* of any tree of	Gen.3.1
Let me *e.* some of that red pottage	Gen.25.30
Only you shall not *e.* the blood	Dt.12.16
These are the animals you may *e.*	Dt.14.4
And the dogs shall *e.* Jezebel	2 Kg.9.10
who *e.* up my people as they *e.* bread	Ps.14.4
you shall *e.* the good of the land	Is.1.19
The fathers have *e.* sour grapes	Jer.31.29
e. this scroll, and go, speak to	Ezek.3.1
be made to *e.* grass like an ox	Dan.4.25
do not be anxious . . . what you shall *e.*	Mt.6.25
your teacher *e.* with tax collectors	Mt.9.11
John came neither *e.* nor drinking	Mt.11.18
Take, *e.*; this is my body	Mt.26.26
Why do you *e.* and drink with tax	Lk.5.30
I have food to *e.* of which you do	Jn.4.32
He who *e.* my flesh and drinks my	Jn.6.56
Rise, Peter; kill and *e.*	Acts 10.13
and he was *e.* by worms and died	Acts 12.23
One believes he may *e.* anything	Rom.14.2
it is right not to *e.* meat or drink	Rom.14.21
I will never *e.* meat, lest I cause	1 Cor.8.13
whether you *e.* or drink, or	1 Cor.10.31
as often as you *e.* this bread	1 Cor.11.26
Let us *e.* and drink, for tomorrow	1 Cor.15.32
I will grant to *e.* of the tree of	Rev.2.7

EBED-MELECH

Ethiopian eunuch, intercedes with king Zedediah for Jeremiah, Jer.38.7–13; deliverance promised to, Jer.39.16–18

EDEN

(1) Garden of, Gen.2.8; Adam driven from, Gen.3.24; mentioned, Is.51.3; Ezek.28.13; 31.9; 36.35; Jl.2.3; (2) 2 Kg.19.12; (3) 2 Chr.29.12

EDIFY

please his neighbor . . . to *e.* him	Rom.15.2
who speaks in a tongue . . . himself	1 Cor.14.4
but the other man is not *e.*	1 Cor.14.17
but only such as is good for *e.*	Eph.4.29

EGG

For she leaves her *e.* to the earth	Job 39.14
They hatch adders' *e.*, they weave	Is.59.5
if he asks for an *e.*, will give	Lk.11.12

EGYPT

Abram goes down into, Gen.12.10; Joseph sold into, Gen.37.36; his advancement, fall, imprisonment, and restoration there, Gen.39–41; Jacob's sons go to buy food in, Gen.42; Jacob and all his descendants go there, Gen.46.6; plagued on account of Israelites, Ex.7–11; children of Israel depart from, Ex.13.17; army of, pursue, and perish in the Red Sea, Ex.14; kings of, harass Judah, 1 Kg.14.25; 2 Kg.23.29; 2 Chr.12.2; 35.20; 36.3; Jer.37.5; the remnant of Judah go there, Jer.43.5–7; Jesus taken to, Mt.2.13

ELDER

the *e.* shall serve the younger	Gen.25.23
Moses called all the *e.* of Israel	Ex.12.21
and seventy of the *e.* of Israel	Ex.24.1
conferred with the *e.* of Israel	2 Sam.3.17
according to the tradition of the *e.*	Mk.7.5
rejected by the *e.* and chief priests	Lk.9.22
Now his *e.* son was in the field	Lk.15.25
called . . . the *e.* of the church	Acts 20.17
Let the *e.* who rule well be	1 Tim.5.17
call for the *e.* of the church	Jas.5.14
as a fellow *e.* and a witness of	1 Pet.5.1
The *e.* to the elect lady and her	2 Jn.1
The *e.* to the beloved Gaius	3 Jn.1

ELEAZAR

(1) son of Aaron, and chief priest, Ex.6.23; 28.1; Num.3.2,32; 4.16; 16.37; 20.26–28; 27.22; 31.13; 34.17; Jos.17.4; 24.33; (2) son of Abinadab, keeps the ark, 1 Sam.7.1; (3) one of David's captains, 2 Sam.23.9; 1 Chr.11.12

ELECT

for the sake of the *e.* those days	Mt.24.22
lead astray, if possible, the *e.*	Mk.13.22
And will not God vindicate his *e.*	Lk.18.7
bring any charge against God's *e.*?	Rom.8.33
of the *e.* angels I charge you	1 Tim.5.21
everything for the sake of the *e.*	2 Tim.2.10
The elder to the *e.* lady and her	2 Jn.1
The children of your *e.* sister greet	2 Jn.13

ELECTION

God's purpose of *e.* might continue	Rom.9.11
as regards *e.* they are beloved	Rom.11.28
to confirm your call and *e.*	2 Pet.1.10

ELI

high priest and judge, blesses Hannah, who bears Samuel, 1 Sam.1.17,20; Samuel brought to, 1 Sam.1.25; wickedness of his sons, 1 Sam. 2.22; rebuked by man of God, 1 Sam.2.27–36; his sons slain, 1 Sam.4.11; his death, 1 Sam.4.18

ELIHU

reproves Job's friends, Job 32, and Job's impatience, Job 33.8–11, and self-righteousness, Job 34.5; declares God's justice, Job 33.12; 34.10; 35.13, power, Job 33–37; and mercy, Job 33.23–28; 34.28

ELIJAH

the Tishbite, prophet, predicts great drought, 1 Kg.17.1; Lk.4.25; Jas.5.17; hides at the brook Cherith, and is fed by ravens, 1 Kg.17.5–6

(19.5); raises the widow's son, 1 Kg.17.21; his sacrifice at Carmel, 1 Kg.18.38; kills the prophets of Baal at the brook Kishon, 1 Kg. 18.40; flees from Jezebel into the wilderness of Beersheba, 1 Kg.19; anoints Elisha, 1 Kg.19.19; by God's command denounces Ahab in Naboth's vineyard, 1 Kg.21.17; his prediction fulfilled, 1 Kg.22.38; 2 Kg.9.36; 10.10; divides Jordan, 2 Kg.2.8; taken up by chariot of fire, 2 Kg.2.11; his mantle taken by Elisha, 2 Kg.2.13; appears at Christ's transfiguration, Mt.17.3; Mk.9.4; Lk.9.30; precursor of John the Baptist, Mal.4.5; Mt.11.14; 16.14; Lk.1.17; 9.8,19; Jn.1.21

ELIPHAZ
reproves Job, Job 4; 5; 15; 22; God's wrath against him, Job 42.7; he offers burnt offering, and Job prays for him, Job 42.8

ELISHA
succeeds Elijah, 1 Kg. 19.16; receives his mantle, and divides Jordan, 2 Kg.2.13–14; bears destroy the children who mock him, 2 Kg.2.24; his miracles: water, 2 Kg.3.16–20; oil, 4.4; Shunammite's son, 4.32; death in the pot, 4.40; feeds a hundred men with twenty loaves, 4.44; Naaman's leprosy, 5.1–14; iron floats, 6.5–7; Syrians struck blind, 6.18; prophesies abundance in Samaria when besieged, 2 Kg.7.1; sends to anoint Jehu, 2 Kg.9.1–3; his death, 2 Kg.13.20; miracle wrought by his bones, 2 Kg.13.21

ELOI
E., *E.*, lama sabachthani?	Mk.15.34

ELOQUENT
Moses said . . . I am not *e.*	Ex.4.10
He was an *e.* man, well versed	Acts 18.24
to preach . . . not with *e.* wisdom	1 Cor.1.17

EMBRACE
Laban . . . *e.* him and kissed him	Gen.29.13
a time to *e.*, and a time to refrain	Ec.3.5
ran and *e.* him and kissed him	Lk.15.20
all wept and *e.* Paul and kissed	Acts 20.37

EMPEROR
custody for the decision of the *e.*	Acts 25.21
he himself appealed to the *e.*	Acts 25.25
be subject . . . to the *e.* as supreme	1 Pet.2.13
Fear God. Honor the *e.*	1 Pet.2.17

EMPTY (adjective)
The pit was *e.*, there was no water	Gen.37.24
And none shall appear before me *e.*	Ex.34.20
the LORD has brought me back *e.*	Ru.1.21
e. vessels and not too few	2 Kg.4.3
Job opens his mouth in *e.* talk	Job 35.16
it shall not return to me *e.*	Is.55.11
he has made me an *e.* vessel	Jer.51.34
in praying do not heap up *e.* phrases	Mt.6.7
when he comes he finds it *e.*	Mt.12.44
the rich he has sent *e.* away	Lk.1.53
Let no one deceive you with *e.* words	Eph.5.6
by philosophy and *e.* deceit	Col.2.8
e. talkers and deceivers	Tit.1.10

ENCAMP
Though a host *e.* against me	Ps.27.3
angel of the LORD *e.* around those	Ps.34.7
And I will *e.* against you	Is.29.3
E. . . . . about her; let no one escape	Jer.50.29

ENCOMPASS
The cords of death *e.* me	Ps.18.4
Many bulls *e.* me, strong bulls of	Ps.22.12
thou dost *e.* me with deliverance	Ps.32.7
The snares of death *e.* me	Ps.116.3

ENCOURAGE
the brethren *e.* him, and wrote to	Acts 18.27
Then they all were *e.* and ate	Acts 27.36
be mutually *e.* by each other's faith	Rom.1.12
that he may *e.* your hearts	Col.4.8
Therefore *e.* one another and build	1 Th.5.11
e. the fainthearted, help the weak	1 Th.5.14
e. one another, and all the more	Heb.10.25

ENCOURAGEMENT
When he . . . had given them much *e.*	Acts 20.2
by the *e.* of the scriptures we	Rom.15.4
the God of steadfastness and *e.*	Rom.15.5
upbuilding and *e.* and consolation	1 Cor.14.3
So if there is any *e.* in Christ	Phil.2.1
have strong *e.* to seize the hope	Heb.6.18

END (noun)
to make an *e.* of all flesh	Gen.6.13
what is my *e.*, that I . . . be patient?	Job 6.11
LORD, let me know my *e.*	Ps.39.4
wars cease to the *e.* of the earth	Ps.46.9
from the *e.* of the earth I call	Ps.61.2
its *e.* is the way to death	Pr.16.25
Better is the *e.* of a thing than	Ec.7.8
Of making many books there is no *e.*	Ec.12.12
LORD of hosts, will make a full *e.*	Is.10.23
my indignation will come to an *e.*	Is.10.25
I will not make a full *e.* of you	Jer.5.18
great houses shall come to an *e.*	Am.3.15
I will make an *e.* of the pride	Zech.9.6
endures to the *e.* will be saved	Mt.10.22
but the *e.* is not yet	Mk.13.7
of his kingdom there will be no *e.*	Lk.1.33
came from the *e.* of the earth	Lk.11.31
For Christ is the *e.* of the law	Rom.10.4
their words to the *e.* of the world	Rom.10.18
Then comes the *e.*, when he	1 Cor.15.24
beginning of days nor *e.* of life	Heb.7.3
The *e.* of all things is at hand	1 Pet.4.7
who keeps my works until the *e.*	Rev.2.26
I am . . . the beginning and the *e.*	Rev.21.6

ENDURANCE
By your *e.* you will gain your lives	Lk.21.19
knowing that suffering produces *e.*	Rom.5.3
e. produces character	Rom.5.4
through great *e.*, in afflictions	2 Cor.6.4
for all *e.* and patience with joy	Col.1.11
For you have need of *e.*	Heb.10.36
the kingdom and the patient *e.*	Rev.1.9
your toil and your patient *e.*	Rev.2.2
a call for the *e.* of the saints	Rev.14.12

ENDURE
his prosperity will not *e.*	Job 20.21
May he live while the sun *e.*	Ps.72.5
his steadfast love *e.* for ever	Ps.100.5
They will perish, but thou dost *e.*	Ps.102.26
the glory of the LORD *e.* for ever	Ps.104.31
faithfulness of the LORD *e.* for ever	Ps.117.2
whatever God does *e.* for ever	Ec.3.14
Who can *e.* the heat of his anger?	Nah.1.6
who can *e.* the day of his coming	Mal.3.2
he has no root . . . but *e.* for a while	Mt.13.21

the food which e. to eternal life Jn.6.27
hopes all things, e. all things· 1 Cor.13.7
Therefore I e. everything 2 Tim.2.10
if we e., we shall also reign 2 Tim.2.12
at Lystra, what persecutions I e. 2 Tim.3.11
he e. as seeing him who is invisible Heb.11.27
e. the cross, despising the shame Heb.12.2

ENEMY
I will be an e. to your e. Ex.23.22
Saul was David's e. continually 1 Sam.18.29
Have you found me, O my e.? 1 Kg.21.20
And Esther said, "A foe and e. Est.7.6
to still the e. and the avenger Ps.8.2
He delivered me from my strong e. Ps.18.17
God arise, let his e. be scattered Ps.68.1
till I make your e. your footstool Ps.110.1
Deliver me, O LORD, from my e. Ps.143.9
If your e. is hungry, give him bread Pr.25.21
Love your e. and pray for those who Mt.5.44
till I put thy e. under thy feet Mk.12.36
that we should be saved from our e. Lk.1.71
while we were e. we were reconciled Rom.5.10
if your e. is hungry, feed him Rom.12.20
The last e. to be destroyed is 1 Cor.15.26

ENJOY
shall rest, and e. its sabbaths Lev.26.34
dwell in the land, and e. security Ps.37.3
that a man should e. his work Ec.3.22
God does not give . . . power to e. them Ec.6.2
E. life with the wife whom you love Ec.9.9
than to e. the . . . pleasures of sin Heb.11.25

ENLIGHTEN
The true light that e. every man Jn.1.9
a zeal for God, but it is not e. Rom.10.2
having the eyes of your hearts e. Eph.1.18
those who have once been e. Heb.6.4
after you were e., you endured Heb.10.32

ENMITY
put e. between you and the woman Gen.3.15
Because you cherished perpetual e. Ezek.35.5
had been at e. with each other Lk.23.12
e., strife, jealousy, anger Gal.5.20
with the world is e. with God? Jas.4.4

ENRAGED
he was angry and greatly e. Neh.4.1
At this the king was e. Est.1.12
the LORD is e. against all the nations Is.34.2
the princes were e. at Jeremiah Jer.37.15
were e. and wanted to kill them Acts 5.33
were e., and . . . ground their teeth Acts 7.54
When they heard this they were e. Acts 19.28

ENRICH
king will e. with great riches 1 Sam.17.25
waterest it, thou greatly e. it Ps.65.9
who trusts in the LORD will be e. Pr.28.25
were e. in him with all speech 1 Cor.1.5
You will be e. in every way 2 Cor.9.11

ENROLLED
All . . . were e. by genealogies 1 Chr.5.17
priests were e. with all their 2 Chr.31.18
the people to be e. by genealogy Neh.7.5
not be e. among the righteous Ps.69.28
that all the world should be e. Lk.2.1
to be e. with Mary, his betrothed Lk.2.5
he was e. with the eleven Acts 1.26

Let a widow be e. if she is not less 1 Tim.5.9
first-born who are e. in heaven Heb.12.23

ENSIGN
stand as an e. to the peoples Is.11.10
will raise an e. for the nations Is.11.12
lift up an e. over the peoples Is.62.10
was your sail, serving as your e. Ezek.27.7

ENSLAVE
so that no one should e. a Jew Jer.34.9
the hand of those who e. them Ezek.34.27
we might no longer be e. to sin Rom.6.6
but I will not be e. by anything 1 Cor.6.12
overcomes a man, to that he is e. 2 Pet.2.19

ENSNARE
that he should not e. the people Job 34.30
the cords of the wicked e. me Ps.119.61
The iniquities of the wicked e. him Pr.5.22
An evil man is e. by the transgression Pr.12.13

ENTANGLE
the cords of Sheol e. me 2 Sam.22.6
counsel how to e. him in his talk Mt.22.15
No soldier . . . gets e. in civilian 2 Tim.2.4
they are again e. in them 2 Pet.2.20

ENTER
not allow the destroyer to e. your Ex.12.23
No . . . Moabite shall e. the assembly Dt.23.3
no one e. the house of the LORD 2 Chr.23.6
E. his gates with thanksgiving Ps.100.4
E. not into judgment with thy Ps.143.2
Do not e. the path of the wicked Pr.4.14
Do not e. the house of mourning Jer.16.5
But the Spirit e. into me and set Ezek.3.24
E. by the narrow gate; for the gate Mt.7.13
and e. no town of the Samaritans Mt.10.5
can one e. a strong man's house Mt.12.29
If you would e. life, keep the Mt.19.17
e. into the joy of your master Mt.25.21
that you may not e. into temptation Mt.26.41
how hard it is to e. the kingdom Mk.10.24
like a child shall not e. it Lk.18.17
a rich man to e. the kingdom of God Lk.18.25
Then Satan e. into Judas Lk.22.3
he cannot e. the kingdom of God Jn.3.5
he who does not e. the sheepfold Jn.10.1
They shall never e. my rest Heb.3.11
But nothing unclean shall e. it Rev.21.27

ENTHRONED
LORD who sits e. above the cherubim 1 Chr.13.6
the LORD sits e. as king for ever Ps.29.10
But thou, O LORD, art e. for ever Ps.102.12

ENTICE
E. your husband to tell us what Jg.14.15
my heart has been secretly e. Job 31.27
if sinners e. you, do not consent Pr.1.10
A man of violence e. his neighbor Pr.16.29
is lured and e. by his own desire Jas.1.14
They e. unsteady souls 2 Pet.2.14
they e. with licentious passions 2 Pet.2.18

ENTREAT
E. the LORD to take away the frogs Ex.8.8
E. me not to leave you or to Ru.1.16
E. now the favor of the LORD 1 Kg.13.6
now e. the favor of God, that he Mal.1.9
His father came out and e. him Lk.15.28
I, Paul . . . e. you, by the meekness 2 Cor.10.1
I e. Euodia and I e. Syntyche Phil.4.2

ENTRUST

Moses . . . is *e*. with all my house	Num.12.7
who will *e*. to you the true riches?	Lk.16.11
Jews are *e*. with the oracles of God	Rom.3.2
I am *e*. with a commission	1 Cor.9.17
e. to us the message of	2 Cor.5.19
Peter had been *e*. with the gospel	Gal.2.7
and *e*. their souls to a faithful	1 Pet.4.19

ENVIOUS

be not *e*. of wrongdoers	Ps.37.1
For I was *e*. of the arrogant	Ps.73.3
Be not *e*. of evil men, nor desire to	Pr.24.1
and be not *e*. of the wicked	Pr.24.19

ENVY (noun)

the anger and *e*. which you showed	Ezek.35.11
out of *e*. that they had delivered	Mt.27.18
e., slander, pride, foolishness	Mk.7.22
Full of *e*., murder, strife, deceit	Rom.1.29
e., drunkenness, carousing	Gal.5.21
preach Christ from *e*. and rivalry	Phil.1.15
passing our days in malice and *e*.	Tit.3.3
insincerity and *e*. and all slander	1 Pet.2.1

EPHESUS

Acts 18.19; 19.35; 1 Cor.15.32; 1 Tim.1.3; Rev.2.1

EPHOD

they shall make the *e*. of gold	Ex.28.6
the skilfully woven band of the *e*.	Lev.8.7
Gideon made an *e*. of it	Jg.8.27
persons who wore the linen *e*.	1 Sam.22.18
David was girded with a linen *e*.	2 Sam.6.14
without *e*. or teraphim	Hos.3.4

EPHRAIM

younger son of Joseph, Gen.41.52; Jacob blesses Ephraim and Manasseh, Gen.48.14; his descendants numbered, Num.1.10,32; 2.18; 26.35; 1 Chr.7.20; their possessions, Jos.16.5; 17.17; Jg.1.29; quarrel with Gideon, Jg.8.1, and Jephthah, Jg.12; revolt from the house of David, 1 Kg.12.25; carried into captivity, 2 Kg.17.5–6; Ps.78.9,67; Jer.7.15

EQUAL

Gold and glass cannot *e*. it	Job 28.17
to whom will you . . . make me *e*.	Is.46.5
have made them *e*. to us who have	Mt.20.12
they *e*. to angels and are sons	Lk.20.36
making himself *e*. with God	Jn.5.18
a faith of *e*. standing with ours	2 Pet.1.1
breadth and height are *e*.	Rev.21.16

EQUALITY

that there may be *e*.	2 Cor.8.14
did not count *e*. with God a thing	Phil.2.6

EQUIPMENT

all the *e*. for their service	Num.4.26
war and the *e*. of his chariots	1 Sam.8.12
for the *e*. of the saints, for the	Eph.4.12
with the *e*. of the gospel of peace	Eph.6.15

ERR

make me understand how I have *e*.	Job 6.24
They are a people who *e*. in heart	Ps.95.10
they *e*. in vision, they stumble in	Is.28.7
and fools shall not *e*. therein	Is.35.8

ERROR

my *e*. remains with myself	Job 19.4
sinned through *e*. or ignorance	Ezek.45.20
no *e*. or fault was found in him	Dan.6.4

the due penalty for their *e*.	Rom.1.27
and for the *e*. of the people	Heb.9.7
By this we know . . . the spirit of *e*.	1 Jn.4.6
abandon themselves . . . to Balaam's *e*.	Jude 11

ESAU

son of Isaac, Gen.25.25 (Mal.1.2; Rom.9.13); sells his birthright, Gen.25.29 (Heb.12.16); deprived of the blessing, Gen.27.38; his anger against Jacob, Gen.27.41, and reconciliation, Gen.33; his riches and descendants, Gen.36; 1 Chr.1.35

ESCAPE (verb)

I am shut in so that I cannot *e*.	Ps.88.8
Let them not *e*. from your sight	Pr.4.21
And we, how shall we *e*.?	Is.20.6
And those who *e*. the sword shall	Jer.44.28
Can a man *e*. who does such things	Ezek.17.15
E. to Zion, you who dwell with the	Zech.2.7
how are you to *e*. being sentenced	Mt.23.33
but he *e*. from their hands	Jn.10.39
were seeking to *e*. from the ship	Acts 27.30
you will *e*. the judgment of God?	Rom.2.3
how shall we *e*. if we neglect such	Heb.2.3
much less shall we *e*. if we reject	Heb.12.25

ESTABLISH

But I will *e*. my covenant with you	Gen.6.18
The LORD will *e*. you as a people	Dt.28.9
that the LORD may *e*. his word	1 Kg.2.4
I will *e*. his kingdom for ever	1 Chr.28.7
the Most High himself will *e*. her	Ps.87.5
and *e*. thou the work of our hands	Ps.90.17
The LORD has *e*. his throne in the	Ps.103.19
In righteousness you shall be *e*.	Is.54.14
I will *e*. with you an everlasting	Ezek.16.60
to *e*. you in your faith and	1 Th.3.2
comfort your hearts and *e*. them	2 Th.2.17
when I will *e*. a new covenant with	Heb.8.8
E. your hearts, for the coming of	Jas.5.8

ESTEEM

so that his name was highly *e*.	1 Sam.18.30
yet we *e*. him stricken, smitten by	Is.53.4
One man *e*. one day as better than	Rom.14.5
who are least *e*. by the church?	1 Cor.6.4

ESTHER

(Hadassah), Est.2.7; made queen in the place of Vashti, Est.2.17; pleads for her people, Est. 7.3–4; the feast of Purim and Mordecai's advancement, Est.9–10

ETERNAL

The *e*. God is your dwelling place	Dt.33.27
What . . . must I do, to have *e*. life?	Mt.19.16
will go away into *e*. punishment	Mt.25.46
but the righteous into *e*. life	Mt.25.46
believes in him may have *e*. life	Jn.3.15
of water welling up to *e*. life	Jn.4.14
the food which endures to *e*. life	Jn.6.27
You have the words of *e*. life	Jn.6.68
this is *e*. life, that they know thee	Jn.17.3
as many as were ordained to *e*.	Acts 13.48
gift of God is *e*. life in Christ	Rom.6.23
the things that are unseen are *e*.	2 Cor.4.18
gave us *e*. comfort and good hope	2 Th.2.16
who through the *e*. Spirit offered	Heb.9.14
by the blood of the *e*. covenant	Heb.13.20
This is the true God and *e*. life	1 Jn.5.20
angels . . . kept by him in *e*. chains	Jude 6

undergoing a punishment of *e.* fire — Jude 7
with an *e.* gospel to proclaim — Rev.14.6

ETERNITY
he has put *e.* into man's mind — Ec.3.11
high and lofty One who inhabits *e.* — Is.57.15
both now and to the day of *e.* — 2 Pet.3.18

ETHIOPIA
Ps.87.4; Jer.46.9; Ezek.30.5; Zeph.3.10

EUNUCH
the seven *e.* who served King — Est.1.10
the chief of the *e.* said to Daniel — Dan.1.10
For there are *e.* who have been so — Mt.19.12
a *e.*, a minister of Candace — Acts 8.27

EUPHRATES
Gen.2.14; Dt.1.7; 2 Sam.10.16; Jer.13.4;
Rev.9.14

EVANGELIST
entered the house of Philip the *e.* — Acts 21.8
some *e.*, some pastors and teachers — Eph.4.11
do the work of an *e.* — 2 Tim.4.5

EVE
created, Gen.1.27; 2.18–22; her fall and fate,
Gen.3; 2 Cor.11.3

EVERLASTING
remember the *e.* covenant between Gen.9.16
the name of the LORD, the *E.* God — Gen.21.33
The enemy have vanished in *e.* ruins — Ps.9.6
from *e.* to *e.* thou art God — Ps.90.2
love of the LORD is from *e.* to *e.* — Ps.103.17
Thy kingdom is an *e.* kingdom — Ps.145.13
Mighty God, *E.* Father, Prince of Peace Is.9.6
The LORD is the *e.* God, the Creator Is.40.28
e. joy shall be upon their heads — Is.51.11
but the LORD will be your *e.* light — Is.60.19
I will make an *e.* covenant with them Is.61.8
I have loved you with an *e.* love — Jer.31.3
His kingdom is an *e.* kingdom — Dan.4.3

EVERMORE
shall be peace from the LORD for *e.* 1 Kg.2.33
in thy right hand are pleasures for *e.* Ps.16.11
from this time forth and for *e.* — Ps.113.2
glory for *e.* through Jesus Christ — Rom.16.27
I died, and behold I am alive for *e.* Rev.1.18

EVIDENCE
to death on the *e.* of witnesses — Num.35.30
speaks the truth gives honest *e.* — Pr.12.17
by the *e.* of two or three witnesses — Mt.18.16
e. of the righteous judgment of God 2 Th.1.5
their rust will be *e.* against you — Jas.5.3

EVIL
of the knowledge of good and *e.* — Gen.2.9
his heart was only *e.* continually — Gen.6.5
Why have you returned *e.* for good? Gen.44.4
And God sent an *e.* spirit between — Jg.9.23
to avert the *e.* design of Haman — Est.8.3
feared God, and turned away from *e.* Job 1.1
Depart from me, all you workers of *e.* Ps.6.8
Keep your tongue from *e.*, and your Ps.34.13
Depart from *e.*, and do good — Ps.34.14
The LORD loves those who hate *e.* — Ps.97.10
The LORD will keep you from all *e.* Ps.121.7
Do not plan *e.* against your neighbor Pr.3.29
to preserve you from the *e.* woman — Pr.6.24
The fear of the LORD is hatred of *e.* Pr.8.13
Be not envious of *e.* men, nor desire Pr.24.1
ointment give off an *e.* odor — Ec.10.1

There is an *e.* which I have seen — Ec.10.5
I will punish the world for its *e.* — Is.13.11
Their feet run to *e.* — Is.59.7
This *e.* people, who refuse to hear Jer.13.10
No *e.* shall come upon you — Jer.23.17
Hate *e.*, and love good — Am.5.15
Do not resist one who is *e.* — Mt.5.39
sun rise on the *e.* and on the good Mt.5.45
who are *e.*, know how to give good Mt.7.11
He who speaks *e.* of father or mother Mt.15.4
Lazarus in like manner *e.* things — Lk.16.25
shouldst keep them from the *e.* one Jn.17.15
some were . . . speaking *e.* of the Way Acts 19.9
deliver us from the present *e.* age — Gal.1.4
Let no *e.* talk come out of your — Eph.4.29
liars, *e.* beasts, lazy gluttons — Tit.1.12
Do not speak *e.* against one another Jas.4.11
you have overcome the *e.* one — 1 Jn.2.14
he who does *e.* has not seen God — 3 Jn.11

EVILDOER
Break thou the arm of the . . . *e.* — Ps.10.15
The face of the LORD is against *e.* — Ps.34.16
Fret not yourself because of *e.* — Pr.24.19
If this man were not an *e.*, we — Jn.18.30
Let the *e.* still do evil, and the — Rev.22.11

EXALT
didst *e.* me above my adversaries 2 Sam.22.49
Be *e.*, O LORD, in thy strength — Ps.21.13
let us *e.* his name together — Ps.34.3
Prize her highly, and she will *e.* you Pr.4.8
Righteousness *e.* a nation, but sin Pr.14.34
Capernaum, will you be *e.* to heaven? Mt.11.23
every one who *e.* himself will be — Lk.14.11
God *e.* him at his right hand — Acts 5.31
Therefore God has highly *e.* him — Phil.2.9
who opposes and *e.* himself against 2 Th.2.4
with unutterable and *e.* joy — 1 Pet.1.8

EXAMINE
Let us test and *e.* our ways — Lam.3.40
if we are being *e.* today concerning Acts 4.9
e. the scriptures daily to see if — Acts 17.11
Let a man *e.* himself, and so eat 1 Cor.11.28
E. yourselves, to see whether you 2 Cor.13.5

EXAMPLE
For I have given you an *e.*, that you Jn.13.15
also follow the *e.* of the faith — Rom.4.12
so live as you have an *e.* in us — Phil.3.17
become an *e.* to all the believers — 1 Th.1.7
in our conduct an *e.* to imitate — 2 Th.3.9
an *e.* in speech and conduct — 1 Tim.4.12
As an *e.* of suffering and patience Jas.5.10
suffered for you, leaving you an *e.* 1 Pet.2.21

EXCELLENT
because an *e.* spirit was in him — Dan.6.3
for you, most *e.* Theophilus — Lk.1.3
by your provision, most *e.* Felix — Acts 24.2
I am not mad, most *e.* Festus — Acts 26.25
and approve what is *e.* — Rom.2.18
show you a still more *e.* way — 1 Cor.12.31
so that you may approve what is *e.* Phil.1.10

EXCUSE (noun)
But they all alike began to make *e.* Lk.14.18
now they have no *e.* for their sin — Jn.15.22
So they are without *e.* — Rom.1.20
Therefore you have no *e.*, O man — Rom.2.1

EXECUTE

to *e*. the LORD's vengeance	Num.31.3
He *e*. justice for the fatherless	Dt.10.18
will *e*. judgment among the nations	Ps.110.6
by fire will the LORD *e*. judgment	Is.66.16
E. justice in the morning, and	Jer.21.12
given him authority to *e*. judgment	Jn.5.27
to *e*. his wrath on the wrongdoer	Rom.13.4

EXERCISE

kings of the Gentiles *e*. lordship	Lk.22.25
if they cannot *e*. self-control	1 Cor.7.9
Every athlete *e*. self-control	1 Cor.9.25
it was allowed to *e*. authority	Rev.13.5

EXHORT

he *e*. them all to remain faithful	Acts 11.23
e. the brethren with many words	Acts 15.32
we beseech and *e*. you in the Lord	1 Th.4.1
we command and *e*. in the Lord	2 Th.3.12
e. and reprove with all authority	Tit.2.15
But *e*. one another every day	Heb.3.13
So I *e*. the elders among you	1 Pet.5.1

EXILE (noun)

He took into *e*. in Babylon those	2 Chr.36.20
of Israel who had returned from *e*.	Ezra 6.21
The survivors . . . who escaped *e*.	Neh.1.3
Prepare yourselves baggage for *e*.	Jer.46.19
Judah has gone into *e*. because of	Lam.1.3
they carried into *e*. a whole people	Am.1.6
take you into *e*. beyond Damascus	Am.5.27
half of the city shall go into *e*.	Zech.14.2
Moses . . . became an *e*. in the land	Acts 7.29
throughout the time of your *e*.	1 Pet.1.17

EXIST

there is one God . . . for whom we *e*.	1 Cor.8.6
must believe that he *e*.	Heb.11.6
jealousy and selfish ambition *e*.	Jas.3.16
by the word of God heavens *e*.	2 Pet.3.5
by thy will they *e*. and were created	Rev.4.11

EXPIATION

sprinkle the water of *e*. upon them	Num.8.7
no *e*. can be made for the land	Num.35.33
e. for the land of his people	Dt.32.43
how shall I make *e*., that	2 Sam.21.3
put forward as an *e*. by his blood	Rom.3.25
make *e*. for the sins of the people	Heb.2.17
he is the *e*. for our sins	1 Jn.2.2
his Son to be the *e*. for our sins	1 Jn.4.10

EXPLAIN

Moses undertook to *e*. the law	Dt.1.5
e. riddles, and solve problems	Dan.5.12
E. to us the parable of the weeds	Mt.13.36
much to say which is hard to *e*.	Heb.5.11

EXTEND

has *e*. to us his steadfast love	Ezra 9.9
thy . . . love . . . *e*. to the heavens	Ps.36.5
the Lord will *e*. his hand yet a	Is.11.11
I will *e*. prosperity to her like a	Is.66.12
as grace *e*. to more and more	2 Cor.4.15

EXTOL

For this I will *e*. thee, O LORD	2 Sam.22.50
and *e*. thy righteousness	Ps.89.16
E. the LORD our God, and worship at	Ps.99.9
E. him, all peoples	Ps.117.1
I will *e*. thee, my God and King	Ps.145.1
e. and honor the King of heaven	Dan.4.37
the name of the Lord Jesus was *e*.	Acts 19.17

EXULT

let the field *e*.	1 Chr.16.32
I will be glad and *e*. in thee	Ps.9.2
let not my enemies *e*. over me	Ps.25.2
how long shall the wicked *e*.?	Ps.94.3
my soul shall *e*. in my God	Is.61.10
their hearts shall *e*. in the LORD	Zech.10.7
rejoice and *e*. and give him glory	Rev.19.7

EYE

Then the *e*. of both were opened	Gen.3.7
as a memorial between your *e*.	Ex.13.9
e. for *e*., tooth for tooth	Ex.21.24
his *e*. was not dim, nor his natural	Dt.34.7
is under the *e*. of the LORD	Jg.18.6
But the *e*. of their God was upon	Ezra 5.5
my *e*. pours out tears to God	Job 16.20
I have made a covenant with my *e*.	Job 31.1
Keep me as the apple of the *e*.	Ps.17.8
LORD is pure, enlightening the *e*.	Ps.19.8
my *e*. grows dim through sorrow	Ps.88.9
who formed the *e*., does he not see?	Ps.94.9
The *e*. of the LORD are in every	Pr.15.3
the *e*. is not satisfied with seeing	Ec.1.8
no *e*. has seen a God besides thee	Is.64.4
touches the apple of his *e*.	Zech.2.8
The *e*. is the lamp of the body	Mt.6.22
speck that is in your brother's *e*.	Mt.7.3
if your *e*. causes you to sin	Mt.18.9
go through the *e*. of a needle	Mt.19.24
What no *e*. has seen, nor ear heard	1 Cor.2.9
Because I am not an *e*.	1 Cor.12.16
in the twinkling of an *e*.	1 Cor.15.52
and every *e*. will see him	Rev.1.7

EYEWITNESS

were *e*. and ministers of the word	Lk.1.2
we were *e*. of his majesty	2 Pet.1.16

EZEKIEL

sent to the house of Israel, Ezek.2–3; 33.7; his visions of God's glory, Ezek.1; 8; 10; 11.22; of the resurrection of dry bones, Ezek.37; his vision of the measuring of the temple, Ezek.40–42; intercedes for Israel, Ezek.9,8; 11.13; his dumbness, Ezek.3.26; 24.27; 33.22; his parables, Ezek.15–17; 19; 23–24; exhorts Israel against idolatry, Ezek.14.1–11; 20.1–44; predicts Israel's and the nations' doom, Ezek.21; 25

EZRA

goes from Babylonia to Jerusalem, Ezra 7.1–6; 8.1; his commission from Artaxerxes to rebuild the temple, Ezra 7.11–26; fast ordered by, Ezra 8.21; reproves the people, Ezra 10.9–11; reads the book of the law, Neh.8; reforms corruptions, Ezra 10; Neh.13

FACE

moving over the *f*. of the waters	Gen.1.2
In the sweat of your *f*. you shall eat	Gen.3.19
Then Abram fell on his *f*.	Gen.17.3
For I have seen God *f*. to *f*.	Gen.32.30
Moses hid his *f*., for he was afraid	Ex.3.6
you cannot see my *f*.	Ex.33.20
the skin of his *f*. shone because	Ex.34.29
put the veil upon his *f*. again	Ex.34.35
The LORD make his *f*. to shine upon	Num.6.25
Hezekiah turned his *f*. to the wall	2 Kg.20.2
not turn away the *f*. of thy anointed	2 Chr.6.42

I . . . blush to lift my *f.* to thee — Ezra 9.6
he will curse thee to thy *f.* — Job 1.11
Thou hast said, "Seek ye my *f.*" — Ps.27.8
Make thy *f.* shine upon thy servant — Ps.119.135
Hide not thy *f.* from me, lest I be — Ps.143.7
A wicked man puts on a bold *f.* — Pr.21.29
As in water *f.* answers to *f.* — Pr.27.19
by grinding the *f.* of the poor? — Is.3.15
wings: with two he covered his *f.* — Is.6.2
I have set my *f.* like a flint — Is.50.7
Then I turned my *f.* to the Lord God — Dan.9.3
anoint your head and wash your *f.* — Mt.6.17
always behold the *f.* of my Father — Mt.18.10
he fell on his *f.* and prayed — Mt.26.39
they spat in his *f.*, and struck — Mt.26.67
his *f.* was like the *f.* of an angel — Acts 6.15
glory of God in the *f.* of Christ — 2 Cor.4.6
I opposed him to his *f.* — Gal.2.11
the *f.* of the Lord is against — 1 Pet.3.12
his *f.* was like the sun shining — Rev.1.16
fell on their *f.* and worshiped God — Rev.11.16
they shall see his *f.* — Rev.22.4

FADE

As the cloud *f.* and vanishes, so he — Job 7.9
For they will soon *f.* like the grass — Ps.37.2
in the evening it *f.* and withers — Ps.90.6
We all *f.* like a leaf, and our — Is.64.6
its brightness, *f.* as this was — 2 Cor.3.7
see the end of the *f.* splendor — 2 Cor.3.13
the rich man *f.* away in the midst — Jas.1.11

FAIL

I will not *f.* you or forsake you — Jos.1.5
shall never *f.* you a man before me — 1 Kg.8.25
My flesh and my heart may *f.* — Ps.73.26
that your faith may not *f.* — Lk.22.32
unless . . . you *f.* to meet the test — 2 Cor.13.5
that no one *f.* to obtain the grace — Heb.12.15
I will never *f.* you nor forsake — Heb.13.5
keeps the . . . law but *f.* in one point — Jas.2.10

FAINT

I call to thee, when my heart is *f.* — Ps.61.2
f. for the courts of the LORD — Ps.84.2
When my spirit is *f.*, thou knowest — Ps.142.3
If you *f.* in the day of adversity — ·Pr.24.10
is sick, and the whole heart *f.* — Is.1.5
He does not *f.* or grow weary — Is.40.28
Even youths shall *f.* and be weary — Is.40.30.
head of Jonah so that he was *f.* — Jon.4.8
hungry, lest they *f.* on the way — Mt.15.32
f. with fear and with foreboding — Lk.21.26

FAIR

saw that the daughters of men were *f.* — Gen.6.2
Queen Vashti . . . was *f.* to behold — Est.1.11
no women so *f.* as Job's daughters — Job 42.15
f. as the moon, bright as the sun — S.of S.6.10
you say, 'It will be *f.* weather — Mt.16.2
treat your slaves justly and *f.* — Col.4.1

FAITH

a breach of *f.* against the LORD — Lev.6.2
by breaking *f.* with the LORD — Num.5.6
have *f.* in him that he will return — Job 39.12
because they had no *f.* in God — Ps.78.22
clothe you, O men of little *f.*? — Mt.6.30
when Jesus saw their *f.* he said to — Mt.9.2
if you have *f.* as a grain of mustard — Mt.17.20
Go . . . your *f.* has made you well — Mk.10.52

f. in his name, has made this man — Acts 3.16
full of *f.* and of the Holy Spirit — Acts 6.5
full of the Holy Spirit and of *f.* — Acts 11.24
for I have *f.* in God that it will — Acts 27.25
he justifies him who has *f.* in Jesus — Rom.3.26
those who share the *f.* of Abraham — Rom.4.16
So *f.* comes from what is heard — Rom.10.17
As for the man who is weak in *f.* — Rom.14.1
whatever . . . not . . . from *f.* is sin — Rom.14.23
f., hope, love abide, these three — 1 Cor.13.13
Be watchful, stand firm in your *f.* — 1 Cor.16.13
for we walk by *f.*, not by sight — 2 Cor.5.7
that we might be justified by *f.* — Gal.3.24
but *f.* working through love — Gal.5.6
one Lord, one *f.*, one baptism — Eph.4.5
provided that you continue in the *f.* — Col.1.23
supply what is lacking in your *f.*? — 1 Th.3.10
Timothy, my true child in the *f.* — 1 Tim.1.2
have made shipwreck of their *f.* — 1 Tim.1.19
Fight the good fight of the *f.* — 1 Tim.6.12
I am reminded of your sincere *f.* — 2 Tim.1.5
my righteous one shall live by *f.* — Heb.10.38
Now *f.* is the assurance of things — Heb.11.1
without *f.* it is impossible to please — Heb.11.6
By *f.* Abraham obeyed when he was — Heb.11.8
By *f.* Moses, when he was grown up — Heb.11.24
that *f.* apart from works is barren? — Jas.2.20
so *f.* apart from works is dead — Jas.2.26
the prayer of *f.* will save the sick — Jas.5.15
your *f.* and hope are in God — 1 Pet.1.21
that overcomes the world, our *f.* — 1 Jn.5.4
contend for the *f.* . . . . once . . . delivered — Jude 3
did not deny my *f.* even in the — Rev.2.13
the endurance and *f.* of the saints — Rev.13.10

FAITHFUL

the *f.* God who keeps covenant and — Dt.7.9
the LORD preserves the *f.*, but — Ps.31.23
The LORD is *f.* in all his words — Ps.145.13
A *f.* witness does not lie, but a — Pr.14.5
F. are the wounds of a friend — Pr.27.6
Who then is the *f.* and wise servant — Mt.24.45
you have been *f.* over a little — Mt.25.23
all to remain *f.* to the Lord — Acts 11.23
God is *f.*, by whom you were called — 1 Cor.1.9
who are also *f.* in Christ Jesus — Eph.1.1
But the Lord is *f.* — 2 Th.3.3
he remains *f.* . . . . he cannot deny — 2 Tim.2.13
a merciful and *f.* high priest — Heb.2.17
but Christ was *f.* over God's house — Heb.3.6
entrust their souls to a *f.* Creator — 1 Pet.4.19
Be *f.* unto death, and I will give — Rev.2.10
He . . . is called *F.* and True — Rev.19.11

FAITHFULNESS

abounding in steadfast love and *f.* — Ex.34.6
A God of *f.* and without iniquity — Dt.32.4
thy *f.* to the clouds — Ps.36.5
thy *f.* is firm as the heavens — Ps.89.2
his *f.* is a shield and buckler — Ps.91.4
the *f.* of the LORD endures forever — Ps.117.2
faithlessness nullify the *f.* of God? — Rom.3.3
patience, kindness, goodness, *f.* — Gal.5.22

FAITHLESS

who were *f.* to the LORD God — 2 Chr.30.7
I look at the *f.* with disgust — Ps.119.158
Return, O *f.* children, says the LORD — Jer.3.14
Why then are we *f.* to one another — Mal.2.10

O *f.* and perverse generation, how	Mt.17.17
do not be *f.*, but believing	Jn.20.27
if we are *f.*, he remains faithful	2 Tim.2.13
as for the cowardly, the *f.*	Rev.21.8

FALL (verb)

The lines have *f.* for me in pleasant	Ps.16.6
though he *f.*, he shall not be cast	Ps.37.24
terrors of death have *f.* upon me	Ps.55.4
May all kings *f.* down before him	Ps.72.11
A thousand may *f.* at your side, ten	Ps.91.7
The LORD upholds all who are *f.*	Ps.145.14
Where . . . is no guidance, a people *f.*	Pr.11.14
He who digs a pit will *f.* into it	Pr.26.27
And the Assyrian shall *f.* by a sword	Is.31.8
and young men shall *f.* exhausted	Is.40.30
whoever does not *f.* down and worship	Dan.3.11
and to the hills, *F.* upon us	Hos.10.8
You will all *f.* away because of me	Mt.26.31
I saw Satan *f.* like lightning from	Lk.10.18
a grain of wheat *f.* into the earth	Jn.12.24
lest I cause my brother to *f.*	1 Cor.8.13
those who desire to be rich *f.*	1 Tim.6.9
if you do this you will never *f.*	2 Pet.1.10
is able to keep you from *f.*	Jude 24
F., f. is Babylon the great, she who	Rev.14.8

FALSE

You shall not bear *f.* witness	Ex.20.16
For he was *f.* to the LORD his God	2 Chr.26.16
Put *f.* ways far from me	Ps.119.29
therefore I hate every *f.* way	Ps.119.104
A *f.* balance is an abomination to	Pr.11.1
A *f.* witness will not go unpunished	Pr.19.5
Beware of *f.* prophets, who come to	Mt.7.15
F. Christs and *f.* prophets will arise	Mk.13.22
many bore *f.* witness against him	Mk.14.56
Jewish *f.* prophet, named Bar-Jesus	Acts 13.6
For such men are *f.* apostles	2 Cor.11.13
f. brethren secretly brought in	Gal.2.4
there will be *f.* teachers among you	2 Pet.2.1
the beast and the *f.* prophet were	Rev.20.10

FALSEHOOD

my lips will not speak *f.*	Job 27.4
I hate and abhor *f.*, but I love	Ps.119.163
A righteous man hates *f.*, but	Pr.13.5
Remove far from me *f.* and lying	Pr.30.8
They have spoken *f.* and divined a	Ezek.13.6
in him there is no *f.*	Jn.7.18
putting away *f.*, let every one speak	Eph.4.25
every one who loves and practices *f.*	Rev.22.15

FAME

the *f.* of David went out into	1 Chr.14.17
heard of the *f.* of Solomon she came	2 Chr.9.1
not heard my *f.* or seen my glory	Is.66.19
tetrarch heard about the *f.* of Jesus	Mt.14.1
And at once his *f.* spread everywhere	Mk.1.28

FAMILY

went forth by *f.* out of the ark	Gen.8.19
These are the *f.* of the sons of	Gen.10.32
O *f.* of the peoples, ascribe to the	Ps.96.7
the God of all the *f.* of Israel	Jer.31.1
known of all the *f.* of the earth	Am.3.2
all the *f.* of the earth be blessed	Acts 3.25
from whom every *f.* . . . is named	Eph.3.15

FAMINE

for the *f.* was severe in the land	Gen.12.10
besides the former *f.* that was in	Gen.26.1
seven years of *f.* began to come	Gen.41.54
three years of *f.* come to you	2 Sam.24.13
Now the *f.* was severe in Samaria	1 Kg.18.2
When he summoned a *f.* on the land	Ps.105.16
Sword and *f.* shall not come	Jer.14.15
against you my deadly arrows of *f.*	Ezek.5.16
not a *f.* of bread, nor a thirst for	Am.8.11
there will be *f.* and earthquakes	Mt.24.7
a great *f.* arose in that country	Lk.15.14
or *f.*, or nakedness, or peril, or	Rom.8.35
pestilence and mourning and *f.*	Rev.18.8

FAMOUS

name of Solomon more *f.* than yours	1 Kg.1.47
f. men, heads of their fathers'	1 Chr.5.24
slew *f.* kings, for his steadfast	Ps.136.18
How the *f.* city is forsaken	Jer.49.25
the brother who is *f.* among all	2 Cor.8.18

FAR

Thus *f.* shall you come, and no	Job 38.11
But thou, O LORD, be not *f.* off	Ps.22.19
Perverseness . . . shall be *f.* from me	Ps.101.4
who looks *f.* down upon the heavens	Ps.113.6
The LORD is *f.* from the wicked	Pr.15.29
Remove *f.* from me falsehood	Pr.30.8
for a comforter is *f.* from me	Lam.1.16
but their heart is *f.* from me	Mt.15.8
You are not *f.* from the kingdom of	Mk.12.34
took his journey into a *f.* country	Lk.15.13
saw Abraham *f.* off and Lazarus	Lk.16.23
he led them out as *f.* as Bethany	Lk.24.50
is able to do *f.* more abundantly	Eph.3.20
with Christ, for that is *f.* better	Phil.1.23

FARMER

he had *f.* and vinedressers in	2 Chr.26.10
the *f.* are ashamed, they cover their	Jer.14.4
shall call the *f.* to mourning	Am.5.16
hard-working *f.* who ought to have	2 Tim.2.6
Behold, the *f.* waits for the precious	Jas.5.7

FAST (verb)

Why have we *f.*, and thou seest it not?	Is.58.3
Though they *f.*, I will not hear	Jer.14.12
And when you *f.*, do not look dismal	Mt.6.16
but your disciples do not *f.*?	Mt.9.14
the disciples of the Pharisees *f.*	Mk.2.18
I *f.* twice a week, I give tithes of	Lk.18.12

FASTING

with *f.* and weeping and lamenting	Est.4.3
I afflicted myself with *f.*	Ps.35.13
F. like yours this day will not	Is.58.4
that their *f.* may be seen by men	Mt.6.16
worshiping with *f.* and prayer	Lk.2.37
Then after *f.* and praying they laid	Acts 13.3
every church, with prayer and *f.*	Acts 14.23

FAT

seven cows sleek and *f.*	Gen.41.2
But Jeshurun waxed *f.*, and kicked	Dt.32.15
Now Eglon was a very *f.* man	Jg.3.17
ate, and were filled and became *f.*	Neh.9.25
Make the heart of this people *f.*	Is.6.10
they have grown *f.* and sleek	Jer.5.28
between the *f.* sheep and the lean	Ezek.34.20
my oxen and my *f.* calves are killed	Mt.22.4

FATE

are visited by the *f.* of all men	Num.16.29
This is the *f.* of those who have	Ps.49.13

since one *f*. comes to all, to the	Ec.9.2	**FAULT**	
grief at the *f*. of all the maidens	Lam.3.51	the people found *f*. with Moses	Ex.17.2
FATHER		I have found no *f*. in him	1 Sam.29.3
a man leaves his *f*. and his mother	Gen.2.24	for no *f*. of mine, they run and make	Ps.59.4
Honor your *f*. and your mother	Ex.20.12	go and tell him his *f*.	Mt.18.15
Whoever curses his *f*. or his mother	Ex.21.17	that no *f*. may be found with our	2 Cor.6.3
my son, know the God of your *f*.	1 Chr.28.9	he finds *f*. with them when he	Heb.8.8
I was a *f*. to the poor	Job 29.16	**FAVOR (noun)**	
F. of the fatherless and protector	Ps.68.5	Noah found *f*. in the eyes of the LORD	Gen.6.8
Thou art my *F*., my God	Ps.89.26	So Joseph found *f*. in his sight	Gen.39.4
As a *f*. pities his children, so the	Ps.103.13	Entreat now the *f*. of the LORD	1 Kg.13.6
A wise son makes a glad *f*.	Pr.15.20	Remember this also in my *f*.	Neh.13.22
A stupid son is a grief to a *f*.	Pr.17.21	Esther found *f*. in the eyes of all	Est.2.15
If one curses his *f*. or his mother	Pr.20.20	cover him with *f*. as with a shield	Ps.5.12
Everlasting *F*., Prince of Peace	Is.9.6	Let the *f*. of the Lord our God be	Ps.90.17
thou, O LORD, art our *F*.	Is.63.16	obtains *f*. from the LORD	Pr.8.35
Yet, O LORD, thou art our *F*.; we are	Is.64.8	A good man obtains *f*. from the LORD	Pr.12.2
The *f*. have eaten sour grapes	Jer.31.29	Good sense wins *f*., but the way	Pr.13.15
Have we not all one *f*.? Has not one	Mal.2.10	Many seek the *f*. of a generous man	Pr.19.6
glory to your *F*. who is in heaven	Mt.5.16	God gave Daniel *f*. and compassion	Dan.1.9
be sons of your *F*. who is in heaven	Mt.5.45	to entreat the *f*. of the LORD	Zech.7.2
Our *F*. who art in heaven, Hallowed	Mt.6.9	for you have found *f*. with God	Lk.1.30
your heavenly *F*. knows that you need	Mt.6.32	and the *f*. of God was upon him	Lk.2.40
I also will deny before my *F*.	Mt.10.33	and in *f*. with God and man	Lk.2.52
F., Lord of heaven and earth	Mt.11.25	praising God and having *f*. with all	Acts 2.47
no one knows the Son except the *F*.	Mt.11.27	**FEAR (noun)**	
Come, O blessed of my *F*., inherit	Mt.25.34	God of Abraham and the *F*. of Isaac	Gen.31.42
comes in the glory of his *F*.	Mk.8.38	Serve the LORD with *f*.	Ps.2.11
nor the Son, but only the *F*.	Mk.13.32	no *f*. of God before his eyes	Ps.36.1
your *f*. and I have been looking	Lk.2.48	The *f*. of the LORD is the beginning	Ps.111.10
merciful . . . as your *F*. is merciful	Lk.6.36	The *f*. of the LORD is the beginning	Pr.1.7
the heavenly *F*. give the Holy Spirit	Lk.11.13	The *f*. of the LORD is hatred of	Pr.8.13
F., give me the share of property	Lk.15.12	The *f*. of the LORD prolongs life	Pr.10.27
F., I have sinned against heaven	Lk.15.21	The *f*. of the LORD leads to life	Pr.19.23
F., if thou art willing, remove	Lk.22.42	Take heart, it is I; have no *f*.	Mk.6.50
And Jesus said, "*F*., forgive them	Lk.23.34	*F*. seized them all; and they glorified	Lk.7.16
F., into thy hands I commit my	Lk.23.46	through *f*. of death were subject	Heb.2.15
Son, who is in the bosom of the *F*.	Jn.1.18	but perfect love casts out *f*.	1 Jn.4.18
worship the *F*. in spirit and truth	Jn.4.23	**FEAR (verb)**	
My *F*. is working . . . and I am working	Jn.5.17	*F*. not, Abram, I am your shield	Gen.15.1
Our *f*. ate the manna in the wilderness	Jn.6.31	*F*. not, stand firm, and see the	Ex.14.13
All that the *F*. gives me will come	Jn.6.37	You shall not *f*. them; for it is the	Dt.3.22
knew me, you would know my *F*. also	Jn.8.19	You shall *f*. the LORD your God	Dt.10.20
as the *F*. knows me and I know the *F*.	Jn.10.15	You shall not *f*. other gods or bow	2 Kg.17.35
I and the *F*. are one	Jn.10.30	Does Job *f*. God for nought?	Job 1.9
He who has seen me has seen the *F*.	Jn.14.9	You who *f*. the LORD, praise him	Ps.22.23
I am in the *F*. and the *F*. in me	Jn.14.11	whom shall I *f*.? The LORD is	Ps.27.1
but I do as the *F*. has commanded me	Jn.14.31	Let all the earth *f*. the LORD	Ps.33.8
All that the *F*. has is mine	Jn.16.15	the LORD pities those who *f*. him	Ps.103.13
Holy *F*., keep them in thy name which	Jn.17.11	*F*. God, and keep his commandments	Ec.12.13
As the *F*. has sent me, even so I send	Jn.20.21	thou didst say, 'Do not *f*.!'	Lam.3.57
from God our *F*. and the Lord Jesus	Rom.1.7	*f*. not, peace be with you	Dan.10.19
When we cry, "Abba! *F*.!"	Rom.8.15	you shall *f*. evil no more	Zeph.3.15
Blessed be the God and *F*. of our	2 Cor.1.3	*F*. not, therefore; you are of more	Mt.10.31
a man shall leave his *f*. and mother	Eph.5.31	But I will warn you whom to *f*.	Lk.12.5
F., do not provoke your children	Col.3.21	*F*. not, little flock, for it is your	Lk.12.32
be subject to the *F*. of spirits	Heb.12.9	Men of Israel, and you that *f*. God	Acts 13.16
coming down from the *F*. of lights	Jas.1.17	*F*. God. Honor the emperor	1 Pet.2.17
we have an advocate with the *F*.	1 Jn.2.1	*F*. not, I am the first and the last	Rev.1.17
No one who denies . . . Son has the *F*.	1 Jn.2.23	**FEARFUL**	
sat down with my *F*. on his throne	Rev.3.21	Whoever is *f*. and trembling, let	Jg.7.3
FATHERLESS		for thou art *f*. and wonderful	Ps.139.14
justice for the *f*. and the widow	Dt.10.18	Say to those who are of a *f*. heart	Is.35.4
thou hast been the helper of the *f*.	Ps.10.14	he shall cause *f*. destruction	Dan.8.24
Father of the *f*. . . . protector of widows	Ps.68.5	a *f*. prospect of judgment ·	Heb.10.27
they judge not . . . cause of the *f*.	Jer.5.28		

It is a *f.* thing to fall into the | Heb.10.31
so *f.* was that plague | Rev.16.21

FEAST (noun)

So he made them a *f.*, and they ate | Gen.26.30
for we must hold a *f.* to the LORD | Ex.10.9
You shall keep the *f.* of unleavened | Ex.23.15
You shall keep the *f.* of harvest | Ex.23.16
shall keep the *f.* of ingathering | Ex.23.16
You shall keep the *f.* of booths | Dt.16.13
f. of weeks, and at the *f.* of booths | Dt.16.16
the yearly *f.* of the LORD at Shiloh | Jg.21.19
Solomon held the *f.* for seven days | 2 Chr.7.8
among the Jews, a *f.* and a holiday | Est.8.17
your appointed *f.* my soul hates | Is.1.14
I hate, I despise your *f.* | Am.5.21
I will turn your *f.* into mourning | Am.8.10
gave a marriage *f.* for his son | Mt.22.2
before . . . the *f.* of Unleavened Bread | Mk.14.1
After this there was a *f.* of the Jews | Jn.5.1
It was the *f.* of the Dedication | Jn.10.22
These are blemishes on your love *f.* | Jude 12

FEEBLE

but the *f.* gird on strength | 1 Sam.2.4
What are these *f.* Jews doing? | Neh.4.2
you have made firm the *f.* knees | Job 4.4
hands, and make firm the *f.* knees | Is.35.3
will melt and all hands will be *f.* | Ezek.21.7

FEED

commanded . . . ravens to *f.* you there | 1 Kg.17.4
commanded a widow there to *f.* you | 1 Kg.17.9
I would *f.* you with the finest of | Ps.81.16
The lips of the righteous *f.* many | Pr.10.21
the mouths of fools *f.* on folly | Pr.15.14
The cow and the bear shall *f.* | Is.11.7
He will *f.* his flock like a shepherd | Is.40.11
Aliens shall stand and *f.* your flocks | Is.61.5
wolf and the lamb shall *f.* together | Is.65.25
I will *f.* them with wormwood | Jer.23.15
should not shepherds *f.* the sheep? | Ezek.34.2
yet your heavenly Father *f.* them | Mt.6.26
when did we see thee hungry and *f.* | Mt.25.37
Jesus said to him, "*F.* my sheep | Jn.21.17
to *f.* the church of the Lord | Acts 20.28
if your enemy is hungry, *f.* him | Rom.12.20

FEET

put off your shoes from your *f.* | Ex.3.5
the great toes of their right *f.* | Lev.8.24
Put off your shoes from your *f.* | Jos.5.15
a son who was crippled in his *f.* | 2 Sam.4.4
He made my *f.* like hinds' *f.* | 2 Sam.22.34
the *f.* and the palms of her hands | 2 Kg.9.35
Thou puttest my *f.* in the stocks | Job 13.27
thou hast put all things under his *f.* | Ps.8.6
they have pierced my hands and *f.* | Ps.22.16
He . . . set my *f.* upon a rock | Ps.40.2
my *f.* had almost stumbled, my steps | Ps.73.2
Thy word is a lamp to my *f.* | Ps.119.105
spreads a net for his *f.* | Pr.29.5
Their *f.* run to evil, and they make | Is.59.7
Son of man, stand upon your *f.* | Ezek.2.1
its *f.* partly of iron and partly of | Dan.2.33
shake off the dust from your *f.* | Mt.10.14
than with two *f.* to be thrown into | Mk.9.45
has anointed my *f.* with ointment | Lk.7.46
sat at the Lord's *f.* and listened | Lk.10.39
began to wash the disciples' *f.* | Jn.13.5

brought up . . . at the *f.* of Gamaliel | Acts 22.3
shod your *f.* with the equipment of | Eph.6.15
whose *f.* are like burnished bronze | Rev.2.18

FELIX

Acts 23.24; 24.2,25,27; 25.14

FELLOW

regard this ill-natured *f.*, Nabal | 1 Sam.25.25
for I set every man against his *f.* | Zech.8.10
have had mercy on your *f.* servant | Mt.18.33
Away with such a *f.* from the earth | Acts 22.22
and *f.* heirs with Christ | Rom.8.17
my *f.* workers in Christ Jesus | Rom.16.3
Timothy, my *f.* worker, greets you | Rom.16.21
For we are *f.* workers for God | 1 Cor.3.9
you are *f.* citizens with the saints | Eph.2.19
among my *f.* workers for the kingdom | Col.4.11
that we may be *f.* workers in the truth | 3 Jn.8
I am a *f.* servant with you | Rev.22.9

FELLOWSHIP

within God's house we walked in *f.* | Ps.55.14
to the apostles' teaching and *f.* | Acts 2.42
were called into the *f.* of his Son | 1 Cor.1.9
and the *f.* of the Holy Spirit | 2 Cor.13.14
gave . . . the right hand of *f.* | Gal.2.9
our *f.* is with the Father and | 1 Jn.1.3

FEMALE

male and *f.*, went into the ark | Gen.7.9
two hundred male and *f.* singers | Ezra 2.65
there is neither male nor *f.* | Gal.3.28

FESTIVAL

thanksgiving, a multitude keeping *f.* | Ps.42.4
do on the day of appointed *f.* | Hos.9.5
celebrate the *f.*, not with the old | 1 Cor.5.8
with regard to a *f.* or a new moon | Col.2.16

FESTUS

Acts 24.27; 25.9,14; 26.24-25

FETTERS

Gaza, and bound him with bronze *f.* | Jg.16.21
of Zedekiah, and bound him in *f.* | 2 Kg.25.7
been bound with *f.* and chains | Mk.5.4
every one's *f.* were unfastened | Acts 16.26
Remember my *f.* | Col.4.18
I am suffering and wearing *f.* | 2 Tim.2.9

FEVER

The LORD will smite you . . . with *f.* | Dt.28.22
mother-in-law lying sick with a *f.* | Mt.8.14
at the seventh hour the *f.* left him | Jn.4.52
lay sick with *f.* and dysentery | Acts 28.8

FEW

from saving by many or by *f.* | 1 Sam.14.6
When they were *f.* in number | 1 Chr.16.19
I and a *f.* men with me | Neh.2.12
born of a woman is of *f.* days | Job 14.1
therefore let your words be *f.* | Ec.5.2
grinders cease because they are *f.* | Ec.12.3
life, and those who find it are *f.* | Mt.7.14
plentiful, but the laborers are *f.* | Mt.9.37
many are called, but *f.* are chosen | Mt.22.14
But I have a *f.* things against you | Rev.2.14
you have still a *f.* names in Sardis | Rev.3.4

FIELD

when no plant of the *f.* was yet in | Gen.2.5
when they were in the *f.*, Cain rose | Gen.4.8
the *f.* of Ephron in Machpelah | Gen.23.17
Six years you shall sow your *f.* | Lev.25.3
gleaned in the *f.* after the reapers | Ru.2.3

Come, let us go out into the *f*.   1 Sam.20.11
oxen, and also the beasts of the *f*.   Ps.8.7
let the *f*. exult, and everything in   Ps.96.12
She considers a *f*. and buys it   Pr.31.16
trees of the *f*. shall clap their hands   Is.55.12
Zion shall be plowed as a *f*.   Jer.26.18
And I bought the *f*. at Anathoth   Jer.32.9
God so clothes the grass of the *f*.   Mt.6.30
the parable of the weeds of the *f*.   Mt.13.36
bought with them the potter's *f*.   Mt.27.7
there were shepherds out in the *f*.   Lk.2.8
Now his elder son was in the *f*.   Lk.15.25
see how the *f*. are already white   Jn.4.35
Akeldama, that is, *F*. of Blood   Acts 1.19
you are God's *f*., God's building   1 Cor.3.9

FIERCE

the *f*. anger of the LORD may turn   Num.25.4
f. wrath of our God . . . be averted   Ezra 10.14
the *f*. anger of the LORD has not   Jer.4.8
He has cut down in *f*. anger all the   Lam.2.3
repent and turn from his *f*. anger   Jon.3.9
after my departure *f*. wolves will   Acts 20.29

FIERY

Then the LORD sent *f*. serpents   Num.21.6
be cast into a burning *f*. furnace   Dan.3.6
surprised at the *f*. ordeal which   1 Pet.4.12

FIG

and they sewed *f*. leaves together   Gen.3.7
And the trees said to the *f*. tree   Jg.9.10
Let them take a cake of *f*.   Is.38.21
every man . . . under his *f*. tree   Mic.4.4
from thorns, or *f*. from thistles?   Mt.7.16
And the *f*. tree withered at once   Mt.21.19
From the *f*. tree learn its lesson   Mk.13.28
I saw you under the *f*. tree   Jn.1.50
Can a *f*. tree, my brethren, yield   Jas.3.12

FIGHT

the LORD your God who *f*. for you   Dt.3.22
I myself will *f*. against you   Jer.21.5
this world, my servants would *f*.   Jn.18.36
F. the good *f*. of the faith   1 Tim.6.12
I have fought the good *f*.   2 Tim.4.7
you covet . . . so you *f*. and wage war   Jas.4.2
beast, and who can *f*. against it?   Rev.13.4

FILL

multiply and *f*. the waters in the   Gen.1.22
F. me with joy and gladness   Ps.51.8
My mouth is *f*. with thy praise   Ps.71.8
Open your mouth . . . I will *f*. it   Ps.81.10
Let the sea roar, and all that *f*. it   Ps.98.7
the hungry he *f*. with good things   Ps.107.9
the wicked are *f*. with trouble   Pr.12.21
he will *f*. Zion with justice   Is.33.5
the glory of the LORD *f*. the temple   Ezek.43.5
glorified God and were *f*. with awe   Lk.5.26
were all *f*. with the Holy Spirit   Acts 2.4
why has Satan *f*. your heart to lie   Acts 5.3
the disciples were *f*. with joy   Acts 13.52
May the God of hope *f*. you with all   Rom.15.13
but be *f*. with the Spirit   Eph.5.18
the temple was *f*. with smoke   Rev.15.8

FIND

Can you *f*. out the deep things of God?   Job 11.7
that I knew where I might *f*. him   Job 23.3
The Almighty–we cannot *f*. him   Job 37.23
under his wings you will *f*. refuge   Ps.91.4

I *f*. my delight in thy commandments   Ps.119.47
So you will *f*. favor and good   Pr.3.4
those who seek me diligently *f*. me   Pr.8.17
A good wife who can *f*.? She is far   Pr.31.10
for you will *f*. it after many days   Ec.11.1
the LORD, but they will not *f*. him   Hos.5.6
seek, and you will *f*.; knock   Mt.7.7
He who *f*. his life will lose it   Mt.10.39
you will *f*. rest for your souls   Mt.11.29
will *f*. a babe wrapped in swaddling   Lk.2.12
on entering you will *f*. a colt tied   Lk.19.30
I *f*. no crime in this man   Lk.23.4
f. grace to help in time of need   Heb.4.16

FINGER

to Pharaoh, "This is the *f*. of God."   Ex.8.19
stone, written with the *f*. of God   Ex.31.18
who had six *f*. on each hand   2 Sam.21.20
thy heavens, the work of thy *f*.   Ps.8.3
the *f*. of a man's hand appeared   Dan.5.5
But if it is by the *f*. of God that   Lk.11.20
Put your *f*. here, and see my hands   Jn.20.27

FINISH

Thus the heavens and the earth were *f*.   Gen.2.1
when Moses had *f*. speaking with them   Ex.34.33
When Moses had *f*. writing the words   Dt.31.24
Solomon built the house, and *f*. it   1 Kg.6.14
So Hiram *f*. all the work that he   1 Kg.7.40
the wall was *f*. on the twenty-fifth   Neh.6.15
When the Lord has *f*. all his work   Is.10.12
And when Jesus *f*. these sayings   Mt.7.28
Jesus . . . said, "It is *f*."   Jn.19.30
I have *f*. the race, I have kept the   2 Tim.4.7
And when they have *f*. their testimony   Rev.11.7

FIRE

the LORD descended upon it in *f*.   Ex.19.18
an offering by *f*. to the LORD   Ex.29.18
burnt offering, an offering by *f*.   Lev.1.13
F. shall be kept burning upon the   Lev.6.13
f. came forth from before the LORD   Lev.9.24
offered unholy *f*. before the LORD   Num.3.4
the *f*. of the LORD burned among them   Num.11.1
And *f*. came forth from the LORD   Num.16.35
the LORD . . . is a devouring *f*.   Dt.4.24
God who answers by *f*., he is God   1 Kg.18.24
after a still small voice   1 Kg.19.12
a chariot of *f*. and horses of *f*.   2 Kg.2.11
f. came down from heaven   2 Chr.7.1
The *f*. of God fell from heaven   Job 1.16
As I mused, the *f*. burned   Ps.39.3
he burns the chariots with *f*.   Ps.46.9
Can a man carry *f*. in his bosom and   Pr.6.27
will heap coals of *f*. on his head   Pr.25.22
For behold, the LORD will come in *f*.   Is.66.15
Is not my word like *f*., says the   Jer.23.29
and *f*. flashing forth continually   Ezek.1.4
walking in the midst of the *f*.   Dan.3.25
he will burn with unquenchable *f*.   Mt.3.12
to be thrown into the eternal *f*.   Mt.18.8
eternal *f*. prepared for the devil   Mt.25.41
with the Holy Spirit and with *f*.   Lk.3.16
I came to cast *f*. upon the earth   Lk.12.49
Sinai, in a flame of *f*. in a bush   Acts 7.30
for our God is a consuming *f*.   Heb.12.29
And the tongue is a *f*.   Jas.3.6
his eyes were like a flame of *f*.   Rev.1.14
the lake of *f*. and brimstone   Rev.20.10

FIRM

stand *f*., and see the salvation of	Ex.14.13
you have made *f*. the feeble knees	Job 4.4
thy faithfulness is *f*. as the heavens	Ps.89.2
my covenant will stand *f*. for him	Ps.89.28
shall stand *f*. and take action	Dan.11.32
stand *f*. in your faith	1 Cor.16.13
But God's *f*. foundation stands	2 Tim.2.19
Resist him, *f*. in your faith	1 Pet.5.9

FIRMAMENT

Let there be a *f*. in the midst of	Gen.1.6
and the *f*. proclaims his handiwork	Ps.19.1
shine like the brightness of the *f*.	Dan.12.3

FIRST

Noah was the *f*. tiller of the soil	Gen.9.20
the *f*. fruits of your labor	Ex.23.16
two tables of stone like the *f*.	Dt.10.3
Your *f*. father sinned, and your	Is.43.27
I am the *f*. and I am the last	Is.44.6
But seek *f*. his kingdom and his	Mt.6.33
You hypocrite, *f*. take the log out	Mt.7.5
But many that are *f*. will be last	Mt.19.30
This is the great and *f*. commandment	Mt.22.38
on the *f*. day of Unleavened Bread	Mt.26.17
the dawn of the *f*. day of the week	Mt.28.1
He *f*. found his brother Simon	Jn.1.41
This, the *f*. of his signs, Jesus did	Jn.2.11
In the *f*. book, O Theophilus, I have	Acts 1.1
were . . . *f*. . . . called Christians	Acts 11.26
On the *f*. day of the week, when we	Acts 20.7
On the *f*. day of every week, each	1 Cor.16.2
we hold our *f*. confidence firm to	Heb.3.14
We love, because he *f*. loved us	1 Jn.4.19
I am the *f*. and the last	Rev.1.17
abandoned the love you had at *f*.	Rev.2.4
This is the *f*. resurrection	Rev.20.5
for the *f*. heaven and the *f*. earth	Rev.21.1

FIRST-BORN

Consecrate to me all the *f*.	Ex.13.2
He smote all the *f*. in Egypt	Ps.78.51
offer by fire all their *f*.	Ezek.20.26
Shall I give my *f*. for my transgression	Mic.6.7
she gave birth to her *f*. son	Lk.2.7
the *f*. of all creation	Col.1.15
assembly of the *f*. who are enrolled	Heb.12.23

FISH (noun)

dominion over the *f*. of the sea	Gen.1.26
and the *f*. of the sea, whatever	Ps.8.8
appointed a great *f*. to swallow up	Jon.1.17
he took the seven loaves and the *f*.	Mt.15.36
they enclosed a great shoal of *f*.	Lk.5.6
instead of a *f*. give him a serpent	Lk.11.11
has five barley loaves and two *f*.	Jn.6.9
hauled the net . . . full of large *f*.	Jn.21.11

FISHERS

Behold, I am sending for many *f*.	Jer.16.16
and I will make you *f*. of men	Mt.4.19
I will make you become *f*. of men	Mk.1.17

FIXED

means that the thing is *f*. by God	Gen.41.32
Thou hast *f*. all the bounds of the	Ps.74.17
thy word is . . . *f*. in the heavens	Ps.119.89
he *f*. their bounds which cannot be	Ps.148.6
a great chasm has been *f*.	Lk.16.26
seasons which the Father has *f*.	Acts 1.7
because he has *f*. a day on which	Acts 17.31

FLAME (noun)

a *f*. comes forth from his mouth	Job 41.21
makest . . . fire and *f*. thy ministers	Ps.104.4
and his Holy One a *f*.	Is.10.17
anger and a *f*. of devouring fire	Is.30.30
his throne was fiery *f*.	Dan.7.9
for I am in anguish in this *f*.	Lk.16.24
winds, and his servants *f*. of fire	Heb.1.7
his eyes were like a *f*. of fire	Rev.1.14

FLASH

His sneezings *f*. forth light	Job 41.18
F. forth the lightning and scatter	Ps.144.6
a light from heaven *f*. about him	Acts 9.3
From the throne issue *f*. of lightning	Rev.4.5
there were *f*. of lightning	Rev.16.18

FLATTER

they *f*. with their tongue	Ps.5.9
But they *f*. him with their mouths	Ps.78.36
and a *f*. mouth works ruin	Pr.26.28
by fair and *f*. words they deceive	Rom.16.18
f. people to gain advantage	Jude 16

FLEE

Should such a man as I *f*.?	Neh.6.11
F. like a bird to the mountains	Ps.11.1
whither . . . *f*. from thy presence?	Ps.139.7
The wicked *f*. when no one pursues	Pr.28.1
To whom will you *f*. for help	Is.10.3
sorrow and sighing shall *f*. away	Is.51.11
both man and beast shall *f*. away	Jer.50.3
But Jonah rose to *f*. to Tarshish	Jon.1.3
f. to Egypt, and remain there till	Mt.2.13
warned you to *f*. from the wrath to	Mt.3.7
persecute you in one town, *f*. to	Mt.10.23
in Judea *f*. to the mountains	Mk.13.14
He *f*. because he is a hireling	Jn.10.13
Resist the devil and he will *f*. from	Jas.4.7

FLEECE

the first of the *f*. of your sheep	Dt.18.4
if there is dew on the *f*. alone	Jg.6.37
it was dry on the *f*. only	Jg.6.40

FLESH

bone of my bones and *f*. of my *f*.	Gen.2.23
all *f*. died that moved upon the earth	Gen.7.21
the life of the *f*. is in the blood	Lev.17.11
My *f*. is clothed with worms and dirt	Job 7.5
then from my *f*. I shall see God	Job 19.26
my *f*. faints for thee, as in a dry	Ps.63.1
My *f*. and my heart may fail, but God	Ps.73.26
He remembered that they were but *f*.	Ps.78.39
he who gives food to all *f*.	Ps.136.25
All *f*. is grass, and all its beauty	Is.40.6
All *f*. shall see that I the LORD	Ezek.20.48
You eat *f*. with the blood	Ezek.33.25
f. and blood has not revealed this	Mt.16.17
spirit . . . is willing . . . *f*. is weak	Mk.14.38
the Word became *f*. and dwelt among	Jn.1.14
That which is born of the *f*. is *f*.	Jn.3.6
you eat the *f*. of the Son of man	Jn.6.53
pour out my Spirit upon all *f*.	Acts 2.17
To set the mind on the *f*. is death	Rom.8.6
we are debtors, not to the *f*.	Rom.8.12
f. and blood cannot inherit the	1 Cor.15.50
a thorn was given me in the *f*.	2 Cor.12.7
Now the works of the *f*. are plain	Gal.5.19
not contending against *f*. and blood	Eph.6.12
we . . . put no confidence in the *f*.	Phil.3.3

He was manifested in the *f.* — 1 Tim.3.16
curtain, that is, through his *f.* — Heb.10.20
since . . . Christ suffered in the *f.* — 1 Pet.4.1

FLOCK

Jacob fed the rest of Laban's *f.* — Gen.30.36
Then we . . . the *f.* of thy pasture — Ps.79.13
will feed his *f.* like a shepherd — Is.40.11
LORD's *f.* has been taken captive — Jer.13.17
as a shepherd keeps his *f.* — Jer.31.10
I will save my *f.*, they shall no — Ezek.34.22
LORD took me from following the *f.* — Am.7.15
Shepherd . . . the *f.* of thy inheritance — Mic.7.14
LORD of hosts cares for his *f.* — Zech.10.3
sheep of the *f.* will be scattered — Mt.26.31
keeping watch over their *f.* — Lk.2.8
Fear not, little *f.*, for it — Lk.12.32
So there shall be one *f.* — Jn.10.16
Take heed . . . to all the *f.* — Acts 20.28
Tend the *f.* of God that is your — 1 Pet.5.2
but being examples to the *f.* — 1 Pet.5.3

FLOOD

I will bring a *f.* of waters upon — Gen.6.17
abroad on the earth after the *f.* — Gen.10.32
Terrors overtake him like a *f.* — Job 27.20
The LORD sits enthroned over the *f.* — Ps.29.10
Let the *f.* clap their hands — Ps.98.8
and the *f.* was round about me — Jon.2.3
the *f.* came, and the winds blew — Mt.7.25
to sweep her away with the *f.* — Rev.12.15

FLOURISH

In his days may righteousness *f.* — Ps.72.7
in the morning it *f.* and is renewed — Ps.90.6
The righteous *f.* like the palm tree — Ps.92.12
he *f.* like a flower of the field — Ps.103.15
the righteous will *f.* like a green — Pr.11.28
the tent of the upright will *f.* — Pr.14.11
they shall *f.* as a garden — Hos.14.7
Grain shall make the young men *f.* — Zech.9.17

FLOW

A river *f.* out of Eden to water — Gen.2.10
a land which *f.* with milk and honey — Num.14.8
caused waters to *f.* down like rivers — Ps.78.16
for from it *f.* the springs of life — Pr.4.23
all the nations shall *f.* to it — Is.2.2
my eyes *f.* with tears — Lam.1.16
and peoples shall *f.* to it — Mic.4.1
waters shall *f.* out from Jerusalem — Zech.14.8
out of his heart shall *f.* rivers of — Jn.7.38

FLOWER

flourishes like a *f.* of the field — Ps.103.15
beauty is like the *f.* of the field — Is.40.6
The grass withers, the *f.* fades — Is.40.8
its *f.* falls . . . its beauty perishes — Jas.1.11
all its glory like the *f.* of grass — 1 Pet.1.24

FLY

and let birds *f.* above the earth — Gen.1.20
He will *f.* away like a dream — Job 20.8
they are soon gone, and we *f.* away — Ps.90.10
I answered, "I see a *f.* scroll — Zech.5.2
living creature like a *f.* eagle — Rev.4.7
saw another angel *f.* in midheaven — Rev.14.6

FOAL

Binding his *f.* to the vine and his — Gen.49.11
on a colt the *f.* of an ass — Zech.9.9
and on a colt, the *f.* of an ass — Mt.21.5

FOE

And Esther said, "A *f.* and enemy — Est.7.6
O LORD, how many are my *f.* — Ps.3.1
hast not let my *f.* rejoice over me — Ps.30.1
Through thee we push down our *f.* — Ps.44.5
But thou hast saved us from our *f.* — Ps.44.7
a man's *f.* will be those of his — Mt.10.36
fire pours . . . and consumes their *f.* — Rev.11.5

FOLLOW

not learn to *f.* the abominable — Dt.18.9
you will *f.* the LORD your God — 1 Sam.12.14
and did not wholly *f.* the LORD — 1 Kg.11.6
mercy shall *f.* me all the days — Ps.23.6
the upright in heart will *f.* it — Ps.94.15
who stubbornly *f.* their own heart — Jer.13.10
F. me, and I will make you fishers — Mt.4.19
I will *f.* you wherever you go — Mt.8.19
his cross and *f.* me is not worthy — Mt.10.38
and take up his cross and *f.* me — Mt.16.24
Jesus . . . said to him, "*F.* me." — Jn.1.43
the sheep *f.* him, for they know his — Jn.10.4
If any one serves me, he must *f.* me — Jn.12.26
but you shall *f.* afterward — Jn.13.36
we did not *f.* cleverly devised — 2 Pet.1.16
as indeed you do *f.* the truth — 3 Jn.3
it is these who *f.* the Lamb — Rev.14.4
labors, for their deeds *f.* them — Rev.14.13

FOLLY

deal with you according to your *f.* — Job 42.8
O God, thou knowest my *f.* — Ps.69.5
but a fool flaunts his *f.* — Pr.13.16
f. is the garland of fools — Pr.14.24
F. is . . . in the heart of a child — Pr.22.15
Answer not a fool according to his *f.* — Pr.26.4
wisdom excels *f.* as light excels — Ec.2.13
the cross is *f.* to those who — 1 Cor.1.18
for they are *f.* to him — 1 Cor.2.14

FOOD

have given every green plant for *f.* — Gen.1.30
saw that the tree was good for *f.* — Gen.3.6
prepare . . . savory *f.* for your father — Gen.27.9
and we loathe this worthless *f.* — Num.21.5
So none of the people tasted *f.* — 1 Sam.14.24
he gives *f.* in abundance — Job 36.31
My tears have been my *f.* day and — Ps.42.3
he sent them *f.* in abundance — Ps.78.25
give them their *f.* in due season — Ps.104.27
He gives to the beasts their *f.* — Ps.147.9
and provides *f.* for her household — Pr.31.15
dust shall be the serpent's *f.* — Is.65.25
the children beg for *f.*, but no one — Lam.4.4
youths who ate the king's rich *f.* — Dan.1.15
that there may be *f.* in my house — Mal.3.10
his *f.* was locusts and wild honey — Mt.3.4
Is not life more than *f.*, and — Mt.6.25
for I was hungry and you gave me *f.* — Mt.25.35
he who has *f.*, let him do likewise — Lk.3.11
I have *f.* to eat of which you do — Jn.4.32
not labor for the *f.* which perishes — Jn.6.27
For my flesh is *f.* indeed — Jn.6.55
they partook of *f.* with glad and — Acts 2.46
the kingdom . . . does not mean *f.* — Rom.14.17
Now concerning *f.* offered to idols — 1 Cor.8.1
F. will not commend us to God — 1 Cor.8.8
But solid *f.* is for the mature — Heb.5.14

FOOL

The *f.* says in his heart, "There is	Ps.14.1
he who utters slander is a *f.*	Pr.10.18
The way of a *f.* is right in his own	Pr.12.15
A *f.* despises his father's instruction	Pr.15.5
Even a *f.* who keeps silent is	Pr.17.28
Answer not a *f.* according to his	Pr.26.4
the wise man dies just like the *f.*	Ec.2.16
and whoever says, 'You *f.!'*	Mt.5.22
But God said to him, '*F.!* This night	Lk.12.20
become a *f.* that he may become	1 Cor.3.18
We are *f.* for Christ's sake	1 Cor.4.10
I have been a *f.!* You forced me	2 Cor.12.11

FOOLISH

A *f.* woman is noisy; she is wanton	Pr.9.13
a *f.* son is a sorrow to his mother	Pr.10.1
a *f.* man despises his mother	Pr.15.20
Woe to the *f.* prophets who follow	Ezek.13.3
Five of them were *f.*, and five were	Mt.25.2
O *f.* men, and slow of heart to	Lk.24.25
God made *f.* the wisdom of the	1 Cor.1.20
You *f.* man! What you sow	1 Cor.15.36
O *f.* Galatians! Who has bewitched	Gal.3.1

FOOT

dove found no place to set her *f.*	Gen.8.9
hand for hand, *f.* for *f.*	Ex.21.24
you strike your *f.* against a stone	Mt.4.6
except to be . . . trodden under *f.* by men	Mt.5.13
And if your *f.* causes you to sin	Mk.9.45
If the *f.* should say, "Because	1 Cor.12.15

FOOTSTOOL

worship at his *f.!* Holy is he	Ps.99.5
till I make your enemies your *f.*	Ps.110.1
says the LORD . . . the earth is my *f.*	Is.66.1
or by the earth, for it is his *f.*	Mt.5.35
Heaven is my throne . . . earth my *f.*	Acts 7.49

FORBEARANCE

In thy *f.* take me not away	Jer.15.15
his kindness and *f.* and patience	Rom.2.4
f., kindness . . . genuine love	2 Cor.6.6
Let all men know your *f.*	Phil.4.5
count the *f.* of our Lord	2 Pet.3.15

FORBID

rebuke him, saying, "God *f.*, Lord	Mt.16.22
Jesus said to him, "Do not *f.* him	Lk.9.50
Can any one *f.* water for baptizing	Acts 10.47
having been *f.* by the Holy Spirit	Acts 16.6
f. marriage and enjoin abstinence	1 Tim.4.3

FOREFATHER

remember the covenant with their *f.*	Lev.26.45
the iniquities of our *f.*	Ps.79.8
back to the iniquities of their *f.*	Jer.11.10
our *f.* according to the flesh?	Rom.4.1
children by one man, our *f.* Isaac	Rom.9.10
beloved for the sake of their *f.*	Rom.11.28

FOREHEAD

It shall be upon Aaron's *f.*	Ex.28.38
baldness on your *f.* for the dead	Dt.14.1
struck the Philistine on his *f.*	1 Sam.17.49
marked on the right hand or the *f.*	Rev.13.16
on her *f.* was written a name of	Rev.17.5

FOREIGN

all the *f.* gods that they had	Gen.35.4
forsake the LORD and serve *f.* gods	Jos.24.20
King Solomon loved many *f.* women	1 Kg.11.1
He took away the *f.* altars	2 Chr.14.3

by marrying *f.* women	Neh.13.27
sing the LORD's song in a *f.* land?	Ps.137.4
and served *f.* gods in your land	Jer.5.19
to be a preacher of *f.* divinities	Acts 17.18
as in a *f.* land, living in tents	Heb.11.9

FOREST

For every beast of the *f.* is mine	Ps.50.10
the beasts of the *f.* creep forth	Ps.104.20
O *f.*, and every tree in it	Is.44.23
Does a lion roar in the *f.*	Am.3.4
How great a *f.* is set ablaze by a	Jas.3.5

FORGET

Take heed lest you *f.* the LORD	Dt.8.11
to Sheol . . . the nations that *f.* God	Ps.9.17
and not *f.* the works of God	Ps.78.7
I will never *f.* thy precepts	Ps.119.93
If I *f.* you, O Jerusalem, let my	Ps.137.5
Can a woman *f.* her sucking child	Is.49.15
f. what lies behind and straining	Phil.3.13

FORGIVE

Now therefore, *f.* my sin, I pray	Ex.10.17
But thou art a God ready to *f.*	Neh.9.17
f. our sins, for thy name's sake	Ps.79.9
I will *f.* their iniquity, and I	Jer.31.34
O LORD, *f.*; O LORD, give heed	Dan.9.19
And *f.* us our debts, As we also have	Mt.6.12
against the Spirit will not be *f.*	Mt.12.31
if you do not *f.* your brother from	Mt.18.35
and if he repents, *f.* him	Lk.17.3
And Jesus said, "Father, *f.* them	Lk.23.34
has *f.* you, so you also must *f.*	Col.3.13
will *f.* our sins and cleanse us	1 Jn.1.9

FORGIVENESS

there is *f.* with thee, that thou	Ps.130.4
to . . . our God belong mercy and *f.*	Dan.9.9
repentance for the *f.* of sins	Lk.3.3
for the *f.* of your sins	Acts 2.38
we have . . . the *f.* of our trespasses	Eph.1.7
we have redemption, the *f.* of sins	Col.1.14

FORGOTTEN

For the needy shall not always be *f.*	Ps.9.18
yet I have not *f.* thy statutes	Ps.119.83
O Israel, you will not be *f.* by me	Is.44.21
But my people have *f.* me	Jer.18.15
you have *f.* me, says the Lord	Ezek.22.12
For Israel has *f.* his Maker	Hos.8.14
not one of them is *f.* before God	Lk.12.6

FORM (noun)

The earth was without *f.* and void	Gen.1.2
and his *f.* beyond that of the sons	Is.52.14
he had no *f.* or comeliness that we	Is.53.2
likeness as it were of a human *f.*	Ezek.1.26
descended upon him in bodily *f.*	Lk.3.22
the *f.* of this world is passing	1 Cor.7.31
who, though he was in the *f.* of God	Phil.2.6
abstain from every *f.* of evil	1 Th.5.22
holding the *f.* of religion but	2 Tim.3.5

FORM (verb)

then the LORD God *f.* man of dust	Gen.2.7
I too was *f.* from a piece of clay	Job 33.6
or ever thou hadst *f.* the earth and	Ps.90.2
For thou didst *f.* my inward parts	Ps.139.13
the thing *f.* say of him who *f.* it	Is.29.16
who *f.* you from the womb and will	Is.44.2
I *f.* light and create darkness	Is.45.7
Before I *f.* you in the womb I knew	Jer.1.5

travail until Christ be *f*. in you	Gal.4.19	**FRANKINCENSE**		
For Adam was *f*. first, then Eve	1 Tim.2.13	pour oil upon it, and put *f*. on it	Lev.2.1	
FORSAKE		the *f*., the vessels, and the tithes	Neh.13.5	
he will not fail you or *f*. you	Dt.31.6	They shall bring gold and *f*.	Is.60.6	
I will not fail you or *f*. you	Jos.1.5	gifts, gold and *f*. and myrrh	Mt.2.11	
If you *f*. the LORD and serve	Jos.24.20	*f*., wine, oil, fine flour	Rev.18.13	
if you *f*. him, he will *f*. you	2 Chr.15.2	**FREE**		
My God, my God, why hast thou *f*. me?	Ps.22.1	The man shall be *f*. from iniquity	Num.5.31	
f. me not, O God of my salvation	Ps.27.9	the LORD answered me and set me *f*.	Ps.118.5	
If his children *f*. my law and do	Ps.89.30	The LORD sets the prisoners *f*.	Ps.146.7	
Do not *f*. the work of thy hands	Ps.138.8	said to him, "Then the sons are *f*.	Mt.17.26	
Do not *f*. her, and she will keep you	Pr.4.6	and the truth will make you *f*.	Jn.8.32	
who *f*. the LORD shall be consumed	Is.1.28	the *f*. gift is not like the trespass	Rom.5.15	
your house is *f*. and desolate	Mt.23.38	and, having been set *f*. from sin	Rom.6.18	
God, my God, why hast thou *f*. me?	Mt.27.46	the *f*. gift of God is eternal life	Rom.6.23	
I will never fail you nor *f*. you	Heb.13.5	I want you to be *f*. from anxieties	1 Cor.7.32	
FORSOOK		I . . . make the gospel *f*. of charge	1 Cor.9.18	
and they *f*. the LORD, the God of	Jg.2.12	But the Jerusalem above is *f*.	Gal.4.26	
they *f*. all the commandments of	2 Kg.17.16	For freedom Christ has set us *f*.	Gal.5.1	
For a brief moment I *f*. you, but	Is.54.7	Live as *f*. men, yet without using	1 Pet.2.16	
all the disciples *f*. him and fled	Mt.26.56	both *f*. and slave, both small and	Rev.19.18	
FORTRESS		**FREED**		
The LORD is my rock, and my *f*.	2 Sam.22.2	you are *f*. from your infirmity	Lk.13.12	
Yea, thou art my rock and my *f*.	Ps.31.3	believes is *f*. from everything	Acts 13.39	
thou . . . art my *f*., the God who shows	Ps.59.17	could not be *f*. by the law of	Acts 13.39	
to the LORD, "My refuge and my *f*.	Ps.91.2	For he who has died is *f*. from sin	Rom.6.7	
All your *f*. are like fig trees with	Nah.3.12	and has *f*. us from our sins by	Rev.1.5	
FORTY		**FREEDOM**		
The flood continued *f*. days upon	Gen.7.17	But if you can gain your *f*.	1 Cor.7.21	
At the end of *f*. days they returned	Num.13.25	where the Spirit . . . is, there is *f*.	2 Cor.3.17	
f. years, and you shall know my	Num.14.34	For *f*. Christ has set us free	Gal.5.1	
F. stripes may be given him, but not	Dt.25.3	For you were called to *f*., brethren	Gal.5.13	
So the land had rest *f*. years	Jg.3.11	using your *f*. as a pretext for evil	1 Pet.2.16	
f. days and *f*. nights to Horeb	1 Kg.19.8	They promise them *f*., but they	2 Pet.2.19	
F. years didst thou sustain them in	Neh.9.21	**FREELY**		
Yet *f*. days, and Nineveh shall be	Jon.3.4	You may *f*. eat of every tree of	Gen.2.16	
he fasted *f*. days and *f*. nights	Mt.4.2	You shall give to him *f*., and your	Dt.15.10	
appearing to them during *f*. days	Acts 1.3	He has distributed *f*., he has given	Ps.112.9	
There were more than *f*. who made	Acts 23.13	I will love them *f*., for my anger	Hos.14.4	
FOUNDATION		and began to talk *f*. about it	Mk.1.45	
to lay the *f*. of the house with	1 Kg.5.17	and to him I speak *f*.	Acts 26.26	
The *f*. was of costly stones, huge	1 Kg.7.10	grace which he *f*. bestowed on us	Eph.1.6	
if the *f*. are destroyed, what can	Ps.11.3	**FRESH**		
thou didst lay the *f*. of the earth	Ps.102.25	thou hast poured over me *f*. oil	Ps.92.10	
I am laying in Zion for a *f*. a stone	Is.28.16	shall obtain *f*. joy in the LORD	Is.29.19	
My hand laid the *f*. of the earth	Is.48.13	waters of the sea may become *f*.	Ezek.47.9	
the day that the *f*. of the LORD's	Hag.2.18	new wine is put into *f*. wineskins	Mt.9.17	
hidden since the *f*. of the world	Mt.13.35	same opening *f*. water and brackish?	Jas.3.11	
a house on the ground without a *f*.	Lk.6.49	**FRIEND**		
lest I build on another man's *f*.	Rom.15.20	as a man speaks to his *f*.	Ex.33.11	
For no other *f*. can any one lay	1 Cor.3.11	Ammon had a *f*., whose name was	2 Sam.13.3	
built upon the *f*. of the apostles	Eph.2.20	Zabud was priest and king's *f*.	1 Kg.4.5	
But God's firm *f*. stands	2 Tim.2.19	the descendants of Abraham thy *f*.	2 Chr.20.7	
before the *f*. of the world	1 Pet.1.20	Job's three *f*. heard of all this	Job 2.11	
from the *f*. of the world	Rev.17.8	Even my bosom *f*. in whom I trusted	Ps.41.9	
the wall of the city had twelve *f*.	Rev.21.14	my companion, my familiar *f*.	Ps.55.13	
FOX		A *f*. loves at all times, and a	Pr.17.17	
if a *f*. goes up on it he will break	Neh.4.3	a *f*. who sticks closer than a brother	Pr.18.24	
Catch us the *f*., the little *f*.	S.of S.2.15	a poor man is deserted by his *f*.	Pr.19.4	
F. have holes, and birds of the air	Mt.8.20	Faithful are the wounds of a *f*.	Pr.27.6	
said to them, "Go and tell that *f*.	Lk.13.32	a *f*. of tax collectors and sinners	Mt.11.19	
FRAGRANT		*F*., lend me three loaves	Lk.11.5	
Aaron shall burn *f*. incense on it	Ex.30.7	may say to you, '*F*., go up higher'	Lk.14.10	
your robes are all *f*. with myrrh	Ps.45.8	that I might make merry with my *f*.	Lk.15.29	
a *f*. offering and sacrifice to God	Eph.5.2	Our *f*. Lazarus has fallen asleep	Jn.11.11	
a *f*. offering . . . pleasing to God	Phil.4.18	You are my *f*. if you do what I	Jn.15.14	

FRIGHTEN

you are not Caesar's *f.*	Jn.19.12
Abraham . . . was called the *f.* of God	Jas.2.23
wishes to be a *f.* of the world	Jas.4.4

FRIGHTEN

be not *f.*, neither be dismayed	Jos.1.9
For they all wanted to *f.* us	Neh.6.9
Terrors *f.* him on every side	Job 18.11
I was *f.* and fell upon my face	Dan.8.17
and as they were *f.* and bowed their	Lk.24.5
But they were startled and *f.*	Lk.24.37
near to the boat. They were *f.*	Jn.6.19
and not *f.* in anything by your	Phil.1.28

FROST

destroyed . . . their sycamores with *f.*	Ps.78.47
snow and *f.*, stormy wind fulfilling	Ps.148.8
heat by day and the *f.* by night	Jer.36.30
there shall be neither cold nor *f.*	Zech.14.6

FRUIT

f. trees bearing *f.* in which is	Gen.1.11
may eat of the *f.* of the trees of	Gen.3.2
The land will yield its *f.*	Lev.25.19
will give back the *f.* of his toil	Job 20.18
that yields its *f.* in its season	Ps.1.3
They still bring forth *f.* in old age	Ps.92.14
the *f.* of the womb a reward	Ps.127.3
all hills, *f.* trees and all cedars	Ps.148.9
My *f.* is better than gold, even fine	Pr.8.19
The *f.* of the righteous is a tree	Pr.11.30
shall eat the *f.* of their deeds	Is.3.10
and yield your *f.* to my people	Ezek.36.8
will bear fresh *f.* every month	Ezek.47.12
And I said, "A basket of summer *f.*"	Am.8.2
Bear *f.* that befits repentance	Mt.3.8
A sound tree cannot bear evil *f.*	Mt.7.18
again of this *f.* of the vine until	Mt.26.29
and gathers *f.* for eternal life	Jn.4.36
but if it dies, it bears much *f.*	Jn.12.24
Every branch of mine that bears no *f.*	Jn.15.2
that we may bear *f.* for God	Rom.7.4
But the *f.* of the Spirit is love	Gal.5.22
bearing *f.* in every good work	Col.1.10
twelve kinds of *f.*, yielding its *f.*	Rev.22.2

FRUITFUL

Be *f.* and multiply and fill the	Gen.1.22
I will make you exceedingly *f.*	Gen.17.6
God has made me *f.* in the land	Gen.41.52
like a *f.* vine within your house	Ps.128.3
and they shall increase and be *f.*	Ezek.36.11
that means *f.* labor for me	Phil.1.22

FULFIL

I will *f.* the number of your days	Ex.23.26
spoken, and will he not *f.* it?	Num.23.19
May the LORD *f.* all your petitions	Ps.20.5
and I will *f.* to you my promise	Jer.29.10
Behold, I will *f.* my words against	Jer.39.16
for us to *f.* all righteousness	Mt.3.15
not to abolish them but to *f.* them	Mt.5.17
loves his neighbor has *f.* the law	Rom.13.8
and so *f.* the law of Christ	Gal.6.2
See that you *f.* the ministry which	Col.4.17
may *f.* every good resolve	2 Th.1.11
of an evangelist, *f.* your ministry	2 Tim.4.5
If you really *f.* the royal law	Jas.2.8
the scripture was *f.* which says	Jas.2.23
until the words of God shall be *f.*	Rev.17.17

FULL

f. of the blessing of the LORD	Dt.33.23
Joshua . . . was *f.* of the spirit of	Dt.34.9
For I am *f.* of words, the spirit	Job 32.18
voice of the LORD is *f.* of majesty	Ps.29.4
the river of God is *f.* of water	Ps.65.9
For my soul is *f.* of troubles	Ps.88.3
the earth is *f.* of thy creatures	Ps.104.24
lest I be *f.*, and deny thee	Pr.30.9
your hands are *f.* of blood	Is.1.15
the whole earth is *f.* of his glory	Is.6.3
earth shall be *f.* of the knowledge	Is.11.9
I will not make a *f.* end of you	Jer.5.18
city shall be *f.* of boys and girls	Zech.8.5
Bring the *f.* tithes into the storehouse	Mal.3.10
whole body will be *f.* of light	Mt.6.22
then the *f.* grain in the ear	Mk.4.28
And Jesus, *f.* of the Holy Spirit	Lk.4.1
Woe to you that are *f.* now	Lk.6.25
the Word . . . *f.* of grace and truth	Jn.1.14
and that your joy may be *f.*	Jn.15.11
And Stephen, *f.* of grace and power	Acts 6.8
She was *f.* of good works and acts	Acts 9.36
until the *f.* number of the Gentiles	Rom.11.25
realizing the *f.* assurance of hope	Heb.6.11
f. of mercy and good fruits	Jas.3.17
They have eyes *f.* of adultery	2 Pet.2.14
with golden bowls *f.* of incense	Rev.5.8
golden bowls *f.* of the wrath of God	Rev.15.7

FULNESS

best gifts of the earth and its *f.*	Dt.33.16
in thy presence there is *f.* of joy	Ps.16.11
is the LORD'S and the *f.* thereof	Ps.24.1
And from his *f.* have we all received	Jn.1.16
in the *f.* of the blessing of Christ	Rom.15.29
a plan for the *f.* of time, to unite	Eph.1.10
the *f.* of him who fills all in all	Eph.1.23
the stature of the *f.* of Christ	Eph.4.13
For in him all the *f.* of God was	Col.1.19
in him the whole *f.* of deity dwells	Col.2.9

FURNACE

went up like the smoke of a *f.*	Gen.19.28
smoke, and my bones burn like a *f.*	Ps.102.3
us from the burning fiery *f.*	Dan.3.17
throw them into the *f.* of fire	Mt.13.42
smoke like the smoke of a great *f.*	Rev.9.2

FURY

I will walk contrary to you in *f.*	Lev.26.28
he will . . . terrify them in his *f.*	Ps.2.5
to render his anger in *f.*	Is.66.15
So will I satisfy my *f.* on you	Ezek.16.42
Thou didst bestride the earth in *f.*	Hab.3.12
But they were filled with *f.* and	Lk.6.11
there will be wrath and *f.*	Rom.2.8
a *f.* of fire which will consume	Heb.10.27
the cup of the *f.* of his wrath	Rev.16.19
the *f.* of the wrath of God	Rev.19.15

FUTILE

they became *f.* in their thinking	Rom.1.21
the thoughts of the wise are *f.*	1 Cor.3.20
your faith is *f.* and you are	1 Cor.15.17
for they are unprofitable and *f.*	Tit.3.9
from the *f.* ways inherited from	1 Pet.1.18

FUTURE

Surely there is a *f.*, and your hope	Pr.23.18
for the evil man has no *f.*	Pr.24.20

There is hope for your *f.*	Jer.31.17
present or the *f.*, all are yours	1 Cor.3.22
a good foundation for the *f.*	1 Tim.6.19

GABRIEL
Dan.8.16; 9.21; Lk.1.19,26

GAIN (noun)

every one is greedy for unjust *g.*	Jer.6.13
the dishonest *g.* which you have	Ezek.22.13
to live is Christ, and to die is *g.*	Phil.1.21
But whatever *g.* I had, I counted as	Phil.3.7
There is great *g.* in godliness	1 Tim.6.6
by teaching for base *g.* what they	Tit.1.11
we will . . . trade and get *g.*	Jas.4.13

GAIN (verb)

to *g.* the whole world and forfeit	Mk.8.36
Whoever seeks to *g.* his life will	Lk.17.33
What do I *g.* if, humanly speaking	1 Cor.15.32
in order that I may *g.* Christ	Phil.3.8
merchants . . . who *g.* wealth from her	Rev.18.15

GALATIA
Acts 16.6; 1 Cor.16.1; 2 Tim.4.10; 1 Pet.1.1

GALILEE
Is.9.1; Mt.3.13; Mk.1.9; Lk.3.1; Jn.1.43; 21.2

GAMALIEL
(1) Num.1.10; 10.23; (2) Acts 5.34; 22.3

GARDEN

the LORD God planted a *g.* in Eden	Gen.2.8
Let my beloved come to his *g.*	S.of S.4.16
her desert like the *g.* of the LORD	Is.51.3
you shall be like a watered *g.*	Is.58.11
as a *g.* causes what is sown in it	Is.61.11
has become like the *g.* of Eden	Ezek.36.35
where he was crucified . . . was a *g.*	Jn.19.41
in the *g.* a new tomb where no one	Jn.19.41

GARMENT

the LORD God made . . . *g.* of skins	Gen.3.21
coverest . . . with light as with a *g.*	Ps.104.2
the earth will wear out like a *g.*	Is.51.6
clothed me with the *g.* of salvation	Is.61.10
rend your hearts and not your *g.*	Jl.2.13
Remove the filthy *g.* from him	Zech.3.4
Now John wore a *g.* of camel's hair	Mt.3.4
to herself, "If I only touch his *g.*	Mt.9.21
saw a man who had no wedding *g.*	Mt.22.11
of unshrunk cloth on an old *g.*	Mk.2.21
throwing their *g.* on the colt they	Lk.19.35
They parted my *g.* among them	Jn.19.24
they will all grow old like a *g.*	Heb.1.11
hating even the *g.* spotted by the	Jude 23

GATE

and this is the *g.* of heaven	Gen.28.17
Enter his *g.* with thanksgiving	Ps.100.4
This is the *g.* of the LORD	Ps.118.20
and turn aside the needy in the *g.*	Am.5.12
Enter by the narrow *g.*	Mt.7.13
at the Beautiful *G.* of the temple	Acts 3.10
Peter was standing at the *g.*	Acts 12.14
outside the *g.* in order to sanctify	Heb.13.12
and its *g.* shall never be shut	Rev.21.25

GATHER

I will *g.* you to your fathers	2 Kg.22.20
and *g.* us from among the nations	Ps.106.47
and a time to *g.* stones together	Ec.3.5
and *g.* his wheat into the granary	Mt.3.12
neither sow nor . . . *g.* into barns	Mt.6.26

G. the weeds first and bind them	Mt.13.30
two or three are *g.* in my name	Mt.18.20
often would I have *g.* your children	Mt.23.37
he who does not *g.* with me scatters	Lk.11.23
as a hen *g.* her brood under her	Lk.13.34
G. up the fragments left over, that	Jn.6.12

GENEALOGY

of Noah, according to their *g.*	Gen.10.32
not enrolled in the *g.* according to	1 Chr.5.1
So all Israel was enrolled by *g.*	1 Chr.9.1
this is the *g.* of those who went up	Ezra 8.1
the people to be enrolled by *g.*	Neh.7.5
The book of the *g.* of Jesus Christ	Mt.1.1

GENERATION

that you may tell the next *g.*	Ps.48.13
be recorded for a *g.* to come	Ps.102.18
One *g.* shall laud thy works to	Ps.145.4
A *g.* goes, and a *g.* comes, but the	Ec.1.4
to what shall I compare this *g.*?	Mt.11.16
adulterous *g.* seeks for a sign	Mt.16.4
this *g.* will not pass away till all	Mt.24.34
O faithless *g.*, how long am I to	Mk.9.19
henceforth all *g.* will call me blessed	Lk.1.48
from early *g.* Moses has had in	Acts 15.21
glory . . . in Christ Jesus to all *g.*	Eph.3.21
the mystery hidden for ages and *g.*	Col.1.26

GENEROUS

the righteous is *g.* and gives	Ps.37.21
Many seek the favor of a *g.* man	Pr.19.6
partook of food with glad and *g.* hearts	Acts 2.46
in good deeds, liberal and *g.*	1 Tim.6.18

GENTILE

in his name will the *G.* hope	Mt.12.21
be . . . as a *G.* and a tax collector	Mt.18.17
a light for revelation to the *G.*	Lk.2.32
the times of the *G.* are fulfilled	Lk.21.24
Why did the *G.* rage, and the	Acts 4.25
set you to be a light for the *G.*	Acts 13.47
how God first visited the *G.*	Acts 15.14
From now on I will go to the *G.*	Acts 18.6
Is he not the God of *G.* also?	Rom.3.29
the full number of the *G.* come in	Rom.11.25
if the *G.* have come to share in	Rom.15.27
I might preach him among the *G.*	Gal.1.16
you compel the *G.* to live like Jews	Gal.2.14
how the *G.* are fellow heirs, members	Eph.3.6
preach to the *G.* the unsearchable	Eph.3.8

GENTLE

A *g.* tongue is a tree of life, but	Pr.15.4
I was like a *g.* lamb led to the	Jer.11.19
for I am *g.* and lowly in heart	Mt.11.29
be *g.*, and . . . show perfect courtesy	Tit.3.2
g., open to reason, full of mercy	Jas.3.17

GENTLENESS

by the meekness and *g.* of Christ	2 Cor.10.1
g., self-control; against such	Gal.5.23
restore him in a spirit of *g.*	Gal.6.1
correcting his opponents with *g.*	2 Tim.2.25

GETHSEMANE
Mt.26.36; Mk.14.32

GIANTS

one of the descendants of the *g.*	2 Sam.21.16
were descended from the *g.* in Gath	1 Chr.20.8

GIBEAH
(1) a city of Judah, Jos.15.57; (2) a city of Benjamin, Jg.19.14; sin of its inhabitants,

Jg.19.22; their punishment, Jg.20; the city of Saul, 1 Sam.10.26; 11.4; 14.2; 15.34; 2 Sam. 21.6

GIBEON
situated about five miles north of Jerusalem Jos.9.3; its inhabitants deceive Joshua, Jos.9; delivered by him from the five kings, Jos.10; Saul persecutes them, 2 Sam.21.1; David makes atonement, 2 Sam.21.3–9; Solomon's dream at, 1 Kg.3.5; site of the tabernacle under David and Solomon, 1 Chr.16.39; 21.29; 2 Chr.1.3–6

GIDEON
God appoints him to deliver Israel from the Midianites, Jg.6.11,14; destroys the altar and grove of Baal, Jg.6.25–27; called Jerubbaal, Jg.6.32; God gives him two signs, Jg.6.36–40; his army reduced, and selected by a test of water, Jg.7.2–7; his stratagem, Jg.7.16; subdues the Midianites, Jg.7.19–8.28; makes an ephod of the spoil, Jg.8.24-27; his death, Jg.8.32

GIFT
he shall offer his g. to the LORD	Num.6.14
A g. in secret averts anger	Pr.21.14
it is God's g. to man that every	Ec.3.13
to give good g. to your children	Lk.11.13
her, "If you knew the g. of God	Jn.4.10
receive the g. of the Holy Spirit	Acts 2.38
the free g. is not like the trespass	Rom.5.15
the free g. of God is eternal life	Rom.6.23
Having g. that differ according to	Rom.12.6
Now concerning spiritual g.	1 Cor.12.1
to God for his inexpressible g.	2 Cor.9.15
to the measure of Christ's g.	Eph.4.7
Do not neglect the g. you have	1 Tim.4.14
who have tasted the heavenly g.	Heb.6.4
every perfect g. is from above	Jas.1.17
As each has received a g.	1 Pet.4.10

GIRD
G. up your loins like a man	Job 40.7
the God who g. me with strength	Ps.18.32
the mountains, being g. with might	Ps.65.6
G. yourselves with sackcloth	Jer.49.3
Let your loins be g. and your	Lk.12.35
the towel with which he was g.	Jn.13.5
having g. your loins with truth	Eph.6.14
g. up your minds, be sober	1 Pet.1.13

GIRL
and have sold a g. for wine	Jl.3.3
boys and g. playing in its streets	Zech.8.5
her by the hand, and the g. arose	Mt.9.25
Little g., I say to you, arise	Mk.5.41
a slave g. . . . who had a spirit	Acts 16.16

GLAD
Let the heavens be g., and let	1 Chr.16.31
The righteous see it and are g.	Job 22.19
dost make him g. with the joy of	Ps.21.6
Be g. in the LORD, and rejoice	Ps.32.11
let the afflicted hear and be g.	Ps.34.2
streams make g. the city of God	Ps.46.4
Let the nations be g. and sing for	Ps.67.4
Make us g. as many days as thou	Ps.90.15
I was g. when they said to me, "Let	Ps.122.1
A wise son makes a g. father	Pr.10.1
by sadness . . . the heart is made g.	Ec.7.3
let us be g. and rejoice in his	Is.25.9

Rejoice and be g., O daughter of	Lam.4.21
Rejoice and be g., for your reward	Mt.5.12
see my day; he saw it and was g.	Jn.8.56
disciples were g. when they saw	Jn.20.20
I am g. and rejoice with you all	Phil.2.17

GLADNESS
anointed you with the oil of g.	Ps.45.7
Serve the LORD with g.! Come into	Ps.100.2
they shall obtain joy and g.	Is.51.11
And you will have joy and g.	Lk.1.14

GLEAN
you shall not g. it afterward	Dt.24.21
When she rose to g., Boaz instructed	Ru.2.15
as when one g. the ears of grain	Is.17.5
G. thoroughly as a vine	Jer.6.9
as when the vintage has been g.	Mic.7.1

GLOOM
Some sat in darkness and in g.	Ps.107.10
and your g. be as the noonday	Is.58.10
turns it into g. and makes it deep	Jer.13.16
a day of darkness and g.	Jl.2.2
darkness, and g., and a tempest	Heb.12.18
for them the nether g. of darkness	2 Pet.2.17

GLORIFY
I will g. thy name for ever	Ps.86.12
they g. God, who had given such	Mt.9.8
he taught . . . being g. by all	Lk.4.15
they g. God, saying, "A great	Lk.7.16
for the Son of man to be g.	Jn.12.23
the Father may be g. in the Son	Jn.14.13
I g. thee . . . having accomplished	Jn.17.4
thine are mine, and I am g. in them	Jn.17.10
they g. God, saying, "Then to	Acts 11.18
So g. God in your body	1 Cor.6.20
you will g. God by your obedience	2 Cor.9.13
Who shall not fear and g. thy name	Rev.15.4

GLORIOUS
terrible in g. deeds, doing wonders	Ex.15.11
Blessed be his g. name for ever	Ps.72.19
G. things are spoken of you, O city	Ps.87.3
the g. splendor of thy kingdom	Ps.145.12
the branch of the LORD shall be . . . g.	Is.4.2
to make for thyself a g. name	Is.63.14
A g. throne set on high	Jer.17.12
will . . . obtain the g. liberty of the	Rom.8.21
the riches of his g. inheritance	Eph.1.18
lowly body to be like his g. body	Phil.3.21
the g. gospel of the blessed God	1 Tim.1.11

GLORY (noun)
The g. of the LORD settled on Mount	Ex.24.16
I pray thee, show me thy g.	Ex.33.18
Then the g. of the LORD appeared	Num.14.10
The g. has departed from Israel	1 Sam.4.21
Declare his g. among the nations	1 Chr.16.24
Thou whose g. above the heavens is	Ps.8.1
Who is the King of g.? The LORD	Ps.24.8
Ascribe to the LORD the g. of his	Ps.29.2
May the g. of the LORD endure for	Ps.104.31
not to us, but to thy name give g.	Ps.115.1
A hoary head is a crown of g.	Pr.16.31
It is the g. of God to conceal	Pr.25.2
They shall see the g. of the LORD	Is.35.2
My g. I will not give to another	Is.48.11
lo, the g. of the LORD stood	Ezek.3.23
Ephraim's g. shall fly away like a	Hos.9.11
knowledge of the g. of the LORD	Hab.2.14

When the Son of man comes in his *g*.	Mt.25.31
G. to God in the highest, and on	Lk.2.14
Yet I do not seek my own *g*.	Jn.8.50
you would see the *g*. of God	Jn.11.40
The *g*. which thou hast given me	Jn.17.22
and fall short of the *g*. of God	Rom.3.23
not have crucified the Lord of *g*.	1 Cor.2.8
he is the image and *g*. of God	1 Cor.11.7
the Father of *g*., may give you a	Eph.1.17
To our God . . . be *g*. for ever	Phil.4.20
Christ in you, the hope of *g*.	Col.1.27
For you are our *g*. and joy	1 Th.2.20
the *g*. of our great God and Savior	Tit.2.13
He reflects the *g*. of God and bears	Heb.1.3
To him belong *g*. and dominion for	1 Pet.4.11
Blessing and *g*. and wisdom and	Rev.7.12
Fear God and give him *g*.	Rev.14.7
for the *g*. of God is its light	Rev.21.23

GLUTTON

he is a *g*. and a drunkard	Dt.21.20
the *g*. will come to poverty	Pr.23.21
Behold, a *g*. and a drunkard	Mt.11.19
always liars, evil beasts, lazy *g*.	Tit.1.12

GOAT

but the *g*. on which the lot fell	Lev.16.10
he who lets the *g*. go to Azazel	Lev.16.26
separates the sheep from the *g*.	Mt.25.32
the blood of *g*. and bulls and with	Heb.9.13
went about in skins of . . . *g*.	Heb.11.37

GOD

In the beginning *G*. created the	Gen.1.1
So *G*. created man in his own image	Gen.1.27
the LORD *G*. planted a garden in	Gen.2.8
But *G*. remembered Noah and all the	Gen.8.1
G. said to Moses, "I AM WHO I AM."	Ex.3.14
a *G*. merciful and gracious, slow to	Ex.34.6
I am the LORD your *G*., who brought	Lev.25.38
is a devouring fire, a jealous *G*.	Dt.4.24
a people holy to the LORD your *G*.	Dt.14.2
A *G*. of faithfulness and without	Dt.32.4
O Lord *G*., remember me, I pray thee	Jg.16.28
the spirit of *G*. is in my nostrils	Job 27.3
Behold, *G*. does all these things	Job 33.29
By the breath of *G*. ice is given	Job 37.10
Answer me . . . O *G*. of my right	Ps.4.1
G. is a righteous judge, and a	Ps.7.11
My *G*., my *G*., why hast thou forsaken	Ps.22.1
G. is our refuge and strength	Ps.46.1
Behold, *G*. is my helper; the Lord is	Ps.54.4
Our *G*. is a *G*. of salvation	Ps.68.20
but *G*. is the strength of my heart	Ps.73.26
When *G*. heard, he was full of wrath	Ps.78.59
For the LORD *G*. is a sun and shield	Ps.84.11
It is the glory of *G*. to conceal	Pr.25.2
G. will judge the righteous and the	Ec.3.17
for the LORD *G*. is my strength	Is.12.2
The Spirit of the Lord *G*. is upon me	Is.61.1
I will be their *G*., and they shall	Jer.31.33
for I am *G*. and not man, the Holy	Hos.11.9
thou art a gracious *G*. and merciful	Jon.4.2
and to walk humbly with your *G*.?	Mic.6.8
LORD is a jealous *G*. and avenging	Nah.1.2
Emmanuel" (which means, *G*. with us)	Mt.1.23
You cannot serve *G*. and mammon	Mt.6.24
No one is good but *G*. alone	Lk.18.19
Word was with *G*., and the Word was *G*.	Jn.1.1

For *G*. so loved the world that he	Jn.3.16
G. is spirit, and those who worship	Jn.4.24
I proceeded and came forth from *G*.	Jn.8.42
answered him, "My Lord and my *G*.	Jn.20.28
For *G*. shows no partiality	Rom.2.11
Is he not the *G*. of Gentiles also?	Rom.3.29
But *G*. shows his love for us in	Rom.5.8
the free gift of *G*. is eternal life	Rom.6.23
in everything *G*. works for good	Rom.8.28
G. is faithful, by whom you were	1 Cor.1.9
G. is faithful, and he will not	1 Cor.10.13
G. was in Christ reconciling	2 Cor.5.19
G. is not mocked, for whatever a man	Gal.6.7
one *G*. and Father of us all, who is	Eph.4.6
He is the image of the invisible *G*.	Col.1.15
For there is one *G*., and there	1 Tim.2.5
of our great *G*. and Savior Jesus	Tit.2.13
for our *G*. is a consuming fire	Heb.12.29
for *G*. cannot be tempted with evil	Jas.1.13
G. opposes the proud, but gives	Jas.4.6
G. is light and in him is no darkness	1 Jn.1.5
G. is love, and he who abides in	1 Jn.4.16
the Lord *G*. Almighty, who was and is	Rev.4.8
and *G*. will wipe away every tear	Rev.7.17

GODLINESS

great gain in *g*. with contentment	1 Tim.6.6
the truth which accords with *g*.	Tit.1.1
and *g*. with brotherly affection	2 Pet.1.7

GODLY

has set apart the *g*. for himself	Ps.4.3
Preserve my life, for I am *g*.	Ps.86.2
g. grief produces a repentance	2 Cor.7.10
to live a *g*. life in Christ Jesus	2 Tim.3.12
how to rescue the *g*. from trial	2 Pet.2.9

GOG

1 Chr.5.4; Ezek.38.2; 39.1; Rev.20.8

GOLD

More to be desired are they than *g*.	Ps.19.10
and its profit better than *g*.	Pr.3.14
To get wisdom is better than *g*.	Pr.16.16
like apples of *g*. in a setting of	Pr.25.11
g. like the dirt of the streets	Zech.9.3
think that the Deity is like *g*.	Acts 17.29
builds on the foundation with *g*.	1 Cor.3.12
the street of the city was pure *g*.	Rev.21.21

GOLGOTHA

Mt.27.33; Mk.15.22; Jn.19.17

GOLIATH

1 Sam.17.4; 21.9; 2 Sam.21.19; 1 Chr.20.5

GOOD (adjective)

And God saw that the light was *g*.	Gen.1.4
It is not *g*. that the man should	Gen.2.18
but God meant it for *g*.	Gen.50.20
God is bringing you into a *g*. land	Dt.8.7
Be strong and of *g*. courage	Dt.31.23
the *g*. hand of my God was upon me	Neh.2.8
G. and upright is the LORD	Ps.25.8
who seek the LORD lack no *g*. thing	Ps.34.10
Truly God is *g*. to the upright	Ps.73.1
The LORD is *g*. to all, and his	Ps.145.9
A cheerful heart is a *g*. medicine	Pr.17.22
A *g*. name is to be chosen rather	Pr.22.1
A *g*. wife who can find? She is	Pr.31.10
He has showed you, O man, what is *g*.	Mic.6.8
how to give *g*. gifts to your	Mt.7.11
Why do you ask me about what is *g*.?	Mt.19.17

No one is *g*. but God alone   Mk.10.18
Mary has chosen the *g*. portion   Lk.10.42
I am the *g*. shepherd   Jn.10.11
She was full of *g*. works and acts   Acts 9.36
a *g*. man, full of the Holy Spirit   Acts 11.24
Bad company ruins *g*. morals   1 Cor.15.33
everything created by God is *g*.   1 Tim.4.4
Fight the *g*. fight of the faith   1 Tim.6.12
I have fought the *g*. fight, I have   2 Tim.4.7
Every *g*. endowment . . . is from above   Jas.1.17
Maintain *g*. conduct among the   1 Pet.2.12

GOOD (noun)
we receive *g*. at the hand of God   Job 2.10
I have no *g*. apart from thee   Ps.16.2
one sinner destroys much *g*.   Ec.9.18
God works for *g*. with those who   Rom.8.28
let us do *g*. to all men . . . especially   Gal.6.10
has the world's *g*. and sees his   1 Jn.3.17
He who does *g*. is of God   3 Jn.11

GOODNESS
make all my *g*. pass before you   Ex.33.19
Surely *g*. and mercy shall follow me   Ps.23.6
O how abundant is thy *g*., which   Ps.31.19
thy *g*., O God, thou didst provide   Ps.68.10
be radiant over the *g*. of the LORD   Jer.31.12
but when the *g*. and loving kindness   Tit.3.4
tasted the *g*. of the word of God   Heb.6.5

GOSPEL
preaching the *g*. of the kingdom   Mt.4.23
beginning of the *g*. of Jesus Christ   Mk.1.1
they departed . . . preaching the *g*.   Lk.9.6
For I am not ashamed of the *g*.   Rom.1.16
my ambition to preach the *g*.   Rom.15.20
woe . . . if I do not preach the *g*.   1 Cor.9.16
want to pervert the *g*. of Christ   Gal.1.7
to proclaim the mystery of the *g*.   Eph.6.19
by God to be entrusted with the *g*.   1 Th.2.4
during my imprisonment for the *g*.   Philem.13
with an eternal *g*. to proclaim to   Rev.14.6

GOSSIP (noun)
the talk and evil *g*. of the people   Ezek.36.3
deceit, malignity, they are *g*.   Rom.1.29
g., conceit, and disorder   2 Cor.12.20
not only idlers but *g*.   1 Tim.5.13

GRACE
g. is poured upon your lips   Ps.45.2
g. and truth came through Jesus   Jn.1.17
When he came and saw the *g*. of God   Acts 11.23
to the gospel of the *g*. of God   Acts 20.24
g. abounded all the more   Rom.5.20
there is a remnant, chosen by *g*.   Rom.11.5
G. to you and peace from God our   2 Cor.1.2
For you know the *g*. of our Lord   2 Cor.8.9
My *g*. is sufficient for you   2 Cor.12.9
you have fallen away from *g*.   Gal.5.4
For by *g*. you have been saved   Eph.2.8
G., mercy, and peace from God   1 Tim.1.2
strong in the *g*. that is in Christ   2 Tim.2.1
draw near to the throne of *g*.   Heb.4.16
be strengthened by *g*., not by foods   Heb.13.9
But grow in the *g*. and knowledge   2 Pet.3.18
who pervert the *g*. of our God into   Jude 4
The *g*. of the Lord Jesus be with   Rev.22.21

GRACIOUS
g. and merciful, slow to anger and   Neh.9.17
Be *g*. to me . . . for I am languishing   Ps.6.2

May God be *g*. to us and bless us   Ps.67.1
G. is the LORD, and righteous   Ps.116.5
A *g*. woman gets honor   Pr.11.16
for he is *g*. and merciful, slow to   Jl.2.13
Father, for such was thy *g*. will   Mt.11.26
Let your speech always be *g*.   Col.4.6

GRAIN
seven ears of *g*., plump and good   Gen.41.5
a cereal offering of new *g*. to   Num.28.26
thou providest their *g*., for so thou   Ps.65.9
valleys deck themselves with *g*.   Ps.65.13
and gave them the *g*. of heaven   Ps.78.24
it was I who gave her the *g*.   Hos.2.8
threshing floors shall be full of *g*.   Jl.2.24
on good soil and brought forth *g*.   Mt.13.8
is like a *g*. of mustard seed which   Mt.13.31
have faith as a *g*. of mustard seed   Mt.17.20
unless a *g*. of wheat falls into the   Jn.12.24

GRANT
may God Almighty *g*. you mercy   Gen.43.14
may the LORD *g*. you discretion   1 Chr.22.12
O *g*. us help against the foe   Ps.60.11
G. us to sit, one at your right   Mk.10.37
May the Lord *g*. mercy to the   2 Tim.1.16
I will *g*. him to sit with me on my   Rev.3.21

GRAPE
you may eat your fill of *g*.   Dt.23.24
When I looked for it to yield *g*.   Is.5.4
The fathers have eaten sour *g*.   Jer.31.29
you shall tread *g*., but not drink   Mic.6.15
Are *g*. gathered from thorns, or figs   Mt.7.16

GRASS
For they will soon fade like the *g*.   Ps.37.2
like *g*. which is renewed in the   Ps.90.5
As for man, his days are like *g*.   Ps.103.15
All flesh is *g*., and all its beauty   Is.40.6
Nebuchadnezzar . . . ate *g*. like an ox   Dan.4.33
like showers upon the *g*.   Mic.5.7
God so clothes the *g*. of the field   Mt.6.30
Now there was much *g*. in the place   Jn.6.10
the flower of *g*. The *g*. withers   1 Pet.1.24

GRAVE (noun)
man was cast into the *g*. of Elisha   2 Kg.13.21
come to your *g*. in ripe old age   Job 5.26
straight to the *g*. they descend   Ps.49.14
jealousy is cruel as the *g*.   S.of S.8.6
you are like *g*. which are not seen   Lk.11.44
Their throat is an open *g*.   Rom.3.13

GRAVEN
not make for yourself a *g*. image   Ex.20.4
set up Micah's *g*. image which he   Jg.18.31
he makes it a *g*. image and falls   Is.44.15

GREECE
Dan.11.2; Zech.9.13; Acts 20.2

GREED
His *g*. is as wide as Sheol   Hab.2.5
he is guilty of immorality or *g*.   1 Cor.5.11
as you know, or a cloak for *g*.   1 Th.2.5
They have hearts trained in *g*.   2 Pet.2.14

GREEK
Now the woman was a G.   Mk.7.26
in Hebrew, in Latin, and in G.   Jn.19.20
Timothy . . . his father was a G.   Acts 16.1
of the devout G. and not a few of   Acts 17.4
to the Jew first and also to the G.   Rom.1.16
There is neither Jew nor G.   Gal.3.28

GREEN

have given every *g*. plant for food	Gen.1.30
he makes me lie down in *g*. pastures	Ps.23.2
I the LORD . . . dry up the *g*. tree	Ezek.17.24
they do this when the wood is *g*.	Lk.23.31

GRIEF

My eye has grown dim from *g*.	Job 17.7
A stupid son is a *g*. to a father	Pr.17.21
man of sorrows . . . acquainted with *g*.	Is.53.3
has borne our *g*. and carried our	Is.53.4
godly *g*. produces a repentance	2 Cor.7.10
but worldly *g*. produces death	2 Cor.7.10

GRIEVE

Was not my soul *g*. for the poor?	Job 30.25
rebelled and *g*. his holy Spirit	Is.63.10
not willingly . . . *g*. the sons of men	Lam.3.33
g. at their hardness of heart	Mk.3.5
Peter was *g*. because he said to	Jn.21.17
because you were *g*. into repenting	2 Cor.7.9
do not *g*. the Holy Spirit of God	Eph.4.30

GROAN

despoiled, because the needy *g*.	Ps.12.5
the wicked rule, the people *g*.	Pr.29.2
gates are desolate, her priests *g*.	Lam.1.4
has been *g*. in travail together	Rom.8.22
Here indeed we *g*., and long to put	2 Cor.5.2

GROW

God made to *g*. every tree that is	Gen.2.9
he makes grass *g*. upon the hills	Ps.147.8
He does not faint or *g*. weary	Is.40.28
Consider the lilies, how they *g*.	Lk.12.27
let us not *g*. weary in well-doing	Gal.6.9
may not *g*. weary or fainthearted	Heb.12.3
But *g*. in the grace and knowledge	2 Pet.3.18

GUARD (verb)

to *g*. the way to the tree of life	Gen.3.24
will *g*. the feet of his faithful	1 Sam.2.9
G. them and keep them until you	Ezra 8.29
Oh *g*. my life, and deliver me	Ps.25.20
G. me, O LORD, from the hands of	Ps.140.4
understanding will *g*. you	Pr.2.11
G. your steps when you go to the	Ec.5.1
angels charge of you, to *g*. you	Lk.4.10
I have *g*. them, and none of them is	Jn.17.12
strengthen you and *g*. you from evil	2 Th.3.3
g. what has been entrusted	1 Tim.6.20
g. the truth . . . entrusted to you	2 Tim.1.14

GUARDIAN

the *g*. cherub drove you out	Ezek.28.16
the Holy Spirit has made you *g*.	Acts 20.28
but he is under *g*. and trustees	Gal.4.2
the Shepherd and *G*. of your souls	1 Pet.2.25

GUIDE (verb)

or can you *g*. the Bear with its	Job 38.32
thy name's sake lead me and *g*. me	Ps.31.3
thou dost . . . *g*. the nations upon earth	Ps.67.4
and *g*. them with skilful hand	Ps.78.72
the LORD will *g*. you continually	Is.58.11
to *g*. our feet into the way of peace	Lk.1.79
he will *g*. you into all the truth	Jn.16.13
he will *g*. them to springs of	Rev.7.17

GUILE

said, "Your brother came with *g*.	Gen.27.35
Israelite indeed, in whom is no *g*.	Jn.1.47
keep . . . his lips from speaking *g*.	1 Pet.3.10

GUILT

less than your *g*. deserves	Job 11.6
Make them bear their *g*., O God	Ps.5.10
pardon my *g*., for it is great	Ps.25.11
didst forgive the *g*. of my sin	Ps.32.5
your *g*. is taken away, and your sin	Is.6.7
inhabitants suffer for their *g*.	Is.24.6
Because your *g*. is great	Jer.30.15
is full of *g*. against the Holy One	Jer.51.5
were blind, you would have no *g*.	Jn.9.41

GUILTY

who will by no means clear the *g*.	Ex.34.7
although thou knowest that I am not *g*.	Job 10.7
of him who walks in his *g*. ways	Ps.68.21
The way of the *g*. is crooked	Pr.21.8
who will declare me *g*.? Behold, all	Is.50.9
LORD will by no means clear the *g*.	Nah.1.3
but is *g*. of an eternal sin	Mk.3.29
I did not find this man *g*. of any	Lk.23.14
commits sin is *g*. of lawlessness	1 Jn.3.4

HABITATION

Look down from thy holy *h*.	Dt.26.15
I love the *h*. of thy house, and the	Ps.26.8
made . . . the Most High your *h*.	Ps.91.9
O *h*. of righteousness, O holy hill	Jer.31.23
receive you into the eternal *h*.	Lk.16.9
Let his *h*. become desolate, and let	Acts 1.20
asked leave to find a *h*. for the	Acts 7.46

HAGAR

Gen.16.1; 21.9; 25.12; Gal.4.24

HAIL (noun)

I will cause very heavy *h*. to fall	Ex.9.18
He destroyed their vines with *h*.	Ps.78.47
like a storm of *h*., a destroying	Is.28.2
with blight and mildew and *h*.	Hag.2.17
and there followed *h*. and fire	Rev.8.7
an earthquake, and heavy *h*.	Rev.11.19
cursed . . . for the plague of the *h*.	Rev.16.21

HAIR

Do not let the *h*. of your heads	Lev.10.6
the *h*. of his head began to grow	Jg.16.22
sling a stone at a *h*., and not miss	Jg.20.16
the *h*. of my flesh stood up	Job 4.15
are more than the *h*. of my head	Ps.40.12
beauty of old men is their gray *h*.	Pr.20.29
Now John wore a garment of camel's *h*.	Mt.3.4
cannot make one *h*. white or black	Mt.5.36
the *h*. of your head are all numbered	Lk.12.7
not a *h*. of your head will perish	Lk.21.18
and wiped his feet with her *h*.	Jn.11.2
At Cenchreae he cut his *h*.	Acts 18.18
his head and his *h*. were white as	Rev.1.14

HALLOW

blessed the seventh day and *h*. it	Gen.2.3
And you shall *h*. the fiftieth year	Lev.25.10
which he had *h*. in Jerusalem	2 Chr.36.14
who art in heaven, *H*. be thy name	Mt.6.9

HAM

Gen.5.32; 14.5; Ps.78.51; 106.22

HAMAN

Est.3.1; 5.5; 6.11; 7.8,10; 9.14

HAND

Do not lay your *h*. on the lad or	Gen.22.12
h. for *h*., foot for foot	Ex.21.24
he shall lay his *h*. upon the head	Lev.1.4

LORD has given Sisera into your *h.*   Jg.4.14
The *h.* of God was very heavy there   1 Sam.5.11
I have taken my life in my *h.*   − 1 Sam.28.21
His right *h.* and his holy arm have   Ps.98.1
I hold my life in my *h.*   Ps.119.109
LORD is your shade on your right *h.*   Ps.121.5
Whatever your *h.* finds to do, do it   Ec.9.10
for the kingdom of heaven is at *h.*   Mt.3.2
do not let your left *h.* know what   Mt.6.3
And if your *h.* or your foot causes   Mt.18.8
to my Lord, Sit at my right *h.*   Mt.22.44
The Teacher says, My time is at *h.*   Mt.26.18
has dipped his *h.* in the dish with   Mt.26.23
seated at the right *h.*   Mt.26.64
standing at the right *h.* of God   Acts 7.55
And the *h.* of the Lord was with   Acts 11.21
gave . . . the right *h.* of fellowship   Gal.2.9
at his right *h.* in the heavenly   Eph.1.20
the coming of the Lord is at *h.*   Jas.5.8
under the mighty *h.* of God   1 Pet.5.6
But he laid his right *h.* upon me   Rev.1.17

HANG
Pharaoh will . . . *h.* you on a tree   Gen.40.19
for a *h.* man is accursed by God   Dt.21.23
So they *h.* Haman on the gallows   Est.7.10
and he went and *h.* himself   Mt.27.5
criminals who were *h.* railed at him   Lk.23.39
you killed by *h.* him on a tree   Acts 5.30

HANNAH
1 Sam.1.2,13; 2.1,21

HAPPY
Behold, *h.* is the man whom God   Job 5.17
H. the people whose God is the LORD Ps.144.15
H. is the man who finds wisdom   Pr.3.13
h. are those who keep my ways   Pr.8.32
but *h.* is he who is kind to the poor   Pr.14.21
and *h.* is he who trusts in the LORD Pr.16.20
h. is he who has no reason to judge Rom.14.22
we call those *h.* who were steadfast Jas.5.11

HARD
Is anything too *h.* for the LORD?   Gen.18.14
I weep for him whose day was *h.*?   Job 30.25
Disaster follows *h.* on disaster   Jer.4.20
Nothing is too *h.* for thee   Jer.32.17
gate is narrow and the way is *h.*   Mt.7.14
it will be *h.* for a rich man to   Mt.19.23
Master, I knew you to be a *h.* man Mt.25.24
Many . . . said, "This is a *h.* saying Jn.6.60
But by your *h.* and impenitent heart Rom.2.5
I am *h.* pressed between the two   Phil.1.23
much to say which is *h.* to explain Heb.5.11
things in them *h.* to understand   2 Pet.3.16

HARDEN
but I will *h.* his heart, so that he   Ex.4.21
you shall not *h.* your heart or shut Dt.15.7
H. not your hearts, as at Meribah   Ps.95.8
err from thy ways and *h.* our heart Is.63.17
he *h.* the heart of whomever he   Rom.9.18
But their minds were *h.*   2 Cor.3.14
do not *h.* your hearts as in the   Heb.3.8

HARDNESS
for your *h.* of heart Moses allowed Mt.19.8
grieved at their *h.* of heart   Mk.3.5
due to their *h.* of heart   Eph.4.18

HARLOT
They shall not marry a *h.* or a woman Lev.21.7

shall not bring the hire of a *h.*   Dt.23.18
only Rahab the *h.* and all who are Jos.6.17
Israel . . . played the *h.* after the Baals Jg.8.33
For a *h.* is a deep pit   Pr.23.27
How the faithful city has become a *h.* Is.1.21
have left their God to play the *h.* Hos.4.12
tax collectors and the *h.* go into the Mt.21.31
has devoured your living with *h.*   Lk.15.30
was not . . . Rahab the *h.* justified by Jas.2.25
the judgment of the great *h.* who Rev.17.1

HARM (noun)
he feared that *h.* might befall him   Gen.42.4
If any *h.* follows, then you shall   Ex.21.23
for I will no more do you *h.*   1 Sam.26.21
will do us more *h.* than Absalom   2 Sam.20.6
on the sabbath to do good or to do *h.* Mk.3.4
the demon . . . having done him no *h.* Lk.4.35

HARMONY
Live in *h.* with one another   Rom.12.16
live in such *h.* with one another   Rom.15.5
everything together in perfect *h.*   Col.3.14

HARP
from the high place with *h.*   1 Sam.10.5
with the *h.* for thy faithfulness   Ps.71.22
a ten-stringed *h.* I will play to   Ps.144.9
praise him with lute and *h.*   Ps.150.3
h., bagpipe, and every kind of music Dan.3.5
such as the flute or the *h.*   1 Cor.14.7
before the Lamb, each holding a *h.* Rev.5.8

HARVEST (noun)
seedtime and *h.*, cold and heat   Gen.8.22
You shall keep the feast of *h.*   Ex.23.16
fruits of your *h.* to the priest   Lev.23.10
gathers her sustenance in *h.*   Pr.6.8
son who sleeps in *h.* brings shame Pr.10.5
Like . . . snow in the time of *h.* is Pr.25.13
The *h.* is past, the summer is ended Jer.8.20
Put in the sickle, for the *h.* is ripe Jl.3.13
pray therefore the Lord of the *h.*   Mt.9.38
because the *h.* has come   Mk.4.29
The *h.* is plentiful, but the laborers Lk.10.2
fields are already white for *h.*   Jn.4.35
the *h.* of your righteousness   2 Cor.9.10
the *h.* of righteousness is sown   Jas.3.18

HATE (verb)
You shall not *h.* your brother in   Lev.19.17
those who *h.* the righteous will   Ps.34.21
The LORD loves those who *h.* evil   Ps.97.10
therefore I *h.* every false way   Ps.119.104
Do I not *h.* them that *h.* thee   Ps.139.21
How long will . . . fools *h.* knowledge? Pr.1.22
a time to love, and a time to *h.*   Ec.3.8
I *h.* robbery and wrong   Is.61.8
H. evil, and love good   Am.5.15
you who *h.* the good and love the   Mic.3.2
these things I *h.*, says the LORD   Zech.8.17
For I *h.* divorce, says the LORD   Mal.2.16
love your neighbor and *h.* your enemy Mt.5.43
either he will *h.* the one and love Mt.6.24
Blessed are you when men *h.* you   Lk.6.22
do good to those who *h.* you   Lk.6.27
you will be *h.* by all for my name's Lk.21.17
The world cannot *h.* you, but it   Jn.7.7
h. what is evil, hold fast to what   Rom.12.9

HAUGHTY
upon the *h.* to bring them down   2 Sam.22.28

HAZAEL

and a *h.* spirit before a fall — Pr.16.18
the eyes of the *h.* are humbled — Is.5.15
They were *h.,* and did abominable — Ezek.16.50
h., boastful, inventors of evil — Rom.1.30
do not be *h.,* but associate with — Rom.12.16
charge them not to be *h.* — 1 Tim.6.17

HAZAEL

king of Syria, 1 Kg.19.15; Elisha's prediction, 2 Kg.8.7–10; slays Ben-hadad, 2 Kg.8.15; oppresses Israel, 2 Kg.9.14; 10.32; 12.17; 13.22

HEAD

he shall bruise your *h.,* and you — Gen.3.15
his blood shall be upon his *h.* — Jos.2.19
Sisera a blow, she crushed his *h.* — Jg.5.26
them over to me, I will be your *h.* — Jg.11.9
No razor shall come upon his *h.* — Jg.13.5
of oil and poured it on his *h.* — 1 Sam.10.1
took the *h.* of the Philistine — 1 Sam.17.54
to his father, "Oh, my *h.,* my *h.!*" — 2 Kg.4.19
his axe *h.* fell into the water — 2 Kg.6.5
Behold, God is with us at our *h.* — 2 Chr.13.12
his foot to the crown of his *h.* — Job 2.7
thou anointest my *h.* with oil — Ps.23.5
A hoary *h.* is a crown of glory — Pr.16.31
will heap coals of fire on his *h.* — Pr.25.22
And do not swear by your *h.* — Mt.5.36
Son of man has nowhere to lay his *h.* — Mt.8.20
Give me the *h.* of John the Baptist — Mt.14.8
has become the *h.* of the corner — Mt.21.42
a crown of thorns . . . on his *h.* — Mt.27.29
not a hair of your *h.* will perish — Lk.21.18
he bowed his *h.* and gave up his — Jn.19.30
heap burning coals upon his *h.* — Rom.12.20
the *h.* of every man is Christ — 1 Cor.11.3
and the *h.* of Christ is God — 1 Cor.11.3
made him the *h.* over all things — Eph.1.22
husband is the *h.* of the wife as — Eph.5.23
He is the *h.* of the body, the church — Col.1.18
his *h.* and his hair were white as — Rev.1.14

HEAL

forgive their sin and *h.* their — 2 Chr.7.14
h. me, for my bones are troubled — Ps.6.2
who *h.* all your diseases — Ps.103.3
He *h.* the brokenhearted, and binds — Ps.147.3
with his stripes we are *h.* — Is.53.5
H. me, O LORD, and I shall be *h.* — Jer.17.14
I will *h.* their faithlessness — Hos.14.4
H. the sick, raise the dead, cleanse — Mt.10.8
Is it lawful to *h.* on the sabbath? — Mt.12.10
proverb, 'Physician, *h.* yourself — Lk.4.23
thou stretchest out thy hand to *h.* — Acts 4.30
By his wounds you have been *h.* — 1 Pet.2.24

HEALING (noun)

I will bring to it health and *h.* — Jer.33.6
cured those who had need of *h.* — Lk.9.11
this sign of *h.* was performed — Acts 4.22
gifts of *h.* by the one Spirit — 1 Cor.12.9
Do all possess gifts of *h.?* — 1 Cor.12.30
were for the *h.* of the nations — Rev.22.2

HEAP (verb)

will *h.* coals of fire on his head — Pr.25.22
do not *h.* up empty phrases — Mt.6.7
h. burning coals upon his head — Rom.12.20
for her sins are *h.* high as heaven — Rev.18.5

HEAR

God does not *h.* an empty cry — Job 35.13
But thou didst *h.* my supplications — Ps.31.22
H. my prayer, O LORD, and give ear — Ps.39.12
O thou who *h.* prayer! To thee shall — Ps.65.2
They have ears, but do not *h.* — Ps.115.6
h., that your soul may live — Is.55.3
tell John what you *h.* and see — Mt.11.4
He who has ears to *h.,* let him *h.* — Mt.11.15
H., O Israel: The Lord our God — Mk.12.29
when you *h.* of wars and tumults — Lk.21.9
when the dead will *h.* the voice of — Jn.5.25
My sheep *h.* my voice, and I know — Jn.10.27
Let every man be quick to *h.,* slow — Jas.1.19
we know that he *h.* us in whatever — 1 Jn.5.15

HEART

imagination . . . of his *h.* was only evil — Gen.6.5
LORD hardened the *h.* of Pharaoh — Ex.9.12
with all your *h.* and with all your — Dt.4.29
The fool says in his *h.,* ". . . no God." — Ps.14.1
meditation of my *h.* be acceptable — Ps.19.14
He who has clean hands and a pure *h.* — Ps.24.4
For he knows the secrets of the *h.* — Ps.44.21
Create in me a clean *h.,* O God — Ps.51.10
a broken and contrite *h.,* O God — Ps.51.17
Search me, O God, and know my *h.* — Ps.139.23
for wisdom will come into your *h.* — Pr.2.10
Trust in the LORD with all your *h.* — Pr.3.5
Anxiety in a man's *h.* weighs him — Pr.12.25
Hope deferred makes the *h.* sick — Pr.13.12
A glad *h.* makes a cheerful — Pr.15.13
A wise man's *h.* inclines him toward — Ec.10.2
Say to those who are of a fearful *h.* — Is.35.4
when you seek me with all your *h.* — Jer.29.13
Let not your *h.* faint, and be not — Jer.51.46
How lovesick is your *h.,* says — Ezek.16.30
Blessed are the pure in *h.* — Mt.5.8
out of the *h.* come evil thoughts — Mt.15.19
love the Lord . . . with all your *h.* — Mt.22.37
kept all these things in her *h.* — Lk.2.51
ought always to pray and not lose *h.* — Lk.18.1
Let not your *h.* be troubled — Jn.14.1
in singleness of *h.,* as to Christ — Eph.6.5
doing the will of God from the *h.* — Eph.6.6
Refresh my *h.* in Christ — Philem.20
God is greater than our *h.* — 1 Jn.3.20
I am he who searches mind and *h.* — Rev.2.23

HEAVEN

God created the *h.* and the earth — Gen.1.1
And God called the firmament *H.* — Gen.1.8
Most High, maker of *h.* and earth — Gen.14.19
Elijah up to *h.* by a whirlwind — 2 Kg.2.1
the LORD's throne is in *h.* — Ps.11.4
Let *h.* and earth praise him — Ps.69.34
the LORD, who made *h.* and earth — Ps.121.2
If I ascend to *h.,* thou art there — Ps.139.8
Who has ascended to *h.* and come down? — Pr.30.4
I create new *h.* and a new earth — Is.65.17
H. is my throne and the earth is — Is.66.1
for the kingdom of *h.* is at hand — Mt.3.2
a voice from *h.,* saying, "This is my — Mt.3.17
for the kingdom of *h.* is at hand — Mt.4.17
for your reward is great in *h.* — Mt.5.12
till *h.* and earth pass away, not an — Mt.5.18
Our Father who art in *h.* — Mt.6.9
before my Father who is in *h.* — Mt.10.32

I thank thee . . . Lord of *h*. and earth   Mt.11.25
H. and earth will pass away, but my   Mt.24.35
the Spirit descend as a dove from *h*.   Jn.1.32
He gave them bread from *h*. to eat   Jn.6.31
H. is my throne, and earth my   Acts 7.49
Then I saw a new *h*. and a new earth   Rev.21.1

HEAVENLY
O *h*. beings, ascribe to the LORD   Ps.29.1
as your *h*. Father is perfect   Mt.5.48
multitude of the *h*. host praising   Lk.2.13
believe if I tell you *h*. things?   Jn.3.12
not disobedient to the *h*. vision   Acts 26.19
and save me for his *h*. kingdom   2 Tim.4.18
copies of the *h*. things . . . purified   Heb.9.23
h. Jerusalem, and to innumerable   Heb.12.22

HEAVY
Your father made our yoke *h*.   1 Kg.12.4
his hand is *h*. in spite of my   Job 23.2
Thy wrath lies *h*. upon me   Ps.88.7
all who labor and are *h*. laden   Mt.11.28
They bind *h*. burdens, hard to bear   Mt.23.4
sleeping, for their eyes were *h*.   Mt.26.43
their ears are *h*. of hearing   Acts 28.27

HEBRON
a city about 19 miles southwest of Jerusalem;
Abraham dwells there, Gen.13.18; 23.2; the
spies come to, Num.13.22; captured, Jos.10.36–
37; given to Caleb, Jos.14.13; 15.13; David
reigns there, 2 Sam.2.1; 3.2; 5.1; 1 Chr.11;
12.38; 29.27

HEED (noun)
Take *h*. lest you forget the LORD   Dt.8.11
thou hast taken *h*. of my adversities   Ps.31.7
Take *h*. what you hear   Mk.4.24
he stands take *h*. lest he fall   1 Cor.10.12

HEED (verb)
wise of heart will *h*. commandments   Pr.10.8
he who *h*. reproof is honored   Pr.13.18
h. the word of the LORD   Jer.2.31
they have not all *h*. the gospel   Rom.10.16
h. my appeal, agree with one   2 Cor.13.11

HEIFER
bring you a red *h*. without defect   Num.19.2
If you had not plowed with my *h*.   Jg.14.18
A beautiful *h*. is Egypt   Jer.46.20
Like a stubborn *h*., Israel is   Hos.4.16
Ephraim was a trained *h*.   Hos.10.11
the ashes of a *h*. sanctifies for   Heb.9.13

HEIR
shall not be *h*. with my son Isaac   Gen.21.10
Has Israel no sons? Has he no *h*.?   Jer.49.1
and if children, then *h*., *h*. of God   Rom.8.17
offspring, *h*. according to promise   Gal.3.29
and if a son then an *h*.   Gal.4.7
he appointed the *h*. of all things   Heb.1.2
are joint *h*. of the grace of life   1 Pet.3.7

HELL
shall be liable to the *h*. of fire   Mt.5.22
destroy both soul and body in *h*.   Mt.10.28
twice as much a child of *h*. as   Mt.23.15
has power to cast into *h*.   Lk.12.5
The tongue is . . . set on fire by *h*.   Jas.3.6
God . . . cast them into *h*.   2 Pet.2.4

HELMET
Ephraim is my *h*.; Judah is my scepter   Ps.60.7
a *h*. of salvation upon his head   Is.59.17

And take the *h*. of salvation   Eph.6.17
and for a *h*. the hope of salvation   1 Th.5.8

HELP (noun)
The God of my father was my *h*.   Ex.18.4
In truth I have no *h*. in me   Job 6.13
soul of the wounded cries for *h*.   Job 24.12
there is no *h*. for him in God   Ps.3.2
the LORD; he is our *h*. and shield   Ps.33.20
Thou art my *h*. and my deliverer   Ps.40.17
a very present *h*. in trouble   Ps.46.1
He is their *h*. and their shield   Ps.115.9
My *h*. comes from the LORD, who made   Ps.121.2
Our *h*. is in the name of the LORD   Ps.124.8
the *h*. of the Spirit of Jesus   Phil.1.19

HELP (verb)
God has power to *h*. or to cast   2 Chr.25.8
Fear not, I will *h*. you   Is.41.13
before him, saying, "Lord, *h*. me."   Mt.15.25
said, "I believe; *h*. my unbelief!"   Mk.9.24
He has *h*. his servant Israel   Lk.1.54
toiling one must *h*. the weak   Acts 20.35
Likewise the Spirit *h*. us in our   Rom.8.26
You also must *h*. us by prayer   2 Cor.1.11
h. the weak, be patient with them   1 Th.5.14
find grace to *h*. in time of need   Heb.4.16

HELPER
I will make him a *h*. fit for him   Gen.2.18
hast been the *h*. of the fatherless   Ps.10.14
Behold, God is my *h*.; the Lord is   Ps.54.4
he delivers . . . him who has no *h*.   Ps.72.12
healers, *h*., administrators   1 Cor.12.28
confidently say, "The Lord is my *h*.   Heb.13.6

HERITAGE
For they are thy people and thy *h*.   Dt.9.29
the *h*. decreed for him by God   Job 20.29
yea, I have goodly *h*.   Ps.16.6
given me the *h*. of those who fear   Ps.61.5
he will not abandon his *h*.   Ps.94.14
and he abhorred his *h*.   Ps.106.40
Lo, sons are a *h*. from the LORD   Ps.127.3
gave their land as a *h*.   Ps.135.12
Blessed be . . . Israel my *h*.   Is.19.25
the *h*. of the servants of the LORD   Is.54.17
and made my *h*. an abomination   Jer.2.7
and make not thy *h*. a reproach   Jl.2.17
left his *h*. to jackals of the desert   Mal.1.3
He who conquers shall have this *h*.   Rev.21.7

HEROD
(1) (the Great) king of Judea, Mt.2.1; troubled
at Jesus' birth, Mt.2.3; kills the male children
in Bethlehem, Mt.2.16; (2) (Antipas) reproved
by John the Baptist, imprisons him, Lk.3.19;
beheads him, Mt.14; Mk.6.14–28; desires to
see Jesus, Lk.9.9; scourges him, and is reconciled to Pilate, Lk.23.7–12; Acts 4.27; (3)
(Agrippa I) persecutes the church, Acts 12.1;
his pride and miserable death, Acts 12.23;
(4) (Agrippa II) visit to Festus, Acts 25.13;
Paul's defense before, Acts 26

HEW
H. two tables of stone like the   Dt.10.1
you shall *h*. down the graven images   Dt.12.3
to the rock from which you were *h*.   Is.51.1
h. out cisterns for themselves   Jer.2.13
which had been *h*. out of the rock   Mk.15.46

HEZEKIAH

king of Judah, 2 Kg.16.19–20 (2 Chr.28.27); abolishes idolatry, 2 Kg.18; attacked by the Assyrians, his prayer and deliverance, 2 Kg.19; his life lengthened, shadow of dial goes backward, displays his treasure, Isaiah's prediction, 2 Kg.20 (Is.38); his passover, 2 Chr.30.13; his piety and good reign, 2 Chr.29; his death, 2 Kg.20.20–21

HID

I was naked; and I *h.* myself	Gen.3.10
Moses *h.* his face, for he was afraid	Ex.3.6
You shall be *h.* from the scourge	Job 5.21
It is *h.* from the eyes of all	Job 28.21
let the net which they *h.* ensnare	Ps.35.8
My way is *h.* from the LORD, and my	Is.40.27
in the shadow of his hand he *h.* me	Is.49.2
for thou hast *h.* thy face from us	Is.64.7
Compassion is *h.* from my eyes	Hos.13.14
A city set on a hill cannot be *h.*	Mt.5.14
nothing *h.*, except to come to light	Mk.4.22
now they are *h.* from your eyes	Lk.19.42
Jesus *h.* himself, and went out	Jn.8.59
in whom are *h.* all the treasures of	Col.2.3
your life is *h.* with Christ in God	Col.3.3

HIDE

And when she could *h.* him no longer	Ex.2.3
long wilt thou *h.* thy face from me?	Ps.13.1
h. me in the shadow of thy wings	Ps.17.8
For he will *h.* me in his shelter	Ps.27.5
H. not thy face from thy servant	Ps.69.17
the wicked rise, men *h.* themselves	Pr.28.12
thou art a God who *h.* thyself	Is.45.15
I will not *h.* my face any more	Ezek.39.29
Though they *h.* themselves . . . I will	Am.9.3
he will *h.* his face from them	Mic.3.4
Fall on us and *h.* us from the face	Rev.6.16

HIGH

Is not God *h.* in the heavens?	Job 22.12
He beholds everything that is *h.*	Job 41.34
the name of the LORD, the Most *H.*	Ps.7.17
men of *h.* estate are a delusion	Ps.62.9
the heavens are *h.* above the earth	Ps.103.11
The LORD is *h.* above all nations	Ps.113.4
For though the LORD is *h.*	Ps.138.6
it is *h.*, I cannot attain it	Ps.139.6
is poured upon us from on *h.*	Is.32.15
Lift up your eyes on *h.* and see	Is.40.26
your nest as *h.* as the eagle's	Jer.49.16
and abase that which is *h.*	Ezek.21.26
led them up a *h.* mountain apart	Mt.17.1
day shall dawn upon us from on *h.*	Lk.1.78
mother-in-law . . . ill with a *h.* fever	Lk.4.38
are clothed with power from on *h.*	Lk.24.49
right hand of the Majesty on *h.*	Heb.1.3
have not a *h.* priest who is unable	Heb.4.15
exalt himself to be made a *h.* priest	Heb.5.5
her sins are heaped *h.* as heaven	Rev.18.5

HIGHWAY

we will go by the King's *H.*	Num.21.22
The *h.* of the upright turns aside	Pr.16.17
there will be a *h.* from Assyria	Is.11.16
a *h.* shall be there . . . the Holy Way	Is.35.8
in the desert a *h.* for our God	Is.40.3
Go out to the *h.* and hedges	Lk.14.23

HILKIAH

2 Kg.18.18; 2 Chr.34.9; Is.22.20

HILL

set my king on Zion, my holy *h.*	Ps.2.6
Who shall dwell on thy holy *h.*?	Ps.15.1
Who shall ascend the *h.* of the LORD?	Ps.24.3
the cattle on a thousand *h.*	Ps.50.10
I lift up my eyes to the *h.*	Ps.121.1
before the *h.*, I was brought forth	Pr.8.25
every mountain and *h.* be made low	Is.40.4
weighed . . . the *h.* in a balance?	Is.40.12
their altars, upon every high *h.*	Ezek.6.13
thy city Jerusalem, thy holy *h.*	Dan.9.16
A city set on a *h.* cannot be hid	Mt.5.14
went with haste into the *h.* country	Lk.1.39
through all the *h.* country of Judea	Lk.1.65
mountain and *h.* shall be brought low	Lk.3.5
led him to the brow of the *h.*	Lk.4.29
and to the *h.*, 'Cover us.'	Lk.23.30
Jesus went up into the *h.*	Jn.6.3
the seven heads are seven *h.*	Rev.17.9

HINDER

for nothing can *h.* the LORD from	1 Sam.14.6
who can *h.* him? Who will say	Job 9.12
I work and who can *h.* it?	Is.43.13
children come to me, do not *h.* them	Mk.10.14
who *h.* you from obeying the truth?	Gal.5.7
again and again–but Satan *h.* us	1 Th.2.18
that your prayers may not be *h.*	1 Pet.3.7

HIRAM

2 Sam.5.11; 1 Kg.5.1,8; 1 Chr.14.1

HIRE

wages of a *h.* servant shall not	Lev.19.13
You shall not oppress a *h.* servant	Dt.24.14
early in the morning to *h.* laborers	Mt.20.1
my father's *h.* servants have bread	Lk.15.17

HISS

will be astonished, and will *h.*	1 Kg.9.8
a thing to be *h.* at for ever	Jer.18.16
they *h.*, they gnash their teeth	Lam.2.16
merchants . . . *h.* at you	Ezek.27.36
Every one who passes by her *h.*	Zeph.2.15

HITTITE

Gen.23.10; Ex.23.28; 2 Sam.11.6; 2 Chr.1.17

HOLD

Do you still *h.* fast your integrity?	Job 2.9
I *h.* fast my righteousness	Job 27.6
trembling took *h.* of them there	Ps.48.6
thou dost *h.* my right hand	Ps.73.23
do not *h.* thy peace . . . O God	Ps.83.1
I *h.* my life in my hand	Ps.119.109
H. me up, that I may be safe	Ps.119.117
and thy right hand shall *h.* me	Ps.139.10
Let your heart *h.* fast my words	Pr.4.4
h. fast to love and justice	Hos.12.6
shall take *h.* of the robe of a Jew	Zech.8.23
Do not *h.* me, for I have not yet	Jn.20.17
h. fast to what is good	Rom.12.9
let us *h.* true to what we have	Phil.3.16
in him all things *h.* together	Col.1.17
take *h.* of the eternal life	1 Tim.6.12
let us *h.* fast our confession	Heb.4.14
you *h.* fast my name	Rev.2.13
h. fast what you have, until I	Rev.2.25

HOLINESS

Who is like thee, majestic in *h.*	Ex.15.11

Once for all I have sworn by my *h.*	Ps.89.35
h. befits thy house, O LORD	Ps.93.5
I will manifest my *h.* among you	Ezek.20.41
vindicate my *h.* before their eyes	Ezek.38.16
in *h.* and righteousness before him	Lk.1.75
according to the Spirit of *h.*	Rom.1.4
with *h.* and godly sincerity	2 Cor.1.12
unblamable in *h.* before our God	1 Th.3.13
and love and *h.*, with modesty	1 Tim.2.15
that we may share his *h.*	Heb.12.10
h. without which no one will see	Heb.12.14
lives of *h.* and godliness	2 Pet.3.11

HOLLOW

he touched the *h.* of Jacob's thigh	Gen.32.32
he made it *h.*, with boards	Ex.38.7
waters in the *h.* of his hand	Is.40.12

HOLY

you are standing is *h.* ground	Ex.3.5
the sabbath day, to keep it *h.*	Ex.20.8
He made the *h.* anointing oil also	Ex.37.29
whoever touches them shall become *h.*	Lev.6.18
between the *h.* and the common	Lev.10.10
be *h.*, for I am *h.*	Lev.11.44
wearing the *h.* linen garments	Lev.16.32
Consecrate yourselves . . . and be *h.*	Lev.20.7
the seventh day is a *h.* convocation	Lev.23.8
the place where you stand is *h.*	Jos.5.15
he is a *h.* God; he is a jealous	Jos.24.19
the *h.* race has mixed itself with	Ezra 9.2
The LORD is in his *h.* temple	Ps.11.4
who shall stand in his *h.* place?	Ps.24.3
give thanks to his *h.* name	Ps.30.4
take not thy *h.* Spirit from me	Ps.51.11
Worship the LORD in *h.* array	Ps.96.9
worship at his *h.* mountain	Ps.99.9
he looked down from his *h.* height	Ps.102.19
H. and terrible is his name	Ps.111.9
H., *h.*, *h.*, is the LORD of hosts	Is.6.3
I dwell in the high and *h.* place	Is.57.15
put in the midst . . . his *h.* Spirit	Is.63.11
you have drunk upon my *h.* mountain	Ob.16
But the LORD is in his *h.* temple	Hab.2.20
all the *h.* ones with him	Zech.14.5
conceived in her is of the *H.* Spirit	Mt.1.20
Do not give dogs what is *h.*	Mt.7.6
baptize you with the *H.* Spirit	Mk.1.8
The *H.* Spirit will come upon you	Lk.1.35
the *H.* Spirit was upon him	Lk.2.25
that you are the *H.* One of God	Jn.6.69
H. Father, keep them in thy name	Jn.17.11
said to them, "Receive the *H.* Spirit	Jn.20.22
be baptized with the *H.* Spirit	Acts 1.5
the promise of the *H.* Spirit	Acts 2.33
you are standing is *h.* ground	Acts 7.33
directed by a *h.* angel to send	Acts 10.22
H. Spirit fell on all who heard	Acts 10.44
his prophets in the *h.* scriptures	Rom.1.2
Greet one another with a *h.* kiss	Rom.16.16
For God's temple is *h.*	1 Cor.3.17
called us with a *h.* calling	2 Tim.1.9
as he who called you is *h.*, be *h.*	I Pet.1.15
You shall be *h.*, for I am *h.*	1 Pet.1.16
the Lord came with his *h.* myriads	Jude 14
H., *h.*, *h.*, is the Lord God Almighty	Rev.4.8
For thou alone art *h.*	Rev.15.4
I saw the *h.* city, new Jerusalem	Rev.21.2

HOME

The LORD grant that you may find a *h.*	Ru.1.9
Even the sparrow finds a *h.*	Ps.84.3
because man goes to his eternal *h.*	Ec.12.5
Go *h.* to your friends, and tell them	Mk.5.19
Return to your *h.*, and declare how	Lk.8.39
have left our *h.* and followed you	Lk.18.28
to him and make our *h.* with him	Jn.14.23
rather be . . . at *h.* with the Lord	2 Cor.5.8
So whether we are at *h.* or away	2 Cor.5.9

HONEST

How forceful are *h.* words	Job 6.25
hold it fast in an *h.* and good heart	Lk.8.15
doing *h.* work with his hands	Eph.4.28
to be ready for any *h.* work	Tit.3.1

HONEY

a land flowing with milk and *h.*	Ex.3.8
What is sweeter than *h.*?	Jg.14.18
sweeter than *h.* to my mouth	Ps.119.103
the lips of a loose woman drip *h.*	Pr.5.3
it was in my mouth as sweet as *h.*	Ezek.3.3
his food was locusts and wild *h.*	Mt.3.4
it was sweet as *h.* in my mouth	Rev.10.10

HONOR (noun)

H. and majesty are before him	Ps.96.6
Full of *h.* and majesty is his work	Ps.111.3
humility goes before *h.*	Pr.15.33
so *h.* is not fitting for a fool	Pr.26.1
If . . . I am a father, where is my *h.*?	Mal.1.6
A prophet is not without *h.*	Mk.6.4
h. to whom *h.* is due	Rom.13.7
in *h.* and dishonor, in ill repute	2 Cor.6.8
To him be *h.* and eternal dominion	1 Tim.6.16
Let marriage be held in *h.* among all	Heb.13.4
glory and *h.* at the revelation	1 Pet.1.7
to receive glory and *h.* and power	Rev.4.11
be blessing and *h.* and glory	Rev.5.13

HONOR (verb)

H. your father and your mother	Ex.20.12
H. your father and mother	Mt.19.19
This people *h.* me with their lips	Mk.7.6
He who does not *h.* the Son does not	Jn.5.23
if one member is *h.*, all rejoice	1 Cor.12.26
H. widows who are real widows	1 Tim.5.3
Fear God. *H.* the emperor	1 Pet.2.17

HONORABLE

insolent . . . the base fellow to the *h.*	Is.3.5
call . . . the holy day of the LORD *h.*	Is.58.13
parts of the body . . . less *h.*	1 Cor.12.23
we aim at what is *h.*	2 Cor.8.21
whatever is *h.*, whatever is just	Phil.4.8
they who blaspheme that *h.* name	Jas.2.7

HOOF

not a *h.* shall be left behind	Ex.10.26
that chew the cud or part the *h.*	Lev.11.4
parts the *h.* and has the *h.* cloven	Dt.14.6
their horses' *h.* seem like flint	Is.5.28
I will make . . . your *h.* bronze	Mic.4.13

HOOK

I will put my *h.* in your nose	2 Kg.19.28
beat . . . their spears into pruning *h.*	Is.2.4
I will put my *h.* in your nose	Is.37.29
Beat . . . your pruning *h.* into spears	Jl.3.10
go to the sea and cast a *h.*	Mt.17.27

HOPE (noun)

for what do I wait? My *h.* is in thee	Ps.39.7

H. deferred makes the heart sick	Pr.13.12
Discipline . . . son while there is *h.*	Pr.19.18
your *h.* will not be cut off	Pr.24.14
There is more *h.* for a fool than	Pr.26.12
are dried up, and our *h.* is lost	Ezek.37.11
the Valley of Achor a door of *h.*	Hos.2.15
for this *h.* I am accused by Jews	Acts 26.7
For in this *h.* we were saved	Rom.8.24
Now *h.* that is seen is not *h.*	Rom.8.24
that . . . we might have *h.*	Rom.15.4
May the God of *h.* fill you with	Rom.15.13
So faith, *h.*, love abide	1 Cor.13.13
know what is the *h.* to which	Eph.1.18
having no *h.* and without God	Eph.2.12
Christ in you, the *h.* of glory	Col.1.27
what is our *h.* or joy or crown	1 Th.2.19
grieve as others . . . who have no *h.*	1 Th.4.13
for a helmet the *h.* of salvation	1 Th.5.8
awaiting our blessed *h.*	Tit.2.13
born anew to a living *h.*	1 Pet.1.3
account for the *h.* that is in you	1 Pet.3.15

HOPE (verb)

be upon us, even as we *h.* in thee	Ps.33.22
But I will *h.* continually	Ps.71.14
O Israel, *h.* in the LORD	Ps.131.3
in his name will the Gentiles *h.*	Mt.12.21
those from whom you *h.* to receive	Lk.6.34
if we *h.* for what we do not see	Rom.8.25
in him shall the Gentiles *h.*	Rom.15.12
Love . . . *h.* all things, endures all	1 Cor.13.7
is the assurance of things *h.* for	Heb.11.1
holy women who *h.* in God	1 Pet.3.5
one who thus *h.* in him purifies	1 Jn.3.3

HOREB

a mountain (Sinai), Ex.3.1; 17.6; 33.6; Dt.1.6; laws given, Ex.19; 20; Dt.4–5; 18.16; 1 Kg.8.9; Mal.4.4; Moses twice there for forty days, Ex.24.18; 34.28; Dt.9.9; Elijah there, 1 Kg.19.8

HORN

Fill your *h.* with oil, and go	1 Sam.16.1
and the *h.* of my salvation	Ps.18.2
hast exalted my *h.* like that of	Ps.92.10
his *h.* is exalted in honor	Ps.112.9
has raised up a *h.* for his people	Ps.148.14
a fourth beast . . . had ten *h.*	Dan.7.7
Blow the *h.* in Gibeah	Hos.5.8
has raised up a *h.* of salvation	Lk.1.69
with seven *h.* and with seven eyes	Rev.5.6

HORROR

shall be a *h.* to all the kingdoms	Dt.28.25
he has made them an object of *h.*	2 Chr.29.8
and *h.* overwhelms me	Ps.55.5
My mind reels, *h.* has appalled me	Is.21.4
make them a *h.* to all the kingdoms	Jer.29.18
that Bozrah shall become a *h.*	Jer.49.13
and a taunt, a warning and a *h.*	Ezek.5.15
A cup of *h.* and desolation	Ezek.23.33

HORSE

the *h.* and his rider he has thrown	Ex.15.1
Some boast of chariots . . . some of *h.*	Ps.20.7
Be not like a *h.* or a mule	Ps.32.9
The war *h.* is a vain hope for victory	Ps.33.17
A whip for the *h.*, a bridle for the	Pr.26.3
like a *h.* plunging headlong	Jer.8.6
break in pieces the *h.* and . . . rider	Jer.51.21

behold, a man riding upon a red *h.*	Zech.1.8
I will strike every *h.* with panic	Zech.12.4
a white *h.*, and its rider had a bow	Rev.6.2
and behold, a white *h.*	Rev.19.11

HOSANNA

H. to the Son of David! Blessed be	Mt.21.9
H. in the highest	Mk.11.10
went out to meet him, crying, "*H.*	Jn.12.13

HOST

The LORD of *h.*, he is the King of	Ps.24.10
Though a *h.* encamp against me, my	Ps.27.3
LORD will punish the *h.* of heaven	Is.24.21
who brings out their *h.* by number	Is.40.26
the moon and all the *h.* of heaven	Jer.8.2
h. of heaven cannot be numbered	Jer.33.22
Bring up a *h.* against them	Ezek.23.46
the heavenly *h.* praising God	Lk.2.13
to worship the *h.* of heaven	Acts 7.42
Gaius, who is *h.* to me and to the	Rom.16.23
on high he led a *h.* of captives	Eph.4.8
the spiritual *h.* of wickedness	Eph.6.12

HOT

went out from Pharaoh in *h.* anger	Ex.11.8
dancing, Moses' anger burned *h.*	Ex.32.19
In *h.* anger he went back to his	Jg.14.19
when it is *h.*, they vanish	Job 6.17
my heart became *h.* within me	Ps.39.3
I speak in my *h.* jealousy against	Ezek.36.5
My anger is *h.* against the	Zech.10.3
you are neither cold nor *h.*	Rev.3.15

HOUR

will be given to you in that *h.*	Mt.10.19
of that day and *h.* no one knows	Mt.24.36
And about the ninth *h.* Jesus cried	Mt.27.46
Could you not watch one *h.*?	Mk.14.37
My *h.* has not yet come	Jn.2.4
But the *h.* is coming, and now is	Jn.4.23
Father, save me from this *h.*	Jn.12.27
you know what *h.* it is	Rom.13.11
Why am I in peril every *h.*?	1 Cor.15.30
Children, it is the last *h.*	1 Jn.2.18
the *h.* of his judgment has come	Rev.14.7

HOUSE

is none other than the *h.* of God	Gen.28.17
of Egypt, from the *h.* of bondage	Ex.13.14
and peace be to your *h.*	1 Sam.25.6
I dwell in a *h.* of cedar	2 Sam.7.2
saying, 'I will build you a *h.*'	2 Sam.7.27
The *h.* which King Solomon built	1 Kg.6.2
the glory of the LORD filled the *h.*	1 Kg.8.11
the LORD, 'Set your *h.* in order	2 Kg.20.1
the *h.* appointed for all living	Job 30.23
dwell in the *h.* of the LORD for ever	Ps.23.6
I love the habitation of thy *h.*	Ps.26.8
For zeal for thy *h.* has consumed me	Ps.69.9
doorkeeper in the *h.* of my God	Ps.84.10
holiness befits thy *h.*	Ps.93.5
Wealth and riches are in his *h.*	Ps.112.3
Let us go to the *h.* of the LORD	Ps.122.1
Unless the LORD builds the *h.*	Ps.127.1
Wisdom has built her *h.*, she has	Pr.9.1
the *h.* of the righteous will stand	Pr.12.7
better to go to the *h.* of mourning	Ec.7.2
brought me to the banqueting *h.*	S.ofS.2.4
Woe to those who join *h.* to *h.*	Is.5.8
my *h.* shall be called a *h.* of prayer	Is.56.7

Our holy and beautiful *h.*	Is.64.11
I will drive them out of my *h.*	Hos.9.15
while this *h.* lies in ruins?	Hag.1.4
man who built his *h.* upon the rock	Mt.7.24
As you enter the *h.*, salute it	Mt.10.12
and no city or *h.* divided against	Mt.12.25
My *h.* shall be called a *h.* of prayer	Mt.21.13
your *h.* is forsaken and desolate	Mt.23.38
who has left *h.* or brothers	Mk.10.29
that I must be in my Father's *h.*?	Lk.2.49
make my Father's *h.* a *h.* of trade	Jn.2.16
Zeal for thy *h.* will consume me	Jn.2.17
In my Father's *h.* are many rooms	Jn.14.2
a *h.* not made with hands, eternal	2 Cor.5.1
gadding about from *h.* to *h.*	1 Tim.5.13
For every *h.* is built by some one	Heb.3.4
faithful over God's *h.* as a son	Heb.3.6
yourselves built into a spiritual *h.*	1 Pet.2.5

HOUSEHOLD

into the ark, you and all your *h.*	Gen.7.1
foes will be those of his own *h.*	Mt.10.36
he himself believed, and all his *h.*	Jn.4.53
you will be saved, you and your *h.*	Acts 16.31
those who are of the *h.* of faith	Gal.6.10
He must manage his own *h.* well	1 Tim.3.4
an ark for the saving of his *h.*	Heb.11.7
to begin with the *h.* of God	1 Pet.4.17

HOUSEHOLDER

is like a *h.* who brings out of his	Mt.13.52
is like a *h.* who went out early	Mt.20.1
a *h.* who planted a vineyard	Mt.21.33
if the *h.* had known at what	Lk.12.39
tell the *h.*, 'The Teacher says	Lk.22.11

HOUSETOP

I am like a lonely bird on the *h.*	Ps.102.7
a corner of the *h.* than in a house	Pr.21.9
proclaim upon the *h.*	Mt.10.27
let him who is on the *h.* not go	Mk.13.15
Peter went up on the *h.* to pray	Acts 10.9

HUMAN

was so marred, beyond *h.* semblance	Is.52.14
a stone was cut out by no *h.* hand	Dan.2.34
no *h.* being would be saved; but	Mt.24.22
nor is he served by *h.* hands	Acts 17.25
For no *h.* being will be justified	Rom.3.20
not taught by *h.* wisdom but taught	1 Cor.2.13
but on tablets of *h.* hearts	2 Cor.3.3
Christ from a *h.* point of view	2 Cor.5.16
being found in *h.* form he humbled	Phil.2.8
no *h.* being can tame the tongue	Jas.3.8
a dumb ass spoke with *h.* voice	2 Pet.2.16
their faces were like *h.* faces	Rev.9.7

HUMBLE

He leads the *h.* in what is right	Ps.25.9
he adorns the *h.* with victory	Ps.149.4
but to the *h.* he shows favor	Pr.3.34
Better is a man of *h.* standing	Pr.12.9
who is of a contrite and *h.* spirit	Is.57.15
he that is *h.* and contrite in spirit	Is.66.2
proud, but gives grace to the *h.*	Jas.4.6

HUMBLE (verb)

that we might *h.* ourselves before	Ezra 8.21
Whoever *h.* himself like this child	Mt.18.4
one who exalts himself will be *h.*	Lk.14.11
he *h.* himself and became obedient	Phil.2.8
H. yourselves therefore under the	1 Pet.5.6

HUMILITY

and *h.* goes before honor	Pr.15.33
reward for *h.* . . . . is riches and . . . life	Pr.22.4
serving the Lord with all *h.*	Acts 20.19
in *h.* count others better than	Phil.2.3
with *h.* toward one another	1 Pet.5.5

HUNGER (verb)

Blessed are those who *h.* and thirst	Mt.5.6
he who comes to me shall not *h.*	Jn.6.35
To the present hour we *h.* and	1 Cor.4.11
They shall *h.* no more, neither	Rev.7.16

HUNGRY

If I were *h.*, I would not tell you	Ps.50.12
the *h.* he fills with good things	Ps.107.9
If your enemy is *h.*, give him bread	Pr.25.21
to share your bread with the *h.*	Is.58.7
his disciples were *h.*, and they	Mt.12.1
am unwilling to send them away *h.*	Mt.15.32
for I was *h.* and you gave me food	Mt.25.35
he has filled the *h.* with good things	Lk.1.53
read what David did when he was *h.*	Lk.6.3
if your enemy is *h.*, feed him	Rom.12.20
one is *h.* and another is drunk	1 Cor.11.21
if any one is *h.*, let him eat at	1 Cor.11.34

HUNT

to the field, and *h.* game for me	Gen.27.3
thou dost *h.* me like a lion	Job 10.16
let evil *h.* down the violent man	Ps.140.11
they shall *h.* them from every	Jer.16.16
I have been *h.* like a bird by	Lam.3.52
Will you *h.* down souls belonging	Ezek.13.18

HURT (noun)

who swears to his own *h.* and does	Ps.15.4
those who seek my *h.* speak of ruin	Ps.38.12
brought to dishonor who desire my *h.*	Ps.70.2
while man lords it over man to his *h.*	Ec.8.9
LORD binds up the *h.* of his people	Is.30.26
Your *h.* is incurable	Jer.30.12

HURT (verb)

but a cruel man *h.* himself	Pr.11.17
and nothing shall *h.* you	Lk.10.19
It *h.* . . . . to kick against the goads	Acts 26.14
shall not be *h.* by the second death	Rev.2.11

HUSBAND

bereft of her two sons and her *h.*	Ru.1.5
A good wife is the crown of her *h.*	Pr.12.4
The heart of her *h.* trusts in her	Pr.31.11
For your Maker is your *h.*	Is.54.5
her *h.* Joseph, being a just man	Mt.1.19
if she divorces her *h.* and marries	Mk.10.12
Go, call your *h.*, and come here	Jn.4.16
and each woman her own *h.*	1 Cor.7.2
is consecrated through her *h.*	1 Cor.7.14
is bound to her *h.* as long as he	1 Cor.7.39
as a pure bride to her one *h.*	2 Cor.11.2
For the *h.* is the head of the wife	Eph.5.23
H., love your wives, as Christ loved	Eph.5.25
Wives, be subject to your *h.*	Col.3.18
to love their *h.* and children	Tit.2.4
to be . . . submissive to their *h.*	Tit.2.5
wives, be submissive to your *h.*	1 Pet.3.1
as a bride adorned for her *h.*	Rev.21.2

HYMN

And when they had sung a *h.*	Mt.26.30
come together, each one has a *h.*	1 Cor.14.26

in psalms and *h.* and spiritual   Eph.5.19
psalms and *h.* and spiritual songs   Col.3.16

HYPOCRITE
as the *h.* do in the synagogues   Mt.6.2
Why put me to the test, you *h.*?   Mt.22.18
Woe to you, scribes and . . . *h.*   Mt.23.15
You *h.*, first take the log out of   Lk.6.42
You *h.*! You know how to interpret   Lk.12.56
the Lord answered him, "You *h.*   Lk.13.15

HYSSOP
Take a bunch of *h.* and dip it in   Ex.12.22
then a clean person shall take *h.*   Num.19.18
Purge me with *h.*, and I shall be   Ps.51.7
a sponge full of the vinegar on *h.*   Jn.19.29
with water and scarlet wool and *h.*   Heb.9.19

IDLE
he said, "You are *i.*, you are *i.*   Ex.5.17
an *i.* person will suffer hunger   Pr.19.15
Why do you stand here *i.* all day?   Mt.20.6
these words seemed . . . an *i.* tale   Lk.24.11
admonish the *i.*, encourage the   1 Th.5.14
we were not *i.* when we were with you   2 Th.3.7
their condemnation has not been *i.*   2 Pet.2.3

IDOL
Do not turn to *i.* or . . . molten gods   Lev.19.4
all the gods of the peoples are *i.*   Ps.96.5
make their boast in worthless *i.*   Ps.97.7
The *i.* of the nations are silver   Ps.135.15
who carry about their wooden *i.*   Is.45.20
Their *i.* are like scarecrows in a   Jer.10.5
Ephraim is joined to *i.*   Hos.4.17
abstain from the pollutions of *i.*   Acts 15.20
saw that the city was full of *i.*   Acts 17.16
Now concerning food offered to *i.*   1 Cor.8.1
to eat food offered to *i.*   1 Cor.8.10
you were led astray to dumb *i.*   1 Cor.12.2
how you turned to God from *i.*   1 Th.1.9
children, keep yourselves from *i.*   1 Jn.5.21
to eat food sacrificed to *i.*   Rev.2.20

IDOLATRY
the penalty for your sinful *i.*   Ezek.23.49
i., sorcery, enmity, strife   Gal.5.20
covetousness, which is *i.*   Col.3.5
revels, carousing, and lawless *i.*   1 Pet.4.3

IGNORANCE
has sinned through error or *i.*   Ezek.45.20
I know that you acted in *i.*   Acts 3.17
The times of *i.* God overlooked   Acts 17.30
because of the *i.* that is in them   Eph.4.18
to the passions of your former *i.*   1 Pet.1.14

IGNORANT
I was stupid and *i.*   Ps.73.22
being *i.* of the righteousness   Rom.10.3
we are not *i.* of his designs   2 Cor.2.11
deal gently with the *i.* and wayward   Heb.5.2
which the *i.* and unstable twist   2 Pet.3.16

ILL
No *i.* befalls the righteous   Pr.12.21
Lord, he whom you love is *i.*   Jn.11.3
in *i.* repute and good repute   2 Cor.6.8
because you heard that he was *i.*   Phil.2.26
Indeed he was *i.*, near to death   Phil.2.27
Trophimus I left *i.* at Miletus   2 Tim.4.20

IMAGE
Let us make man in our *i.*   Gen.1.26

for God made man in his own *i.*   Gen.9.6
not make yourself a graven *i.*   Ex.20.4
in Horeb and worshiped a molten *i.*   Ps.106.19
to set up an *i.* that will not move   Is.40.20
be conformed to the *i.* of his Son   Rom.8.29
a man . . . is the *i.* and glory of God   1 Cor.11.7
bear the *i.* of the man of heaven   1 Cor.15.49
He is the *i.* of the invisible God   Col.1.15
after the *i.* of its creator   Col.3.10
not worship the *i.* of the beast   Rev.13.15

IMAGINATION
that every *i.* . . . . was only evil   Gen.6.5
the *i.* of man's heart is evil   Gen.8.21
proud in the *i.* of their hearts   Lk.1.51
representation by the art and *i.*   Acts 17.29

IMITATE
join in *i.* me, and mark those who   Phil.3.17
know how you ought to *i.* us   2 Th.3.7
to give you . . . an example to *i.*   2 Th.3.9
your leaders . . . *i.* their faith   Heb.13.7
Beloved, do not *i.* evil but *i.* good   3 Jn.11

IMITATORS
I urge you, then, be *i.* of me   1 Cor.4.16
Be *i.* of me, as I am of Christ   1 Cor.11.1
be *i.* of God, as beloved children   Eph.5.1
you became *i.* of us and of the Lord   1 Th.1.6
became *i.* of the churches of God   1 Th.2.14
i. of those who . . . inherit the promises   Heb.6.12

IMMORAL
not to associate with *i.* men   1 Cor.5.9
the *i.* man sins against his own   1 Cor.6.18
Be sure . . . that no *i.* or impure man   Eph.5.5
that no one be *i.* or irreligious   Heb.12.16
will judge the *i.* and adulterous   Heb.13.4

IMMORALITY
reported . . . there is *i.* among you   1 Cor.5.1
The body is not meant for *i.*   1 Cor.6.13
Shun *i.* Every other sin   1 Cor.6.18
But *i.* . . . . must not even be named   Eph.5.3
that you abstain from *i.*   1 Th.4.3
she refuses to repent of her *i.*   Rev.2.21
nor did they repent of . . . their *i.*   Rev.9.21

IMMORTALITY
those who . . . seek for . . . honor and *i.*   Rom.2.7
mortal nature must put on *i.*   1 Cor.15.53
when . . . the mortal puts on *i.*   1 Cor.15.54
who alone has *i.* and dwells in   1 Tim.6.16
brought life and *i.* to light   2 Tim.1.10

IMPERISHABLE
a perishable wreath, but we an *i.*   1 Cor.9.25
what is raised is *i.*   1 Cor.15.42
the dead will be raised *i.*   1 Cor.15.52
the perishable puts on the *i.*   1 Cor.15.54
to an inheritance which is *i.*   1 Pet.1.4
not of perishable seed but of *i.*   1 Pet.1.23
the *i.* jewel of a gentle . . . spirit   1 Pet.3.4

IMPOSSIBLE
nothing will be *i.* to you   Mt.17.20
said to them, "With men this is *i.*   Mt.19.26
For with God nothing will be *i.*   Lk.1.37
is *i.* to restore again to repentance   Heb.6.4
i. that God should prove false   Heb.6.18
it is *i.* that the blood of bulls   Heb.10.4
without faith it is *i.* to please him   Heb.11.6

IMPRISONMENT
confiscation of his goods or for *i.*   Ezra 7.26

i. and afflictions await me	Acts 20.23
nothing deserving death or *i.*	Acts 23.29
partakers with me . . . both in my *i.* and	Phil.1.7
thinking to afflict me in my *i.*	Phil.1.17
during my *i.* for the gospel	Philem.13
even chains and *i.*	Heb.11.36

IMPURITY

as in the days of her *i.*	Lev.15.25
takes his brother's wife, it is *i.*	Lev.20.21
approach a woman in her time of *i.*	Ezek.18.6
in the lusts of their hearts to *i.*	Rom.1.24
you once yielded your members to *i.*	Rom.6.19
have not repented of the *i.*	2 Cor.12.21
immorality, *i.*, licentiousness	Gal.5.19
immorality and all *i.*	Eph.5.3
i., passion, evil desire	Col.3.5

INCENSE

Aaron shall burn fragrant *i.* on it	Ex.30.7
laid *i.* on it, and offered unholy	Lev.10.1
i. is an abomination to me	Is.1.13
they burned *i.* upon the mountains	Is.65.7
they have burned *i.* to other gods	Jer.1.16
When we burned *i.* to the queen of	Jer.44.19
in every place *i.* is offered to my	Mal.1.11
praying outside at the hour of *i.*	Lk.1.10
having the golden altar of *i.*	Heb.9.4
with golden bowls full of *i.*	Rev.5.8
smoke of the *i.* rose with the prayers	Rev.8.4

INCLINE

I. thy ear, O LORD, and hear	2 Kg.19.16
he *i.* to me and heard my cry	Ps.40.1
I will *i.* my ear to a proverb	Ps.49.4
I *i.* my heart to perform thy	Ps.119.112
I. thy ear, O LORD, and hear	Is.37.17
O my God, *i.* thy ear and hear	Dan.9.18

INCREASE

the land shall yield its *i.*	Lev.26.4
if riches *i.*, set not your heart on	Ps.62.10
The earth has yielded its *i.*	Ps.67.6
Thou wilt *i.* my honor, and comfort	Ps.71.21
May the LORD give you *i.*	Ps.115.14
he will *i.* in learning	Pr.9.9
when they perish, the righteous *i.*	Pr.28.28
For when dreams *i.*, empty words	Ec.5.7
Of the *i.* of his government and	Is.9.7
who has no might he *i.* strength	Is.40.29
Jesus *i.* in wisdom and in stature	Lk.2.52
said to the Lord, "*I.* our faith!"	Lk.17.5
He must *i.*, but I must decrease	Jn.3.30
but where sin *i.*, grace abounded	Rom.5.20
make you *i.* and abound in love	1 Th.3.12

INDIGNANT

they were *i.* at the two brothers	Mt.20.24
were *i.*, saying, "Why this waste?	Mt.26.8
when Jesus saw it he was *i.*	Mk.10.14
i. because Jesus had healed on the	Lk.13.14
is made to fall, and I am not *i.*?	2 Cor.11.29

INDIGNATION

Pour out thy *i.* upon them	Ps.69.24
put away thy *i.* toward us	Ps.85.4
Hot *i.* seizes me because of the	Ps.119.53
his *i.* is against his enemies	Is.66.14
the nations cannot endure his *i.*	Jer.10.10
Who can stand before his *i.*?	Nah.1.6
see . . . what *i.*, what alarm, what	2 Cor.7.11

INFERIOR

I also know; I am not *i.* to you	Job 13.2
the greater honor to the *i.* part	1 Cor.12.24
I am not at all *i.* to these	2 Cor.12.11
the *i.* is blessed by the superior	Heb.7.7

INFIRMITY

thou healest all his *i.*	Ps.41.3
He took our *i.* and bore our	Mt.8.17
to hear and to be healed of their *i.*	Lk.5.15
had a spirit of *i.* for eighteen	Lk.13.11

INHABITANTS

let all the *i.* of the world stand	Ps.33.8
Give ear, all *i.* of the world	Ps.49.1
its *i.* are like grasshoppers	Is.40.22
known to all the *i.* of Jerusalem	Acts 1.19
its *i.* worship the first beast	Rev.13.12

INHERIT

they shall *i.* it for ever	Ex.32.13
The wise will *i.* honor, but fools	Pr.3.35
my chosen shall *i.* it	Is.65.9
for they shall *i.* the earth	Mt.5.5
a hundredfold, and *i.* eternal life	Mt.19.29
i. the kingdom prepared for you	Mt.25.34
what must I do to *i.* eternal life?	Mk.10.17
will not *i.* the kingdom of God?	1 Cor.6.9
cannot *i.* the kingdom of God	1 Cor.15.50
shall not *i.* the kingdom of God	Gal.5.21
faith and patience *i.* the promises	Heb.6.12
when he desired to *i.* the blessing	Heb.12.17
futile ways *i.* from your fathers	1 Pet.1.18

INHERITANCE

LORD your God gives you for an *i.*	Dt.4.21
the heathen have come into thy *i.*	Ps.79.1
i. gotten hastily in the beginning	Pr.20.21
Wisdom is good with an *i.*	Ec.7.11
Our *i.* . . . . turned over to strangers	Lam.5.2
let us kill him and have his *i.*	Mt.21.38
my brother divide the *i.* with me	Lk.12.13
he gave them their land as an *i.*	Acts 13.19
For if the *i.* is by the law, it is	Gal.3.18
guarantee of our *i.* until we acquire	Eph.1.14
has any *i.* in the kingdom of Christ	Eph.5.5
to share in the *i.* of the saints	Col.1.12
will receive the *i.* as your reward	Col.3.24
receive the promised eternal *i.*	Heb.9.15
to an *i.* which is imperishable	1 Pet.1.4

INIQUITY

visiting the *i.* of the fathers upon	Ex.20.5
for our *i.* have risen higher than	Ezra 9.6
my sins, and blot out all my *i.*	Ps.51.9
Thou hast set our *i.* before thee	Ps.90.8
who forgives all your *i.*	Ps.103.3
If thou . . . shouldst mark *i.*, Lord	Ps.130.3
The *i.* of the wicked ensnare him	Pr.5.22
you have wearied me with your *i.*	Is.43.24
he was bruised for our *i.*	Is.53.5
and he shall bear their *i.*	Is.53.11
but your *i.* have made a separation	Is.59.2
Your *i.* have turned these away	Jer.5.25
Though our *i.* testify against us	Jer.14.7
By the multitude of your *i.*	Ezek.28.18
I will punish you for all your *i.*	Am.3.2
Blessed . . . whose *i.* are forgiven	Rom.4.7
name of the Lord depart from *i.*	2 Tim.2.19
to redeem us from all *i.*	Tit.2.14

I will be merciful toward their *i.* — Heb.8.12
and God has remembered her *i.* — Rev.18.5

INJUSTICE
You shall do no *i.* in judgment — Lev.19.15
than great revenues with *i.* — Pr.16.8
He who sows *i.* will reap calamity — Pr.22.8
i. has blossomed, pride has budded — Ezek.7.10
iniquity, you have reaped *i.* — Hos.10.13
is there *i.* on God's part? — Rom.9.14

INK
I wrote them with *i.* on the scroll — Jer.36.18
not with *i.* but with the Spirit of — 2 Cor.3.3
would rather not use paper and *i.* — 2 Jn.12
rather not write with pen and *i.* — 3 Jn.13

INNER
The *i.* sanctuary he prepared in — 1 Kg.6.19
into the *i.* court of the house — Ezek.8.16
down into the *i.* part of the ship — Jon.1.5
he put them into the *i.* prison — Acts 16.24
our *i.* nature is being renewed — 2 Cor.4.16
through his Spirit in the *i.* man — Eph.3.16
hope . . . enters into the *i.* shrine — Heb.6.19

INNOCENT
Lord, wilt thou slay an *i.* people? — Gen.20.4
takes a bribe to slay an *i.* person — Dt.27.25
who that was *i.* ever perished? — Job 4.7
Though I am *i.*, I cannot answer him — Job 9.15
he mocks at the calamity of the *i.* — Job 9.23
I am *i.*, and God has taken away my — Job 34.5
not take a bribe against the *i.* — Ps.15.5
and *i.* of great transgression — Ps.19.13
they poured out *i.* blood — Ps.106.38
deprive the *i.* of his right — Is.5.23
nor shed *i.* blood in this place — Jer.22.3
wise as serpents and *i.* as doves — Mt.10.16
I am *i.* of this man's blood — Mt.27.24
said, "Certainly this man was *i.*!" — Lk.23.47
that you may be blameless and *i.* — Phil.2.15

INQUIRE
I. of God, we pray thee, that we may — Jg.18.5
I. first for the word of the LORD — 1 Kg.22.5
i. of the LORD for me and for — 2 Chr.34.21
and to *i.* in his temple — Ps.27.4
My people *i.* of a thing of wood — Hos.4.12
do not seek the LORD or *i.* of him — Zeph.1.6
prophets . . . *i.* about this salvation — 1 Pet.1.10

INSCRIBE
Oh that they were *i.* in a book — Job 19.23
i. it in a book, that it may be — Is.30.8
this is the writing that was *i.* — Dan.5.25
i. on the bells of the horses — Zech.14.20
has a name *i.* which no one knows — Rev.19.12

INSCRIPTION
pure gold, and wrote upon it an *i.* — Ex.39.30
the *i.* of the charge against him — Mk.15.26
Whose likeness and *i.* has it? — Lk.20.24
I found also an altar with this *i.* — Acts 17.23

INSIGHT
his words are without *i.* — Job 34.35
understand words of *i.* — Pr.1.2
whatever you get, get *i.* — Pr.4.7
knowledge of the Holy One is *i.* — Pr.9.10
in all wisdom and *i.* the mystery of — Eph.1.9
my *i.* into the mystery of Christ — Eph.3.4

INSOLENT
For *i.* men have risen against me — Ps.54.3

Thou dost rebuke the *i.* — Ps.119.21
the youth will be *i.* to the elder — Is.3.5
You will see no more the *i.* people — Is.33.19
i., haughty, boastful, inventors of — Rom.1.30

INSPIRE
And he has *i.* him to teach — Ex.35.34
I. decisions are on the lips of a — Pr.16.10
David, *i.* by the Spirit, calls him — Mt.22.43
And *i.* by the Spirit he came into — Lk.2.27
which he mightily *i.* within me — Col.1.29
with joy *i.* by the Holy Spirit — 1 Th.1.6
All scripture is *i.* by God — 2 Tim.3.16

INSTRUCT
gavest thy good Spirit to *i.* them — Neh.9.20
I will *i.* you and teach you the way — Ps.32.8
or as his counselor has *i.* him? — Is.40.13
able to *i.* one another — Rom.15.14
mind of the Lord so as to *i.* him? — 1 Cor.2.16
are able to *i.* you for salvation — 2 Tim.3.15
he was *i.* by God, saying, "See that — Heb.8.5

INSTRUCTION
Receive *i.* from his mouth — Job 22.22
fools despise wisdom and *i.* — Pr.1.7
Keep hold of *i.*, do not let go — Pr.4.13
Listen to advice and accept *i.* — Pr.19.20
whatever . . . was written for our *i.* — Rom.15.4
were written down for our *i.* — 1 Cor.10.11
the discipline and *i.* of the Lord — Eph.6.4
be able to give *i.* in sound doctrine — Tit.1.9

INSTRUMENT
the forger of all *i.* of bronze — Gen.4.22
accompanied by the *i.* of David — 2 Chr.29.27
stringed *i.* make you glad — Ps.45.8
he is a chosen *i.* of mine to carry — Acts 9.15
not yield . . . to sin as *i.* of wickedness — Rom.6.13
to God as *i.* of righteousness — Rom.6.13
If even lifeless *i.*, . . . do not give — 1 Cor.14.7

INTEGRITY
He still holds fast his *i.* — Job 2.3
let God know my *i.* — Job 31.6
May *i.* and uprightness preserve me — Ps.25.21
O LORD, for I have walked in my *i.* — Ps.26.1
The *i.* of the upright guides them — Pr.11.3
who walks in *i.* will be delivered — Pr.28.18
in your teaching show *i.*, gravity — Tit.2.7

INTERCEDE
who can *i.* for him? — 1 Sam.2.25
let them *i.* with the LORD of hosts — Jer.27.18
Spirit himself *i.* for us with sighs — Rom.8.26
Christ Jesus . . . indeed *i.* for us? — Rom.8.34

INTERCESSION
made *i.* for the transgressors — Is.53.12
I urge that . . . *i.* . . . be made — 1 Tim.2.1
always lives to make *i.* for them — Heb.7.25

INTEREST
you shall not exact *i.* from him — Ex.22.25
received what was my own with *i.* — Mt.25.27
and his *i.* are divided — 1 Cor.7.34
look not only to his own *i.* — Phil.2.4

INTERPRET
and understanding to *i.* dreams — Dan.5.12
how to *i.* the appearance of the sky — Mt.16.3
he *i.* to them in all the scriptures — Lk.24.27
speak with tongues? Do all *i.*? — 1 Cor.12.30
should pray for the power to *i.* — 1 Cor.14.13

INTERPRETATION

This is its *i*.: the three branches   Gen.40.12
This is its *i*.: the three baskets   Gen.40.18
show me the dream and its *i*.   Dan.2.6
This is the *i*. of the matter: MENE   Dan.5.26
to another the *i*. of tongues   1 Cor.12.10
a revelation, a tongue, or an *i*.   1 Cor.14.26
is a matter of one's own *i*.   2 Pet.1.20

INVISIBLE

his *i*. nature . . . has been . . . perceived   Rom.1.20
He is the image of the *i*. God   Col.1.15
To the King of ages, immortal, *i*.   1 Tim.1.17
he endured as seeing him who is *i*.   Heb.11.27

INVITE

one of you will *i*. his neighbor   Zech.3.10
i. to the marriage feast as many   Mt.22.9
when you are *i*. . . . sit in the lowest   Lk.14.10
i. the poor, the maimed, the lame   Lk.14.13
he *i*. Philip to come up and sit   Acts 8.31
the unbelievers *i*. you to dinner   1 Cor.10.27
those who are *i*. to the marriage   Rev.19.9

INVOKE

the king *i*. the LORD your God   2 Sam.14.11
he began to *i*. a curse on himself   Mt.26.74
By faith Isaac *i*. future blessings   Heb.11.20
you *i*. as Father him who judges   1 Pet.1.17

INWARD

desirest truth in the *i*. being   Ps.51.6
the *i*. mind and heart . . . are deep   Ps.64.6
For thou didst form my *i*. parts   Ps.139.13
shall be hunger in your *i*. parts   Mic.6.14
but *i*. are ravenous wolves   Mt.7.15
He is a Jew who is one *i*.   Rom.2.29
groan *i*. as we wait for adoption   Rom.8.23

IOTA

Not an *i*., not a dot, will pass from   Mt.5.18

IRON

I. is taken out of the earth   Job 28.2
You shall break them with a rod of *i*.   Ps.2.9
I. sharpens *i*.   Pr.27.17
image on its feet of *i*. and clay   Dan.2.34
came to the *i*. gate leading into   Acts 12.10
they had scales like *i*. breastplates   Rev.9.9
he will rule them with a rod of *i*.   Rev.19.15

ISAAC

his birth promised, Gen.17.16,19; 18.10; born, Gen.21.2; offered by Abraham, Gen.22.7–14; marries Rebekah, Gen.24.67; blesses his sons, Gen.27.28–40; dies, Gen.35.29

ISAIAH

prophet, Is.1.1; 2.1; sent to Ahaz, Is.7; sent to Hezekiah, 2 Kg.20.1–19; Is.37.6; 38.5; 39.3; prophesies concerning various nations, Is.7–8; 10; 13–23; 45–47; referred to in Mt.3.3; 4.14; 8.17; 12.17; 13.14; 15.7; Mk.1.2; Jn.1.23; Acts 8.28; Rom.9.27

ISCARIOT

Judas, Mt.10.4; Mk.3.19; his treachery, Mt.26.21–25; Mk.14.18–21; Lk.22.47–48; Jn.18.3; death, Mt.27.5; Acts 1.18

ISHMAEL

(1) son of Abram, Gen.16.15; 17.20; 21.17; 25.17; his descendants, Gen.25.12; 1 Chr.1.29; (2) son of Nethaniah, kills Gedaliah, 2 Kg.25.25; Jer.40.14; 41; (3) others, 1 Chr.8.38; 2 Chr.19.11; Ezra 10.22

ISRAEL

(1) Jacob so named after striving with God, Gen.32.28; 35.10; Hos.12.3; (2) the name of the ten tribes as distinguished from Judah, 2 Sam.2.9

ISSACHAR

(1) son of Jacob, Gen.30.18; 35.23; (2) tribe, Gen.46.13; Jg.5.15; 1 Chr.7.1; (3) territory, occupied by tribe, Jos.19.17; see Gen.49.14; Num.1.28; 26.23; Dt.33.18; Ezek.48.33; Rev.7.7

IVORY

king . . . made a great *i*. throne   1 Kg.10.18
silver, *i*., apes, and peacocks   1 Kg.10.22
From *i*. palaces stringed instruments   Ps.45.8
the houses of *i*. shall perish   Am.3.15
Woe to those who lie upon beds of *i*.   Am.6.4
scented wood, all articles of *i*.   Rev.18.12

JACOB

his birth, Gen.25.26; birthright, Gen.25.33; blessing, Gen.27.27; his vision of the ladder, and vow, Gen.28.10–22; marriages, Gen.29; sons, Gen.29.31–30.24; dealings with Laban, Gen.31; his vision of God's host, Gen.32.1; his prayer, Gen.32.9; wrestles with an angel, Gen.32.24; Hos.12.4; reconciled with Esau, Gen.33; builds an altar at Bethel, Gen.35.1; his grief for Joseph and Benjamin, Gen.37; 42.38; goes down to Egypt, Gen.46; brought before Pharaoh, Gen.47.7; blesses his sons, Gen.48–49; his death, and burial, Gen.49.33; 50; see Ps.105.23; Mal.1.2; Rom.9.10-13; Heb.11.21

JAIRUS

Mk.5.22; Lk.8.41

JAMES

English form of Jacob in the New Testament; (1) (Apostle), son of Zebedee, called, Mt.4.21; Mk.1.19; Lk.5.10; appointed one of the twelve, Mt.10.2; Mk.3.14; Lk.6.13; witnesses Jesus' transfiguration, Mt.17.1–8; Mk.9.2–8; Lk.9.28–36; present at Gethsemane, Mt.26.36–37; Mk.14.32–33; killed by Herod, Acts 12.2; (2) (Apostle), son of Alphaeus, Mt.10.3; Mk.3.18; Lk.6.15; Acts 1.13; (3) (brother of Jesus), Mt.13.55; Mk.6.3; 1 Cor. 15.7; head of church at Jerusalem, Acts 12.17; 15.13; 21.18; Gal.1.19; 2.9; (4) (the father of the Apostle Judas), Lk.6.16; Acts 1.13

JAW

or pierce his *j*. with a hook?   Job 41.2
my tongue cleaves to my *j*.   Ps.22.15
to place on the *j*. of the peoples   Is.30.28
I will put hooks in your *j*.   Ezek.29.4
one who eases the yoke on their *j*.   Hos.11.4

JAWBONE

he found a fresh *j*. of an ass   Jg.15.15
with the *j*. of an ass have I slain   Jg.15.16

JEALOUS

I the LORD your God am a *j*. God   Ex.20.5
God is a devouring fire, a *j*. God   Dt.4.24
I have been very *j*. for the LORD   1 Kg.19.10
The LORD is a *j*. God and avenging   Nah.1.2
am *j*. for Zion with great jealousy   Zech.8.2
love is not *j*. or boastful   1 Cor.13.4

JEALOUSY

This is the law in cases of *j*.   Num.5.29

JEHOAHAZ

stirred me to *j*. with what is no god Dt.32.21
moved him to *j*. with their graven Ps.78.58
not in quarreling and *j*. Rom.13.13
there is *j*. and strife among you 1 Cor.3.3
I feel a divine *j*. for you 2 Cor.11.2
j., anger, selfishness, dissension Gal.5.20
where *j*. and selfish ambition exist Jas.3.16

JEHOAHAZ

(1) son of Jehu, king of Israel, 2 Kg.10.35;
13.4; (2) (Shallum), king of Judah, his evil
reign, 2 Kg.23.31–34; 2 Chr.36.1–3; Jer.22.11–12

JEHOIADA

2 Sam.8.18; high priest, deposes and slays
Athaliah, and restores Jehoash, 2 Kg.11; 2
Chr.23; repairs the temple, 2 Kg.12.7; 2
Chr.24.6–14; abolishes idolatry, 2 Chr.23.16–17

JEHORAM

(1) (son of Jehoshaphat), king of Judah, 1
Kg.22.50; 2 Kg.8.16; his cruelty and death,
2 Chr.21.4,18; (2) (Joram), king of Israel, son
of Ahab, 2 Kg.1.17; 3.1; his evil reign, 2
Kg.3.2; slain by Jehu, 2 Kg.9.24; (3) a priest,
2 Chr.17.8

JEHOSHAPHAT

(1) king of Judah; his good reign, 1 Kg.15.24;
2 Chr.17; his death, 1 Kg.22.50; 2 Chr.21.1;
(2) others, 2 Sam.8.16; 1 Kg.4.17; 2 Kg.9.2;
1 Chr.11.43; 15.24; (3) valley of, Jl.3.2

JEHU

(1) son of Hanani, prophesies against Baasha,
1 Kg.16.1; rebukes Jehoshaphat, 2 Chr.19.2;
20.34; (2) son of Nimshi, to be anointed king of
Israel, 1 Kg.19.16; 2 Kg.9.1–3; his reign, 2
Kg.9.4–10.36; (3) others, 1 Chr.2.38; 4.35;
12.3

JEPHTHAH

Jg.11.1,29; 12.7; 1 Sam.12.11; Heb.11.32

JEREMIAH

(1) prophet, his call and visions, Jer.1; his
mission, Jer.7; his complaint, Jer.20.14; his
message to Zedekiah, Jer.21.3; 34.2; arraigned,
condemned, but delivered, Jer.26; denounces
the false prophet Hananiah, Jer.28.5–17; his
promises of redemption to Israel, Jer.31; dic-
tates a scroll, Jer.36.4; Baruch reads it, Jer.36.8;
imprisoned by Zedekiah, Jer.37–38; released,
Jer.38.7–13; with all the remnant of Israel carried into Egypt, Jer.43.4–7; various predictions,
Jer.46–51; mentioned in Dan.9.2; Mt.2.17;
16.14; 27.9; (2) others, 2 Kg.23.31; 1 Chr.5.24;
12.4,10

JERICHO

15 miles northeast of Jerusalem, in the Jordan
valley, 5 miles from the river, Num.22.1; the
spies at, Jos.2.1; capture of, Jos.6.20 (Heb.
11.30); rebuilt by Hiel, 1 Kg.16.34; *see* Jos.6.26

JEROBOAM I

1 Kg.11.26; promoted by Solomon, 1 Kg.11.28;
Ahijah's prophecy to, 1 Kg.11.29–39; made
king, 1 Kg.12.20 (2 Chr.10); his idolatry,
withered hand, denunciation, 1 Kg.12; 13;
14; death, 1 Kg.14.20; evil example, 1 Kg.15.34

JEROBOAM II

2 Kg.13.13; 14.23–29

JERUSALEM

the religious capital of Palestine; Adoni-zedek,
king of, slain by Joshua, Jos.10; David reigns
there, 2 Sam.5.6–10; the ark brought there, 2
Sam.6; saved from the pestilence, 2 Sam.24.16–
25; temple built at, 1 Kg.5–8; 2 Chr.1–7; sufferings from war, 1 Kg.14.25; 2 Kg.14.14; 25;
2 Chr.12; 25.24; 36; capture and destruction by
Nebuchadrezzar, Jer.52.12–15; captives return,
and rebuilding of the temple begun by Cyrus,
Ezra 1–3; continued by Artaxerxes, Neh.2; wall
rebuilt and dedicated by Nehemiah, Neh.12.38;
abominations there, Ezek.16.2; presentation of
Christ at, Lk.2.22; Christ rides into, Mt.21.1–
11; Mk.11.7–11; Lk.19.28–38; Jn.12.12–15;
laments over it, Mt.23.37–39; Lk.13.34; 19.41;
foretells its destruction, Mt.24; Mk.13; Lk.13.34;
19.43; 21; disciples filled with the Holy Spirit
at, Acts 2.4; the new, Rev.21.2

JESSE

Ru.4.17; 1 Sam.16.10; Ps.72.20; Is.11.1;
Lk.3.32; Rom.15.12

JESUS

(1) his birth foretold, Lk.1.26–38; born,
Mt.1.18–25; Lk.2.1–7; is circumcised and presented in the temple, Lk.2.21–38; visited by
the wise men, Mt.2.1–12; taken to Egypt, Mt.
2.13–18; brought to Nazareth, Mt.2.19–23; Lk.
2.39; visits Jerusalem when twelve years of
age, Lk. 2.41–50; is baptized, Mt.3.13–17;
Mk.1.9–11; Lk.3.21–22; tempted by the devil,
Mt.4.1–11; Mk.1.12–13; Lk.4.1–13; calls his
disciples, Mt. 4.18–22; 9.9; Jn.1.35–51; delivers
the Sermon on the Mount, Mt.5–7; commis-
sions the twelve, Mt.10.1–4; Mk.3.13–19;
Lk.6.12–16; teaches in parables, Mt.13.1–52;
Mk.4.1–34; performs miracles, Mk.4.35–5.43;
Jn.2.1–11; foretells his death and resurrection,
Mt.16.21–26; Mk. 10.32–34; Lk.18.31–34;
is transfigured, Mt.17.1–8; Mk.9.2–8; Lk.
9.28–36; his triumphal entry into Jerusalem,
Mt.21.1–11; Mk.11.1–11; Lk.19.28–44; Jn.
12.12–19; institutes the Lord's supper, Mt.
26.26–29; Mk.14.22–25; Lk.22.15–20; 1 Cor.
11.23–25; farewell discourses to his disciples,
Jn.14–16; his high priestly prayer, Jn.17; is
betrayed, arrested, and forsaken, Mt.26.47–56;
Mk.14.43–50; Lk.22.47–53; Jn.18.2–14; crucified, Mt.27.33–56; Mk.15.22–41; Lk.23.33–49;
Jn.19.17–30; appears to his disciples after his
resurrection, Mt.28.9–20; Mk.16.9–18; Lk.
24.13–49; Jn.20.11–31; Acts 1.3–8; 1 Cor.
15.5–7; the great commission, Mt.28.18–20;
his ascension, Mk.16.19–20; Lk.24.50–53; Acts
1.9–11; *see* CHRIST; (2) Mt.27.16–17 note *k*;
(3) Justus, Col.4.11

JEWEL

for wisdom is better than *j*. Pr.8.11
She is far more precious than *j*. Pr.31.10
like . . . *j*. . . . they shall shine Zech.9.16
imperishable *j*. of a gentle . . . spirit 1 Pet.3.4
were adorned with every *j*. Rev.21.19

JEZEBEL

wife of Ahab, 1 Kg.16.31; kills the prophets, 1
Kg.18.4; 19.2; causes Naboth to be put to
death, 1 Kg.21; her violent death, 2 Kg.9.30–37

JEZREEL

Jos.17.16; 1 Sam.29.11; 2 Sam.4.4; 2 Kg.9.30

JOAB

(1) 2 Sam.2.13; nephew of David, and captain of the host, 2 Sam.8.16; kills Abner, 2 Sam. 3.27; intercedes for Absalom, 2 Sam.14; kills him in an oak, 2 Sam.18.14; reproves David's grief, 2 Sam.19.5–8; kills Amasa, 2 Sam.20.9–10; unwillingly numbers the people, 2 Sam.24.3–9 (1 Chr.21.3–6); joins Adonijah's usurpation, 1 Kg.1.7; killed by Solomon's command, 1 Kg.2.5–34; (2) Othniel's grandson, 1 Chr.4.14; (3) Ezra 2.6; 8.9; Neh.7.11

JOASH

(1) father of Gideon, Jg.6.11; (2) (Jehoash), king of Israel, 2 Kg.13.10; visits Elisha, 2 Kg.13.14; defeats the Syrians, 2 Kg.13.25; defeats Amaziah, 2 Kg.14.8–14; (3) king of Judah, 2 Chr.23.3; 24.1–14; repairs the temple, 2 Kg.12; 2 Chr.24; kills Zechariah, 2 Chr.24.22; killed by his servants, 2 Kg.12.19–21; 2 Chr.24.23–27; (4) others, 1 Kg.22.26; 1 Chr. 4.22; 12.3; 27.28

JOB

his character, Job 1.1,8; 2.3; Ezek.14.14,20; his afflictions and patience, Job 1.13–21; 2.7–10; Jas.5.11; complains of his life, Job 3; reproves his friends, Job 6–7; 9–10; 12–14; 16–17; 19; 21; 23–24; 26–30; solemnly protests his integrity, Job 31; humbles himself, Job 40.3–5; 42.1–6; God accepts and doubly blesses, Job 42.10

JOHN

English form of Johanan; (1) the Apostle, called, Mt.4.21; Mk.1.19; Lk.5.10; reproved, Mt.20. 20–23; Mk.10.35–40; Lk.9.49–50; sent to prepare the passover, Lk.22.8; his care for Mary the mother of Jesus, Jn.19.27; meets for prayer, Acts 1.13; accompanies Peter before the council, Acts 3–4; (2) (Mark) Acts 12.12, 25; see MARK; (3) the Baptist, his birth and circumcision, Lk.1.13–25,57–80; preaching and baptism of, Mt.3; Mk.1; Lk.3; Jn.1.6; 3.26; Acts 1.5; 13.24; imprisoned by Herod, Mt.4.12; Mk.1.14; Lk.3.20; beheaded, Mt.14; Mk.6.25; sends his disciples to Christ, Mt.11.2; Lk.7.19; Christ's testimony concerning, Mt.11.11; 17.12–13; Mk.9.11–13; Lk.7.27–28; his disciples receive the Holy Spirit, Acts 19.3–6; (4) Jewish dignitary, Acts 4.6; (5) the seer, Rev.1.4,9; 22.8

JOIN

I . . . j. words together against you	Job 16.4
Woe to those who j. house to house	Is.5.8
What therefore God has j. together	Mk.10.9
the whole structure is j. together	Eph.2.21
j. and knit together by every joint	Eph.4.16

JONAH

2 Kg.14.25; Jon.1.1; Mt.12.39–40; 16.4; Lk.11.32

JONATHAN

(1) son of Saul, defeats the Philistines, 1 Sam.13.2–3; 14.1–15; his love for David, 1 Sam.18.1; 19; 20; 23.16; killed by the Philistines, 1 Sam.31.2; David's lamentation for, 2 Sam. 1.17–27; (2) son of Abiathar, 2 Sam.15.27; 1 Kg.1.42; (3) one of David's nephews, 2

Sam.21.21; 1 Chr.20.7; (4) son of Gershom, Jg.18.30

JORDAN

river, waters of, divided for the Israelites, Jos.3; 4; Ps.114.3; by Elijah and Elisha, 2 Kg.2.8, 13–14; Naaman's leprosy cured at, 2 Kg.5.10–14; John baptizes there, Mt.3; Mk.1.5; Lk.3.3; see Job 40.23; Ps.42.6; Jer.12.5; 49.19; Zech.11.3

JOSEPH

(1) son of Jacob, Gen.30.24; see Ps.105.17; Acts 7.9; Heb.11.22; his dreams, and the jealousy of his brothers, Gen.37.5; sold to the Ishmaelites, Gen.37.28; slave to Potiphar, Gen.39; resists Potiphar's wife, Gen.39.7–13; interprets the dreams of Pharaoh's servants, Gen.40, and of Pharaoh, predicting famine, Gen.41.25; made ruler of Egypt, Gen.41.39–41; prepares for the famine, Gen.41.48–49; receives his brothers and father, Gen.42–46; gives direction concerning his bones, Gen.50.25; his death, Gen.50.26; (2) of Arimathea, Mt.27.57; Mk.15.42–43; Lk.23.50; Jn.19.38; (3) (Barsabbas), Justus, Acts 1.23; (4) others, Num.13.7; Ezra 10.42; Neh.12.14; Lk.3.24

JOSHUA

son of Nun, Num.14.6; 1 Chr.7.27; Heb.4.8; ministers to Moses, Ex.24.13; 32.17; 33.11; spies out Canaan, Num.13.16; appointed to succeed Moses, Num.27.18–23; 34.17; Dt.1.38; 3.28; 34.9; reassured by God, Jos.1; crosses river Jordan, Jos.3; erects memorial pillars, Jos.4; assaults and destroys Jericho, Jos.6; condemns Achan, Jos.7; subdues Ai, Jos.8; his victories, Jos.10–12; apportions the land, Jos. 14–21; his charge to the Reubenites, Jos.22; exhortation to the people, Jos.23; reminds them of God's mercies, Jos.24; renews the covenant, Jos.24.14–28; his death, Jos.24.29; Jg.2.8; his curse, Jos.6.26, fulfilled, 1 Kg.16.34; (2) others, 1 Sam.6.14; 2 Kg.23.8; Hag.1.1; Zech. 3.1–9

JOSIAH

(1) 2 Kg.21.24; prophecy concerning, 1 Kg.13.2; fulfilled, 2 Kg.23.15–18; reigns well, 2 Kg.22; repairs the temple, 2 Kg.22.3–7; hears the words of the book of the law, 2 Kg.22.8–13; Huldah's message from God to him, 2 Kg.22.14–20; reads the book of the covenant, Kg.23; keeps the passover, 2 Chr.35; slain by Pharaoh Neco at Megiddo, 2 Kg.23.29; (2) son of Zephaniah, Zech.6.10

JOTHAM

(1) son of Jerubbaal (Gideon), Jg.9.5; (2) king of Judah, 2 Kg.15.32; 2 Chr.27

JOY

sing for j. before the LORD	1 Chr.16.33
there was great j. in Jerusalem	2 Chr.30.26
the j. of the LORD is your strength	Neh.8.10
the widow's heart to sing for j.	Job 29.13
all the sons of God shouted for j.?	Job 38.7
in thy presence there is fulness of j.	Ps.16.11
but j. comes with the morning	Ps.30.5
is the j. of all the earth	Ps.48.2
let thy saints shout for j.	Ps.132.9
they shall obtain j. and gladness	Is.35.10

I will turn their mourning into *j.*   Jer.31.13
the *j.* of all the earth?   Lam.2.15
rejoiced exceedingly with great *j.*   Mt.2.10
more *j.* in heaven over one sinner   Lk.15.7
but your sorrow will turn into *j.*   Jn.16.20
my brethren . . . my *j.* and crown   Phil.4.1
For you are our glory and *j.*   1 Th.2.20
Count it all *j.*, my brethren, when   Jas.1.2

JOYFUL

not distinguish . . . the *j.* shout from   Ezra 3.13
for the Lord had made them *j.*   Ezra 6.22
Make a *j.* noise to God, all the earth   Ps.66.1
But let the righteous be *j.*   Ps.68.3
Make a *j.* noise to the Lord, all   Ps.100.1
city is forsaken, the *j.* city   Jer.49.25

JUDAH

(1) son of Jacob, Gen.29.35; his descendants, Gen.38; 46.12; Num.1.26; 26.19; 1 Chr.4; pledges himself for Benjamin, Gen.43.9; his interview with Joseph, Gen.44.18–34; blessed by Jacob, Gen.49.8–12; (2) tribe of, their blessing by Moses, Dt.33.7; their inheritance, Jos.15; they make David king, 2 Sam.2.4; (3) others, Ezra 3.9; 10.23; Neh.11.9

JUDAS

Greek form of Judah, (1) Apostle, son of James, Lk.6.16; Jn.14.22; Acts 1.13; (2) the brother of Jesus, Mt.13.55; Mk.6.3; (3) of Galilee, Acts 5.37; (4) (Barsabbas), Acts 15.22

JUDAS ISCARIOT

Mt.10.4; Mk.3.19; Lk.6.16; Jn.6.70–71; betrays Jesus, Mt.26.14–16,47–56; Mk.14.10,43–50; Lk.22.3–6,47–53; Jn.13.26–30; 18.2–11; kills himself, Mt.27.5; Acts 1.18

JUDEA

Ezra 9.9; Mt.2.5; Mk.1.5; Jn.4.3; Acts 28.21; Gal.1.22

JUDGE (verb)

the Lord *j.* between me and you   1 Sam.24.12
for he comes to *j.* the earth   1 Chr.16.33
j. me . . . according to my righteousness   Ps.7.8
j. the world with righteousness   Ps.96.13
He shall *j.* between the nations   Is.2.4
He shall not *j.* by what his eyes see   Is.11.3
I will *j.* between sheep and   Ezek.34.22
J. not, and you will not be *j.*   Lk.6.37
The Father *j.* no one, but has given   Jn.5.22
You *j.* according to the flesh, I *j.*   Jn.8.15
the ruler of this world is *j.*   Jn.16.11
then how could God *j.* the world?   Rom.3.6
not know that we are to *j.* angels?   1 Cor.6.3
But when we are *j.* by the Lord   1 Cor.11.32
that you may not be *j.*   Jas.5.9
dead were *j.* by what was written   Rev.20.12

JUDGMENT

but I will bring *j.* on the nation   Gen.15.14
You shall do no injustice in *j.*   Lev.19.15
and enters into *j.* with you?   Job 22.4
for any man to go before God in *j.*   Job 34.23
the wicked will not stand in the *j.*   Ps.1.5
but it is God who executes *j.*   Ps.75.7
Teach me good *j.* and knowledge   Ps.119.66
Enter not into *j.* with thy servant   Ps.143.2
God will bring every deed into *j.*   Ec.12.14
By oppression and *j.* he was taken   Is.53.8

the court sat in *j.*, and the books   Dan.7.10
my *j.* goes forth as the light   Hos.6.5
whoever kills shall be liable to *j.*   Mt.5.21
arise at the *j.* with this generation   Lk.11.32
but has given all *j.* to the Son   Jn.5.22
my *j.* is true, for it is not I alone   Jn.8.16
Now is the *j.* of this world   Jn.12.31
God's righteous *j.* will be revealed   Rom.2.5
all stand before the *j.* seat of God   Rom.14.10
die once, and after that comes *j.*   Heb.9.27
yet mercy triumphs over *j.*   Jas.2.13
to be kept until the *j.*   2 Pet.2.4
pronounce a reviling *j.* upon him   Jude 9
In one hour has thy *j.* come   Rev.18.10
for his *j.* are true and just   Rev.19.2

JUST

A full and *j.* weight you shall have   Dt.25.15
Let me be weighed in a *j.* balance   Job 31.6
For thou hast maintained my *j.* cause   Ps.9.4
The Lord is *j.* in all his ways   Ps.145.17
A *j.* balance and scales are the   Pr.16.11
The way of the Lord is not *j.*   Ezek.18.25
rain on the *j.* and on the unjust   Mt.5.45
my judgment is *j.*, because I seek   Jn.5.30
Their condemnation is *j.*   Rom.3.8
commandment is holy and *j.* and good   Rom.7.12
God deems it *j.* to repay with   2 Th.1.6
received a *j.* retribution   Heb.2.2
the spirits of *j.* men made perfect   Heb.12.23
he is faithful and *j.*   1 Jn.1.9
for his judgments are true and *j.*   Rev.19.2

JUSTICE

He executes *j.* for the fatherless   Dt.10.18
You shall not pervert *j.*   Dt.16.19
the Almighty will not pervert *j.*   Job 34.12
to do *j.* to the fatherless   Ps.10.18
For the Lord loves *j.*   Ps.37.28
j. to the weak and the fatherless   Ps.82.3
I will sing of loyalty and of *j.*   Ps.101.1
A worthless witness mocks at *j.*   Pr.19.28
but from the Lord a man gets *j.*   Pr.29.26
seek *j.*, correct oppression   Is.1.17
For the Lord is a God of *j.*   Is.30.18
For I the Lord love *j.*   Is.61.8
Do *j.* and righteousness   Jer.22.3
But let *j.* roll down like waters   Am.5.24
Lord require of you but to do *j.*   Mic.6.8
j. and mercy and faith   Mt.23.23
serves to show the *j.* of God   Rom.3.5

JUSTIFY

so that thou art *j.* in thy sentence   Ps.51.4
Yet wisdom is *j.* by her deeds   Mt.11.19
doers of the law who will be *j.*   Rom.2.13
For if Abraham was *j.* by works   Rom.4.2
since we are *j.* by faith, we have   Rom.5.1
those whom he *j.* he also glorified   Rom.8.30
man is not *j.* by works of the law   Gal.2.16
God would *j.* the Gentiles by faith   Gal.3.8
no man is *j.* before God by the law   Gal.3.11
You see that a man is *j.* by works   Jas.2.24

KEEP

you shall *k.* my covenant, you and   Gen.17.9
would *k.* the passover to the Lord   Ex.12.48
the sabbath day, to *k.* it holy   Ex.20.8
So you shall *k.* my commandments   Lev.22.31

The LORD bless you and *k*. you	Num.6.24
K. back thy servant also from	Ps.19.13
O God, do not *k*. silence	Ps.83.1
nor will he *k*. his anger for ever	Ps.103.9
to those who *k*. his covenant	Ps.103.18
I will *k*. thy law continually	Ps.119.44
The LORD will *k*. you from all evil	Ps.121.7
K. your heart with all vigilance	Pr.4.23
k. my teachings as the apple of	Pr.7.2
Fear God, and *k*. his commandments	Ec.12.13
Thou dost *k*. him in perfect peace	Is.26.3
If you *k*. my commandments	Jn.15.10
Holy Father, *k*. them in thy name	Jn.17.11
the women should *k*. silence	1 Cor.14.34
will *k*. your hearts and your minds	Phil.4.7
let him *k*. his tongue from evil	1 Pet.3.10
All who *k*. his commandments abide	1 Jn.3.24
k. yourselves in the love of God	Jude 21

KIDRON

2 Sam.15.23; 2 Kg.23.6; Jer.31.40; Jn.18.1	

KILL

his brother Abel, and *k*. him	Gen.4.8
heard of it, he sought to *k*. Moses	Ex.2.15
You shall not *k*.	Ex.20.13
Saul my father seeks to *k*. you	1 Sam.19.2
the men of old, 'You shall not *k*.	Mt.5.21
for Herod wants to *k*. you	Lk.13.31
Do not *k*., Do not steal, Do not bear	Lk.18.20
Jews sought all the more to *k*. him	Jn.5.18
passed, the Jews plotted to *k*. him	Acts 9.23
Rise, Peter; *k*. and eat	Acts 10.13

KIN

any one near of *k*. to him	Lev.18.6
for you are next of *k*.	Ru.3.9
the king is near of *k*. to us	2 Sam.19.42
in his own country . . . among his own *k*.	Mk.6.4

KIND

If you will be *k*. to his people	2 Chr.10.7
A man who is *k*. benefits himself	Pr.11.17
He who is *k*. to the poor lends to	Pr.19.17
the Most High . . . is *k*. to the ungrateful	Lk.6.35
Love is patient and *k*.	1 Cor.13.4
k. to one another, tenderhearted	Eph.4.32
it was *k*. of you to share my	Phil.4.14
k., and submissive to their husbands	Tit.2.5
be submissive . . . not only to the *k*.	1 Pet.2.18

KINDLED

Jacob's anger was *k*. against Rachel	Gen.30.2
a fire is *k*. by my anger, and it	Dt.32.22
Eliab's anger was *k*. against David	1 Sam.17.28
of the LORD was *k*. against Uzzah	1 Chr.13.10
My wrath is *k*. against you	Job 42.7
a fire was *k*. against Jacob	Ps.78.21
and would that it were already *k*.	Lk.12.49
heavens will be *k*. and dissolved	2 Pet.3.12

KINDLY

May the LORD deal *k*. with you	Ru.1.8
Julius treated Paul *k*.	Acts 27.3
remember us *k*. and long to see us	1 Th.3.6
be . . . *k*. to every one	2 Tim.2.24

KINDNESS

whose *k*. has not forsaken the living	Ru.2.20
I may show him *k*. for Jonathan's	2 Sam.9.1
He who withholds *k*. from a friend	Job 6.14
For he did not remember to show *k*.	Ps.109.16
and to love *k*., and to walk humbly	Mic.6.8

God's *k*. is meant to lead you	Rom.2.4
Note then . . . God's *k*. to you	Rom.11.22
loving *k*. of God our Savior appeared	Tit.3.4
you have tasted the *k*. of the Lord	1 Pet.2.3

KING

Now there arose a new *k*. over Egypt	Ex.1.8
there was no *k*. in Israel	Jg.18.1
but we will have a a *k*. over us	1 Sam.8.19
shouted, "Long live the *k*.!"	1 Sam.10.24
that the *K*. of glory may come in	Ps.24.9
For God is the *k*. of all the earth	Ps.47.7
O LORD of hosts, my *k*. and my God	Ps.84.3
and a great *K*. above all gods	Ps.95.3
and faithfulness preserve the *k*.	Pr.20.28
In the year that *K*. Uzziah died	Is.6.1
for my eyes have seen the *K*.	Is.6.5
a *k*. will reign in righteousness	Is.32.1
the *K*. of Israel and his Redeemer	Is.44.6
for I am a great *K*., says the LORD	Mal.1.14
who has been born *k*. of the Jews?	Mt.2.2
your *k*. is coming to you, humble and	Mt.21.5
This is Jesus the *K*. of the Jews	Mt.27.37
salute him, "Hail, *K*. of the Jews!"	Mk.15.18
saying that he himself is Christ a *k*.	Lk.23.2
the Lord, even the *K*. of Israel	Jn.12.13
Pilate said . . . "So you are a *k*.?"	Jn.18.37
that there is another *k*., Jesus	Acts 17.7
Wherefore, O *K*. Agrippa, I was	Acts 26.19
K. of ages, immortal, invisible	1 Tim.1.17
k. of Salem, that is, *k*. of peace	Heb.7.2
Just and true . . . O *K*. of the ages	Rev.15.3
K. of kings and Lord of lords	Rev.19.16

KINGDOM

The beginning of his *k*. was Babel	Gen.10.10
come to the *k*. for such a time as	Est.4.14
and his *k*. rules over all	Ps.103.19
the glorious splendor of thy *k*.	Ps.145.12
Thy *k*. is an everlasting *k*.	Ps.145.13
and the *k*. shall be the LORD's	Ob.21
for the *k*. of heaven is at hand	Mt.4.17
Thy *k*. come, Thy will be done	Mt.6.10
the *k*. of God has come upon you	Mt.12.28
the keys of the *k*. of heaven	Mt.16.19
Then the *k*. of heaven shall be	Mt.25.1
if a *k*. is divided against itself	Mk.3.24
The *k*. of God is as if a man should	Mk.4.26
You are not far from the *k*. of God	Mk.12.34
The *k*. of God has come near to you	Lk.10.9
k. of God is in the midst of you	Lk.17.21
as my Father appointed a *k*. for me	Lk.22.29
the *k*. of God does not mean food	Rom.14.17
the *k*. of God does not consist	1 Cor.4.20
delivers the *k*. to God the Father	1 Cor.15.24
who through faith conquered *k*.	Heb.11.33
receiving a *k*. that cannot be	Heb.12.28
made us a *k*., priests to his God	Rev.1.6
The *k*. of the world has become	Rev.11.15

KISS (noun)

profuse are the *k*. of an enemy	Pr.27.6
betray the Son of man with a *k*.?	Lk.22.48
Greet one another with a holy *k*.	Rom.16.16
Greet . . . with the *k*. of love	1 Pet.5.14

KISS (verb)

k. his feet, lest he be angry	Ps.2.12
The one I shall *k*. is the man	Mt.26.48

she has not ceased to *k*. my feet   Lk.7.45
wept and embraced Paul and *k*. him   Acts 20.37
KNEE
cried before him, "Bow the *k*.!"   Gen.41.43
and make firm the feeble *k*.   Is.35.3
To me every *k*. shall bow   Is.45.23
who have not bowed the *k*. to Baal   Rom.11.4
every *k*. shall bow to me   Rom.14.11
name of Jesus every *k*. should bow   Phil.2.10
KNEW
and they *k*. that they were naked   Gen.3.7
that I *k*. where I might find him   Job 23.3
Before I formed you . . . I *k*. you   Jer.1.5
I declare to them, 'I never *k*. you   Mt.7.23
You *k*. that I reap where I have not   Mt.25.26
But he *k*. their thoughts, and he   Lk.6.8
yet the world *k*. him not   Jn.1.10
For Jesus *k*. from the first who   Jn.6.64
For he *k*. who was to betray him   Jn.13.11
although they *k*. God they did not   Rom.1.21
made him to be sin who *k*. no sin   2 Cor.5.21
KNOCK
k., and it will be opened to you   Mt.7.7
Behold, I stand at the door and *k*.   Rev.3.20
KNOW
that you may *k*. that I am the LORD   Ex.8.22
Moses did not *k*. that the skin of   Ex.34.29
Now Samuel did not yet *k*. the LORD   1 Sam.3.7
Make me *k*. my transgression and my   Job 13.23
For I *k*. that my Redeemer lives   Job 19.25
I *k*. that thou canst do all things   Job 42.2
Make me to *k*. thy ways, O LORD   Ps.25.4
Be still, and *k*. that I am God   Ps.46.10
K. that the LORD is God! It is he   Ps.100.3
For he *k*. our frame; he remembers   Ps.103.14
Search me, O God, and *k*. my heart   Ps.139.23
Therefore my people shall *k*. my name   Is.52.6
'*K*. the LORD,' for they shall all   Jer.31.34
your left hand *k*. what your right   Mt.6.3
no one *k*. the Son except the Father   Mt.11.27
I say to you, I do not *k*. you   Mt.25.12
k. how to give good gifts to your   Lk.11.13
saying, "Woman, I do not *k*. him."   Lk.22.57
Nathanael said . . . "How do you *k*. me?" Jn.1.48
you will *k*. the truth, and the truth   Jn.8.32
We *k*. that God does not listen to   Jn.9.31
I *k*. my own and my own *k*. me   Jn.10.14
I *k*. that he will rise again   Jn.11.24
they *k*. that everything that thou   Jn.17.7
We *k*. that in everything God works   Rom.8.28
Now I *k*. in part; then I shall   1 Cor.13.12
and to *k*. the love of Christ which   Eph.3.19
that I may *k*. him and the power of   Phil.3.10
I *k*. how to be abased, and I *k*.   Phil.4.12
for I *k*. whom I have believed   2 Tim.1.12
The Lord *k*. those who are his   2 Tim.2.19
They profess to *k*. God, but   Tit.1.16
'*K*. the Lord,' for all shall *k*. me   Heb.8.11
you do not *k*. about tomorrow   Jas.4.14
who says "I *k*. him" but disobeys   1 Jn.2.4
who does not love does not *k*. God   1 Jn.4.8
KNOWLEDGE
the tree of the *k*. of good and evil   Gen.2.9
for the LORD is a God of *k*.   1 Sam.2.3
he multiplies words without *k*.   Job 35.16
Such *k*. is too wonderful for me   Ps.139.6

by *k*. the righteous are delivered   Pr.11.9
The tongue of the wise dispenses *k*.   Pr.15.2
God gives wisdom and *k*. and joy   Ec.2.26
give *k*. of salvation to his people   Lk.1.77
through the law comes *k*. of sin   Rom.3.20
"*K*." puffs up, but love builds up   1 Cor.8.1
understand all mysteries and all *k*.   1 Cor.13.2
love of Christ which surpasses *k*.   Eph.3.19
of what is falsely called *k*.   1 Tim.6.20
the grace and *k*. of our Lord   2 Pet.3.18

LABAN
(1) hospitality of, Gen.24.29; gives Jacob his
two daughters, Gen.29; envies and oppresses
him, Gen.30.27; 31.1; his dream, Gen.31.24;
his covenant with Jacob, Gen.31.43–50; (2) city,
Dt.1.1
LABOR (verb)
Six days you shall *l*., and do all   Ex.20.9
those who build it *l*. in vain   Ps.127.1
all who *l*. and are heavy-laden   Mt.11.28
reap that for which you did not *l*.   Jn.4.38
Do not *l*. for the food which perishes   Jn.6.27
we *l*., working with our own hands   1 Cor.4.12
but rather let him *l*.   Eph.4.28
did not run in vain or *l*. in vain   Phil.2.16
those who *l*. in preaching   1 Tim.5.17
LABORER
Sweet is the sleep of a *l*.   Ec.5.12
is plentiful, but the *l*. are few   Mt.9.37
The *l*. deserves his wages   1 Tim.5.18
wages of the *l*. who mowed your   Jas.5.4
LAMB
Your *l*. shall be without blemish   Ex.12.5
But if he cannot afford a *l*.   Lev.5.7
The wolf shall dwell with the *l*.   Is.11.6
like a *l*. . . . led to the slaughter   Is.53.7
send you out as *l*. in the midst of   Lk.10.3
L. of God, who takes away the sin   Jn.1.29
or a *l*. before its shearer is dumb   Acts 8.32
paschal *l*., has been sacrificed   1 Cor.5.7
like that of a *l*. without blemish   1 Pet.1.19
I saw a *L*. standing, as though it   Rev.5.6
Worthy is the *L*. who was slain   Rev.5.12
the throne of God and of the *L*.   Rev.22.1
LAME
he fell, and became *l*.   2 Sam.4.4
then shall the *l*. man leap like a   Is.35.6
to enter life *l*. than with two feet   Mk.9.45
the *l*. walk, lepers are cleansed   Lk.7.22
And a man *l*. from birth was being   Acts 3.2
LAMENT
year by year to *l*. the daughter of   Jg.11.40
Gird on sackcloth and *l*., O priests   Jl.1.13
of women who bewailed and *l*. him   Lk.23.27
I say to you, you will weep and *l*.   Jn.16.20
LAMP
thou art my *l*., O LORD   2 Sam.22.29
Yea, thou dost light my *l*.   Ps.18.28
Thy word is a *l*. to my feet and a   Ps.119.105
spirit of man is the *l*. of the LORD   Pr.20.27
l. of the wicked will be put out   Pr.24.20
Nor do men light a *l*. and put it   Mt.5.15
For when the foolish took their *l*.   Mt.25.3
Your eye is the *l*. of your body   Lk.11.34
be girded and your *l*. burning   Lk.12.35

as to a *l*. shining in a dark	2 Pet.1.19	**LAZARUS**
they need no light of *l*. or sun	Rev.22.5	(1) a poor man, Lk.16.20; (2) brother of
LANGUAGE		Mary and Martha, raised from the dead,
people, and they have all one *l*.	Gen.11.6	Jn.11; 12.1
from a people of strange *l*.	Ps. 114.1	**LEAD**
heard them speaking in his own *l*.	Acts 2.6	let them *l*. me, let them bring me to · Ps.43.3
not know the meaning of the *l*.	1 Cor.14.11	*L*. thou me to the rock that is higher · Ps.61.2
LAODICEA		*l*. me in the way everlasting · Ps.139.24
Col.2.1; 4.16; Rev.1.11; 3.14		a little child shall *l*. them · Is.11.6
LAST		gently *l*. those that are with young · Is.40.11
at *l*. he will stand upon the earth	Job 19.25	And *l*. us not into temptation · Mt.6.13
But many that are first will be *l*.	Mt.19.30	Can a blind man *l*. a blind man? · Lk.6.39
a loud cry, and breathed his *l*.	Mk.15.37	in Christ always *l*. us in triumph · 2 Cor.2.14
I will raise him up at the *l*. day	Jn.6.40	repentance that *l*. to salvation · 2 Cor.7.10
The *l*. enemy to be destroyed is	1 Cor.15.26	to *l*. a life worthy of God · 1 Th.2.12
the *l*. Adam became a life-giving	1 Cor.15.45	that we may *l*. a quiet . . . life · 1 Tim.2.2
at the *l*. trumpet	1 Cor.15.52	**LEADER**
I am the first and the *l*.	Rev.1.17	the *l*. of the people of Judah being · Num.2.3
bowls full of the seven *l*. plagues	Rev.21.9	take one *l*. of every tribe · Num.34.18
LAUGH (verb)		to Jephthah, "Come and be our *l*. · Jg.11.6
Abraham fell on his face and *l*.	Gen.17.17	for he chose Judah as *l*. · 1 Chr.28.4
He who sits in the heavens *l*.	Ps.2.4	a *l*. and commander for the peoples · Is.55.4
a time to weep, and a time to *l*.	Ec.3.4	the *l*. as one who serves · Lk.22.26
And they *l*. at him	Mt.9.24	at his right hand as *L*. and Savior · Acts 5.31
Woe to you that *l*. now	Lk.6.25	Remember your *l*., those who spoke · Heb.13.7
LAUGHTER		Obey your *l*. and submit to them · Heb.13.17
Then our mouth was filled with *l*.	Ps.126.2	Greet all your *l*. and all the saints · Heb.13.24
Even in *l*. the heart is sad	Pr.14.13	**LEAF**
Sorrow is better than *l*.	Ec.7.3	a freshly plucked olive *l*. · Gen.8.11
Let your *l*. be turned to mourning	Jas.4.9	its *l*. does not wither · Ps.1.3
LAW		be like an oak whose *l*. withers · Is.1.30
This is the *l*. which Moses set	Dt.4.44	We all fade like a *l*. · Is.64.6
This book of the *l*. shall not	Jos.1.8	in the distance a fig tree in *l*. · Mk.11.13
delight is in the *l*. of the LORD	Ps.1.2	**LEAH**
The *l*. of the LORD is perfect	Ps.19.7	Gen.29.16,30; 30.19; 49.31; Ru.4.11
refused to walk according to his *l*.	Ps.78.10	**LEAP**
wondrous things out of thy *l*.	Ps.119.18	by my God I can *l*. over a wall · Ps.18.29
I will keep thy *l*. continually	Ps.119.44	then shall the lame man *l*. like a hart · Is.35.6
Oh, how I love thy *l*.! It is my	Ps.119.97	*l*. for joy, for behold, your reward · Lk.6.23
Great peace . . . who love thy *l*.	Ps.119.165	And *l*. up he stood and walked · Acts 3.8
He who keeps the *l*. is a wise son	Pr.28.7	**LEARN**
out of Zion shall go forth the *l*.	Is.2.3	that you may *l*. to fear the LORD · Dt.14.23
I will put my *l*. within them	Jer.31.33	that I may *l*. thy commandments · Ps.119.73
out of Zion shall go forth the *l*.	Mic.4.2	O simple ones, *l*. prudence · Pr.8.5
For the *l*. was given through Moses	Jn.1.17	*l*. to do good; seek justice · Is.1.17
doers of the *l*. . . . will be justified	Rom.2.13	neither shall they *l*. war any more · Mic.4.3
For the *l*. brings wrath, but where	Rom.4.15	Take my yoke . . . and *l*. from me · Mt.11.29
L. came in, to increase the trespass	Rom.5.20	From the fig tree *l*. its lesson · Mk.13.28
That the *l*. is sin? By no means	Rom.7.7	I have *l*., in whatever state I am · Phil.4.11
Apart from the *l*. sin lies dead	Rom.7.8	Let a woman *l*. in silence · 1 Tim.2.11
For I delight in the *l*. of God	Rom.7.22	he *l*. obedience through what he · Heb.5.8
For Christ is the end of the *l*.	Rom.10.4	No one could *l*. that song except · Rev.14.3
does he dare go to *l*. before the	1 Cor.6.1	**LEAST**
but the *l*. does not rest on faith	Gal.3.12	I am the *l*. in my family · Jg.6.15
So that the *l*. was our custodian	Gal.3.24	one of the *l*. of these commandments · Mt.5.19
and so fulfil the *l*. of Christ	Gal.6.2	yet he who is *l*. in the kingdom · Lk.7.28
Now we know that the *l*. is good	1 Tim.1.8	from the *l*. to the greatest · Acts 8.10
since the *l*. has but a shadow of	Heb.10.1	For I am the *l*. of the apostles · 1 Cor.15.9
he who looks into the perfect *l*.	Jas.1.25	I am the very *l*. of all the saints · Eph.3.8
If you really fulfil the royal *l*.	Jas.2.8	**LEAVEN** (noun)
keeps the whole *l*. but fails in one	Jas.2.10	put away *l*. out of your houses · Ex.12.15
LAWYER		is like *l*. which a woman took · Mt.13.33
a *l*., asked him a question, to test	Mt.22.35	Beware of the *l*. of the Pharisees · Mt.16.11
behold a *l*. stood up to put him	Lk.10.25	Cleanse out the old *l*. that you · 1 Cor.5.7
Woe to you *l*.! for you have taken	Lk.11.52	the *l*. of malice and evil · 1 Cor.5.8
speed Zenas the *l*. and Apollos on	Tit.3.13	a little *l*. leavens the whole lump · Gal.5.9

LEBANON

Dt.1.7; **2** Chr.2.8; Ps.29.5; Is.35.2; Hos.14.6

LEND

You shall not *l.* him your money   Lev.25.37
I have *l.* him to the LORD   1 Sam.1.28
is kind to the poor *l.* to the LORD   Pr.19.17
and *l.*, expecting nothing in return   Lk.6.35

LENTILS

gave Esau bread and pottage of *l.*   Gen.25.34
parched grain, beans and *l.*   2 Sam.17.28
a plot of ground full of *l.*   2 Sam.23.11
beans and *l.*, millet and spelt   Ezek.4.9

LEPER

the law of the *l.* for . . . his cleansing   Lev.14.2
a . . . man of valor, but he was a *l.*   2 Kg.5.1
Uzziah was a *l.* to the day of   2 Chr.26.21
in the house of Simon the *l.*   Mt.26.6
And a *l.* came to him beseeching him   Mk.1.40
l. are cleansed, and the deaf hear   Lk.7.22
he was met by ten *l.*   Lk.17.12

LEPROSY

pronounce him unclean; it is *l.*   Lev.13.8
that you may cure him of his *l.*   2 Kg.5.6
And immediately the *l.* left him   Lk.5.13

LETTER

Hezekiah received the *l.* from the   Is.37.14
I Tertius, the writer of this *l.*   Rom.16.22
l. of recommendation to you   2 Cor.3.1
His *l.* are weighty and strong   2 Cor.10.10
See with what large *l.* I am writing   Gal.6.11
speaking . . . as . . . in all his *l.*   2 Pet.3.16

LEVI

(1) son of Jacob, Gen.29.34; avenges Dinah, Gen.34.25; 49.5; (2) same as Matthew, Mk.2.14; (3) others, Lk.3.24,29

LEVITES

descendants of Levi, Ex.6.25; 32.26; their service, Ex.38.21; appointed over the tabernacle, Num.1.50; their divisions, Gershonites, Kohathites, Merarites, Num.3; duties of, Num.4; 8.23–26; 18; their consecration, Num.8.5; inheritance of, Num.35; Dt.18; Jos.21; not to be forsaken, Dt.12.19; 14.27; their genealogies, 1 Chr.6; 9; charged with the temple service, 1 Chr.23–27; organized into divisions by David, 1 Chr.23.6; redivided by Ezra, Ezra 6.18; their sin censured, Ezek.22.26; Mal.1.2

LIAR

a poor man is better than a *l.*   Pr.19.22
he is a *l.* and the father of lies   Jn.8.44
one . . . said, "Cretans are always *l.*   Tit.1.12
Who is the *l.* but he who denies   1 Jn.2.22
not believe God, has made him a *l.*   1 Jn.5.10
and all *l.*, their lot shall be in   Rev.21.8

LIBATION

you shall pour no *l.* thereon   Ex.30.9
there were the *l.* for the burnt   2 Chr.29.35
their *l.* of blood I will not pour   Ps.16.4
as a *l.* upon the sacrificial   Phil.2.17

LIBERTY

proclaim *l.* throughout the land   Lev.25.10
to proclaim *l.* to the captives   Is.61.1
to set at *l.* those who are oppressed   Lk.4.18
the glorious *l.* of the children of   Rom.8.21

why should my *l.* be determined   1 Cor.10.29
to be judged under the law of *l.*   Jas.2.12

LICENTIOUSNESS

not in debauchery and *l.*   Rom.13.13
immorality, impurity, *l.*   Gal.5.19
have given themselves up to *l.*   Eph.4.19
distressed by the *l.* of the wicked   2 Pet.2.7

LIFE

everything that has the breath of *l.*   Gen.1.30
the tree of *l.* also in the midst of   Gen.2.9
I have set before you *l.* and death   Dt.30.19
therefore choose *l.*; that you and   Dt.30.19
The LORD kills and brings to *l.*   1 Sam.2.6
Elisha had restored the dead to *l.*   2 Kg.8.5
Are not the days of my *l.* few?   Job 10.20
Deliver my *l.* from the wicked   Ps.17.13
follow me all the days of my *l.*   Ps.23.6
For my *l.* is spent with sorrow   Ps.31.10
The years of our *l.* are threescore   Ps.90.10
With long *l.* I will satisfy him   Ps.91.16
who redeems your *l.* from the Pit   Ps.103.4
give me *l.* according to thy promise   Ps.119.154
for from it flow the springs of *l.*   Pr.4.23
he who finds me finds *l.*   Pr.8.35
The fear of the LORD prolongs *l.*   Pr.10.27
A gentle tongue is a tree of *l.*   Pr.15.4
So I hated *l.*, because what is done   Ec.2.17
In my vain *l.* I have seen everything   Ec.7.15
awake, some to everlasting *l.*   Dan.12.2
didst bring up my *l.* from the Pit   Jon.2.6
Is not *l.* more than food   Mt.6.25
He who finds his *l.* will lose it   Mt.10.39
loses his *l.* for my sake will find   Mt.16.25
If you would enter *l.*, keep the   Mt.19.17
must I do to inherit eternal *l.*?   Mk.10.17
can add a cubit to his span of *l.*?   Lk.12.25
In him was *l.*, and the *l.* was the   Jn.1.4
believes in the Son has eternal *l.*   Jn.3.36
the Son gives *l.* to whom he will   Jn.5.21
said to them, "I am the bread of *l.*   Jn.6.35
I lay down my *l.* for the sheep   Jn.10.15
I am the resurrection and the *l.*   Jn.11.25
this is eternal *l.*, that they know   Jn.17.3
and killed the Author of *l.*   Acts 3.15
ordained to eternal *l.* believed   Acts 13.48
to eternal *l.* through Jesus Christ   Rom.5.21
who risked their necks for my *l.*   Rom.16.4
but the Spirit gives *l.*   2 Cor.3.6
whose names are in the book of *l.*   Phil.4.3
your *l.* is hid with Christ in God   Col.3.3
God who gives *l.* to all things   1 Tim.6.13
become heirs in hope of eternal *l.*   Tit.3.7
have passed out of death into *l.*   1 Jn.3.14
he who has not the Son . . . has not *l.*   1 Jn.5.12
grant to eat of the tree of *l.*   Rev.2.7
written in the Lamb's book of *l.*   Rev.21.27
take the water of *l.* without price   Rev.22.17

LIFETIME

Absalom in his *l.* had taken   2 Sam.18.18
and his favor is for a *l.*   Ps.30.5
my *l.* is as nothing in thy sight   Ps.39.5
you in your *l.* received your good   Lk.16.25

LIFT

The LORD *l.* up his countenance upon   Num.6.26
I cannot *l.* up my head, for I am   Job 10.15
L. up the light of thy countenance   Ps.4.6

L. up your heads, O gates! and be	Ps.24.7	She makes *l.* garments and sells	Pr.31.24
To thee, O LORD, I *l.* up my soul	Ps.25.1	Go and buy a *l.* waistcloth, and put	Jer.13.1
I *l.* up my eyes to the hills	Ps.121.1	he said to the man clothed in *l.*	Ezek.10.2
L. up your eyes on high and see	Is.40.26	and behold, a man clothed in *l.*	Dan.10.5
as Moses *l.* up the serpent in the	Jn.3.14	wrapped it in a clean *l.* shroud	Mt.27.59
when I am *l.* up from the earth	Jn.12.32	but he left the *l.* cloth and ran	Mk.14.52
he was *l.* up, and a cloud took him	Acts 1.9	was clothed in purple and fine *l.*	Lk.16.19
l. holy hands without anger or	1 Tim.2.8	tomb; he saw the *l.* cloths lying	Jn.20.6
LIGHT		for the fine *l.* is the righteous	Rev.19.8
"Let there be *l.*"; and there was *l.*	Gen.1.3	**LION**	
Israel had *l.* where they dwelt	Ex.10.23	honey from the carcass of the *l.*	Jg.14.9
a pillar of fire to give them *l.*	Ex.13.21	Save me from the mouth of the *l.*	Ps.22.21
The Jews had *l.* and gladness	Est.8.16	will tread on the *l.* and the adder	Ps.91.13
They grope in the dark without *l.*	Job 12.25	the righteous are bold as a *l.*	Pr.28.1
and *l.* will shine on your ways	Job 22.28	a living dog is better than a dead *l.*	Ec.9.4
Lift up the *l.* of thy countenance	Ps.4.6	the *l.* shall eat straw like the ox	Is.11.7
The LORD is my *l.* and my salvation	Ps.27.1	I was rescued from the *l.* mouth	2 Tim.4.17
Oh send out thy *l.* and thy truth	Ps.43.3	stopped the mouths of *l.*	Heb.11.33
L. dawns for the righteous	Ps.97.11	prowls around like a roaring *l.*	1 Pet.5.8
L. rises in the darkness for the	Ps.112.4	lo, the *L.* of the tribe of Judah	Rev.5.5
to my feet and a *l.* to my path	Ps.119.105	**LIPS**	
L. is sweet, and it is pleasant for	Ec.11.7	Job did not sin with his *l.*	Job 2.10
I form *l.* and create darkness	Is.45.7	my *l.* will not speak falsehood	Job 27.4
And nations shall come to your *l.*	Is.60.3	the LORD cut off all flattering *l.*	Ps.12.3
my judgment goes forth as the *l.*	Hos.6.5	Let the lying *l.* be dumb	Ps.31.18
He will bring me forth to the *l.*	Mic.7.9	My *l.* will pour forth praise	Ps.119.171
You are the *l.* of the world	Mt.5.14	Truthful *l.* endure for ever	Pr.12.19
Let your *l.* so shine before men	Mt.5.16	Lying *l.* are an abomination to the	Pr.12.22
a *l.* for revelation to the Gentiles	Lk.2.32	The *l.* of the wise spread knowledge	Pr.15.7
lest the *l.* in you be darkness	Lk.11.35	for I am a man of unclean *l.*	Is.6.5
and the life was the *l.* of men	Jn.1.4	This people honors me with their *l.*	Mt.15.8
I am the *l.* of the world	Jn.8.12	he confesses with his *l.*	Rom.10.10
Walk while you have the *l.*	Jn.12.35	no guile was found on his *l.*	1 Pet.2.22
a *l.* to those who are in darkness	Rom.2.19	**LISTEN**	
Let *l.* shine out of darkness	2 Cor.4.6	but they did not *l.* to Moses	Ex.6.9; 16.20
walk as children of *l.*	Eph.5.8	Hear my cry, O God, *l.* to my prayer	Ps.61.1
walk in the *l.*, as he is in the *l.*	1 Jn.1.7	O that my people would *l.* to me	Ps.81.13
By its *l.* shall the nations walk	Rev.21.24	*L.* to advice and accept instruction	Pr.19.20
for the Lord God will be their *l.*	Rev.22.5	*L.* to me, my people, and give ear	Is.51.4
LIGHTNING		melody of your harps I will not *l.*	Am.5.23
he scatters his *l.* about him	Job 36.30	This is my beloved Son; *l.* to him	Mk.9.7
his face like the appearance of *l.*	Dan.10.6	that God does not *l.* to sinners	Jn.9.31
His appearance was like *l.*	Mt.28.3	sent to the Gentiles; they will *l.*	Acts 28.28
I saw Satan fall like *l.* from heaven	Lk.10.18	Whoever knows God *l.* to us	1 Jn.4.6
And there were flashes of *l.*	Rev.16.18	**LITTLE**	
LIKENESS		hast made him *l.* less than God	Ps.8.5
man in our image, after our *l.*	Gen.1.26	Better is a *l.* that the righteous	Ps.37.16
or any *l.* of anything that is in	Ex.20.4	Better is a *l.* with righteousness	Pr.16.8
own Son in the *l.* of sinful flesh	Rom.8.3	so a *l.* folly outweighs wisdom	Ec.10.1
of Christ, who is the *l.* of God	2 Cor.4.4	and a *l.* child shall lead them	Is.11.6
being born in the *l.* of men	Phil.2.7	here a *l.*, there a *l.*	Is.28.13
who are made in the *l.* of God	Jas.3.9	You have sown much, and harvested *l.*	Hag.1.6
LILY		more clothe you, O men of *l.* faith?	Mt.6.30
of Sharon, a *l.* of the valleys	S.of S.2.1	but he who is forgiven *l.*, loves *l.*	Lk.7.47
as a *l.* among brambles, so is my	S.of S.2.2	Fear not *l.* flock, for it is your	Lk.12.32
he shall blossom as the *l.*	Hos.14.5	*L.* children, yet a *l.* while I am	Jn.13.33
Consider the *l.* of the field	Mt.6.28	A *l.* while, and you will not see me	Jn.16.19
LINE		but use a *l.* wine for the sake of	1 Tim.5.23
Or who stretched the *l.* upon it?	Job 38.5	who for a *l.* while was made lower	Heb.2.9
His *l.* shall endure for ever	Ps.89.36	He had a *l.* scroll open in his hand	Rev.10.2
l. upon *l.*, *l.* upon *l.*	Is.28.10	**LIVE**	
eastward with a *l.* in his hand	Ezek.47.3	tree of life, and . . . *l.* for ever	Gen.3.22
with a plumb *l.* in his hand	Am.7.7	Long *l.* the king! Long *l.* the	2 Sam.16.16
with a measuring *l.* in his hand	Zech.2.1	If a man die, shall he *l.* again?	Job 14.14
LINEN		For I know that my Redeemer *l.*	Job 19.25
David was girded with a *l.* ephod	2 Sam.6.14	So I will bless thee as long as I *l.*	Ps.63.4

What man can *l.* and never see death?	Ps.89.48
praise the LORD as long as I *l.*	Ps.146.2
hear, that your soul may *l.*	Is.55.3
by whose observance man shall *l.*	Ezek.20.13
Son of man, can these bones *l.?*	Ezek.37.3
Seek the LORD and *l.,* lest he break	Am.5.6
Man shall not *l.* by bread alone	Mt.4.4
who eats me will *l.* because of me	Jn.6.57
though he die, yet shall he *l.*	Jn.11.25
because I *l.,* you will *l.* also	Jn.14.19
In him we *l.* and move and have	Acts 17.28
L. in harmony with one another	Rom.12.16
If we *l.,* we *l.* to the Lord	Rom.14.8
no longer I who *l.,* but Christ	Gal.2.20
if we *l.* by the Spirit, let us also	Gal.5.25
For to me to *l.* is Christ, and to	Phil.1.21
wake or sleep we might *l.* with him	1 Th.5.10
L. as free men, yet without using	1 Pet.2.16
l. considerately with your wives	1 Pet.3.7
God who *l.* for ever and ever	Rev.15.7

LIVING

Divide the *l.* child in two	1 Kg.3.25
blotted out of the book of the *l.*	Ps.69.28
no man *l.* is righteous before thee	Ps.143.2
a *l.* dog is better than a dead lion	Ec.9.4
For the *l.* know that they will die	Ec.9.5
see the LORD in the land of the *l.*	Is.38.11
the Christ, the Son of the *l.* God	Mt.16.16
not God of the dead, but of the *l.*	Mk.12.27
where do you get that *l.* water?	Jn.4.11
I am the *l.* bread which came down	Jn.6.51
he received *l.* oracles to give	Acts 7.38
your bodies as a *l.* sacrifice	Rom.12.1
we are the temple of the *l.* God	2 Cor.6.16
born anew to a *l.* hope through the	1 Pet.1.3
guide them to springs of *l.* water	Rev.7.17

LOAVES

these stones to become *l.* of bread	Mt.4.3
taking the five *l.* and the two fish	Mt.14.19
he took the seven *l.* and the fish	Mt.15.36
to him, 'Friend, lend me three *l.*	Lk.11.5
you ate your fill of the *l.*	Jn.6.26

LOCUST

the *l.* came up over all the land	Ex.10.14
It will devour you like the *l.*	Nah.3.15
his food was *l.* and wild honey	Mt.3.4
In appearance the *l.* were like horses	Rev.9.7

LOINS

Gird up your *l.* like a man	Job 40.7
didst lay affliction on our *l.*	Ps.66.11
faithfulness the girdle of his *l.*	Is.11.5
Let your *l.* be girded and your	Lk.12.35
having girded your *l.* with truth	Eph.6.14

LONG (verb)

who *l.* for death, but it comes not	Job 3.21
As a hart *l.* for . . . streams, so *l.*	Ps.42.1
My soul *l.,* yea, faints for the	Ps.84.2
righteous men *l.* to see what you	Mt.13.17
and *l.* to put on our heavenly	2 Cor.5.2
brethren, whom I love and *l.* for	Phil.4.1
remember us kindly and *l.* to see us	1 Th.3.6
l. for the pure spiritual milk	1 Pet.2.2
will *l.* to die, and death will fly	Rev.9.6

LOOK

for he was afraid to *l.* at God	· Ex.3.6
L. down from thy holy habitation	Dt.26.15

L., Hebrews are coming out of	1 Sam.14.11
But when I *l.* for good, evil came	Job 30.26
When I *l.* at thy heavens, the work of	Ps.8.3
L. to him, and be radiant	Ps.34.5
L. down from heaven, and see	Ps.80.14
l. upon the face of thine anointed	Ps.84.9
so our eyes *l.* to the LORD our God	Ps.123.2
l. to the rock from which you were	Is.51.1
no . . . comeliness that we should *l.* at	Is.53.2
L. down from heaven and see	Is.63.15
L. and see if there is any sorrow	Lam.1.12
I will *l.* to the LORD, I will wait	Mic.7.7
one who *l.* at a woman lustfully	Mt.5.28
he *l.* around at them with anger	Mk.3.5
Bring me a coin, and let me *l.* at it	Mk.12.15
L. at the fig tree, and all the	Lk.21.29
They shall *l.* on him whom they	Jn.19.37
Let each of you *l.* not only to his	Phil.2.4
he *l.* forward to the city which	Heb.11.10

LOOSE

or *l.* the cords of Orion?	Job 38.31
to *l.* the bonds of wickedness	Is.58.6
whatever you *l.* on earth shall be *l.*	Mt.16.19
having *l.* the pangs of death	Acts 2.24
Satan will be *l.* from his prison	Rev.20.7

LORD

day that the *L.* God made the earth	Gen.2.4
the *L.,* a God merciful and gracious	Ex.34.6
you might know that the *L.* is God	Dt.4.35
The *L.* our God is one *L.*	Dt.6.4
the *L.* gave, and the *L.* has taken	Job 1.21
O *L.,* our *L.,* how majestic is thy name	Ps.8.1
For who is God, but the *L.?*	Ps.18.31
Great is the *L.* and greatly to be	Ps.48.1
For the *L.* God is a sun and shield	Ps.84.11
kneel before the *L.,* our Maker	Ps.95.6
Know that the *L.* is God! It is he	Ps.100.3
on that day the *L.* will be one and	Zech.14.9
one after another, "Is it I, *L.?*"	Mt.26.22
Son of man is *L.* even of the sabbath	Mk.2.28
said, "My soul magnifies the *L.*	Lk.1.46
You call me Teacher and *L.*	Jn.13.13
answered him, "My *L.* and my God!"	Jn.20.28
has made him both *L.* and Christ	Acts 2.36
if you confess . . . that Jesus is *L.*	Rom.10.9
no one can say "Jesus is *L.*"	1 Cor12.3
be accursed. Our *L.,* come	1 Cor.16.22
the *L.* is the Spirit, and where	2 Cor.3.17
one *L.,* one faith, one baptism	Eph.4.5
confess that Jesus Christ is *L.*	Phil.2.11
For the *L.* himself will descend	1 Th.4.16
The *L.* be with your spirit	2 Tim.4.22
If the *L.* wills, we shall live and	Jas.4.15
O Sovereign *L.,* holy and true	Rev.6.10
King of kings and *L.* of lords	Rev.19.16
Amen. Come, *L.* Jesus	Rev.22.20

LOSE

a time to seek, and a time to *l.*	Ec.3.6
better that you *l.* one of your members	Mt.5.29
He who finds his life will *l.* it	Mt.10.39
what woman . . . if she *l.* one coin	Lk.15.8
seeks to gain his life will *l.* it	Lk.17.33
shall reap, if we do not *l.* heart	Gal.6.9
nor *l.* courage when . . . punished	Heb.12.5

LOST

asses that were *l.* three days ago	1 Sam.9.20

LOT

I have gone astray like a *l.* sheep   Ps.119.176
but the memory of them is *l.*   Ec.9.5
but if salt has *l.* its taste   Mt.5.13
only to the *l.* sheep of the house   Mt.15.24
I have found my sheep which was *l.*   Lk.15.6
came to seek and to save the *l.*   Lk.19.10
none of them is *l.* but the son of   Jn.17.12

LOT

Abram's nephew, Gen.11.27; separates from Abram, Gen.13.10–12; captured by four kings, and rescued by Abram, Gen.14; entertains angel visitors, Gen.19.1–3; saved from Sodom, Gen. 19.16; 2 Pet.2.7; his wife turned into a pillar of salt, Gen.19.26; Lk.17.28,32

LOTS

they cast *l.* for their duties   1 Chr.25.8
and for my raiment they cast *l.*   Ps.22.18
let us cast *l.*, that we may know   Jon.1.7
cast *l.* . . . to see whose it shall be   Jn.19.24
And they cast *l.* for them   Acts 1.26

LOVE (noun)

but *l.* covers all offenses   Pr.10.12
his banner over me was *l.*   S. of S.2.4
for *l.* is strong as death   S.of S.8.6
loved you with an everlasting *l.*   Jer.31.3
the abundance of his steadfast *l.*   Lam.3.32
most men's *l.* will grow cold   Mt.24.12
have not the *l.* of God within you   Jn.5.42
Greater *l.* has no man than this   Jn.15.13
L. does no wrong to a neighbor   Rom.13.10
L. is patient and kind   1 Cor.13.4
L. never ends; as for prophecies   1 Cor.13.8
For the *l.* of Christ controls us   2 Cor.5.14
But the fruit of the Spirit is *l.*   Gal.5.22
and to know the *l.* of Christ which   Eph.3.19
the *l.* of money is the root of   1 Tim.6.10
Let brotherly *l.* continue   Heb.13.1
Keep your life free from *l.* of money   Heb.13.5
since *l.* covers a multitude of sins   1 Pet.4.8
know God; for God is *l.*   1 Jn.4.8
but perfect *l.* casts out fear   1 Jn.4.18
abandoned the *l.* you had at first   Rev.2.4

LOVE (verb)

you shall *l.* your neighbor as yourself   Lev.19.18
you shall *l.* the LORD your God   Dt.6.5
I *l.* thee, O LORD, my strength   Ps.18.1
I *l.* the habitation of thy house   Ps.26.8
L. the LORD, all you his saints   Ps.31.23
I *l.* the LORD, because he has heard   Ps.116.1
Oh, how I *l.* thy law! It is my   Ps.119.97
peace have those who *l.* thy law   Ps.119.165
The LORD preserves all who *l.* him   Ps.145.20
all who hate me *l.* death   Pr.8.36
a time to *l.*, and a time to hate   Ec.3.8
I the LORD *l.* justice, I hate robbery   Is.61.8
to *l.* kindness, and to walk humbly   Mic.6.8
L. your enemies and pray for those   Mt.5.44
You shall *l.* the Lord your God   Mt.22.37
You shall *l.* your neighbor as   Mk.12.31
scribes . . . *l.* salutations in the market   Lk.20.46
God so *l.* the world that he gave   Jn.3.16
If you *l.* me, you will keep my   Jn.14.15
As the Father has *l.* me, so have I *l.*   Jn.15.9
I command you, to *l.* one another   Jn.15.17
do you *l.* me more than these?   Jn.21.15
Jacob I *l.*, but Esau I hated   Rom.9.13

taught by God to *l.* one another   1 Th.4.9
Lord disciplines him whom he *l.*   Heb.12.6
Without having seen him you *l.* him   1 Pet.1.8
l. one another earnestly from the   1 Pet.1.22
Do not *l.* the world or the things   1 Jn.2.15
that we should *l.* one another   1 Jn.3.11
We *l.*, because he first *l.* us   1 Jn.4.19
To him who *l.* us and has freed us   Rev.1.5
Those whom I *l.*, I reprove and   Rev.3.19

LOW

when I was brought *l.*, he saved me   Ps.116.6
who remembered us in our *l.* estate   Ps.136.23
the sound of the grinding is *l.*   Ec.12.4
every mountain and hill be made *l.*   Is.40.4
regarded the *l.* estate of his   Lk.1.48
and exalted those of *l.* degree   Lk.1.52
God chose what is *l.* and despised   1 Cor.1.28

LOWLY

he sets on high those who are *l.*   Job 5.11
the LORD is high, he regards the *l.*   Ps.138.6
for I am gentle and *l.* in heart   Mt.11.29
but associate with the *l.*   Rom.12.16
will change our *l.* body to be like   Phil.3.21

LOYALTY

I will sing of *l.* and of justice   Ps.101.1
Let not *l.* and faithfulness forsake   Pr.3.3
What is desired in a man is *l.*   Pr.19.22
L. and faithfulness preserve the   Pr.20.28
Those . . . forsake their true *l.*   Jon.2.8

LUKE

Col.4.14; 2 Tim.4.11; Philem.24

LUST (noun)

are taken captive by their *l.*   Pr.11.6
is corrupt through deceitful *l.*   Eph.4.22
not in the passion of *l.* like   1 Th.4.5
in the *l.* of defiling passion   2 Pet.2.10
l. of the flesh and the *l.* of   1 Jn.2.16
and indulged in unnatural *l.*   Jude 7

LYDIA

Acts 16.14,40

LYING

the LORD has put a *l.* spirit in   1 Kg.22.23
Let the *l.* lips be dumb   Ps.31.18
speaking against me with *l.* tongues   Ps.109.2
haughty eyes, a *l.* tongue   Pr.6.17
He who conceals hatred has *l.* lips   Pr.10.18
L. lips are an abomination to the   Pr.12.22
Remove far from me falsehood and *l.*   Pr.30.8
there is swearing, *l.*, killing   Hos.4.2

LYRE

all those who play the *l.* and pipe   Gen.4.21
My *l.* is turned to mourning   Job 30.31
Praise the LORD with the *l.*   Ps.33.2
Awake, O harp and *l.*   Ps.57.8
Sing praises to the LORD with the *l.*   Ps.98.5
make melody to our God upon the *l.*   Ps.147.7

MACEDONIA

Acts 16.9; Rom.15.26; 1 Cor.16.5; Phil.4.15; 1 Tim.1.3

MAD

He has a demon, and he is *m.*   Jn.10.20
I am not *m.*, most excellent Festus   Acts 26.25
will they not say that you are *m.*?   1 Cor.14.23

MADE

God saw everything that he had *m.*   Gen.1.31

God *m.* man in his own image	Gen.9.6
I have *m.* a covenant with my eyes	Job 31.1
The sea is his, for he *m.* it	Ps.95.5
This is the day . . . the LORD has *m.*	Ps.118.24
The LORD has *m.* everything for its	Pr.16.4
He has *m.* everything beautiful in	Ec.3.11
God *m.* man upright, but they	Ec.7.29
The sabbath was *m.* for man	Mk.2.27
God *m.* them male and female	Mk.10.6
all things were *m.* through him	Jn.1.3
For our sake he *m.* him to be sin	2 Cor.5.21
Christ Jesus has *m.* me his own	Phil.3.12
he had to be *m.* like his brethren	Heb.2.17

MAGICIAN

he . . . called for all the *m.* of Egypt	Gen.41.8
Then the king commanded that the *m.*	Dan.2.2
But Elymas the *m.* . . . withstood them	Acts 13.8

MAGNIFY

O *m.* the LORD with me, and let us	Ps.34.3
And you *m.* yourselves against me	Ezek.35.13
And Mary said, "My soul *m.* the Lord	Lk.1.46
to the Gentiles, I *m.* my ministry	Rom.11.13

MAIDEN

The *m.* was very fair to look upon	Gen.24.16
Then Boaz said . . . "Whose *m.* is this?"	Ru.2.5
Young men and *m.* together, old men	Ps.148.12
and the way of a man with a *m.*	Pr.30.19
ten *m.* who took their lamps	Mt.25.1

MAINTAIN

m. the right of the afflicted	Ps.82.3
LORD *m.* the cause of the afflicted	Ps.140.12
eager to *m.* the unity of the Spirit	Eph.4.3
M. good conduct among the Gentiles	1 Pet.2.12

MAJESTIC

m. in holiness, terrible in glorious	Ex.15.11
how *m.* is thy name in all the earth	Ps.8.1
I will make you *m.* for ever	Is.60.15
was borne to him by the *M.* Glory	2 Pet.1.17

MAJESTY

Honor and *m.* are before him	1 Chr.16.27
God is clothed with terrible *m.*	Job 37.22
the voice of the LORD is full of *m.*	Ps.29.4
The LORD reigns; he is robed in *m.*	Ps.93.1
were astonished at the *m.* of God	Lk.9.43
the right hand of the *M.* on high	Heb.1.3
we were eyewitnesses of his *m.*	2 Pet.1.16
m., dominion, and authority	Jude 25

MAKER

Can a man be pure before his *M.*?	Job 4.17
let us kneel before the LORD, our *M.*	Ps.95.6
Let Israel be glad in his *M.*	Ps.149.2
He who mocks the poor insults his *M.*	Pr.17.5
the LORD is the *m.* of them all	Pr.22.2
Woe to him who strives with his *M.*	Is.45.9
For Israel has forgotten his *M.*	Hos.8.14
whose builder and *m.* is God	Heb.11.10

MALICE

They scoff and speak with *m.*	Ps.73.8
But Jesus, aware of their *m.*	Mt.22.18
the leaven of *m.* and evil	1 Cor.5.8
be put away from you, with all *m.*	Eph.4.31
m., slander, and foul talk	Col.3.8
passing our days in *m.* and envy	Tit.3.3
So put away all *m.* and all guile	1 Pet.2.1

MAN

So God created *m.* in his own image	Gen.1.27
God is not *m.*, that he should lie	Num.23.19
Can a *m.* be pure before his Maker?	Job 4.17
how can a *m.* be just before God?	Job 9.2
If a *m.* die, shall he live again?	Job 14.14
what is *m.* that thou art mindful of	Ps.8.4
The steps of a *m.* are from the LORD	Ps.37.23
for vain is the help of *m.*	Ps.60.11
for no *m.* living is righteous	Ps.143.2
A faithful *m.* will abound with	Pr.28.20
Turn away from *m.* in whose nostrils	Is.2.22
Who is the *m.* so wise that he can	Jer.9.12
Cursed is the *m.* who trusts in *m.*	Jer.17.5
I am God and not *m.*, the Holy One	Hos.11.9
M. shall not live by bread alone	Mt.4.4
No *m.* ever spoke like this *m.*	Jn.7.46
each *m.* take care how he builds	1 Cor.3.10
the head of every *m.* is Christ	1 Cor.11.3
For each *m.* will have to bear his	Gal.6.5
Blessed is the *m.* who endures trial	Jas.1.12
No *m.* has ever seen God	1 Jn.4.12

MANASSEH

(1) first-born son of Joseph, Gen.41.51; his blessing, Gen.48.20; his descendants numbered, Num.1.34; 26.29; Jos.22.1; 1 Chr.5.23; 7.14; their inheritance, Num.32.33; 34.14; Jos.13.29; 17.1; desert to David's cause, 1 Chr. 12.19; 2 Chr.15.9; 30.11; (2) king of Judah, his reign, 2 Kg.21; 2 Chr.33; (3) others, Jg.18.30 note *z*; Ezra 10.30,33

MANIFEST

Let thy work be *m.* to thy servants	Ps.90.16
I will *m.* my glory in the midst	Ezek.28.22
will love him and *m.* myself to him	Jn.14.21
each man's work will become *m.*	1 Cor.3.13
that the life of Jesus may be *m.*	2 Cor.4.11
He was *m.* in the flesh, vindicated	1 Tim.3.16

MANNA

house of Israel called its name *m.*	Ex.16.31
Israel ate the *m.* forty years	Ex.16.35
Now the *m.* was like coriander seed	Num.11.7
he rained down upon them *m.* to eat	Ps.78.24
Your fathers ate the *m.* in the	Jn.6.49
a golden urn holding the *m.*	Heb.9.4
I will give some of the hidden *m.*	Rev.2.17

MARCH

the Egyptians were *m.* after them	Ex.14.10
You shall *m.* around the city	Jos.6.3
M. on, my soul, with might	Jg.5.21
the sound of *m.* in the tops of	1 Chr.14.15
thou didst *m.* through the wilderness	Ps.68.7
m. in the greatness of his strength	Is.63.1

MARK (John Mark)

(Evangelist), Acts 12.12; goes with Paul and Barnabas, Acts 12.25; 13.5; leaves them at Perga, Acts 13.13; contention about him, Acts 15.37; proves his usefulness, 2 Tim.4.11

MARK (noun)

And the LORD put a *m.* on Cain	Gen.4.15
It shall be as a *m.* on your hand	Ex.13.16
put a *m.* upon the foreheads of	Ezek.9.4
my finger in the *m.* of the nails	Jn.20.25
I bear on my body the *m.* of Jesus	Gal.6.17
buy or sell unless he has the *m.*	Rev.13.17
receives a *m.* on his forehead	Rev.14.9
who bore the *m.* of the beast	Rev.16.2
received its *m.* on their foreheads	Rev.20.4

MARKET

children sitting in the *m.* places	Mt.11.16
standing idle in the *m.* place	Mt.20.3
and salutations in the *m.* places	Mt.23.7
whatever is sold in the meat *m.*	1 Cor.10.25

MARRIAGE

a king who gave a *m.* feast for his	Mt.22.2
neither marry nor are given in *m.*	Mk.12.25
there was a *m.* at Cana in Galilee	Jn.2.1
free from a wife? Do not seek *m.*	1 Cor.7.27
who forbid *m.* and enjoin abstinence	1 Tim.4.3
Let *m.* be held in honor among all	Heb.13.4
for the *m.* of the Lamb has come	Rev.19.7

MARRY

They shall not *m.* a harlot or a	Lev.21.7
and *m.* another, commits adultery	Mt.19.9
they neither *m.*, nor are given in	Mk.12.25
I have *m.* a wife, and . . . cannot come	Lk.14.20
those who *m.* will have worldly	1 Cor.7.28
So I would have younger widows *m.*	1 Tim.5.14

MARTHA

Lk.10.38; Jn.11.1,19,39; 12.2

MARVEL

When the disciples saw it they *m.*	Mt.21.20
And he *m.* because of their unbelief	Mk.6.6
Do not *m.* that I said to you	Jn.3.7
Do not *m.* at this; for the hour is	Jn.5.28

MARVELOUS

his *m.* works among all the peoples	1 Chr.16.24
and *m.* things without number	Job 9.10
for he has done *m.* things	Ps.98.1
and it is *m.* in our eyes	Mk.12.11
out of darkness into his *m.* light	1 Pet.2.9

MARY

Greek form of Miriam, (1) the Virgin, mother of Jesus, visited by the angel Gabriel, Lk.1.26–38; believes, and magnifies the Lord, Lk.1.38, 46; Jn.2.5; Jesus born of, Mt.1.18; Lk.2.5–7; witnesses the miracle at Cana, Jn.2.1–11; desires to speak with Jesus, Mt.12.46; Mk.3.31; Lk.8.19; commended to John by Jesus at his crucifixion, Jn.19.25–26; (2) MAGDALENE, Lk. 8.2; at the cross, Mt.27.56; Mk.15.40; Jn.19.25; Jesus appears first to, Jn.20.1–18; (3) sister of Lazarus, commended, Lk.10.42; Jesus' love for, Jn.11.5; anoints Jesus' feet, Jn.12.3; (4) mother of John Mark, Acts 12.12; (5) a Roman Christian, Rom.16.6

MASTER

no one can serve two *m.*; for either	Mt.6.24
for you have one *m.*, the Christ	Mt.23.10
M., you delivered to me five	Mt.25.20
betrayed him, said, "Is it I, *M.*?"	Mt.26.25
Jesus, *M.*, have mercy on us	Lk.17.13
a servant is not greater than his *m.*	Jn.13.16
the *M.* is able to make him stand	Rom.14.4
like a skilled *m.* builder I laid	1 Cor.3.10
M., treat your slaves justly	Col.4.1
you also have a *M.* in heaven	Col.4.1
denying the *M.* who bought them	2 Pet.2.1

MATTHEW

Mt.9.9; Mk.3.18; Lk.6.15; Acts 1.13

MATURE

among the *m.* we do impart wisdom	1 Cor.2.6
but in thinking be *m.*	1 Cor.14.20
let . . . us who are *m.* be thus minded	Phil.3.15

may present every man *m.* in Christ	Col.1.28
But solid food is for the *m.*	Heb.5.14

MEAL

The jar of *m.* shall not be spent	1 Kg.17.12
and hid in three measures of *m.*	Mt.13.33
one goes ahead with his own *m.*	1 Cor.11.21
sold his birthright for a single *m.*	Heb.12.16

MEASURE (noun)

Correct me, O LORD, but in just *m.*	Jer.10.24
I will chasten you in just *m.*	Jer.46.28
the scant *m.* that is accursed	Mic.6.10
m. you give will be the *m.* you get	Mt.7.2
good *m.*, pressed down, shaken	Lk.6.38
might become sinful beyond *m.*	Rom.7.13
according to the *m.* of faith which	Rom.12.3
according to the *m.* of Christ's gift	Eph.4.7

MEASURE (verb)

Who has *m.* the waters in the hollow	Is.40.12
If the heavens above can be *m.*	Jer.31.37
can be neither *m.* nor numbered	Hos.1.10
He stood and *m.* the earth	Hab.3.6
To *m.* Jerusalem, to see what is its	Zech.2.2
they *m.* themselves by one another	2 Cor.10.12
Rise and *m.* the temple of God	Rev.11.1
he *m.* the city with his rod	Rev.21.16

MEAT

and said, "O that we had *m.* to eat	Num.11.4
no *m.* or wine entered my mouth	Dan.10.3
not to eat *m.* or drink wine or do	Rom.14.21
I will never eat *m.*, lest I cause	1 Cor.8.13

MEDIATOR

a *m.*, one of the thousand	Job 33.23
there is one *m.* between God and	1 Tim.2.5
he is the *m.* of a new covenant	Heb.9.15
Jesus, the *m.* of a new covenant	Heb.12.24

MEDITATE

Isaac went out to *m.* in the field	Gen.24.63
you shall *m.* on it day and night	Jos.1.8
and on his law he *m.* day and night	Ps.1.2
I will *m.* on all thy work, and muse	Ps.77.12
I will *m.* on thy wondrous works	Ps.119.27
not to *m.* beforehand how to answer	Lk.21.14

MEDITATION

the *m.* of my heart be acceptable	Ps.19.14
m. of my heart . . . be understanding	Ps.49.3
May my *m.* be pleasing to him	Ps.104.34
thy law! It is my *m.* all the day	Ps.119.97
for thy testimonies are my *m.*	Ps.119.99

MEEK

Now the man Moses was very *m.*	Num.12.3
thou wilt hear the desire of the *m.*	Ps.10.17
But the *m.* shall possess the land	Ps.37.11
The *m.* shall obtain fresh joy	Is.29.19
Blessed are the *m.*, for they shall	Mt.5.5

MEEKNESS

the *m.* and gentleness of Christ	2 Cor.10.1
with all lowliness and *m.*	Eph.4.2
receive with *m.* the implanted word	Jas.1.21
show his works in the *m.* of wisdom	Jas.3.13

MEET

The rich and the poor *m.* together	Pr.22.2
went to *m.* the bridegroom	Mt.25.1
When you *m.* together, it is not	1 Cor.11.20
to *m.* the Lord in the air	1 Th.4.17
not neglecting to *m.* together	Heb.10.25
when you *m.* various trials	Jas.1.2

MELCHIZEDEK
Gen.14,18; Ps.110.4; Heb.5.6,10; 6.20; 7.1–17
MELODY
I will make *m.* to the LORD Jg.5.3
I will sing and make *m.* Ps.57.7
make *m.* to our God upon the lyre Ps.147.7
to the *m.* of your harps I will not Am.5.23
singing and making *m.* to the Lord Eph.5.19
MELT
he utters his voice, the earth *m.* Ps.46.6
The mountains *m.* like wax before Ps.97.5
the elements will *m.* with fire 2 Pet.3.12
MEMBERS
Do not yield your *m.* to sin Rom.6.13
now yield your *m.* to righteousness Rom.6.19
For as in one body we have many *m.* Rom.12.4
your bodies are *m.* of Christ? 1 Cor.6.15
If one *m.* suffers, all suffer 1 Cor.12.26
for we are *m.* one of another Eph.4.25
the tongue is a little *m.* and boasts Jas.3.5
passions that are at war in your *m.*? Jas.4.1
MEMORIAL
This day shall be for you a *m.* day Ex.12.14
Write this as a *m.* in a book Ex.17.14
it shall be to the LORD for a *m.* Is.55.13
have ascended as a *m.* before God Acts 10.4
MEMORY
His *m.* perishes from the earth Job 18.17
may his *m.* be cut off from the Ps.109.15
The *m.* of the righteous is a blessing Pr.10.7
will be told in *m.* of her Mt.26.13
MEN
At that time *m.* began to call upon Gen.4.26
So these three *m.* ceased to answer Job 32.1
He recounts to *m.* his salvation Job 33.26
nations know that they are but *m.* Ps.9.20
You are the fairest of the sons of *m.* Ps.45.2
nevertheless, you shall die like *m.* Ps.82.7
M. are all a vain hope Ps.116.11
Deliver me, O LORD, from evil *m.* Ps.140.1
Young *m.* and maidens . . . old *m.* Ps.148.12
the hearts of *m.* are full of evil Ec.9.3
young *m.* shall fall exhausted Is.40.30
He was despised and rejected by *m.* Is.53.3
behold, wise *m.* from the East came to Mt.2.1
God is stronger than *m.* 1 Cor.1.25
So let no one boast of *m.* 1 Cor.3.21
let us do good to all *m.* Gal.6.10
Let all *m.* know your forbearance Phil.4.5
who desires all *m.* to be saved 1 Tim.2.4
spirits of just *m.* made perfect Heb.12.23
Honor all *m.* Love the brotherhood 1 Pet.2.17
the dwelling of God is with *m.* Rev.21.3
MENTION
Among those who know me I *m.* Ps.87.4
We must not *m.* the name of the LORD Am.6.10
without ceasing I *m.* you always Rom.1.9
made *m.* of the exodus of the Heb.11.22
MEPHIBOSHETH
2 Sam.4.4; 9.11; 16.1; 19.30; 21.7
MERCHANDISE
perceives that her *m.* is profitable Pr.31.18
Her *m.* . . . . will be dedicated Is.23.18
vessels of bronze for your *m.* Ezek.27.13
your *m.* and all your crew have Ezek.27.34

MERCHANT
the fragrant powders of the *m.*? S.of S.3.6
you ware the *m.* of the nations Is.23.3
set it in a city of *m.* Ezek.17.4
you increased your *m.* more than Nah.3.16
like a *m.* in search of fine pearls Mt.13.45
And the *m.* of the earth weep and Rev.18.11
thy *m.* were the great men of Rev.18.23
MERCIFUL
a God *m.* and gracious, slow to anger Ex.34.6
gracious and *m.*, slow to anger and Neh.9.17
Be *m.* to me, O God, be *m.* to me Ps.57.1
thou art a gracious God and *m.* Jon.4.2
Blessed are the *m.*, for they Mt.5.7
Be *m.*, even as your Father is *m.* Lk.6.36
For I will be *m.* toward their Heb.8.12
the Lord is compassionate and *m.* Jas.5.11
MERCY
shall make a *m.* seat of pure gold Ex.25.17
show *m.* on whom I will show *m.* Ex.33.19
LORD, for his *m.* is very great 1 Chr.21.13
Surely goodness and *m.* shall follow Ps.23.6
Be mindful of thy *m.*, O LORD Ps.25.6
Have *m.* on me, O God, according to Ps.51.1
Great is thy *m.*, O LORD Ps.119.156
his *m.* never come to an end Lam.3.22
in wrath remember *m.* Hab.3.2
'I desire *m.*, and not sacrifice.' Mt.9.13
Lord, have *m.* on my son, for he is Mt.17.15
his *m.* is on those who fear him Lk.1.50
the Lord had shown great *m.* to her Lk.1.58
perform the *m.* promised to our Lk.1.72
have *m.* upon me, and send Lazarus Lk.16.24
Jesus, Master, have *m.* on us Lk.17.13
I will have *m.* on whom I have *m.* Rom.9.15
by the *m.* of God, to present your Rom.12.1
the Father of *m.* and God of all 2 Cor.1.3
But God, who is rich in *m.* Eph.2.4
I received *m.* because I had 1 Tim.1.13
By his great *m.* we have been born 1 Pet.1.3
Grace, *m.*, and peace will be with us 2 Jn.3
MERE
think that *m.* words are strategy 2 Kg.18.20
surely every man is a *m.* breath Ps.39.11
but *m.* talk tends only to want Pr.14.23
think that *m.* words are strategy Is.36.5
They utter *m.* words; with empty Hos.10.4
m. busybodies, not doing any work 2 Th.3.11
MERRY
King David dancing and making *m.* 1 Chr.15.29
heart of the king was *m.* with wine Est.1.10
the voices of those who make *m.* Jer.30.19
young men and the old shall be *m.* Jer.31.13
take your ease, eat, drink, be *m.* Lk.12.19
And they began to make *m.* Lk.15.24
make *m.* and exchange presents Rev.11.10
MESHACH
Dan.1.7; 2.49; 3.12,30
MESOPOTAMIA
Gen.24.10; 1 Chr.19.6; Acts 2.9; 7.2
MESSAGE
sends a *m.* by the hand of a fool Pr.26.6
to the people with the LORD's *m.* Hag.1.13
sent the *m.* of this salvation Acts 13.26
to us the *m.* of reconciliation 2 Cor.5.19
for he strongly opposed our *m.* 2 Tim.4.15

For if the *m.* declared by angels | Heb.2.2
This is the *m.* we have heard from | 1 Jn.1.5

MESSENGER
who makest the winds thy *m.* | Ps.104.4
Haggai, the *m.* of the Lord, spoke | Hag.1.13
I send my *m.* to prepare the way | Mal.3.1
the *m.* of the covenant in whom you | Mal.3.1
I send my *m.* before thy face | Mt.11.10
they are *m.* of the churches | 2 Cor.8.23
a *m.* of Satan, to harass me | 2 Cor.12.7

MESSIAH
We have found the *M.* | Jn.1.41
I know that *M.* is coming | Jn.4.25

METHUSELAH
Gen.5.21,27; 1 Chr.1.3; Lk.3.37

MICAIAH
1 Kg.22.8; 2 Chr.13.2; Jer.36.11

MICHAEL
Dan.10.13; 12.1; Jude 9; Rev.12.7

MIDNIGHT
About *m.* I will go forth in . . . Egypt | Ex.11.4
At *m.* the LORD smote all the | Ex.12.29
At *m.* I rise to praise thee | Ps.119.62
But at *m.* there was a cry, 'Behold | Mt.25.6
go to him at *m.* and say to him | Lk.11.5
But about *m.* Paul and Silas were | Acts 16.25
he prolonged his speech until *m.* | Acts 20.7

MIDST
the LORD in the *m.* of the earth | Ex.8.22
went into the *m.* of the sea on dry | Ex.14.22
art in the *m.* of this people | Num.14.14
God speaking out of the *m.* of fire | Dt.5.26
God walks in the *m.* of your camp | Dt.23.14
The sun stayed in the *m.* of heaven | Jos.10.13
God is in the *m.* of her, she shall | Ps.46.5
Though I walk in the *m.* of trouble | Ps.138.7
I dwell in the *m.* of a people of | Is.6.5
I will dwell in their *m.* for ever | Ezek.43.9
Is not the LORD in the *m.* of us? | Mic.3.11
and I will dwell in the *m.* of you | Zech.2.10
there am I in the *m.* of them | Mt.18.20
kingdom of God is in the *m.* of you | Lk.17.21
the Lamb in the *m.* of the throne | Rev.7.17

MIGHT (noun)
all your soul, and with all your *m.* | Dt.6.5
power and the *m.* of my hand have | Dt.8.17
In thy hand are power and *m.* | 2 Chr.20.6
With God are wisdom and *m.* | Job 12.13
Do you give the horse his *m.*? | Job 39.19
But I will sing of thy *m.* | Ps.59.16
Thou didst divide the sea by thy *m.* | Ps.74.13
Stir up thy *m.*, and come to save us | Ps.80.2
proclaim the *m.* of thy terrible | Ps.145.6
I say that wisdom is better than *m.* | Ec.9.16
Behold, the Lord GOD comes with *m.* | Is.40.10
Not by *m.*, nor by power, but by my | Zech.4.6
the working of his great *m.* | Eph.1.19
strengthened with *m.* through his | Eph.3.16
according to his glorious *m.* | Col.1.11
and from the glory of his *m.* | 2 Th.1.9
glory and *m.* for ever and ever | Rev.5.13
power and *m.* be to our God for | Rev.7.12

MIGHTY
These were the *m.* men that were of | Gen.6.4
Like Nimrod a *m.* hunter before the | Gen.10.9
has brought you out with a *m.* hand | Dt.7.8

The *M.* One, God, the LORD | Jos.22.22
How are the *m.* fallen | 2 Sam.1.25
All the leaders and the *m.* men | 1 Chr.29.24
a *m.* man of valor, with two | 2 Chr.17.17
So Jotham became *m.*, because he | 2 Chr.27.6
God is *m.*, and does not despise any | Job 36.5
strong and *m.*, the LORD, *m.* in battle | Ps.24.8
who is *m.* as thou art, O LORD | Ps.89.8
M. King, lover of justice, thou hast | Ps.99.4
Praise him for his *m.* deeds | Ps.150.2
M. God, Everlasting Father, Prince of | Is.9.6
The LORD goes forth like a *m.* man | Is.42.13
your Redeemer, the *M.* One of Jacob | Is.49.26
O great and *m.* God whose name is | Jer.32.18
and do many *m.* works in your name? | Mt.7.22
And he could do no *m.* work there | Mk.6.5
he was *m.* in his words and deeds | Acts 7.22
under the *m.* hand of God | 1 Pet.5.6
Then a *m.* angel took up a stone | Rev.18.21

MILK
not boil a kid in its mother's *m.* | Ex.34.26
a land flowing with *m.* and honey | Lev.20.24
m. from the flock, with fat of lambs | Dt.32.14
He asked water and she gave him *m.* | Jg.5.25
buy wine and *m.* without money | Is.55.1
I fed you with *m.*, not solid food | 1 Cor.3.2
You need *m.*, not solid food | Heb.5.12
long for the pure spiritual *m.* | 1 Pet.2.2

MILLSTONE
cast an upper *m.* upon him from | 2 Sam.11.21
to have a great *m.* fastened round | Mt.18.6
better for him if a *m.* were hung | Lk.17.2
like a great *m.* and threw it into | Rev.18.21
sound of the *m.* shall be heard in | Rev.18.22

MIND
man in whose *m.* the LORD had put | Ex.36.2
For the people had a *m.* to work | Neh.4.6
test my heart and my *m.* | Ps.26.2
the inward *m.* and heart of a man | Ps.64.6
Men of perverse *m.*. . . . an abomination | Pr.11.20
Apply your *m.* to instruction | Pr.23.12
who trusts in his own *m.* is a fool | Pr.28.26
the *m.* of a wise man will know | Ec.8.5
whose *m.* is stayed on thee | Is.26.3
I the LORD search the *m.* and try | Jer.17.10
let a beast's *m.* be given to him | Dan.4.16
Settle it therefore in your *m.* | Lk.21.14
he opened their *m.* to understand | Lk.24.45
serve the law of God with my *m.* | Rom.7.25
who has known the *m.* of the Lord | Rom.11.34
But we have the *m.* of Christ | 1 Cor.2.16
blinded the *m.* of the unbelievers | 2 Cor.4.4
Have this *m.* among yourselves | Phil.2.5
Set your *m.* on things that are above | Col.3.2
a tender heart and a humble *m.* | 1 Pet.3.8
I am he who searches *m.* and heart | Rev.2.23

MINDFUL
m. of his covenant for ever | 1 Chr.16.15
what is man that thou art *m.* of him | Ps.8.4
Be *m.* of thy mercy, O LORD, and of | Ps.25.6
He is *m.* of his covenant for ever | Ps.105.8
God will be *m.* of them and restore | Zeph.2.7

MINGLE
and *m.* tears with my drink | Ps.102.9
offered him wine *m.* with myrrh | Mk.15.23

whose blood Pilate had *m.* with their   Lk.13.1
to be a sea of glass *m.* with fire   Rev.15.2

MINISTER (noun)

Joshua . . . the *m.* of Moses, one of   Num.11.28
for the authorities are *m.* of God   Rom.13.6
to be *m.* of a new covenant   2 Cor.3.6
was made a *m.* according to the gift   Eph.3.7
He is a faithful *m.* of Christ on our   Col.1.7
of which I, Paul, became a *m.*   Col.1.23
will be a good *m.* of Christ Jesus   1 Tim.4.6
a *m.* in the sanctuary and the true   Heb.8.2

MINISTER (verb)

they come near the altar to *m.*   Ex.30.20
that is blameless shall *m.* to me   Ps.101.6
behold, angels came and *m.* to him   Mt.4.11
in prison, and did not *m.* to thee?   Mt.25.44
these hands *m.* to my necessities   Acts 20.34

MINISTERING

Samuel was *m.* before the LORD   1 Sam.2.18
the Shunammite was *m.* to the king   1 Kg.1.15
many women there . . . *m.* to him   Mt.27.55
Are they not all *m.* spirits sent   Heb.1.14

MINISTRY

Jesus, when he began his *m.*   Lk.3.23
to prayer and to the *m.* of the word   Acts 6.4
I magnify my *m.*   Rom.11.13
having this *m.* by the mercy of God   2 Cor.4.1
gave us the *m.* of reconciliation   2 Cor.5.18
no fault may be found with our *m.*   2 Cor.6.3
for the work of *m.*, for building up   Eph.4.12
fulfil the *m.* which you have   Col.4.17
an evangelist, fulfil your *m.*   2 Tim.4.5
Christ has obtained a *m.* which is as   Heb.8.6

MIRACLE

Prove yourselves by working a *m.*   Ex.7.9
seeing signs and great *m.*   Acts 8.13
extraordinary *m.* by . . . Paul   Acts 19.11
to another the working of *m.*   1 Cor.12.10
third teachers, then workers of *m.*   1 Cor.12.28
Do all work *m.*?   1 Cor.12.29
supplies the Spirit . . . and works *m.*   Gal.3.5
bore witness by . . . various *m.*   Heb.2.4

MIRE

God has cast me into the *m.*   Job 30.19
I sink in deep *m.*, where there is   Ps.69.2
rescue me from sinking in the *m.*   Ps.69.14
and Jeremiah sank in the *m.*   Jer.38.6
that your feet are sunk in the *m.*   Jer.38.22
washed only to wallow in the *m.*   2 Pet.2.22

MIRIAM

Ex.15.20; Num.12.1,15; 20.1; Mic.6.4

MIRTH

sent you away with *m.* and songs   Gen.31.27
heart of fools is in the house of *m.*   Ec.7.4
The *m.* of the timbrels is stilled   Is.24.8
I will put an end to all her *m.*   Hos.2.11

MISCHIEF

They conceive *m.* and bring forth   Job 15.35
His *m.* returns upon his own head   Ps.7.16
He plots *m.* while on his bed   Ps.36.4
let the *m.* of their lips overwhelm   Ps.140.9
their lips talk of *m.*   Pr.24.2
they conceive *m.* and bring forth   Is.59.4
their minds shall be bent on *m.*   Dan.11.27

MISERY

You will forget your *m.*   Job 11.16

my strength fails because of my *m.*   Ps.31.10
in their paths are ruin and *m.*   Rom.3.16
howl for the *m.* that are coming   Jas.5.1

MISSION

the LORD sent you on a *m.*   1 Sam.15.18
when they had fulfilled their *m.*   Acts 12.25
in their boasted *m.* they work   2 Cor.11.12
Peter for the *m.* to the circumcised   Gal.2.8

MIST

but a *m.* went up from the earth   Gen.2.6
he distils his *m.* in rain   Job 36.27
he makes the *m.* rise from the ends   Jer.10.13
Immediately *m.* and darkness fell   Acts 13.11
For you are a *m.* that appears for a   Jas.4.14

MIXED

A *m.* multitude also went up with   Ex.12.38
the holy race has *m.* itself with   Ezra 9.2
and drink of the wine I have *m.*   Pr.9.5
those who go to try *m.* wine   Pr.23.30
you saw the iron *m.* with miry clay   Dan.2.43
for her in the cup she *m.*   Rev.18.6

MIZPAH

Gen.31.49; Jg.10.17; 1 Sam.7.5; 2 Chr.16.6;
Jer.40.10

MOAB

Gen.19.37; Dt.1.5; Ru.1.1; 2 Kg.3.4; Is.15.1;
Zeph.2.9

MOABITE

Dt.23.3; Jg.3.28; 2 Sam.8.2; 2 Kg.13.20

MOAN

noon I utter my complaint and *m.*   Ps.55.17
I think of God, and I *m.*   Ps.77.3
Therefore my soul *m.* like a lyre   Is.16.11
we *m.* and *m.* like doves   Is.59.11

MOANING

I am weary with my *m.*; every night   Ps.6.6
there shall be *m.* and lamentation   Is.29.2
all of them *m.*, every one over his   Ezek.7.16
m. like doves, and beating their   Nah.2.7

MOCK

has sent to *m.* the living God   2 Kg.19.4
All who see me *m.* at me   Ps.22.7
He who *m.* the poor insults his   Pr.17.5
he has sent to *m.* the living God   Is.37.17
they will *m.* him, and spit upon   Mk.10.34
all who see it begin to *m.* him   Lk.14.29
The soldiers also *m.* him   Lk.23.36
Now when they heard . . . some *m.*   Acts 17.32
God is not *m.*, for whatever a man   Gal.6.7

MOCKING

gloated over her, *m.* at her downfall   Lam.1.7
others *m.* said, "They are filled   Acts 2.13
Others suffered *m.* and scourging   Heb.11.36

MOLECH

Lev.18.21; 1 Kg.11.7; 2 Kg.23.10; Jer.32.35

MOLTEN

have made for themselves a *m.* calf   Ex.32.8
destroy all their *m.* images   Num.33.52
m. images, provoking me to anger   1 Kg.14.9
their *m.* images are empty wind   Is.41.29
who say to *m.* images, "You are our   Is.42.17

MOMENT

that I may consume them in a *m.*   Num.16.21
In a *m.* they die; at midnight   Job 34.20
For his anger is but for a *m.*   Ps.30.5
For a brief *m.* I forsook you, but   Is.54.7

servant was healed at that very *m.* Mt.8.13
in a *m.*, in the twinkling of 1 Cor.15.52
For the *m.* all discipline seems Heb.12.11

MONEY

If you lend *m.* to any of my people Ex.22.25
does not put out his *m.* at interest Ps.15.5
will not be satisfied with *m.* Ec.5.10
and *m.* answers everything Ec.10.19
you shall be redeemed without *m.* Is.52.3
he who has no *m.*, come, buy and eat Is.55.1
Show me the *m.* for the tax Mt.22.19
gave a sum of *m.* to the soldiers Mt.28.12
Pharisees, who were lovers of *m.* Lk.16.14
because Judas had the *m.* box Jn.13.29
obtain the gift of God with *m.* Acts 8.20
the love of *m.* is the root of 1 Tim.6.10
lovers of *m.*, proud, arrogant 2 Tim.3.2
Keep your life free from love of *m.* Heb.13.5

MONEY-CHANGERS

tables of the *m.* and the seats of Mt.21.12
and the *m.* at their business Jn.2.14

MONUMENT

he set up a *m.* for himself 1 Sam.15.12
called Absalom's *m.* to this day 2 Sam.18.18
to set up his *m.* at the river 1 Chr.18.3
adorn the *m.* of the righteous Mt.23.29

MOON

the *m.* stayed, until the nation Jos.10.13
the *m.* and the stars which thou hast Ps.8.3
by day, nor the *m.* by night Ps.121.6
sun and *m.*, praise him, all you Ps.148.3
the *m.* shall not give its light Ezek.32.7
there will be signs in sun and *m.* Lk.21.25
and the *m.* into blood Acts 2.20
with the *m.* under her feet Rev.12.1
no need of sun or *m.* to shine Rev.21.23

MORDECAI

Ezra 2.2; Est.2.5; 3.2; 5.9; 9.4; 10.3

MORIAH

Gen.22.2; 2 Chr.3.1

MORNING

but joy comes with the *m.* Ps.30.5
Evening and *m.* and at noon I utter Ps.55.17
in the *m.* my prayer comes before Ps.88.13
If I take the wings of the *m.* Ps.139.9
early in the *m.* to hire laborers Mt.20.1
were at the tomb early in the *m.* Lk.24.22
the *m.* star rises in your hearts 2 Pet.1.19
I will give him the *m.* star Rev.2.28

MORSEL

or have eaten my *m.* alone Job 31.17
He casts forth his ice like *m.* Ps.147.17
Better is a dry *m.* with quiet than Pr.17.1
he to whom I shall give this *m.* Jn.13.26
Then after the *m.*, Satan entered Jn.13.27

MORTAL

Can *m.* man be righteous before God? Job 4.17
resembling *m.* man or birds or Rom.1.23
this *m.* nature must put on 1 Cor.15.53
may be manifested in our *m.* flesh 2 Cor.4.11
Here tithes are received by *m.* men Heb.7.8
committing what is not a *m.* sin 1 Jn.5.16
There is sin which is *m.* 1 Jn.5.16
but its *m.* wound was healed Rev.13.3

MOSES

born and hidden, Ex.2 (Acts 7.20; Heb.11.23);

escapes to Midian, Ex.2.25; revelation from
God, Ex.3; confirmed by signs, Ex.4; returns to
Egypt, Ex.4.20; intercedes with Pharaoh for
Israel, Ex.5–12; leads Israel forth, Ex.14;
meets God on Mount Sinai, Ex.19.3 (24.18);
brings the law to the people, Ex.19.25; 20–23;
35.1; Lev.1; Num.5–6; 15; 27–30; 36; Dt.12–
26; instructed to build the tabernacle, Ex.25–31;
35; 40; his grief at Israel's idolatry, Ex.32.10;
his intercession, Ex.32.11–14; again meets
God on the mount, Ex.34.2; skin of his face
shines, Ex.34.29 (2 Cor.3.7,13); sets apart
Aaron, Lev.8–9; numbers the people, Num.1;
26; sends out the spies to Canaan, Num.13;
intercedes for the murmuring people, Num.
14.13; Korah's sedition against, Num.16; for
his unbelief not allowed to enter Canaan,
Num.20.12; 27.12–14; Dt.1.37; 3.23–27; his
government of Israel in the wilderness, Num.
20–21; makes the bronze serpent, Num.21.9 (Jn.
3.14); his charge to Joshua, Dt.3.28; 31.7,23; his
death, Dt.34.5; his body, Jude 9; seen at Jesus'
transfiguration, Mt.17.3; Mk.9.4; Lk.9.30; his
meekness, Num.12.3; distinction, Dt.34.10;
faithfulness, Num.12.7; Heb.3.2

MOTH

the *m.* will eat them up Is.50.9
For the *m.* will eat them up like a Is.51.8
where *m.* and rust consume and where Mt.6.19
where . . . no *m.* destroys Lk.12.33

MOTHER

she was the *m.* of all living Gen.3.20
she shall be a *m.* of nations Gen.17.16
Honor your father and your *m.* Ex.20.12
father and my *m.* have forsaken me Ps.27.10
in sin did my *m.* conceive me Ps.51.5
a foolish son is a sorrow to his *m.* Pr.10.1
If one curses his father or his *m.* Pr.20.20
As one whom his *m.* comforts Is.66.13
took the child and his *m.* by night Mt.2.14
loves father or *m.* more than me is Mt.10.37
He who speaks evil of father or *m.* Mt.15.4
the *m.* of Jesus was there Jn.2.1
to the disciple, "Behold, your *m.*" Jn.19.27
the Jerusalem above . . . is our *m.* Gal.4.26

MOTHER-IN-LAW

and Orpah kissed her *m.* Ru.1.14
Then Naomi her *m.* said to her Ru.3.1
a daughter-in-law against her *m.* Mt.10.35
Simon's *m.* was ill with a high fever Lk.4.38

MOUNT OF OLIVES

Zech.14.4; Mt.21.1; Mk.11.1; Lk.19.37

MOUNTAIN

he was encamped at the *m.* of God Ex.18.5
Then Moses went up on the *m.* Ex.24.15
though the *m.* shake in the heart of Ps.46.2
Before the *m.* were brought forth Ps.90.2
and worship at his holy *m.* Ps.99.9
As the *m.* are round about Jerusalem Ps.125.2
Get you up to a high *m.*, O Zion Is.40.9
was cut from a *m.* by no human hand Dan.2.45
let us go up to the *m.* of the LORD Mic.4.2
devil took him to a very high *m.* Mt.4.8
who are in Judea flee to the *m.* Mt.24.16
every *m.* and hill shall be brought low Lk.3.5
Our fathers worshiped on this *m.* Jn.4.20

MOURN

we were with him on the holy *m*.	2 Pet.1.18
every *m*. and island was removed	Rev.6.14

MOURN

those who *m*. are lifted to safety	Job 5.11
a time to *m*., and a time to dance	Ec.3.4
to comfort all who *m*.	Is.61.2
shall *m*. for him, as one *m*. for	Zech.12.10
Blessed are those who *m*., for they	Mt.5.4
for you shall *m*. and weep	Lk.6.25
Ought you not rather to *m*.?	1 Cor.5.2

MOURNING (noun)

My lyre is turned to *m*.	Job 30.31
turned for me my *m*. into dancing	Ps.30.11
your days of *m*. shall be ended	Is.60.20
the oil of gladness instead of *m*.	Is.61.3
I will turn their *m*. into joy	Jer.31.13
I will turn your feasts into *m*.	Am.8.10

MOUTH

He will yet fill your *m*. with laughter	Job 8.21
by the *m*. of babes and infants, thou	Ps.8.2
Let the words of my *m*. and the	Ps.19.14
My *m*. shall speak wisdom	Ps.49.3
Open your *m*. wide, and I will fill	Ps.81.10
tongue cleave to the roof of my *m*.	Ps.137.6
My *m*. will speak the praise of	Ps.145.21
He who guards his *m*. preserves his	Pr.13.3
He who keeps his *m*. and his tongue	Pr.21.23
Be not rash with your *m*.	Ec.5.2
And he touched my *m*., and said	Is.6.7
the *m*. of the LORD has commanded	Is.34.16
He made my *m*. like a sharp sword	Is.49.2
is dumb, so he opened not his *m*.	Is.53.7
And he opened his *m*. and taught	Mt.5.2
I will open my *m*. in parables	Mt.13.35
abundance of the heart his *m*. speaks	Lk.6.45
I will give you a *m*. and wisdom	Lk.21.15
no evil talk come out of your *m*.	Eph.4.29
I was rescued from the lion's *m*.	2 Tim.4.17
I will spew you out of my *m*.	Rev.3.16
From his *m*. issues a sharp sword	Rev.19.15

MOVE

does these things shall never be *m*.	Ps.15.5
I shall not be greatly *m*.	Ps.62.2
For the righteous will never be *m*.	Ps.112.6
'M. hence to yonder place,' and it	Mt.17.20
M. with pity, he stretched out his	Mk.1.41
he was deeply *m*. in spirit	Jn.11.33
in him we live and *m*. and have	Acts 17.28
men *m*. by the Holy Spirit spoke	2 Pet.1.21

MULE

Absalom was riding upon his *m*.	2 Sam.18.9
Solomon to ride on King David's *m*.	1 Kg.1.38
Be not like a horse or a *m*.	Ps.32.9

MULTIPLY

Be fruitful and *m*. and fill the	Gen.1.22
I will *m*. your descendants as the	Gen.26.4
And when you have *m*. and increased	Jer.3.16
disciples *m*. greatly in Jerusalem	Acts 6.7
But the word of God grew and *m*.	Acts 12.24
May grace and peace be *m*. to you	1 Pet.1.2

MULTITUDE

be the father of a *m*. of nations	Gen.17.4
A mixed *m*. also went up with them	Ex.12.38
Should a *m*. of words go unanswered	Job 11.2
a *m*. keeping festival	Ps.42.4
M., *m*., in the valley of decision	Jl.3.14

a great *m*. from Galilee followed	Mk.3.7
because all the *m*. was astonished	Mk.11.18
In these lay a *m*. of invalids	Jn.5.3
since love covers a *m*. of sins	1 Pet.4.8
a great *m*. which no man could number	Rev.7.9

MURDER

fornication, theft, *m*., adultery	Mk.7.21
had committed *m*. in the insurrection	Mk.15.7
breathing threats and *m*. against	Acts 9.1
Full of envy, *m*., strife, deceit	Rom.1.29

MURDERER

the *m*. shall be put to death	Num.35.18
He was a *m*. from the beginning	Jn.8.44
and asked for a *m*. to be granted	Acts 3.14
let none of you suffer as a *m*.	1 Pet.4.15
one who hates his brother is a *m*.	1 Jn.3.15
know that no *m*. has eternal life	1 Jn.3.15
fornicators and *m*. and idolaters	Rev.22.15

MURMUR

And the people *m*. against Moses	Ex.15.24
what are we, that you *m*. against us?	Ex.16.7
the Pharisees and the scribes *m*.	Lk.15.2
Do not *m*. among yourselves	Jn.6.43
Hellenists *m*. against the Hebrews	Acts 6.1

MUSIC

leader of the *m*. of the singers	1 Chr.15.27
instruments for *m*. to the LORD	2 Chr.7.6
to the *m*. of the lute and the harp	Ps.92.3
I will stop the *m*. of your songs	Ezek.26.13
for themselves instruments of *m*.	Am.6.5
he heard *m*. and dancing	Lk.15.25

MUSTARD

have faith as a grain of *m*. seed	Mt.17.20
It is like a grain of *m*. seed	Mk.4.31

MYRRH

fragrant with *m*. and aloes	Ps.45.8
perfumed with *m*. and frankincense	S.of S.3.6
gold and frankincense and *m*.	Mt.2.11
offered him wine mingled with *m*.	Mk.15.23
bringing a mixture of *m*. and aloes	Jn.19.39
m., frankincense, wine, oil	Rev.18.13

MYRTLE

instead of . . . shall come up the *m*.	Is.55.13
was standing among the *m*. trees	Zech.1.11

MYSTERY

Then the *m*. was revealed to Daniel	Dan.2.19
I want you to understand this *m*.	Rom.11.25
if I . . . understand all *m*. and all	1 Cor.13.2
I tell you a *m*. We shall not all	1 Cor.15.51
my insight into the *m*. of Christ	Eph.3.4
the plan of the *m*. hidden for ages	Eph.3.9
to declare the *m*. of Christ	Col.4.3
the *m*. of lawlessness is . . . at work	2 Th.2.7
As for the *m*. of the seven stars	Rev.1.20

MYTHS

with *m*. and endless genealogies	1 Tim.1.4
turn away . . . and wander into *m*.	2 Tim.4.4
giving heed to Jewish *m*.	Tit.1.14
not follow cleverly devised *m*.	2 Pet.1.16

NAAMAN

2 Kg.5.1,11,27; Lk.4.27

NABAL

1 Sam.25.3; 30.5; 2 Sam.2.2

NAILS

like *n*. firmly fixed are . . . sayings	Ec.12.11

his *n*. were like birds' claws   Dan.4.33
my finger in the mark of the *n*.   Jn.20.25

NAKED

the man and his wife were both *n*.   Gen.2.25
N. I came from my mother's womb   Job 1.21
I was *n*. and you clothed me   Mt.25.36
left the linen cloth and ran away *n*.   Mk.14.52
we may not be found *n*.   2 Cor.5.3
they will make her desolate and *n*.   Rev.17.16

NAKEDNESS

covered the *n*. of their father   Gen.9.23
not uncover the *n*. of your father   Lev.18.7
so openly and flaunted her *n*.   Ezek.23.18
or *n*., or peril, or sword?   Rom.8.35
shame of your *n*. from being seen   Rev.3.18

NAME (noun)

Abram called on the *n*. of the LORD   Gen.13.4
this is my *n*. for ever, and thus I   Ex.3.15
the LORD is his *n*.   Ex.15.3
blasphemed the *N*., and cursed   Lev.24.11
what wilt thou do for thy great *n*.?   Jos.7.9
My *n*. shall be there   1 Kg.8.29
in thy *n*. we have come against   2 Chr.14.11
thou didst get thee a *n*.   Neh.9.10
blessed be the *n*. of the LORD   Job 1.21
how majestic is thy *n*. in all the earth   Ps.8.1
let us exalt his *n*. together   Ps.34.3
May his *n*. endure for ever   Ps.72.17
Ascribe . . . the glory due his *n*.   Ps.96.8
Give thanks to him, bless his *n*.   Ps.100.4
all . . . within me, bless his holy *n*.   Ps.103.1
Holy and terrible is his *n*.   Ps.111.9
Our help is in the *n*. of the LORD   Ps.124.8
Thy *n*., O LORD, endures for ever   Ps.135.13
A good *n*. is to be chosen rather   Pr.22.1
A good *n*. is better than precious   Ec.7.1
and shall call his *n*. Immanuel   Is.7.14
I am the LORD, that is my *n*.   Is.42.8
the LORD of hosts is his *n*.   Is.48.2
whose *n*. is Holy: "I dwell in the   Is.57.15
our Redeemer from of old is thy *n*.   Is.63.16
no one that calls upon thy *n*.   Is.64.7
walk in the *n*. of the LORD our God   Mic.4.5
How have we despised thy *n*.?   Mal.1.6
you shall call his *n*. Jesus   Mt.1.21
who art in heaven, Hallowed be thy *n*.   Mt.6.9
in his *n*. will the Gentiles hope   Mt.12.21
two or three are gathered in my *n*.   Mt.18.20
because you bear the *n*. of Christ   Mk.9.41
that your *n*. are written in heaven   Lk.10.20
works that I do in my Father's *n*.   Jn.10.25
Whatever you ask in my *n*., I will   Jn.14.13
I made known to them thy *n*.   Jn.17.26
is no other *n*. under heaven given   Acts 4.12
carry my *n*. before the Gentiles   Acts 9.15
the *n*. which is above every *n*.   Phil.2.9
whose *n*. are in the book of life   Phil.4.3
reproached for the *n*. of Christ   1 Pet.4.14
not blot his *n*. out of the book of   Rev.3.5

NAOMI

Ru.1.2,11,20; 4.5,17

NAPHTALI

(1) son of Jacob, Gen.30.8; 35.25; 46.24; 49.21;
Dt.33.23; (2) tribe of, numbered, Num.1.42;
10.27; 13.14; 26.48; subdue the Canaanites,

Jg.4.10; 5.18; 6.35; carried captive, 2 Kg.15.29;
see Is.9.1; Mt.4.13-15

NARD

my *n*. gave forth its fragrance   S.of S.1.12
alabaster jar of ointment of pure *n*.   Mk.14.3
Mary took . . . ointment of pure *n*.   Jn.12.3

NARROW

covering too *n*. to wrap oneself in   Is.28.20
The place is too *n*. for me   Is.49.20
the gate is *n*. and the way is hard   Mt.7.14
Strive to enter by the *n*. door   Lk.13.24

NATHAN

(1) the prophet, 2 Sam.7; 1 Chr.29.29; 2 Chr.
9.29; reproves David for his sin, 2 Sam.12.1–15;
anoints Solomon king, 1 Kg.1.34; (2) son of
David, 2 Sam.5.14; Zech.12.12; Lk.3.31; (3)
others, 2 Sam.23.36; 1 Kg.4.5; Ezra 8.16; 10.39

NATHANAEL

Jn.1.45-49; 21.2

NATION

I will make of you a great *n*.   Gen.12.2
A *n*. which you have not known shall   Dt.28.33
Blessed is the *n*. whose God is the   Ps.33.12
Let the *n*. be glad and sing for joy   Ps.67.4
Declare his glory among the *n*.   Ps.96.3
The LORD is high above all *n*.   Ps.113.4
not dealt thus with any other *n*.   Ps.147.20
Righteousness exalts a *n*.   Pr.14.34
Against a godless *n*. I send him   Is.10.6
n. . . . not lift up sword against *n*.   Mic.4.3
robbing me; the whole *n*. of you   Mal.3.9
For *n*. will rise against *n*.   Mt.24.7
make disciples of all *n*.   Mt.28.19
a house of prayer for all the *n*.   Mk.11.17
that Jesus should die for the *n*.   Jn.11.51
men from every *n*. under heaven   Acts 2.5
he made from one every *n*. of men   Acts 17.26
In you shall all the *n*. be blessed   Gal.3.8
a holy *n*., God's own people   1 Pet.2.9
from every . . . tongue and people and *n*.   Rev.5.9
over every . . . people and tongue and *n*.   Rev.13.7
All *n*. shall come and worship thee   Rev.15.4
were for the healing of the *n*.   Rev.22.2

NATIVE

return no more to see his *n*. land   Jer.22.10
each of us in his own *n*. language   Acts 2.8
a *n*. of Pontus, lately come from   Acts 18.2
Apollos, a *n*. of Alexandria, came   Acts 18.24

NATURAL

not dim, nor his *n*. force abated   Dt.34.7
women exchanged *n*. relations for   Rom.1.26
because of your *n*. limitations   Rom.6.19
God did not spare the *n*. branches   Rom.11.21
observes his *n*. face in a mirror   Jas.1.23

NATURE

Does not *n*. itself teach you   1 Cor.11.14
this perishable *n*. must put on   1 Cor.15.53
our outer *n*. is wasting away   2 Cor.4.16
so we were by *n*. children of wrath   Eph.2.3
Put off your old *n*. which belongs   Eph.4.22
have put on the new *n*.   Col.3.10
become partakers of the divine *n*.   2 Pet.1.4
for God's *n*. abides in him   1 Jn.3.9

NAVE

in front of the *n*. of the house   1 Kg.6.3
The *n*. he lined with cypress   2 Chr.3.5

Then he brought me to the *n.* Ezek.41.1
doorposts of the *n.* were squared Ezek.41.21
NAZARENE
Mt.2.23; Mk.14.67; Acts 24.5
NAZARETH
Mt.2.23; 21.11; Lk.2.39; Jn.1.46; Acts 22.8
NAZIRITE
the vow of a *N.*, to separate Num.6.2
I have been a *N.* to God from my Jg.16.17
But you made the *N.* drink wine Am.2.12
NEBUCHADNEZZAR
same as Nebuchadrezzar; King of Babylon, Jer.
21; 25; 27–28; 32; 34; Ezek.26.7; 29.19; cap-
tures Jerusalem, 2 Kg.24–25; 2 Chr.36; Jer.37–
39; 52; Dan.1.1; his dreams, Dan.2; 4; sets up
a golden image, Dan.3; his madness, Dan.4.33;
his restoration and confession, Dan.4.34
NECESSARY
For it is *n.* that temptations come Mt.18.7
Was it not *n.* that the Christ Lk.24.26
hence it is *n.* for this priest also Heb.8.3
I found it *n.* to write appealing to Jude 3
NECK
stiffened his *n.* and hardened 2 Chr.36.13
stiffened their *n.* and would not Neh.9.29
bind them about your *n.*, write them Pr.3.3
stiffens his *n.* will suddenly be Pr.29.1
round his *n.* and to be drowned in Mt.18.6
yoke upon the *n.* of the disciples Acts 15.10
who risked their *n.* for my life Rom.16.4
NECROMANCER
a medium, or a wizard, or a *n.* Dt.18.11
NEED (noun)
Those who are well have no *n.* of Mk.2.17
distributed them . . . as any had *n.* Acts 2.45
to the feet, "I have no *n.* of you 1 Cor.12.21
supply every *n.* of yours according Phil.4.19
find grace to help in time of *n.* Heb.4.16
For you have *n.* of endurance Heb.10.36
sees his brother in *n.* 1 Jn.3.17
the city has no *n.* of sun or moon Rev.21.23
NEED (verb)
knows what you *n.* before you ask him Mt.6.8
who has bathed does not *n.* to wash Jn.13.10
You *n.* milk, not solid food Heb.5.12
I have prospered, and I *n.* nothing Rev.3.17
NEEDLE
easier . . . through the eye of a *n.* than Mk.10.25
NEEDY
he lifts the *n.* from the ash heap 1 Sam.2.8
the *n.* shall not always be forgotten Ps.9.18
As for me, I am poor and *n.* Ps.40:17
For the LORD hears the *n.* Ps.69.33
He has pity on the weak and the *n.* Ps.72.13
to turn aside the *n.* from justice Is.10.2
they sell . . . the *n.* for a pair of shoes Am.2.6
you who trample upon the *n.* Am.8.4
was not a *n.* person among them Acts 4.34
NEGEB
Gen.12.9; Num.13.17; Jos.10.40; Jg.1.9; Ps.
126.4; Ezek.20.46
NEGLECT (verb)
will not *n.* the house of our God Neh.10.39
n. justice and the love of God Lk.11.42
their widows were *n.* in the daily Acts 6.1

Do not *n.* the gift you have 1 Tim.4.14
how shall we escape if we *n.* such Heb.2.3
NEHEMIAH
(1) Ezra 2.2; (2) Neh.3.16; (3) son of Hacali-
ah, his grief for Jerusalem, Neh.1.1–3; his
prayer for, Neh.1.5–11; his visit to, Neh.2.5,
11; his work at, Neh.4–6; 8–10; 13
NEIGHBOR
bear false witness against your *n.* Ex.20.16
not oppress your *n.* or rob him Lev.19.13
you shall love your *n.* as yourself Lev.19.18
takes up a reproach against his *n.* Ps.15.3
He who despises his *n.* is a sinner Pr.14.21
and every man against his *n.* Is.19.2
shall love your *n.* and hate your Mt.5.43
You shall love your *n.* as yourself Mt.22.39
said to Jesus, "And who is my *n.?*" Lk.10.29
Love does no wrong to a *n.* Rom.13.10
who are you that you judge your *n.?* Jas.4.12
NEIGHBORHOOD
women of the *n.* gave him a name Ru.4.17
beg Jesus to depart from their *n.* Mk.5.17
in the *n.* of that place were lands Acts 28.7
NEST
Like an eagle that stirs up its *n.* Dt.32.11
and the swallow a *n.* for herself Ps.84.3
Like a bird that strays from its *n.* Pr.27.8
birds of the air have *n.* Mt.8.20
NET
will pluck my feet out of the *n.* Ps.25.15
take me out of the *n.* which is Ps.31.4
They set a *n.* for my steps Ps.57.6
in vain is a *n.* spread in the sight Pr.1.17
he spread a *n.* for my feet Lam.1.13
they spread their *n.* over him Ezek.19.8
Immediately they left their *n.* and Mt.4.20
is like a *n.* which was thrown into Mt.13.47
Cast the *n.* on the right side of Jn.21.6
NETHER
heart . . . hard as the *n.* millstone Job 41.24
committed their to pits of *n.* gloom 2 Pet.2.4
the *n.* gloom of darkness 2 Pet.2.17
kept . . . in . . . chains in the *n.* gloom Jude 6
NEW
Now there arose a *n.* king over Egypt Ex.1.8
Sing to him a *n.* song Ps.33.3
Sing to the LORD a *n.* song Ps.149.1
there is nothing *n.* under the sun Ec.1.9
I create *n.* heavens and a *n.* earth Is.65.17
they are *n.* every morning Lam.3.23
A *n.* heart I will give you Ezek.36.26
Neither is *n.* wine put into old Mt.9.17
when I drink it *n.* with you in my Mt.26.29
A *n.* commandment I give to you Jn.13.34
in the garden a *n.* tomb where no Jn.19.41
They are filled with *n.* wine Acts 2.13
know what this *n.* teaching is Acts 17.19
This cup is the *n.* covenant in 1 Cor.11.25
in Christ, he is a *n.* creation 2 Cor.5.17
is the mediator of a *n.* covenant Heb.9.15
I am writing you a *n.* commandment 1 Jn.2.8
the *n.* Jerusalem which comes down Rev.3.12
I saw a *n.* heaven and a *n.* earth Rev.21.1
said, "Behold, I make all things *n.*" Rev.21.5
NEWS
This day is a day of good *n.* 2 Kg.7.9

told the glad *n.* of deliverance	Ps.40.9
poor have good *n.* preached to them	Mt.11.5
bring you good *n.* of a great joy	Lk.2.10
the good *n.* of the kingdom of God	Lk.8.1
he told him the good *n.* of Jesus	Acts 8.35
feet of those who preach good *n.*	Rom.10.15
For good *n.* came to us just as to	Heb.4.2

NICODEMUS
Jn.3.1,9; 7.50; 19.39

NICOLAITANS
Rev.2.6, 15

NIGHT

on his law he meditates day and *n.*	Ps.1.2
and *n.* to *n.* declares knowledge	Ps.19.2
Weeping may tarry for the *n.*	Ps.30.5
I commune with my heart in the *n.*	Ps.77.6
fire to give light by *n.*	Ps.105.39
nor the moon by *n.*	Ps.121.6
Upon my bed by *n.* I sought him	S. of S.3.1
Watchman, what of the *n.*?	Is.21.11
this very *n.*, before the cock crows	Mt.26.34
N. and day among the tombs	Mk.5.5
watch over their flock by *n.*	Lk.2.8
we toiled all *n.* and took nothing	Lk.5.5
This *n.* your soul is required	Lk.12.20
But if any one walks in the *n.*	Jn.11.10
on the *n.* when he was betrayed	1 Cor.11.23
will come like a thief in the *n.*	1 Th.5.2
prayers *n.* and day	1 Tim.5.5
And *n.* shall be no more	Rev.22.5

NILE
Gen.41.1; Ex.1.22; Is.18.2; Ezek.29.3; Zech.
10.11

NIMROD
Gen.10.8; 1 Chr.1.10; Mic.5.6

NINEVEH
Gen.10.11; 2 Kg.19.36; Jon.1.2; 4.11; Zeph.
2.13; Mt.12.41

NOAH
son of Lamech, Gen.5.29; finds favor with God,
Gen.6.8; ordered to build the ark, Gen.6.14;
with his family and animals enters into the ark,
Gen.7; God blesses and makes a covenant with,
Gen.9.8–17; is drunken, and mocked by Ham,
Gen.9.22; his death, Gen.9.29

NOBLE

Hear, for I will speak *n.* things	Pr.8.6
he who is *n.* devises *n.* things	Is.32.8
these Jews were more *n.* than	Acts 17.11
what is *n.* in the sight of all	Rom.12.17
of bishop, he desires a *n.* task	1 Tim.3.1

NOISE

There is a *n.* of war in the camp	Ex.32.17
by the *n.* of the enemy	Ps.55.3
Make a joyful *n.* to God, all the	Ps.66.1
The *n.* of battle is in the land	Jer.50.22
Take away . . . the *n.* of your songs	Am.5.23
was like the *n.* of many chariots	Rev.9.9

NOISY

A foolish woman is *n.*; she is wanton	Pr.9.13
N. one who lets the hour go by	Jer.46.17
a *n.* multitude of men	Mic.2.12
am a *n.* gong or a clanging cymbal	1 Cor.13.1

NOON
called . . . Baal from morning until *n.* 1 Kg.18.26

I will make the sun go down at *n.*	Am.8.9
about *n.* a great light from heaven	Acts 22.6

NOONDAY

you shall grope at *n.*	Dt.28.29
your life . . . brighter than the *n.*	Job 11.17
the destruction that wastes at *n.*	Ps.91.6
your gloom be as the *n.*	Is.58.10

NOSE

Can you put a rope in his *n.*	Job 41.2
pressing the *n.* produces blood	Pr.30.33
Your *n.* is like a tower	S.of S.7.4
my hook in your *n.* and my bit in	Is.37.29

NOSTRILS

breathed into his *n.* the breath of	Gen.2.7
Smoke went out from his *n.*	2 Sam.22.9
the spirit of God is in my *n.*	Job 27.3
from man in whose *n.* is breath	Is.2.22

NOWHERE

Go *n.* among the Gentiles, and enter	Mt.10.5
Son of man has *n.* to lay his head	Lk.9.58
for I have *n.* to store my crops?	Lk.12.17

NUMBER (verb)

Go, *n.* Israel and Judah	2 Sam.24.1
Who can *n.* the clouds by wisdom?	Job 38.37
go round about her, *n.* her towers	Ps.48.12
So teach us to *n.* our days that we	Ps.90.12
God has *n.* the days of your kingdom	Dan.5.26
the hairs of your head are all *n.*	Mt.10.30
For he was *n.* among us	Acts 1.17
multitude which no man could *n.*	Rev.7.9

NURSE

Rebekah's *n.* died, and . . . was buried	Gen.35.8
a *n.* from the Hebrew women	Ex.2.7
as a *n.* carries the sucking child	Num.11.12

OATH

Joshua laid an *o.* upon them	Jos.6.26
Saul laid an *o.* on the people	1 Sam.14.24
They took *o.* to the LORD with a	2 Chr.15.14
have sworn an *o.* and confirmed	Ps.119.106
may perform the *o.* which I swore	Jer.11.5
promised with an *o.* to give her	Mt.14.7
again he denied it with an *o.*	Mt.26.72
the *o.* which he swore to our father	Lk.1.73
bound themselves by an *o.*	Acts 23.12
do not swear . . . with any other *o.*	Jas.5.12

OBADIAH
(1) prophet, his prediction, Ob.1–21; (2)
Levite, gatekeeper in the temple, Neh.12.25; (3)
sent by Ahab to find water, 1 Kg.18.3; meets
Elijah, 1 Kg.18.7; hid a hundred prophets, 1 Kg.
18.4,13; (4) others, 1 Chr.7.3; 8.38; 9.16; 12.9;
27.19; 2 Chr.17.7; 34.12; Ezra 8.9

OBEDIENCE

by one man's *o.* many will be made	Rom.5.19
while your *o.* is known to all	Rom.16.19
Confident of your *o.*, I write to	Philem.21
learned *o.* through what he suffered	Heb.5.8

OBEDIENT

If you are willing and *o.*	Is.1.19
to Nazareth, and was *o.* to them	Lk.2.51
many . . . priests were *o.* to the faith	Acts 6.7
Slaves, be *o.* to those who are your	Eph.6.5
o. children, do not be conformed	1 Pet.1.14

OBEISANCE
they bowed their heads and made *o.* Gen.43.28

he fell to the ground and did *o*.	2 Sam.1.2
Bathsheba bowed and did *o*. to	1 Kg.1.16
Mordecai did not bow down or do *o*.	Est.3.2

OBEY

o. the commandments of the LORD	Dt.11.27
serve, and his voice we will *o*.	Jos.24.24
to *o*. is better than sacrifice	1 Sam.15.22
did not *o*. the voice of the LORD	Ps.106.25
O. now the voice of the LORD in	Jer.38.20
that even winds and sea *o*. him?	Mt.8.27
unclean spirits, and they *o*. him	Mk.1.27
he who does not *o*. the Son shall	Jn.3.36
We must *o*. God rather than men	Acts 5.29
are slaves of the one whom you *o*.	Rom.6.16
o. your parents in everything	Col.3.20
By faith Abraham *o*. when he was	Heb.11.8
O. your leaders and submit to them	Heb.13.17
formerly did not *o*., when God's	1 Pet.3.20
love God and *o*. his commandments	1 Jn.5.2

OBSERVE

O. what I command you this day	Ex.34.11
O. the sabbath day, to keep it	Dt.5.12
good care to *o*. the commandment	Jos.22.5
o. and seek . . . the commandments	1 Chr.28.8
Blessed are they who *o*. justice	Ps.106.3
that I may *o*. thy testimonies	Ps.119.146
o. carefully what is before you	Pr.23.1
He who *o*. the wind will not sow	Ec.11.4
so practice and *o*. whatever they	Mt.23.3
teaching them to *o*. all that I have	Mt.28.20
All these I have *o*. from my youth	Lk.18.21
You *o*. days, and months, and	Gal.4.10
like a man who *o*. his natural face	Jas.1.23

OBSTACLE

an *o*. in the way of the gospel	1 Cor.9.12
We put no *o*. in any one's way	2 Cor.6.3
We destroy . . . every proud *o*.	2 Cor.10.5

OBTAIN

lowly in spirit will *o*. honor	Pr.29.23
they shall *o*. joy and gladness	Is.35.10
merciful, for they shall *o*. mercy	Mt.5.7
Through him we have *o*. access to	Rom.5.2
So run that you may *o*. it	1 Cor.9.24
to *o*. salvation through our Lord	1 Th.5.9
you will *o*. the unfading crown of	1 Pet.5.4

OCCASION

seeking an *o*. against the Philistines	Jg.14.4
as fits the *o*., that it may impart	Eph.4.29
give the enemy no *o*. to revile	1 Tim.5.14
would have been no *o*. for a second	Heb.8.7

OCCUPATION

Pharaoh . . . says, 'What is your *o*.?'	Gen.46.33
What is your *o*.? And whence do	Jon.1.8
with the workmen of like *o*.	Acts 19.25

OCCUPY

Let us go up at once, and *o*. it	Num.13.30
they also *o*. the land which the	Dt.3.20
I do not *o*. myself with things too	Ps.131.1
nor to *o*. themselves with myths	1 Tim.1.4

ODOR

the LORD smelled the pleasing *o*.	Gen.8.21
by fire, a pleasing *o*. to the LORD	Lev.1.9
a burnt offering of pleasing *o*.	Num.28.13
pleasing *o*. to all their idols	Ezek.6.13
by this time there will be an *o*.	Jn.11.39

OFFENSE

but love covers all *o*.	Pr.10.12
it is his glory to overlook an *o*.	Pr.19.11
And they took *o*. at him. But Jesus	Mt.13.57
And they took *o*. at him	Mk.6.3
blessed is he who takes no *o*. at me	Lk.7.23
Give no *o*. to Jews or to Greeks	1 Cor.10.32

OFFER

when they *o*. unholy fire	Num.3.4
that the people *o*. themselves	Jg.5.2
I will *o*. in his tent sacrifices	Ps.27.6
O. . . . . a sacrifice of thanksgiving	Ps.50.14
When you *o*. your gifts	Ezek.20.31
Even though you *o*. me your burnt	Am.5.22
And when you *o*. those that are lame	Mal.1.8
o. the gift that Moses commanded	Mt.8.4
to *o*. a sacrifice according to	Lk.2.24
Now concerning food *o*. to idols	1 Cor.8.1
to *o*. gifts and sacrifices for sins	Heb.5.1
Jesus *o*. up prayers and supplications	Heb.5.7
By faith Abel *o*. to God a more	Heb.11.4
By faith Abraham . . . *o*. up Isaac	Heb.11.17
to *o*. spiritual sacrifices	1 Pet.2.5

OFFERING (noun)

had regard for Abel and his *o*.	Gen.4.4
continual burnt *o*. throughout your	Ex.29.42
Sacrifice and *o*. thou dost not	Ps.40.6
With a freewill *o*. I will sacrifice	Ps.54.6
I will render thank *o*. to thee	Ps.56.12
come into thy house with burnt *o*.	Ps.66.13
bring an *o*., and come into his	Ps.96.8
he makes himself an *o*. for sin	Is.53.10
offer burnt *o*. and cereal *o*.	Jer.14.12
not accept an *o*. from your hand	Mal.1.10
make an *o*. for your cleansing	Lk.5.14
that the *o*. of the Gentiles may	Rom.15.16
write . . . about the *o*. for the saints	2 Cor.9.1
the sacrificial *o*. of your faith	Phil.2.17
the gifts you sent, a fragrant *o*.	Phil.4.18
by a single *o*. he has perfected	Heb.10.14

OFFICE

Matthew sitting at the tax *o*.	Mt.9.9
His *o*. let another take	Acts 1.20
the divine *o*. which was given to me	Col.1.25
one aspires to the *o*. of bishop	1 Tim.3.1
took their *o*. without an oath	Heb.7.21

OFFSPRING

Behold, thou hast given me no *o*.	Gen.15.3
All the *o*. of Jacob were seventy	Ex.1.5
Should women eat their *o*.	Lam.2.20
Being then God's *o*., we ought not	Acts 17.29
then you are Abraham's *o*.	Gal.3.29
I am the root and the *o*. of David	Rev.22.16

OFTEN

How *o*. they rebelled against him	Ps.78.40
He who is *o*. reproved, yet stiffens	Pr.29.1
for *o*. he falls into the fire	Mt.17.15
how *o*. shall my brother sin against	Mt.18.21
How *o*. would I have gathered your	Lk.13.34
For as *o*. as you eat this bread	1 Cor.11.26
o. without food, in cold and	2 Cor.11.27

OG

	Num.21.33; Dt.1.4; Jos.2.10; 1 Kg.4.19; Ps. 135.11

OIL

the cruse of *o*. shall not fail	1 Kg.17.14

thou anointest my head with *o.* Ps.23.5
anointed you with the *o.* of gladness Ps.45.7
o. to make his face shine Ps.104.15
like the precious *o.* upon the head Ps.133.2
and her speech is smoother than *o.* Pr.5.3
O. and perfume make the heart glad Pr.27.9
lamps, they took no *o.* with them Mt.25.3
Give us some of your *o.* Mt.25.8
You did not anoint my head with *o.* Lk.7.46
his wounds, pouring on *o.* and wine Lk.10.34

OINTMENT
good name is better than precious *o.* Ec.7.1
Why was the *o.* thus wasted? Mk.14.4
and anointed them with the *o.* Lk.7.38
pound of costly *o.* of pure nard Jn.12.3
Why was this *o.* not sold for three Jn.12.5

OLD
Now Abraham and Sarah were *o.* Gen.18.11
I have been young and now am *o.* Ps.37.25
I will remember thy wonders of *o.* Ps.77.11
thy throne is established from of *o.* Ps.93.2
child shall die a hundred years *o.* Is.65.20
your *o.* men shall dream dreams Jl.2.28
new wine put into *o.* wineskins Mt.9.17
Elizabeth in her *o.* age has also Lk.1.36
can a man be born when he is *o.*? Jn.3.4
Cleanse out the *o.* leaven 1 Cor.5.7
the *o.* has passed away, behold 2 Cor.5.17
Put off your *o.* nature Eph.4.22
God spoke of *o.* to our fathers Heb.1.1
will all grow *o.* like a garment Heb.1.11
an *o.* commandment which you had 1 Jn.2.7

OLIVE
there are two *o.* trees by it Zech.4.3
you, a wild *o.* shoot . . . grafted in Rom.11.17
Can a fig tree . . . yield *o.* Jas.3.12
These are the two *o.* trees Rev.11.4

OLIVET
Lk.19.29; 21.37; Acts 1.12

OMEGA
I am the Alpha and the *O.* Rev.1.8
is done! I am the Alpha and the *O.* Rev.21.6
the Alpha and the *O.*, the first Rev.22.13

OMEN
the men were watching for an *o.* 1 Kg.20.33
for they are men of good *o.* Zech.3.8
This is a clear *o.* to them of Phil.1.28

ONESIMUS
Col.4.9; Philem.10

ONIONS
the leeks, the *o.*, and the garlic Num.11.5

ONYX
bdellium and *o.* stone are there Gen.2.12
And you shall take two *o.* stones Ex.28.9
valued . . . in precious *o.* or sapphire Job 28.16
o., sapphire, carbuncle Ezek.28.13
the fifth *o.*, the sixth carnelian Rev.21.20

OPEN (verb)
Then the eyes of both were *o.* Gen.3.7
if he shuts a man in, none can *o.* Job 12.14
o. thou my lips, and my mouth Ps.51.15
O. your mouth wide, and I will fill it Ps.81.10
O. my eyes, that I may behold Ps.119.18
Thou *o.* thy hand, thou satisfiest Ps.145.16
O. your mouth, judge righteously Pr.31.9
to *o.* the eyes that are blind Is.42.7

if I will not *o.* the windows of Mal.3.10
saying, 'Lord, lord, *o.* to us Mt.25.11
And their eyes were *o.* and they Lk.24.31
hears my voice and *o.* the door Rev.3.20
Then God's temple in heaven was *o.* Rev.11.19

OPENING (noun)
with a woven binding around the *o.* Ex.28.32
Its *o.* was within a crown which 1 Kg.7.31
from the same *o.* fresh water and Jas.3.11

OPHIR
Gen.10.29; 1 Kg.9.28; Ps.45.9; Is.13.12

OPINION
go limping with two different *o.* 1 Kg.18.21
afraid to declare my *o.* to you Job 32.6
but not for disputes over *o.* Rom.14.1
but I give my *o.* as one who by 1 Cor.7.25

OPPORTUNITY
he sought an *o.* to betray him Mt.26.16
freedom, avail yourself of the *o.* 1 Cor.7.21
as we have *o.*, let us do good to all Gal.6.10
give no *o.* to the devil Eph.4.27

OPPOSE
when Cephas came . . . I *o.* him Gal.2.11
so these men also *o.* the truth 2 Tim.3.8
God *o.* the proud, but gives grace Jas.4.6
God *o.* the proud, but gives 1 Pet.5.5

OPPRESS
You shall not *o.* a stranger Ex.23.9
You shall not *o.* a hired servant Dt.24.14
The LORD is a stronghold for the *o.* Ps.9.9
Let the *o.* see it and be glad Ps.69.32
let not the godless *o.* me Ps.119.122
I will punish all who *o.* them Jer.30.20
who *o.* the poor, who crush the needy Am.4.1
not *o.* the widow, the fatherless Zech.7.10
who *o.* the hireling in his wages Mal.3.5
to set at liberty those who are *o.* Lk.4.18
Is it not the rich who *o.* you Jas.2.6

OPPRESSION
I have seen the *o.* with which the Ex.3.9
for he saw the *o.* of Israel 2 Kg.13.4
o. and fraud do not depart from its Ps.55.11
Redeem me from man's *o.* Ps.119.134
who despises the gain of *o.* Is.33.15

OPPRESSOR
Ransom me from the hand of *o.* Job 6.23
give deliverance . . . and crush the *o.* Ps.72.4
The poor man and the *o.* meet Pr.29.13
the rod of his *o.*, thou hast broken Is.9.4
And where is the fury of the *o.*? Is.51.13

ORACLE
The *o.* of Balaam the son of Beor Num.24.3
The *o.* concerning Babylon which Is.13.1
This *o.* concerns the prince in Ezek.12.10
An *o.* concerning Nineveh Nah.1.1
The *o.* of God which Habakkuk Hab.1.1
The *o.* of the word of the LORD to Mal.1.1
he received living *o.* to give to us Acts 7.38
are entrusted with the *o.* of God Rom.3.2
as one who utters *o.* of God 1 Pet.4.11

ORDAIN
Thus you shall *o.* Aaron and his sons Ex.29.9
thou wilt *o.* peace for us Is.26.12
the one *o.* by God to be judge Acts 10.42
as many as were *o.* to eternal life Acts 13.48
it was *o.* by angels through an Gal.3.19

ORDER
the LORD, 'Set your house in *o*.   2 Kg.20.1
for ever after the *o*. of Melchizedek   Ps.110.4
be done decently and in *o*.   1 Cor.14.40
But each in his own *o*.   1 Cor.15.23
priest after the *o*. of Melchizedek   Heb.5.10

ORDINANCE
This is the *o*. of the passover   Ex.12.43
the *o*. of the LORD are true   Ps.19.9
O LORD, and teach me thy *o*.   Ps.119.108
commandments and *o*. of the Lord   Lk.1.6
the law of commandments and *o*.   Eph.2.15

ORIGIN
city whose *o*. is from days of old   Is.23.7
in the land of your *o*.   Ezek.21.30
whose *o*. is from of old   Mic.5.2
who are sanctified have all one *o*.   Heb.2.11

ORPAH
Ru.1.4,14

ORPHAN
shall not afflict any widow or *o*.   Ex.22.22
In thee the *o*. finds mercy   Hos.14.3
who oppress . . . the widow and the *o*.   Mal.3.5
to visit *o*. and widows in their   Jas.1.27

OSTRICH
The wings of the *o*. wave proudly   Job 39.13
haunt of jackals, an abode for *o*.   Is.34.13
and *o*. shall dwell in her   Jer.50.39
jackals, and mourning like the *o*.   Mic.1.8

OUGHT
these you *o*. to have done   Lk.11.42
you also *o*. to wash one another's   Jn.13.14
we *o*. not to think that the Deity   Acts 17.29
more highly than he *o*. to think   Rom.12.3
We who are strong *o*. to bear with   Rom.15.1
declare it boldly, as I *o*. to speak   Eph.6.20
My brethren, this *o*. not to be so   Jas.3.10
Instead you *o*. to say, "If the Lord   Jas.4.15
we also *o*. to love one another   1 Jn.4.11

OUTER
cast him into the *o*. darkness   Mt.22.13
Though our *o*. nature is wasting   2 Cor.4.16
go continually into the *o*. tent   Heb.9.6

OUTSIDE
mother and his brothers stood *o*.   Mt.12.46
you cleanse the *o*. of the cup   Mt.23.25
into a man from *o*. cannot defile   Mk.7.18
But Mary stood weeping *o*. the tomb   Jn.20.11
that I might win those *o*. the law   1 Cor.9.21
let us go forth to him *o*. the camp   Heb.13.13
O. are the dogs and sorcerers   Rev.22.15

OUTSIDER
An *o*. shall not eat of a holy thing   Lev.22.10
how can . . . an *o*. say the "Amen"   1 Cor.14.16
and an unbeliever or *o*. enters   1 Cor.14.24
Conduct yourselves wisely towards *o*.   Col.4.5
you may command the respect of *o*.   1 Th.4.12
he must be well thought of by *o*.   1 Tim.3.7

OUTWARDLY
tombs, which *o*. appear beautiful   Mt.23.27
So you also *o*. appear righteous   Mt.23.28
he is not a real Jew who is one *o*.   Rom.2.28

OVEN
as a blazing *o*. when you appear   Ps.21.9
For like an *o*. their hearts burn   Hos.7.6

the day comes, burning like an *o*.   Mal.4.1
and tomorrow is thrown into the *o*.   Lk.12.28

OVERCOME
and the darkness has not *o*. it   Jn.1.5
of good cheer, I have *o*. the world   Jn.16.33
Do not be *o*. by evil, but *o*. evil   Rom.12.21
Who is it that *o*. the world but he   1 Jn.5.5

OVERFLOW
the Red Sea *o*. them as they   Dt.11.4
my head with oil, my cup *o*.   Ps.23.5
My heart *o*. with a goodly theme   Ps.45.1
shall again *o*. with prosperity   Zech.1.17
pour down for you an *o*. blessing   Mal.3.10

OVERPOWER
by what means we may *o*. him   Jg.16.5
the lions *o*. them and broke all   Dan.6.24
o. them, so that they fled out   Acts 19.16
are . . . entangled in them and *o*.   2 Pet.2.20

OVERSHADOW
o. the mercy seat with their wings   Ex.25.20
a cloud *o*. them, and a voice came out   Mk.9.7
power of the Most High will *o*. you   Lk.1.35
cherubim of glory *o*. the mercy seat   Heb.9.5

OVERTAKE
Terrors *o*. him like a flood   Job 27.20
let thy burning anger *o*. them   Ps.69.24
say, 'Evil shall not *o*. or meet us.'   Am.9.10
the plowman shall *o*. the reaper   Am.9.13
lest the darkness *o*. you   Jn.12.35
No temptation has *o*. you that   1 Cor.10.13
if a man is *o*. in any trespass, you   Gal.6.1

OVERTHROW
confront them, *o*. them! Deliver my   Ps.17.13
I will *o*. the wicked; I will cut off   Zeph.1.3
you will not be able to *o*. them   Acts 5.39
Do we . . . *o*. the law by this faith?   Rom.3.31

OVERWHELM
thou dost *o*. me with all thy waves   Ps.88.7
by thy wrath we are *o*.   Ps.90.7
the mischief of their lips *o*. them   Ps.140.9
Wrath is cruel, anger is *o*.; but   Pr.27.4
he may be *o*. by excessive sorrow   2 Cor.2.7

OWE
he said, 'Pay what you *o*.'   Mt.18.28
'And how much do you *o*.?'   Lk.16.7
O. no one anything, except to love   Rom.13.8

OWL
the *o*., the cormorant, the ibis   Lev.11.17
like an *o*. of the waste places   Ps.102.6
the *o*. and the raven shall dwell in   Is.34.11
the *o*. shall hoot in the window   Zeph.2.14

OWNER
the *o*. of the ox shall be clear   Ex.21.28
the *o*. of the vineyard said to his   Mt.20.8
What will the *o*. of the vineyard do?   Mk.12.9
paid . . . attention . . . to the *o*. of   Acts 27.11
he is the *o*. of all the estate   Gal.4.1

OX
all sheep and *o*., and also the beasts   Ps.8.7
an ass or an *o*. that has fallen   Lk.14.5
Is it for *o*. that God is concerned?   1 Cor.9.9
not muzzle an *o*. when . . . treading   1 Tim.5.18

PAGANS
that is not found even among *p*.   1 Cor.5.1
imply that what *p*. sacrifice   1 Cor.10.20

PAIN

in *p*. you shall bring forth children — Gen.3.16
chastened with *p*. upon his bed — Job 33.19
How long must I bear *p*. in my soul — Ps.13.2
But I am afflicted and in *p*. — Ps.69.29
For all his days are full of *p*. — Ec.2.23
Why is my *p*. unceasing — Jer.15.18
if I cause you *p*., who is there — 2 Cor.2.2
nor crying nor *p*. any more — Rev.21.4

PAINFUL

not to make you another *p*. visit — 2 Cor.2.1
discipline seems *p*. rather than — Heb.12.11

PAIR

Take with you seven *p*. of all clean — Gen.7.2
sell . . . the needy for a *p*. of shoes — Am.2.6
buy . . . the needy for a *p*. of sandals — Am.8.6
a *p*. of turtledoves, or two young — Lk.2.24

PALACE

burned all its *p*. with fire — 2 Chr.36.19
as they enter the *p*. of the king — Ps.45.15
roof of the royal *p*. of Babylon — Dan.4.29
led him away inside the *p*. — Mk.15.16

PALE

no more shall his face grow *p*. — Is.29.22
Why has every face turned *p*.? — Jer.30.6
Hearts faint . . . all faces grow *p*. — Nah.2.10
I saw . . . a *p*. horse, and its rider's — Rev.6.8

PALLET

Rise, take up your *p*. and walk — Mk.2.9
to bring sick people on their *p*. — Mk.6.55
laid them on beds and *p*. — Acts 5.15

PALM

there were . . . seventy *p*. trees — Ex.15.27
righteous flourish like the *p*. tree — Ps.92.12
graven you on the *p*. of my hands — Is.49.16
a *p*. tree between cherub and — Ezek.41.18
they took branches of *p*. trees and — Jn.12.13
with *p*. branches in their hands — Rev.7.9

PAMPHYLIA

Acts 2.10; 14.24; 15.38; 27.5

PANGS·

Many are the *p*. of the wicked — Ps.32.10
the *p*. of Sheol laid hold on me — Ps.116.3
having loosed the *p*. of death — Acts 2.24
pierced their hearts with many *p*. — 1 Tim.6.10

PANIC

threw them into a *p*. before Israel — Jos.10.10
there was a *p*. in the camp — 1 Sam.14.15
I will mock when *p*. strikes you — Pr.1.26
Do not be afraid of sudden *p*. — Pr.3.25
a great *p*. from the LORD shall — Zech.14.13

PARABLE

I will open my mouth in a *p*. — Ps.78.2
Hear then the *p*. of the sower — Mt.13.18
said nothing to them without a *p*. — Mt.13.34
With many such *p*. he spoke the word — Mk.4.33
but for others they are in *p*. — Lk.8.10

PARADISE

today you will be with me in *P*. — Lk.23.43
this man was caught up into *P*. — 2 Cor.12.3
tree of life . . . in the *p*. of God — Rev.2.7

PARALYZED

my servant is lying *p*. at home — Mt.8.6
bringing on a bed a man who was *p*. — Lk.5.18
of invalids, blind, lame, *p*. — Jn.5.3

many who were *p*. or lame were healed — Acts 8.7
bedridden for . . . years and was *p*. — Acts 9.33

PARCHED

my throat is *p*. My eyes grow dim — Ps.69.3
thirsts for thee like a *p*. land — Ps.143.6
the river will be *p*. and dry — Is.19.5
their tongue is *p*. with thirst — Is.41.17

PARDON

p. our iniquity and our sin — Ex.34.9
P. the iniquity of this people — Num.14.19
dost thou not *p*. my transgression — Job 7.21
LORD, *p*. my guilt, for it is great — Ps.25.11
is ended, that her iniquity is *p*. — Is.40.2
our God, for he will abundantly *p*. — Is.55.7
I will *p*. those whom I leave — Jer.50.20

PARENT

his *p*. went to Jerusalem every year — Lk.2.41
wife or brothers or *p*. or children — Lk.18.29
who sinned, this man or his *p*. — Jn.9.2
Children, obey your *p*. in the Lord — Eph.6.1
abusive, disobedient to their *p*. — 2 Tim.3.2
who loves the *p*. loves the child — 1 Jn.5.1

PART

dwell in the uttermost *p*. of the sea — Ps.139.9
brought only a *p*. and laid it at — Acts 5.2
You have neither *p*. nor lot in — Acts 8.21
hardening has come upon *p*. of — Rom.11.25
there are many *p*., yet one body — 1 Cor.12.20
Now I know in *p*.; then I shall — 1 Cor.13.12
when each *p*. is working properly — Eph.4.16

PARTAKERS

p. of the promise in Christ — Eph.3.6
for you are all *p*. with me of grace — Phil.1.7
have become *p*. of the Holy Spirit — Heb.6.4
become *p*. of the divine nature — 2 Pet.1.4

PARTIALITY

I will not show *p*. to any person — Job 32.21
P. in judging is not good — Pr.24.23
show no *p*., but truly teach the — Lk.20.21
I perceive that God shows no *p*. — Acts 10.34
For God shows no *p*. — Rom.2.11
there is no *p*. with him — Eph.6.9
But if you show *p*., you commit sin — Jas.2.9

PARTNER

to their *p*. in the other boat — Lk.5.7
not want you to be *p*. with demons — 1 Cor.10.20
he is my *p*. and fellow worker — 2 Cor.8.23
So if you consider me your *p*. — Philem.17

PARTY

the circumcision *p*. criticized him — Acts 11.2
belonged to the *p*. of the Pharisees — Acts 15.5
fearing the circumcision *p*. — Gal.2.12
selfishness, dissension, *p*. spirit — Gal.5.20

PASS

I will *p*. over you, and no plague — Ex.12.13
all our days *p*. away under thy wrath — Ps.90.9
When you *p*. through the waters — Is.43.2
till heaven and earth *p*. away — Mt.5.18
but my words will not *p*. away — Mt.24.35
the hour might *p*. from him — Mk.14.35
those who would *p*. from here to you — Lk.16.26
but has *p*. from death to life — Jn.5.24
all *p*. through the sea — 1 Cor.10.1
as for prophecies, they will *p*. away — 1 Cor.13.8
let no one *p*. judgment on you — Col.2.16
like . . . the grass he will *p*. away — Jas.1.10

heavens will *p*. away with a loud 2 Pet.3.10
we have *p*. out of death into life 1 Jn.3.14
for the former things have *p*. away Rev.21.4
PASSION
but *p*. makes the bones rot Pr.14.30
alive after his *p*. by many proofs Acts 1.3
consumed with *p*. for one another Rom.1.27
our sinful *p*., aroused by the law Rom.7.5
the flesh with its *p*. and desires Gal.5.24
once lived in the *p*. of our flesh Eph.2.3
So shun youthful *p*. and aim at 2 Tim.2.22
wrongly, to spend it on your *p*. Jas.4.3
p., drunkenness, revels, carousing 1 Pet.4.3
malcontents, following their own *p*. Jude 16
PASSOVER
This is the ordinance of the *p*. Ex.12.43
they kept the *p*. in the first month Num.9.5
keep the *p*. to the LORD your God Dt.16.1
Keep the *p*. to the LORD your God 2 Kg.23.21
Josiah kept a *p*. to the LORD 2 Chr.35.1
No *p*. like it had been kept in 2 Chr.35.18
I will keep the *p*. at your house Mt.26.18
Go and prepare the *p*. for us Lk.22.8
The *P*. of the Jews was at hand Jn.2.13
Now the *P*., the feast of the Jews Jn.6.4
Six days before the *P*., Jesus came Jn.12.1
intending after the *P*. to bring Acts 12.4
he kept the *P*. and sprinkled the Heb.11.28
PASTORS
evangelists, some *p*. and teachers Eph.4.11
PASTURE
he makes me lie down in green *p*. Ps.23.2
we thy people, the flock of thy *p*. Ps.79.13
the sheep of his *p*. Ps.100.3
and scatter the sheep of my *p*. Jer.23.1
I will restore Israel to his *p*. Jer.50.19
he . . . will go in and out and find *p*. Jn.10.9
PATH
Thou dost show me the *p*. of life Ps.16.11
He leads me in *p*. of righteousness Ps.23.3
lead me on a level *p*. because of my Ps.27.11
Thy word is . . . a light to my *p*. Ps.119.105
Thou searchest out my *p*. and my Ps.139.3
he will make straight your *p*. Pr.3.6
the *p*. of the upright is a level Pr.15.19
as he sowed, some fell along the *p*. Lk.8.5
make straight *p*. for your feet Heb.12.13
PATIENCE
and bring forth fruit with *p*. Lk.8.15
do not see, we wait for it with *p*. Rom.8.25
p., kindness, goodness Gal.5.22
with *p*., forbearing one another Eph.4.2
for all endurance and *p*. with joy Col.1.11
his perfect *p*. for an example 1 Tim.1.16
be unfailing in *p*. and in teaching 2 Tim.4.2
faith and *p*. inherit the promises Heb.6.12
As an example of suffering and *p*. Jas.5.10
God's *p*. waited in the days of 1 Pet.3.20
PATIENT
the *p*. in spirit is better than Ec.7.8
be *p*. in tribulation, be constant Rom.12.12
Love is *p*. and kind; love is not 1 Cor.13.4
help the weak, be *p*. with them all 1 Th.5.14
Be *p*., therefore, brethren, until . Jas.5.7
I know . . . your *p*. endurance Rev.2.2
have kept my word of *p*. endurance Rev.3.10

PATIENTLY
before the LORD and wait *p*. for him Ps.37.7
I waited *p*. for the LORD Ps.40.1
I beg you to listen to me *p*. Acts 26.3
you *p*. endure the same sufferings 2 Cor.1.6
I know you are enduring *p*. Rev.2.3
PATMOS
Rev.1.9
PATTERN
concerning the *p*. of the tabernacle Ex.25.9
Follow the *p*. of the sound words 2 Tim.1.13
according to the *p*. which was shown Heb.8.5
PAUL
as a persecutor, Acts 7.58; 8.1; 9.1; 22.4; 26.9;
1 Cor.15.9; Gal.1.13; Phil.3.6; 1 Tim.1.13; as a
convert to the gospel, Acts 9.3–19; 22.6–16;
26.12–18; as a preacher, Acts 9.19–29; 13.1–15;
17.18; stoned at Lystra, Acts 14.8,19; is persecuted at Philippi, Acts 16; restores Eutychus,
Acts 20.10; his charge to the elders of Ephesus,
at Miletus, Acts 20.17; his return to Jerusalem,
and persecution there, Acts 21; his defense
before the people and the council, Acts 22–23;
before Felix, Acts 24; Festus, Acts 25; Agrippa,
Acts 26; appeals to Caesar at Rome, Acts
25.11; his voyage and shipwreck, Acts 27; at
Rome, reasons with the Jews, Acts 28.17–20; his
sufferings, 1 Cor.4.9; 2 Cor.11.23–28; 12.7;
Phil.1.12; 2 Tim.3.11; defends his apostleship,
1 Cor.9; 2 Cor.11–12; 2 Tim.3.10; rebukes
Peter, Gal.2.14; his letters mentioned in 2
Pet.3.15-16
PAVEMENT
as it were a *p*. of sapphire stone Ex.24.10
silver on a mosaic *p*. of porphyry Est.1.6
thirty chambers fronted on the *p*. Ezek.40.17
at a place called The *P*. Jn.19.13
PAY (verb)
thief is found, he shall *p*. double Ex.22.7
Go, sell the oil and *p*. your debts 2 Kg.4.7
my vows I will *p*. before those who Ps.22.24
I will *p*. my vows to the LORD in Ps.116.15
PAYMENT
whether in *p*. of a vow or as a Lev.22.18
all that he had, and *p*. to be made Mt.18.25
I have received full *p*., and more Phil.4.18
PEACE
The LORD . . . give you *p*. Num.6.26
I give to him my covenant of *p*. Num.25.12
P. be to you, and *p*. be to 1 Sam.25.6
In *p*. I will both lie down and Ps.4.8
do good; seek *p*., and pursue it Ps.34.14
Great *p*. have those who love thy Ps.119.165
Pray for the *p*. of Jerusalem Ps.122.6
his enemies to be at *p*. with him Pr.16.7
Everlasting Father, Prince of *P*. Is.9.6
Thou dost keep him in perfect *p*. Is.26.3
"There is no *p*.," says the LORD Is.48.22
who publishes *p*., who brings good Is.52.7
'*P*., *p*.,' when there is no *p*. Jer.6.14
I have not come to bring *p*., but a Mt.10.34
said to the sea, "*P*.! Be still!" Mk.4.39
be at *p*. with one another Mk.9.50
guide our feet into the way of *p*. Lk.1.79
on earth *p*. among men with whom Lk.2.14
lettest thou thy servant depart in *p*. Lk.2.29

PEACEABLE

P. in heaven and glory in the	Lk.19.38
P. I leave with you; my *p.* I give	Jn.14.27
we have *p.* with God through our	Rom.5.1
The God of *p.* be with you all	Rom.15.33
For he is our *p.*, who has made us	Eph.2.14
the *p.* of God, which passes all	Phil.4.7
let the *p.* of Christ rule in your	Col.3.15
Be at *p.* among yourselves	1 Th.5.13
Strive for *p.* with all men	Heb.12.14
Now may the God of *p.* who brought	Heb.13.20

PEACEABLE

those who are *p.* and faithful	2 Sam.20.19
we may lead a quiet and *p.* life	1 Tim.2.2
then *p.*, gentle, open to reason	Jas.3.17

PEACEFUL

will abide in a *p.* habitation	Is.32.18
p. understanding shall be between	Zech.6.13
the *p.* fruit of righteousness	Heb.12.11

PEACEMAKERS

Blessed are the *p.*	Mt.5.9

PEARL

the price of wisdom is above *p.*	Job 28.18
do not throw your *p.* before swine	Mt.7.6
finding one *p.* of great value	Mt.13.46
or gold or *p.* or costly attire	1 Tim.2.9
the twelve gates were twelve *p.*	Rev.21.21

PENALTY

man of great wrath will pay the *p.*	Pr.19.19
You bear the *p.* of your lewdness	Ezek.16.58
no reason for the death *p.*	Acts 28.18
receiving . . . due *p.* for their error	Rom.1.27

PENTECOST

When the day of *P.* had come	Acts 2.1
if possible, on the day of *P.*	Acts 20.16
I will stay in Ephesus until *P.*	1 Cor.16.8

PERCEIVE

see and see, but do not *p.*	Is.6.9
they may indeed see but not *p.*	Mk.4.12
lest they . . . *p.* with their heart	Jn.12.40
Truly I *p.* that God shows no	Acts 10.34
they should *p.* with their eyes	Acts 28.27
been clearly *p.* in the things that	Rom.1.20
they *p.* the grace that was given	Gal.2.9

PERDITION

the torrents of *p.* assailed me	Ps.18.4
none . . . is lost but the son of *p.*	Jn.17.12
is revealed, the son of *p.*	2 Th.2.3
The beast . . . is to . . . go to *p.*	Rev.17.8

PERFECT

This God–his way is *p.*	2 Sam.22.31
of him who is *p.* in knowledge	Job 37.16
The law of the LORD is *p.*, reviving	Ps.19.7
Thou dost keep him in *p.* peace	Is.26.3
be *p.*, as your heavenly Father is *p.*	Mt.5.48
what is good and acceptable and *p.*	Rom.12.2
when the *p.* comes, the imperfect	1 Cor.13.10
my power is made *p.* in weakness	2 Cor.12.9
make . . . *p.* through suffering	Heb.2.10
the spirits of just men made *p.*	Heb.12.23
every *p.* gift is from above	Jas.1.17
But he who looks into the *p.* law	Jas.1.25
but *p.* love casts out fear	1 Jn.4.18
I have not found your works *p.*	Rev.3.2

PERFECTION

the *p.* of beauty, God shines forth	Ps.50.2
I have seen a limit to all *p.*	Ps.119.96

PERSECUTE

which was called the *p.* of beauty	Lam.2.15
Now if *p.* had been attainable	Heb.7.11

PERFORM

to *p.* the words of the covenant	2 Chr.34.31
My vows to thee I must *p.*, O God	Ps.56.12
make vows to the LORD and *p.* them	Is.19.21
am watching over my word to *p.* it	Jer.1.12
that I may *p.* the oath which I	Jer.11.5
turn to God and *p.* deeds worthy	Acts 26.20

PERIL

our bread at the *p.* of our lives	Lam.5.9
or nakedness, or *p.*, or sword?	Rom.8.35
Why am I in *p.* every hour?	1 Cor.15.30
delivered us from so deadly a *p.*	2 Cor.1.10

PERISH

Let the day *p.* wherein I was born	Job 3.3
all flesh would *p.* together	Job 34.15
but the way of the wicked will *p.*	Ps.1.6
he is like the beasts that *p.*	Ps.49.12
who are far from thee shall *p.*	Ps.73.27
They will *p.*, but thou dost endure	Ps.102.26
A false witness will *p.*	Pr.21.28
LORD our God has doomed us to *p.*	Jer.8.14
all who take the sword will *p.*	Mt.26.52
Teacher, do you not care if we *p.*?	Mk.4.38
But not a hair of your head will *p.*	Lk.21.18
should not *p.* but have eternal life	Jn.3.16
Do not labor for the food which *p.*	Jn.6.27
will also *p.* without the law	Rom.2.12
is folly to those who are *p.*	1 Cor.1.18
not wishing that any should *p.*	2 Pet.3.9

PERISHABLE

They do it to receive a *p.* wreath	1 Cor.9.25
nor does the *p.* inherit the	1 Cor.15.50
not of *p.* seed but of imperishable	1 Pet.1.23

PERMIT

he will never *p.* the righteous to	Ps.55.22
he would not *p.* the demons to speak	Mk.1.34
time with you, if the Lord *p.*	1 Cor.16.7
I *p.* no woman to teach or to have	1 Tim.2.12
And this we will do if God *p.*	Heb.6.3
its rider was *p.* to take peace from	Rev.6.4

PERPETUAL

keep the sabbath . . . as a *p.* covenant	Ex.31.16
shall be to you for a *p.* statute	Num.10.8
the covenant of a *p.* priesthood	Num.25.13
a *p.* barrier which it cannot pass	Jer.5.22
everlasting reproach and *p.* shame	Jer.23.40
shall sleep a *p.* sleep and not wake	Jer.51.57
I will make you a *p.* desolation	Ezek.35.9

PERPLEXED

When he heard him, he was much *p.*	Mk.6.20
While they were *p.* about this	Lk.24.4
all were amazed and *p.*	Acts 2.12
for I am *p.* about you	Gal.4.20

PERSECUTE

Princes *p.* me without cause	Ps.119.161
Let those be put to shame who *p.*	Jer.17.18
pray for those who *p.* you	Mt.5.44
When they *p.* you in one town, flee	Mt.10.23
If they *p.* me, they will *p.* you	Jn.15.20
Saul, Saul, why do you *p.* me?	Acts 9.4
Bless those who *p.* you; bless and	Rom.12.14
when *p.*, we endure	1 Cor.4.12
I *p.* the church of God violently	Gal.1.13
live a godly life . . . will be *p.*	2 Tim.3.12

PERSECUTION

tribulation or *p*. arises on account	Mt.13.21
great *p*. arose against the church	Acts 8.1
or *p*., or famine, or nakedness	Rom.8.35
in all your *p*. and in the afflictions	2 Th.1.4
my *p*., my sufferings	2 Tim.3.11

PERSECUTOR

from the hand of my enemies and *p*.	Ps.31.15
Many are my *p*. and my adversaries	Ps.119.157
Deliver me from my *p*.	Ps.142.6
take vengeance for me on my *p*.	Jer.15.15
as to zeal a *p*. of the church	Phil.3.6

PERSIA

2 Chr.36.20; Ezra 1.1; Est.1.3; Ezek.27.10; Dan.8.20

PERSUADE

the elders *p*. the people to ask for	Mt.27.20
This man is *p*. men to worship God	Acts 18.13
for I am *p*. that none of these	Acts 26.26
I know and am *p*. in the Lord Jesus	Rom.14.14
the fear of the Lord, we *p*. men	2 Cor.5.11

PERVERSE

the *p*. tongue will be cut off	Pr.10.31
Men of *p*. mind are an abomination	Pr.11.20
A *p*. man spreads strife	Pr.16.28
and your mind utter *p*. things	Pr.23.33
O faithless and *p*. generation	Lk.9.41
will arise men speaking *p*. things	Acts 20.30
a crooked and *p*. generation	Phil.2.15

PERVERSENESS

P. of heart shall be far from me	Ps.101.4
delight in the *p*. of evil	Pr.2.14
and trust in oppression and *p*.	Is.30.12

PERVERT

You shall not *p*. the justice due	Ex.23.6
the Almighty will not *p*. justice	Job 34.12
We found this man *p*. our nation	Lk.23.2
and want to *p*. the gospel of Christ	Gal.1.7
such a person is *p*. and sinful	Tit.3.11
persons who *p*. the grace of our God	Jude 4

PESTILENCE

lest he fall upon us with *p*.	Ex.5.3
the Lord sent a *p*. upon Israel	1 Chr.21.14
he will deliver . . . from the deadly *p*.	Ps.91.3
nor the *p*. that stalks in darkness	Ps.91.6
by the sword, by famine, and by *p*.	Jer.14.12
I sent among you a *p*. after the	Am.4.10
in various places famines and *p*.	Lk.21.11
p. and mourning and famine	Rev.18.8

PETER

Apostle, called, Mt.4.18; Mk.1.16; Lk.5.1–11; Jn.1.35; sent forth, Mt.10.2–5; Mk.3.16; Lk. 6.14; tries to walk to Jesus on the sea, Mt.14.29; confesses Jesus to be the Christ, Mt.16.16; Mk.8.29; Lk.9.20; witnesses the transfiguration, Mt.17; Mk.9; Lk.9.28–36 (2 Pet.1.16–17); his self-confidence reproved, Lk.22.31; Jn.13.36; thrice denies Jesus, Mt.26.69–74; Mk.14.66–71; Lk.22.57–61; Jn.18.17; his repentance, Mt. 26.75; Mk.14.72; Lk.22.62; sermon at Pentecost, Acts 2.14–36; brought before the council, Acts 4; condemns Ananias and Sapphira, Acts 5; denounces Simon the magician, Acts 8.20–23; sent for by Cornelius, Acts 10; instructed in a vision not to despise the Gentiles, Acts 10.9–16; imprisoned, and liberated by an angel, Acts 12; his

decision about circumcision, Acts 15.7–11; rebuked by Paul, Gal.2.14

PHARAOH

when the princes of *P*. saw her	Gen.12.15
P. was angry with his two officers	Gen.40.2
P. dreamed that he was standing by	Gen.41.1
Then *P*. said to Joseph, "Behold	Gen.41.17
they built for *P*. store-cities	Ex.1.11
Then *P*. called Moses and Aaron	Ex.8.25
But *P*. hardened his heart this time	Ex.8.32
the Lord hardened the heart of *P*.	Ex.9.12
Then *P*. called Moses, and said, "Go	Ex.10.24
your God did to *P*. and to all Egypt	Dt.7.18
Joseph's family became known to *P*.	Acts 7.13
For the scripture says to *P*.	Rom.9.17

PHARISEES

notable Pharisees: Nicodemus, Jn.3.1; Simon, Lk.7.36–47; Gamaliel, Acts 5.34; Saul of Tarsus, Acts 23.6; 26.5; Phil.3.5; Jesus entertained by, Lk.7.36; 11.37; 14.1; Jesus utters woes against, Mt.23.13; Lk.11.42; Jesus questioned by, about: divorce, Mt.19.3; eating, Mt.9.11; 15.1; Mk.2.16; Lk.5.30; forgiveness of sin, Lk.5.21; sabbath, Mt.12.2,10; fasting, Mk.2.18; taxes, Mt.22.17; murmur against Jesus, Mt.9.34; Lk.15.2; denounced by Jesus, Mt.5.20; 16.6; 21.43; 23; Lk.11.39; people cautioned against, Mk.8.15; Lk.12.1; seek a sign from Jesus, Mt.12.38; 16.1; take counsel against Jesus, Mt.12.14; Mk.3.6; Nicodemus remonstrates with, Jn.7.51; cast out the man cured of blindness, Jn.9.34; dissensions among, Jn.9.16; send officers to arrest Jesus, Jn.7.32; contend about circumcision, Acts 15.5; their belief in the resurrection, Acts 23.8; and tax collector, Lk.18.10–14

PHILIP

(1) Apostle, called, Jn.1.43; sent forth, Mt.10.3; Mk.3.18; Lk.6.14; Jn.12.22; Acts 1.13; remonstrated with by Jesus, Jn.14.8; (2) the evangelist, Acts 6.5; preaches in Samaria, Acts 8.5; baptizes the Ethiopian, Acts 8.38; his four daughters prophesy, Acts 21.8–9; (3) Herod Philip, half-brother of Herod Antipas, and tetrarch of Trachonitis, Lk.3.1; (4) half-brother of (3) and of Herod Antipas, first husband of Herodias, and father of Salome, Mt.14.3; Mk.6.17; Lk.3.19

PHILIPPI

Mt.16.13; Acts 16.12; Phil.1.1; 1 Th.2.2

PHILISTIA

Ex.15.14; Ps.83.7, 108.9; Zech.9.6

PHILISTINES

Gen.10.14; Ex.13.17; Jos.13.2; 1 Sam.4.2; 18.27; 1 Chr.1.12; Zeph.2.5

PHILOSOPHERS

Epicurean and Stoic *p*. met him	Acts 17.18

PHILOSOPHY

makes a prey of you by *p*. and	Col.2.8

PHOENICIA

Ob.20; Acts 11.19; 15.3; 21.2

PHYSICIAN

who are well have no need of a *p*.	Mt.9.12
had suffered much under many *p*.	Mk.5.26
this proverb, '*P*., heal yourself	Lk.4.23

who are well have no need of a *p.* Lk.5.31
Luke the beloved *p.* and Demas greet Col.4.14

PIECES
dash them in *p.* like a potter's vessel Ps.2.9
thou that didst cut Rahab in *p.* Is.51.9
little ones shall be dashed in *p.* Hos.13.16
they paid him thirty *p.* of silver Mt.26.15
twelve baskets of broken *p.* Lk.9.17
on planks or on *p.* of the ship Acts 27.44

PIERCE
they have *p.* my hands and feet Ps.22.16
look on him whom they have *p.* Zech.12.10
a sword will *p.* through your own soul Lk.2.35
soldiers *p.* his side with a spear Jn.19.34
will see him, every one who *p.* him Rev.1.7

PIGEON
a turtledove, and a young *p.* Gen.15.9
or young *p.* such as he can afford Lev.14.30
and the seats of those who sold *p.* Mt.21.12
he told those who sold the *p.* Jn.2.16

PILATE
Pontius, governor of Judea during Jesus' ministry, sufferings, and death, Lk.3.1; admonished by his wife, examines Jesus, washes his hands, but delivers him to be crucified, Mt.27; Mk.15; Lk.23; Jn.18–19; grants request of Joseph of Arimathea, Mt.27.57–60; Mk.15.42–46; Lk. 23.50–53; Jn.19.38; *see* Acts 3.13; 4.27; 13.28; 1 Tim.6.13

PILLAR
Lot's wife . . . became a *p.* of salt Gen.19.26
p. of cloud by day . . . *p.* of fire Ex.13.22
erect no graven image or *p.* Lev.26.1
And you shall not set up a *p.* Dt.16.22
He spoke to them in the *p.* of cloud Ps.99.7
who were reputed to be *p.* Gal.2.9
the *p.* and bulwark of the truth 1 Tim.3.15
I will make him a *p.* in the temple Rev.3.12

PISGAH
Num.21.20; Dt.3.17; Jos.12.3; 13.20

PIT
The *p.* was empty, there was no Gen.37.24
His soul draws near the *P.* Job 33.22
like those who go down to the *P.* Ps.28.1
He drew me up from the desolate *p.* Ps.40.2
who redeems your life from the *P.* Ps.103.4
He who digs a *p.* will fall into it Pr.26.27
falls into a *p.* on the sabbath Mt.12.11
Will they not both fall into a *p.*? Lk.6.39
the shaft of the bottomless *p.* Rev.9.1

PITY (noun)
I looked for *p.*, but there was none Ps.69.20
He has *p.* on the weak and the needy Ps.72.13
wilt arise and have *p.* on Zion Ps.102.13
in his *p.* he redeemed them Is.63.9
And Jesus in *p.* touched their eyes Mt.20.34
Moved with *p.*, he stretched out his Mk.1.41

PITY (verb)
so the LORD *p.* those who fear him Ps.103.13
said to him, "Call her name Not *p.* Hos.1.6
And should not I *p.* Nineveh Jon.4.11
we are of all men most to be *p.* 1 Cor.15.19

PLACE (noun)
for the *p.* on which you are standing Ex.3.5
And who shall stand in his holy *p.*? Ps.24.3
the *p.* where thy glory dwells Ps.26.8

How lovely is thy dwelling *p.* Ps.84.1
our dwelling *p.* in all generations Ps.90.1
The eyes of the LORD are in every *p.* Pr.15.3
I dwell in the high and holy *p.* Is.57.15
and said, "This is a lonely *p.* Mt.14.15
(which means the *p.* of a skull) Mt.27.33
Come, see the *p.* where he lay Mt.28.6
Jerusalem is the *p.* where men ought Jn.4.20
that I go to prepare a *p.* for you? Jn.14.2
they were all together in one *p.* Acts 2.1
who in every *p.* call on the name 1 Cor.1.2
his right hand in the heavenly *p.* Eph.1.20
a dwelling *p.* of God in the Spirit Eph.2.22
enters the Holy *P.* yearly with Heb.9.25

PLAGUE (noun)
the LORD sent a *p.* upon the people Ex.32.35
companions stand aloof from my *p.* Ps.38.11
diseases and *p.* and evil spirits Lk.7.21
the seven angels with the seven *p.* Rev.15.6
add to him the *p.* described in Rev.22.18

PLAIN (adjective)
make it *p.* upon tablets, so he may Hab.2.2
what can be known about God is *p.* Rom.1.19
we have made this *p.* to you 2 Cor.11.6
Now the works of the flesh are *p.* Gal.5.19
for their folly will be *p.* to all 2 Tim.3.9
that it might be *p.* that they all 1 Jn.2.19

PLAN (noun)
understands every *p.* and thought 1 Chr.28.9
that God had frustrated their *p.* Neh.4.15
the definite *p.* and foreknowledge Acts 2.23
whatever . . . thy *p.* had predestined Acts 4.28
as a *p.* for the fulness of time Eph.1.10
see what is the *p.* of the mystery Eph.3.9

PLANT (noun)
have given every green *p.* for food Gen.1.30
p. for man to cultivate, that he Ps.104.14
grew up before him like a young *p.* Is.53.2
Every *p.* which my heavenly Father Mt.15.13

PLANT (verb)
the LORD God *p.* a garden in Eden Gen.2.8
He is like a tree *p.* by streams of Ps.1.3
but them thou didst *p.* Ps.44.2
a time to *p.*, and a time to pluck Ec.3.2
I will *p.* you, and not pluck you up Jer.42.10
I will *p.* them upon their land Am.9.15
Father has not *p.* will be rooted up Mt.15.13
A man *p.* a vineyard, and set a hedge Mk.12.1
I *p.*, Apollos watered, but God gave 1 Cor.3.6

PLATTER
the head of John . . . here on a *p.* Mt.14.8

PLAYING
while David was *p.* the lyre 1 Sam.18.10
will make you stop *p.* the harlot Ezek.16.41
boys and girls *p.* in its streets Zech.8.5
sound of harpers *p.* on their harps Rev.14.2

PLEAD
Arise, O God, *p.* thy cause Ps.74.22
P. my cause and redeem me Ps.119.154
for the LORD will *p.* their cause Pr.22.23
p. for the widow Is.1.17
how he *p.* with God against Israel? Rom.11.2

PLEASANT
every tree that is *p.* to the sight Gen.2.9
have fallen for me in *p.* places Ps.16.6
how good and *p.* it is when brothers Ps.133.1

bread eaten in secret is *p.*   Pr.9.17
P. words are like a honeycomb   Pr.16.24
you have planted *p.* vineyards   Am.5.11
the *p.* land was made desolate   Zech.7.14
seems painful rather than *p.*   Heb.12.11

PLEASE
Be *p.,* O God, to deliver me   Ps.70.1
When a man's ways *p.* the LORD   Pr.16.7
my . . . Son, with whom I am well *p.*   Mt.3.17
For Christ did not *p.* himself   Rom.15.3
I try to *p.* all men in everything   1 Cor.10.33
the fulness of God was *p.* to dwell   Col.1.19
without faith . . . impossible to *p.* him   Heb.11.6
such sacrifices are *p.* to God   Heb.13.16

PLEASURE
thy right hand are *p.* for evermore   Ps.16.11
Do good to Zion in thy good *p.*   Ps.51.18
I kept my heart from no *p.*   Ec.2.10
you will say, "I have no *p.* in them"   Ec.12.1
from doing your *p.* on my holy day   Is.58.13
For I have no *p.* in the death of   Ezek.18.32
Father's good *p.* to give you the   Lk.12.32
lovers of *p.* rather than lovers of   2 Tim.3.4
than to enjoy the fleeting *p.* of sin   Heb.11.25

PLEDGE (noun)
take your neighbor's garment in *p.*   Ex.22.26
an oath to bind himself by a *p.*   Num.30.2
they take the widow's ox for a *p.*   Job 24.3
A man without sense gives a *p.*   Pr.17.18
exacts no *p.,* commits no robbery   Ezek.18.16
having violated their first *p.*   1 Tim.5.12

PLEIADES
the *P.* and the chambers of the south   Job 9.9
Can you bind the chains of the *P.*   Job 38.31
He who made the *P.* and Orion   Am.5.8

PLENTEOUS
during the seven *p.* years   Gen.41.34
with him is *p.* redemption   Ps.130.7
the ground . . . will be rich and *p.*   Is.30.23

PLENTY
seven years of *p.* that prevailed   Gen.41.53
your barns will be filled with *p.*   Pr.3.10
You shall eat in *p.* and be satisfied   Jl.2.26
the secret of facing *p.* and hunger   Phil.4.12

PLOT (verb)
why do . . . the peoples *p.* in vain?   Ps.2.1
The wicked *p.* against the righteous   Ps.37.12
What do you *p.* against the LORD?   Nah.1.9
the Jews *p.* to kill him   Acts 9.23

PLOW
shall not *p.* with an ox and an ass   Dt.22.10
If you had not *p.* with my heifer   Jg.14.18
sluggard does not *p.* in the autumn   Pr.20.4
Does one *p.* the sea with oxen?   Am.6.12
his hand to the *p.* and looks back   Lk.9.62

PLOWMAN
the *p.* shall overtake the reaper   Am.9.13
the *p.* should plow in hope   1 Cor.9.10

PLOWSHARES
shall beat their swords into *p.*   Is.2.4
Beat your *p.* into swords, and your   Jl.3.10
shall beat their swords into *p.*   Mic.4.3

PLUCK
he will *p.* my feet out of the net   Ps.25.15
and a time to *p.* up what is planted   Ec.3.2
I will *p.* up the house of Judah   Jer.12.14

I will plant you, and not *p.* you up   Jer.42.10
a brand *p.* from the fire?   Zech.3.2
p. it out and throw it away   Mt.5.29
disciples began to *p.* ears of grain   Mk.2.23
eye causes you to sin, *p.* it out   Mk.9.47

PLUNDER (verb)
may strangers *p.* the fruits of his   Ps.109.11
shall *p.* the people of the east   Is.11.14
all who *p.* her shall be sated   Jer.50.10
your strongholds shall be *p.*   Am.3.11
Because you have *p.* many nations   Hab.2.8
Then indeed he may *p.* his house   Mt.12.29

POINT (noun)
Hezekiah . . . was at the *p.* of death   Is.38.1
my . . . daughter is at the *p.* of death   Mk.5.23
son, for he was at the *p.* of death   Jn.4.47
Christ from a human *p.* of view   2 Cor.5.16
The *p.* is this: he who sows   2 Cor.9.6
Now the *p.* in what we are saying is   Heb.8.1
to the *p.* of shedding your blood   Heb.12.4
fails in one *p.* has become guilty   Jas.2.10
remains and is on the *p.* of death   Rev.3.2

POISON (noun)
They gave me *p.* for food   Ps.69.21
under their lips is the *p.* of vipers   Ps.140.3
you have turned justice into *p.*   Am.6.12
a restless evil, full of deadly *p.*   Jas.3.8

POLLUTE
You shall not thus *p.* the land   Num.35.33
the land was *p.* with blood   Ps.106.38
You have *p.* the land with your vile   Jer.3.2
and *p.* yourself with their idols   Ezek.23.30
And you say, 'How have we *p.* it?'   Mal.1.7

POMP
splendor and *p.* of his majesty   Est.1.4
Man cannot abide in his *p.*   Ps.49.12
Your *p.* is brought down to Sheol   Is.14.11
Bernice came with great *p.*   Acts 25.23

POOR
be partial to a *p.* man in his suit   Ex.23.3
But if he is *p.* and cannot afford   Lev.14.21
For the *p.* will never cease out of   Dt.15.11
The LORD makes *p.* and makes rich   1 Sam.2.7
but he took the *p.* man's lamb   2 Sam.12.4
Was not my soul grieved for the *p.*   Job 30.25
This *p.* man cried, and the LORD heard   Ps.34.6
As for me, I am *p.* and needy   Ps.40.17
Blessed is he who considers the *p.*   Ps.41.1
He raises the *p.* from the dust   Ps.113.7
He who mocks the *p.* insults his   Pr.17.5
The rich and the *p.* meet together   Pr.22.2
Better is a *p.* man who walks in his   Pr.28.6
He who gives to the *p.* will not   Pr.28.27
or lest I be *p.,* and steal, and   Pr.30.9
Yet no one remembered that *p.* man   Ec.9.15
by grinding the face of the *p.?*   Is.3.15
hast been a stronghold to the *p.*   Is.25.4
Blessed are the *p.* in spirit   Mt.5.3
and the *p.* have good news preached   Mt.11.5
you always have the *p.* with you   Mt.26.11
a *p.* widow came, and put in two   Mk.12.42
at his gate lay a *p.* man . . . Lazarus   Lk.16.20
as *p.,* yet making many rich   2 Cor.6.10
yet for your sake he became *p.*   2 Cor.8.9
and a *p.* man in shabby clothing   Jas.2.2
pitiable, *p.,* blind, and naked   Rev.3.17

PORTION

I am your *p*. and your inheritance	Num.18.20
For the LORD's *p*. is his people	Dt.32.9
This is the *p*. of a wicked man	Job 27.13
The LORD is my chosen *p*. and my cup	Ps.16.5
my *p*. in the land of the living	Ps.142.5
divide him a *p*. with the great	Is.53.12
Mary has chosen the good *p*.	Lk.10.42

POSITION

you do not regard the *p*. of men	Mt.22.16
one in the *p*. of an outsider	1 Cor.14.16
pride themselves on a man's *p*.	2 Cor.5.12
kings and all who are in high *p*.	1 Tim.2.2

POSSESS

to give you this land to *p*.	Gen.15.7
God has given you this land to *p*.	Dt.3.18
and his children shall *p*. the land	Ps.25.13
The righteous shall *p*. the land	Ps.37.29
your descendants will *p*. the nations	Is.54.3
many who were *p*. with demons	Mt.8.16
sell what you *p*. and give to them	Mt.19.21
any of the things which he *p*. was	Acts 4.32
truths to those who *p*. the Spirit	1 Cor.2.13
However, not all *p*. this knowledge	1 Cor.8.7
having nothing, and yet *p*.	2 Cor.6.10

POSSESSION

of Canaan, for an everlasting *p*.	Gen.17.8
the ends of the earth your *p*.	Ps.2.8
for himself, Israel as his own *p*.	Ps.135.4
no *p*. in Israel; I am their *p*.	Ezek.44.28
my special *p*. on the day when I act	Mal.3.17
sorrowful; for he had great *p*.	Mt.19.22
they sold their *p*. and goods	Acts 2.45
inheritance until we acquire *p*. of	Eph.1.14
had a better *p*. and an abiding one	Heb.10.34

POSSIBLE

but with God all things are *p*.	Mt.19.26
if it be *p*., let this cup pass from me	Mt.26.39
it was not *p*. for him to be held	Acts 2.24
If *p*., so far as it depends upon	Rom.12.18
if *p*., you would have plucked out	Gal.4.15
that if *p*. I may attain the	Phil.3.11

POSTERITY

the *p*. of the wicked shall be cut off	Ps.37.38
May his *p*. be cut off	Ps.109.13
to Abraham and to his *p*. for ever	Lk.1.55
in your *p*. shall all . . . be blessed	Acts 3.25
Of this man's *p*. God has brought	Acts 13.23

POTIPHAR

	Gen.37.36; 39.1

POTTER

we are the clay, and thou art our *p*.	Is.64.8
as it seemed good to the *p*. to do	Jer.18.4
bought with them the *p*. field	Mt.27.7
Has the *p*. no right over the clay	Rom.9.21

POUND

your *p*. has made ten *p*. more	Lk.19.16
here is your *p*., which I kept	Lk.19.20
Mary took a *p*. of costly ointment	Jn.12.3
aloes, about a hundred *p*. weight	Jn.19.39

POUR

I am *p*. out like water, and all my	Ps.22.14
as I *p*. out my soul	Ps.42.4
P. out thy indignation upon them	Ps.69.24
My lips will *p*. forth praise	Ps.119.171
The mouths of fools *p*. out folly	Pr.15.2

because he *p*. out his soul to death	Is.53.12
P. out your heart like water before	Lam.2.19
I *p*. out my Spirit upon . . . Israel	Ezek.39.29
p. down for you an overflowing	Mal.3.10
I will *p*. out my Spirit upon all	Acts 2.17
love has been *p*. into our hearts	Rom.5.5
if I am to be *p*. as a libation	Phil.2.17
which he *p*. out upon us richly	Tit.3.6
Does a spring *p*. forth from the	Jas.3.11
p. out on the earth the seven bowls	Rev.16.1

POVERTY

A slack hand causes *p*.	Pr.10.4
Love not sleep, lest you come to *p*.	Pr.20.13
give me neither *p*. nor riches	Pr.30.8
she out of her *p*. put in all . . . she had	Lk.21.4
so that by his *p*. you might become	2 Cor.8.9
I know . . . your *p*. (but you are rich)	Rev.2.9

POWER

Thy right hand . . . glorious in *p*.	Ex.15.6
let the *p*. of the LORD be great as	Num.14.17
he who gives you *p*. to get wealth	Dt.8.18
save us from the *p*. of our enemies	1 Sam.4.3
God has *p*. to help or to cast down	2 Chr.25.8
you have helped him who has no *p*.	Job 26.2
Behold, God is exalted in his *p*.	Job 36.22
ransom my soul from the *p*. of Sheol	Ps.49.15
thy saving *p*. among all nations	Ps.67.2
he might make known his mighty *p*.	Ps.106.8
Great is our LORD . . . abundant in *p*.	Ps.147.5
No man has *p*. to retain the spirit	Ec.8.8
He gives *p*. to the faint	Is.40.29
he who made the earth by his *p*.	Jer.51.15
Daniel from the *p*. of the lions	Dan.6.27
nor by *p*., but by my Spirit	Zech.4.6
seated at the right hand of *P*.	Mt.26.64
p. of the Most High will overshadow	Lk.1.35
the *p*. of the Lord was with him	Lk.5.17
in a cloud with *p*. and great glory	Lk.21.27
he gave *p*. to become children of God	Jn.1.12
hast given him *p*. over all flesh	Jn.17.2
By what *p*. or by what name did you	Acts 4.7
And Stephen, full of grace and *p*.	Acts 6.8
p. of signs and wonders, by the *p*.	Rom.15.19
will also raise us up by his *p*.	1 Cor.6.14
my *p*. is made perfect in weakness	2 Cor.12.9
May you be strengthened with all *p*.	Col.1.11
upholding the universe by his . . . *p*.	Heb.1.3
with angels . . . and *p*. subject to him	1 Pet.3.22
honor and *p*. and might be to	Rev.7.12
glory and *p*. belong to our God	Rev.19.1

POWERFUL

The voice of the LORD is *p*.	Ps.29.4
like a *p*. army drawn up for battle	Jl.2.5
not many were *p*., not many were	1 Cor.1.26
He is not weak . . . but is *p*. in you	2 Cor.13.3

PRACTICE (verb)

You shall not *p*. augury or	Lev.19.26
I am the LORD who *p*. steadfast love	Jer.9.24
those who *p*. magic arts brought	Acts 19.19
refuse to *p*. cunning or to tamper	2 Cor.4.2
to *p*. every kind of uncleanness	Eph.4.19
P. these duties, devote yourself	1 Tim.4.15
P. hospitality ungrudgingly	1 Pet.4.9

PRACTICES (noun)

people still followed corrupt *p*.	2 Chr.27.2
Esther fixed these *p*. of Purim	Est.9.32

confessing and divulging their *p.* — Acts 19.18
put off the old nature with its *p.* — Col.3.9

PRAETORIUM

inside the palace (that is, the *p.*) — Mk.15.16
Pilate entered the *p.* again — Jn.18.33
to be guarded in Herod's *p.* — Acts 23.35

PRAISE (noun)

He is your *p.*; he is your God — Dt.10.21
in Sheol who can give thee *p.?* — Ps.6.5
his *p.* shall continually be in my — Ps.34.1
P. is due to thee, O God, in Zion — Ps.65.1
My mouth is filled with thy *p.* — Ps.71.8
you shall call . . . your gates *P.* — Is.60.18
the mantle of *p.* instead of a faint — Is.61.3
and the earth was full of his *p.* — Hab.3.3
His *p.* is not from men but from God — Rom.2.29
to live for the *p.* of his glory — Eph.1.12

PRAISE (verb)

P. his people, O you nations — Dt.32.43
You who fear the LORD, *p.* him — Ps.22.23
for I shall again *p.* him, my help — Ps.42.5
Let the peoples *p.* thee, O God — Ps.67.3
the wrath of men shall *p.* thee — Ps.76.10
Seven times a day I *p.* thee — Ps.119.164
the LORD, and greatly to be *p.* — Ps.145.3
P. our God, all you his servants — Rev.19.5

PRAY

will *p.* for you, and you shall live — Gen.20.7
So Moses *p.* for the people — Num.21.7
I will *p.* to the LORD for you — 1 Sam.7.5
by ceasing to *p.* for you — 1 Sam.12.23
p. and seek my face, and turn — 2 Chr.7.14
what profit do we get if we *p.* — Job 21.15
P. for the peace of Jerusalem — Ps.122.6
Then Jonah *p.* to the LORD his God — Jon.2.1
And when you *p.*, you must not be like — Mt.6.5
P. then like this: Our Father who art — Mt.6.9
Watch and *p.* that you may not enter — Mt.26.41
teach us to *p.*, as John taught his — Lk.11.1
Two men went up into the temple to *p.* — Lk.18.10
I will *p.* with the mind also — 1 Cor.14.15
P. at all times in the Spirit — Eph.6.18
p. constantly — 1 Th.5.17
P. for us, for we are sure that — Heb.13.18
p. for one another, that you may — Jas.5.16

PRAYER

my ears attentive to the *p.* — 2 Chr.7.15
and the LORD accepted Job's *p.* — Job 42.9
Hear my *p.*, O LORD, and give ear to — Ps.39.12
O thou who hearest *p.!* To thee shall — Ps.65.2
May *p.* be made for him continually — Ps.72.15
Let my *p.* come before thee — Ps.88.2
Let my *p.* be counted as incense — Ps.141.2
he hears the *p.* of the righteous — Pr.15.29
whatever you ask in *p.*, you will — Mt.21.22
with fasting and *p.* night and day — Lk.2.37
My house shall be a house of *p.* — Lk.19.46
devoted themselves to *p.* — Acts 1.14
every church, with *p.* and fasting — Acts 14.23
in tribulation, be constant in *p.* — Rom.12.12
You also must help us by *p.* — 2 Cor.1.11
everything by *p.* and supplication — Phil.4.6
Continue steadfastly in *p.* — Col.4.2
The *p.* of a righteous man has great — Jas.5.16
his ears are open to their *p.* — 1 Pet.3.12
which are the *p.* of the saints — Rev.5.8

PRAYING

she continued *p.* before the LORD — 1 Sam.1.12
And whenever you stand *p.*, forgive — Mk.11.25
as he was *p.*, the appearance of — Lk.9.29
where many . . . were *p.* — Acts 12.12
p. earnestly night and day — 1 Th.3.10

PREACH

From that time Jesus began to *p.* — Mt.4.17
the poor have good news *p.* to them — Mt.11.5
they *p.*, but do not practice — Mt.23.3
anointed me to *p.* good news — Lk.4.18
so I am eager to *p.* the gospel to — Rom.1.15
how can men *p.* unless they are — Rom.10.14
but we *p.* Christ crucified — 1 Cor.1.23
what we *p.* is not ourselves, but — 2 Cor.4.5
p. to the Gentiles the unsearchable — Eph.3.8
Some indeed *p.* Christ from envy — Phil.1.15
p. the word, be urgent in season — 2 Tim.4.2
he . . . *p.* to the spirits in prison — 1 Pet.3.19

PREACHER

The words of the *P.*, the son of David — Ec.1.1
he would be the *p.* for this people — Mic.2.11
how are they to hear without a *p.?* — Rom.10.14
I was appointed a *p.* and apostle — 1 Tim.2.7
I was appointed a *p.* and apostle — 2 Tim.1.11

PREACHING (noun)

they repented at the *p.* of Jonah — Mt.12.41
Paul was occupied with *p.* — Acts 18.5
then our *p.* is in vain and your — 1 Cor.15.14
famous . . . for his *p.* of the gospel — 2 Cor.8.18
who labor in *p.* and teaching — 1 Tim.5.17
through the *p.* with which I have — Tit.1.3

PRECEPT

the *p.* of the LORD are right — Ps.19.8
Make me understand . . . thy *p.* — Ps.119.27
Through . . . *p.* I get understanding — Ps.119.104
For it is *p.* upon *p.*, *p.* upon *p.* — Is.28.10
Not all men can receive this *p.* — Mt.19.11
teaching as doctrines the *p.* of men — Mk.7.7
uncircumcised keeps . . . *p.* of the law — Rom.2.26
according to human *p.* and doctrines — Col.2.22

PRECIOUS

How *p.* is thy steadfast love, O God — Ps.36.7
P. in the sight of the LORD is the — Ps.116.15
How *p.* to me are thy thoughts — Ps.139.17
She is more *p.* than jewels — Pr.3.15
She is far more *p.* than jewels — Pr.31.10
good name is better than *p.* ointment — Ec.7.1
p. cornerstone, of a sure foundation — Is.28.16
Because you are *p.* in my eyes — Is.43.4
p. stones, wood, hay, stubble — 1 Cor.3.12
but with the *p.* blood of Christ — 1 Pet.1.19
To you . . . who believe, he is *p.* — 1 Pet.2.7
his *p.* and very great promises — 2 Pet.1.4

PREDESTINED

thy plan had *p.* to take place — Acts 4.28
those whom he foreknew he also *p.* — Rom.8.29
And those whom he *p.* he also called — Rom.8.30

PREPARE

Thou *p.* a table before me in the — Ps.23.5
he *p.* rain for the earth — Ps.147.8
p. to meet your God, O Israel — Am.4.12
P. the way of the Lord, make his — Mt.3.3
eternal fire *p.* for the devil and — Mt.25.41
has done it to *p.* me for burial — Mt.26.12
go before the Lord to *p.* his ways — Lk.1.76

PRESENCE

Go and *p*. the passover for us	Lk.22.8
when I go and *p*. a place for you	Jn.14.3
affliction is *p*. for us an eternal	2 Cor.4.17
Always be *p*. to make a defense to	1 Pet.3.15
p. as a bride adorned for her	Rev.21.2

PRESENCE

went away from the *p*. of the LORD	Gen.4.16
My *p*. will go with you, and I will	Ex.33.14
went forth from the *p*. of the LORD	Job 1.12
in thy *p*. there is fulness of joy	Ps.16.11
Cast me not away from thy *p*.	Ps.51.11
Come into his *p*. with singing	Ps.100.2
whither shall I flee from thy *p*.?	Ps.139.7
mountains might quake at thy *p*.	Is.64.1
Gabriel, who stand in the *p*. of God	Lk.1.19
say, 'We ate and drank in your *p*.	Lk.13.26
bring us with you into his *p*.	2 Cor.4.14
In the *p*. of God and of Christ	1 Tim.5.21
the table and the bread of the P.	Heb.9.2
will shelter them with his *p*.	Rev.7.15
from his *p*. earth and sky fled	Rev.20.11

PRESENT (adjective)

God is . . . a very *p*. help in trouble	Ps.46.1
nor things *p*., nor things to come	Rom.8.38
absent in body I am *p*. in spirit	1 Cor.5.3
to deliver us from the *p*. evil age	Gal.1.4
corresponds to the *p*. Jerusalem	Gal.4.25
world rulers of this *p*. darkness	Eph.6.12

PRESENT (verb)

Seven days you shall *p*. offerings	Lev.23.36
they *p*. themselves before God	Jos.24.1
To them he *p*. himself alive after	Acts 1.3
to *p*. your bodies as a living	Rom.12.1
to *p*. you as a pure bride	2 Cor.11.2
he might *p*. the church to himself	Eph.5.27
to *p*. you holy and blameless	Col.1.22
Do your best to *p*. yourself to God	2 Tim.2.15

PRESERVE

God sent me before you to *p*. life	Gen.45.5
that he might *p*. us alive	Dt.6.24
P. me, O God, for in thee I take	Ps.16.1
p. my life from dread of the enemy	Ps.64.1
P. my life according to thy	Ps.119.159
he who guards his way *p*. his life	Pr.16.17
whoever loses his life will *p*. it	Lk.17.33
he . . . *p*. Noah, a herald of	2 Pet.2.5

PRESS (verb)

let us *p*. on to know the LORD	Hos.6.3.
I will *p*. you down in your place	Am.2.13
good measure, *p*. down	Lk.6.38
the Pharisees began to *p*. him hard	Lk.11.53
but I *p*. on to make it my own	Phil.3.12
I *p*. on toward the goal for the	Phil.3.14

PRETEND

why do you *p*. to be another?	1 Kg.14.6
There are friends who *p*. to be	Pr.18.24
sent spies, who *p*. to be sincere	Lk.20.20
with *p*. signs and wonders	2 Th.2.9

PREVAIL

When our transgressions *p*. over us	Ps.65.3
they shall not *p*. against you	Jer.1.19
He strove with the angel and *p*.	Hos.12.4
death shall not *p*. against it	Mt.16.18
the word of the Lord grew and *p*.	Acts 19.20
and *p*. when thou art judged	Rom.3.4

PREY (noun)

Who provides for the raven its *p*.	Job 38.41
The young lions roar for their *p*.	Ps.104.21
not given us as *p*. to their teeth	Ps.124.6
slothful man will not catch his *p*.	Pr.12.27
makes a *p*. of you by philosophy	Col.2.8

PRICE

the *p*. of wisdom is above pearls	Job 28.18
give to God the *p*. of his life	Ps.49.7
milk without money and without *p*.	Is.55.1
p. of him on whom a *p*. had been set	Mt.27.9
You were bought with a *p*.	1 Cor.7.23
take the water of life without *p*.	Rev.22.17

PRIDE

let them be trapped in their *p*.	Ps.59.12
P. goes before destruction	Pr.16.18
A man's *p*. will bring him low	Pr.29.23
the *p*. of men shall be humbled	Is.2.11
We have heard of the *p*. of Moab	Is.16.6
I spoil the *p*. of Judah	Jer.13.9
bring to nought the *p*. of Egypt	Ezek.32.12
I abhor the *p*. of Jacob, and hate	Am.6.8
The *p*. of your heart has deceived	Ob.3
p. of Assyria shall be laid low	Zech.10.11
who *p*. themselves on a man's	2 Cor.5.12
I have great *p*. in you	2 Cor.7.4
our confidence and *p*. in our hope	Heb.3.6
lust of the eyes and the *p*. of life	I Jn.2.16

PRIEST

he was *p*. of God Most High	Gen.14.18
You are a *p*. ever after the order	Ps.110.4
as with the people, so with the *p*.	Is.24.2
Both prophet and *p*. are ungodly	Jer.23.11
No *p*. shall drink wine	Ezek.44.21
struck the slave of the high *p*.	Mt.26.51
but go, show yourself to the *p*.	Mk.1.44
there was a *p*. named Zechariah	Lk.1.5
Now by chance a *p*. was going down	Lk.10.31
Would you revile God's high *p*.?	Acts 23.4
high *p*. of our confession	Heb.3.1
have not a high *p*. who is unable	Heb.4.15
that we should have such a high *p*.	Heb.7.26
we have a great *p*. over the house	Heb.10.21
a kingdom and *p*. to our God	Rev.5.10

PRIESTHOOD

I give your *p*. as a gift	Num.18.7
but he holds his *p*. permanently	Heb.7.24
be a holy *p*., to offer spiritual	1 Pet.2.5
a royal *p*., a holy nation	1 Pet.2.9

PRINCE

Who made you a *p*. and a judge over	Ex.2.14
a *p*. and a great man has fallen	2 Sam.3.38
die like men, and fall like any *p*.	Ps.82.7
P. persecute me without cause	Ps.119.161
Put not your trust in *p*.	Ps.146.3
p. and all rulers of the earth	Ps.148.11
by me *p*. rule, and nobles govern	Pr.8.16
Everlasting Father, P. of Peace	Is.9.6
shall even rise up against the P. of	Dan.8.25
The *p*. of the kingdom of Persia	Dan.10.13
the *p*. of Greece will come	Dan.10.20
Your *p*. are like grasshoppers	Nah.3.17
by the *p*. of demons he casts out	Mk.3.22
the *p*. of the power of the air	Eph.2.2

PRINCIPALITIES

nor *p*., nor things present, nor	Rom.8.38

the *p.* and powers in the heavenly — Eph.3.10
we are . . . contending . . . against the *p.* Eph.6.12
dominions or *p.* or authorities — Col.1.16
He disarmed the *p.* and powers — Col.2.15

PRISCA (PRISCILLA)
Acts 18.2; Rom.16.3; 1 Cor.16.19; 2 Tim.4.19

PRISON
the *p.* where Joseph was confined — Gen.40.3
he ground at the mill in the *p.* — Jg.16.21
Bring me out of *p.*, that I may — Ps.142.7
from the *p.* those . . . in darkness — Is.42.7
opening of the *p.* to those . . . bound — Is.61.1
for he had not yet been put in *p.* — Jer.37.4
John heard in *p.* about the deeds — Mt.11.2
I was in *p.* and you came to me — Mt.25.36
went and beheaded him in the *p.* — Mk.6.27
delivering you up to the . . . *p.* — Lk.21.12
to go with you to *p.* and to death — Lk.22.33
an angel . . . opened the *p.* doors — Acts 5.19
So Peter was kept in *p.* — Acts 12.5
foundations of the *p.* were shaken — Acts 16.26
a favor, Felix left Paul in *p.* — Acts 24.27
on account of which I am in *p.* — Col.4.3
Remember those who are in *p.* — Heb.13.3
preached to the spirits in *p.* — 1 Pet.3.19
Satan will be loosed from his *p.* — Rev.20.7

PRISONER
groans of the *p.* come before thee — Ps.79.11
p. in affliction and in irons — Ps.107.10
The LORD sets the *p.* free — Ps.146.7
they had then a notorious *p.* — Mt.27.16
a *p.* for Christ Jesus on behalf of — Eph.3.1
Aristarchus my fellow *p.* greets you — Col.4.10
Paul, a *p.* for Christ Jesus — Philem.1
you had compassion on the *p.* — Heb.10.34

PRIZE
shall have his life as a *p.* of war — Jer.21.9
but only one receives the *p.*? — 1 Cor.9.24
for the *p.* of the upward call — Phil.3.14

PROCEED
for they *p.* from evil to evil — Jer.9.3
every word that *p.* from the mouth — Mt.4.4
what comes out of the mouth *p.* — Mt.15.18
I *p.* and came forth from God — Jn.8.42
Spirit of truth . . . *p.* from the — Jn.15.26
does not *p.* from faith is sin — Rom.14.23

PROCLAIM
will *p.* before you my name — Ex.33.19
p. liberty throughout the land — Lev.25.10
the firmament *p.* his handiwork — Ps.19.1
I will *p.* thy name, for it is good — Ps.52.9
The heavens *p.* his righteousness — Ps.97.6
shall *p.* the praise of the LORD — Is.60.6
to *p.* liberty to the captives — Is.61.1
P. this among the nations: Prepare — Jl.3.9
p. to it the message that I tell you — Jon.3.2
p. upon the housetops — Mt.10.27
he shall *p.* justice to the Gentiles — Mt.12.18
go and *p.* the kingdom of God — Lk.9.60
forgiveness of sins is *p.* to you — Acts 13.38
p. to you the way of salvation — Acts 16.17
those who *p.* the gospel — 1 Cor.9.14
you *p.* the Lord's death until he — 1 Cor.11.26
to *p.* the mystery of the gospel — Eph.6.19
Him we *p.*, warning every man — Col.1.28
I will *p.* thy name to my brethren — Heb.2.12

p. to you the eternal life — 1 Jn.1.2
to *p.* to those who dwell on earth — Rev.14.6

PRODUCE (verb)
pressing anger *p.* strife — Pr.30.33
The earth *p.* of itself, first the — Mk.4.28
suffering *p.* endurance — Rom.5.3
godly grief *p.* a repentance — 2 Cor.7.10
p. envy, dissension, slander — 1 Tim.6.4
your faith *p.* steadfastness — Jas.1.3

PROFANE (verb)
you shall not *p.* my holy name — Lev.22.32
steal, and *p.* the name of my God — Pr.30.9
shall no more *p.* with your gifts — Ezek.20.39
Forces . . . appear and *p.* the temple — Dan.11.31
you *p.* it when you say that the — Mal.1.12
how . . . the priests . . . *p.* the sabbath — Mt.12.5
He even tried to *p.* the temple — Acts 24.6
guilty of *p.* the body and blood — 1 Cor.11.27
p. the blood of the covenant by — Heb.10.29

PROFIT (verb)
things which cannot *p.* or save — 1 Sam.12.21
Riches do not *p.* in the day of wrath — Pr.11.4
that which does not *p.* — Jer.2.11
what does it *p.* a man if he gains — Lk.9.25
What does it *p.*, my brethren, if a — Jas.2.14

PROFITABLE
Can a man be *p.* to God? — Job 22.2
an image, that is *p.* for nothing — Is.44.10
All scripture is . . . *p.* for teaching — 2 Tim.3.16
these are excellent and *p.* to men — Tit.3.8

PROLONG
that you may *p.* your days in the land — Dt.4.40
P. the life of the king — Ps.61.6
The fear of the LORD *p.* life — Pr.10.27
neither will he *p.* his days like a — Ec.8.13
he shall *p.* his days — Is.53.10
their lives were *p.* for a season — Dan.7.12
he *p.* his speech until midnight — Acts 20.7

PROMISE (noun)
the *p.* of the LORD proves true — 2 Sam.22.31
Confirm to thy servant thy *p.* — Ps.119.38
Uphold me according to thy *p.* — Ps.119.116
that I may meditate upon thy *p.* — Ps.119.148
I send the *p.* of my Father upon you — Lk.24.49
to wait for the *p.* of the Father — Acts 1.4
For the *p.* is to you and to your — Acts 2.39
p. to Abraham and his descendants — Rom.4.13
all the *p.* of God find their Yes — 2 Cor.1.20
receive the *p.* of the Spirit — Gal.3.14
heirs according to *p.* — Gal.3.29
strangers to the covenants of *p.* — Eph.2.12
the first commandment with a *p.* — Eph.6.2
not slow about his *p.* as some count — 2 Pet.3.9

PROMISE (verb)
and I *p.* that I will bring you up — Ex.3.17
I *p.* to keep thy words — Ps.119.57
so that he *p.* with an oath to give — Mt.14.7
perform the mercy *p.* to our fathers — Lk.1.72
which he *p.* beforehand through his — Rom.1.2
sealed with the *p.* Holy Spirit — Eph.1.13
God, who never lies, *p.* ages ago — Tit.1.2
receive the *p.* eternal inheritance — Heb.9.15
considered him faithful who had *p.* — Heb.11.11
which God has *p.* to those who love — Jas.1.12
They *p.* them freedom, but they — 2 Pet.2.19

PROMOTE

King Ahasuerus *p*. Haman the Agagite   Est.3.1
Then the king *p*. Shadrach, Meshach   Dan.3.30
to *p*. good order and to secure   1 Cor.7.35
genealogies which *p*. speculations   1 Tim.1.4
your faith may *p*. the knowledge of   Philem.6

PRONOUNCE

By you Israel will *p*. blessing   Gen.48.20
for he could not *p*. it right   Jg.12.6
judgment you *p*. you will be judged   Mt.7.2
Is this blessing *p*. only upon the   Rom.4.9
do not *p*. judgment before the time   1 Cor.4.5
do not *p*. a reviling judgment   2 Pet.2.11

PROOF

Why do you put the LORD to the *p*.?   Ex.17.2
put me to the *p*. these ten times   Num.14.22
tested me, and put me to the *p*.   Ps.95.9
for a *p*. to the people   Mk.1.44
alive after his passion by many *p*.   Acts 1.3
give *p*., before the churches, of   2 Cor.8.24
since you desire *p*. that Christ   2 Cor.13.3

PROPER

their food at the *p*. time   Mt.24.45
is it *p*. for a woman to pray   1 Cor.11.13
be made manifest at the *p*. time   1 Tim.6.15
but left their *p*. dwelling   Jude 6

PROPERTY

met him at the *p*. of Naboth   2 Kg.9.21
and entrusted to them his *p*.   Mt.25:14
squandered his *p*. in loose living   Lk.15.13
wife Sapphira sold a piece of *p*.   Acts 5.1
accepted the plundering of your *p*.   Heb.10.34

PROPHECY

Where there is no *p*. the people   Pr.29.18
fulfilled the *p*. of Isaiah which   Mt.13.14
if *p*., in proportion to our faith   Rom.12.6
as for *p*., they will pass away   1 Cor.13.8
no *p*. of scripture is a matter   2 Pet.1.20
reads aloud the words of the *p*.   Rev.1.3
the testimony . . . is the spirit of *p*.   Rev.19.10
the words of the book of this *p*.   Rev.22.19

PROPHESY

spirit rested upon them, they *p*.   Num.11.25
other messengers . . . also *p*.   1 Sam.19.21
And all the prophets *p*. so   2 Chr.18.11
they *p*. by Baal and led my people   Jer.23.13
as I *p*., there was a noise   Ezek.37.7
sons and your daughters shall *p*.   Jl.2.28
did we not *p*. in your name, and cast   Mt.7.22
prophets and the law *p*. until John   Mt.11.13
his father Zechariah . . . *p*.   Lk.1.67
that year he *p*. that Jesus should   Jn.11.51
they spoke with tongues and *p*.   Acts 19.6
four unmarried daughters, who *p*.   Acts 21.9
but he who *p*. edifies the church   1 Cor.14.4
The prophets who *p*. of the grace   1 Pet.1.10

PROPHET

Aaron your brother shall be your *p*.   Ex.7.1
that all the LORD's people were *p*.   Num.11.29
If a *p*. arises among you, or a   Dt.13.1
the LORD sent a *p*. to the people   Jg.6.8
established as a *p*. of the LORD   1 Sam.3.20
sent a message by Nathan the *p*.   2 Sam.12.25
I only, am left a *p*. of the LORD   1 Kg.18.22
Is there no *p*. of the LORD here   2 Kg.3.11
there is no longer any *p*.   Ps.74.9

my anointed ones, do my *p*. no harm   Ps.105.15
I am no *p*., nor a *p*.'s son   Am.7.14
I am no *p*., I am a tiller of the   Zech.13.5
Elijah the *p*. before the great   Mal.4.5
come to abolish the law and the *p*.   Mt.5.17
Beware of false *p*., who come to you   Mt.7.15
receives a *p*. because he is a *p*.   Mt.10.41
A *p*. is not without honor except   Mt.13.57
This is the *p*. Jesus from Nazareth   Mt.21.11
mouth of his holy *p*. from of old   Lk.1.70
be called the *p*. of the Most High   Lk.1.76
A great *p*. has arisen among us   Lk.7.16
"Are you the *p*.?" And he answered   Jn.1.21
Sir, I perceive that you are a *p*.   Jn.4.19
God will raise up for you a *p*.   Acts 3.7
a *p*. named Agabus came down from   Acts 21.10
If any one thinks that he is a *p*.   1 Cor.14.37
foundation of the apostles and *p*.   Eph.2.20
the beast and the false *p*. were   Rev.20.10

PROPHETESS

Miriam, the *p*., the sister of Aaron   Ex.15.20
Now Deborah, a *p*., the wife of   Jg.4.4
Asaiah went to Huldah the *p*.   2 Kg.22.14
also the *p*. Noadiah and the rest of   Neh.6.14
I went to the *p*., and she conceived   Is.8.3
And there was a *p*., Anna   Lk.2.36
calls herself a *p*. and is teaching   Rev.2.20

PROPHETIC

through the *p*. writings is made   Rom.16.26
if I have *p*. powers, and   1 Cor.13.2
p. utterances which pointed to   1 Tim.1.18
given you by *p*. utterance when   1 Tim.4.14
we have the *p*. word made more   2 Pet.1.19

PROSPER

all that he did to *p*. in his hands   Gen.39.3
I know that the LORD will *p*. me   Jg.17.13
you will *p*. if you are careful   1 Chr.22.13
The God of heaven will make us *p*.   Neh.2.20
In all that he does, he *p*.   Ps.1.3
May they *p*. who love you   Ps.122.6
he who keeps understanding will *p*.   Pr.19.8
p. in the thing for which I sent it   Is.55.11
her enemies *p*., because the LORD   Lam.1.5
I have *p*., and I need nothing   Rev.3.17

PROSPERITY

the LORD will make you abound in *p*.   Dt.28.11
in *p*. the destroyer will come upon   Job 15.21
my *p*. has passed away like a cloud   Job 30.15
I said in my *p*., "I shall never be   Ps.30.6
when I saw the *p*. of the wicked   Ps.73.3
May you see the *p*. of Jerusalem   Ps.128.5
In the day of *p*. be joyful   Ec.7.14
abundance of *p*. and security   Jer.33.6
shall again overflow with *p*.   Zech.1.17

PROSTITUTE

be no cult *p*. of the daughters of   Dt.23.17
also male cult *p*. in the land   1 Kg.14.24
harlots, and sacrifice with cult *p*.   Hos.4.14
make them members of a *p*.?   1 Cor.6.15

PROSTRATE

Then I lay *p*. before the LORD   Dt.9.18
There the evildoers lie *p*.   Ps.36.12
I am utterly bowed down and *p*.   Ps.38.6
princes . . . shall *p*. themselves   Is.49.7

PROTECT

For my sake *p*. the young man   2 Sam.18.12

The name of the God of Jacob *p*. you   Ps.20.1
the LORD *p*. him and keeps him alive   Ps.41.2
I will *p*. him, because he knows my   Ps.91.14
he will *p*. and deliver it   Is.31.5
The LORD of hosts will *p*. them   Zech.9.15

PROUD
when he was strong he grew *p*.   2 Chr.26.16
God abases the *p*., but he saves   Job 22.29
Look on every one that is *p*.   Job 40.12
to divide the spoil with the *p*.   Pr.16.19
against all that is *p*. and lofty   Is.2.12
be not *p*., for the LORD has spoken   Jer.13.15
The *p*. one shall stumble and fall   Jer.50.32
scattered the *p*. in the imagination   Lk.1.51
So do not become *p*., but stand in   Rom.11.20
p., arrogant, abusive, disobedient   2 Tim.3.2
it says, "God opposes the *p*.   Jas.4.6

PROVE
for God has come to *p*. you   Ex.20.20
P. me, O LORD, and try me   Ps.26.2
Which . . . *p*. neighbor to the man who   Lk.10.36
and so *p*. to be my disciples   Jn.15.8
that you may *p*. what is the will of   Rom.12.2
impossible that God should *p*. false   Heb.6.18
which comes upon you to *p*. you   1 Pet.4.12

PROVERB
a *p*., and a byword among all the   Dt.28.37
He also uttered three thousand *p*.   1 Kg.4.32
Your maxims are *p*. of ashes   Job 13.12
I will incline my ear to a *p*.   Ps.49.4
The *p*. of Solomon, son of David   Pr.1.1
this *p*. shall no more be used by   Ezek.18.3
you will quote to me this *p*.   Lk.4.23
to them according to the true *p*.   2 Pet.2.22

PROVIDE
God will *p*. himself the lamb for a   Gen.22.8
thou *p*. their grain, for so thou   Ps.65.9
O God, thou didst *p*. for the needy   Ps.68.10
will also *p*. the way of escape   1 Cor.10.13
God is able to *p*. you with every   2 Cor.9.8
one does not *p*. for his relatives   1 Tim.5.8

PROVOCATION
because of the *p*. of his sons   Dt.32.19
all the *p*. with which Manasseh   2 Kg.23.26
my eye dwells on their *p*.   Job 17.2
a fool's *p*. is heavier than both   Pr.27.3
Ephraim has given bitter *p*.   Hos.12.14

PROVOKE
so as to *p*. him to anger   Dt.4.25
Ahab did more to *p*. the LORD   1 Kg.16.33
a people who *p*. me to my face   Is.65.3
when your fathers *p*. me to wrath   Zech.8.14
his spirit was *p*. within him as   Acts 17.16
Shall we *p*. the Lord to jealousy?   1 Cor.10.22
do not *p*. your children to anger   Eph.6.4
with whom was he *p*. forty years?   Heb.3.17

PRUDENCE
O simple ones, learn *p*.; O foolish   Pr.8.5
I, wisdom, dwell in *p*.   Pr.8.12
replied with *p*. and discretion to   Dan.2.14
the dishonest steward for his *p*.   Lk.16.8

PRUDENT
p. in speech, and a man of good   1 Sam.16.18
A son who gathers in summer is *p*.   Pr.10.5
he who restrains his lips is *p*.   Pr.10.19
but the *p*. man ignores an insult   Pr.12.16

but a *p*. wife is from the LORD   Pr.19.14
A *p*. man sees danger and hides   Pr.22.3

PRUNING
beat . . . their spears into *p*. hooks   Is.2.4
cut off the shoots with *p*. hooks   Is.18.5
Beat . . . your *p*. hooks into spears   Jl.3.10
beat . . . their spears into *p*. hooks   Mic.4.3

PSALM
sing praises with a *p*.   Ps.47.7
prophets and the *p*. must be fulfilled   Lk.24.44
addressing one another in *p*. and   Eph.5.19
as you sing *p*. and hymns and   Col.3.16

PUBLIC
from the *p*. square of Beth-shan   2 Sam.21.12
truth has fallen in the *p*. squares   Is.59.14
powerfully confuted the Jews in *p*.   Acts 18.28
teaching you in *p*. and from house to   Acts 20.20
and made a *p*. example of them   Col.2.15
the *p*. reading of scripture   1 Tim.4.13

PUBLISH
p. it not in . . . Ashkelon   2 Sam.1.20
they should *p*. and proclaim in all   Neh.8.15
who *p*. peace, who brings good tidings   Is.52.7
who *p*. salvation, who says to Zion   Is.52.7

PUFFED
that none of you may be *p*. up   1 Cor.4.6
p. up without reason by his sensuous   Col.2.18
he may be *p*. up with conceit   1 Tim.3.6
he is *p*. up with conceit   1 Tim.6.4

PUNISH
then I will *p*. their transgression   Ps.89.32
I will *p*. the world for its evil   Is.13.11
Behold, I will *p*. them   Jer.11.22
I will *p*. you for all your iniquities   Am.3.2
will *p*. him, and put him with the   Mt.24.51
ready to *p*. every disobedience   2 Cor.10.6
governors . . . to *p*. those who   1 Pet.2.14

PUNISHMENT
My *p*. is greater than I can bear   Gen.4.13
Add to them *p*. upon *p*.   Ps.69.27
The days of *p*. have come, the days   Hos.9.7
they will go away into eternal *p*.   Mt.25.46
what longing, what zeal, what *p*.   2 Cor.7.11
How much worse *p*. do you think   Heb.10.29
unrighteous under *p*. until the day   2 Pet.2.9
For fear has to do with *p*.   1 Jn.4.18

PURE
with the *p*. . . . . show thyself *p*.   2 Sam.22.27
Can a man be *p*. before his Maker?   Job 4.17
the commandment of the LORD is *p*.   Ps.19.8
who has clean hands and a *p*. heart   Ps.24.4
How can a young man keep his way *p*.?   Ps.119.9
ways of a man are *p*. in his own eyes   Pr.16.2
those who are *p*. in their own eyes   Pr.30.12
Thou who art of *p*. eyes than to   Hab.1.13
of the peoples to a *p*. speech   Zeph.3.9
Blessed are the *p*. in heart   Mt.5.8
ointment of *p*. nard and anointed   Jn.12.3
may be *p*. and blameless for the   Phil.1.10
whatever is *p*., whatever is lovely   Phil.4.8
keep yourself *p*.   1 Tim.5.22
call upon the Lord from a *p*. heart   2 Tim.2.22
To the *p*. all things are *p*., but   Tit.1.15
Religion that is *p*. and undefiled   Jas.1.27
the street of the city was *p*. gold   Rev.21.21

PURIFY

they should *p*. themselves and come   Neh.13.22
Many shall *p*. themselves, and make   Dan.12.10
not eat unless they *p*. themselves   Mk.7.4
take these men and *p*. yourself   Acts 21.24
p. your conscience from dead works   Heb.9.14
almost everything is *p*. with blood   Heb.9.22
p. your hearts, you men of double   Jas.4.8
p. himself as he is pure   1 Jn.3.3

PURITY

He who loves *p*. of heart, and whose   Pr.22.11
by *p*., knowledge, forbearance   2 Cor.6.6
in love, in faith, in *p*.   1 Tim.4.12
women like sisters, in all *p*.   1 Tim.5.2

PURPLE

Daniel was clothed with *p*.   Dan.5.29
they clothed him in a *p*. cloak   Mk.15.17
was clothed in *p*. and fine linen   Lk.16.19
crown of thorns and the *p*. robe   Jn.19.5
a seller of *p*. goods, who was a   Acts 16.14
was arrayed in *p*. and scarlet   Rev.17.4

PURPOSE (noun)

no *p*. of thine can be thwarted   Job 42.2
to God who fulfils his *p*. for me   Ps.57.2
The LORD will fulfil his *p*. for me   Ps.138.8
has made everything for its *p*.   Pr.16.4
p. of the LORD will be established   Pr.19.21
for I was sent for this *p*.   Lk.4.43
No, for this *p*. I have come to this   Jn.12.27
who are called according to his *p*.   Rom.8.28
that God's *p*. of election might   Rom.9.11
will disclose the *p*. of the heart   1 Cor.4.5
according to the *p*. of his will   Eph.1.5
the eternal *p*. which he has realized   Eph.3.11
unchangeable character of his *p*.   Heb.6.17
you have seen the *p*. of the Lord   Jas.5.11

PURSE

we will all have one *p*.   Pr.1.14
Those who lavish gold from the *p*.   Is.46.6
Carry no *p*., no bag, no sandals   Lk.10.4
let him who has a *p*. take it   Lk.22.36

PURSUE

in hot anger *p*. the manslayer   Dt.19.6
Why do you, like God, *p*. me?   Job 19.22
do good; seek peace, and *p*. it   Ps.34.14
The wicked flee when no one *p*.   Pr.28.1
Thou wilt *p*. them in anger   Lam.3.66
Let us . . . *p*. what makes for peace   Rom.14.19
let him seek peace and *p*. it   1 Pet.3.11

QUAILS

In the evening *q*. came up and   Ex.16.13
it brought *q*. from the sea   Num.11.31
the next day, and gathered the *q*.   Num.11.32
They asked, and he brought *q*.   Ps.105.40

QUAKE

the whole mountain *q*. greatly   Ex.19.18
The mountains *q*. before the LORD   Jg.5.5
Thou hast made the land to *q*.   Ps.60.2
mountains might *q*. at thy presence   Is.64.1
all . . . shall *q*. at my presence   Ezek.38.20

QUALIFIED

able men *q*. for the service   1 Chr.26.8
who has *q*. us to be ministers of   2 Cor.3.6
q. us to share in the inheritance   Col.1.12

QUARREL (verb)

said to them, "Do not *q*. on the way."   Gen.45.24
When men *q*. and one strikes the   Ex.21.18
they *q*. with one another in the   2 Sam.14.6
you fast only to *q*. and to fight   Is.58.4

QUARRELING (noun)

a wife's *q*. is a continual . . . rain   Pr.19.13
where . . . is no whisperer, *q*. ceases   Pr.26.20
not in *q*. and jealousy   Rom.13.13
that there is *q*. among you   1 Cor.1.11
holy hands without anger or *q*.   1 Tim.2.8
to avoid *q*., to be gentle, and to   Tit.3.2

QUARRELSOME

so is a *q*. man for kindling strife   Pr.26.21
not *q*., and no lover of money   1 Tim.3.3
must not be *q*. but kindly to   2 Tim.2.24

QUEEN

when the *q*. of Sheba had seen   1 Kg.10.4
But *Q*. Vashti refused to come at   Est.1.12
What is your petition, *Q*. Esther?   Est.7.2
stands the *q*. in gold of Ophir   Ps.45.9
and their *q*. your nursing mothers   Is.49.23
The *q*. of the South will arise at   Mt.12.42
Candace the *q*. of the Ethiopians   Acts 8.27
A *q*. I sit, I am no widow, mourning   Rev.18.7

QUENCH

lest you *q*. the lamp of Israel   2 Sam.21.17
Many waters cannot *q*. love   S.of S.8.7
dimly burning wick he will not *q*.   Is.42.3
or *q*. a smoldering wick   Mt.12.20
not die, and the fire is not *q*.   Mk.9.48
you can *q*. all the flaming darts   Eph.6.16
Do not *q*. the Spirit   1 Th.5.19
q. raging fire, escaped the edge   Heb.11.34

QUESTION (noun)

And Solomon answered all her *q*.   2 Chr.9.2
I also will ask you a *q*.   Mt.21.24
asked him a *q*., to test him   Mt.22.35
no one dared to ask him any *q*.   Mk.12.34
listening to them and asking them *q*.   Lk.2.46
in *q*. of food and drink or   Col.2.16

QUESTION (verb)

Why do you *q*. thus in your hearts?   Mk.2.8
and all men *q*. in their hearts   Lk.3.15
you . . . need none to *q*. you   Jn.16.30
And the high priest *q*. them   Acts 5.27

QUICK

A man of *q*. temper acts foolishly   Pr.14.17
Be not *q*. to anger, for anger lodges   Ec.7.9
Make friends *q*. with your accuser   Mt.5.25
not to be *q*. shaken in mind or   2 Th.2.2
Let every man be *q*. to hear   Jas.1.19

QUIET

Be *q*., for this day is holy   Neh.8.11
Better is a dry morsel with *q*. than   Pr.17.1
shall return and have *q*. and ease   Jer.30.10
like the sea which cannot be *q*.   Jer.49.23
should wait *q*. for the salvation   Lam.3.26
aspire to live *q*., to mind your   1 Th.4.11
may lead a *q*. and peaceable life   1 Tim.2.2
jewel of a gentle and *q*. spirit   1 Pet.3.4

QUIVER

Upon him rattle the *q*., the   Job 39.23
the man who has his *q*. full of them   Ps.127.5
in his *q*. he hid me away   Is.49.2

Their *q.* is like an open tomb — Jer.5.16
into my heart the arrows of his *q.* — Lam.3.13

RABBI
you are not to be called *r.* — Mt.23.8
"*R.*" (which means Teacher), "where — Jn.1.38
R., we know that you are a teacher — Jn.3.2
R., who sinned, this man or his — Jn.9.2

RACE
the holy *r.* has mixed itself — Ezra 9.2
the *r.* is not to the swift — Ec.9.11
my brethren, my kinsmen by *r.* — Rom.9.3
in a *r.* all the runners compete — 1 Cor.9.24
I have finished the *r.* — 2 Tim.4.7
run with perseverance the *r.* — Heb.12.1
But you are a chosen *r.*, a royal — 1 Pet.2.9

RACHEL
Gen.29.6; 30.1; 35.19; Jer.31.15; Mt.2.18

RADIANT
Look to him, and be *r.* — Ps.34.5
My beloved is all *r.* and ruddy — S.of S.5.10
Then you shall see and be *r.* — Is.60.5
they shall be *r.* over the goodness — Jer.31.12

RAGE
The nations *r.*, the kingdoms totter — Ps.46.6
his heart *r.* against the LORD — Pr.19.3
The sword shall *r.* against their — Hos.11.6
The chariots *r.* in the streets — Nah.2.4
Why did the Gentiles *r.* — Acts 4.25
quenched *r.* fire, escaped the edge — Heb.11.34
The nations *r.*, but thy wrath came — Rev.11.18

RAHAB
Jos.2.1; 6.17; Mt.1.5; Heb.11.31; Jas.2.25

RAIMENT
and for my *r.* they cast lots — Ps.22.18
Thou changest them like *r.* — Ps.102.26
his *r.* was white as snow — Dan.7.9
To see a man clothed in soft *r.*? — Mt.11.8
and his *r.* white as snow — Mt.28.3
his *r.* became dazzling white — Lk.9.29

RAIN (noun)
I will send *r.* upon the earth — Gen.7.4
he made a decree for the *r.* — Job 28.26
Has the *r.* a father, or who has — Job 38.28
the early *r.* also covers it with — Ps.84.6
he prepares *r.* for the earth — Ps.147.8
If the clouds are full of *r.* — Ec.11.3
For as the *r.* and the snow come — Is.55.10
withheld the *r.* from you when — Am.4.7
Ask *r.* from the LORD in the season — Zech.10.1
sends *r.* on the just and on the — Mt.5.45
the *r.* fell, and the floods came — Mt.7.25

RAIN (verb)
not caused it to *r.* upon the earth — Gen.2.5
Then the LORD *r.* on Sodom and — Gen.19.24
On the wicked he will *r.* coals of — Ps.11.6
he *r.* down upon them manna to — Ps.78.24
let the skies *r.* down righteousness — Is.45.8
fire and brimstone *r.* from heaven — Lk.17.29
he prayed . . . that it might not *r.* — Jas.5.17

RAISE
I will *r.* up for them a prophet — Dt.18.18
He has *r.* up a horn for his people — Ps.148.14
Heal the sick, *r.* the dead, cleanse — Mt.10.8
and *r.* up children for his brother — Mk.12.19
has *r.* up a horn of salvation — Lk.1.69

able . . . to *r.* up children to Abraham — Lk.3.8
will you *r.* it up in three days? — Jn.2.20
I will *r.* him up at the last day — Jn.6.44
This Jesus God *r.* up, and of that — Acts 2.32
God will *r.* up for you a prophet — Acts 7.37
whom he did not *r.* if it is true — 1 Cor.15.15
will *r.* us also with Jesus — 2 Cor.4.14
who for their sake died and was *r.* — 2 Cor.5.15
Father, who *r.* him from the dead — Gal.1.1
r. us up with him, and made us — Eph.2.6
you were also *r.* with him through — Col.2.12
If then you have been *r.* with Christ — Col.3.1
the Lord will *r.* him up — Jas.5.15
who *r.* him from the dead and gave — 1 Pet.1.21

RAISINS
a hundred clusters of *r.* — 1 Sam.25.18
portion of meat, and a cake of *r.* — 2 Sam.6.19
clusters of *r.*, and wine and oil — 1 Chr.12.40
Sustain me with *r.*, refresh me — S.of S.2.5
to other gods and love cakes of *r.* — Hos.3.1

RAMPART
it stood against the *r.* — 2 Sam.20.15
consider well her *r.*, go through — Ps.48.13
her *r.* a sea, and water her wall? — Nah.3.8
Tyre has built herself a *r.* — Zech.9.3

RANSOM
R. me from the hand of oppressors — Job 6.23
God will *r.* my soul from . . . Sheol — Ps.49.15
the *r.* of the LORD shall return — Is.35.10
Shall I *r.* them from the power of — Hos.13.14
to give his life as a *r.* for many — Mt.20.28
who gave himself as a *r.* for all — 1 Tim.2.6
that you were *r.* from the futile — 1 Pet.1.18
by thy blood didst *r.* men for God — Rev.5.9

RASH
therefore my words have been *r.* — Job 6.3
he spoke words that were *r.* — Ps.106.33
There is one whose *r.* words are — Pr.12.18
Be not *r.* with your mouth, nor let — Ec.5.2
to be quiet and do nothing *r.* — Acts 19.36

RAVEN
sent forth a *r.* . . . it went to and fro — Gen.8.7
commanded the *r.* to feed you there — 1 Kg.17.4
Who provides for the *r.* its prey — Job 38.41
food . . . to the young *r.* which cry — Ps.147.9
the owl and the *r.* shall dwell in — Is.34.11
Consider the *r.*: they neither sow — Lk.12.24

RAZOR
No *r.* shall come upon his head — Jg.13.5
A *r.* has never come upon my head — Jg.16.17
Your tongue is like a sharp *r.* — Ps.52.2
shave with a *r.* which is hired — Is.7.20
as a barber's *r.* and pass it over — Ezek.5.1

REACH
his head *r.* to the clouds — Job 20.6
waters, they shall not *r.* him — Ps.32.6
thy praise *r.* to the ends of the — Ps.48.10
thy faithfulness *r.* to the clouds — Ps.108.4
r. out her hands to the needy — Pr.31.20
salvation may *r.* to the end of the — Is.49.6
that all should *r.* repentance — 2 Pet.3.9

READ
afterward he *r.* all the words — Jos.8.34
he *r.* from the book of the law of — Neh.8.18
So Baruch *r.* it to them — Jer.36.15
so he may run who *r.* it — Hab.2.2

sabbath day. And he stood up to *r.*	Lk.4.16		harden your hearts as in the *r.*	Heb.3.8
prophets . . . are *r.* every sabbath	Acts 13.27		and perish in Korah's *r.*	Jude 11
to be known and *r.* by all men	2 Cor.3.2		**REBELLIOUS**	
when they *r.* the old covenant	2 Cor.3.14		You have been *r.* against the LORD	Dt.9.24
this letter has been *r.* among you	Col.4.16		This our son is stubborn and *r.*	Dt.21.20
this letter be *r.* to all the brethren	1 Th.5.27		let not the *r.* exalt themselves	Ps.66.7
READING			a stubborn and *r.* generation	Ps.78.8
that the people understood the *r.*	Neh.8.8		"Woe to the *r.* children," says the	Is.30.1
When you finish *r.* this book	Jer.51.63		has a stubborn and *r.* heart	Jer.5.23
Do you understand what you are *r.?*	Acts 8.30		be not *r.* like that *r.* house	Ezek.2.8
After the *r.* of the law and the	Acts 13.15		for they are a *r.* house. Therefore	Ezek.12.3
to the public *r.* of scripture	1 Tim.4.13		Woe to her that is *r.* and defiled	Zeph.3.1
READY			they that heard and yet were *r.?*	Heb.3.16
the grave is *r.* for me	Job 17.1		**REBUILD**	
is like the pen of a *r.* scribe	Ps.45.1		*r.* the walls of Jerusalem	Ps.51.18
blown the trumpet and made all *r.*	Ezek.7.14		*r.* them as they were at first	Jer.33.7
Therefore you also must be *r.*	Mt.24.44		and they shall *r.* the ruined cities	Am.9.14
Come; for all is now *r.*	Lk.14.17		I will *r.* the dwelling of David	Acts 15.16
r. for any good work	2 Tim.2.21		**REBUKE (verb)**	
a salvation *r.* to be revealed	1 Pet.1.5		He will surely *r.* you if in secret	Job 13.10
his Bride has made herself *r.*	Rev.19.7		O LORD, *r.* me not in thy anger	Ps.6.1
REAP			*R.* the beasts that dwell among the	Ps.68.30
sow in tears *r.* with shouts of joy	Ps.126.5		He *r.* the Red Sea, and it became dry	Ps.106.9
who sows injustice will *r.* calamity	Pr.22.8		Thou dost *r.* the insolent	Ps.119.21
who regards the clouds will not *r.*	Ec.11.4		lest he *r.* you, and you be found a	Pr.30.6
they shall *r.* the whirlwind	Hos.8.7		The LORD *r.* you, O Satan	Zech.3.2
neither sow nor *r.* nor gather into	Mt.6.26		Behold, I will *r.* your offspring	Mal.2.3
and *r.* what you did not sow	Lk.19.21		I will *r.* the devourer for you so	Mal.3.11
I sent you to *r.* that for which you	Jn.4.38		Peter took him and began to *r.* him	Mt.16.22
sparingly will also *r.* sparingly	2 Cor.9.6		he *r.* Peter, and said, "Get behind	Mk.8.33
a man sows, that he will also *r.*	Gal.6.7		But Jesus *r.* the unclean spirit	Lk.9.42
REAPER			to him, "Teacher, *r.* your disciples."	Lk.19.39
gleaned in the field after the *r.*	Ru.2.3		Do not *r.* an older man but exhort	1 Tim.5.1
the plowman shall overtake the *r.*	Am.9.13		Therefore *r.* them sharply	Tit.1.13
of the age, and the *r.* are angels	Mt.13.39		but said, "The Lord *r.* you."	Jude 9
that sower and *r.* may rejoice	Jn.4.36		**RECEIVE**	
REASON (noun)			He will *r.* blessing from the LORD	Ps.24.5
or even by *r.* of strength foursore	Ps.90.10		afterward thou wilt *r.* me to glory	Ps.73.24
Do not contend with a man for no *r.*	Pr.3.30		let your ear *r.* the word of his	Jer.9.20
my *r.* returned to me, and I blessed	Dan.4.34		the Most High shall *r.* the kingdom	Dan.7.18
For this *r.* a man shall leave his	Mk.10.7		a prophet shall *r.* a prophet's	Mt.10.41
For this *r.* the Father loves me	Jn.10.17		Not all men can *r.* this precept	Mt.19.11
there was no *r.* for the death	Acts 28.18		will *r.* the greater condemnation	Mk.12.40
The *r.* the Son of God appeared was	1 Jn.3.8		the blind *r.* their sight, the lame	Lk.7.22
REASON (verb)			Whoever *r.* this child in my name *r.*	Lk.9.48
you shall *r.* with your neighbor	Lev.19.17		For every one who asks *r.*	Lk.11.10
an upright man could *r.* with him	Job 23.7		and his own people *r.* him not	Jn.1.11
let us *r.* together, says the LORD	Is.1.18		from his fulness have we all *r.*	Jn.1.16
like a child, I *r.* like a child	1 Cor.13.11		I do not *r.* glory from men	Jn.5.41
REBEKAH			said to them, "*R.* the Holy Spirit	Jn.20.22
Gen.24.15; 25.28; 26.35; 27.5; 49.31			you shall *r.* power when the Holy	Acts 1.8
REBEL (verb)			more blessed to give than to *r.*	Acts 20.35
Only, do not *r.* against the LORD	Num.14.9		Brother Saul, *r.* your sight	Acts 22.13
that we should *r.* against the LORD	Jos.22.29		What have you that you did not *r.?*	1 Cor.4.7
The king of Moab has *r.* against me	2 Kg.3.7		I *r.* from the Lord what I also	1 Cor.11.23
Zedekiah *r.* against the king of	2 Kg.24.20		that each one may *r.* good or evil	2 Cor.5.10
How often they *r.* against him in	Ps.78.40		that we may *r.* mercy and find grace	Heb.4.16
for they had *r.* against the words	Ps.107.11		You ask and do not *r.*, because you	Jas.4.3
But they *r.* and grieved his holy	Is.63.10		If we *r.* the testimony of men, the	1 Jn.5.9
You have all *r.* against me, says	Jer.2.29		to *r.* power and wealth and wisdom	Rev.5.12
We have transgressed and *r.*	Lam.3.42		**RECHABITES**	
wickedly *r.* against my ordinances	Ezek.5.6		Jer.35.2, 18	
they *r.* against me	Hos.7.14		**RECKON**	
REBELLION			he *r.* it to him as righteousness	Gen.15.6
An evil man seeks only *r.*	Pr.17.11		He shall *r.* with him who bought	Lev.25.50
unless the *r.* comes first	2 Th.2.3		And he was *r.* with transgressors	Lk.22.37

it was *r*. to him as righteousness — Rom.4.3
whom the Lord will not *r*. his sin — Rom.4.8

RECOGNIZE
immediately the people *r*. him — Mk.6.54
eyes were opened and they *r*. him — Lk.24.31
did not *r*. him nor understand — Acts 13.27
we *r*. no other practice, nor do — 1 Cor.11.16
If any one does not *r*. this, he — 1 Cor.14.38

RECOMPENSE (noun)
and see the *r*. of the wicked — Ps.91.8
is with him, and his *r*. before him — Is.62.11
for the LORD is a God of *r*. — Jer.51.56
bringing my *r*., to repay every one — Rev.22.12

RECONCILE
if while . . . enemies we were *r*. to God — Rom.5.10
God was in Christ *r*. the world to — 2 Cor.5.19
on behalf of Christ, be *r*. to God — 2 Cor.5.20
and might *r*. us both to God in one — Eph.2.16
and through him to *r*. to himself — Col.1.20

RECONCILIATION
through whom we . . . received our *r*. — Rom.5.11
means the *r*. of the world — Rom.11.15
and gave us the ministry of *r*. — 2 Cor.5.18
entrusting to us the message of *r*. — 2 Cor.5.19

RECORDER
the son of Ahilud was *r*. — 2 Sam.8.16
Joah the son of Asaph, the *r*. — Is.36.3

RECOUNT
that I may *r*. all thy praises — Ps.9.14
we will *r*. thy praise — Ps.79.13
r. the deeds of the LORD — Ps.118.17
I will *r*. the steadfast love of the — Is.63.7

RECOVER
Shall I *r*. from this sickness? — 2 Kg.8.8
lay it on the boil, that he may *r*. — 2 Kg.20.7
you shall die, you shall not *r*. — Is.38.1
if he has fallen asleep, he will *r*. — Jn.11.12

RED
and drove them into the *R*. Sea — Ex.10.19
to bring you a *r*. heifer without — Num.19.2
He rebuked the *R*. Sea, and it became — Ps.106.9
Do not look at wine when it is *r*. — Pr.23.31
though they are *r*. like crimson — Is.1.18
Why is thy apparel *r*., and thy — Is.63.2
a man riding upon a *r*. horse — Zech.1.8
for the sky is *r*. and threatening — Mt.16.3
out came another horse, bright *r*. — Rev.6.4
behold, a great *r*. dragon — Rev.12.3

REDEEM
I will *r*. you with an outstretched — Ex.6.6
all the first-born of my sons I *r*. — Ex.13.15
I cannot *r*. it for myself, lest I — Ru.4.6
In famine he will *r*. you from death — Job 5.20
R. Israel, O God, out of all his — Ps.25.22
who *r*. your life from the Pit — Ps.103.4
Let the *r*. of the LORD say so — Ps.107.2
And he will *r*. Israel from all his — Ps.130.8
hand shortened, that it cannot *r*.? — Is.50.2
you shall be *r*. without money — Is.52.3
the LORD will *r*. you from the hand — Mic.4.10
he was the one to *r*. Israel — Lk.24.21
Christ *r*. us from the curse of the — Gal.3.13
to *r*. those who were under the law — Gal.4.5
to *r*. us from all iniquity — Tit.2.14

REDEEMER
For I know that my *R*. lives — Job 19.25

O LORD, my rock and my *r*. — Ps.19.14
the Most High God their *r*. — Ps.78.35
their *R*. is strong; he will plead — Pr.23.11
your *R*. is the Holy One of Israel — Is.41.14
Their *R*. is strong; the LORD of — Jer.50.34

REDEMPTION
shall give for the *r*. of his life — Ex.21.30
you shall grant a *r*. of the land — Lev.25.24
Moses gave the *r*. money to Aaron — Num.3.51
He sent *r*. to his people — Ps.111.9
and with him is plenteous *r*. — Ps.130.7
and my year of *r*. has come — Is.63.4
through the *r*. which is in Christ — Rom.3.24
the *r*. of our bodies — Rom.8.23
and sanctification and *r*. — 1 Cor.1.30
In him we have *r*. through his blood — Eph.1.7
you were sealed for the day of *r*. — Eph.4.30
in whom we have *r*., the forgiveness — Col.1.14
blood, thus securing an eternal *r*. — Heb.9.12

REED
seven cows . . . fed in the *r*. grass — Gen.41.2
among the *r*. at the river's brink — Ex.2.3
a bruised *r*. he will not break — Is.42.3
A *r*. shaken by the wind? — Mt.11.7
took the *r*. and struck him on — Mt.27.30
put it on a *r*. and gave it to him — Mk.15.36

REFINE
I will *r*. them and test them — Jer.9.7
r. them as one *r*. silver — Zech.13.9
r. them like gold and silver — Mal.3.3
bronze, *r*. as in a furnace — Rev.1.15
to buy from me gold *r*. by fire — Rev.3.18

REFRAIN
R. from anger, and forsake wrath — Ps.37.8
he who *r*. from marriage will do — 1 Cor.7.38
will *r*. from burdening you in — 2 Cor.11.9

REFRESH
that you may *r*. yourselves — Gen.18.5
and good news *r*. the bones — Pr.15.30
with joy and be *r*. in your company — Rom.15.32
they *r*. my spirit as well as yours — 1 Cor.16.18
Onesiphorus, for he often *r*. me — 2 Tim.1.16
R. my heart in Christ — Philem.20

REFUGE
shall be the six cities of *r*. — Num.35.6
This God is my strong *r*. — 2 Sam.22.33
O LORD my God, in thee do I take *r*. — Ps.7.1
Preserve me . . . for in thee I take *r*. — Ps.16.1
In thee, O LORD, do I seek *r*. — Ps.31.1
God is our *r*. and strength, a very — Ps.46.1
shadow of thy wings I will take *r*. — Ps.57.1
under his wings you will find *r*. — Ps.91.4
But the LORD is a *r*. to his people — Jl.3.16
he knows those who take *r*. in him — Nah.1.7
we who have fled for *r*. might — Heb.6.18

REFUSE
Pharaoh stubbornly *r*. to let us go — Ex.13.15
but *r*. to walk according to his law — Ps.78.10
I have called and you *r*. to listen — Pr.1.24
But if you *r*. and rebel, you shall — Is.1.20
do not *r*. him who would borrow — Mt.5.42
Our fathers *r*. to obey him — Acts 7.39
If any one *r*. to obey what we say — 2 Th.3.14
See that you do not *r*. him who is — Heb.12.25

REGARD (verb)
I *r*. not myself; I loathe my life — Job 9.21

nor *r.* the rich more than the poor — Job 34.19
will *r.* the prayer of the destitute — Ps.102.17
what is man that thou dost *r.* him — Ps.144.3
In that day men will *r.* their Maker — Is.17.7
for he has *r.* the low estate of his — Lk.1.48
I neither fear God nor *r.* man — Lk.18.4
we *r.* no one from a human point — 2 Cor.5.16
do not *r.* lightly the discipline of — Heb.12.5

REHOBOAM
1 Kg.11.43; 14.21; 2 Chr.9.31; 11.5; 12.16

REIGN (verb)
The LORD will *r.* for ever and ever — Ex.15.18
No, but a king shall *r.* over us — 1 Sam.12.12
Solomon your son shall *r.* after me — 1 Kg.1.13
Say among the nations, "The LORD *r.* — Ps.96.10
The LORD *r.*; let the peoples tremble — Ps.99.1
The LORD will *r.* for ever, thy God — Ps.146.10
But thou, O LORD, dost *r.* for ever — Lam.5.19
he will *r.* over the house of Jacob — Lk.1.33
death *r.* through that one man — Rom.5.17
Let not sin . . . *r.* in your . . . bodies — Rom.6.12
he must *r.* until he has put all — 1 Cor.15.25
if we endure, we shall also *r.* — 2 Tim.2.12
and he shall *r.* for ever and ever — Rev.11.15
r. with Christ a thousand years — Rev.20.4

REJECT
God will not *r.* a blameless man — Job 8.20
and *r.* not your mother's teaching — Pr.1.8
He was despised and *r.* by men — Is.53.3
You have *r.* me, says the LORD — Jer.15.6
I *r.* you from being a priest to me — Hos.4.6
and be *r.* by the elders and chief — Lk.9.22
stone which was *r.* by you builders — Acts 4.11
commands of men who *r.* the truth — Tit.1.14
shall we escape if we *r.* him who — Heb.12.25
The . . . stone which the builders *r.* — 1 Pet.2.7

REJOICE
And you shall *r.* before the LORD — Dt.12.12
r., O righteous, and shout for joy — Ps.32.11
Then my soul shall *r.* in the LORD — Ps.35.9
Only let them not *r.* over me — Ps.38.16
The righteous will *r.* when he sees — Ps.58.10
But the king shall *r.* in God — Ps.63.11
that we may *r.* and be glad all our — Ps.90.14
R. in the LORD, O you righteous — Ps.97.12
r. at thy word like one who finds — Ps.119.162
and *r.* in the wife of your youth — Pr.5.18
Do not *r.* when your enemy falls — Pr.24.17
the desert shall *r.* and blossom — Is.35.1
R. and exult with all your heart — Zeph.3.14
Sing and *r.*, O daughter of Zion — Zech.2.10
R. greatly, O daughter of Zion — Zech.9.9
R. and be glad, for your reward is — Mt.5.12
and my spirit *r.* in God my Savior — Lk.1.47
R. in that day, and leap for joy — Lk.6.23
but *r.* that your names are written — Lk.10.20
Your father Abraham *r.* that he was — Jn.8.56
you . . . lament, but the world will *r.* — Jn.16.20
we *r.* in our sufferings, knowing — Rom.5.3
R. in your hope, be patient in — Rom.12.12
R. with those who *r.*, weep with — Rom.12.15
it does not *r.* at wrong, but — 1 Cor.13.6
R. in the Lord always; again . . . *R.* — Phil.4.4
Now I *r.* in my sufferings for your — Col.1.24
But *r.* in so far as you share — 1 Pet.4.13
R. . . . O heaven and you that dwell — Rev.12.12

RELEASE (verb)
accustomed to *r.* for the crowd any — Mt.27.15
therefore chastise him and *r.* him — Lk.23.16
once more, desiring to *r.* Jesus — Lk.23.20
Upon this Pilate sought to *r.* him — Jn.19.12
When they were *r.* they went to — Acts 4.23
our brother Timothy has been *r.* — Heb.13.23
R. the four angels who are bound — Rev.9.14

RELIEF
the Jews got *r.* from their enemies — Est.9.22
to send *r.* to the brethren who — Acts 11.29
taking part in the *r.* of the saints — 2 Cor.8.4

RELIGION
as befits women who profess *r.* — 1 Tim.2.10
Great . . . is the mystery of our *r.* — 1 Tim.3.16
holding the form of *r.* but denying — 2 Tim.3.5
R. that is pure and undefiled — Jas.1.27

RELIGIOUS
in every way you are very *r.* — Acts 17.22
learn their *r.* duty to their own — 1 Tim.5.4
If any one thinks he is *r.* — Jas.1.26

RELY
we *r.* on thee, and in thy name — 2 Chr.14.11
and do not *r.* on your own insight — Pr.3.5
We *r.* on the LORD our God — Is.36.7
when you *r.* on Egypt for chariots — Is.36.9
if you . . . *r.* upon the law and boast — Rom.2.17
to make us *r.* not on ourselves — 2 Cor.1.9
For all who *r.* on works of the law — Gal.3.10

REMAIN
While the earth *r.*, seedtime and — Gen.8.22
r. every man of you in his place — Ex.16.29
his body shall not *r.* all night — Dt.21.23
even to death; *r.* here, and watch — Mk.14.34
you see the Spirit descend and *r.* — Jn.1.33
Every one should *r.* in the state — 1 Cor.7.20
But to *r.* in the flesh is more — Phil.1.24
that what cannot be shaken may *r.* — Heb.12.27
strengthen what *r.* and is on the — Rev.3.2

REMEMBER
I will *r.* my covenant which is — Gen.9.15
the chief butler did not *r.* Joseph — Gen.40.23
R. the sabbath day, to keep it holy — Ex.20.8
R. what the LORD your God did to — Dt.24.9
R. now, O LORD, I beseech thee — 2 Kg.20.3
R. that thou hast made me of clay — Job 10.9
R. not the sins of my youth, or my — Ps.25.7
Do not *r.* against us the iniquities — Ps.79.8
he *r.* that we are dust — Ps.103.14
sat down and wept, when we *r.* Zion — Ps.137.1
Yet no one *r.* that poor man — Ec.9.15
R. also your Creator in the days of — Ec.12.1
R. my affliction and my bitterness — Lam.3.19
And Peter *r.* the saying of Jesus — Mt.26.75
and to *r.* his holy covenant — Lk.1.72
R. Lot's wife — Lk.17.32
R. the word that I said to you — Jn.15.20
only they would have us *r.* the poor — Gal.2.10
and I will *r.* their sins no more — Heb.8.12
R. those who are in prison — Heb.13.3
R. your leaders, those who spoke — Heb.13.7

REMEMBRANCE
For in death there is no *r.* of thee — Ps.6.5
a book of *r.* was written before him — Mal.3.16
in *r.* of his mercy — Lk.1.54

Do this in r. of me   1 Cor.11.24
I thank my God in all my r. of you   Phil.1.3
REMIND
to r. you of my ways in Christ   1 Cor.4.17
I r. you to rekindle the gift   2 Tim.1.6
R. them to be submissive to rulers   Tit.3.1
Now I desire to r. you, though you   Jude 5
REMINDER
have written to you . . . by way of r.   Rom.15.15
there is a r. of sin year after   Heb.10.3
to arouse you by way of r.   2 Pet.1.13
aroused your . . . mind by way of r.   2 Pet.3.1
REMNANT
to preserve for you a r. on earth   Gen.45.7
one of the r. of the Rephaim   Jos.12.4
but of the r. of the Amorites   2 Sam.21.2
prayer for the r. that is left   2 Kg.19.4
A r. will return, the r. of Jacob   Is.10.21
out of Jerusalem shall go forth a r.   Is.37.32
I will take the r. of Judah who   Jer.44.12
I will cut off . . . the r. of Baal   Zeph.1.4
only a r. of them will be saved   Rom.9.27
at the present time there is a r.   Rom.11.5
REMOVE
R. thy stroke from me; I am spent   Ps.39.10
so far does he r. our transgressions   Ps.103.12
The righteous will never be r.   Pr.10.30
Do not r. an ancient landmark or   Pr.23.10
R. far from me falsehood and lying   Pr.30.8
r. this cup from me; nevertheless   Lk.22.42
I will . . . r. your lampstand   Rev.2.5
REND
lest like a lion they r. me   Ps.7.2
a time to r., and a time to sew   Ec.3.7
O that thou wouldst r. the heavens   Is.64.1
r. your hearts and not your garments   Jl.2.13
RENDER
I will r. thank offerings to thee   Ps.56.12
What shall I r. to the LORD for   Ps.116.12
R. true judgments, show kindness   Zech.7.9
Then r. to Caesar the things that   Lk.20.25
he will r. to every man according   Rom.2.6
RENEW
go to Gilgal and . . . r. the kingdom   1 Sam.11.14
like grass which is r. in the morning   Ps.90.5
your youth is r. like the eagle's   Ps.103.5
the LORD shall r. their strength   Is.40.31
be restored! R. our days as of old   Lam.5.21
In the midst of the years r. it   Hab.3.2
inner nature is being r. every day   2 Cor.4.16
be r. in the spirit of your minds   Eph.4.23
which is being r. in knowledge   Col.3.10
RENOUNCE
Why does the wicked r. God, and say   Ps.10.13
Thou hast r. the covenant with thy   Ps.89.39
have r. disgraceful, underhanded   2 Cor.4.2
training us to r. irreligion and   Tit.2.12
REPAIR
And he r. the altar of the LORD   1 Kg.18.30
let them r. the house wherever   2 Kg.12.5
quarried stone to r. the house   2 Kg.22.6
r. the house of the LORD his God   2 Chr.34.8
they shall r. the ruined cities   Is.61.4
REPAY
given to me, that I should r. him?   Job 41.11
Do not say, "I will r. evil"   Pr.20.22

I will r., yea, I will r. into their   Is.65.6
then he will r. every man for what   Mt.16.27
blessed, because they cannot r. you   Lk.14.14
R. no one evil for evil, but take   Rom.12.17
See that none of you r. evil for evil   1 Th.5.15
Vengeance is mine, I will r.   Heb.10.30
and r. her double for her deeds   Rev.18.6
REPENT
I r. that I have made Saul king   1 Sam.15.11
is not a man, that he should r.   1 Sam.15.29
I . . . r. in dust and ashes   Job 42.6
God r. of the evil which he had   Jon.3.10
R., for the kingdom of heaven is   Mt.3.2
and preached that men should r.   Mk.6.12
if he . . . says, 'I r.,' you must forgive   Lk.17.4
R., and be baptized every one of   Acts 2.38
commands all men everywhere to r.   Acts 17.30
R. then. If not, I will come   Rev.2.16
so be zealous and r.   Rev.3.19
they did not r. and give him glory   Rev.16.9
REPENTANCE
Bear fruit that befits r.   Mt.3.8
a baptism of r. for the forgiveness   Mk.1.4
not . . . the righteous, but sinners to r.   Lk.5.32
that r. and forgiveness of sins   Lk.24.47
give r. to Israel and forgiveness   Acts 5.31
perform deeds worthy of their r.   Acts 26.20
kindness is meant to lead you to r.   Rom.2.4
grief produces a r. that leads to   2 Cor.7.10
impossible to restore again to r.   Heb.6.4
but that all should reach r.   2 Pet.3.9
REPORT (noun)
You shall not utter a false r.   Ex.23.1
brought up an evil r. of the land   Num.14.37
in anguish over the r. about Tyre   Is.23.5
She had heard the r. about Jesus   Mk.5.27
a r. concerning him went out   Lk.4.14
Lord, who has believed our r.   Jn.12.38
REPROACH (noun)
takes away the r. from Israel?   1 Sam.17.26
nor takes up a r. against his   Ps.15.3
for thy sake . . . I have borne r.   Ps.69.7
but sin is a r. to any people   Pr.14.34
fear not the r. of men, and be not   Is.51.7
everlasting r. and perpetual shame   Jer.23.40
You shall be a r. and a taunt   Ezek.5.15
to take away my r. among men   Lk.1.25
Now a bishop must be above r.   1 Tim.3.2
so that they may be without r.   1 Tim.5.7
REPROOF
Give heed to my r.; behold, I will   Pr.1.23
he who rejects r. goes astray   Pr.10.17
he who hates r. will die   Pr.15.10
scripture is . . . profitable . . . for r.   2 Tim.3.16
REPROVE
Behold, happy is the man whom God r.   Job 5.17
r. a wise man, and he will love you   Pr.9.8
He who is often r., yet stiffens his   Pr.29.1
exhort and r. with all authority   Tit.2.15
Those whom I love, I r. and chasten   Rev.3.19
REPUTE
LORD gave Solomon great r.   1 Chr.29.25
pick out . . . seven men of good r.   Acts 6.3
in ill r. and good r.   2 Cor.6.8
who were of r. added nothing to me   Gal.2.6

REQUEST

O that I might have my r.	Job 6.8
not withheld the r. of his lips	Ps.21.2
let your r. be made known to God	Phil.4.6
have obtained the r. made of him	1 Jn.5.15

REQUIRE

I will surely r. a reckoning	Gen.9.5
sin offering thou hast not r.	Ps.40.6
there our captors r. of us songs	Ps.137.3
what does the LORD r. of you but to	Mic.6.8
This night your soul is r. of you	Lk.12.20
is given, of him will much be r.	Lk.12.48
do by nature what the law r.	Rom.2.14

REQUITE

LORD r. the evildoer according	2 Sam.3.39
They r. me evil for good; my soul	Ps.35.12
thou dost r. a man according to	Ps.62.12
nor r. us according to our iniquities	Ps.103.10
R. her according to her deeds	Jer.50.29
Thou wilt r. them, O LORD	Lam.3.64
will r. your deeds upon your head	Ezek.16.43
I will r. your deed upon your own	Jl.3.4
the Lord will r. him for his deeds	2 Tim.4.14

RESCUE

Incline thy ear to me, r. me speedily	Ps.31.2
R. the weak and the needy	Ps.82.4
I will r. my sheep from their	Ezek.34.10
r. him out of all his afflictions	Acts 7.10
So I was r. from the lion's mouth	2 Tim.4.17
Lord will r. me from every evil	2 Tim.4.18
knows how to r. the godly from	2 Pet.2.9

RESIST

Do not r. one who is evil. But if	Mt.5.39
you always r. the Holy Spirit	Acts 7.51
who r. the authorities r. what God	Rom.13.2
R. the devil and he will flee from	Jas.4.7
R. him, firm in your faith	1 Pet.5.9

RESPECT (verb)

Do not r. their offering	Num.16.15
saying, 'They will r. my son.'	Mk.12.6
wife see that she r. her husband	Eph.5.33
to r. those who labor among you	1 Th.5.12
to discipline us and we r. them	Heb.12.9

REST (noun)

until the LORD gives r. to your	Jos.1.15
LORD gave them r. on every side	Jos.21.44
I have no r.; but trouble comes	Job 3.26
I would fly away and be at r.	Ps.55.6
Return, O my soul, to your r.	Ps.116.7
the Spirit of the LORD gave them r.	Is.63.14
heavy laden, and I will give you r.	Mt.11.28
our bodies had no r. but we were	2 Cor.7.5
They shall never enter my r.	Heb.3.11
a sabbath r. for the people of God	Heb.4.9
therefore strive to enter that r.	Heb.4.11
and they have no r., day or night	Rev.14.11

REST (verb)

on the seventh day you shall r.	Ex.34.21
in the night his mind does not r.	Ec.2.23
to a lonely place, and r. a while	Mk.6.31
power of Christ may r. upon me	2 Cor.12.9
that they may r. from their labor	Rev.14.13

RESTORE

the LORD r. the fortunes of Job	Job 42.10
he r. my soul. He leads me in paths	Ps.23.3
R. to me the joy of thy salvation	Ps.51.12

thou didst r. the fortunes of Jacob	Ps.85.1
I will r. your judges as at the first	Is.1.26
R. us to thyself, O LORD, that we	Lam.5.21
I will r. the fortunes of Jacob	Ezek.39.25
Elijah . . . is to r. all things	Mt.17.11
if I . . . defrauded . . . I r. it fourfold	Lk.19.8
Lord, will you . . . r. the kingdom	Acts 1.6
impossible to r. again to repentance	Heb.6.4

RESTRAIN

Therefore I will not r. my mouth	Job 7.11
he does not r. the lightnings	Job 37.4
he r. his anger often, and did not	Ps.78.38
he who r. his lips is prudent	Pr.10.19
He who r. his words has knowledge	Pr.17.27
Who can r. her lust? None who	Jer.2.24
only he who now r. it will do so	2 Th.2.7

RESURRECTION

in the r. they neither marry nor	Mt.22.30
In the r. whose wife will she be?	Mk.12.23
done evil, to the r. of judgment	Jn.5.29
to her, "I am the r. and the life	Jn.11.25
proclaiming . . . the r. from the dead	Acts 4.2
he preached Jesus and the r.	Acts 17.18
Sadducees say that there is no r.	Acts 23.8
united with him in a r. like his	Rom.6.5
So is it with the r. of the dead	1 Cor.15.42
know him and the power of his r.	Phil.3.10
that the r. is past already	2 Tim.2.18
Women received their dead by r.	Heb.11.35
through the r. of Jesus Christ	1 Pet.3.21
were ended. This is the first r.	Rev.20.5

RETURN (verb)

we will r. with you to your people	Ru.1.10
and man would r. to dust	Job 34.15
Like a dog that r. to his vomit is	Pr.26.11
the spirit r. to God who gave it	Ec.12.7
A remnant will r., the remnant of	Is.10.21
the ransomed of the LORD shall r.	Is.51.11
let him r. to the LORD, that he may	Is.55.7
my word . . . shall not r. to me empty	Is.55.11
they have refused to r. to me	Hos.11.5
R., O Israel, to the LORD your God	Hos.14.1
R. to me, and I will r. to you	Mal.3.7
not worthy, let your peace r. to you	Mt.10.13
r. to the Shepherd and Guardian	1 Pet.2.25
Do not r. evil for evil or	1 Pet.3.9

REUBEN

Gen.29.32; 37.21; Dt.33.6; Jg.5.15; Rev.7.5

REVEAL

there God had r. himself to him	Gen.35.7
have been able to r. this mystery	Dan.2.47
to whom the Son chooses to r. him	Mt.11.27
Nothing . . . that will not be r.	Lk.12.2
After this Jesus r. himself again	Jn.21.1
wrath of God is r. from heaven	Rom.1.18
God has r. to us through the Spirit	1 Cor.2.10
because it will be r. with fire	1 Cor.3.13
was pleased to r. his Son to me	Gal.1.16
God will r. that also to you	Phil.3.15
then the lawless one will be r.	2 Th.2.8
ready to be r. in the last time	1 Pet.1.5

REVELATION

a light for r. to the Gentiles	Lk.2.32
according to the r. of the mystery	Rom.16.25
a r. . . . or an interpretation	1 Cor.14.26
too elated by the abundance of r.	2 Cor.12.7

came through a *r.* of Jesus Christ Gal.1.12
honor at the *r.* of Jesus Christ 1 Pet.1.7
The *r.* of Jesus Christ, which God Rev.1.1

REVENUE
the royal *r.* will be impaired Ezra 4.13
than great *r.* with injustice Pr.16.8
your *r.* was the grain of Shihor Is.23.3
r. to whom *r.* is due Rom.13.7

REVERENCE (noun)
shall not pay *r.* to the gods of the Jg.6.10
Be subject . . . out of *r.* for Christ Eph.5.21
acceptable worship, with *r.* and awe Heb.12.28
yet do it with gentleness and *r.* 1 Pet.3.15

REVILE
You shall not *r.* God, nor curse a Ex.22.28
when men *r.* you and persecute you Mt.5.11
when they exclude you and *r.* you Lk.6.22
When *r.*, we bless; when persecuted 1 Cor.4.12
give the enemy no occasion to *r.* us 1 Tim.5.14
those who *r.* your good behavior 1 Pet.3.16
not afraid to *r.* the glorious ones 2 Pet.2.10

REVILING (noun)
and be not dismayed at their *r.* Is.51.7
heard all the *r.* which you uttered Ezek.35.12
of Moab and the *r.* of the Ammonites Zeph.2.8
not return evil for evil or *r.* for *r.* 1 Pet.3.9

REVIVE
Wilt thou not *r.* us again, that thy Ps.85.6
r. me according to thy word Ps.119.25
to *r.* the heart of the contrite Is.57.15
After two days he will *r.* us Hos.6.2
commandment came, sin *r.* and I died Rom.7.9
you have *r.* your concern for me Phil.4.10

REWARD (noun)
in keeping them there is great *r.* Ps.19.11
The *r.* for humility and fear of the Pr.22.4
behold, his *r.* is with him, and his Is.40.10
who love you, what *r.* have you? Mt.5.46
he shall not lose his *r.* Mt.10.42
your *r.* is great in heaven Lk.6.23
survives, he will receive a *r.* 1 Cor.3.14

REWARD (verb)
may the LORD *r.* you with good 1 Sam.24.19
The LORD *r.* me according to my Ps.18.20
So they *r.* me evil for good Ps.109.5
and the LORD will *r.* you Pr.25.22
who sees in secret will *r.* you Mt.6.4
God . . . *r.* those who seek him Heb.11.6

RICH
The LORD makes poor and makes *r.* 1 Sam.2.7
The *r.* man had very many flocks 2 Sam.12.2
nor regards the *r.* more than the Job 34.19
low and high, *r.* and poor together Ps.49.2
The blessing of the LORD makes *r.* Pr.10.22
the *r.* has many friends Pr.14.20
The *r.* and the poor meet together Pr.22.2
A *r.* man is wise in his own eyes Pr.28.11
and with a *r.* man in his death Is.53.9
hard for a *r.* man to enter the Mt.19.23
came a *r.* man from Arimathea Mt.27.57
Many *r.* people put in large sums Mk.12.41
the *r.* he has sent empty away Lk.1.53
But woe to you that are *r.* Lk.6.24
The land of a *r.* man brought forth Lk.12.16
and is not *r.* toward God Lk.12.21
The *r.* man also died and was buried Lk.16.22

Christ . . . though he was *r.*, yet for 2 Cor.8.9
God, who is *r.* in mercy, out of the Eph.2.4
who desire to be *r.* fall into 1 Tim.6.9
So will the *r.* man fade away in the Jas.1.11
both *r.* and poor, both free and Rev.13.16

RICHES
Both *r.* and honor come from thee 1 Chr.29.12
if *r.* increase, set not your heart Ps.62.10
Wealth and *r.* are in his house Ps.112.3
in her left hand are *r.* and honor Pr.3.16
R. do not profit in the day of wrath Pr.11.4
He who trusts in his *r.* will wither Pr.11.28
good name . . . rather than great *r.* Pr.22.1
for *r.* do not last for ever Pr.27.24
give me neither poverty nor *r.* Pr.30.8
the delight in *r.* choke the word Mt.13.22
to make known the *r.* of his glory Rom.9.23
O the depth of the *r.* and wisdom Rom.11.33
immeasurable *r.* of his grace in Eph.2.7
the unsearchable *r.* of Christ Eph.3.8
Your *r.* have rotted and your Jas.5.2

RIDDLE
Let me now put a *r.* to you Jg.14.12
she told the *r.* to her countrymen Jg.14.17
I will solve my *r.* to the music of Ps.49.4
propound a *r.* . . . speak an allegory Ezek.17.2
to . . . explain *r.*, and solve problems Dan.5.12

RIDE
Solomon to *r.* on King David's mule 1 Kg.1.38
So he had him *r.* in his chariot 2 Kg.10.16
In your majesty *r.* forth victoriously Ps.45.4
didst let men *r.* over our heads Ps.66.12
to him who *r.* in the heavens Ps.68.33
I will make you *r.* upon the heights Is.58.14

RIDER
horse and his *r.* he has thrown into Ex.15.1
both *r.* and horse lay stunned Ps.76.6
overthrow the chariots and their *r.* Hag.2.22
white horse, and its *r.* had a bow Rev.6.2

RIGHT (adjective)
Thy *r.* hand, O LORD, glorious in Ex.15.6
Let us choose what is *r.*; let us Job 34.4
in thy *r.* hand are pleasures for Ps.16.11
the precepts of the LORD are *r.* Ps.19.8
He leads the humble in what is *r.* Ps.25.9
put a new and *r.* spirit within me Ps.51.10
His *r.* hand and his holy arm have Ps.98.1
Sit at my *r.* hand, till I make your Ps.110.1
a way which seems *r.* to a man Pr.16.25
if any one strikes you on the *r.* cheek Mt.5.39
seated at the *r.* hand of Power Mt.26.64
and cut off his *r.* ear Lk.22.50
your heart is not *r.* before God Acts 8.21
at the *r.* time Christ died for the Rom.5.6
I can will what is *r.*, but I cannot Rom.7.18
gave . . . the *r.* hand of fellowship Gal.2.9
he sat down at the *r.* hand of God Heb.10.12
in his *r.* hand he held seven stars Rev.1.16

RIGHT (noun)
does the Almighty pervert the *r.*? Job 8.3
God has taken away my *r.* Job 34.5
and your *r.* as the noonday Ps.37.6
yet surely my *r.* is with the LORD Is.49.4
Do we not have the *r.* to be 1 Cor.9.5
we have not made use of this *r.* 1 Cor.9.12

but rejoices in the *r.*	1 Cor.13.6
have the *r.* to the tree of life	Rev.22.14

RIGHTEOUS

find at Sodom fifty *r.* in the city	Gen.18.26
to David, "You are more *r.* than	1 Sam.24.17
The *r.* see it and are glad	Job 22.19
How then can man be *r.* before God?	Job 25.4
the LORD knows the way of the *r.*	Ps.1.6
are destroyed, what can the *r.* do"?	Ps.11.3
eyes of the LORD are toward the *r.*	Ps.34.15
The *r.* shall see, and fear	Ps.52.6
Light dawns for the *r.*, and joy	Ps.97.11
For the *r.* will never be moved	Ps.112.6
no man living is *r.* before thee	Ps.143.2
LORD does not let the *r.* go hungry	Pr.10.3
but the *r.* is established for ever	Pr.10.25
The *r.* is delivered from trouble	Pr.11.8
The thoughts of the *r.* are just	Pr.12.5
he hears the prayer of the *r.*	Pr.15.29
Be not *r.* overmuch, and do not make	Ec.7.16
by his knowledge shall the *r.* one	Is.53.11
I will cause a *r.* Branch to spring	Jer.33.15
But when a *r.* man turns away from	Ezek.18.24
Then the *r.* will shine like the sun	Mt.13.43
I have not come to call the *r.*	Lk.5.32
O *r.* Father, the world has not known	Jn.17.25
But you denied the Holy and *R.* One	Acts 3.14
The prayer of a *r.* man has great	Jas.5.16
eyes of the Lord are upon the *r.*	1 Pet.3.12

RIGHTEOUSNESS

he reckoned it to him as *r.*	Gen.15.6
Not because of your *r.* or the	Dt.9.5
recompensed . . . according to my *r.*	2 Sam.22.25
ascribe *r.* to my Maker	Job 36.3
He loves *r.* and justice	Ps.33.5
May he judge thy people with *r.*	Ps.72.2
r. and peace will kiss each other	Ps.85.10
his *r.* to children's children	Ps.103.17
Let thy priests be clothed with *r.*	Ps.132.9
The *r.* of the upright delivers them	Pr.11.6
R. exalts a nation, but sin is a	Pr.14.34
To do *r.* and justice is more	Pr.21.3
R. shall be the girdle of his waist	Is.11.5
Behold, a king will reign in *r.*	Is.32.1
the effect of *r.* will be peace	Is.32.17
He put on *r.* as a breastplate	Is.59.17
be called: 'The LORD is our *r.*'	Jer.23.6
to bring in everlasting *r.*	Dan.9.24
those who hunger and thirst for *r.*	Mt.5.6
unless your *r.* exceeds that of the	Mt.5.20
seek first his kingdom and his *r.*	Mt.6.33
of sin and of *r.* and of judgment	Jn.16.8
the *r.* of God has been manifested	Rom.3.21
God reckons *r.* apart from works	Rom.4.6
we might become the *r.* of God	2 Cor.5.21
partnership have *r.* and iniquity?	2 Cor.6.14
put on the breastplate of *r.*	Eph.6.14
loved *r.* and hated lawlessness	Heb.1.9
yields the peaceful fruit of *r.* to	Heb.12.11
the harvest of *r.* is sown in peace	Jas.3.18
might die to sin and live to *r.*	1 Pet.2.24
a new earth in which *r.* dwells	2 Pet.3.13
in *r.* he judges and makes war	Rev.19.11

RING

seal it with the king's *r.*	Est.8.8
Like a gold *r.* in a swine's snout	Pr.11.22

put a *r.* on his hand, and shoes	Lk.15.22
a man with gold *r.* and in fine	Jas.2.2

RISE

a scepter shall *r.* out of Israel	Num.24.17
from those who *r.* up against me	Ps.59.1
R. up, O judge of the earth	Ps.94.2
At midnight I *r.* to praise thee	Ps.119.62
Her children *r.* up and call her	Pr.31.28
your light *r.* in the darkness	Is.58.10
the sun of righteousness shall *r.*	Mal.4.2
For nation will *r.* against nation	Mt.24.7
after three days he will *r.*	Mk.10.34
r., take up your bed and go home	Lk.5.24
Nation will *r.* against nation	Lk.21.10
no prophet is to *r.* from Galilee	Jn.7.52
I know that he will *r.* again in the	Jn.11.24
the dead in Christ will *r.* first	1 Th.4.16
morning star *r.* in your hearts	2 Pet.1.19

RIVER

A *r.* flowed out of Eden to water	Gen.2.10
r. of Damascus, better than all	2 Kg.5.12
There is a *r.* whose streams make	Ps.46.4
baptized by him in the *r.* Jordan	Mk.1.5
shall flow *r.* of living water	Jn.7.38
the *r.* of the water of life	Rev.22.1

ROAR

though its waters *r.* and foam	Ps.46.3
Let the sea *r.*, and all that fills	Ps.98.7
The LORD will *r.* from on high	Jer.25.30
The LORD *r.* from Zion, and utters	Am.1.2
devil prowls around like a *r.* lion	1 Pet.5.8

ROB

Do not *r.* the poor, because he is	Pr.22.22
Will man *r.* God? Yet you are	Mal.3.8
R. no one by violence or by false	Lk.3.14
who abhor idols, do you *r.* temples?	Rom.2.22

ROBBER

But you have made it a den of *r.*	Mk.11.17
Have you come out as against a *r.*	Mk.14.48
to Jericho, and he fell among *r.*	Lk.10.30
Now Barabbas was a *r.*	Jn.18.40
nor *r.* will inherit the kingdom	1 Cor.6.10

ROBBERY

shall restore what he took by *r.*	Lev.6.4
set no vain hopes on *r.*	Ps.62.10
I the LORD love justice, I hate *r.*	Is.61.8
commits no *r.*, but gives his	Ezek.18.16
gives back what he had taken by *r.*	Ezek.33.15

ROBE

he made him a long *r.* with sleeves	Gen.37.3
he has covered me with the *r.* of	Is.61.10
put a scarlet *r.* upon him	Mt.27.28
Bring quickly the best *r.*	Lk.15.22
crown of thorns and the purple *r.*	Jn.19.5
Who are these, clothed in white *r.*	Rev.7.13
He is clad in a *r.* dipped in blood	Rev.19.13

ROCK

struck the *r.* with his rod	Num.20.11
scoffed at the *R.* of his salvation	Dt.32.15
The LORD is my *r.*, and my fortress	Ps.18.2
Be thou a *r.* of refuge for me	Ps.31.2
He only is my *r.* and my salvation	Ps.62.2
look to the *r.* from which you were	Is.51.1
hide it there in a cleft of the *r.*	Jer.13.4
who built his house upon the *r.*	Mt.7.24

some fell on the *r.* — Lk.8.6
the *R.* was Christ — 1 Cor.10.4

ROD

But Aaron's *r.* swallowed up their — Ex.7.12
shall break them with a *r.* of iron — Ps.2.9
thy *r.* and thy staff, they comfort — Ps.23.4
He who spares the *r.* hates his son — Pr.13.24
if you beat him with a *r.,* he will — Pr.23.13
I said, "I see a *r.* of almond." — Jer.1.11
Aaron's *r.* that budded, and the — Heb.9.4
he measured the city with his *r.* — Rev.21.16

ROLL (verb)

the skies *r.* up like a scroll — Is.34.4
But let justice *r.* down like waters — Am.5.24
Who will *r.* away the stone for us — Mk.16.3
like a mantle thou wilt *r.* them up — Heb.1.12
like a scroll that is *r.* up — Rev.6.14

ROMAN

the *R.* will come and destroy both — Jn.11.48
of Macedonia, and a *R.* colony — Acts 16.12
men who are *R.* citizens, and have — Acts 16.37
scourge a man who is a *R.* citizen — Acts 22.25
learned that he was a *R.* citizen — Acts 23.27

ROME

Acts 2.10; 28.16; Rom.1.7; 2 Tim.1.17

ROOM

go into your *r.* and shut the door — Mt.6.6
Teacher says, Where is my guest *r.* — Mk.14.14
In my Father's house are many *r.* — Jn.14.2
they went up to the upper *r.* — Acts 1.13
prepare a guest *r.* for me — Philem.22

ROOT (noun)

the *r.* of the righteous stands firm — Pr.12.12
Judah shall again take *r.* downward — Is.37.31
like a *r.* out of dry ground — Is.53.2
axe is laid to the *r.* of the trees — Mt.3.10
they have no *r.* in themselves — Mk.4.17
if the *r.* is holy, so are the — Rom.11.16
of money is the *r.* of all evils — 1 Tim.6.10
the *R.* of David, has conquered — Rev.5.5

ROPE

Can you put a *r.* in his nose — Job 41.2
instead of a girdle, a *r.* — Is.3.24
who draw sin as with cart *r.* — Is.5.18
to Jeremiah in the cistern by *r.* — Jer.38.11

ROT

but the name of the wicked will *r.* — Pr.10.7
passion makes the bones *r.* — Pr.14.30
All the host of heaven shall *r.* away — Is.34.4
tongues shall *r.* in their mouths — Zech.14.12
Your riches have *r.* and your — Jas.5.2

ROUGH

level, and the *r.* places a plain — Is.40.4
the *r.* places into level ground — Is.42.16
the *r.* ways shall be made smooth — Lk.3.5

ROUTED

the LORD *r.* the Egyptians in the — Ex.14.27
And the LORD *r.* Sisera and all his — Jg.4.15
they were *r.* before Israel — 1 Sam.7.10
flashed . . . lightnings, and *r.* them — Ps.18.14

ROYAL

Your *r.* scepter is a scepter of — Ps.45.6
thy righteousness to the *r.* son — Ps.72.1
a *r.* diadem in the hand of your God — Is.62.3
spread his *r.* canopy over them — Jer.43.10
the LORD, and shall bear *r.* honor — Zech.6.13

If you really fulfil the *r.* law — Jas.2.8
a *r.* priesthood, a holy nation — 1 Pet.2.9
who have not yet received *r.* power — Rev.17.12

RUIN (noun)

Let *r.* come upon them unawares — Ps.35.8
they have laid Jerusalem in *r.* — Ps.79.1
way of the wicked he brings to *r.* — Ps.146.9
but a prating fool will come to *r.* — Pr.10.8
A foolish son is *r.* to his father — Pr.19.13
For vast as the sea is your *r.* — Lam.2.13
A *r., r., r.* I will make it — Ezek.21.27
Jerusalem shall become a heap of *r.* — Mic.3.12
a day of *r.* and devastation — Zeph.1.15
in their paths are *r.* and misery — Rom.3.16
plunge men into *r.* and destruction — 1 Tim.6.9

RULE (noun)

we might share the *r.* with you — 1 Cor.4.8
This is my *r.* in all the churches — 1 Cor.7.17
be upon all who walk by this *r.* — Gal.6.16
the head of all *r.* and authority — Col.2.10
to keep these *r.* without favor — 1 Tim.5.21

RULE (verb)

the greater light to *r.* the day — Gen.1.16
husband, and he shall *r.* over you — Gen.3.16
his kingdom *r.* over all — Ps.103.19
stars to *r.* over the night — Ps.136.9
The hand of the diligent will *r.* — Pr.12.24
he who rises to *r.* the Gentiles — Rom.15.12
peace of Christ *r.* in your hearts — Col.3.15
Let the elders who *r.* well be — 1 Tim.5.17
he will *r.* them with a rod of iron — Rev.19.15

RULER

I will make him *r.* all the days — 1 Kg.11.34
A *r.* who lacks understanding is a — Pr.28.16
Many seek the favor of a *r.* — Pr.29.26
is our judge, the LORD is our *r.* — Is.33.22
a *r.* who will govern my people Israel — Mt.2.6
said to the *r.* of the synagogue — Mk.5.36
Nicodemus, a *r.* of the Jews — Jn.3.1
the *r.* of this world is coming — Jn.14.30
in ignorance, as did also your *r.* — Acts 3.17
For *r.* are not a terror to good — Rom.13.3
None of the *r.* of this age — 1 Cor.2.8
world *r.* of this present darkness — Eph.6.12
submissive to *r.* and authorities — Tit.3.1
Jesus Christ . . . the *r.* of kings on earth — Rev.1.5

RUMOR

he shall hear a *r.* and return to — 2 Kg.19.7
We have heard a *r.* of it with our — Job 28.22
Hark, a *r.*! Behold, it comes — Jer.10.22
you will hear of wars and *r.* of wars — Mt.24.6

RUN

r. in the way of thy commandments — Ps.119.32
their feet *r.* to evil, and they make — Pr.1.16
All streams *r.* to the sea, but the — Ec.1.7
that they may *r.* after strong drink — Is.5.11
Many shall *r.* to and fro — Dan.12.4
prize? So *r.* that you may obtain — 1 Cor.9.24
lest somehow I . . . had *r.* in vain — Gal.2.2
let us *r.* with perseverance the — Heb.12.1

RUSH (verb)

an evil spirit . . . *r.* upon Saul — 1 Sam.18.10
r. to and fro through the squares — Nah.2.4
the whole herd *r.* down the steep — Mt.8.32
he called for lights and *r.* in — Acts 16.29

RUST (noun)

Its *r*. is your filthy lewdness	Ezek.24.13
earth, where moth and *r*. consume	Mt.6.19
their *r*. will be evidence against	Jas.5.3

RUTHLESS

r. men seek my life; they do not	Ps.54.3
a band of *r*. men seek my life	Ps.86.14
redeem you from the grasp of the *r*.	Jer.15.21
foolish, faithless, heartless, *r*.	Rom.1.31

SABBATH

The LORD has given you the *s*.	Ex.16.29
Remember the *s*. day, to keep it holy	Ex.20.8
The *s*. of the land shall provide	Lev.25.6
On the *s*. day two male lambs	Num.28.9
It is neither new moon nor *s*.	2 Kg.4.23
do not bear a burden on the *s*. day	Jer.17.21
to keep the *s*. day holy, and not	Jer.17.27
on the *s*. day it shall be opened	Ezek.46.1
And the *s*., that we may offer wheat	Am.8.5
through the grainfields on the *s*. day	Mt.12.1
the Son of man is lord of the *s*.	Mt.12.8
it is lawful to do good on the *s*.	Mt.12.12
The *s*. was made for man, not man for	Mk.2.27
And when the *s*. was past, Mary	Mk.16.1
what is not lawful to do on the *s*.?	Lk.6.2
because Jesus had healed on the *s*.	Lk.13.14
On the *s*. they rested according to	Lk.23.56
you circumcise a man upon the *s*.	Jn.7.22
Now it was a *s*. day when Jesus made	Jn.9.14
(for that *s*. was a high day)	Jn.19.31
a *s*. day's journey away	Acts 1.12
prophets which are read every *s*.	Acts 13.27
is read every *s*. in the synagogues	Acts 15.21
argued in the synagogue every *s*.	Acts 18.4
a festival or a new moon or a *s*.	Col.2.16
there remains a *s*. rest for the	Heb.4.9

SACKCLOTH

put *s*. upon his loins, and mourned	Gen.37.34
assembled with fasting and in *s*.	Neh.9.1
Mordecai . . . put on *s*. and ashes	Est.4.1
I have sewed *s*. upon my skin	Job 16.15
thou hast loosed my *s*. and girded me	Ps.30.11
I wore *s*., I afflicted myself with	Ps.35.13
in the streets they gird on *s*.	Is.15.3
to spread *s*. and ashes under him	Is.58.5
Gird yourselves with *s*., lament	Jer.49.3
with fasting and *s*. and ashes	Dan.9.3
put on *s*., from the greatest of	Jon.3.5
repented long ago in *s*. and ashes	Mt.11.21
the sun became black as *s*.	Rev.6.12

SACRED

make of these a *s*. anointing oil	Ex.30.25
fields . . . shall be *s*. to the LORD	Jer.31.40
her priests profane what is *s*.	Zeph.3.4
or the altar that makes the gift *s*.?	Mt.23.19
acquainted with the *s*. writings	2 Tim.3.15

SACRIFICE (noun)

Jacob offered a *s*. on the mountain	Gen.31.54
It is the *s*. of the LORD's passover	Ex.12.27
you offer a *s*. of peace offerings	Lev.19.5
offer to the LORD the yearly *s*.	1 Sam.1.21
to obey is better than *s*.	1 Sam.15.22
The *s*. acceptable to God is a broken	Ps.51.17
s. of the wicked is an abomination	Pr.21.27
They love *s*. . . . but the LORD	Hos.8.13

'I desire mercy, and not *s*.'	Mt.9.13
wanted to offer *s*. with the people	Acts 14.13
present your bodies as a living *s*.	Rom.12.1
This has been offered in *s*.	1 Cor.10.28
a fragrant offering and *s*. to God	Eph.5.2
put away sin by the *s*. of himself	Heb.9.26
a more acceptable *s*. than Cain	Heb.11.4
offer up a *s*. of praise to God	Heb.13.15
such *s*. are pleasing to God	Heb.13.16
offer spiritual *s*. acceptable to	1 Pet.2.5

SACRIFICE (verb)

for we shall *s*. to the LORD our God	Ex.8.26
freewill offering I will *s*. to thee	Ps.54.6
Therefore he *s*. to his net and	Hab.1.16
already on the point of being *s*.	2 Tim.4.6

SACRIFICIAL

let their *s*. feasts be a trap	Ps.69.22
Can vows and *s*. flesh avert your	Jer.11.15
share in the *s*. offerings?	1 Cor.9.13
the *s*. offering of your faith	Phil.2.17

SAD

her countenance was no longer *s*.	1 Sam.1.18
Why should not my face be *s*.	Neh.2.3
I will put off my *s*. countenance	Job 9.27
Even in laughter the heart is *s*.	Pr.14.13
when he heard this he became *s*.	Lk.18.23
they stood still, looking *s*.	Lk.24.17

SADDUCEES

their controversies with Jesus, Mt.16.1; 22.23;
Mk.12.18; Lk.20.27; with the apostles, Acts
4.1; with Paul, Acts 23.6; their beliefs, Mt.22.23;
Mk.12.18; Acts 23.8

SADNESS

nothing else but *s*. of the heart	Neh.2.2
by *s*. of countenance the heart is	Ec.7.3

SAFE

I shall be *s*., though I walk in	Dt.29.19
God . . . has made my way *s*.	2 Sam.22.33
Their houses are *s*. from fear	Job 21.9
Oh to be *s*. under the shelter of	Ps.61.4
that I may be *s*. and have regard	Ps.119.117
righteous man runs into it and is *s*.	Pr.18.10
he who trusts in the LORD is *s*.	Pr.29.25
not irksome to me, and is *s*. for you	Phil.3.1

SAFELY

And Jacob came *s*. to the city of	Gen.33.18
He pursues them and passes on *s*.	Is.41.3
seize him and lead him away *s*.	Mk.14.44
charging the jailer to keep them *s*.	Acts 16.23
bring him *s*. to Felix the governor	Acts 23.24

SAFETY

The beloved . . . dwells in *s*. by him	Dt.33.12
those who mourn are lifted to *s*.	Job 5.11
thou . . . O LORD, makest me dwell in *s*.	Ps.4.8
He led them in *s*., so that they	Ps.78.53
Flee for *s*., O people of Benjamin	Jer.6.1
I will make them dwell in *s*.	Jer.32.37
I will make you lie down in *s*.	Hos.2.18

SAINT

As for the *s*. in the land, they are	Ps.16.3
O you his *s*., and give thanks to	Ps.30.4
he preserves the lives of his *s*.	Ps.97.10
Precious . . . is the death of his *s*.	Ps.116.15
the *s*. of the Most High shall	Dan.7.18
much evil he has done to thy *s*.	Acts 9.13

also to the *s.* that lived at Lydda — Acts 9.32
in Rome, who are called to be *s.* — Rom.1.7
Contribute to the needs of the *s.* — Rom.12.13
the *s.* will judge the world — 1 Cor.6.2
to the service of the *s.* — 1 Cor.16.15
glorious inheritance in the *s.* — Eph.1.18
the *s.* and members of the household — Eph.2.19
among you, as is fitting among *s.* — Eph.5.3
Greet every *s.* in Christ Jesus — Phil.4.21
the inheritance of the *s.* in light — Col.1.12
our Lord Jesus with all his *s.* — 1 Th.3.13
that day to be glorified in his *s.* — 2 Th.1.10
washed the feet of the *s.* — 1 Tim.5.10
hearts of the *s.* have been refreshed — Philem.7
faith . . . once for all delivered to the *s.* — Jude 3
which are the prayers of the *s.* — Rev.5.8
thy servants, the prophets and *s.* — Rev.11.18
make war on the *s.* and to conquer — Rev.13.7
is the righteous deeds of the *s.* — Rev.19.8
the Lord Jesus be with all the *s.* — Rev.22.21

SAKE

Are you jealous for my *s.*? — Num.11.29
show . . . kindness for Jonathan's *s.*? — 2 Sam.9.1
for David's *s.* the LORD . . . gave — 1 Kg.15.4
of righteousness for his name's *s.* — Ps.23.3
for the *s.* of thy steadfast love — Ps.115.1
persecuted for righteousness' *s.* — Mt.5.10
loses his life for my *s.* will find — Mt.10.39
for the *s.* of your tradition? — Mt.15.3
for the *s.* of the elect, whom he — Mk.13.20
for your *s.* I am glad that I was — Jn.11.15
for their *s.* I consecrate myself — Jn.17.19
accursed . . . for the *s.* of my brethren — Rom.9.3
but also for the *s.* of conscience — Rom.13.5
We are fools for Christ's *s.* — 1 Cor.4.10
do it all for the *s.* of the gospel — 1 Cor.9.23
For our *s.* he made him to be sin — 2 Cor.5.21
For the *s.* of Christ, then, I am — 2 Cor.12.10
. afflictions for his body — Col.1.24
for love's *s.* I prefer to appeal — Philem.9
suffer for righteousness' *s.* — 1 Pet.3.14
your sins are forgiven for his *s.* — 1 Jn.2.12
bearing up for my name's *s.* — Rev.2.3

SALE

within a whole year after its *s.* — Lev.25.29
from the *s.* of his patrimony — Dt.18.8
yourselves for *s.* to your enemies — Dt.28.68
that we may offer wheat for *s.* — Am.8.5

SALEM

Gen.14.18; Ps.76.2; Heb.7.1

SALT

and she became a pillar of *s.* — Gen.19.26
the whole land brimstone and *s.* — Dt.29.23
his sons by a covenant of *s.* — 2 Chr.13.5
is tasteless be eaten without *s.* — Job 6.6
shall sprinkle *s.* upon them — Ezek.43.24
Have *s.* in yourselves, and be at — Mk.9.50
.S. is good; but if *s.* has lost — Lk.14.34
your speech . . . seasoned with *s.* — Col.4.6
No more can *s.* water yield fresh — Jas.3.12

SALUTE

And thus you shall *s.* him — 1 Sam.25.6
If you meet any one, do not *s.* him — 2 Kg.4.29
And if you *s.* only your brethren — Mt.5.47
As you enter the house, *s.* it — Mt.10.12

they began to *s.* him, "Hail, King — Mk.15.18
and *s.* no one on the road — Lk.10.4

SALVATION

I wait for thy *s.*, O LORD — Gen.49.18
see the *s.* of the LORD, which he — Ex.14.13
my song, and he has become my *s.* — Ex.15.2
scoffed at the Rock of his *s.* — Dt.32.15
be my God, the rock of my *s.* — 2 Sam.22.47
Tell of his *s.* from day to day — 1 Chr.16.23
my heart shall rejoice in thy *s.* — Ps.13.5
for thou art the God of my *s.* — Ps.25.5
The LORD is my light and my *s.* — Ps.27.1
The *s.* of the righteous is from the — Ps.37.39
Restore to me the joy of thy *s.* — Ps.51.12
O God of our *s.*, who art the hope — Ps.65.5
Our God is a God of *s.*; and to God — Ps.68.20
tell . . . of thy deeds of *s.* all the — Ps.71.15
working *s.* in the midst of the earth — Ps.74.12
Surely his *s.* is at hand for those — Ps.85.9
joyful noise to the rock of our *s.* — Ps.95.1
tell of his *s.* from day to day — Ps.96.2
I will lift up the cup of *s.* and — Ps.116.13
he has become my *s.* — Ps.118.14
My soul languishes for thy *s.* — Ps.119.81
S. is far from the wicked, for — Ps.119.155
Behold, God is my *s.*; I will trust — Is.12.2
draw water from the wells of *s.* — Is.12.3
our *s.* in the time of trouble — Is.33.2
by the LORD with everlasting *s.* — Is.45.17
in a day of *s.* I have helped you — Is.49.8
LORD our God is the *s.* of Israel — Jer.3.23
wait quietly for the *s.* of the LORD — Lam.3.26
I will joy in the God of my *s.* — Hab.3.18
has raised up a horn of *s.* for us — Lk.1.69
for mine eyes have seen thy *s.* — Lk.2.30
Today *s.* has come to this house — Lk.19.9
for *s.* is from the Jews — Jn.4.22
And there is *s.* in no one else — Acts 4.12
power of God for *s.* to every one — Rom.1.16
s. is nearer to us now than when — Rom.13.11
behold, now is the day of *s.* — 2 Cor.6.2
heard . . . the gospel of your *s.* — Eph.1.13
And take the helmet of *s.* — Eph.6.17
work out your own *s.* with fear 'and — Phil.2.12
destined us . . . to obtain *s.* through — 1 Th.5.9
may obtain the *s.* which in Christ — 2 Tim.2.10
for the sake of those who . . . obtain *s.*? — Heb.1.14
if we neglect such a great *s.*? — Heb.2.3
eternal *s.* to all who obey him — Heb.5.9
better things that belong to *s.* — Heb.6.9
you obtain the *s.* of your souls — 1 Pet.1.9
that by it you may grow up to *s.* — 1 Pet.2.2
to write to you of our common *s.* — Jude 3
S. belongs to our God who sits — Rev.7.10

SAMARIA

(1) the district between Judea and Galilee, Lk.17.11; Jn.4; (2) the city built by Omri, king of Israel, 1 Kg.16.24; 20.1; 2 Kg.6.24; destroyed by the Assyrians, 722–721 B.C., and rebuilt by Herod

SAMARITAN

high places which the *S.* had made — 2 Kg.17.29
But a *S.*, as he journeyed, came to — Lk.10.33
Now he was a *S.* — Lk.17.16
For Jews have no dealings with *S.* — Jn.4.9
gospel to many villages of the *S.* — Acts 8.25

SAMSON
Jg.13–16; delivered up to Philistines, Jg.16.21; his death, Jg.16.30

SAMUEL
born, and presented to the Lord, 1 Sam.1.19–20, 26–28; the Lord speaks to, 1 Sam.3.11; judges Israel, 1 Sam.7; 8.1; Acts 13.20; anoints Saul king, 1 Sam.10.1; rebukes Saul for sin, 1 Sam.13.13; 15.16; anoints David, 1 Sam.16; his death, 1 Sam.25.1; 28.3; his spirit consulted by Saul, 1 Sam.28.12; as a prophet, Acts 3.24

SANCTIFICATION
members to righteousness for *s.*	Rom.6.19
He is . . . righteousness and *s.*	1 Cor.1.30
your *s.*: that you abstain from	1 Th.4.3
through *s.* by the Spirit	2 Th.2.13

SANCTIFY
it shall be *s.* by my glory	Ex.29.43
I the LORD, who *s.* you, am holy	Lev.21.8
said to the people, "*S.* yourselves	Jos.3.5
the Levites *s.* themselves to	1 Chr.15.14
And the priests *s.* themselves in	2 Chr.30.24
they will *s.* the Holy One of Jacob	Is.29.23
Those who *s.* and purify themselves	Is.66.17
S. them in the truth; thy word is	Jn.17.17
those who are *s.* by faith in me	Acts 26.18
acceptable, *s.* by the Holy Spirit	Rom.15.16
to those *s.* in Christ Jesus	1 Cor.1.2
you were *s.*, you were justified	1 Cor.6.11
he might *s.* her, having cleansed	Eph.5.26
God of peace himself *s.* you wholly	1 Th.5.23
those who are *s.* have all one origin	Heb.2.11
s. by the Spirit for obedience	1 Pet.1.2

SANCTUARY
the *s.*, O LORD, which thy hands have	Ex.15.17
And let them make me a *s.*	Ex.25.8
reverence my *s.*: I am the LORD	Lev.19.30
May he send you help from the *s.*	Ps.20.2
I have looked upon thee in the *s.*	Ps.63.2
of my God, my King, into the *s.*	Ps.68.24
Terrible is God in his *s.*	Ps.68.35
until I went into the *s.* of God	Ps.73.17
built his *s.* like the high heavens	Ps.78.69
strength and beauty are in his *s.*	Ps.96.6
Praise God in his *s.*; praise him in	Ps.150.1
he will become a *s.*, and a stone	Is.8.14
to beautify the place of my *s.*	Is.60.13
beginning is the place of our *s.*	Jer.17.12
scorned his altar, disowned his *s.*	Lam.2.7
I have been a *s.* to them	Ezek.11.16
the place of his *s.* was overthrown	Dan.8.11
at Bethel, for it is the king's *s.*	Am.7.13
between the *s.* and the altar	Mt.23.35
copy and shadow of the heavenly *s.*	Heb.8.5
to enter the *s.* by the blood of	Heb.10.19

SAND
as the *s.* which is on the seashore	Gen.22.17
descendants as the *s.* of the sea	Gen.32.12
be heavier than the *s.* of the sea	Job 6.3
s. is weighty, but a fool's	Pr.27.3
shall be like the *s.* of the sea	Hos.1.10
who built his house upon the *s.*	Mt.7.26
sons of Israel be as the *s.* of the sea	Rom.9.27
grains of *s.* by the seashore	Heb.11.12

SANDAL
| pull his *s.* off his foot | Dt.25.9 |

drew off his *s.* and gave it to the	Ru.4.7
two tunics, nor *s.*, nor a staff	Mt.10.10
to wear *s.* and not put on two tunics	Mk.6.9
with no purse or bag or *s.*	Lk.22.35
thong of whose *s.* I am not worthy	Jn.1.27

SANG
the people of Israel *s.* this song to	Ex.15.1
And Miriam *s.* to them: "Sing to the	Ex.15.21
they *s.* responsively, praising	Ezra 3.11
the singers *s.* with Jezrahiah	Neh.12.42
when the morning stars *s.* together	Job 38.7
they *s.* a new song, saying, "Worthy	Rev.5.9

SAPPHIRE
as it were a pavement of *s.* stone	Ex.24.10
Its stones are the place of *s.*	Job 28.6
the beauty of their form was like *s.*	Lam.4.7
above them something like a *s.*	Ezek.10.1
the color of fire and of *s.*	Rev.9.17
the second *s.*, the third agate	Rev.21.19

SARAH
Gen.17.15; 18.10; 20.2; 21.1–6; 23.1; Heb.11.11

SATAN
S. stood up against Israel	1 Chr.21.1
LORD said to *S.*, "Whence have you	Job 1.7
if *S.* casts out *S.*, he is divided	Mt.12.26
rebuked Peter . . . "Get behind me, *S.*	Mk.8.33
I saw *S.* fall like lightning from	Lk.10.18
Then *S.* entered into Judas	Lk.22.3
why has *S.* filled your heart to lie	Acts 5.3
from the power of *S.* to God	Acts 26.18
will soon crush *S.* under your feet	Rom.16.20
you are to deliver this man to *S.*	1 Cor.5.5
keep *S.* from gaining the advantage	2 Cor.2.11
a messenger of *S.*, to harass me	2 Cor.12.7
the activity of *S.* . . . with all power	2 Th.2.9
whom I have delivered to *S.*	1 Tim.1.20
some call the deep things of *S.*	Rev.2.24
S. will be loosed from his prison	Rev.20.7

SATISFY
you shall eat, and not be *s.*	Lev.26.26
I shall be *s.* with beholding thy	Ps.17.15
The afflicted shall eat and be *s.*	Ps.22.26
with honey . . . I would *s.* you	Ps.81.16
S. us in the morning with thy	Ps.90.14
With long life I will *s.* him	Ps.91.16
Sheol and Abaddon are never *s.*	Pr.27.20
see . . . travail of his soul and be *s.*	Is.53.11
labor for that which does not *s.*?	Is.55.2
shall be *s.* with my goodness	Jer.31.14
They shall eat, but not be *s.*	Hos.4.10
righteousness, for they shall be *s.*	Mt.5.6
And they all ate and were *s.*	Mt.15.37
show us the Father . . . we shall be *s.*	Jn.14.8

SATYR
no more slay their sacrifices for *s.*	Lev.17.7
appointed . . . priests . . . for the *s.*	2 Chr.11.15
the *s.* shall cry to his fellow	Is.34.14

SAUL
(1) king of Israel, his parentage, anointing by Samuel, prophesying, and acknowledgment as king, 1 Sam.9–10; his disobedience, and rejection by God, 1 Sam.14.31–15.35; possessed by an evil spirit, quieted by David, 1 Sam.16.14, 15,23; favors David, 1 Sam.18.5; seeks to kill him, 1 Sam.18.10–11; pursues him, 1 Sam.20; 23–24; 26; inquires of the witch of Endor, 1

Sam.28.7; his ruin and suicide, 1 Sam.28.15; 31; 1 Chr.10; his posterity, 1 Chr.8.33; (2) of Tarsus, *see* PAUL

SAVE

s. us, and help us; for all the	Jos.10.6
said, "How can this man *s.* us?"	1 Sam.10.27
S. me, O God, by thy name	Ps.54.1
call upon God; and the LORD will *s.*	Ps.55.16
S. us, we beseech thee, O LORD	Ps.118.25
I am thine, *s.* me; for I have	Ps.119.94
I will *s.* the lame and gather	Zeph.3.19
to sink he cried out, "Lord, *s.* me."	Mt.14.30
For whoever would *s.* his life will	Mt.16.25
it in three days, *s.* yourself	Mt.27.40
to *s.* life or to kill?" But they were	Mk.3.4
He *s.* others; he cannot *s.* himself	Mk.15.31
to *s.* life or to destroy it?	Lk.6.9
s. me from this hour'? No, for this	Jn.12.27
day by day those who were being *s.*	Acts 2.47
among men by which we must be *s.*	Acts 4.12
Men, what must I do to be *s.*?	Acts 16.30
shall we be *s.* by his life	Rom.5.10
For in this hope we were *s.*	Rom.8.24
only a remnant of them will be *s.*	Rom.9.27
confesses with his lips . . . so is *s.*	Rom.10.10
and so all Israel will be *s.*	Rom.11.26
that his spirit may be *s.* in	1 Cor.5.5
(by grace you have been *s.*)	Eph.2.5
came into the world to *s.* sinners	1 Tim.1.15
The Lord will . . . *s.* me for his	2 Tim.4.18
the . . . word . . . is able to *s.* your souls	Jas.1.21
Can his faith *s.* him?	Jas.2.14

SAVIOR

the LORD gave Israel a *s.*	2 Kg.13.5
They forgot God, their *S.*, who	Ps.106.21
the Holy One of Israel, your *S.*	Is.43.3
know that I am the LORD your *S.*	Is.49.26
my spirit rejoices in God my *S.*	Lk.1.47
to you is born this day . . . a *S.*	Lk.2.11
at his right hand as Leader and *S.*	Acts 5.31
God has brought to Israel a *S.*	Acts 13.23
as Christ . . . is himself its *S.*	Eph.5.23
is the *S.* of all men, especially	1 Tim.4.10
appearing of our *S.* Christ Jesus	2 Tim.1.10
adorn the doctrine of God our *S.*	Tit.2.10
our great God and *S.* Jesus Christ	Tit.2.13
through Jesus Christ our *S.*	Tit.3.6
our God and *S.* Jesus Christ	2 Pet.1.1
the commandment of the Lord and *S.*	2 Pet.3.2
our Lord and *S.* Jesus Christ	2 Pet.3.18
his Son as the *S.* of the world	1 Jn.4.14
our *S.* through Jesus Christ our	Jude 25

SAYINGS

I will utter dark *s.* from of old	Ps.78.2
These also are *s.* of the wise	Pr.24.23
The *s.* of the wise are like goads	Ec.12.11
when Jesus finished these *s.*	Mt.7.28
If any one hears my *s.* and does	Jn.12.47

SCALES

in the waters that has fins and *s.*	Lev.11.9
just balance and *s.* are the LORD's	Pr.16.11
weighed the mountains in *s.*	Is.40.12
something like *s.* fell from his eyes	Acts 9.18
They had *s.* like iron breastplates	Rev.9.9

SCARLET

bound on his hand a *s.* thread	Gen.38.28
blue and purple and *s.* stuff	Ex.25.4
bind this *s.* cord in the window	Jos.2.18
though your sins are like *s.*	Is.1.18
and put a *s.* robe upon him	Mt.27.28
with water and *s.* wool and hyssop	Heb.9.19
a woman sitting on a *s.* beast	Rev.17.3

SCATTER

the LORD *s.* them abroad from there	Gen.11.8
So the people were *s.* abroad	Ex.5.12
I will *s.* you among the nations	Lev.26.33
God will *s.* the bones of the ungodly	Ps.53.5
Let God arise, let his enemies be *s.*	Ps.68.1
all evildoers shall be *s.*	Ps.92.9
and all their flock is *s.*	Jer.10.21
I will *s.* you like chaff driven by	Jer.13.24
that the sheep may be *s.*	Zech.13.7
the sheep of the flock will be *s.*	Mt.26.31
has *s.* the proud in the imagination	Lk.1.51
children of God who are *s.* abroad	Jn.11.52
all who followed him were *s.*	Acts 5.37

SCEPTER

The *s.* shall not depart from Judah	Gen.49.10
a *s.* shall rise out of Israel	Num.24.17
held out the golden *s.* to Esther	Est.8.4
Your royal *s.* is a *s.* of equity	Ps.45.6
How the mighty *s.* is broken	Jer.48.17
righteous *s.* is the *s.* of thy kingdom	Heb.1.8

SCOFF

s. at the Rock of his salvation	Dt.32.15
They *s.* and speak with malice	Ps.73.8
remember how the impious *s.* at thee	Ps.74.22
Now therefore do not *s.*, lest your	Is.28.22
heard all this, and they *s.* at him	Lk.16.14
but the rulers *s.* at him	Lk.23.35

SCOFFER

nor sits in the seat of *s.*	Ps.1.1
How will *s.* delight in their	Pr.1.22
"*S.*" is the name of the proud	Pr.21.24
Drive out a *s.*, and strife will go	Pr.22.10
hear . . . you *s.*, who rule this people	Is.28.14
Behold, you *s.*, and wonder	Acts 13.41
s. will come in the last days	2 Pet.3.3
In the last time there will be *s.*	Jude 18

SCORN (noun)

I am the *s.* of all my adversaries	Ps.31.11
derision and *s.* of those about us	Ps.44.13
the LORD is to them an object of *s.*	Jer.6.10
shall bear the *s.* of the peoples	Mic.6.16

SCORPION

serpents and *s.* and thirsty ground	Dt.8.15
to tread upon serpents and *s.*	Lk.10.19
asks for an egg, will give him a *s.*?	Lk.11.12
was like the torture of a *s.*	Rev.9.5

SCOURGE (verb)

some you will *s.* in your synagogues	Mt.23.34
having *s.* Jesus, he delivered him	Mk.15.15
they will *s.* him and kill him	Lk.18.33
Is it lawful . . . to *s.* a . . . Roman	Acts 22.25

SCRIBE

a man of understanding and a *s.*	1 Chr.27.32
Shimshai the *s.* wrote a letter	Ezra 4.8
Ezra the *s.* stood on a wooden pulpit	Neh.8.4
and gave it to Baruch the *s.*	Jer.36.32
a *s.* came up and said to him	Mt.8.19
Therefore every *s.* who has been	Mt.13.52
teaching he said, "Beware of the *s.*	Mk.12.38

Beware of the *s.*, who like to go	Lk.20.46
elders and *s.* were gathered	Acts 4.5
Where is the *s.*?	1 Cor.1.20

SCRIPTURE

Today this *s.* has been fulfilled	Lk.4.21
this *s.* must be fulfilled	Lk.22.37
Has not the *s.* said that the Christ	Jn.7.42
it is that the *s.* may be fulfilled	Jn.13.18
This was to fulfil the *s.*	Jn.19.24
for as yet they did not know the *s.*	Jn.20.9
the *s.* had to be fulfilled	Acts 1.16
the *s.* which he was reading was	Acts 8.32
examining the *s.* daily to see if	Acts 17.11
showing by the *s.* that the Christ	Acts 18.28
For what does the *s.* say?	Rom.4.3
may learn . . . to live according to *s.*	1 Cor.4.6
And the *s.*, foreseeing that God	Gal.3.8
attend to the public reading of *s.*	1 Tim.4.13
All *s.* is inspired by God	2 Tim.3.16
no prophecy of *s.* is a matter of	2 Pet.1.20

SCROLL

a *s.* was found on which this was	Ezra 6.2
the skies roll up like a *s.*	Is.34.4
Take a *s.* and write on it all the	Jer.36.2
I wrote them with ink on the *s.*	Jer.36.18
and saw, and behold, a flying *s.*	Zech.5.1
on the throne a *s.* written within	Rev.5.1
sky vanished like a *s.* that is rolled	Rev.6.14
He had a little *s.* open in his hand	Rev.10.2

SEA

dominion over the fish of the *s.*	Gen.1.26
LORD drove the *s.* back by a strong	Ex.14.21
didst divide the *s.* before them	Neh.9.11
By his power he stilled the *s.*	Job 26.12
Or who shut in the *s.* with doors	Job 38.8
He turned the *s.* into dry land	Ps.66.6
May he have dominion from *s.* to *s.*	Ps.72.8
Thou dost rule the raging of the *s.*	Ps.89.9
mightier than the waves of the *s.*	Ps.93.4
The *s.* is his, for he made it	Ps.95.5
Israel be as the sand of the *s.*	Is.10.22
by my rebuke I dry up the *s.*	Is.50.2
who brought up out of the *s.* the	Is.63.11
Your branches passed over the *s.*	Jer.48.32
our sins into the depths of the *s.*	Mic.7.19
He rebukes the *s.* and makes it dry	Nah.1.4
he . . . dwelt in Capernaum by the *s.*	Mt.4.13
As he walked by the *S.* of Galilee	Mt.4.18
he . . . rebuked the winds and the *s.*	Mt.8.26
of the house and sat beside the *s.*	Mt.13.1
he came to them, walking on the *s.*	Mt.14.25
Be taken up and cast into the *s.*	Mt.21.21
Moses in the cloud and in the *s.*	1 Cor.10.2
there is as it were a *s.* of glass	Rev.4.6
I saw a beast rising out of the *s.*	Rev.13.1
And the *s.* gave up the dead in it	Rev.20.13
passed away, and the *s.* was no more	Rev.21.1

SEAL (noun)

on him has God the Father set his *s.*	Jn.6.27
a sign or *s.* of the righteousness	Rom.4.11
he has put his *s.* upon us	2 Cor.1.22
bearing this *s.*: "The Lord knows	2 Tim.2.19
Lamb opened one of the seven *s.*	Rev.6.1

SEAL (verb)

s. the teaching among my disciples	Is.8.16
s. up the vision, for it pertains	Dan.8.26

were *s.* with the promised Holy Spirit	Eph.1.13
in whom you were *s.* for the day of	Eph.4.30
And I heard the number of the *s.*	Rev.7.4

SEARCH (verb)

thou dost . . . *s.* for my sin	Job 10.6
Who can *s.* out our crimes?	Ps.64.6
I meditate and *s.* my spirit	Ps.77.6
S. me, O God, and know my heart	Ps.139.23
glory of kings is to *s.* things out	Pr.25.2
to seek and to *s.* out by wisdom	Ec.1.13
I the LORD *s.* the mind and try the	Jer.17.10
I myself will *s.* for my sheep	Ezek.34.11
there I will *s.* out and take them	Am.9.3
I will *s.* Jerusalem with lamps	Zeph.1.12
Go and *s.* diligently for the child	Mt.2.8
You *s.* the scriptures, because you	Jn.5.39
he who *s.* the hearts of men	Rom.8.27
For the Spirit *s.* everything	1 Cor.2.10
I am he who *s.* mind and heart	Rev.2.23

SEASHORE

as the sand which is on the *s.*	Gen.22.17
saw the Egyptians dead upon the *s.*	Ex.14.30
as the sand which is upon the *s.*	Jg.7.12
against the *s.* he has appointed it	Jer.47.7
grains of sand by the *s.*	Heb.11.12

SEASON

let them be for signs and for *s.*	Gen.1.14
that yields its fruit in its *s.*	Ps.1.3
For everything there is a *s.*	Ec.3.1
God, who gives the rain in its *s.*	Jer.5.24
its saltness, how will you *s.* it?	Mk.9.50
for in due *s.* we shall reap, if we	Gal.6.9
be urgent in *s.* and out of *s.*	2 Tim.4.2

SEAT

shall make a mercy *s.* of pure gold	Ex.25.17
set the mercy *s.* above on the ark	Ex.40.20
that I might come even to his *s.*	Job 23.3
I prepared my *s.* in the square	Job 29.7
nor sits in the *s.* of scoffers	Ps.1.1
bring near the *s.* of violence?	Am.6.3
the Pharisees sit on Moses' *s.*	Mt.23.2
love the best *s.* in the synagogues	Lk.11.43
sat down on the judgment *s.* at	Jn.19.13
Herod . . . took his *s.* upon the throne	Acts 12.21
before the judgment *s.* of God	Rom.14.10
before the judgment *s.* of Christ	2 Cor.5.10
glory overshadowing the mercy *s.*	Heb.9.5

SECRET (noun)

So the *s.* of his strength was not	Jg.16.9
For he knows the *s.* of the heart	Ps.44.21
when I was being made in *s.*	Ps.139.15
bread eaten in *s.* is pleasant	Pr.9.17
A gift in *s.* averts anger	Pr.21.14
do not disclose another's *s.*	Pr.25.9
I did not speak in *s.*	Is.45.19
I have not spoken in *s.*	Is.48.16
revealing his *s.* to his servants	Am.3.7
who sees in *s.* will reward you	Mt.6.4
pray to your Father who is in *s.*	Mt.6.6
been given the *s.* of the kingdom	Mk.4.11
For no man works in *s.* if he seeks	Jn.7.4
the things that they do in *s.*	Eph.5.12
I have learned the *s.* of facing	Phil.4.12

SECRETARY

the king's *s.* and the high priest	2 Kg.12.10
Shaphan the *s.* came to the king	2 Kg.22.9

Hilkiah said to Shaphan the *s.* 2 Chr.34.15
Then the king's *s.* were summoned Est.3.12
Baruch the *s.* and Jeremiah Jer.36.26

SECRETLY
For you did it *s.*; but I will 2 Sam.12.12
Herod summoned the wise men *s.* Mt.2.7
but *s.*, for fear of the Jews Jn.19.38
Then they *s.* instigated men, who Acts 6.11
false brethren *s.* brought in Gal.2.4
false teachers . . . will *s.* bring in 2 Pet.2.1
admission has been *s.* gained by some Jude 4

SECURE (adjective)
you will be *s.*, and will not fear Job 11.15
thy servants shall dwell *s.* Ps.102.28
You felt *s.* in your wickedness Is.47.10
And they shall dwell *s.* Mic.5.4
go, make it as *s.* as you can Mt.27.65

SECURITY
He gives them *s.*, and they are Job 24.23
dwell in the land, and enjoy *s.* Ps.37.3
I am oppressed; be thou my *s.* Is.38.14
abundance of prosperity and *s.* Jer.33.6
people say, "There is peace and *s.*" 1 Th.5.3

SEED
and between your *s.* and her *s.* Gen.3.15
tithe all the yield of your *s.* Dt.14.22
shall carry much *s.* into the field Dt.28.38
bearing the *s.* for sowing, Ps.126.6
In the morning sow your *s.* Ec.11.6
rain for the *s.* with which you sow Is.30.23
giving *s.* to the sower and bread to Is.55.10
a choice vine, wholly of pure *s.* Jer.2.21
He who sows the good *s.* is the Son Mt.13.37
faith as a grain of mustard *s.* Mt.17.20
A sower went out to sow his *s.* Lk.8.5
to each kind of *s.* its own body 1 Cor.15.38
He who supplies *s.* to the sower 2 Cor.9.10
born anew, not of perishable *s.* 1 Pet.1.23

SEEK
from there you will *s.* the LORD your Dt.4.29
have set your heart to *s.* God 2 Chr.19.3
never *s.* their peace or prosperity Ezra 9.12
I would *s.* God, and to God would I Job 5.8
the generation of those who *s.* him Ps.24.6
Thou hast said, "*S.* ye my face." Ps.27.8
In thee, O LORD, do I *s.* refuge Ps.31.1
do good; *s.* peace, and pursue it Ps.34.14
S. the LORD and his strength Ps.105.4
I applied my mind to *s.* and to Ec.1.13
a time to *s.*, and a time to lose Ec.3.6
s. justice, correct oppression Is.1.17
S. the LORD while he may be found Is.55.6
when you *s.* me with all your heart Jer.29.13
do you *s.* great things for yourself? Jer.45.5
they will *s.* peace, but there shall Ezek.7.25
I will *s.* the lost, and I will Ezek.34.16
return and *s.* the LORD their God Hos.3.5
S. the LORD and live, lest he break Am.5.6
S. good, and not evil, that you may Am.5.14
S. the LORD, all you humble of the Zeph.2.3
But *s.* first his kingdom and his Mt.6.33
s., and you will find; knock, and Mt.7.7
Why do you *s.* the living among the Lk.24.5
I *s.* not my own will but Jn.5.30
You will *s.* me and you will not find Jn.7.36
they should *s.* God, in the hope Acts 17.27

demand signs and Greeks *s.* wisdom 1 Cor.1.22
Let no one *s.* his own good 1 Cor.10.24
s. the things that are above, where Col.3.1
nor did we *s.* glory from men 1 Th.2.6
that he rewards those who *s.* him Heb.11.6
let him *s.* peace and pursue it 1 Pet.3.11

SEER
a prophet was formerly called a *s.* 1 Sam.9.9
Samuel answered . . . "I am the *s.* 1 Sam.9.19
spoke to Gad, David's *s.*, saying 1 Chr.21.9
the visions of Iddo the *s.* 2 Chr.9.29
Hanani the *s.* went out to meet 2 Chr.19.2
words . . . of Asaph the *s.* 2 Chr.29.30

SEIZE
S. the prophets of Baal; let not 1 Kg.18.40
he lurks that he may *s.* the poor Ps.10.9
May the creditor *s.* all that he has Ps.109.11
Pangs and agony will *s.* them Is.13.8
Have you come to *s.* spoil? Ezek.38.13
They covet fields, and *s.* them Mic.2.2
The one I . . . kiss is the man; *s.* him Mt.26.48
For Herod had sent and *s.* John Mk.6.17
And amazement *s.* them all, and they Lk.5.26
they *s.* one Simon of Cyrene Lk.23.26
they *s.* Paul and dragged him out Acts 21.30
that no one may *s.* your crown Rev.3.11

SELF
thou didst swear by thine own *s.* Ex.32.13
our old *s.* was crucified with him Rom.6.6
For men will be lovers of *s.* 2 Tim.3.2
your owing me even your own *s.* Philem.19

SELF-CONTROL
A man without *s.* is like a city Pr.25.28
Satan tempt you through lack of *s.* 1 Cor.7.5
athlete exercises *s.* in all things 1 Cor.9.25
s.; against such there is no law Gal.5.23
a spirit of power and love and *s.* 2 Tim.1.7
s. with steadfastness 2 Pet.1.6

SELFISHNESS
s., slander, gossip, conceit 2 Cor.12.20
anger, *s.*, dissension, party spirit Gal.5.20
Do nothing from *s.* or conceit Phil.2.3

SELL
"First *s.* me your birthright." Gen.25.31
Buy truth, and do not *s.* it Pr.23.23
they *s.* the righteous for silver Am.2.6
s. what you possess and give to the Mt.19.21
has no sword *s.* his mantle and buy Lk.22.36

SELLER
as with the buyer, so with the *s.* Is.24.2
Lydia . . . a *s.* of purple goods Acts 16.14

SEND
he will *s.* his angel before you Gen.24.7
May he *s.* you help from the sanctuary Ps.20.2
Oh *s.* out thy light and thy truth Ps.43.3
I said, "Here am I! *S.* me." Is.6.8
he will *s.* them a savior Is.19.20
to *s.* out laborers into his harvest Mt.9.38
Behold, I *s.* you out as sheep in Mt.10.16
The Son of man will *s.* his angels Mt.13.41
Therefore I *s.* you prophets and Mt.23.34
behold, I *s.* you out as lambs in Lk.10.3
I *s.* the promise of my Father Lk.24.49
whom the Father will *s.* in my name Jn.14.26
but if I go, I will *s.* him to you Jn.16.7
believed that thou didst *s.* me Jn.17.8

Christ did not *s.* me to baptize — 1 Cor.1.17
God *s.* upon them a strong delusion — 2 Th.2.11

SENNACHERIB

2 Kg.18.13; 2 Chr.32.1; Is.36.1; 37.37

SENSE

they gave the *s.*, so that the people — Neh.8.8
He who commits adultery has no *s.* — Pr.6.32
but fools die for lack of *s.* — Pr.10.21
Good *s.* makes a man slow to anger — Pr.19.11
like a dove, silly and without *s.* — Hos.7.11
where would be the *s.* of smell? — 1 Cor.12.17

SENSELESS

O foolish and *s.* people, who have — Jer.5.21
their *s.* minds were darkened — Rom.1.21
into many *s.* and hurtful desires — 1 Tim.6.9
with stupid, *s.* controversies — 2 Tim.2.23

SENTENCE

This man deserves the *s.* of death — Jer.26.11
So Pilate gave *s.* that their demand — Lk.23.24
asking for *s.* against him — Acts 25.15
are summed up in this *s.* — Rom.13.9
we had received the *s.* of death — 2 Cor.1.9

SEPARATE

S. yourself from me. If you take — Gen.13.9
s. yourselves from the peoples of — Ezra 10.11
he will *s.* them one from another — Mt.25.32
shall *s.* us from the love of Christ? — Rom.8.35
be *s.* from them, says the Lord — 2 Cor.6.17
s. from sinners, exalted above the — Heb.7.26

SEPULCHRE

will withhold from you his *s.* — Gen.23.6
their throat is an open *s.* — Ps.5.9
there, sitting opposite the *s.* — Mt.27.61
made the *s.* secure by sealing — Mt.27.66
the other Mary went to see the *s.* — Mt.28.1

SERIOUS

or has any *s.* blemish whatever — Dt.15.21
Deacons likewise must be *s.* — 1 Tim.3.8
The women likewise must be *s.* — 1 Tim.3.11
s., sensible, sound in faith — Tit.2.2

SERPENT

Now the *s.* was more subtle than any — Gen.3.1
The LORD God said to the *s.* — Gen.3.14
Moses made a bronze *s.*, and set it — Num.21.9
They have venom like . . . a *s.* — Ps.58.4
At the last it bites like a *s.* — Pr.23.32
If the *s.* bites before it is charmed — Ec.10.11
punish Leviathan the fleeing *s.* — Is.27.1
there I will command the *s.* — Am.9.3
be wise as *s.* and innocent as doves — Mt.10.16
You *s.*, you brood of vipers, how — Mt.23.33
instead of a fish give him a *s.* — Lk.11.11
lifted up the *s.* in the wilderness — Jn.3.14
the *s.* deceived Eve by his cunning — 2 Cor.11.3
fly from the *s.* into the wilderness — Rev.12.14
that ancient *s.*, who is the Devil — Rev.20.2

SERVANT

Moreover by them is thy *s.* warned — Ps.19.11
O LORD, I am thy *s.*; I am thy *s.* — Ps.116.16
the *s.* like his master. If they — Mt.10.25
Well done, good and faithful *s.* — Mt.25.21
great among you must be your *s.* — Mk.10.43
lettest thy *s.* depart in peace — Lk.2.29
that *s.* who knew his master's will — Lk.12.47
No *s.* can serve two masters — Lk.16.13
the *s.* does not know what his master — Jn.15.15

I should not be a *s.* of Christ — Gal.1.10
taking the form of a *s.* — Phil.2.7
makes . . . his *s.* flames of fire — Heb.1.7
S., be submissive to your masters — 1 Pet.2.18
have sealed the *s.* of our God — Rev.7.3
all you his *s.*, you who fear him — Rev.19.5
to show his *s.* what must soon take — Rev.22.6

SERVE

the elder shall *s.* the younger — Gen.25.23
I will *s.* you seven years for your — Gen.29.18
that they may *s.* the LORD their God — Ex.10.7
not bow down to them or *s.* them — Dt.5.9
Because you did not *s.* the LORD — Dt.28.47
choose this day whom you will *s.* — Jos.24.15
The LORD our God we will *s.* — Jos.24.24
s. him faithfully with all your — 1 Sam.12.24
and also *s.* their graven images — 2 Kg.17.41
s. him with a whole heart and — 1 Chr.28.9
Almighty, that we should *s.* him? — Job 21.15
S. the LORD with fear, with trembling — Ps.2.11
S. the LORD with gladness — Ps.100.2
not go after other gods to *s.* them — Jer.35.15
Go *s.* every one of you his idols — Ezek.20.39
God, whom you *s.* . . . deliver you — Dan.6.16
No one can *s.* two masters — Mt.6.24
Lo, these many years I have *s.* you — Lk.15.29
You cannot *s.* God and mammon — Lk.16.13
Martha *s.*, and Lazarus was one of — Jn.12.2
nor is he *s.* by human hands, as — Acts 17.25
God . . . whom I *s.* with my spirit in — Rom.1.9
with my flesh I *s.* the law of sin — Rom.7.25
to *s.* a living and true God — 1 Th.1.9
whom I *s.* with a clear conscience — 2 Tim.1.3
dead works to *s.* the living God — Heb.9.14
s. him day and night within his — Rev.7.15

SERVICE

What do you mean by this *s.*? — Ex.12.26
all the *s.* of the house of God — 1 Chr.28.21
think he is offering *s.* to God — Jn.16.2
there are varieties of *s.* — 1 Cor.12.5
and fellow worker in your *s.* — 2 Cor.8.23
rendering *s.* with a good will — Eph.6.7
high priest in the *s.* of God — Heb.2.17
whoever renders *s.*, as one who — 1 Pet.4.11

SEVENTY

offspring of Jacob were *s.* persons — Ex.1.5
Gather for me *s.* men of the elders — Num.11.16
serve the king of Babylon *s.* years — Jer.25.11
seven times, but *s.* times seven — Mt.18.22
the Lord appointed *s.* others — Lk.10.1

SEVERE

Now the famine was *s.* in the land — Gen.43.1
a very *s.* plague upon your cattle — Ex.9.3
Why is the decree of the king so *s.*? — Dan.2.15
because you are a *s.* man — Lk.19.21
for in a *s.* test of affliction — 2 Cor.8.2

SHADE (noun)

Do the *s.* rise up to praise thee? — Ps.88.10
LORD is your *s.* on your right hand — Ps.121.5
It will be for a *s.* by day — Is.4.6
s. of a great rock in a weary land — Is.32.2
He sat under it in the *s.* — Jon.4.5

SHADOW

for our days on earth are a *s.* — Job 8.9
all my members are like a *s.* — Job 17.7
hide me in the *s.* of thy wings — Ps.17.8

the valley of the *s.* of death	Ps.23.4	their beards *s.* and their clothes	Jer.41.5
take refuge in the *s.* of thy wings	Ps.36.7	so that they may *s.* their heads	Acts 21.24
abides in the *s.* of the Almighty	Ps.91.1	the same as if her head were *s.*	1 Cor.11.5
in the *s.* of his hand he hid me	Is.49.2	**SHEBA**	
the region and *s.* of death	Mt.4.16	(1) men, Gen.25.3; 2 Sam.20.1; (2) places,	
in darkness and in the *s.* of death	Lk.1.79	Job 6.19; Ps.72.10; Jer.6.20; Ezek.27.22; 38.13;	
a copy and *s.* of the heavenly	Heb.8.5	queen of, visits Solomon, 1 Kg.10; 2 Chr.9;	
no variation or *s.* due to change	Jas.1.17	Mt.12.42	
SHADRACH		**SHED**	
Dan.1.7; 2.49; 3.12,30		by man shall his blood be *s.*	Gen.9.6
SHAKE		lest innocent blood be *s.*	Dt.19.10
trembling . . . made all my bones *s.*	Job 4.14	having *s.* blood without cause	1 Sam.25.31
my foes rejoice because I am *s.*	Ps.13.4	You have *s.* much blood and have	1 Chr.22.8
foundations of the earth are *s.*	Ps.82.5	My eyes *s.* streams of tears	Ps.119.136
earth will be *s.* out of its place	Is.13.13	they make haste to *s.* blood	Pr.1.16
your walls will *s.* at the noise	Ezek.26.10	all the righteous blood *s.* on earth	Mt.23.35
I am about to *s.* the heavens and	Hag.2.21	Their feet are swift to *s.* blood	Rom.3.15
s off the dust from your feet as	Mt.10.14	For men have *s.* the blood of saints	Rev.16.6
I will *s.* not only the earth but	Heb.12.26	**SHEEP**	
SHAME (noun)		Now Abel was a keeper of *s.*	Gen.4.2
let me not be put to *s.*	Ps.25.2	He was shearing his *s.* in Carmel	1 Sam.25.2
let the wicked be put to *s.*	Ps.31.17	He had seven thousand *s.*	Job 1.3
s. has covered my face	Ps.44.15	all *s.* and oxen, and also the beasts	Ps.8.7
Let not the downtrodden be put to *s.*	Ps.74.21	accounted as *s.* for the slaughter	Ps.44.22
His enemies I will clothe with *s.*	Ps.132.18	we are . . . the *s.* of his pasture	Ps.100.3
she who brings *s.* is like rottenness	Pr.12.4	All we like *s.* have gone astray	Is.53.6
You have devised *s.* to your house	Hab.2.10	My people have been lost *s.*	Jer.50.6
all his adversaries were put to *s.*	Lk.13.17	go . . . to the lost *s.* of the house of	Mt.10.6
I say this to your *s.*	1 Cor.6.5	If a man has a hundred *s.*, and one	Mt.18.12
I shall not be put to *s.*	2 Cor.10.8	and the *s.* will be scattered	Mk.14.27
they glory in their *s.*	Phil.3.19	selling oxen and *s.* and pigeons	Jn.2.14
SHAMEFUL		calls his own *s.* by name and leads	Jn.10.3
it is a *s.* thing, and they shall	Lev.20.17	I lay down my life for the *s.*	Jn.10.15
he has done a *s.* thing in Israel	Jos.7.15	I have other *s.*, that are not	Jn.10.16
s. for a woman to speak in church	1 Cor.14.35	Jesus said to him, "Feed my *s.*"	Jn.21.17
not for *s.* gain but eagerly	1 Pet.5.2	went about in skins of *s.* and goats	Heb.11.37
SHAMEFULLY		Jesus, the great shepherd of the *s.*	Heb.13.20
wicked man acts *s.* and disgracefully	Pr.13.5	**SHEEPFOLD**	
will rule over a son who acts *s.*	Pr.17.2	We will build *s.* here for our	Num.32.16
treated them *s.*, and killed them	Mt.22.6	Why did you tarry among the *s.*	Jg.5.16
mocked and *s.* treated and spit upon	Lk.18.32	though they stay among the *s.*	Ps.68.13
we had . . . been *s.* treated at Philippi	1 Th.2.2	took him from the *s.*	Ps.78.70
SHARE (verb)		not enter the *s.* by the door but	Jn.10.1
will *s.* the inheritance as one	Pr.17.2	**SHEKEL**	
Is it not to *s.* your bread with the	Is.58.7	twenty gerahs shall make a *s.*	Lev.27.25
let him *s.* with him who has none	Lk.3.11	a measure of fine meal for a *s.*	2 Kg.7.18
those who *s.* the faith of Abraham	Rom.4.16	the ephah small and the *s.* great	Am.8.5
to *s.* the richness of the olive	Rom.11.17	open its mouth you will find a *s.*	Mt.17.27
that I may *s.* in its blessings	1 Cor.9.23	**SHELTER (noun)**	
s. abundantly in Christ's sufferings	2 Cor.1.5	cling to the rock for want of *s.*	Job 24.8
may *s.* his sufferings, becoming	Phil.3.10	will hide me in his *s.* in the day of	Ps.27.5
we *s.* in Christ, if only we hold	Heb.3.14	be safe under the *s.* of thy wings	Ps.61.4
choosing rather to *s.* ill-treatment	Heb.11.25	dwells in the *s.* of the Most High	Ps.91.1
as you *s.* Christ's sufferings	1 Pet.4.13	a refuge and a *s.* from the storm	Is.4.6
he who *s.* in the first resurrection	Rev.20.6	a *s.* from the storm and a shade	Is.25.4
SHARP		**SHEM**	
Your tongue is like a *s.* razor	Ps.52.2	Gen.5.32; 10.1; 1 Chr.1.4; Lk.3.36	
their tongue *s.* as a serpent's	Ps.140.3	**SHEOL**	
their arrows are *s.*, all their bows	Is.5.28	I shall go down to *S.* to my son	Gen.37.35
And there arose a *s.* contention	Acts 15.39	it burns to the depths of *S.*	Dt.32.22
s. than any two-edged sword	Heb.4.12	Deeper than *S.*—what can you know?	Job 11.8
from his mouth issues a *s.* sword	Rev.19.15	Will it go down to the bars of *S.*?	Job 17.16
SHAVE		*S.* is naked before God	Job 26.6
then he shall *s.* his head	Num.6.9	The wicked shall depart to *S.*	Ps.9.17
Nazirite shall *s.* his consecrated	Num.6.18	the cords of *S.* entangled me	Ps.18.5
had him *s.* off the seven locks	Jg.16.19	let them go down to *S.* alive	Ps.55.15

my life draws near to *S.*	Ps.88.3	ring on his hand, and *s.* on his feet	Lk.15.22
If I make my bed in *S.*, thou art	Ps.139.8	Take off the *s.* from your feet	Acts 7.33
Her house is the way to *S.*	Pr.7.27	SHOOT (noun)	
S. and Abaddon are never satisfied	Pr.27.20	come forth a *s.* from the stump of	Is.11.1
Your pomp is brought down to *S.*	Is.14.11	the *s.* of my planting, the work of	Is.60.21
For *S.* cannot thank thee	Is.38.18	as the earth brings forth its *s.*	Is.61.11
ransom them from the power of *S.?*	Hos.13.14	you, a wild olive *s.*, were grafted in	Rom.11.17
out of the belly of *S.* I cried	Jon.2.2	SHORT	
His greed is as wide as *S.*	Hab.2.5	Thou hast cut *s.* the days of his	Ps.89.45
SHEPHERD (noun)		For the bed is too *s.* to stretch	Is.28.20
The LORD is my *s.*, I shall not want	Ps.23.1	In a *s.* time you think to make me	Acts 26.28
Give ear, O *S.* of Israel, thou who	Ps.80.1	devil . . . knows that his time is *s.*	Rev.12.12
He will feed his flock like a *s.*	Is.40.11	SHOUT (verb)	
I myself will be the *s.* of my sheep	Ezek.34.15	all the sons of God *s.* for joy?	Job 38.7
are afflicted for want of a *s.*	Zech.10.2	*s.* for joy, all you upright in heart	Ps.32.11
Woe to my worthless *s.*	Zech.11.17	My lips will *s.* for joy, when I	Ps.71.23
they were like sheep without a *s.*	Mk.6.34	*S.* aloud, O daughter of Jerusalem	Zech.9.9
there were *s.* out in the field	Lk.2.8	they *s.* out, "Crucify, crucify him!"	Lk.23.21
the *s.* said to one another, "Let us	Lk.2.15	Rejoice . . . break forth and *s.*	Gal.4.27
I am the good *s.* The good *s.* lays	Jn.10.11	SHOWER	
Jesus, the great *s.* of the sheep	Heb.13.20	to the *s.* and the rain	Job 37.6
returned to the *S.* and Guardian	1 Pet.2.25	its ridges, softening it with *s.*	Ps.65.10
when the chief *S.* is manifested	1 Pet.5.4	like *s.* that water the earth	Ps.72.6
the Lamb . . . will be their *s.*	Rev.7.17	Therefore the *s.* have been withheld	Jer.3.3
SHIBBOLETH		send down the *s.* in their season	Ezek.34.26
"Then say *S.*" . . . he said, "Sibboleth"	Jg.12.6	like *s.* upon the grass	Mic.5.7
SHIELD		you say at once, 'A *s.* is coming'	Lk.12.54
Fear not, Abram, I am your *s.*	Gen.15.1	SHRINK	
he is a *s.* for all those who	2 Sam.22.31	for I did not *s.* from declaring	Acts 20.27
thou . . . art a *s.* about me, my glory	Ps.3.3	if he *s.* back, my soul has no	Heb.10.38
he is a *s.* for all those who take	Ps.18.30	those who *s.* back and are destroyed	Heb.10.39
The LORD is my strength and my *s.*	Ps.28.7	not *s.* from him in shame	1 Jn.2.28
For the LORD God is a sun and *s.*	Ps.84.11	SHUT	
he is a *s.* to those who take refuge	Pr.30.5	I am *s.* in so that I cannot escape	Ps.88.8
above all taking the *s.* of faith	Eph.6.16	his angel and *s.* the lions' mouths	Dan.6.22
SHILOH		your room and *s.* the door and pray	Mt.6.6
Jos.18.1; Jg.18.31; 1 Sam.1.3; Ps.78.60;		The doors were *s.*, but Jesus came	Jn.20.26
Jer.26.6		who opens and no one shall *s.*	Rev.3.7
SHINE		SICK	
LORD make his face to *s.* upon you	Num.6.25	Hope deferred makes the heart *s.*	Pr.13.12
light will *s.* on your ways	Job 22.28	The whole head is *s.*, and the	Is.1.5
Let thy face *s.* on thy servant	Ps.31.16	Heal the *s.*, raise the dead, cleanse	Mt.10.8
make his face to *s.* upon us	Ps.67.1	I was *s.* and you visited me	Mt.25.36
Make thy face *s.* upon thy servant	Ps.119.135	prayer of faith will save the *s.*	Jas.5.15
A man's wisdom makes his face *s.*	Ec.8.1	SICKNESS	
Arise, *s.*; for your light has come	Is.60.1	I will take *s.* away from . . . you	Ex.23.25
wise shall *s.* like the brightness	Dan.12.3	Shall I recover from this *s.?*	2 Kg.8.8
Let your light so *s.* before men	Mt.5.16	A man's spirit will endure *s.*	Pr.18.14
the righteous will *s.* like the sun	Mt.13.43	Hezekiah . . . had recovered from his *s.*	Is.38.9
The light *s.* in the darkness	Jn.1.5	*s.* and wounds are ever before me	Jer.6.7
Let light *s.* out of darkness	2 Cor.4.6	SIDON	
among whom you *s.* as lights in the	Phil.2.15	Gen.10.15; Is.23.2; Jer.25.22; Mt.11.21; Acts	
no need of sun or moon to *s.* upon	Rev.21.23	12.20	
SHIP		SIGHT	
There go the *s.*, and Leviathan	Ps.104.26	the earth was corrupt in God's *s.*	Gen.6.11
Some went down to the sea in *s.*	Ps.107.23	turn aside and see this great *s.*	Ex.3.3
the way of a *s.* on the high seas	Pr.30.19	the stars are not clean in his *s.*	Job 25.5
and found a *s.* going to Tarshish	Jon.1.3	precious is their blood in his *s.*	Ps.72.14
centurion found a *s.* of Alexandria	Acts 27.6	Precious in the *s.* of the LORD is	Ps.116.15
on planks or on pieces of the *s.*	Acts 27.44	And I will cast you out of my *s.*	Jer.7.15
Look at the *s.* also; though they	Jas.3.4	Jesus said to him, "Receive your *s.*	Lk.18.42
SHOES		Brother Saul, receive your *s.*	Acts 22.13
put off your *s.* from your feet	Ex.3.5	walk by faith, not by *s.*	2 Cor.5.7
Put off your *s.* from your feet	Jos.5.15	is acceptable in the *s.* of God	1 Tim.5.4
sell . . . the needy for a pair of *s.*	Am.2.6	in God's *s.* chosen and precious	1 Pet.2.4

SIGN (noun)

it shall be a *s.* of the covenant	Gen.9.13
The blood shall be a *s.* for you	Ex.12.13
It is a *s.* for ever between me and	Ex.31.17
This is the *s.* that the LORD has	1 Kg.13.3
those who dwell . . . are afraid at thy *s.*	Ps.65.8
when he wrought his *s.* in Egypt	Ps.78.43
Show me a *s.* of thy favor	Ps.86.17
the Lord himself will give you a *s.*	Is.7.14
Thus shall Ezekiel be to you a *s.*	Ezek.24.24
no *s.* . . . . except the *s.* of Jonah	Mt.16.4
then will appear the *s.* of the Son	Mt.24.30
the betrayer had given them a *s.*	Mk.14.44
hoping to see some *s.* done by him	Lk.23.8
was now the second *s.* that Jesus did	Jn.4.54
they saw the *s.* which he did on	Jn.6.2
For this man performs many *s.*	Jn.11.47
did many other *s.* in the presence	Jn.20.30
circumcision as a *s.* or seal of	Rom.4.11
with *s.* and wonders and mighty	2 Cor.12.12
bore witness by *s.* and wonders	Heb.2.4
It works great *s.*, even making fire	Rev.13.13

SILAS

Acts 15.22; 16.19; 18.5

SILENCE

For God alone my soul waits in *s.*	Ps.62.5
O God, do not keep *s.*; do not hold	Ps.83.1
a time to keep *s.*, and a time	Ec.3.7
all the earth keep *s.* before him	Hab.2.20
should keep *s.* in the churches	1 Cor.14.34
Let a woman learn in *s.* with all	1 Tim.2.11
there was *s.* in heaven for about	Rev.8.1

SILENT

if thou be *s.* to me, I become like	Ps.28.1
be not *s.*! O Lord, be not far	Ps.35.22
I was dumb and *s.*, I held my peace	Ps.39.2
For Zion's sake I will not keep *s.*	Is.62.1
Be *s.*, all flesh, before the LORD	Zech.2.13
Jesus was *s.* And the high priest	Mt.26.63
if these were *s.*, the very stones	Lk.19.40
speak and do not be *s.*	Acts 18.9

SILLY

s. and without sense, calling to	Hos.7.11
nor *s.* talk, nor levity, which are	Eph.5.4
to do with godless and *s.* myths	1 Tim.4.7

SILVANUS

2 Cor.1.19; 1 Th.1.1; 2 Th.1.1; 1 Pet.5.12

SILVER

the *s.* cup, in the mouth of the sack	Gen.44.2
Though he heap up *s.* like dust	Job 27.16
thou hast tried us as *s.* is tried	Ps.66.10
Take my instruction instead of *s.*	Pr.8.10
apples of gold in a setting of *s.*	Pr.25.11
before the *s.* cord is snapped	Ec.12.6
they sell the righteous for *s.*	Am.2.6
they paid him thirty pieces of *s.*	Mt.26.15
I have no *s.* and gold, but I give	Acts 3.6
who made *s.* shrines of Artemis	Acts 19.24
perishable things such as *s.* or gold	1 Pet.1.18

SIMEON

(1) son of Jacob, Gen.29.33; 34.25; 42.24; his descendants, Gen.46.10; Ex.6.15; Num.1.22; 26.12; 1 Chr.4.24; 12.25; prophecy concerning, Gen.49.5; (2) blesses Christ, Lk.2.25–32; (3) (Niger), Acts 13.1

SIMON

(1) brother of Jesus, Mt.13.55; Mk.6.3; (2) Apostle, Mt.10.4; Mk.3.18; Lk.6.15; (3) (Pharisee), reproved, Lk.7.36–47; (4) (leper), Mt.26.6; Mk.14.3; (5) (of Cyrene), bears the cross of Jesus, Mt.27.32; Mk.15.21; Lk.23.26; (6) (a tanner), Peter's vision in his house, Acts 9.43; 10.6; (7) (a sorcerer), baptized, Acts 8.9–13; rebuked by Peter, Acts 8.18; (8) Peter, *see* PETER

SIN (noun)

s. is couching at the door	Gen.4.7
forgive my *s.*, I pray you	Ex.10.17
make atonement for him for his *s.*	Lev.4.26
I acknowledged my *s.* to thee	Ps.32.5
cleanse me from my *s.*	Ps.51.2
in *s.* did my mother conceive me	Ps.51.5
s. is a reproach to any people	Pr.14.34
that they may add *s.* to *s.*	Is.30.1
of my body for the *s.* of my soul?	Mic.6.7
but is guilty of an eternal *s.*	Mk.3.29
who takes away the *s.* of the world	Jn.1.29
who commits *s.* is a slave to *s.*	Jn.8.34
do not hold this *s.* against them	Acts 7.60
to continue in *s.* that grace may	Rom.6.1
Let not *s.* therefore reign in your	Rom.6.12
For the wages of *s.* is death	Rom.6.23
but *s.* which dwells within me	Rom.7.20
does not proceed from faith is *s.*	Rom.14.23
The sting of death is *s.*	1 Cor.15.56
gave himself for our *s.* to deliver	Gal.1.4
redemption, the forgiveness of *s.*	Col.1.14
s. of some men are conspicuous	1 Tim.5.24
he had made purification for *s.*	Heb.1.3
confess your *s.* to one another	Jas.5.16
bore our *s.* in his body on the tree	1 Pet.2.24
If we confess our *s.*, he is faithful	1 Jn.1.9
freed us from our *s.* by his blood	Rev.1.5

SIN (verb)

there is no man who does not *s.*	1 Kg.8.46
foreign women made even him to *s.*	Neh.13.26
Job did not *s.* or charge God with	Job 1.22
that I may not *s.* with my tongue	Ps.39.1
that I might not *s.* against thee	Ps.119.11
And if your eye causes you to *s.*	Mt.18.9
S. no more, that nothing worse	Jn.5.14
who *s.*, this man or his parents	Jn.9.2
all who have *s.* under the law will	Rom.2.12
all have *s.* and fall short of the	Rom.3.23
Be angry but do not *s.*	Eph.4.26
For if we *s.* deliberately after	Heb.10.26
he cannot *s.* because he is born of	1 Jn.3.9

SINAI

Ex.16.1; 19.20; Lev.7.38; Num.1.1; Ps.68.8; Gal.4.24

SINCERE

sent spies, who pretended to be *s.*	Lk.20.20
a good conscience and *s.* faith	1 Tim.1.5
I am reminded of your *s.* faith	2 Tim.1.5
for a *s.* love of the brethren	1 Pet.1.22
I have aroused your *s.* mind	2 Pet.3.1

SINCERITY

serve him in *s.* and in faithfulness	Jos.24.14
unleavened bread of *s.* and truth	1 Cor.5.8
with holiness and godly *s.*	2 Cor.1.12
men of *s.*, as commissioned by God	2 Cor.2.17

SINFUL
were sick through their *s*. ways — Ps.107.17
Ah, *s*. nation, a people laden with — Is.1.4
this adulterous and *s*. generation — Mk.8.38
from me, for I am a *s*. man, O Lord — Lk.5.8
delivered into the hands of *s*. men — Lk.24.7
our *s*. passions, aroused by the law — Rom.7.5

SING
S. to the LORD, for he has triumphed — Ex.15.21
and *s*. praises to thy name — 2 Sam.22.50
rejoice, let them ever *s*. for joy — Ps.5.11
S. to him a new song, play skilfully — Ps.33.3
How shall we *s*. the LORD's song in — Ps.137.4
S. for joy, O heavens, and exult — Is.49.13
I will *s*. with the mind also — 1 Cor.14.15
day and night they never cease to *s*. — Rev.4.8
they *s*. a new song before the throne — Rev.14.3

SINGERS
Therefore the ballad *s*. say — Num.21.27
these are the *s*., the heads of — 1 Chr.9.33
the *s*. sang, and the trumpeters — 2 Chr.29.28
The *s*.: the sons of Asaph, a hundred — Neh.7.44
portions for the *s*. and the — Neh.12.47
the *s*. in front, the minstrels last — Ps.68.25
S. and dancers alike say, "All my — Ps.87.7

SINK
make my assailants *s*. under me — Ps.18.39
I *s*. in deep mire, where there is no — Ps.69.2
Thus shall Babylon *s*. — Jer.51.64
beginning to *s*. he cried out — Mt.14.30
Let these words *s*. into your ears — Lk.9.44

SINNER
nor stands in the way of *s*. — Ps.1.1
Let *s*. be consumed from the earth — Ps.104.35
My son, if *s*. entice you, do not — Pr.1.10
Let not your heart envy *s*. — Pr.23.17
a friend of tax collectors and *s*. — Mt.11.19
Even *s*. lend to *s*., to receive — Lk.6.34
God, be merciful to me a *s*. — Lk.18.13
know that God does not listen to *s*. — Jn.9.31
while we were yet *s*. Christ died for us — Rom.5.8
came into the world to save *s*. — 1 Tim.1.15
Cleanse your hands, you *s*. — Jas.4.8
which ungodly *s*. have spoken — Jude 15

SISERA
Jg.4.2; 5.20; 1 Sam.12.9; Ps.83.9

SISTER
Say you are my *s*., that it may go — Gen.12.13
And his *s*. stood at a distance — Ex.2.4
the worm, 'My mother,' or 'My *s*.' — Job 17.14
We have a little *s*., and she has — S.of S.8.8
and are not his *s*. here with us? — Mk.6.3
village of Mary and her *s*. Martha — Jn.11.1
I commend to you our *s*. Phoebe — Rom.16.1
Apphia our *s*. and Archippus our — Philem.2
If a brother or *s*. is ill-clad and — Jas.2.15

SKILFUL
Esau was a *s*. hunter — Gen.25.27
s. in playing, a man of valor — 1 Sam.16.18
Do you see a man *s*. in his work? — Pr.22.29
he seeks out a *s*. craftsman to set — Is.40.20
send for the *s*. women to come — Jer.9.17
handsome and *s*. in all wisdom — Dan.1.4

SKILL
every willing man who has *s*. — 1 Chr.28.21
showed good *s*. in the service — 2 Chr.30.22

toiled with . . . knowledge and *s*. — Ec.2.21
learning and *s*. in all letters — Dan.1.17

SKIN
Satan answered . . . "*S*. for *s*.! All that — Job 2.4
have escaped by the *s*. of my teeth — Job 19.20
Can the Ethiopian change his *s*. — Jer.13.23
the new wine will burst the *s*. — Lk.5.37

SKULL
Abimelech's head, and crushed his *s*. — Jg.9.53
found no more of her than the *s*. — 2 Kg.9.35
the place which is called The *S*. — Lk.23.33

SKY
righteousness . . . down from the *s*. — Ps.85.11
be fair weather; for the *s*. is red — Mt.16.2
lights up the *s*. from one side to — Lk.17.24
sacred stone that fell from the *s*. — Acts 19.35
the *s*. vanished like a scroll that — Rev.6.14

SLACK
he will not be *s*. with him who — Dt.7.10
care not to be *s*. in this matter — Ezra 4.22
A *s*. hand causes poverty — Pr.10.4
He who is *s*. in his work is a — Pr.18.9

SLAIN
I have *s*. a man for wounding me — Gen.4.23
for thy sake we are *s*. all the day — Ps.44.22
breathe upon these *s*. — Ezek.37.9
Worthy is the Lamb who was *s*. — Rev.5.12

SLANDER (noun)
uttering *s*. against me — Ps.27.2
he who utters *s*. is a fool — Pr.10.18
envy, *s*., pride, foolishness — Mk.7.22
s., gossip, conceit — 2 Cor.12.20
insincerity and envy and all *s*. — 1 Pet.2.1

SLANDERERS
s., haters of God, insolent — Rom.1.30
no *s*., but temperate, faithful in all — 1 Tim.3.11
s., profligates, fierce, haters of good — 2 Tim.3.3
not to be *s*. or slaves to drink — Tit.2.3

SLAUGHTER (noun)
Thou hast made us like sheep for *s*. — Ps.44.11
as an ox goes to the *s*. — Pr.7.22
like a lamb that is led to the *s*. — Is.53.7
As a sheep led to the *s*. or — Acts 8.32
fattened your hearts in a day of *s*. — Jas.5.5

SLAVE
Cast out this *s*. woman with her — Gen.21.10
became a *s*. at forced labor — Gen.49.15
When a man strikes the eye of his *s*. — Ex.21.26
borrower is the *s*. of the lender — Pr.22.7
would be first . . . must be your *s*. — Mt.20.27
one who commits sin is a *s*. to sin — Jn.8.34
I have made myself a *s*. to all — 1 Cor.9.19
there is neither *s*. nor free — Gal.3.28
S., obey in everything those who — Col.3.22
not to be slanderers or *s*. to drink — Tit.2.3
no longer as a *s*. but more than a *s*. — Philem.16

SLAVERY
did not receive the spirit of *s*. — Rom.8.15
for she is in *s*. with her children — Gal.4.25
not submit again to a yoke of *s*. — Gal.5.1
all . . . under the yoke of *s*. regard — 1 Tim.6.1

SLAY
whoever finds me will *s*. me — Gen.4.14
took the knife to *s*. his son — Gen.22.10
Behold, he will *s*. me; I have no — Job 13.15
O that thou wouldst *s*. the wicked — Ps.139.19

SLEEP (noun)

God caused a deep s. to fall upon the   Gen.2.21
he gives to his beloved s.   Ps.127.2
A little s., a little slumber   Pr.6.10
Love not s., lest you come to   Pr.20.13
Sweet is the s. of a laborer   Ec.5.12

SLEEP (verb)

Rouse thyself! Why s. thou, O Lord?   Ps.44.23
a son who s. in harvest brings shame   Pr.10.5
he said to them, "Why do you s.?   Lk.22.46
We shall not all s., but we shall   1 Cor.15.51

SLING (noun)

his s. was in his hand   1 Sam.17.40
David prevailed . . . with a s.   1 Sam.17.50
as from the hollow of a s.   1 Sam.25.29
one who binds the stone in the s.   Pr.26.8

SLIP

ready for those whose feet s.   Job 12.5
and my feet did not s.   Ps.18.36
his steps do not s.   Ps.37.31
has not let our feet s.   Ps.66.9
who s. in to spy out our freedom   Gal.2.4

SLOTHFUL

the s. will be put to forced labor   Pr.12.24
A s. man will not catch his prey   Pr.12.27
You wicked and s. servant   Mt.25.26

SLOW

I am s. of speech and of tongue   Ex.4.10
The Lord is s. to anger, and   Num.14.18
Good sense makes a man s. to anger   Pr.19.11
The Lord is s. to anger and of   Nah.1.3
s. of heart to believe all that   Lk.24.25
quick to hear, s. to speak, s. to   Jas.1.19
Lord is not s. about his promise   2 Pet.3.9

SLUGGARD

Go to the ant, O s.; consider her   Pr.6.6
The s. buries his hand in the dish   Pr.19.24
The s. does not plow in the autumn   Pr.20.4
The s. is wiser in his own eyes   Pr.26.16

SLUMBER (verb)

he who keeps you will not s.   Ps.121.3
will neither s. nor sleep   Ps.121.4
dreaming, lying down, loving to s.   Is.56.10
O king of Assyria; your nobles s.   Nah.3.18
was delayed, they all s. and slept   Mt.25.5

SMALL

after the fire a still s. voice   1 Kg.19.12
fear the Lord, both s. and great   Ps.115.13
I am s. and despised, yet I   Ps.119.141
because he was s. of stature   Lk.19.3

SMELL (noun)

s. of my son is as the s. of a field   Gen.27.27
no s. of fire had come upon them   Dan.3.27
where would be the sense of s.?   1 Cor.12.17

SMITE

I will s. all the first-born in   Ex.12.12
The sun shall not s. you by day   Ps.121.6
lest I come and s. the land with a   Mal.4.6
to s. the earth with every plague   Rev.11.6

SMITH

Now there was no s. to be found   1 Sam.13.19
all the craftsmen and the s.   2 Kg.24.14
the s. who blows the fire   Is.54.16
Then the Lord showed me four s.   Zech.1.20

SMOKE (noun)

Mount Sinai was wrapped in s.   Ex.19.18

Out of his nostrils comes forth s.   Job 41.20
For my days pass away like s.   Ps.102.3
the house was filled with s.   Is.6.4
the s. of their torment goes up   Rev.14.11

SMOOTH

is a hairy man, and I am a s. man   Gen.27.11
the s. tongue of the adventuress   Pr.6.24
thou dost make s. the path of the   Is.26.7
speak to us s. things, prophesy   Is.30.10
the rough ways shall be made s.   Lk.3.5

SNARE (noun)

their gods shall be a s. to you   Jg.2.3
from the s. of the fowler   Ps.91.3
The s. of death encompassed me   Ps.116.3
fall into . . . the s. of the devil   1 Tim.3.7
escape from the s. of the devil   2 Tim.2.26

SNATCH

were s. away before their time   Job 22.16
who seek to s. away my life   Ps.40.14
one comes and s. away what is sown   Mt.13.19
no one shall s. them out of my hand   Jn.10.28

SNOW

If I wash myself with s.   Job 9.30
entered the storehouses of the s.   Job 38.22
wash me . . . I shall be whiter than s.   Ps.51.7
they shall be as white as s.   Is.1.18

SOBER

but let us keep awake and be s.   1 Th.5.6
to live s., upright, and godly lives   Tit.2.12
be s., set your hope fully upon   1 Pet.1.13
Be s., be watchful. Your adversary   1 Pet.5.8

SODOM

Gen.10.19; its iniquity and destruction, Gen.
13.13; 18.20; 19.4–24; Lot's deliverance from,
Gen.19; a warning, Dt.29.23; 32.32; Is.1.9;
13.19; Lam.4.6; Mt.10.15; Lk.17.29; Jude 7;
Rev.11.8

SOFT

Will he speak to you s. words?   Job 41.3
A s. answer turns away wrath, but a   Pr.15.1
a s. tongue will break a bone   Pr.25.15
A man clothed in s. raiment?   Lk.7.25

SOIL

Noah was the first tiller of the s.   Gen.9.20
wash away the s. of the earth   Job 14.19
Be confounded, O tillers of the s.   Jl.1.11
I am a tiller of the s.   Zech.13.5
fell on good s. and brought forth   Mt.13.8

SOJOURN (verb)

Abram went down to Egypt to s. there   Gen.12.10
We have come to s. in the land   Gen.47.4
evil may not s. with thee   Ps.5.4
O Lord, who shall s. in thy tent?   Ps.15.1
the outcasts of Moab s. among you   Is.16.4
the strangers that s. in Israel   Ezek.14.7
By faith he s. in the land of promise   Heb.11.9

SOJOURNER

I am a stranger and a s. among you   Gen.23.4
I have been a s. in a foreign land   Ex.2.22
the s. who is within your gates   Ex.20.10
Love the s. therefore; for you were   Dt.10.19
perverts the justice due to the s.   Dt.27.19
They slay the widow and the s.   Ps.94.6
I am a s. on earth; hide not thy   Ps.119.19
those who thrust aside the s.   Mal.3.5
you are no longer strangers and s.   Eph.2.19

SOLD

s. his birthright to Jacob	Gen.25.33
And the LORD *s.* them into the hand	Jg.4.2
for your iniquities you were *s.*	Is.50.1
Are not two sparrows *s.* for a penny?	Mt.10.29
they *s.*, they planted, they built	Lk.17.28
he told those who *s.* the pigeons	Jn.2.16
they *s.* their possessions	Acts 2.45
Sapphira *s.* a piece of property	Acts 5.1
but I am carnal, *s.* under sin	Rom.7.14
s. his birthright for a single meal	Heb.12.16

SOLDIER

to them, "You have a guard of *s.*	Mt.27.65
his *s.* treated him with contempt	Lk.23.11
When the *s.* had crucified Jesus	Jn.19.23
Peter was sleeping between two *s.*	Acts 12.6
fellow worker and fellow *s.*	Phil.2.25
as a good *s.* of Christ Jesus	2 Tim.2.3
No *s.* on service gets entangled in	2 Tim.2.4

SOLEMN

the first day shall be a *s.* rest	Lev.23.39
Sanctify a *s.* assembly for Baal	2 Kg.10.20
Thy *s.* processions are seen, O God	Ps.68.24
Sanctify a fast, call a *s.* assembly	Jl.1.14
take no delight in your *s.* assemblies	Am.5.21

SOLOMON

2 Sam.5.14; king of Israel, 2 Sam.12.24; 1 Kg.1; 2.24; 1 Chr.28.9; 29; asks of God wisdom, 1 Kg.3.9 (4.29); 2 Chr.1.10; the wise judgment of, 1 Kg.3.16–28; his league with Hiram for building the temple, 1 Kg.5; 2 Chr.2; builds the temple, (2 Sam.7.13; 1 Chr.17.12); 1 Kg.6–7; 2 Chr. 3–5; the dedication, 1 Kg.8; 2 Chr.6; God's covenant with, 1 Kg.9; 2 Chr.7.12; the queen of Sheba visits, 1 Kg.10; 2 Chr.9; Mt. 6.29; 12.42; his idolatry, rebuke, and death, 1 Kg.11; 2 Chr.9.29; Neh.13.26

SON

my *s.*, today I have begotten you	Ps.2.7
and the *s.* of man that thou dost	Ps.8.4
My *s.*, if sinners entice you, do not	Pr.1.10
My *s.*, do not forget my teaching	Pr.3.1
My *s.*, be attentive to my words	Pr.4.20
He who spares the rod hates his *s.*	Pr.13.24
Discipline your *s.* while there is	Pr.19.18
Discipline your *s.*, and he will	Pr.29.17
woman shall conceive and bear a *s.*	Is.7.14
a child is born, to us a *s.* is given	Is.9.6
out of Egypt I called my *s.*	Hos.11.1
saying, "This is my beloved *S.*	Mt.3.17
one knows the *S.* except the Father	Mt.11.27
The *S.* of man will send his angels	Mt.13.41
My *s.*, your sins are forgiven	Mk.2.5
Boanerges, that is, *s.* of thunder	Mk.3.17
her first-born *s.* and wrapped him	Lk.2.7
as of the only *S.* from the Father	Jn.1.14
so loved . . . that he gave his only *S.*	Jn.3.16
his mother, "Woman, behold your *s.*!"	Jn.19.26
conformed to the image of his *S.*	Rom.8.29
I live by faith in the *S.* of God	Gal.2.20
to wait for his *S.* from heaven	1 Th.1.10
For you are all *s.* of light	1 Th.5.5
God is treating you as *s.*	Heb.12.7
He who has the *S.* has life	1 Jn.5.12
one like a *s.* of man	Rev.1.13

SONG

The LORD is my strength and my *s.*	Ex.15.2
So Moses wrote this *s.* the same day	Dt.31.22
at night his *s.* is with me	Ps.42.8
O sing to the LORD a new *s.*	Ps.96.1
psalms and hymns and spiritual *s.*	Eph.5.19
they sing a new *s.* before the	Rev.14.3
and the *s.* of the Lamb, saying	Rev.15.3

SORCERER

summoned the wise men and the *s.*	Ex.7.11
soothsayer, or an augur, or a *s.*	Dt.18.10
will consult the idols and the *s.*	Is.19.3
enchanters, the *s.*, and the Chaldeans	Dan.2.2
be a swift witness against the *s.*	Mal.3.5
s., idolaters and all liars	Rev.21.8
the dogs and *s.* and fornicators	Rev.22.15

SORCERY

used divination and *s.*	2 Kg.17.17
soothsaying and augury and *s.*	2 Chr.33.6
I will cut off *s.* from your hand	Mic.5.12
idolatry, *s.*, enmity, strife	Gal.5.20
nations were deceived by thy *s.*	Rev.18.23

SORROW

my eye grows dim through *s.*	Ps.88.9
a foolish son is a *s.* to his mother	Pr.10.1
Who has *s.*? Who has strife?	Pr.23.29
S. is better than laughter, for by	Ec.7.3
s. and sighing shall flee away	Is.35.10
a man of *s.*, and acquainted with	Is.53.3
borne our griefs and carried our *s.*	Is.53.4
found them sleeping for *s.*	Lk.22.45
s. has filled your hearts	Jn.16.6
have great *s.* and unceasing anguish	Rom.9.2
lest I should have *s.* upon *s.*	Phil.2.27

SORROWFUL

a very great and *s.* lamentation	Gen.50.10
they were very *s.*, and began	Mt.26.22
countenance fell . . . he went away *s.*	Mk.10.22
They began to be *s.*, and to say to	Mk.14.19
My soul is very *s.*, even to death	Mk.14.34
as *s.*, yet always rejoicing	2 Cor.6.10

SORRY

the LORD was *s.* that he had made man	Gen.6.6
I am *s.* for my sin	Ps.38.18
the king was exceedingly *s.*	Mk.6.26
if I made you *s.* with my letter	2 Cor.7.8

SOUL

March on, my *s.*, with might	Jg.5.21
now my *s.* is poured out within	Job 30.16
LORD is perfect, reviving the *s.*	Ps.19.7
he restores my *s.* He leads me	Ps.23.3
My *s.* thirsts for God	Ps.42.2
O my *s.* . . . . why are you disquieted	Ps.43.5
Awake, my *s.*! Awake, O harp and	Ps.57.8
My *s.* longs, yea, faints for the	Ps.84.2
Bless the LORD, O my *s.*	Ps.103.1
The *s.* of the wicked desires evil	Pr.21.10
My *s.* yearns for thee in the night	Is.26.9
he poured out his *s.* to death	Is.53.12
destroy both *s.* and body in hell	Mt.10.28
My *s.* is very sorrowful, even to	Mk.14.34
said, "My *s.* magnifies the Lord	Lk.1.46
I will say to my *s.*, S., you have	Lk.12.19
Now is my *s.* troubled. And what	Jn.12.27
spirit and *s.* and body be kept	1 Th.5.23
which is able to save your *s.*	Jas.1.21

Shepherd and Guardian of your *s*.	1 Pet.2.25	**SPEECH**	
I know that it is well with your *s*.	3 Jn.2	may not understand one another's *s*.	Gen.11.7
I saw the *s*. of those who had	Rev.20.4	but I am slow of *s*. and of tongue	Ex.4.10
SOUND (noun)		Day to day pours forth *s*.	Ps.19.2
they heard the *s*. of the LORD	Gen.3.8	Put away from you crooked *s*.	Pr.4.24
Hearken to the *s*. of my cry, my King	Ps.5.2	to a pure *s*., that all . . . may call	Zeph.3.9
when the *s*. of the grinding is low	Ec.12.4	Let your *s*. always be gracious	Col.4.6
suddenly a *s*. came from heaven	Acts 2.2	sound *s*. that cannot be censured	Tit.2.8
the *s*. of a trumpet, and a voice	Heb.12.19	**SPEED** (verb)	
was like the *s*. of harpers playing	Rev.14.2	let him *s*. his work that we may see	Is.5.19
SOUND (adjective)		that you may *s*. me on my journey	1 Cor.16.6
My son, keep *s*. wisdom and discretion	Pr.3.21	*S*. him on his way in peace·	1 Cor.16.11
if your eye is *s*., your whole body	Mt.6.22	the word of the Lord may *s*. on	2 Th.3.1
A *s*. tree cannot bear evil fruit	Mt.7.18	Do your best to *s*. Zenas the lawyer	Tit.3.13
body be kept *s*. and blameless at	1 Th.5.23	**SPEND**	
is contrary to *s*. doctrine	1 Tim.1.10	Why do you *s*. your money for that	Is.55.2
the pattern of the *s*. words which	2 Tim.1.13	and whatever more you *s*.	Lk.10.35
s. in faith, in love, and in	Tit.2.2	I will most gladly *s*. and be *s*.	2 Cor.12.15
SOVEREIGN		**SPEW**	
S. Lord, who didst make the heaven	Acts 4.24	I will *s*. you out of my mouth	Rev.3.16
by the blessed and only *S*.	1 Tim.6.15	**SPICES**	
O *S*. Lord, holy and true, how long	Rev.6.10	*s*. for the anointing oil and for	Ex.25.6
SOW (verb)		a very great quantity of *s*.	1 Kg.10.10
you shall *s*. your seed in vain	Lev.26.16	His cheeks are like beds of *s*.	S.of S.5.13
May those who *s*. in tears reap with	Ps.126.5	prepared *s*. and ointments	Lk.23.56
He who observes the wind will not *s*.	Ec.11.4	in linen cloths with the *s*.	Jn.19.40
S. for yourselves righteousness	Hos.10.12	**SPIES**	
Listen! A sower went out to *s*.	Mk.4.3	We are honest men, we are not *s*.	Gen.42.31
One *s*. and another reaps	Jn.4.37	men secretly from Shittim as *s*.	Jos.2.1
he who *s*. sparingly will also reap	2 Cor.9.6	David sent out *s*., and learned of	1 Sam.26.4
whatever a man *s*. . . . will also reap	Gal.6.7	*s*., who pretended to be sincere	Lk.20.20
SPAIN		given friendly welcome to the *s*.	Heb.11.31
	Rom.15.24,28	**SPIRIT**	
SPARE		the *S*. of God was moving over	Gen.1.2
In thy steadfast love *s*. my life	Ps.119.88	My *s*. shall not abide in man for	Gen.6.3
He who *s*. the rod hates his son	Pr.13.24	Then the *S*. of the LORD came upon	Jg.11.29
I will *s*. them as a man *s*. his son	Mal.3.17	evil *s*. from God was upon Saul	1 Sam.16.23
He who did not *s*. his own Son but	Rom.8.32	inherit a double share of your *s*.	2 Kg.2.9
For if God did not *s*. the angels	2 Pet.2.4	The *s*. of Elijah rests on Elisha	2 Kg.2.15
SPARROW		A *s*. glided past my face; the hair	Job 4.15
Even the *s*. finds a home	Ps.84.3	Into thy hand I commit my *s*.	Ps.31.5
Like a *s*. in its flitting, like a swallow	Pr.26.2	take not thy holy *S*. from me	Ps.51.11
Are not two *s*. sold for a penny?	Mt.10.29	Whither shall I go from thy *S*.?	Ps.139.2
you are of more value than many *s*.	Lk.12.7	but the LORD weighs the *s*.	Pr.16.7
SPEAK		The *s*. of man is the lamp of the	Pr.20.27
LORD used to *s*. to Moses face to	Ex.33.11	No man has power to retain the *s*.	Ec.8.8
S., LORD, for thy servant hears	1 Sam.3.9	the ·*s*. returns to God who gave it	Ec.12.7
My mouth will *s*. the praise of	Ps.145.21·	Who has directed the *S*. of the LORD	Is.40.13
to keep silence, and a time to *s*.	Ec.3.7	the *S*. entered into me and set me	Ezek.2.2
s. to us smooth things, prophesy	Is.30.10	I will pour out my *s*. on all flesh	Jl.2.28
S. tenderly to Jerusalem, and cry to	Is.40.2	Blessed are the poor in *s*.	Mt.5.3
S. the truth to one another	Zech.8.16	will baptize you with the Holy *S*.	Mk.1.8
Woe . . . when all men *s*. well of you	Lk.6.26	my *s*. rejoices in God my Savior	Lk.1.47
abundance of the heart his mouth *s*.	Lk.6.45	The *S*. of the Lord is upon me	Lk.4.18
began to *s*. in other tongues	Acts 2.4	the Holy *S*. will teach you in	Lk.12.12
If I *s*. in the tongues of men and	1 Cor.13.1	into thy hands I commit my *s*.	Lk.23.46
Rather, *s*. the truth in love	Eph.4.15	God is *s*., and those who worship him	Jn.4.24
slow to *s*., slow to anger	Jas.1.19	When the *S*. of truth comes, he will	Jn.16.13
SPEAR		said to them, "Receive the Holy *S*.	Jn.20.22
LORD saves not with sword and *s*.	1 Sam.17.47	will pour out my *S*. upon all flesh	Acts 2.17
pin David to the wall with the *s*.	1 Sam.19.10	prayed, "Lord Jesus, receive my *s*."	Acts 7.59
whose *s*. weighed three hundred	2 Sam.21.16	shall be baptized with the Holy *S*.	Acts 11.16
beat . . . their *s*. into pruning hooks	Is.2.4	Now the Lord is the *S*.	2 Cor.3.17
Beat . . . your pruning hooks into *s*.	Jl.3.10	walk by the *S*., and do not gratify	Gal.5.16
soldiers pierced his side with a *s*.	Jn.19.34	But the fruit of the *S*. is love	Gal.5.22
		do not grieve the Holy *S*. of God	Eph.4.30

Do not quench the *S*.	1 Th.5.19
Christ . . . through the eternal *S*.	Heb.9.14
because the *S*. is the truth	1 Jn.5.7
I was in the *S*. on the Lord's day	Rev.1.10
The *S*. and the Bride say, "Come."	Rev.22.17

SPIRITS

and he cast out the *s*. with a word	Mt.8.16
seven other *s*. more evil than	Mt.12.45
authority over the unclean *s*.	Mk.6.7
diseases and plagues and evil *s*.	Lk.7.21
unclean *s*. came out of many who	Acts 8.7
ability to distinguish between *s*.	1 Cor.12.10
the weak and beggarly elemental *s*.	Gal.4.9
giving heed to deceitful *s*.	1 Tim.4.1
the *s*. of just men made perfect	Heb.12.23
preached to the *s*. in prison	1 Pet.3.19
test the *s*. to see whether they	1 Jn.4.1
three foul *s*. like frogs	Rev.16.13
they are demonic *s*., performing	Rev.16.14

SPIRITUAL

to God, which is your *s*. worship	Rom.12.1
interpreting *s*. truths to those	1 Cor.2.13
Now concerning *s*. gifts, brethren	1 Cor.12.1
there is also a *s*. body	1 Cor.15.44
you who are *s*. should restore him	Gal.6.1
against the *s*. hosts of wickedness	Eph.6.12
yourselves built into a *s*. house	1 Pet.2.5

SPIT

I am one before whom men *s*.	Job 17.6
when he had *s*. on his eyes	Mk.8.23
s. upon him, and scourge him	Mk.10.34
And some began to *s*. on him	Mk.14.65
shamefully treated and *s*. upon	Lk.18.32

SPLENDOR

clothe yourself with glory and *s*.	Job 40.10
the glorious *s*. of thy kingdom	Ps.145.12
The latter *s*. of this house shall	Hag.2.9
earth was made bright with his *s*.	Rev.18.1

SPOIL (noun)

shall enjoy the *s*. of your enemies	Dt.20.14
But the people took of the *s*.	1 Sam.15.21
to divide the *s*. with the proud	Pr.16.19
divide the *s*. with the strong	Is.53.12
will make a *s*. of your riches	Ezek.26.12
and divides his *s*.	Lk.11.22

SPOT

his skin or the leopard his *s*.?	Jer.13.23
without *s*. or wrinkle or any such	Eph.5.27
a lamb without blemish or *s*.	1 Pet.1.19
found by him without *s*. or blemish	2 Pet.3.14

SPREAD

O LORD; I *s*. out my hands to thee	Ps.88.9
The lips of the wise *s*. knowledge	Pr.15.7
So his fame *s*. throughout all Syria	Mt.4.24
many *s*. their garments on the road	Mk.11.8
so death *s*. to all men because	Rom.5.12

SPRING (noun)

of Baca they make it a place of *s*.	Ps.84.6
from it flow the *s*. of life	Pr.4.23
become in him a *s*. of water	Jn.4.14
Does a *s*. pour forth from the same	Jas.3.11
These are waterless *s*. and mists	2 Pet.2.17
guide them to *s*. of living water	Rev.7.17

SPRING (verb)

sang this song: "*S*. up, O well	Num.21.17
Faithfulness will *s*. up from the	Ps.85.11

before they *s*. forth I tell you of	Is.42.9
a . . . Branch to *s*. forth for David	Jer.33.15

SPURN

if you *s*. my statutes, and if your	Lev.26.15
s. the counsel of the Most High	Ps.107.11
Do not *s*. us, for thy name's sake	Jer.14.21
the man who has *s*. the Son of God	Heb.10.29

SPY (verb)

Send men to *s*. out the land	Num.13.2
whom Joshua sent to *s*. out Jericho	Jos.6.25
overthrow and to *s*. out the land?	1 Chr.19.3
slipped in to *s*. out our freedom	Gal.2.4

STAFF

lay my *s*. upon the . . . child	2 Kg.4.29
thy rod and thy *s*., they comfort me	Ps.23.4
has broken the *s*. of the wicked	Is.14.5
I took my *s*. Grace, and I broke it	Zech.11.10
no *s*., nor bag, nor bread, nor money	Lk.9.3

STAND (verb)

to *s*. before the LORD to minister	Dt.10.8
you cannot *s*. before your enemies	Jos.7.13
Who is able to *s*. before the LORD	1 Sam.6.20
at last he will *s*. upon the earth	Job 19.25
Why dost thou *s*. afar off, O LORD?	Ps.10.1
And who shall *s*. in his holy place?	Ps.24.3
he will *s*. before kings	Pr.22.29
but who can *s*. before jealousy?	Pr.27.4
word of our God will *s*. for ever	Is.40.8
And he shall *s*. and feed his flock	Mic.5.4
Who can *s*. before his indignation?	Nah.1.6
they love to *s*. and pray in the	Mt.6.5
why do you *s*. looking into heaven?	Acts 1.11
shall all *s*. before the judgment	Rom.14.10
s. firm thus in the Lord	Phil.4.1
Behold, I *s*. at the door and knock	Rev.3.20

STANDARD

shall encamp each by his own *s*.	Num.2.2
Raise a *s*. toward Zion, flee for	Jer.4.6
Set up a *s*. against the walls of	Jer.51.12
obedient . . . to the *s*. of teaching	Rom.6.17
were wise according to worldly *s*.	1 Cor.1.26

STAR

he made the *s*. also	Gen.1.16
descendants as the *s*. of heaven	Ex.32.13
a *s*. shall come forth out of Jacob	Num.24.17
when the morning *s*. sang together	Job 38.7
the *s*. which thou hast established	Ps.8.3
He determines the number of the *s*.	Ps.147.4
we have seen his *s*. in the East	Mt.2.2
the seven *s*. are the angels of the	Rev.1.20

STATURE

we saw in it . . . men of great *s*.	Num.13.32
an Egyptian, a man of great *s*.	1 Chr.11.23
increased in wisdom and in *s*.	Lk.2.52
because he was small of *s*.	Lk.19.3
measure of the *s*. of the fulness	Eph.4.13

STATUTE

And it shall be a *s*. to you for	Lev.16.29
for a perpetual *s*. throughout your	Num.10.8
shall keep his *s*. and commandments	Dt.4.40
I will observe thy *s*.; O forsake	Ps.119.8
I will meditate on thy *s*.	Ps.119.48
you have turned aside from my *s*.	Mal.3.7

STEADFAST

Thou hast led in thy *s*. love the	Ex.15.13
Remember thy *s*. love for David	2 Chr.6.42

hast granted me life and *s.* love	Job 10.12
But I have trusted in thy *s.* love	Ps.13.5
Thy *s.* love, O LORD, extends to the	Ps.36.5
Their heart was not *s.* toward him	Ps.78.37
his *s.* love endures for ever	Ps.100.5
thank the LORD for his *s.* love	Ps.107.8
He who is *s.* in righteousness will	Pr.11.19
be *s.*, immovable, always	1 Cor.15.58
as a sure and *s.* anchor of the soul	Heb.6.19

STEADFASTNESS

the God of *s.* and encouragement	Rom.15.5
my patience, my love, my *s.*	2 Tim.3.10
testing of your faith produces *s.*	Jas.1.3
You have heard of the *s.* of Job	Jas.5.11

STEAL

You shall not *s.*	Ex.20.15
where thieves break in and *s.*	Mt.6.19
Do not *s.*, Do not bear false	Mk.10.19
preach against stealing, do you *s.?*	Rom.2.21
Let the thief no longer *s.*	Eph.4.28

STEPHEN

Acts 6.5; 7.2; 8.2; 11.19; 22.20

STEPS

The *s.* of a man are from the LORD	Ps.37.23
they lurk, they watch my *s.*	Ps.56.6
Keep steady my *s.* according to	Ps.119.133
A man's *s.* are ordered by the LORD	Pr.20.24
the dial of Ahaz turn back ten *s.*	Is.38.8
that you should follow in his *s.*	1 Pet.2.21

STEWARD

owner of the vineyard said to his *s.*	Mt.20.8
There was a rich man who had a *s.*	Lk.16.1
When the *s.* of the feast tasted the	Jn.2.9
is required of *s.* that they be	1 Cor.4.2
as good *s.* of God's varied grace	1 Pet.4.10

STIFF-NECKED

and behold, it is a *s.* people	Ex.32.9
Israel, 'You are a *s.* people	Ex.33.5
Do not now be *s.* as your fathers	2 Chr.30.8
You *s.* people, uncircumcised in	Acts 7.51

STILL

after the fire a *s.* small voice	1 Kg.19.12
He leads me beside *s.* waters	Ps.23.2
Be *s.*, and know that I am God	Ps.46.10
"Peace! Be *s.!*" And the wind	Mk.4.39
My Father is working *s.*	Jn.5.17

STIR (verb)

S. up thy might, and come to save us	Ps.80.2
s. up the spirit of a destroyer	Jer.51.1
He *s.* up the people, teaching	Lk.23.5
s. up persecution against Paul	Acts 13.50
your zeal has *s.* up most of them	2 Cor.9.2
consider how to *s.* up one another	Heb.10.24

STOCKS

Thou puttest my feet in *s.*	Job 13.27
he puts my feet in the *s.*	Job 33.11
released Jeremiah from the *s.*	Jer.20.3
fastened their feet in the *s.*	Acts 16.24

STONE (noun)

And they had brick for *s.*	Gen.11.3
So Jacob took a *s.*, and set it up	Gen.31.45
LORD gave me the two tables of *s.*	Dt.9.11
His heart is hard as a *s.*	Job 41.24
lest you dash your foot against a *s.*	Ps.91.12
The *s.* which the builders rejected	Ps.118.22
a tested *s.*, a precious cornerstone	Is.28.16

you saw that a *s.* was cut from a	Dan.2.45
asks . . . for bread, will give him a *s.?*	Mt.7.9
they found the *s.* rolled away	Lk.24.2
sacred *s.* that fell from the sky	Acts 19.35
Come to him, to that living *s.*	1 Pet.2.4
I will give him a white *s.*	Rev.2.17

STONE (verb)

you shall *s.* that man or woman	Dt.17.5
We *s.* you for no good work but for	Jn.10.33
they *s.* Paul and dragged him out	Acts 14.19
They were *s.* . . . were sawn in two	Heb.11.37

STOREHOUSE

Have you entered the *s.* of the snow	Job 38.22
brings forth the wind from his *s.*	Ps.135.7
Bring the full tithes into the *s.*	Mal.3.10
they have neither *s.* nor barn	Lk.12.24

STORM

he made the *s.* be still	Ps.107.29
when panic strikes you like a *s.*	Pr.1.27
a shelter from the *s.* and rain	Is.4.6
Behold, the *s.* of the LORD! Wrath	Jer.23.19
And a great *s.* of wind arose	Mk.4.37

STRAIGHT

make thy way *s.* before me	Ps.5.8
he will make *s.* your paths	Pr.3.6
What is crooked cannot be made *s.*	Ec.1.15
make *s.* in the desert a highway for	Is.40.3
immediately she was made *s.*	Lk.13.13
go to the street called *S.*	Acts 9.11

STRANGE

There shall be no *s.* god among you	Ps.81.9
Your eyes will see *s.* things	Pr.23.33
We have seen *s.* things today	Lk.5.26
led . . . by diverse and *s.* teachings	Heb.13.9

STRANGER

You shall not oppress a *s.*	Ex.23.9
if a *s.* sojourns among you	Num.9.14
I have become a *s.* to my brethren	Ps.69.8
A *s.* they will not follow, but they	Jn.10.5
s. to the covenants of promise	Eph.2.12
show hospitality to *s.*	Heb.13.2

STRAW

no longer give . . . *s.* to make bricks	Ex.5.7
No *s.* is given to your servants	Ex.5.16
they are like *s.* before the wind	Job 21.18
the lion shall eat *s.* like the ox	Is.65.25

STREAM (noun)

like a tree planted by *s.* of water	Ps.1.3
As a hart longs for flowing *s.*	Ps.42.1
a river whose *s.* make glad the city	Ps.46.4
fountain of wisdom is a gushing *s.*	Pr.18.4
All *s.* run to the sea, but the sea	Ec.1.7

STREET

Wisdom cries aloud in the *s.*	Pr.1.20
boys and girls playing in its *s.*	Zech.8.5
in the synagogues and at the *s.* corners	Mt.6.5
go to the *s.* called Straight	Acts 9.11
the *s.* of the city was pure gold	Rev.21.21

STRENGTH

the God who girded me with *s.*	Ps.18.32
May the LORD give *s.* to his people	Ps.29.11
God is our refuge and *s.*	Ps.46.1
gives power and *s.* to his people	Ps.68.35
They go from *s.* to *s.*	Ps.84.7
s. and beauty are in his sanctuary	Ps.96.6
the LORD GOD is my *s.* and my song	Is.12.2

STRENGTHEN

for the LORD shall renew their *s.*	Is.40.31
O LORD, my *s.* and my stronghold	Jer.16.19
He has shown *s.* with his arm	Lk.1.51
not . . . be tempted beyond your *s.*	1 Cor.10.13

STRENGTHEN

but now, O God, *s.* thou my hands	Neh.6.9
s. me according to thy word	Ps.119.28
lengthen . . . cords and *s.* . . . stakes	Is.54.2
s. your brethren	Lk.22.32
the churches were *s.* in the faith	Acts 16.5
is able to *s.* you according to	Rom.16.25
can do all things in him who *s.* me	Phil.4.13
May you be *s.* with all power	Col.1.11
he will *s.* you and guard you from	2 Th.3.3

STRIFE

Let there be no *s.* between you and	Gen.13.8
deliver me from *s.* with the peoples	Ps.18.43
Hatred stirs up *s.*, but love covers	Pr.10.12
A perverse man spreads *s.*	Pr.16.28
Who has *s.*? Who has complaining?	Pr.23.29
there is jealousy and *s.* among you	1 Cor.3.3
s., jealousy, anger, selfishness	Gal.5.20

STRIKE

you shall *s.* the rock, and water	Ex.17.6
Let a good man *s.* or rebuke me in	Ps.141.5
But if any one *s.* you on the right	Mt.5.39
lest you *s.* your foot against a stone	Lk.4.11
God shall *s.* you, you whitewashed	Acts 23.3
the sun shall not *s.* them, nor any	Rev.7.16

STRIPE

wound for wound, *s.* for *s.*	Ex.21.25
Forty *s.* may be given him, but not	Dt.25.3
and with his *s.* we are healed	Is.53.5

STRIPPED

Hezekiah *s.* the gold from the	2 Kg.18.16
stouthearted were *s.* of their spoil	Ps.76.5
I will go *s.* and naked; I will make	Mic.1.8
they *s.* him of the purple cloak	Mk.15.20
s. him and beat him, and departed	Lk.10.30

STRIVE

Woe to him who *s.* with his Maker	Is.45.9
S. to enter by the narrow door	Lk.13.24
For to this end we toil and *s.*	1 Tim.4.10
Let us therefore *s.* to enter that	Heb.4.11
S. for peace with all men	Heb.12.14

STRONG

Drink no wine nor *s.* drink	Lev.10.9
Be *s.* and of good courage	Dt.31.7
Out of the *s.* came something sweet	Jg.14.14
He delivered me from my *s.* enemy	Ps.18.17
be *s.*, and let your heart take	Ps.27.14
Wine is a mocker; *s.* drink a brawler	Pr.20.1
for love is *s.* as death	S.of S.8.6
shall divide the spoil with the *s.*	Is.53.12
And he shall make a *s.* covenant	Dan.9.27
can one enter a *s.* man's house	Mt.12.29
shall drink no wine nor *s.* drink	Lk.1.15
We who are *s.* ought to bear with	Rom.15.1
when I am weak, then I am *s.*	2 Cor.12.10

STRONGHOLD

The LORD is a *s.* for the oppressed	Ps.9.9
my *s.* and my deliverer, my shield	Ps.144.2
The LORD is a *s.* to him whose way	Pr.10.29
O LORD, my strength and my *s.*	Jer.16.19
have divine power to destroy *s.*	2 Cor.10.4

STUBBLE

to gather *s.* for straw	Ex.5.12
Clubs are counted as *s.*; he laughs	Job 41.29
tempest carries them off like *s.*	Is.40.24
they are consumed, like dry *s.*	Nah.1.10
all evildoers will be *s.*	Mal.4.1
precious stones, wood, hay, *s.*	1 Cor.3.12

STUBBORN

for you are a *s.* people	Dt.9.6
This our son is *s.* and rebellious	Dt.21.20
I gave them over to their *s.* hearts	Ps.81.12
Like a *s.* heifer, Israel is *s.*	Hos.4.16
when some were *s.* and disbelieved	Acts 19.9

STUMBLE

they shall *s.* and fall	Ps.27.2
as for me, my feet had almost *s.*	Ps.73.2
and if you run, you will not *s.*	Pr.4.12
a stone that will make men *s.*	Rom.9.33
anything that makes your brother *s.*	Rom.14.21
for they *s.* because they disobey	1 Pet.2.8

STUPID

I was *s.* and ignorant, I was like a	Ps.73.22
A *s.* son is a grief to a father	Pr.17.21
man is *s.* and without knowledge	Jer.10.14
nothing to do with *s.*, senseless	2 Tim.2.23
avoid *s.* controversies, genealogies	Tit.3.9

SUBDUE

fill the earth and *s.* it	Gen.1.28
I would soon *s.* their enemies	Ps.81.14
no one had the strength to *s.* him	Mk.5.4
I pommel my body and *s.* it	1 Cor.9.27

SUBJECT

the demons are *s.* to us	Lk.10.17
the creation was *s.* to futility	Rom.8.20
Let every person be *s.* to the	Rom.13.1
As the church is *s.* to Christ	Eph.5.24
Wives, be *s.* to your husbands	Col.3.18
younger be *s.* to the elders	1 Pet.5.5

SUBJECTION

brought into *s.* under their power	Ps.106.42
brought them into *s.* as slaves	Jer.34.11
all things in *s.* under his feet	1 Cor.15.27
everything in *s.* under his feet	Heb.2.8

SUBMISSIVE

his children *s.* and respectful in	1 Tim.3.4
Bid slaves to be *s.* to their masters	Tit.2.9
Remind them to be *s.* to rulers	Tit.3.1
be *s.* to your husbands, so that	1 Pet.3.1

SUBMIT

did not *s.* to God's righteousness	Rom.10.3
do not *s.* again to a yoke of slavery	Gal.5.1
Obey your leaders and *s.* to them	Heb.13.17
S. yourselves therefore to God	Jas.4.7

SUCCEED

devise mischief, they will not *s.*	Ps.21.11
with many advisers they *s.*	Pr.15.22
a man who shall not *s.* in his days	Jer.22.30
says the LORD . . . you shall not *s.*	Jer.32.5
Will he *s.*? Can a man escape	Ezek.17.15

SUCCESS

the LORD your God granted me *s.*	Gen.27.20
may have good *s.* wherever you go	Jos.1.7
had *s.* in all his undertakings	1 Sam.18.14
so that their hands achieve no *s.*	Job 5.12
LORD, we beseech thee, give us *s.*	Ps.118.25

SUCCOTH
Gen.33.17; Num.33.5; Jg.8.5; Ps.60.6

SUFFER
The young lions *s*. want and hunger	Ps.34.10
the simple go on, and *s*. for it	Pr.22.3
the Son of man must *s*. many things	Mk.8.31
that the Christ must *s*.	Acts 26.23
if one member *s*., all *s*. together	1 Cor.12.26
So Jesus also *s*. outside the gate	Heb.13.12
is better to *s*. for doing right	1 Pet.3.17
Do not fear what you are . . . to *s*.	Rev.2.10

SUFFERING (noun)
saw that his *s*. was very great	Job 2.13
knowing that *s*. produces endurance	Rom.5.3
your share of *s*. for the gospel	2 Tim.1.8
As an example of *s*. and patience	Jas.5.10
so far as you share Christ's *s*.	1 Pet.4.13

SUFFICIENT
and lend him *s*. for his need	Dt.15.8
own trouble be *s*. for the day	Mt.6.34
Who is *s*. for these things?	2 Cor.2.16
My grace is *s*. for you, for my	2 Cor.12.9

SUMMER
s. and winter, day and night	Gen.8.22
thou hast made *s*. and winter	Ps.74.17
A son who gathers in *s*. is prudent	Pr.10.5
behold, a basket of *s*. fruit	Am.8.1
know that the *s*. is already near	Lk.21.30

SUN
S., stand thou still at Gibeon	Jos.10.12
In them he has set a tent for the *s*.	Ps.19.4
the LORD God is a *s*. and shield	Ps.84.11
The *s*. shall not smite you by day	Ps.121.6
Praise him, *s*. and moon, praise him	Ps.148.3
there is nothing new under the *s*.	Ec.1.9
So the *s*. turned back on the dial	Is.38.8
the *s*. beat upon the head of Jonah	Jon.4.8
he makes his *s*. rise on the evil	Mt.5.45
when the *s*. rose it was scorched	Mk.4.6
signs in *s*. and moon and stars	Lk.21.25
a woman clothed with the *s*.	Rev.12.1

SUPPER
There they made him a *s*.; Martha	Jn.12.2
rose from *s*., laid aside his garments	Jn.13.4
after *s*., saying, "This cup is	1.Cor.11.25
to the marriage *s*. of the Lamb	Rev.19.9

SUPPLICATION
The LORD has heard my *s*.	Ps.6.9
and hide not thy self from my *s*.	Ps.55.1
Let my *s*. come before thee	Ps.119.170
making *s*. for all the saints	Eph.6.18
by prayer and *s*. with thanksgiving	Phil.4.6
continues in *s*. and prayers night	1 Tim.5.5
Jesus offered up prayers and *s*.	Heb.5.7

SUPPLY
their abundance may *s*. your want	2 Cor.8.14
by every joint with which it is *s*.	Eph.4.16
my God will *s*. every need of yours	Phil.4.19
s. what is lacking in your faith?	1 Th.3.10
by the strength which God *s*.	1 Pet.4.11

SUPPORT
the land could not *s*. both of them	Gen.13.6
Those who *s*. Egypt shall fall	Ezek.30.6
it is not you that *s*. the root	Rom.11.18
So we ought to *s*. such men	3 Jn.8

SURE
the testimony of the LORD is *s*.	Ps.19.7
All thy commandments are *s*.	Ps.119.86
then all your ways will be *s*.	Pr.4.26
like a peg in a *s*. place	Is.22.23
plans formed of old, faithful and *s*.	Is.25.1
Temptations to sin are *s*. to come	Lk.17.1
I am *s*. that neither death, nor	Rom.8.38
The saying is *s*. and worthy of	1 Tim.1.15
The saying is *s*. I desire you to	Tit.3.8
the prophetic word made more *s*.	2 Pet.1.19

SURETY
I will be *s*. for him; of my hand	Gen.43.9
Be *s*. for thy servant for good	Ps.119.122
He who gives *s*. for a stranger will	Pr.11.15
This makes Jesus the *s*. of a better	Heb.7.22

SURROUND
steadfast love *s*. him who trusts	Ps.32.10
They *s*. me, *s*. me on every side	Ps.118.11
you see Jerusalem *s*. by armies	Lk.21.20
we are *s*. by so great a cloud of	Heb.12.1

SURVIVE
those who *s*. will be very few	Is.16.14
in this city who *s*. the pestilence	Jer.21.7
anger of the LORD none escaped or *s*.	Lam.2.22
Then every one that *s*. of all the	Zech.14.16
work . . . built on the foundation *s*.	1 Cor.3.14

SUSTAIN
thou *s*. them in the wilderness	Neh.9.21
The LORD *s*. him on his sickbed	Ps.41.3
on the LORD, and he will *s*. you	Ps.55.22
may know how to *s*. with a word him	Is.50.4
who will *s*. you to the end	1 Cor.1.8

SWALLOW (verb)
But Aaron's rod *s*. up their rods	Ex.7.12
opened its mouth and *s*. them up	Num.16.32
LORD will *s*. them up in his wrath	Ps.21.9
a great fish to *s*. up Jonah	Jon.1.17
Death is *s*. up in victory	1 Cor.15.54
what is mortal may be *s*. up by life	2 Cor.5.4

SWEAR
you shall not *s*. by my name	Lev.19.12
who *s*. to his own hurt and does not	Ps.15.4
Do not *s*. at all, either by heaven	Mt.5.34
a curse on himself and to *s*.	Mt.26.74
had no one greater by whom to *s*.	Heb.6.13
do. not *s*., either by heaven or by	Jas.5.12

SWEAT
In the *s*. of your face you shall	Gen.3.19
with anything that causes *s*.	Ezek.44.18
his *s*. became like great drops	Lk.22.44

SWEEP
S. me not away with sinners	Ps.26.9
Thou dost *s*. men away	Ps.90.5
Then they *s*. by like the wind	Hab.1.11
light a lamp and *s*. the house	Lk.15.8
to *s*. her away with the flood	Rev.12.15

SWEET
and the water became *s*.	Ex.15.25
the *s*. psalmist of Israel	2 Sam.23.1
wickedness is *s*. in his mouth	Job 20.12
How *s*. are thy words to my taste	Ps.119.103
Stolen water is *s*., and bread	Pr.9.17
S. is the sleep of a laborer	Ec.5.12

SWIFT
My days are *s*. than a weaver's	Job 7.6

the race is not to the *s.* — Ec.9.11
Flight shall perish from the *s.* — Am.2.14
Their feet are *s.* to shed blood — Rom.3.15
upon themselves *s.* destruction — 2 Pet.2.1

SWINE
Like a gold ring in a *s.* snout is a — Pr.11.22
do not throw your pearls before *s.* — Mt.7.6
Now a great herd of *s.* was feeding — Mk.5.11
sent him into his fields to feed *s.* — Lk.15.15

SWORD
a flaming *s.* which turned every — Gen.3.24
Put every man his *s.* on his side — Ex. 32.27
not draw the *s.* out of his belly — Jg.3.22
LORD saves not with *s.* and spear — 1 Sam.17.47
The *s.* of Goliath the Philistine — 1 Sam.21.9
Deliver my soul from the *s.* — Ps.22.20
Rescue me from the cruel *s.* — Ps.144.11
rash words are like *s.* thrusts — Pr.12.18
beat their *s.* into plowshares — Is.2.4
not lift up *s.* against nation — Is.2.4
Ah, *s.* of the LORD! How long till — Jer.47.6
Beat your plowshares into *s.* — Jl.3.10
not come to bring peace, but a *s.* — Mt.10.34
a *s.* will pierce through your own soul — Lk.2.35
Put your *s.* into its sheath — Jn.18.11
the *s.* of the Spirit, which is — Eph.6.17
the *s.* that issues from his mouth — Rev.19.21

SYCAMORE
as the *s.* of the Shephelah — 1 Kg.10.27
and a dresser of *s.* trees — Am.7.14
climbed up into a *s.* tree to see him — Lk.19.4

SYNAGOGUE
he entered the *s.* and taught — Mk.1.21
Then came one of the rulers of the *s.* — Mk.5.22
he went to the *s.*, as his custom — Lk.4.16
he was to be put out of the *s.* — Jn.9.22
belonged to the *s.* of the Freedmen — Acts 6.9
letters to the *s.* at Damascus — Acts 9.2
he argued in the *s.* every sabbath — Acts 18.4
Sosthenes, the ruler of the *s.* — Acts 18.17
in every *s.* I imprisoned — Acts 22.19
and are not, but are a *s.* of Satan — Rev.2.9

SYRIA
Jg.10.6; 1 Kg.10.29; 1 Chr.18.6; Mt.4.24; Gal.
1.21

SYROPHOENICIAN
the woman was a Greek, a *S.* by birth — Mk.7.26

TABERNACLE
concerning the pattern of the *t.* — Ex.25.9
anoint the *t.* and all that is in it — Ex.40.9
Moses erected the *t.*; he laid its — Ex.40.18
the glory of the LORD filled the *t.* — Ex.40.35
anointed the *t.* and all that was in — Lev.8.10
and the feast of *t.* — 2 Chr.8.13
the Jews' feast of *T.* was at hand — Jn.7.2

TABLE
So Moses cut two *t.* of stone like — Ex.34.4
he wrote them upon two *t.* of stone — Dt.5.22
Thou preparest a *t.* before me in — Ps.23.5
and sit at *t.* with Abraham — Mt.8.11
dogs under the *t.* eat the children's — Mk.7.28
the *t.* of the moneychangers — Mk.11.15
was sitting at *t.* in the Pharisee's — Lk.7.37
Now no one at the *t.* knew why he — Jn.13.28

at *t.* in an idol's temple — 1 Cor.8.10
t. of the Lord and the *t.* of demons — 1 Cor.10.21

TABLET
write them on the *t.* of your heart — Pr.7.3
make it plain upon *t.*, so he may run — Hab.2.2
And he asked for a writing *t.* — Lk.1.63
not on *t.* of stone but on *t.* of — 2 Cor.3.3

TABOR
Jos.19.22; Jg.4.6; 1 Chr.6.77; Ps.89.12; Hos.5.1

TALENT
Of a *t.* of pure gold shall it be — Ex.25.39
weight of it was a *t.* of gold — 2 Sam.12.30
else you shall pay a *t.* of silver — 1 Kg.20.39
who owed him ten thousand *t.* — Mt.18.24
But he who had received the one *t.* — Mt.25.18
take the *t.* from him, and give it — Mt.25.28

TALK (noun)
Job opens his mouth in empty *t.* — Job 35.16
I am the *t.* of those who sit in the — Ps.69.12
put devious *t.* far from you — Pr.4.24
how to entangle him in his *t.* — Mt.22.15
not consist in *t.* but in power — 1 Cor.4.20
Let no evil *t.* come out of your — Eph.4.29
nor silly *t.*, nor levity — Eph.5.4
foul *t.* from your mouth — Col.3.8

TALK (verb)
because he had been *t.* with God — Ex.34.29
T. no more so very proudly — 1 Sam.2.3
my tongue will *t.* of thy . . . help — Ps.71.24
their lips *t.* of mischief — Pr.24.2
while he *t.* to us on the road — Lk.24.32
I will no longer *t.* much with you — Jn.14.30
to see you and *t.* with you face to — 2 Jn.12

TARRY
Weeping may *t.* for the night — Ps.30.5
my deliverer; O LORD, do not *t.* — Ps.70.5
Those who *t.* long over wine — Pr.23.30
my salvation will not *t.* — Is.46.13
one shall come and shall not *t.* — Heb.10.37

TARSHISH
Gen.10.4; Ps.48.7; Is.2.16; Jer.10.9; Jon.1.3

TARSUS
Acts 9.11; 11.25; 21.39; 22.3

TASK
all your *t.* of making bricks — Ex.5.14
each to his *t.* and to his burden — Num.4.19
Arise, for it is your *t.* — Ezra 10.4
it seemed to me a wearisome *t.* — Ps.73.16
Whatever your *t.*, work heartily — Col.3.23
he desires a noble *t.* — 1 Tim.3.1

TASTE (verb)
O *t.* and see that the LORD is good — Ps.34.8
How sweet are thy words to my *t.* — Ps.119.103
who will not *t.* death before — Lk.9.27
he will never *t.* death — Jn.8.52
Do not *t.*, Do not touch — Col.2.21
he might *t.* death for every one — Heb.2.9
have *t.* the kindness of the Lord — 1 Pet.2.3

TAUGHT
from my youth thou hast *t.* me — Ps.71.17
I have *t.* you the way of wisdom — Pr.4.11
your sons shall be *t.* by the LORD — Is.54.13
he entered the synagogue and *t.* — Lk.6.6
And they shall all be *t.* by God — Jn.6.45
speak thus as the Father *t.* me — Jn.8.28
in words not *t.* by human wisdom — 1 Cor.2.13

Let him who is *t*. the word share   Gal.6.6
have been *t*. by God to love one   1 Th.4.9

TAX
Do not even the *t*. collectors do   Mt.5.46
Matthew sitting at the *t*. office   Mt.9.9
the *t*. collectors and the harlots   Mt.21.31
Is it lawful to pay *t*. to Caesar   Mk.12.14
But the *t*. collector, standing far   Lk.18.13
t. to whom *t*. are due, revenue to   Rom.13.7

TEACH
will *t*. you what you shall do   Ex.4.15
you shall *t*. them diligently to   Dt.6.7
Will any *t*. God knowledge   Job 21.22
T. me thy way, O LORD; and lead me   Ps.27.11
I will *t*. you the fear of the LORD   Ps.34.11
I will *t*. transgressors thy ways   Ps.51.13
t. the way of God truthfully   Mt.22.16
Spirit will *t*. you in that very hour   Lk.12.12
he will *t*. you all things   Jn.14.26
charged you not to *t*. in this name   Acts 5.28
Command and *t*. these things   1 Tim.4.11
will be able to *t*. others also   2 Tim.2.2
no need that any one should *t*. you   1 Jn.2.27

TEACHER
more understanding than all my *t*.   Ps.119.99
A disciple is not above his *t*.   Mt.10.24
fully taught will be like his *t*.   Lk.6.40
said to him, "Rabbi" (which means *T*.)   Jn.1.38
You call me *T*. and Lord   Jn.13.13
dignified, hospitable, an apt *t*.   1 Tim.3.2
by this time you ought to be *t*.   Heb.5.12
Let not many of you become *t*.   Jas.3.1
there will be false *t*. among you   2 Pet.2.1

TEACHING (noun)
Give ear, O my people, to my *t*.   Ps.78.1
My son, do not forget my *t*.   Pr.3.1
The *t*. of the wise is a fountain of   Pr.13.14
they were astonished at his *t*.   Mt.22.33
A new *t*.! With authority   Mk.1.27
Mary . . . listened to his *t*.   Lk.10.39
My *t*. is not mine, but his who sent   Jn.7.16
Take heed to yourself and to your *t*.   1 Tim.4.16
All scripture . . . profitable for *t*.   2 Tim.3.16
people will not endure sound *t*.   2 Tim.4.3
who hold the *t*. of Balaam   Rev.2.14

TEAR (noun)
My *t*. have been my food day and   Ps.42.3
put thou my *t*. in thy bottle   Ps.56.8
who sow in *t*. reap with shouts of   Ps.126.5
my eyes a fountain of *t*.   Jer.9.1
my eyes flow with rivers of *t*.   Lam.3.48
began to wet his feet with her *t*.   Lk.7.38
to admonish every one with *t*.   Acts 20.31
anguish of heart and with many *t*.   2 Cor.2.4
with loud cries and *t*.   Heb.5.7
though he sought it with *t*.   Heb.12.17
wipe away every *t*. from their eyes   Rev.21.4

TEETH
have escaped by the skin of my *t*.   Job 19.20
dost break the *t*. of the wicked   Ps.3.7
gnashing at me with their *t*.   Ps.35.16
his *t*. shall be set on edge   Jer.31.30
the children's *t*. are set on edge   Ezek.18.2
men will weep and gnash their *t*.   Mt.13.50
they ground their *t*. against him   Acts 7.54
and their *t*. like lions' *t*.   Rev.9.8

TEKOA
2 Sam.14.2; 2 Chr.11.6; Jer.6.1; Am.1.1

TEMPERATE
t., sensible, dignified   1 Tim.3.2
t., faithful in all things   1 Tim.3.11
Bid the older men be *t*., serious   Tit.2.2

TEMPEST
t. carries them off like stubble   Is.40.24
a *t*. in the day of the whirlwind   Am.1.14
there was a mighty *t*. on the sea   Jon.1.4
and no small *t*. lay on us   Acts 27.20
darkness and gloom, and a *t*.   Heb.12.18

TEMPLE
were building a *t*. to the LORD   Ezra 4.1
The LORD is in his holy *t*.   Ps.11.4
the LORD, and to inquire in his *t*.   Ps.27.4
they have defiled thy holy *t*.   Ps.79.1
and his train filled the *t*.   Is.6.1
their backs to the *t*. of the LORD   Ezek.8.16
The songs of the *t*. shall become   Am.8.3
I again look upon thy holy *t*.?   Jon.2.4
will suddenly come to his *t*.   Mal.3.1
set him on the pinnacle of the *t*.   Mt.4.5
greater than the *t*. is here   Mt.12.6
curtain of the *t*. was torn in two   Mk.15.38
She did not depart from the *t*.   Lk.2.37
Two men went up into the *t*. to pray   Lk.18.10
But he spoke of the *t*. of his body   Jn.2.21
at the Beautiful Gate of the *t*.   Acts 3.10
You who abhor idols, do you rob *t*.?   Rom.2.22
God's *t*. is holy, and that *t*. you   1 Cor.3.17
we are the *t*. of the living God   2 Cor.6.16
him a pillar in the *t*. of my God   Rev.3.12
Then God's *t*. in heaven was opened   Rev.11.19
for its *t*. is the Lord God   Rev.21.22

TEMPT
You shall not *t*. the Lord your God   Lk.4.12
to *t*. the Spirit of the Lord?   Acts 5.9
lest Satan *t*. you through lack of   1 Cor.7.5
not . . . be *t*. beyond your strength   1 Cor.10.13
is able to help those who are *t*.   Heb.2.18
in every respect . . . *t*. as we are   Heb.4.15
God cannot be *t*. with evil   Jas.1.13

TEMPTATION
And lead us not into *t*., But deliver   Mt.6.13
woe to the man by whom the *t*. comes   Mt.18.7
pray that you may not enter into *t*.   Mk.14.38
when the devil had ended every *t*.   Lk.4.13
T. to sin are sure to come; but woe   Lk.17.1
No *t*. has overtaken you that is   1 Cor.10.13
who desire to be rich fall into *t*.   1 Tim.6.9

TEMPTER
And the *t*. came and said to him, "If   Mt.4.3
for fear that somehow the *t*. had   1 Th.3.5

TEND
his sons shall *t*. it from evening   Ex.27.21
And I *t*. the sheep   Zech.11.7
He said to him, "*T*. my sheep."   Jn.21.16
Who *t*. a flock without getting some   1 Cor.9.7
T. the flock of God that is your   1 Pet.5.2

TENDER
no more be called *t*. and delicate   Is.47.1
amid the *t*. grass of the field   Dan.4.15
branch becomes *t*. and puts forth   Mt.24.32
through the *t*. mercy of our God   Lk.1.78
a *t*. heart and a humble mind   1 Pet.3.8

TENDERLY

he loved the maiden and spoke *t*.	Gen.34.3
Speak *t*. to Jerusalem, and cry to	Is.40.2
and speak *t*. to her	Hos.2.14

TENT

every man to his *t*., O Israel	2 Sam.20.1
In them he has set a *t*. for the sun	Ps.19.4
Let me dwell in thy *t*. for ever	Ps.61.4
than dwell in the *t*. of wickedness	Ps.84.10
stretched out the heavens like a *t*.	Ps.104.2
if the earthly *t*. we live in is	2 Cor.5.1
the true *t*. which is set up	Heb.8.2
go continually into the outer *t*.	Heb.9.6

TERRIBLE

t. in glorious deeds, doing wonders?	Ex.15.11
the *t*. God, who is not partial	Dt.10.17
the angel of God, very *t*.	Jg.13.6
the Lord, who is great and *t*.	Neh.4.14
God is clothed with *t*. majesty	Job 37.22
Say to God, "How *t*. are thy deeds	Ps.66.3
T. is God in his sanctuary	Ps.68.35
Holy and *t*. is his name	Ps.111.9
the day of the LORD is . . . very *t*.	Jl.2.11
the great and *t*. day of the LORD	Mal.4.5

TERRIFY

when he rises to *t*. the earth	Is.2.19
they were *t*., saying, "It is a ghost!"	Mt.14.26
of wars and tumults, do not be *t*.	Lk.21.9
do right and let nothing *t*. you	1 Pet.3.6
the rest were *t*. and gave glory to	Rev.11.13

TERROR

a *t*. from God fell upon the cities	Gen.35.5
I will send my *t*. before you	Ex.23.27
I will appoint over you sudden *t*.	Lev.26.16
For I was in *t*. of calamity from	Job 31.23
There they shall be in great *t*.	Ps.14.5
You will not fear the *t*. of the night	Ps.91.5
T., and the pit, and the snare	Is.24.17
T., pit, and snare are before you	Jer.48.43
there will be *t*. and great signs	Lk.21.11
are not a *t*. to good conduct	Rom.13.3

TEST (noun)

said to them, "Why put me to the *t*.?	Mk.12.15
We must not put the Lord to the *t*.	1 Cor.10.9
for in a severe *t*. of affliction	2 Cor.8.2
has stood the *t*. he will receive	Jas.1.12

TEST (verb)

After these things God *t*. Abraham	Gen.22.1
he might humble you and *t*. you	Dt.8.16
The LORD *t*. the righteous and the	Ps.11.5
T. your servants for ten days	Dan.1.12
This he said to *t*. him, for he . . . knew	Jn.6.6
T. yourselves. Do you not realize	2 Cor.13.5
But let each one *t*. his own work	Gal.6.4
t. everything; hold fast what is good	1 Th.5.21
though perishable is *t*. by fire	1 Pet.1.7
t. the spirits to see whether	1 Jn.4.1

TESTIFY

and our sins *t*. against us	Is.59.12
Though our iniquities *t*. against us	Jer.14.7
many things they *t*. against you?	Mt.27.13
I *t*. of it that its works are evil	Jn.7.7
t. to the gospel of the grace of God	Acts 20.24
we *t*. of God that he raised Christ	1 Cor.15.15
I *t*. again to every man who receives	Gal.5.3

have seen and *t*. that the Father	1 Jn.4.14
He who *t*. to these things says	Rev.22.20

TESTIMONY

placed it before the *t*., to be kept	Ex.16.34
these are the *t*., the statutes	Dt.4.45
the *t*. of the LORD is sure, making	Ps.19.7
Thy *t*. are wonderful; therefore	Ps.119.129
Bind up the *t*., seal the teaching	Is.8.16
To the teaching and to the *t*.	Is.8.20
sought false *t*. against Jesus	Mt.26.59
for a *t*. against them	Mk.6.11
to bear *t*. before them	Mk.13.9
a time for you to bear *t*.	Lk.21.13
And this is the *t*. of John	Jn.1.19
But the *t*. which I have is greater	Jn.5.36
the *t*. of two men is true	Jn.8.17
gave their *t*. to the resurrection	Acts 4.33
in his *t*. before Pontius Pilate	1 Tim.6.13
the *t*. of God is greater	1 Jn.5.9
And this is the *t*., that God gave	1 Jn.5.11
For the *t*. of Jesus is the spirit	Rev.19.10

TESTING (noun)

They were for the *t*. of Israel	Jg.3.4
For it will not be a *t*.	Ezek.21.13
on the day of *t*. in the wilderness	Heb.3.8
know that the *t*. of your faith	Jas.1.3

TETRARCH

Herod the *t*. heard about the fame of	Mt.14.1
Philip *t*. of the region of Ituraea	Lk.3.1
Now Herod the *t*. heard of all that	Lk.9.7
court of Herod the *t*., and Saul	Acts 13.1

THADDAEUS

James the son of Alphaeus, and *T*.	Mt.10.3
and *T*., and Simon the Cananaean	Mk.3.18

THANK

I will *t*. thee for ever, because	Ps.52.9
I *t*. thee, Father, Lord of heaven	Mt.11.25
I *t*. thee that I am not like other	Lk.18.11
I *t*. thee that thou hast heard me	Jn.11.41
I *t*. my God in all my remembrance	Phil.1.3
I *t*. him who has given me strength	1 Tim.1.12

THANKFUL

I am *t*. that I baptized none of	1 Cor.1.14
t. for . . . partnership in the gospel	Phil.1.5
And be *t*.	Col.3.15

THANKFULNESS

If I partake with *t*., why am I	1 Cor.10.30
with *t*. in your hearts to God	Col.3.16

THANKS

O give *t*. to the LORD, for he	1 Chr.16.34
We give *t*. to thee, O God; we give *t*.	Ps.75.1
we may give *t*. to thy holy name	Ps.106.47
All thy works shall give *t*. to thee	Ps.145.10
I give *t*. and praise, for thou hast	Dan.2.23
having given *t*. he broke them	Mk.8.6
that very hour she gave *t*. to God	Lk.2.38
and when he had given *t*.	Jn.6.11
T. be to God through Jesus Christ	Rom.7.25
But *t*. be to God, who gives us	1 Cor.15.57
T. be to God for his inexpressible	2 Cor.9.15
We give *t*. to God always for you	1 Th.1.2
bound to give *t*. to God always for	2 Th.2.13
honor and *t*. to him who is seated	Rev.4.9

THANKSGIVING

the leader to begin the *t*. in prayer	Neh.11.17
Offer to God a sacrifice of *t*.	Ps.50.14

come into his presence with *t.*	Ps.95.2
Enter his gates with *t.*, and his	Ps.100.4
Sing to the LORD with *t.*	Ps.147.7
say the "Amen" to your *t.*	1 Cor.14.16
by . . . supplication with *t.* let your	Phil.4.6
I urge that . . . *t.* be made for all	1 Tim.2.1
wisdom and *t.* and honor and	Rev.7.12

THEOPHILUS

account for you, most excellent *T.*	Lk.1.3
O *T.*, I have dealt with all that	Acts 1.1

THESSALONICA

Acts 17.1; 27.2; Phil.4.16; 2 Tim.4.10

THIEF

If a *t.* is found breaking in, and is	Ex.22.2
where *t.* break in and steal	Mt.6.19
part of the night the *t.* was coming	Mt.24.43
where no *t.* approaches and no moth	Lk.12.33
that man is a *t.* and a robber	Jn.10.1
but because he was a *t.*	Jn.12.6
Let the *t.* no longer steal, but	Eph.4.28
that day to surprise you like a *t.*	1 Th.5.4
a *t.*, or a wrongdoer, or a	1 Pet.4.15
Lo, I am coming like a *t.*	Rev.16.15

THIGH

Put your hand under my *t.*	Gen.24.2
Jacob's *t.* was put out of joint	Gen.32.25
the *t.* of the priests' portion	Ex.29.27
Gird your sword upon your *t.*	Ps.45.3
Smite therefore upon your *t.*	Ezek.21.12
on his *t.* he has a name inscribed	Rev.19.16

THING

You shall not eat any abominable *t.*	Dt.14.3
I know that thou canst do all *t.*	Job 42.2
hast put all *t.* under his feet	Ps.8.6
One *t.* have I asked of the LORD	Ps.27.4
No good *t.* does the LORD withhold	Ps.84.11
Behold, I am doing a new *t.*	Is.43.19
she has done a beautiful *t.* to me	Mt.26.10
and said to him, "You lack one *t.*	Mk.10.21
for all *t.* are possible with God	Mk.10.27
to Caesar the *t.* that are Caesar's	Mk.12.17
she has done a beautiful *t.* to me	Mk.14.6
one *t.* is needful. Mary has chosen	Lk.10.42
one *t.* I know, that though I was	Jn.9.25
but I do the very *t.* I hate	Rom.7.15
one *t.* I do, forgetting what	Phil.3.13
It is a fearful *t.* to fall into	Heb.10.31
with perishable *t.* such as silver	1 Pet.1.18
The end of all *t.* is at hand	1 Pet.4.7
said, "Behold, I make all *t.* new."	Rev.21.5

THINK

man that thou dost *t.* of him?	Ps.144.3
T. not that I have come to abolish	Mt.5.17
Why do you *t.* evil in your hearts?	Mt.9.4
What do you *t.* of the Christ?	Mt.22.42
Do not *t.* that I shall accuse you	Jn.5.45
short time you *t.* to make me a	Acts 26.28
more highly than he ought to *t.*	Rom.12.3
For if any one *t.* he is something	Gal.6.3
more . . . than all that we ask or *t.*	Eph.3.20

THIRD

he will be raised on the *t.* day	Mt.17.23
he . . . prayed for the *t.* time	Mt.26.44
the *t.* hour, when they crucified	Mk.15.25
crucified, and on the *t.* day rise	Lk.24.7

it is only the *t.* hour of the day	Acts 2.15
was caught up to the *t.* heaven	2 Cor.12.2

THIRST (verb)

My soul *t.* for God, for the living	Ps.42.2
who hunger and *t.* for righteousness	Mt.5.6
whoever drinks . . . will never *t.*	Jn.4.14
If any one *t.*, let him come to me	Jn.7.37
(to fulfil the scripture), "I *t.*"	Jn.19.28
hunger no more, neither *t.* any more	Rev.7.16

THISTLE

thorns and *t.* it shall bring forth	Gen.3.18
A *t.* on Lebanon sent to a cedar	2 Kg.14.9
Thorn and *t.* shall grow up on their	Hos.10.8
gathered from thorns, or figs from *t.*?	Mt.7.16
But if it bears thorns and *t.*	Heb.6.8

THOMAS

Mt.10.3; Jn.11.16; 14.5; 20.24; 21.2; Acts 1.13

THORN

as the crackling of *t.* under a pot	Ec.7.6
Instead of the *t.* shall come up the	Is.55.13
Are grapes gathered from *t.*	Mt.7.16
Other seeds fell upon *t.*	Mt.13.7
the soldiers plaited a crown of *t.*	Jn.19.2
a *t.* was given me in the flesh	2 Cor.12.7

THOUGHT (noun)

but the Lord takes *t.* for me	Ps.40.17
there is no work or *t.* . . . . in Sheol	Ec.9.10
For my *t.* are not your *t.*, neither	Is.55.8
For out of the heart come evil *t.*	Mt.15.19
But he knew their *t.*, and he said	Lk.6.8
but take *t.* for what is noble in	Rom.12.17
take every *t.* captive to obey	2 Cor.10.5
discerning the *t.* and intentions	Heb.4.12
arm yourselves with the same *t.*	1 Pet.4.1

THOUGHT (verb)

We have *t.* on thy steadfast love	Ps.48.9
feared the LORD and *t.* on his name	Mal.3.16
on the sea they *t.* it was a ghost	Mk.6.49
Why is it *t.* incredible by any of	Acts 26.8
I *t.* like a child, I reasoned	1 Cor.13.11

THREAD

I would not take a *t.* or a sandal	Gen.14.23
he snapped the ropes . . . like a *t.*	Jg.16.12
Your lips are like a scarlet *t.*	S.of S.4.3
the *t.* of your life is cut	Jer.51.13

THREEFOLD

A *t.* cord is not quickly broken	Ec.4.12

THRESHING

a fleece of wool on the *t.* floor	Jg.6.37
To buy the *t.* floor of you	2 Sam.24.21
is not threshed with a *t.* sledge	Is.28.27
The *t.* floors shall be full of	Jl.2.24
will clear his *t.* floor and gather	Mt.3.12

THREW

the blood and *t.* it upon the people	Ex.24.8
Moses *t.* the blood upon the altar	Lev.8.24
took up Jonah and *t.* him into the	Jon.1.15
into vessels but *t.* away the bad	Mt.13.48
millstone and *t.* it into the sea	Rev.18.21
t. him into the pit, and shut it	Rev.20.3

THROAT

their *t.* is an open sepulchre	Ps.5.9
my *t.* is parched. My eyes grow dim	Ps.69.3
and seizing him by the *t.* he said	Mt.18.28
Their *t.* is an open grave	Rom.3.13

THRONE

set up the *t.* of David over	2 Sam.3.10
the LORD'S *t.* is in heaven	Ps.11.4
God sits on his holy *t.*	Ps.47.8
thy *t.* is established from of old	Ps.93.2
established his *t.* in the heavens	Ps.103.19
I saw the Lord sitting upon a *t.*	Is.6.1
Heaven is my *t.* and the earth is	Is.66.1
A glorious *t.* set on high	Jer.17.12
he will sit on his glorious *t.*	Mt.25.31
give to him the *t.* of his father	Lk.1.32
put down the mighty from their *t.*	Lk.1.52
Thy *t.*, O God, is for ever and ever	Heb.1.8
at the right hand of the *t.* of God	Heb.12.2
sat down with my Father on his *t.*	Rev.3.21
Round the *t.* were twenty-four.	Rev.4.4
Therefore are they before the *t.*	Rev.7.15
a great white *t.* and him who sat	Rev.20.11
from the *t.* of God and of the Lamb	Rev.22.1

THRONG (noun)

in the mighty *t.* I will praise thee	Ps.35.18
praise him in the midst of the *t.*	Ps.109.30
As he went ashore he saw a great *t.*	Mt.14.14
And the great *t.* heard him gladly	Mk.12.37

THRUST

your God has *t.* them out before you	Dt.9.4
They only plan to *t.* him down from	Ps.62.4
they will be *t.* into thick darkness	Is.8.22
and you yourselves *t.* out	Lk.13.28
which God *t.* out before our fathers	Acts 7.45

THUNDER (noun)

the LORD sent *t.* and hail	Ex.9.23
But the *t.* of his power who can	Job 26.14
Hearken to the *t.* of his voice	Job 37.2
The crash of thy *t.* was in the	Ps.77.18
Mightier than the *t.* of many waters	Ps.93.4
at the sound of thy *t.* they	Ps.104.7
Boanerges, that is, sons of *t.*	Mk.3.17
say, as with a voice of *t.*, "Come!"	Rev.6.1
and like the sound of loud *t.*	Rev.14.2

THYATIRA

Acts 16.14; Rev.1.11; 2.18,24

TIBERIAS

Jn.6.1,23; 21.1

TIGRIS (Hiddekel)

Gen.2.14; Dan.10.4

TIMBRELS

after her with *t.* and dancing	Ex.15.20
meet him with *t.* and with dances	Jg.11.34
between them maidens playing *t.*	Ps.68.25
The mirth of the *t.* is stilled	Is.24.8
you shall adorn yourself with *t.*	Jer.31.4

TIME

the kingdom for such a *t.* as this?	Est.4.14
reserved for the *t.* of trouble	Job 38.23
My *t.* are in thy hand; deliver me	Ps.31.15
their refuge in the *t.* of trouble	Ps.37.39
has appointed a *t.* for every matter	Ec.3.17
For man does not know his *t.*	Ec.9.12
the *t.* of singing has come	S.of S.2.12
it is the *t.* to seek the LORD	Hos.10.12
interpret the signs of the *t.*	Mt.16.3
not . . . seven *t.*, but seventy *t.* seven	Mt.18.22
The Teacher says, My *t.* is at hand	Mt.26.18
The *t.* is fulfilled, and the kingdom	Mk.1.15
you will deny me three *t.*	Mk.14.72

how to interpret the present *t.*?	Lk.12.56
saying . . . 'The *t.* is at hand!'	Lk.21.8
until the *t.* of the Gentiles are	Lk.21.24
for my *t.* has not yet fully come	Jn.7.8
will you at this *t.* restore the	Acts 1.6
In a short *t.* you think to make me	Acts 26.28
Behold, now is the acceptable *t.*	2 Cor.6.2
when the *t.* had fully come, God	Gal.4.4
as a plan for the fulness of *t.*	Eph.1.10
the *t.* is coming when people	2 Tim.4.3
t. would fail me to tell of Gideon	Heb.11.32
the *t.* has come for judgment to	1 Pet.4.17
In the last *t.* there will be scoffers	Jude 18
written therein; for the *t.* is near	Rev.1.3

TIMOTHY

Paul's fellow worker, Acts 16.3; 17.14–15; Rom. 16.21; 2 Cor.1.1,19; commended, 1 Cor.16.10; Phil.2.19

TITHE (noun)

all the *t.* of herds and flocks	Lev.27.32
to the LORD, a *t.* of the *t.*	Num.18.26
paying all the *t.* of your produce	Dt.26.12
when the Levites receive the *t.*	Neh.10.38
Bring the full *t.* into the storehouse	Mal.3.10
I give *t.* of all that I get	Lk.18.12
Levi . . . who receives *t.*, paid *t.*	Heb.7.9

TITUS

Gal.2.3; Paul's love for, 2 Cor.2.13; 7.6,13

TODAY

my son, *t.* I have begotten you	Ps.2.7
O that *t.* you would hearken to his	Ps.95.7
which *t.* is alive and tomorrow is	Mt.6.30
t. you will be with me in Paradise	Lk.23.43
T., when you hear his voice	Heb.3.7
same yesterday and *t.* and for ever	Heb.13.8
T. or tomorrow we will go into	Jas.4.13

TOIL (noun)

in *t.* you shall eat of it all the days	Gen.3.17
their span is but *t.* and trouble	Ps.90.10
In all *t.* there is profit	Pr.14.23
yet there is no end to all his *t.*	Ec.4.8
remember our labor and *t.*, brethren	1 Th.2.9
your *t.* and your patient endurance	Rev.2.2

TOIL (verb)

make them *t.* at the brickkilns	2 Sam.12.31
Do not *t.* to acquire wealth	Pr.23.4
by a man who did not *t.* for it	Ec.2.21
they neither *t.* nor spin	Mt.6.28
we *t.* all night and took nothing	Lk.5.5
to this end we *t.* and strive	1 Tim.4.10

TOMB

it is the pillar of Rachel's *t.*	Gen.35.20
It is the *t.* of the man of God	2 Kg.23.17
Their quiver is like an open *t.*	Jer.5.16
for you are like whitewashed *t.*	Mt.23.27
you build the *t.* of the prophets·	Mt.23.29
the *t.* also were opened, and many	Mt.27.52
who lived among the *t.*; and no one	Mk.5.3
a stone against the door of the *t.*	Mk.15.46
already been in the *t.* four days	Jn.11.17
Magdalene came to the *t.* early	Jn.20.1
outran Peter and reached the *t.* first·	Jn.20.4

TOMORROW

Do not boast about *t.*, for you do not	Pr.27.1
Therefore do not be anxious about *t.*	Mt.6.34
field today and *t.* is thrown into	Lk.12.28

eat and drink, for *t*. we die	1 Cor.15.32
whereas you do not know about *t*.	Jas.4.14

TONGUE

Keep your *t*. from evil	Ps.34.13
my *t*. is like the pen of a ready	Ps.45.1
Your *t*. is like a sharp razor	Ps.52.2
Let my *t*. cleave to the roof of my	Ps.137.6
Even before a word is on, my *t*.	Ps.139.4
a lying *t*. is but for a moment	Pr.12.19
answer of the *t*. is from the LORD	Pr.16.1
and the *t*. of the dumb sing for joy	Is.35.6
have taught their *t*. to speak lies	Jer.9.5
his *t*. was released, and he spoke	Mk.7.35
and began to speak in other *t*.	Acts 2.4
If I speak in the *t*. of men	1 Cor.13.1
He who speaks in a *t*. edifies	1 Cor.14.4
and every *t*. confess that Jesus	Phil.2.11
not bridle his *t*. but deceives his	Jas.1.26
And the *t*. is a fire	Jas.3.6

TOOTH

t. for *t*., hand for hand	Ex.21.24; Dt.19.21
If he knocks out the *t*. of his slave	Ex.21.27
An eye for an eye and a *t*. for a *t*.	Mt.5.38

TORMENT

come here to *t*. us before the time?	Mt.8.29
being in *t*., he lifted up his eyes	Lk.16.23
smoke of their *t*. goes up for ever	Rev.14.11
they will be *t*. day and night for	Rev.20.10

TOTTER

The nations rage, the kingdoms *t*.	Ps.46.6
make them *t*. by thy power	Ps.59.11
When the earth *t*., and all its	Ps.75.3
my steps *t*. beneath me	Hab.3.16

TOUCH

neither shall you *t*. it	Gen.3.3
T. not my anointed ones	1 Chr.16.22
there shall no evil *t*. you	Job 5.19
t. no unclean thing; go out from	Is.52.11
If I only *t*. his garment, I shall	Mt.9.21
Do not taste, Do not *t*.	Col.2.21
looked upon and *t*. with our hands	1 Jn.1.1
the evil one does not *t*. him	1 Jn.5.18

TOWER

a *t*. with its top in the heavens	Gen.11.4
go round about her, number her *t*.	Ps.48.12
a strong *t*. against the enemy	Ps.61.3
The name of the LORD is a strong *t*.	Pr.18.10
Your neck is like an ivory *t*.	S.of S.7.4
built a *t*., and let it out to tenants	Mk.12.1
upon whom the *t*. in Siloam fell	Lk.13.4
desiring to build a *t*.	Lk.14.28

TRADE

by your great wisdom in *t*. you	Ezek.28.5
my Father's house a house of *t*.	Jn.2.16
for by *t*. they were tentmakers	Acts 18.3
all whose *t*. is on the sea	Rev.18.17

TRADITION

transgress the *t*. of the elders	Mt.15.2
observing the *t*. of the elders	Mk.7.3
and hold fast the *t*. of men	Mk.7.8
deceit, according to human *t*.	Col.2.8
hold to the *t*. which you were	2 Th.2.15

TRAIN (verb)

who were *t*. in singing to the LORD	1 Chr.25.7
T. up a child in the way he should	Pr.22.6
T. yourself in godliness	1 Tim.4.7

t. the young women to love	Tit.2.4
those who have been *t*. by it	Heb.12.11

TRAMPLE

my enemies *t*. upon me all day long	Ps.56.2
T. under foot those who lust after	Ps.68.30
the serpent you will *t*. under foot	Ps.91.13
they that *t*. the head of the poor	Am.2.7
lest they *t*. them under foot	Mt.7.6
they will *t*. over the holy city	Rev.11.2

TRANSGRESS

if you *t*. the covenant of the LORD	Jos.23.16
my mouth does not *t*.	Ps.17.3
We have *t*. and rebelled, and thou	Lam.3.42
All Israel has *t*. thy law	Dan.9.11
Come to Bethel, and *t*.; to Gilgal	Am.4.4
why do you *t*. the commandment	Mt.15.3

TRANSGRESSION

forgiving iniquity and *t*. and sin	Ex.34.7
Make me know my *t*. and my sin	Job 13.23
blameless, and innocent of great *t*.	Ps.19.13
Blessed is he whose *t*. is forgiven	Ps.32.1
I know my *t*., and my sin is ever	Ps.51.3
so far does he remove our *t*. from	Ps.103.12
But he was wounded for our *t*.	Is.53.5
What is the *t*. of Jacob? Is it not	Mic.1.5
Shall I give my first-born for my *t*.	Mic.6.7
sins were not like the *t*. of Adam	Rom.5.14
was rebuked for his own *t*.	2 Pet.2.16

TRANSGRESSOR

t. shall be altogether destroyed	Ps.37.38
Then I will teach *t*. thy ways	Ps.51.13
but *t*. stumble in them	Hos.14.9
the woman . . . became a *t*.	1 Tim.2.14
you have become a *t*. of the law	Jas.2.11

TRAP

Arrogant men have hidden a *t*.	Ps.140.5
Keep me from the *t*. which they have	Ps.141.9
a *t*. and a snare to the inhabitants	Is.8.14
They set a *t*.; they catch men	Jer.5.26
Let their feast become . . . a *t*.	Rom.11.9

TRAVAIL

anguish as of a woman in *t*.	Ps.48.6
groaning in *t*. together until now	Rom.8.22
I am again in *t*. until Christ be	Gal.4.19
upon them as *t*. comes upon a woman	1 Th.5.3

TREACHEROUS

be ashamed who are wantonly *t*.	Ps.25.3
crookedness of the *t*. destroys them	Pr.11.3
the *t*. are taken captive by their lust	Pr.11.6
For the *t*. deal treacherously	Is.24.16
Why do all who are *t*. thrive?	Jer.12.1
t., reckless, swollen with conceit	2 Tim.3.4

TREACHERY

What is this *t*. which you have	Jos.22.16
and meditate *t*. all the day long	Ps.38.12
their houses are full of *t*.	Jer.5.27
all the *t*. they have practiced	Ezek.39.26

TREAD

t. down the wicked where they	Job 40.12
it is he who will *t*. down our foes	Ps.60.12
will *t*. on the lion and the adder	Ps.91.13
you shall *t*. down the wicked	Mal.4.3
authority to *t*. upon serpents	Lk.10.19
an ox when it is *t*. out the grain	1 Cor.9.9
he will *t*. the wine press	Rev.19.15

TREASURE (noun)

T. gained by wickedness do not	Pr.10.2
the t. of all nations shall come in	Hag.2.7
For where your t. is, there will	Mt.6.21
is like t. hidden in a field	Mt.13.44
you will have t. in heaven	Mk.10.21
out of the good t. of his heart	Lk.6.45
we have this t. in earthen vessels	2 Cor.4.7
in whom are hid all the t. of wisdom	Col.2.3
greater wealth than the t. of Egypt	Heb.11.26
have laid up t. for the last days	Jas.5.3

TREE

every t. with seed in its fruit	Gen.1.29
the t. of the knowledge of good	Gen.2.17
to guard the way to the t. of life	Gen.3.24
And the t. said to the fig t.	Jg.9.10
He is like a t. planted by streams	Ps.1.3
She is a t. of life to those who	Pr.3.18
a desire fulfilled is a t. of life	Pr.13.12
in the place where the t. falls	Ec.11.3
who say to a t., 'You are my father'	Jer.2.27
A sound t. cannot bear evil fruit	Mt.7.18
the fig t. withered at once	Mt.21.19
From the fig t. learn its lesson	Mk.13.28
axe is laid to the root of the t.	Lk.3.9
you could say to this sycamine t.	Lk.17.6
they took him down from the t.	Acts 13.29
bore our sins in his body on the t.	1 Pet.2.24
grant to eat of the t. of life	Rev.2.7
leaves of the t. were for the healing	Rev.22.2

TREMBLE

The pillars of heaven t.	Job 26.11
the mountains t. with its tumult	Ps.46.3
t. before him, all the earth	Ps.96.9
let the peoples t.	Ps.99.1
Do you not t. before me?	Jer.5.22
The inhabitants of Samaria t. for	Hos.10.5
the guards t. and became like dead	Mt.28.4
Moses t. and did not dare to look	Acts 7.32
Moses said, "I t. with fear."	Heb.12.21

TREMBLING (noun)

Serve the LORD with fear, with t.	Ps.2.11
t. took hold of them there, anguish	Ps.48.6
came in fear and t. and fell down	Mk.5.33
I was . . . in much fear and t.	1 Cor.2.3
with fear and t., in singleness of	Eph.6.5
your own salvation with fear and t.	Phil.2.12

TRESPASS (noun)

if you do not forgive men their t.	Mt.6.15
Father . . . may forgive you your t.	Mk.11.25
many died through one man's t.	Rom.5.15
Law came in, to increase the t.	Rom.5.20
Now if their t. means riches for	Rom.11.12
if a man is overtaken in any t.	Gal.6.1
when we were dead through our t.	Eph.2.5
having forgiven us all our t.	Col.2.13

TRIAL

have continued with me in my t.	Lk.22.28
I stand here on t. for hope in the	Acts 26.6
Blessed is the man who endures t.	Jas.1.12
you may have to suffer various t.	1 Pet.1.6
how to rescue the godly from t.	2 Pet.2.9
the hour of t. which is coming on	Rev.3.10

TRIBES

these are the twelve t. of Israel	Gen.49.28
according to the twelve t. of Israel	Ex.24.4
the t. of the LORD, as was decreed	Ps.122.4
judging the twelve t. of Israel	Lk.22.30
To the twelve t. in the Dispersion	Jas.1.1
from all t. and peoples and tongues	Rev.7.9

TRIBULATION

may he deliver me out of all t.	1 Sam.26.24
For then there will be great t.	Mt.24.21
when t. or persecution arises	Mk.4.17
In the world you have t.; but be	Jn.16.33
through many t. we must enter the	Acts 14.22
Shall t., or distress, or persecution	Rom.8.35
be patient in t., be constant in	Rom.12.12
who have come out of the great t.	Rev.7.14

TRIBUTE

May the kings . . . render him t.	Ps.72.10
where is he who weighed the t.?	Is.33.18
do kings of the earth take toll or t.?	Mt.17.25
lawful for us to give t. to Caesar	Lk.20.22

TRIUMPH (verb)

the LORD, for he has t. gloriously	Ex.15.1
thou wilt not let them t.	Job 17.4
my enemy has not t. over me	Ps.41.11
When the righteous t., there is	Pr.28.12
Israel shall t. and glory	Is.45.25
a public example of them, t. over	Col.2.15
yet mercy t. over judgment	Jas.2.13

TROAS

Acts 16.8; 20.5; 2 Cor.2.12; 2 Tim.4.13

TROUBLE (noun)

The LORD brings t. on you today	Jos.7.25
those who . . . sow t. reap the same	Job 4.8
man is born to t. as the sparks fly	Job 5.7
Man . . . is of few days, and full of t.	Job 14.1
The LORD answer you in the day of t.	Ps.20.1
their refuge in the time of t.	Ps.37.39
call upon me in the day of t.	Ps.50.15
They are not in t. as other men are	Ps.73.5
I will be with him in t.	Ps.91.15
T. and anguish have come upon me	Ps.119.143
his tongue keeps himself out of t.	Pr.21.23
the day's own t. be sufficient for	Mt.6.34
who marry will have worldly t.	1 Cor.7.28

TROUBLE (verb)

my spirit is t. to know the dream	Dan.2.3
he was t., and all Jerusalem with him	Mt.2.3
he began to be sorrowful and t.	Mt.26.37
Why t. the Teacher any further?	Mk.5.35
anxious and t. about many things	Lk.10.41
Now is my soul t. And what shall I	Jn.12.27
Let not your hearts be t.	Jn.14.1
some who t. you and want to pervert	Gal.1.7

TRUE

thou art God, and thy words are t.	2 Sam.7.28
Israel was without the t. God	2 Chr.15.3
right ordinances and t. laws	Neh.9.13
the ordinances of the LORD are t.	Ps.19.9
that the word of the LORD is t.	Ps.141.6
But the LORD is the t. God	Jer.10.10
Teacher, we know that you are t.	Mt.22.16
The t. light that enlightens every	Jn.1.9
when the t. worshipers will worship	Jn.4.23
gives you the t. bread from heaven	Jn.6.32
the testimony of two men is t.	Jn.8.17
I am the t. vine, and my Father is	Jn.15.1
they know thee the only t. God	Jn.17.3
whatever is t., whatever is	Phil.4.8

to serve a living and *t*. God — 1 Th.1.9
draw near with a *t*. heart — Heb.10.22
This is the *t*. God and eternal life — 1 Jn.5.20
Just and *t*. are thy ways, O King of — Rev.15.3
He . . . is called Faithful and *T*. — Rev.19.11
These words are trustworthy and *t*. — Rev.22.6
TRUMPET
lift up your voice like a *t*. — Is.58.1
Give heed to the sound of the *t*. — Jer.6.17
Blow the *t*. in Zion; sanctify a fast — Jl.2.15
sound no *t*. before you — Mt.6.2
in a moment . . . at the last *t*. — 1 Cor.15.52
the sound of a *t*., and a voice — Heb.12.19
I heard . . . a loud voice like a *t*. — Rev.1.10
seven *t*. were given to them — Rev.8.2
Then the seventh angel blew his *t*. — Rev.11.15
TRUST (verb)
T. in the LORD, and do good — Ps.37.3
I *t*. in the steadfast love of God — Ps.52.8
blessed is the man who *t*. in thee — Ps.84.12
He who *t*. in his own mind is a fool — Pr.28.26
T. in the LORD for ever — Is.26.4
to some who *t*. in themselves that — Lk.18.9
Jesus did not *t*. himself to them — Jn.2.24
t. him who justifies the ungodly — Rom.4.5
TRUTH
Oh send out thy light and thy *t*. — Ps.43.3
thou desirest *t*. in the inward being — Ps.51.6
to all who call upon him in *t*. — Ps.145.18
Buy *t*., and do not sell it — Pr.23.23
and no one speaks the *t*. — Jer.9.5
therefore love *t*. and peace — Zech.8.19
grace and *t*. came through Jesus — Jn.1.17
must worship in spirit and *t*. — Jn.4.24
and the *t*. will make you free — Jn.8.32
the Spirit of *t*., whom the world — Jn.14.17
Pilate said to him, "What is *t*.?" — Jn.18.38
speaking the *t*. in love — Eph.4.15
the pillar and bulwark of the *t*. — 1 Tim.3.15
the *t*. that has been entrusted — 2 Tim.1.14
rightly handling the word of *t*. — 2 Tim.2.15
the way of *t*. will be reviled — 2 Pet.2.2
because the Spirit is the *t*. — 1 Jn.5.7
we may be fellow workers in the *t*. — 3 Jn.8
TUMULT
the *t*. in the camp . . . increased — 1 Sam.14.19
the mountains tremble with its *t*. — Ps.46.3
a day of *t*. and trampling — Is.22.5
my soul is in *t*. — Lam.2.11
lest there be a *t*. among the people — Mt.26.5
Why do you make a *t*. and weep? — Mk.5.39
when you hear of wars and *t*. — Lk.21.9
TURN
he is unchangeable . . . who can *t*. him? — Job 23.13
T. not thy servant away in anger — Ps.27.9
Let them be *t*. back and confounded — Ps.35.4
T. back, O children of men — Ps.90.3
I do not *t*. aside from thy — Ps.119.102
T. to me and be gracious to me — Ps.119.132
to *t*. aside the needy from justice — Is.10.2
T. to me and be saved, all the ends — Is.45.22
we have *t*. every one to his own way — Is.53.6
I will *t*. their mourning into joy — Jer.31.13
I will *t*. to you, and you shall — Ezek.36.9
The sun shall be *t*. to darkness — Jl.2.31
But you have *t*. justice into poison — Am.6.12

they shall *t*. in dread to the LORD — Mic.7.17
he will *t*. the hearts of children — Mal.4.6
unless you *t*. and become like — Mt.18.3
to *t*. the hearts of the fathers to — Lk.1.17
men who have *t*. the world upside — Acts 17.6
that they may *t*. from darkness to — Acts 26.18
let him *t*. away from evil — 1 Pet.3.11
TURTLEDOVE
if he cannot afford two *t*. — Lev.5.11
pigeon or a *t*. for a sin offering — Lev.12.6
the voice of the *t*. is heard — S.of S.2.12
a pair of *t*., or two young pigeons — Lk.2.24
TWELVE
these are the *t*. tribes of Israel — Gen.49.28
The names of the *t*. apostles are — Mt.10.2
more than *t*. legions of angels? — Mt.26.53
And they took up *t*. baskets full — Mk.6.43
appeared to Cephas, then to the *t*. — 1 Cor.15.5
the *t*. gates were *t*. pearls — Rev.21.21
TYCHICUS
Acts 20.4; Eph.6.21; Col.4.7; 2 Tim.4.12; Tit. 3.12
TYRE
Jos.19.29; 1 Kg.5.1; Ps.45.12; Jer.25.22; Mt. 11.21; Acts 12.20

UNBELIEF
he marveled because of their *u*. — Mk.6.6
I believe; help my *u*. — Mk.9.24
broken off because of their *u*. — Rom.11.20
I had acted ignorantly in *u*. — 1 Tim.1.13
were unable to enter because of *u*. — Heb.3.19
UNBELIEVER
has a wife who is an *u*. — 1 Cor.7.12
If one of the *u*. invites you to — 1 Cor.10.27
if . . . an *u*. or outsider enters — 1 Cor.14.24
a believer in common with an *u*.? — 2 Cor.6.15
is worse than an *u*. — 1 Tim.5.8
UNCHASTITY
except on the ground of *u*. — Mt.5.32
except for *u*., and marries another — Mt.19.9
abstain . . . from *u*. and from — Acts 15.20
from what is strangled and from *u*. — Acts 21.25
UNCIRCUMCISED
Any *u*. male who is not circumcised — Gen.17.14
the house of Israel is *u*. in heart — Jer.9.26
if a man who is *u*. keeps the . . . law — Rom.2.26
entrusted with the gospel to the *u*. — Gal.2.7
UNCIRCUMCISION
your circumcision becomes *u*. — Rom.2.25
neither circumcision . . . nor *u*. — 1 Cor.7.19
nor *u*., but a new creation — Gal.6.15
dead in . . . the *u*. of your flesh — Col.2.13
UNCLEAN
if any one touches an *u*. thing — Lev.5.2
Thus they became *u*. by their acts — Ps.106.39
I am a man of *u*. lips, and I dwell — Is.6.5
go out thence, touch no *u*. thing — Is.52.11
gave them authority over *u*. spirits — Mt.10.1
he commands even the *u*. spirits — Mk.1.27
not call any man common or *u*. — Acts 10.28
it is *u*. for . . . one who thinks it *u*. — Rom.14.14
be separate . . . and touch nothing *u*. — 2 Cor.6.17
nothing *u*. shall enter it — Rev.21.27
UNDERSTAND
thunder of his power who can *u*.? — Job 26.14

I have uttered what I did not *u.*	Job 42.3
Make me *u.* the way of thy precepts	Ps.119.27
I *u.* more than the aged, for I	Ps.119.100
Evil men do not *u.* justice	Pr.28.5
those who are wise shall *u.*	Dan.12.10
You shall indeed hear but never *u.*	Mt.13.14
they did not *u.* the saying	Mk.9.32
opened . . . minds to *u.* the scriptures	Lk.24.45
Why do you *u.* what I say?	Jn.8.43
Do you *u.* what you are reading?	Acts 8.30
I do not *u.* my own actions	Rom.7.15
and *u.* all mysteries and all	1 Cor.13.2
By faith we *u.* that the world was	Heb.11.3
some things in them hard to *u.*	2 Pet.3.16

UNDERSTANDING (noun)

But I have *u.* as well as you	Job 12.3
Through thy precepts I get *u.*	Ps.119.104
his *u.* is beyond measure	Ps.147.5
from his mouth come knowledge and *u.*	Pr.2.6
He who is slow to anger has great *u.*	Pr.14.29
A ruler who lacks *u.* is a cruel	Pr.28.16
The shepherds also have no *u.*	Is.56.11
hidden . . . from the wise and *u.*	Lk.10.21
they are darkened in their *u.*	Eph.4.18
peace of God, which passes all *u.*	Phil.4.7
all the riches of assured *u.*	Col.2.2
will grant you *u.* in everything	2 Tim.2.7
the Son of God . . . has given us *u.*	1 Jn.5.20

UNFAITHFUL

he was *u.* to the LORD in that he	1 Chr.10.13
If you are *u.*, I will scatter you	Neh.1.8
the master . . . put him with the *u.*	Lk.12.46
What if some were *u.*?	Rom.3.3
U. creatures! Do you not know that	Jas.4.4

UNFRUITFUL

choke the word, and it proves *u.*	Mk.4.19
my spirit prays but my mind is *u.*	1 Cor.14.14
Take no part in the *u.* works of	Eph.5.11
ineffective or *u.* in the knowledge	2 Pet.1.8

UNGODLINESS

to practice *u.*, to utter error	Is.32.6
against all *u.* and wickedness	Rom.1.18
lead people into more and more *u.*	2 Tim.2.16
deeds of *u.* which they have done	Jude 15

UNGODLY

God gives me up to the *u.*	Job 16.11
will scatter the bones of the *u.*	Ps.53.5
Both prophet and priest are *u.*	Jer.23.11
right time Christ died for the *u.*	Rom.5.6
the law is . . . for the *u.* and sinners	1 Tim.1.9
u. persons who pervert the grace of	Jude 4
things which *u.* sinners have spoken	Jude 15

UNHOLY

shall offer no *u.* incense thereon	Ex.30.9
offered *u.* fire before the LORD	Lev.10.1
they offered *u.* fire before the LORD	Num.3.4
law is . . . for the *u.* and profane	1 Tim.1.9
disobedient . . . ungrateful, *u.*	2 Tim.3.2

UNITE

u. my heart to fear thy name	Ps.86.11
if we have been *u.* with him in	Rom.6.5
But he who is *u.* to the Lord	1 Cor.6.17
to *u.* all things in him, things in	Eph.1.10

UNITY

good . . . when brothers dwell in *u.*	Ps.133.1

eager to maintain the *u.* of the	Eph.4.3
have *u.* of spirit, sympathy, love	1 Pet.3.8

UNJUST

from deceitful and *u.* men deliver me	Ps.43.1
he who hates *u.* gain will prolong	Pr.28.16
every one is greedy for *u.* gain	Jer.6.13
sends rain on the just and on the *u.*	Mt.5.45
For God is not so *u.* as to overlook	Heb.6.10

UNLEAVENED

Seven days you shall eat *u.* bread	Ex.13.6
shall keep the feast of *u.* bread	Ex.23.15
on the first day of *U.* Bread	Mk.14.12
after the days of *U.* Bread	Acts 20.6
with the *u.* bread of sincerity	1 Cor.5.8

UNPUNISHED

an evil man will not go *u.*	Pr.11.21
A false witness will not go *u.*	Pr.19.9
hastens to be rich will not go *u.*	Pr.28.20
You shall not go *u.*, for I am	Jer.25.29
I will by no means leave you *u.*	Jer.46.28

UNRIGHTEOUS

and the *u.* man his thoughts	Is.55.7
by means of *u.* mammon	Lk.16.9
Hear what the *u.* judge says	Lk.18.6
The tongue is an *u.* world among	Jas.3.6
the righteous for the *u.*	1 Pet.3.18

UNRIGHTEOUSNESS

there is no *u.* in him	Ps.92.15
Woe . . . who builds his house by *u.*	Jer.22.13
but had pleasure in *u.*	2 Th.2.12
cleanse us from all *u.*	1 Jn.1.9

UNSEARCHABLE

the number of his years is *u.*	Job 36.26
his greatness is *u.*	Ps.145.3
his understanding is *u.*	Is.40.28
How *u.* are his judgments and how	Rom.11.33
to preach . . . the *u.* riches of Christ	Eph.3.8

UNSEEN

yet thy footprints were *u.*	Ps.77.19
the things that are *u.* are eternal	2 Cor.4.18
warned . . . concerning events as yet *u.*	Heb.11.7

UPHOLD

and *u.* me with a willing spirit	Ps.51.12
The LORD *u.* all who are falling	Ps.145.14
he *u.* the widow and the fatherless	Ps.146.9
Behold my servant, whom I *u.*	Is.42.1
On the contrary, we *u.* the law	Rom.3.31
u. the universe by his word of power	Heb.1.3

UPRIGHT

may the LORD be with the *u.*	2 Chr.19.11
Or where were the *u.* cut off?	Job 4.7
God, who saves the *u.* in heart	Ps.7.10
Good and *u.* is the LORD	Ps.25.8
For the word of the LORD is *u.*	Ps.33.4
joy for the *u.* in heart	Ps.97.11
Light . . . in the darkness for the *u.*	Ps.112.4
but the *u.* enjoy his favor	Pr.14.9
the prayer of the *u.* is his delight	Pr.15.8
I found, that God made man *u.*	Ec.7.29
an *u.* and God-fearing man	Acts 10.22
u., holy, and self-controlled	Tit.1.8

UR

Gen.11.28; 15.7; 1 Chr.11.35; Neh.9.7

URIAH

2 Sam.11.3,17; 12.10; 1 Kg.15.5; Mt.1.6

URIM

shall put the *U*. and the Thummim Ex.28.30
he put the *U*. and the Thummim Lev.8.8
judgment of the *U*. before the LORD Num.27.21
O LORD, God of Israel, give *U*. 1 Sam.14.41
a priest to consult *U*. and Thummim Ezra 2.63
a priest with *U*. and Thummim Neh.7.65

UTTERANCE

speak . . . as the Spirit gave them *u*. Acts 2.4
to another the *u*. of knowledge 1 Cor.12.8
that *u*. may be given me in opening Eph.6.19

UZ

(1) Gen.10.23; (2) Gen.36.28; (3) Job 1.1;
Jer.25.20; Lam.4.21

UZZIAH

2 Kg.15.13; 2 Chr.26.1; Is.1.1; 6.1; Am.1.1

VAIN

guiltless who takes his name in *v*. Ex.20.7
How long will you love *v*. words Ps.4.2
for *v*. is the help of man Ps.108.12
Men are all a *v*. hope Ps.116.11
It is in *v*. that you rise up early Ps.127.2
beauty is *v*., but a woman who Pr.31.30
But I said, "I have labored in *v*. Is.49.4
the peoples imagine *v*. things Acts 4.25
turn from these *v*. things to Acts 14.15
in the Lord your labor is not in *v*. 1 Cor.15.58
did not run in *v*. or labor in *v*. Phil.2.16
this man's religion is *v*. Jas.1.26

VALIANT

only be *v*. for me and fight the 1 Sam.18.17
Be courageous and be *v*. 2 Sam.13.28
having an army of *v*. men of war 2 Chr.13.3
v. men in mixing strong drink Is.5.22

VALLEY

the *v*. of the shadow of death Ps.23.4
the *v*. deck themselves with grain Ps.65.13
As they go through the *v*. of Baca Ps.84.6
Every *v*. shall be lifted up Is.40.4
the *v*. shall perish, and the plain Jer.48.8
in the midst of the *v*. . . . of bones Ezek.37.1
multitudes, in the *v*. of decision Jl.3.14
Every *v*. shall be filled Lk.3.5

VALUE

on finding one pearl of great *v*. Mt.13.46
you are of more *v*. than many sparrows Lk.12.7
Of how much more *v*. are you than Lk.12.24
Or what is the *v*. of circumcision? Rom.3.1
godliness is of *v*. in every way 1 Tim.4.8

VANISH

for the heavens will *v*. like smoke Is.51.6
and he *v*. out of their sight Lk.24.31
growing old is ready to *v*. away Heb.8.13
the sky *v*. like a scroll that is Rev.6.14

VANITY

Turn my eyes from looking at *v*. Ps.119.37
v. of *v*.! All is *v*. Ec.1.2; 12.8
Everything before them is *v*. Ec.9.1
All that comes is *v*. Ec.11.8

VASHTI

Est.1.9; 2.1,17

VEGETATION

Let the earth put forth *v*. Gen.1.11
devoured all the *v*. in their land Ps.105.35
brings forth *v*. useful to those Heb.6.7

VEIL

shall make a *v*. of blue and purple Ex.26.31
Your *v*. also I will tear off Ezek.13.21
ought to have a *v*. on her head 1 Cor.11.10
a *v*. lies over their minds 2 Cor.3.15

VENGEANCE

v. shall be taken on him sevenfold Gen.4.15
V. is mine, and recompense Dt.32.35
thou God of *v*., shine forth Ps.94.1
Behold, your God will come with *v*. Is.35.4
the day of *v*. of our God Is.61.2
this is the time of the LORD's *v*. Jer.51.6
for these are days of *v*. Lk.21.22
V. is mine, I will repay, says the Rom.12.19

VESSEL

them in pieces like a potter's *v*. Ps.2.9
I have become like a broken *v*. Ps.31.12
the *v*. he was making of clay Jer.18.4
like a *v*. for which no one cares Jer.48.38
lighting a lamp covers it with a *v*. Lk.8.16
to make . . . one *v*. for beauty and Rom.9.21
have this treasure in earthen *v*. 2 Cor.4.7
he will be a *v*. for noble use 2 Tim.2.21

VEXATION

Surely *v*. kills the fool Job 5.2
O that my *v*. were weighed Job 6.2
The *v*. of a fool is known at once Pr.12.16
For in much wisdom is much *v*. Ec.1.18
Remove *v*. from your mind Ec.11.10

VICTORY

Thy right hand is filled with *v*. Ps.48.10
and his holy arm have gotten him *v*. Ps.98.1
All . . . have seen the *v*. of our God Ps.98.3
but the *v*. belongs to the LORD Pr.21.31
then his own arm brought him *v*. Is.59.16
till he brings justice to *v*. Mt.12.20
Death is swallowed up in *v*. 1 Cor.15.54
O death, where is thy *v*.? 1 Cor.15.55
this is the *v*. that overcomes 1 Jn.5.4

VILE

do not do this *v*. thing Jg.19.23
make them like *v*. figs which are Jer.29.17
see the *v*. abominations that Ezek.8.9
disorder and every *v*. practice Jas.3.16

VINDICATE

V. me, O God, and defend my cause Ps.43.1
For the LORD will *v*. his people Ps.135.14
he who *v*. me is near Is.50.8
And will not God *v*. his elect Lk.18.7
v. in the Spirit, seen by angels 1 Tim.3.16

VINDICATION

Turn now, my *v*. is at stake Job 6.29
v. from the God of his salvation Ps.24.5
bring forth your *v*. as the light Ps.37.6
The LORD works *v*. and justice for Ps.103.6
her *v*. goes forth as brightness Is.62.1
The nations shall see your *v*. Is.62.2
The LORD has brought forth our *v*. Jer.51.10

VINE

a fruitful *v*. within your house Ps.128.3
every one . . . will eat of his own *v*. Is.36.16
Yet I planted you a choice *v*. Jer.2.21
it became a *v*., and brought forth Ezek.17.6
every man under his *v*. and under Mic.4.4
not drink again of the fruit of the *v*. Mk.14.25.
I am the *v*., you are the branches Jn.155

VINEGAR

they gave me *v.* to drink	Ps.69.21
Like *v.* to the teeth, and smoke to	Pr.10.26
filling a sponge full of *v.*	Mk.15.36
a sponge full of the *v.* on hyssop	Jn.19.29

VINEYARD

possession of the *v.* of Naboth	1 Kg.21.15
shall plant *v.* and eat their fruit	Is.65.21
though they plant *v.*, they shall not	Zeph.1.13
to hire laborers for his *v.*	Mt.20.1
A man planted a *v.*, and set a hedge	Mk.12.1
Who plants a *v.* without eating any	1 Cor.9.7

VIOLENCE

my savior; thou savest me from *v.*	2 Sam.22.3
there is no *v.* in my hands	Job 16.17
didst deliver me from men of *v.*	Ps.18.48
From oppression and *v.* he redeems	Ps.72.14
A man of *v.* entices his neighbor	Pr.16.29
V. shall no more be heard in your	Is.60.18
do no wrong or *v.* to the alien	Jer.22.3
Put away *v.* and oppression	Ezek.45.9
For the *v.* done to your brother	Ob.10
Your rich men are full of *v.*	Mic.6.12
kingdom of heaven has suffered *v.*	Mt.11.12
great city be thrown down with *v.*	Rev.18.21

VIOLENT

I have avoided the ways of the *v.*	Ps.17.4
preserve me from *v.* men	Ps.140.1
the king laid *v.* hands upon some	Acts 12.1
not *v.* but gentle, not quarrelsome	1 Tim.3.3
a drunkard or *v.* or greedy for gain	Tit.1.7

VIPER

under their lips is the poison of *v.*	Ps.140.3
You brood of *v.*! how can you speak	Mt.12.34
you brood of *v.*, how are you to	Mt.23.33
a *v.* came out because of the heat	Acts 28.3

VIRGIN

If a man seduces a *v.* who is not	Ex.22.16
beautiful young *v.* to the harem	Est.2.3
how then could I look upon a *v.*?	Job 31.1
the *v.* daughter of my people is	Jer.14.17
Fallen, no more to rise, is the *v.*	Am.5.2
Behold, a *v.* shall conceive and	Mt.1.23
a *v.* betrothed to a man whose name	Lk.1.27

VISION

the LORD came to Abram in a *v.*	Gen.15.1
there was no frequent *v.*	1 Sam.3.1
thou dost . . . terrify me with *v.*	Job 7.14
chased away like a *v.* of the night	Job 20.8
speak in a *v.* to thy faithful one	Ps.89.19
The *v.* of Isaiah the son of Amoz	Is.1.1
prophets obtain no *v.* from the LORD	Lam.2.9
I saw in my *v.* by night, and behold	Dan.7.2
had understanding of the *v.*	Dan.10.1
The *v.* of Obadiah. Thus says the	Ob.1
The book of the *v.* of Nahum	Nah.1.1
commanded them, "Tell no one the *v.*	Mt.17.9
he had seen a *v.* in the temple	Lk.1.22
they had even seen a *v.* of angels	Lk.24.23
Lord said to him in a *v.*, "Ananias."	Acts 9.10
And a *v.* appeared to Paul	Acts 16.9
not disobedient to the heavenly *v.*	Acts 26.19
I will go on to *v.* and revelations	2 Cor.12.1
taking his stand on *v.*	Col.2.18

VISIT (verb)

I will *v.* their sin upon them	Ex.32.34
v. the iniquity of the fathers upon	Dt.5.9
Thou *v.* the earth and waterest it	Ps.65.9
the LORD will *v.* Tyre, and she will	Is.23.17
sick or in prison and *v.* thee?	Mt.25.39
he has *v.* and redeemed his people	Lk.1.68
return and *v.* the brethren in	Acts 15.36
I will *v.* you after passing through	1 Cor.16.5
I wanted to *v.* you on my way to	2 Cor.1.16
to *v.* orphans and widows in their	Jas.1.27

VOICE

The *v.* is Jacob's *v.*, but the	Gen.27.22
saw no form; there was only a *v.*	Dt.4.12
if you obey the *v.* of the LORD	Dt.15.5
after the fire a still small *v.*	1 Kg.19.12
there was silence, then . . . a *v.*	Job 4.16
God thunders wondrously with his *v.*	Job 37.5
their *v.* is not heard	Ps.19.3
Hear the *v.* of my supplication	Ps.28.2
The *v.* of the LORD flashes forth	Ps.29.7
he utters his *v.*, the earth melts	Ps.46.6
hearkening to the *v.* of his word	Ps.103.20
Give ear to my *v.*, when I call	Ps.141.1
one rises up at the *v.* of a bird	Ec.12.4
the *v.* of the turtledove is heard	S. of S.2.12
And I heard the *v.* of the Lord	Is.6.8
A *v.* cries: "In the wilderness	Is.40.3
He will not cry or lift up his *v.*	Is.42.2
lift up your *v.* like a trumpet	Is.58.1
A *v.* is heard in Ramah, lamentation	Jer.31.15
I heard the *v.* of one speaking	Ezek.1.28
lo, a *v.* from heaven, saying	Mt.3.17
Jesus cried with a loud *v.*	Mt.27.46
a *v.* came out of the cloud	Lk.9.35
will hear the *v.* of the Son of God	Jn.5.25
My sheep hear my *v.*	Jn.10.27
Then a *v.* came from heaven	Jn.12.28
hearing the *v.* but seeing no one	Acts 9.7
His *v.* then shook the earth	Heb.12.26
one hears my *v.* and opens the door	Rev.3.20
I heard a great *v.* from the throne	Rev.21.3

VOID

The earth was without form and *v.*	Gen.1.2
stretches out the north over the *v.*	Job 26.7
you have made *v.* the word of God	Mt.15.6
one dot of the law to become *v.*	Lk.16.17
faith is null and the promise is *v.*	Rom.4.14
so as to make the promise *v.*	Gal.3.17

VOMIT (noun)

a drunken man staggers in his *v.*	Is.19.14
For all tables are full of *v.*	Is.28.8
Moab shall wallow in his *v.*	Jer.48.26
The dog turns back to his own *v.*	2 Pet.2.22

VOMIT (verb)

the land *v.* out its inhabitants	Lev.18.25
be drunk and *v.*, fall and rise no	Jer.25.27
it *v.* out Jonah upon the dry land	Jon.2.10

VOW (noun)

the *v.* of a Nazirite, to separate	Num.6.2
Jephthah made a *v.* to the LORD	Jg.11.30
pay your *v.* to the Most High	Ps.50.14
to thee shall *v.* be performed	Ps.65.1
he cut his hair, for he had a *v.*	Acts 18.18

WAGE (noun)

w. of the righteous leads to life	Pr.10.16
the laborers and pay them their *w.*	Mt.20.8

and be content with your _w._   Lk.3.14
his _w._ are not reckoned as a gift   Rom.4.4
For the _w._ of sin is death   Rom.6.23
The laborer deserves his _w._   1 Tim.5.18
Behold, the _w._ of the laborers who   Jas.5.4

WAGE (verb)
that _w._ war against Jerusalem   Zech.14.12
you may _w._ the good warfare   1 Tim.1.18
so you fight and _w._ war   Jas.4.2
that _w._ war against your soul   1 Pet.2.11

WAIL
_W._, for the day of the LORD is near   Is.13.6
_W._, you shepherds, and cry   Jer.25.34
Cry and _w._, son of man, for it is   Ezek.21.12
and _w._, all you drinkers of wine   Jl.1.5
we _w._, and you did not mourn   Mt.11.17
the earth will _w._ on account of him   Rev.1.7
kings . . . will weep and _w._ over her   Rev.18.9

WAILING (noun)
the _w._ reaches to Beer-elim   Is.15.8
For a sound of _w._ is heard   Jer.9.19
in all vineyards there shall be _w._   Am.5.17
_w._ and loud lamentation, Rachel   Mt.2.18

WAIT
I _w._ for thy salvation, O LORD   Gen.49.18
_W._ for the LORD; be strong   Ps.27.14
_w._ patiently for him; fret not   Ps.37.7
The wicked lie in _w._ to destroy me   Ps.119.95
I _w._ for the LORD, my soul _w._   Ps.130.5
_w._ for the LORD, and he will help   Pr.20.22
but they who _w._ for the LORD shall   Is.40.31
For the coastlands shall _w._ for me   Is.60.9
LORD is good to those who _w._ for him   Lam.3.25
will _w._ for the God of my salvation   Mic.7.7
the creation _w._ with eager longing   Rom.8.19
we _w._ for the hope of righteousness   Gal.5.5
to _w._ for his Son from heaven   1 Th.1.10
God's patience _w._ in the days of   1 Pet.3.20
_w._ for the mercy of our Lord Jesus   Jude 21

WALK
Enoch _w._ with God; and he was not   Gen.5.24
_w._ before me, and be blameless   Gen.17.1
keep my statutes and _w._ in them   Lev.18.4
I will _w._ among you, and will be   Lev.26.12
And if you will _w._ in my ways   1 Kg.3.14
Blessed is the man who _w._ not in   Ps.1.1
though I _w._ through the valley of   Ps.23.4
_W._ about Zion, go round about her   Ps.48.12
from those who _w._ uprightly   Ps.84.11
Though I _w._ in the midst of trouble   Ps.138.7
do not _w._ in the way of evil men   Pr.4.14
let us _w._ in the light of the LORD   Is.2.5
The people who _w._ in darkness have   Is.9.2
they shall _w._ and not faint   Is.40.31
Do two _w._ together, unless they   Am.3.3
and to _w._ humbly with your God?   Mic.6.8
So Peter . . . _w._ on the water   Mt.14.29
or to say, 'Rise and _w._'?   Lk.5.23
follows me will not _w._ in darkness   Jn.8.12
_W._ while you have the light, lest   Jn.12.35
for we _w._ by faith, not by sight   2 Cor.5.7
_w._ by the Spirit, and do not gratify   Gal.5.16
_w._ in love, as Christ loved us   Eph.5.2
if we _w._ in the light, as he is   1 Jn.1.7
By its light shall the nations _w._   Rev.21.24

WALL
waters being a _w._ to them on their   Ex.14.22
the _w._ of the city will fall   Jos.6.5
let us build the _w._ of Jerusalem   Neh.2.17
Now when the _w._ had been built   Neh.7.1
by my God I can leap over a _w._   Ps.18.29
Peace be within your _w._   Ps.122.7
Hezekiah turned his face to the _w._   Is.38.2
the dividing _w._ of hostility   Eph.2.14
By faith the _w._ of Jericho fell   Heb.11.30
the _w._ of the city had twelve   Rev.21.14

WANDER
let me not _w._ from thy commandments   Ps.119.10
Therefore the people _w._ like sheep   Zech.10.2
Certain persons . . . have _w._ away   1 Tim.1.6
turn away . . . and _w._ into myths   2 Tim.4.4
if any one . . . _w._ from the truth   Jas.5.19

WANTON
do not do this _w._ folly   2 Sam.13.12
But they had a _w._ craving   Ps.106.14
she is _w._ and knows no shame   Pr.9.13
Her prophets are _w._, faithless men   Zeph.3.4
when they grow _w._ against Christ   1 Tim.5.11
glorified herself and played the _w._   Rev.18.7

WAR (noun)
The LORD is a man of _w._   Ex.15.3
in the Book of the _W._ of the LORD   Num.21.14
He trains my hands for _w._   Ps.18.34
though _w._ arise against me, yet I   Ps.27.3
yet _w._ was in his heart   Ps.55.21
but when I speak, they are for _w._   Ps.120.7
a time for _w._, and a time for peace   Ec.3.8
Wisdom is better than weapons of _w._   Ec.9.18
neither shall they learn _w._ any more   Is.2.4
Prepare the nations for _w._ against   Jer.51.28
to Sheol with their weapons of _w._   Ezek.32.27
neither shall they learn _w._ any more   Mic.4.3
when you hear of _w._ and rumors of _w._   Mk.13.7
another law at _w._ with the law of   Rom.7.23
your passions that are at _w._   Jas.4.1
that wage _w._ against your soul   1 Pet.2.11
Now _w._ arose in heaven, Michael and   Rev.12.7
allowed to make _w._ on the saints   Rev.13.7

WARFARE
cry to her that her _w._ is ended   Is.40.2
weapons of our _w._ are not worldly   2 Cor.10.4
by them you may wage the good _w._   1 Tim.1.18

WARN
I solemnly _w._ you this day that you   Dt.8.19
didst _w._ them by thy Spirit   Neh.9.30
But if you _w._ the wicked, and he   Ezek.3.19
being _w._ in a dream not to return   Mt.2.12
Who _w._ you to flee from the wrath   Lk.3.7
But I will _w._ you whom to fear   Lk.12.5
I _w._ you, as I _w._ you before   Gal.5.21
I _w._ every one who hears the words   Rev.22.18

WASH
let them _w._ their garments   Ex.19.10
They shall _w._ their hands and their   Ex.30.21
_W._ me thoroughly from my iniquity   Ps.51.2
_w._ me, and I shall be whiter than   Ps.51.7
_W._ yourselves; make yourselves clean   Is.1.16
anoint your head and _w._ your face   Mt.6.17
not eat unless they _w._ their hands   Mk.7.3
began to _w._ the disciples' feet   Jn.13.5
_w._ away your sins, calling on   Acts 22.16

you were *w*., you were sanctified — 1 Cor.6.11
w. the feet of the saints — 1 Tim.5.10
our bodies *w*. with pure water — Heb.10.22
Blessed are those who *w*. their robes — Rev.22.14

WASTE
the destruction that *w*. at noonday — Ps.91.6
the LORD will lay *w*. the earth — Is.24.1
earth and lo, it was *w*. and void — Jer.4.23
made my flesh and my skin *w*. away — Lam.3.4
indignant, saying, "Why this *w*.? — Mt.26.8
But Saul laid *w*. the church — Acts 8.3
In one hour she has been laid *w*. — Rev.18.19

WATCH (noun)
whose eyes keep *w*. on the nations — Ps.66.7
or as a *w*. in the night — Ps.90.4
keep *w*. over the door of my lips — Ps.141.3
keeping *w*. on the evil and the good — Pr.15.3
keeping *w*. over their flock by night — Lk.2.8

WATCH (verb)
The LORD *w*. between you and me — Gen.31.49
love and faithfulness *w*. over him — Ps.61.7
those who *w*. for my life consult — Ps.71.10
Unless the LORD *w*. over the city — Ps.127.1
so I will *w*. over them to build — Jer.31.28
I will take my stand to *w*. — Hab.2.1
W. therefore, for you know neither — Mt.25.13
Could you not *w*. one hour? — Mk.14.37
the scribes and the Pharisees *w*. him — Lk.6.7

WATCHFUL
Be *w*., stand firm in your faith — 1 Cor.16.13
being *w*. in it with thanksgiving — Col.4.2
Be sober, be *w*. — 1 Pet.5.8

WATCHMAN
the *w*. stays awake in vain — Ps.127.1
more than *w*. for the morning — Ps.130.6
W., what of the night? *W*., what of — Is.21.11
His *w*. are blind, they are all — Is.56.10
if the *w*. sees the sword coming — Ezek.33.6

WATER (noun)
Unstable as *w*., you shall not have — Gen.49.4
how he made the *w*. of the Red Sea — Dt.11.4
a tree planted by streams of *w*. — Ps.1.3
I am poured out like *w*., and all my — Ps.22.14
He leads me beside still *w*. — Ps.23.2
He opened the rock, and *w*. gushed — Ps.105.41
Stolen *w*. is sweet, and bread eaten — Pr.9.17
As in *w*. face answers to face, so — Pr.27.19
Cast your bread upon the *w*. — Ec.11.1
you will draw *w*. from the wells of — Is.12.3
broken cisterns, that can hold no *w*. — Jer.2.13
LORD, the fountain of living *w*. — Jer.17.13
But let justice roll down like *w*. — Am.5.24
gives . . . even a cup of cold *w*. — Mt.10.42
he took *w*. and washed his hands — Mt.27.24
he commands even wind and *w*. — Lk.8.25
his finger in *w*. and cool my tongue — Lk.16.24
tasted the *w*. now become wine — Jn.2.9
unless one is born of *w*. and the — Jn.3.5
Then he poured *w*. into a basin — Jn.13.5
there came out blood and *w*. — Jn.19.34
the washing of *w*. with the word — Eph.5.26
No longer drink only *w*. — 1 Tim.5.23
guide them to springs of living *w*. — Rev.7.17
the river of the *w*. of life — Rev.22.1

WAVE (noun)
shall your proud *w*. be stayed'? — Job 38.11

all thy *w*. and thy billows have — Ps.42.7
boat was being swamped by the *w*. — Mt.8.24
rebuked the wind and the raging *w*. — Lk.8.24
he who doubts is like a *w*. of the sea — Jas.1.6

WAY
corrupted their *w*. upon the earth — Gen.6.12
wilt prosper the *w*. which I go — Gen.24.42
This God–his *w*. is perfect — 2 Sam.22.31
I shall go the *w*. whence I shall not — Job 16.22
But he knows the *w*. that I take — Job 23.10
LORD knows the *w*. of the righteous — Ps.1.6
Teach me thy *w*., O LORD — Ps.27.11
Commit your *w*. to the LORD — Ps.37.5
that thy *w*. may be known upon earth — Ps.67.2
Teach me thy *w*., O LORD — Ps.86.11
He made known his *w*. to Moses — Ps.103.7
How can a . . . man keep his *w*. pure? — Ps.119.9
lead me in the *w*. everlasting — Ps.139.24
I walk in the *w*. of righteousness — Pr.8.20
The *w*. of a fool is right in his — Pr.12.15
Train up a child in the *w*. he should — Pr.22.6
This is the *w*., walk in it — Is.30.21
let the wicked forsake his *w*. — Is.55.7
Prepare the *w*. of the LORD, make his — Mt.3.3
gate is wide and the *w*. is easy — Mt.7.13
guide our feet into the *w*. of peace — Lk.1.79
Make straight the *w*. of the Lord — Jn.1.23
I am the *w*., and the truth, and the — Jn.14.6
the *w*. of God more accurately — Acts 18.26
no little stir concerning the *W*. — Acts 19.23
I persecuted this *W*. to the death — Acts 22.4
the *w*. of peace they do not know — Rom.3.17
and how inscrutable his *w*. — Rom.11.33
will also provide the *w*. of escape — 1 Cor.10.13
show you a . . . more excellent *w*. — 1 Cor.12.31
Love does not insist on its own *w*. — 1 Cor.13.5
new and living *w*. which he opened — Heb.10.20
unstable in all his *w*. — Jas.1.7
were ransomed from the futile *w*. — 1 Pet.1.18
Just and true are thy *w*., O King of — Rev.15.3

WEAK
Leah's eyes were *w*., but Rachel was — Gen.29.17
you have strengthened the *w*. hands — Job 4.3
He has pity on the *w*. and the needy — Ps.72.13
all knees be *w*. as water — Ezek.21.7
spirit . . . is willing . . . flesh is *w*. — Mk.14.38
toiling one must help the *w*. — Acts 20.35
As for the man who is . . . *w*. in faith — Rom.14.1
God chose what is *w*. in the world — 1 Cor.1.27
To the *w*. I became *w*., that — 1 Cor.9.22
when I am *w*., then I am strong — 2 Cor.12.10
help the *w*., be patient with them — 1 Th.5.14
and strengthen your *w*. knees — Heb.12.12

WEAKNESS
the Spirit helps us in our *w*. — Rom.8.26
the *w*. of God is stronger than men — 1 Cor.1.25
It is sown in *w*., it is raised — 1 Cor.15.43
my power is made perfect in *w*. — 2 Cor.12.9
unable to sympathize with our *w*. — Heb.4.15

WEALTH
his *w*. will not endure — Job 15.29
leave their *w*. to others — Ps.49.10
W. and riches are in his house — Ps.112.3
A rich man's *w*. is his strong city — Pr.10.15
W. hastily gotten will dwindle — Pr.13.11
W. brings many new friends — Pr.19.4

God has given *w*. and possessions Ec.5.19
the *w*. of the nations shall come to Is.60.5
you have gotten *w*. for yourself Ezek.28.4
put an end to the *w*. of Egypt Ezek.30.10
and hurl her *w*. into the sea Zech.9.4
power and *w*. and wisdom and might Rev.5.12
ships at sea grew rich by her *w*. Rev.18.19

WEAPON
every man with his *w*. in his hand 2 Kg.11.11
he goes out to meet the *w*. Job 39.21
he has prepared his deadly *w*. Ps.7.13
Wisdom is better than *w*. of war Ec.9.18
You are my hammer and *w*. of war Jer.51.20
with the *w*. of righteousness 2 Cor.6.7
the *w*. of our warfare are not 2 Cor.10.4

WEAR
Your clothing did not *w*. out upon you Dt.8.4
will all *w*. out like a garment Ps.102.26
the earth will *w*. out like a garment Is.51.6
or 'What shall we *w*.?' Mt.6.31
Jesus . . . *w*. the crown of thorns Jn.19.5
I am suffering and *w*. fetters 2 Tim.2.9
to the one who *w*. the fine clothing Jas.2.3

WEARY
I am *w*. with my moaning Ps.6.6
as in a dry and *w*. land where no Ps.63.1
lest he become *w*. of you and hate Pr.25.17
that you *w*. my God also? Is.7.13
shade of a great rock in a *w*. land Is.32.2
Even youths shall faint and be *w*. Is.40.30
let us not grow *w*. in well-doing Gal.6.9
you may not grow *w*. or fainthearted Heb.12.3

WEDDING
crowned him on the day of his *w*. S.of S.3.11
The *w*. is ready, but those invited Mt.22.8
a man who had no *w*. garment Mt.22.11
Can the *w*. guests fast while the Mk.2.19

WEEK
you shall observe the feast of *w*. Ex.34.22
dawn of the first day of the *w*. Mt.28.1
I fast twice a *w*., I give tithes of all Lk.18.12
But on the first day of the *w*. Lk.24.1
that day, the first day of the *w*. Jn.20.19
On the first day of the *w*. Acts 20.7
On the first day of every *w*. 1 Cor.16.2

WEEP
a time to *w*., and a time to laugh Ec.3.4
For these things I *w*. Lam.1.16
there men will *w*. and gnash their Mt.8.12
Why do you make a tumult and *w*.? Mk.5.39
do not *w*. for me, but *w*. for Lk.23.28
w. with those who *w*. Rom.12.15
you rich, *w*. and howl for the miseries Jas.5.1
one of the elders said to me, "*W*. not Rev.5.5

WEEPING (noun)
My face is red with *w*. Job 16.16
the LORD has heard the sound of my *w*. Ps.6.8
W. may tarry for the night, but joy Ps.30.5
sound of *w*. and the cry of distress Is.65.19
Take up *w*. and wailing for the Jer.9.10

WEIGH
Let me be *w*. in a just balance Job 31.6
w. like a burden too heavy for me Ps.38.4
Anxiety in a man's heart *w*. him down Pr.12.25
but the LORD *w*. the spirit .Pr.16.2
let the others *w*. what is said 1 Cor.14.29

WEIGHT
A full and just *w*. you shall have Dt.25.15
but a just *w*. is his delight Pr.11.1
food which you eat shall be by *w*. Ezek.4.10
aloes, about a hundred pounds' *w*. Jn.19.39
an eternal *w*. of glory 2 Cor.4.17
let us also lay aside every *w*. Heb.12.1

WELCOME (verb)
Hezekiah *w*. them, and he showed 2 Kg.20.13
a stranger and you did not *w*. me Mt.25.43
the Galileans *w*. him, having seen Jn.4.45
they were *w*. by the church Acts 15.4
W. one another, therefore, as Christ Rom.15.7
he refuses . . . to *w*. the brethren 3 Jn.10

WELFARE
they asked each other of their *w*. Ex.18.7
he sought the *w*. of his people Est.10.3
delights in the *w*. of his servant Ps.35.27
not pray for the *w*. of this people Jer.14.11
seek the *w*. of the city where Jer.29.7
be genuinely anxious for your *w*. Phil.2.20

WELL (noun)
sang this song: "Spring up, O *w*. Num.21.17
a *w*. of living water S.of S.4.15
water from the *w*. of salvation Is.12.3
or an ox that has fallen into a *w*. Lk.14.5
Jacob's *w*. was there, and so Jesus Jn.4.6

WEPT
Joseph *w*. when they spoke to him Gen.50.17
You fasted and *w*. for the child 2 Sam.12.21
I sat down and *w*. Neh.1.4
Babylon, there we sat down and *w*. Ps.137.1
Peter . . . went out and *w*. bitterly Mt.26.75
when he . . . saw the city he *w*. over it Lk.19.41
Jesus *w*. Jn.11.35
I *w*. much that no one was found Rev.5.4

WHEAT
let thorns grow instead of *w*. Job 31.40
feed you with the finest of the *w*. Ps.81.16
gather his *w*. into the granary Mt.3.12
enemy . . . sowed weeds among the *w*. Mt.13.25
that he might sift you like *w*. Lk.22.31
a grain of *w*. falls into the earth Jn.12.24

WHEEL
or the *w*. broken at the cistern Ec.12.6
as it were a *w*. within a *w*. Ezek.1.16
the *w*. were full of eyes round Ezek.10.12
rumble of *w*., galloping horse Nah.3.2

WHIRLWIND
Elijah went up by a *w*. into heaven 2 Kg.2.11
the LORD answered Job out of the *w*. Job 40.6
your calamity comes like a *w*. Pr.1.27
they shall reap the *w*. Hos.8.7

WHITE
I shall be *w*. than snow Ps.51.7
they shall be as *w*. as snow Is.1.18
cannot make one hair *w*. or black Mt.5.36
a young man . . . dressed in a *w*. robe Mk.16.5
his raiment became dazzling *w*. Lk.9.29
she saw two angels in *w*. Jn.20.12
two men stood by them in *w*. robes Acts 1.10
hair . . . *w*. as *w*. wool, *w*. as snow Rev.1.14
a great multitude . . . clothed in *w*. robes Rev.7.9
Then I saw a great *w*. throne Rev.20.11

WHOLE
may his glory fill the *w*. earth Ps.72.19

thanks to the Lord with my *w*. heart   Ps.111.1
for this is the *w*. duty of man   Ec.12.13
The *w*. head is sick, and the *w*. heart   Is.1.5
the *w*. earth is full of his glory   Is.6.3
your *w*. body will be full of light   Mt.6.22
it was restored, *w*. like the other   Mt.12.13
to gain the *w*. world and forfeit   Mk.8.36
gospel is preached in the *w*. world   Mk.14.9
the *w*. creation has been groaning   Rom.8.22
he is bound to keep the *w*. law   Gal.5.3
Put on the *w*. armor of God   Eph.6.11
the Head, from whom the *w*. body   Col.2.19
also for the sins of the *w*. world   1 Jn.2.2

WICKED
Yea, the light of the *w*. is put out   Job 18.5
walks not in the counsel of the *w*.   Ps.1.1
On the *w*. he will rain coals of fire   Ps.11.6
Many are the pangs of the *w*.   Ps.32.10
how long shall the *w*. exult?   Ps.94.3
The *w*. have laid a snare for me   Ps.119.110
see if there be any *w*. way in me   Ps.139.24
but the name of the *w*. will rot   Pr.10.7
house of the *w*. will be destroyed   Pr.14.11
The soul of the *w*. desires evil   Pr.21.10
be not envious of the *w*.   Pr.24.19
The *w*. flee when no one pursues   Pr.28.1
they made his grave with the *w*.   Is.53.9
let the *w*. forsake his way, and the   Is.55.7
no peace, says my God, for the *w*.   Is.57.21
Why does the way of the *w*. prosper?   Jer.12.1
no pleasure in the death of the *w*.   Ezek.33.11
the *w*. turns from his wickedness   Ezek.33.19
You *w*. and slothful servant   Mt.25.26
Drive out the *w*. person from   1 Cor.5.13

WICKEDLY
I have sinned, and I have done *w*.   2 Sam.24.17
we . . . have acted perversely and *w*.   1 Kg.8.47
Of a truth, God will not do *w*.   Job 34.12
committed iniquity, we have done *w*.   Ps.106.6
we have sinned, we have done *w*.   Dan.9.15

WICKEDNESS
Lord saw that the *w*. of man was great   Gen.6.5
Out of the wicked comes forth *w*.   1 Sam.24.13
let not *w*. dwell in your tents   Job 11.14
thou art not a God who delights in *w*.   Ps.5.4
you love righteousness and hate *w*.   Ps.45.7
w. is an abomination to my lips   Pr.8.7
A man is not established by *w*.   Pr.12.3
Jerusalem, wash your heart from *w*.   Jer.4.14
when the wicked turns from his *w*.   Ezek.33.19
who devise *w*. and work evil upon   Mic.2.1
because *w*. is multiplied, most men's   Mt.24.12
coveting, *w*., deceit, licentiousness   Mk.7.22
you are full of extortion and *w*.   Lk.11.39
were filled with all manner of *w*.   Rom.1.29
hosts of *w*. in the heavenly places   Eph.6.12
put away all . . . rank growth of *w*.   Jas.1.21

WIDOW
I caused the *w*. heart to sing for   Job 29.13
he upholds the *w*. and the fatherless   Ps.146.9
How like a *w*. has she become   Lam.1.1
devour *w*. houses and for a pretense   Mk.12.40
a poor *w*. came, and put in two   Mk.12.42
as a *w*. till she was eighty-four   Lk.2.37
there was a *w*. in that city who   Lk.18.3
because their *w*. were neglected in   Acts 6.1

If a *w*. has children or   1 Tim.5.4
She who is a real *w*., and is left   1 Tim.5.5
orphans and *w*. in their affliction   Jas.1.27

WIFE
a man leaves . . . and cleaves to his *w*.   Gen.2.24
And Abram took Sarai his *w*.   Gen.12.5
shall not covet your neighbor's *w*.   Ex.20.17
When the *w*. of Uriah heard that   2 Sam.11.26
Then his *w*. said to him, "Do you   Job 2.9
rejoice in the *w*. of your youth   Pr.5.18
good *w*. is the crown of her husband   Pr.12.4
He who finds a *w*. finds a good   Pr.18.22
a prudent *w*. is from the Lord   Pr.19.14
A good *w*. who can find?   Pr.31.10
does not defile his neighbor's *w*.   Ezek.18.15
Go, take to yourself a *w*. of harlotry   Hos.1.2
do not fear to take Mary your *w*.   Mt.1.20
Whoever divorces his *w*., let him give   Mt.5.31
to which of the seven will she be *w*.?   Mt.22.28
Whoever divorces his *w*. and marries   Mk.10.11
your *w*. Elizabeth will bear you   Lk.1.13
Remember Lot's *w*.   Lk.17.32
a man is living with his father's *w*.   1 Cor.5.1
husband should not divorce his *w*.   1 Cor.7.11
is consecrated through his *w*.   1 Cor.7.14
the husband is the head of the *w*.   Eph.5.23
W., be subject to your husbands, as   Col.3.18
take a *w*. for himself in holiness   1 Th.4.4
live considerately with your *w*.   1 Pet.3.7
the Bride, the *w*. of the Lamb   Rev.21.9

WILD
say that a *w*. beast has devoured   Gen.37.20
but it yielded *w*. grapes   Is.5.2
Go, assemble all the *w*. beasts   Jer.12.9
Even the *w*. beasts cry to thee   Jl.1.20
Now John . . . ate locusts and *w*. honey   Mk.1.6
you, a *w*. olive . . . were grafted in   Rom.11.17
w. waves of the sea, casting up   Jude 13

WILDERNESS
may hold a feast to me in the *w*.   Ex.5.1
they came into the *w*. of Sinai   Ex.19.1
shall let the goat go in the *w*.   Lev.16.22
have led you forty years in the *w*.   Dt.29.5
The voice of the Lord shakes the *w*.   Ps.29.8
Can God spread a table in the *w*.?   Ps.78.19
guided them in the *w*. like a flock   Ps.78.52
who led his people through the *w*.   Ps.136.16
In the *w*. prepare the way of the   Is.40.3
I will cast you forth into the *w*.   Ezek.29.5
It was I who knew you in the *w*.   Hos.13.5
did you go out into the *w*. to behold?   Mt.11.7
John the baptizer appeared in the *w*.   Mk.1.4
The voice of one crying in the *w*.   Lk.3.4
for forty days in the *w*., tempted by   Lk.4.2
leave the ninety-nine in the *w*.   Lk.15.4
lifted up the serpent in the *w*.   Jn.3.14
Our fathers ate the manna in the *w*.   Jn.6.31
they were overthrown in the *w*.   1 Cor.10.5
on the day of testing in the *w*.   Heb.3.8

WILES
have harassed you with their *w*.   Num.25.18
their craftiness in deceitful *w*.   Eph.4.14
stand against the *w*. of the devil   Eph.6.11

WILL (noun)
I delight to do thy *w*., O my God   Ps.40.8

WISE

established the world by his *w*.	Jer.51.15
full of *w*. and perfect in beauty	Ezek.28.12
he gives *w*. to the wise	Dan.2.21
Yet *w*. is justified by her deeds	Mt.11.19
What is the *w*. given to him?	Mk.6.2
Jesus increased in *w*. and in stature	Lk.2.52
Therefore also the *W*. of God said	Lk.11.49
for I will give you a mouth and *w*.	Lk.21.15
I will destroy the *w*. of the wise	1 Cor.1.19
demand signs and Greeks seek *w*.	1 Cor.1.22
For the *w*. of this world is folly	1 Cor.3.19
teaching every man in all *w*.	Col.1.28
If any of you lacks *w*., let him ask	Jas.1.5
But the *w*. from above is first pure	Jas.3.17
glory and *w*. and thanksgiving	Rev.7.12

WISE

was to be desired to make one *w*.	Gen.3.6
It is not the old that are *w*.	Job 32.9
is sure, making *w*. the simple	Ps.19.7
Whoever is *w*., let him give heed	Ps.107.43
Be not *w*. in your own eyes	Pr.3.7
reprove a *w*. man, and he will love	Pr.9.8
A *w*. son makes a glad father	Pr.10.1
the fool will be servant to the *w*.	Pr.11.29
The *w*. man's path leads upward to	Pr.15.24
who keeps silent is considered *w*.	Pr.17.28
A *w*. man is mightier than a strong	Pr.24.5
lest he be *w*. in his own eyes	Pr.26.5
I said, "I will be *w*."	Ec.7.23
The sayings of the *w*. are like goads	Ec.12.11
wisdom of their *w*. men shall perish	Is.29.14
Then all the king's *w*. men came in	Dan.5.8
w. men from the East came to Jerusalem	Mt.2.1
so be *w*. as serpents and innocent	Mt.10.16
hast hidden these things from the *w*.	Mt.11.25
five were foolish, and five were *w*.	Mt.25.2
both to the *w*. and to the foolish	Rom.1.14
Lest you be *w*. in your own conceits	Rom.11.25
foolishness of God is *w*. than men	1 Cor.1.25
the thoughts of the *w*. are futile	1 Cor.3.20
Who is *w*. and understanding among	Jas.3.13

WISH (verb)

So whatever you *w*. that men would	Mt.7.12
Sir, we *w*. to see Jesus	Jn.12.21
could *w*. that I myself were accursed	Rom.9.3
I *w*. those who unsettle you would	Gal.5.12
Therefore whoever *w*. to be a friend	Jas.4.4
not *w*. that any should perish	2 Pet.3.9

WITHER

its leaf does not *w*.	Ps.1.3
O Jerusalem, let my right hand *w*.	Ps.137.5
The grass *w*., the flower fades	Is.40.7
since they had no root they *w*. away	Mt.13.6
a man was there who had a *w*. hand	Mk.3.1
the fig tree *w*. away to its roots	Mk.11.20
grass *w*., and the flower falls	1 Pet.1.24

WITHHOLD

you may not *w*. your help	Dt.22.3
Do not . . . *w*. thy mercy from me	Ps.40.11
Do not *w*. good from those to whom	Pr.3.27
Do not *w*. discipline from a child	Pr.23.13
do not *w*. your coat as well	Lk.6.29

WITHSTAND

could no longer *w*. their enemies	Jg.2.14
so that none is able to *w*. thee	2 Chr.20.6

But they could not *w*. the wisdom	Acts 6.10
who was I that I could *w*. God?	Acts 11.17
may be able to *w*. in the evil day	Eph.6.13

WITNESS (noun)

This heap is a *w*. between you and	Gen.31.48
not bear false *w*. against your	Ex.20.16
only on the evidence of two *w*.	Dt.19.15
A truthful *w*. saves lives	Pr.14.25
A false *w*. will not go unpunished	Pr.19.9
who bears false *w*. against his	Pr.25.18
I made him a *w*. to the peoples	Is.55.4
You shall not bear false *w*.	Mt.19.18
For many bore false *w*. against him	Mk.14.56
to bear *w*. to the light	Jn.1.7
Father who sent me bears *w*. to me	Jn.8.18
you shall be my *w*. in Jerusalem	Acts 1.8
from the dead. To this we are *w*.	Acts 3.15
the *w*. laid down their garments	Acts 7.58
did not leave himself without *w*.	Acts 14.17
blood of Stephen thy *w*. was shed	Acts 22.20
For God is my *w*., whom I serve with	Rom.1.9
my conscience bears me *w*.	Rom.9.1
For God is my *w*., how I yearn for	Phil.1.8
Holy Spirit also bears *w*. to us	Heb.10.15
surrounded by so great a cloud of *w*.	Heb.12.1
There are three *w*., the Spirit	1 Jn.5.8

WOE

If I am wicked, *w*. to me	Job 10.15
Who has *w*.? Who has sorrow?	Pr.23.29
W. to those who rise early in the	Is.5.11
And I said: "*W*. is me! For I am lost	Is.6.5
W. to the shepherds who destroy	Jer.23.1
W. to the foolish prophets who	Ezek.13.3
W. to you, Chorazin! *W*. to you	Mt.11.21
W. to the world for temptations	Mt.18.7
W. to you, scribes and Pharisees	Mt.23.15
w. to that man by whom the Son of	Mk.14.21
w. to you that are rich	Lk.6.24
W. to you, when all men speak well	Lk.6.26
W. to me if I do not preach the	1 Cor.9.16
W., *w*., *w*. to those who dwell on	Rev.8.13

WOLF

The *w*. shall dwell with the lamb	Is.11.6
but inwardly are ravenous *w*.	Mt.7.15
out as lambs in the midst of *w*.	Lk.10.3
sees the *w*. coming and leaves the	Jn.10.12
fierce *w*. will come in among you	Acts 20.29

WOMAN

the rib . . . he made into a *w*.	Gen.2.22
The *w*. said, "The serpent beguiled	Gen.3.13
men say of me, 'A *w*. killed him.'	Jg.9.54
Man . . . born of a *w*. is of few days	Job 14.1
the lips of a loose *w*. drip honey	Pr.5.3
A foolish *w*. is noisy; she is wanton	Pr.9.13
a house shared with a contentious *w*.	Pr.21.9
a *w*. who fears the LORD is . . . praised	Pr.31.30
a young *w*. shall conceive and bear	Is.7.14
one who looks at a *w*. lustfully has	Mt.5.28
instantly the *w*. was made well	Mt.9.22
O *w*., great is your faith	Mt.15.28
Two *w*. will be grinding at the mill	Mt.24.41
a *w*. came with an alabaster jar of	Mk.14.3
a *w*. named Martha received him	Lk.10.38
leaven which a *w*. took and hid in	Lk.13.21
whose wife will the *w*. be?	Lk.20.33

There came a *w.* of Samaria to draw | Jn.4.7
he said . . ."*W.*, behold, your son!" | Jn.19.26
the devout *w.* of high standing | Acts 13.50
the head of a *w.* is her husband | 1 Cor.11.3
but *w.* is the glory of man | 1 Cor.11.7
these *w.* are two covenants | Gal.4.24
Let a *w.* learn in silence | 1 Tim.2.11
a *w.* clothed with the sun | Rev.12.1
and I saw a *w.* sitting on a scarlet | Rev.17.3

WOMB
to her, "Two nations are in your *w.* | Gen.25.23
Naked I came from my mother's *w.* | Job 1.21
From whose *w.* did the ice come | Job 38.29
he who took me from my mother's *w.* | Ps.71.6
From the *w.* of the morning like dew | Ps.110.3
The LORD called me from the *w.* | Is.49.1
Before I formed you in the *w.* I knew | Jer.1.5
blessed is the fruit of your *w.* | Lk.1.42
Blessed is the *w.* that bore you | Lk.11.27
into his mother's *w.* and be born? | Jn.3.4

WONDER (verb)
w. and be astounded. For I am doing | Hab.1.5
Pilate *w.* if he were already dead | Mk.15.44
they *w.* at his delay in the temple | Lk.1.21
w. at the gracious words which | Lk.4.22
why do you *w.* at this, or why do | Acts 3.12
Do not *w.* . . . that the world hates | 1 Jn.3.13

WONDERFUL
Why . . . ask my name, seeing it is *w.*? | Jg.13.18
I have uttered things too *w.* for me | Job 42.3
Remember the *w.* works that he has | Ps.105.5
his *w.* works to the sons of men | Ps.107.15
Such knowledge is too *w.* for me | Ps.139.6
for thou art fearful and *w.* | Ps.139.14
Three things are too *w.* for me | Pr.30.18
his name will be called "*W.* Counselor | Is.9.6
what *w.* stones and what *w.* buildings | Mk.13.1
Great and *w.* are thy deeds, O Lord | Rev.15.3

WONDERS
did all these *w.* before Pharaoh | Ex.11.10
the LORD showed signs and *w.* | Dt.6.22
mindful of the *w.* which thou didst | Neh.9.17
Thou art the God who workest *w.* | Ps.77.14
Let the heavens praise thy *w.* | Ps.89.5
to him who alone does great *w.* | Ps.136.4
he works signs and *w.* in heaven | Dan.6.27
will arise and show signs and *w.* | Mk.13.22
Unless you see signs and *w.* you will | Jn.4.48
many *w.* and signs were done | Acts 2.43
signs and *w.* and mighty works | 2 Cor.12.12
by signs and *w.* and various miracles | Heb.2.4

WONDROUS
consider the *w.* works of God | Job 37.14
telling all thy *w.* deeds | Ps.26.7
thou art great and doest *w.* things | Ps.86.10
I may behold *w.* things out of thy | Ps.119.18
I will meditate on thy *w.* works | Ps.119.27

WOOL
a fleece of *w.* on the threshing floor | Jg.6.37
He gives snow like *w.* | Ps.147.16
the hair of his head like pure *w.* | Dan.7.9
white as white *w.*, white as snow | Rev.1.14

WORD
the *w.* of the LORD came to him | Gen.15.4
the LORD put a *w.* in Balaam's | Num.23.5

Let the *w.* of my mouth and the | Ps.19.14
By the *w.* of the LORD the heavens | Ps.33.6
he sent forth his *w.*, and healed | Ps.107.20
I have laid up thy *w.* in my heart | Ps.119.11
Thy *w.* is a lamp to my feet | Ps.119.105
Even before a *w.* is on my tongue | Ps.139.4
but a harsh *w.* stirs up anger | Pr.15.1
a *w.* in season, how good it is | Pr.15.23
A *w.* fitly spoken is like apples of | Pr.25.11
Every *w.* of God proves true | Pr.30.5
The *w.* which Isaiah the son of Amoz | Is.2.1
but the *w.* of our God will stand | Is.40.8
so shall my *w.* be that goes forth | Is.55.11
Now the *w.* of the LORD came to me | Jer.1.4
but by every *w.* that proceeds from | Mt.4.4
for every careless *w.* they utter | Mt.12.36
the delight in riches choke the *w.* | Mt.13.22
thus making void the *w.* of God | Mk.7.13
The seed is the *w.* of God | Lk.8.11
is ashamed of me and of my *w.* | Lk.9.26
all the people hung upon his *w.* | Lk.19.48
but my *w.* will not pass away | Lk.21.33
In the beginning was the *W.* | Jn.1.1
And the *W.* became flesh and dwelt | Jn.1.14
You have the *w.* of eternal life | Jn.6.68
If you continue in my *w.* | Jn.8.31
a man loves me, he will keep my *w.* | Jn.14.23
thy *w.* is truth | Jn.17.17
And the *w.* of God increased | Acts 6.7
the *w.* of God grew and multiplied | Acts 12.24
received the *w.* with all eagerness | Acts 17.11
the *w.* of the cross is folly to | 1 Cor.1.18
Let the *w.* of Christ dwell in you | Col.3.16
in every good work and *w.* | 2 Th.2.17
But the *w.* of God is not fettered | 2 Tim.2.9
the *w.* of God is living and active | Heb.4.12
world was created by the *w.* of God | Heb.11.3
be doers of the *w.*, and not hearers | Jas.1.22
the *w.* of the Lord abides for ever | 1 Pet.1.25
the prophetic *w.* made more sure | 2 Pet.1.19
let us not love in *w.* or speech but | 1 Jn.3.18
he is called . . . The *W.* of God | Rev.19.13

WORK (noun)
God finished his *w.* which he had | Gen.2.2
Let heavier *w.* be laid upon the men | Ex.5.9
shall labor, and do all your *w.* | Ex.20.9
Thus all the *w.* that Solomon did | 2 Chr.5.1
this *w.* goes on diligently | Ezra 5.8
the *w.* of thy fingers, the moon and | Ps.8.3
establish thou the *w.* of our hands | Ps.90.17
the heavens are the *w.* of thy hands | Ps.102.25
Commit your *w.* to the LORD, and your | Pr.16.3
that a man should enjoy his *w.* | Ec.3.22
then I saw all the *w.* of God | Ec.8.17
bow down to the *w.* of their hands | Is.2.8
he could do no mighty *w.* there | Mk.6.5
does a mighty *w.* in my name will | Mk.9.39
This is the *w.* of God, that you | Jn.6.29
We must work the *w.* of him who sent | Jn.9.4
The *w.* that I do in my Father's name | Jn.10.25
greater *w.* than these will he do | Jn.14.12
by faith apart from *w.* of law | Rom.3.28
cast off the *w.* of darkness | Rom.13.12
If any man's *w.* is burned up | 1 Cor.3.15
But let each one test his own *w.* | Gal.6.4

WORK		WORLDLY	
for the *w.* of ministry	Eph. 4.12	wise according to *w.* standards	1 Cor.1.26
he who began a good *w.* in you will	Phil.1.6	but *w.* grief produces death	2 Cor.7.10
do the *w.* of an evangelist	2 Tim.4.5	we are not carrying on a *w.* war	2 Cor.10.3
faith apart from *w.* is barren?	Jas.2.20	renounce irreligion and *w.* passions	Tit.2.12
so faith apart from *w.* is dead	Jas.2.26	*w.* people, devoid of the Spirit	Jude 19
was to destroy the *w.* of the devil	1 Jn.3.8	**WORM**	
do the *w.* you did at first	Rev.2.5	it bred *w.* and became foul	Ex.16.20
WORK (verb)		if I say . . . to the *w.*, 'My mother	Job 17.14
deliver me from those who *w.* evil	Ps.59.2	But I am a *w.*, and no man	Ps.22.6
I *w.* and who can hinder it?	Is.43.13	God appointed a *w.* which attacked	Jon.4.7
night comes, when no one can *w.*	Jn.9.4	where their *w.* does not die	Mk.9.48
to one who does not *w.* but trusts	Rom.4.5	he was eaten by *w.* and died	Acts 12.23
in everything God *w.* for good	Rom.8.28	**WORMWOOD**	
Do all *w.* miracles?	1 Cor.12.29	but in the end she is bitter as *w.*	Pr.5.4
w. out your own salvation	Phil.2.12	I will feed this people with *w.*	Jer.9.15
w. heartily, as serving the Lord	Col.3.23	O you who turn justice to *w.*	Am.5.7
command: If any one will not *w.*	2 Th.3.10	The name of the star is *W.*	Rev.8.11
WORKER		A third of the waters became *w.*	Rev.8.11
Depart from me, all you *w.* of evil	Ps.6.8	**WORSHIP (verb)**	
those who are *w.* of evil	Ps.28.3	you shall *w.* no other god	Ex.34.14
What gain has the *w.* from his toil?	Ec.3.9	that I may *w.* the LORD your God	1 Sam.15.30
Timothy, my fellow *w.*, greets you	Rom.16.21	I will *w.* toward thy holy temple	Ps.5.7
fellow *w.* in your service	2 Cor.8.23	O come, let us *w.* and bow down	Ps.95.6
fellow *w.* and fellow soldier	Phil.2.25	let us *w.* at his footstool	Ps.132.7
Demas, and Luke, my fellow *w.*	Philem.24	Egyptians will *w.* with the Assyrians	Is.19.23
that we may be fellow *w.* in the truth	3 Jn.8	enter these gates to *w.* the LORD	Jer.7.2
WORKMAN		fall down and *w.* the golden image	Dan.3.10
I was beside him, like a master *w.*	Pr.8.30	we . . . have come to *w.* him	Mt.2.2
with the *w.* of like occupation	Acts 19.25	if you will fall down and *w.* me	Mt.4.9
For we are fellow *w.* for God	1 Cor.3.9	in vain do they *w.* me, teaching as	Mk.7.7
such men are . . . deceitful *w.*	2 Cor.11.13	You shall *w.* the Lord your God	Lk.4.8
w. who has no need to be ashamed	2 Tim.2.15	will *w.* the Father in spirit	Jn.4.23
WORLD		fell down at his feet and *w.* him	Acts 10.25
he judges the *w.* with righteousness	Ps.9.8	what therefore you *w.* as unknown	Acts 17.23
the *w.* and those who dwell therein	Ps.24.1	*w.* him who made heaven and earth	Rev.14.7
hadst formed the earth and the *w.*	Ps.90.2	*W.* God. For the testimony of	Rev.19.10
judge the *w.* with righteousness	Ps.96.13	**WORTHLESS**	
established the *w.* by his wisdom	Jer.10.12	Now the sons of Eli were *w.* men	1 Sam.2.12
You are the light of the *w.*	Mt.5.14	A *w.* man plots evil, and his speech	Pr.16.27
the field is the *w.*, and the good	Mt.13.38	A *w.* witness mocks at justice	Pr.19.28
gain the whole *w.* and forfeit his	Mk.8.36	They are *w.*, a work of delusion	Jer.51.18
the *w.* was made through him	Jn.1.10	Woe to my *w.* shepherd, who deserts	Zech.11.17
God so loved the *w.* that he gave his	Jn.3.16	cast the *w.* servant into the outer	Mt.25.30
is indeed the Savior of the *w.*	Jn.4.42	it is *w.* and near to being cursed	Heb.6.8
saying, "I am the light of the *w.*	Jn.8.12	**WORTHY**	
Now is the judgment of this *w.*	Jn.12.31	I am not *w.* of the least of all	Gen.32.10
not as the *w.* gives do I give to	Jn.14.27	the LORD, who is *w.* to be praised	Ps.18.3
In the *w.* you have tribulation	Jn.16.33	whose sandals I am not *w.* to carry	Mt.3.11
My kingship is not of this *w.*	Jn.18.36	if the house is *w.*, let your peace	Mt.10.13
have turned the *w.* upside down	Acts 17.6	for I am not *w.* to have you come	Lk.7.6
sin came into the *w.* through one	Rom.5.12	whose sandal I am not *w.* to untie	Jn.1.27
made foolish the wisdom of the *w.*?	1 Cor.1.20	deeds *w.* of their repentance	Acts 26.20
wisdom of this *w.* is folly with God	1 Cor.3.19	lead a life *w.* of the calling	Eph.4.1
the saints will judge the *w.*?	1 Cor.6.2	let your . . . life be *w.* of the gospel	Phil.1.27
the god of this *w.* has blinded	2 Cor.4.4	if there is anything *w.* of praise	Phil.4.8
no hope and without God in the *w.*	Eph.2.12	lead a life *w.* of God, who calls you	1 Th.2.12
you shine as lights in the *w.*	Phil.2.15	God may make you *w.* of his call	2 Th.1.11
came into the *w.* to save sinners	1 Tim.1.15	of whom the world was not *w.*	Heb.11.38
we brought nothing into the *w.*	1 Tim.6.7	*W.* art thou, our Lord and God, to	Rev.4.11
of whom the *w.* was not worthy	Heb.11.38	*W.* is the Lamb who was slain, to	Rev.5.12
keep oneself unstained from the *w.*	Jas.1.27	**WOUND (noun)**	
Do not love the *w.* or the things	1 Jn.2.15	Who has *w.* without cause?	Pr.23.29
the *w.* passes away, and the lust	1 Jn.2.17	like vinegar on a *w.*	Pr.25.20
God sent his only Son into the *w.*	1 Jn.4.9	Faithful are the *w.* of a friend	Pr.27.6
kingdom of the *w.* has become the	Rev.11.15		

healed the *w*. of my people lightly   Jer.8.11
Why is . . . my *w*. incurable, refusing   Jer.15.18
her *w*. is incurable; and it has   Mic.1.9
By his *w*. you have been healed   1 Pet.2.24

WOUND (verb)
I *w*. and I heal; and there is none   Dt.32.39
But he was *w*. for our transgressions   Is.53.5
they *w*. him in the head   Mk.12.4
by means of them they *w*.   Rev.9.19

WRAP
Mount Sinai was *w*. in smoke   Ex.19.18
too narrow to *w*. oneself in it   Is.28.20
Thou hast *w*. thyself with anger   Lam.3.43
w. him in the linen shroud   Mk.15.46
find a babe *w*. in swaddling cloths   Lk.2.12

WRATH
my *w*. will burn, and I will kill you   Ex.22.24
why does thy *w*. burn hot against   Ex.32.11
w. has gone forth from the LORD   Num.16.46
you provoked the LORD to *w*.   Dt.9.22
w. fell upon all the congregation   Jos.22.20
great is the *w*. of the LORD   2 Kg.22.13
my *w*. will be poured out   2 Chr.34.25
He has kindled his *w*. against me   Job 19.11
My *w*. is kindled against you   Job 42.7
Then he will speak to them in his *w*.   Ps.2.5
nor chasten me in thy *w*.   Ps.38.1
the *w*. of men shall praise thee   Ps.76.10
all our days pass away under thy *w*.   Ps.90.9
A soft answer turns away *w*.   Pr.15.1
A man of *w*. stirs up strife   Pr.29.22
the bowl of my *w*. you shall drink   Is.51.22
for in my *w*. I smote you   Is.60.10
Pour out thy *w*. upon the nations   Jer.10.25
will soon pour out my *w*. upon you   Ezek.7.8
I will pour out my *w*. like water   Hos.5.10
His *w*. is poured out like fire   Nah.1.6
in *w*. remember mercy   Hab.3.2
to flee from the *w*. to come?   Mt.3.7
the *w*. of God rests upon him   Jn.3.36
For the *w*. of God is revealed from   Rom.1.18
For the law brings *w*.   Rom.4.15
if God, desiring to show his *w*.   Rom.9.22
we were by nature children of *w*.   Eph.2.3
delivers us from the *w*. to come   1 Th.1.10
For God has not destined us for *w*.   1 Th.5.9
hide us . . . from the *w*. of the Lamb   Rev.6.16
the seven bowls of the *w*. of God   Rev.16.1

WRATHFUL
nor go with a *w*. man   Pr.22.24
upon them with *w*. chastisements   Ezek.25.17
the LORD is avenging and *w*.   Nah.1.2

WRETCHED
W. man that I am! Who will deliver   Rom.7.24
Be *w*. and mourn and weep   Jas.4.9
not knowing that you are *w*.   Rev.3.17

WRITE
W. this as a memorial in a book   Ex.17.14
LORD said to Moses, "*W*. these words   Ex.34.27
W. each man's name upon his rod   Num.17.2
I will *w*. on the tables the words   Dt.10.2
Now therefore *w*. this song   Dt.31.19
we make a firm covenant and *w*. it   Neh.9.38
w. them on the tablet of your heart   Pr.7.3
W. in a book all the words that I   Jer.30.2

I will *w*. it upon their hearts   Jer.31.33
take a stick and *w*. on it   Ezek.37.16
the LORD answered me: "*W*. the vision   Hab.2.2
Do not *w*., 'The King of the Jews'   Jn.19.21
I, Paul, *w*. this greeting with my   Col.4.18
it is the way I *w*.   2 Th.3.17
I had much to *w*. to you, but I would   3 Jn.13
saying, "*W*. what you see in a book   Rev.1.11
W. this: Blessed are those who are   Rev.19.9

WRITINGS
But if you do not believe his *w*.   Jn.5.47
through the prophetic *w*. is made   Rom.16.26
with the sacred *w*. which are able   2 Tim.3.15

WRONG (noun)
Is there any *w*. on my tongue?   Job 6.30
had declared Job to be in the *w*.   Job 32.3
who also do no *w*., but walk in his   Ps.119.3
I hate robbery and *w*.   Is.61.8
no *w*. was found on his lips   Mal.2.6
but this man has done nothing *w*.   Lk.23.41
We find nothing *w*. in this man   Acts 23.9
But if you do *w*., be afraid   Rom.13.4
it does not rejoice at *w*.   1 Cor.13.6
suffering *w*. for their wrongdoing   2 Pet.2.13

WRONGDOER
be not envious of *w*.   Ps.37.1
If then I am a-*w*., and have   Acts 25.11
to execute his wrath on the *w*.   Rom.13.4
the *w*. will be paid back for   Col.3.25
or a *w*., or a mischief-maker   1 Pet.4.15

WRONGDOING
but an avenger of their *w*.   Ps.99.8
say what *w*. they found when I   Acts 24.20
who loved gain from *w*.   2 Pet.2.15
All *w*. is sin, but there is sin   1 Jn.5.17

WROUGHT
Jacob and Israel, 'What has God *w*.!'   Num.23.23
the LORD has *w*. deliverance in   1 Sam.11.13
he has *w*. desolations in the earth   Ps.46.8
I muse on what thy hands have *w*.   Ps.143.5
thou hast *w*. for us all our works   Is.26.12
mighty works are *w*. by his hands   Mk.6.2
his deeds have been *w*. in God   Jn.3.21
what Christ has *w*. through me   Rom.15.18

YEAR
three times in the *y*. shall all   Ex.23.17
atonement upon its horns once a *y*.   Ex.30.10
a lamb a *y*. old for a burnt offering   Lev.12.6
you shall hallow the fiftieth *y*.   Lev.25.10
bought it until the *y*. of jubilee   Lev.25.28
As a servant hired *y*. by *y*. shall   Lev.25.53
at the time appointed every *y*.   Est.9.27
rejoice among the days of the *y*.   Job 3.6
crownest the *y*. with thy bounty   Ps.65.11
For a thousand *y*. in thy sight are   Ps.90.4
The *y*. of our life are threescore   Ps.90.10
the *y*. draw nigh, when you will   Ec.12.1
In the *y*. that King Uzziah died   Is.6.1
to proclaim the *y*. of the LORD's   Is.61.2
my *y*. of redemption has come   Is.63.4
offerings, with calves a *y*. old?   Mic.6.6
go up *y*. after *y*. to worship   Zech.14.16
the acceptable *y*. of the Lord   Lk.4.19
priest goes, and he but once a *y*.   Heb.9.7

continually offered *y*. after *y*.   Heb.10.1
spend a *y*. there and trade   Jas.4.13
and a thousand *y*. as one day   2 Pet.3.8
and bound him for a thousand *y*.   Rev.20.2

YES
what you say be simply 'Y.' or 'No'   Mt.5.37
ready to say Y. and No at once?   2 Cor.1.17
promises of God find their Y.   2 Cor.1.20
but let your *y*. be *y*. and your no   Jas.5.12

YESTERDAY
we are but of *y*., and know nothing   Job 8.9
are but as *y*. when it is past   Ps.90.4
Y. at the seventh hour the fever   Jn.4.52
the same *y*. and today and for ever   Heb.13.8

YIELD
but *y*. yourselves to the LORD   2 Chr.30.8
The earth has *y*. its increase   Ps.67.6
our land will *y*. its increase   Ps.85.12
a loud voice and *y*. up his spirit   Mt.27.50
Do not *y*. your members to sin   Rom.6.13
y. your members to righteousness   Rom.6.19
later it *y*. the peaceful fruit of   Heb.12.11
No more can salt water *y*. fresh   Jas.3.12
y. its fruit each month   Rev.22.2

YOKE
Your father made our *y*. heavy   1 Kg.12.4
you made your *y*. exceedingly heavy   Is.47.6
I break the *y*. of Nebuchadnezzar   Jer.28.11
that he bear the *y*. in his youth   Lam.3.27
but I will put Ephraim to the *y*.   Hos.10.11
Take my *y*. upon you, and learn from   Mt.11.29
For my *y*. is easy, and my burden is   Mt.11.30
I have bought five *y*. of oxen   Lk.14.19
by putting a *y*. upon the neck of   Acts 15.10
not submit again to a *y*. of slavery   Gal.5.1

YOUNG
I am *y*. in years, and you are aged   Job 32.6
The *y*. lions suffer want and hunger   Ps.34.10
I have been *y*., and now am old   Ps.37.25
How can a *y*. man keep his way pure?   Ps.119.9
Rejoice, O *y*. man, in your youth   Ec.11.9
Behold, a *y*. woman shall conceive   Is.7.14
their *y*. shall lie down together   Is.11.7
Spare not her *y*. men   Jer.51.3
y. men and maidens, little children   Ezek.9.6
Does a *y*. lion cry out from his den   Am.3.4
The *y*. man said . . . "All these I   Mt.19.20
Y. man, I say to you, arise   Lk.7.14
at the feet of a *y*. man named Saul   Acts 7.58
a *y*. man named Eutychus was   Acts 20.9
so train the *y*. women to love   Tit.2.4
y. men, because you are strong   1 Jn.2.14

YOUTH
man's heart is evil from his *y*.   Gen.8.21
a man of war from his *y*.   1 Sam.17.33
have revered the LORD from my *y*.   1 Kg.18.12
Remember not the sins of my *y*.   Ps.25.7
O God, from my *y*. thou hast taught   Ps.71.17
so that your *y*. is renewed like   Ps.103.5
your Creator in . . . your *y*.   Ec.12.1
Even *y*. shall faint and be weary   Is.40.30
that he bear the yoke in his *y*.   Lam. 3.27
these I have observed from my *y*.   Mk.10.20
My manner of life from my *y*.   Acts 26.4
Let no one despise your *y*. '   1 Tim.4.12

ZACCHAEUS
Lk.19.2,5,8

ZEAL
The *z*. of the LORD will do this   2 Kg.19.31
z. for thy house has consumed me   Ps.69.9
Z. for thy house will consume me   Jn.2.17
they have a *z*. for God, but   Rom.10.2
Never flag in *z*., be aglow with   Rom.12.11
as to *z*. a persecutor of the church   Phil.3.6

ZEALOUS
they are all *z*. for the law   Acts 21.20
being *z*. for God as you all are   Acts 22.3
so extremely *z*. was I for the   Gal.1.14
who are *z*. for good deeds   Tit.2.14
if you are *z*. for what is right?   1 Pet.3.13
the more *z*. to confirm your call   2 Pet.1.10
be *z*. to be . . . without spot   2 Pet.3.14
so be *z*. and repent   Rev.3.19

ZEBEDEE
Mt.4.21; 20.20; Mk.1.20; Jn.21.2

ZECHARIAH
(1) king of Israel; begins to reign, 2 Kg.14.29;
killed by Shallum, who succeeds him, 2
Kg.15.10; (2) father of Abi, Hezekiah's
mother, 2 Kg.18.2; (3) prophet, Zech.1.1; (4)
father of John the Baptist, Lk.1.5; is promised
a son, Lk.1.13; doubting, is stricken with dumbness, Lk.1.22; his recovery and song, Lk.1.64,
68–79; (5) others, 2 Chr.26.5; Ezra 8.16; Neh.
11.12; Is.8.2

ZEDEKIAH
(1) false prophet, 1 Kg.22.11; 2 Chr.18.10,23;
(2) another, Jer.29.22; (3) (Mattaniah), king
of Judah, 2 Kg.24.17; 25; 2 Chr.36.10–11;
Jer.37–39; 52

ZEPHANIAH
(1) priest, 2 Kg.25.18; Jer.29.25; 37.3; (2)
prophet, Zeph.1–3; (3) others, 1 Chr.6.36;
Zech. 6.10, 14

ZERUBBABEL
prince of Judah, Ezra 2.2; restores the worship
of God, Ezra 3.2; Neh.12.47; Hag.1.1,14;
2.2; Zech.4.6

ZION
David took the stronghold of Z.   2 Sam.5.7
the city of David, which is Z.   2 Chr.5.2
let Mount Z. be glad! Let the   Ps.48.11
Walk about Z., go round about her   Ps.48.12
Do good to Z. in thy good pleasure   Ps.51.18
in whose heart are the highways to Z.   Ps.84.5
The LORD is great in Z.   Ps.99.2
For the LORD will build up Z.   Ps.102.16
May all who hate Z. be put to shame   Ps.129.5
For the LORD has chosen Z.   Ps.132.13
and wept, when we remembered Z.   Ps.137.1
Sing us one of the songs of Z.   Ps.137.3
let the sons of Z. rejoice in their   Ps.149.2
For out of Z. shall go forth the law   Is.2.3
I am laying in Z. for a foundation   Is.28.16
For the LORD will comfort Z.   Is.51.3
and come to Z. with singing   Is.51.11
awake, put on your strength, O Z.   Is.52.1
sound of wailing is heard from Z.   Jer.9.19
for Mount Z. which lies desolate   Lam.5.18
the LORD roars from Z., and utters   Jl.3.16

Woe to those who are at ease in Z.	Am.6.1	I am laying in Z. a stone that	Rom.9.33
I am jealous for Z. with great	Zech.8.2	The Deliverer will come from Z.	Rom.11.26
I will brandish your sons, O Z.	Zech.9.13	come to Mount Z. and to the city	Heb.12.22
Tell the daughter of Z., Behold	Mt.21.5	Behold, I am laying in Z. a stone	1 Pet.2.6
Fear not, daughter of Z.	Jn.12.15	on Mount Z. stood the Lamb	Rev.14.1

5.69
2½.69 N6½

ſ